Ernest Mandel

Ernest Mandel

A Rebel's Dream Deferred

———————◆———————

Translated by
CHRISTOPHER BECK and PETER DRUCKER

V
VERSO
London • New York

This edition first published by Verso 2009
© Jan Willem Stutje 2007
Translation Christopher Beck and Peter Drucker 2009
First published as *Ernest Mandel: Rebel tussen droom en daad, 1923–1995 Houtekiet/Amsab-ISG*, Antwerpen/Gent, 2007

The translation of this work was made possible by support from the Netherlands Organization for Scientific Research (NWO)

1 3 5 7 9 10 8 6 4 2

Verso
UK: 6 Meard Street, London W1F 0EG
US: 20 Jay Street, Suite 1010, Brooklyn, NY 11201
www.versobooks.com

Verso is the imprint of New Left Books

ISBN-13: 978-1-84467-316-2

British Library Cataloguing in Publication Data
A catalogue record for this book is available from the British Library

Library of Congress Cataloging-in-Publication Data
A catalog record for this book is available from the Library of Congress

Typeset by Hewer Text UK Ltd, Edinburgh
Printed in the US by Maple Vail

Contents

List of Illustrations

The author and publisher would like to thank all those who have kindly supplied permission for the following illustrations to be reproduced in this work.

- Henry and Rosa Mandel and their sons, Antwerp, September 1937. (Source: Michel Mandel.)
- On the eve the Second World Congress of the Fourth International, theatre on Rue de l'Arbre Sec, the French Trotskyist HQ, Paris, April 1948. (Source: Rudolphe Prager Archive, IISH, Amsterdam.)
- Letter from Ernest Mandel after his release, 'somewhere in Germany', April 1945. (Source: Henri Mandel Archive, IISH Amsterdam.)
- Ernest Mandel and Pierre Le Grève selling *La Gauche*, early 1960s. (Source: Anne Mandel-Sprimont.)
- Sherry Mangan, ca. 1950. (Source: Rudolphe Prager Archive, IISH, Amsterdam.)
- Ernest Mandel and Pierre Le Grève (with pipe) at the founding conference of the Union de la Gauche Socialiste, 1964. (Source: Anne Mandel-Sprimont.)
- Ernest Mandel at work on *Late Capitalism*, 1970. (Source: Anne Mandel-Sprimont.)
- Ernest Mandel the professor. (Photo by Herman Selleslags.)
- Rudi Dutschke. (Source: IISH, Amsterdam.)
- Clandestine press conference with Tariq Ali, Alain Krivine and Ernest Mandel. (Source: private collection.)
- Ernest Bloch, mid 1970s. (Source: IISH, Amsterdam.)
- Gisela Scholtz, late 1970s. (Source: IISH, Amsterdam.)
- Verso dinner celebrating the publication of Mandel's *The Meaning of the Second World War*, 1986. (Source: Anne Mandel-Sprimont.)

Foreword

Ernest Mandel was one of the most creative and independent-minded revolutionary thinkers of the postwar world. His writings on political theory, world history and Marxist economics have been translated into more than forty languages. In a series of specialist works – *Late Capitalism* (1975), *The Second Slump* (1978), *The Long Waves of Capitalist Development* (revised and re-issued in 1995) – he analyzed how capitalism functioned in the West, and far from being surprised by the Wall Street crash of 2008, he would have been able to situate his analysis of it within Marxist theory. From the late 1950s onwards, he was a prominent leader and theoretician of the Fourth International, the Brussels-based Trotskyist movement, while working on his two-volume classic, *Marxist Economic Theory*. A skilful orator who could speak several languages, he became a much admired figure during the 1960s, especially after 1968. Even those on the left not sympathetic to his politics acknowledged his influence and demonstrated a respect for his razor-sharp intelligence. He was one of the theoreticians most respected by the West German SDS, in particular the late Rudi Dutschke.

No serious biography or intellectual history of Mandel has appeared to date – Jan Willem Stutje's thoroughly researched account is a good start, an attempt to explain not only Mandel's ideas but also their development within the context of his personal history, and the details he gives of his subject's private life might surprise some of those who knew Ernest Mandel only as a revolutionary leader. Stutje not only took full advantage of being the first to gain complete access to Mandel's archives, he also conducted a broad range of interviews with those who knew the man and those who knew the thinker and activist, and has managed to situate Mandel within the intellectual and political upheavals of his time, tracing his evolution as both scholar and revolutionary from childhood, through the Second World War and the events of '68, right up to his death in 1995.

Ernest Mandel was born in Belgium and educated at the Roya Athae-
naeum in Antwerp and later at the University of Brussels. His father, Henri
Mandel, a Polish-born left-wing socialist, had opposed the First World War
and fled from Belgium to Holland to avoid conscription into the Austrian
army, subsequently moving to Germany with the communist Wilhelm
Pieck after the Kaiser's fall. Working in Berlin as a journalist with the newly
organized Soviet Press Agency, Henri befriended Karl Radek, the Bolshevik
emissary dispatched by Lenin to promote the German revolution, but the
repression that followed the execution of Rosa Luxemburg and Karl
Liebknecht demoralized him, and he remained a member of the German
Communist Party for only a few years longer. He dropped out of active
politics and moved to Antwerp, where his first son, Ezra, or Ernest, was
born.

Ernest was ten when Hitler rose to absolute power, in 1933. Years later,
we would speak of those events and he would describe his memories of that
era. 'My father made some very sharp comments at the time on the
incapacity of the Social Democrats and the Communists to resist fascism,'
he told me. 'I remember him saying "This will end very badly. It could be
the end for our people." '

In 1939, Mandel joined a small Trotskyist group in Antwerp and became
active in resisting the Occupation. The leader of the Belgian Socialist Party,
who was also the deputy prime minister at the time, publicly appealed for
collaboration with the Nazis and was supported by an important section of
the trade union apparatus – a move that left Mandel feeling outraged and
disgusted. Meanwhile, the official Communists basked in the deadly rays of
the Stalin-Hitler pact.

Mandel was first arrested for distributing seditious leaflets to the occupying German soldiers. A revolutionary and a Jew, he subsequently went into
hiding, yet he continued to observe the uniformed Germans, noting how
they were affected by the anti-fascist propaganda. When he was finally
caught, he was sent to a transit camp for prisoners – normally a stop en route
to Auschwitz – where he began talking to the warders, veteran employees of
the German state who were considered subhuman by the other Belgian and
French prisoners. Mandel saw them otherwise, and he sought to convince
them of the merits of socialism, in the process discovering that some of them
had been members of the now-banned Social Democratic and Communist
parties in Germany. The admiration of these men for the precocity of the
sixteen-year-old Mandel inspired them to help in his escape. These events,
as Stutje describes them, marked a critical turning point in Mandel's
evolution as a revolutionary and an intellectual. Although he was re-arrested
soon after, it was through this experience that he became a true inter-

nationalist. He realized that whole nations and peoples could not be condemned for the crimes of their leaders.

He rarely spoke of the Holocaust; one of the few occasions that I heard him refer to it was in the telling of a semi-comic anecdote. Two Nigerian Trotskyists had arrived in Brussels to attend a meeting, getting into the airport late at night. They had gone straight to Mandel's house (the only address they had), but he was at a meeting, as was his wife, Gisela. His aged mother heard loud knocks on the front door and opened it, then, when she saw the African comrades, slammed it shut. They were incredibly amused and understanding, but when Mandel heard about the episode he lost his temper, shouting at his mother and reminding her that similar views had led to most of their own relations being killed in the camps. A number of us told him that this analogy had been cruel and far-fetched. He wouldn't listen. 'Unacceptable behaviour. Unacceptable.' Moreover, like Abram Leon, Ygael Gluckstein [Tony Cliff] and many other Bolsheviks of Jewish origin, Mandel was utterly hostile to Zionism and the idea of an Israeli state. He was, like the Israeli Socialist Organisation founded by Akiva Orr, Moshe Machover and Haim Hanegbi, committed to a single state with equal rights for all. On this he was implacable.

Following the Second World War, Mandel devoted much energy to building the Fourth International as a world party for the socialist revolution, a party whose distance from the crimes of Stalinism and the capitulations of social democracy would result in success. It is easier now than it was at the time to see that this was a utopian project. Ralph Miliband, sympathetic on many levels, was always convinced that the Fourth International was a road to nowhere and cut off some fine comrades from the broader movement. During the 1960s and 1970s Mandel, fluent in the major European languages, was much in demand as a speaker all over the world. His polemical and oratorical skills led to him being barred from entering the United States, France, West Germany, Switzerland and Australia. Paranoid governments deemed him a threat to national security – a phrase that echoes loudly in our political climate today.

These restrictions on his movements sent him back to the typewriter. Mandel produced pamphlets and books at an amazing speed, without loss of quality or relevance – his *Introduction to Marxist Economic Theory* sold half a million copies. Yet his preoccupation with producing these written works never interfered with his observation of the plethora of Trotskyist movements that were organizing around the world. When I would ring him during the '70s, asking a polite 'How are you?' the reply was never the same: 'I'm just finishing off a draft reply to the sectarians in Ceylon on the Tamil question' or 'Fine. Have you read my reply to the IS Group on state capitalism?' or 'Those sectarian idiots in Argentina have caved in to Peronism. Crazy people. Don't they understand?' They never did, but Mandel never stopped trying to convince 'crazy people' to tread the true revolutionary road. He was thinking of new projects right up until the end. 'I can't decide what book to write,' he told me shortly before his death. 'A history of the European workers' movement or the permanent and eternal links between capitalism and crime?' In the end, he wasn't able to write either.

His motto was Optimism of the Will, Optimism of the Intellect, and in his last years he refused to accept the scale of the defeat that socialism had suffered in 1989. To his great irritation, I sometimes reminded him that Trotsky's prescience in *The Revolution Betrayed* was much closer to the mark than his own rejection of reality. The exiled Bolshevik had written in 1936 that the Soviet regime was transitory; that it would either be pushed forward by a political revolution from below, triggered by new revolutions elsewhere in the world, or it would atrophy and regress, paving the way for a capitalist restoration in which many of the leading socialist bureaucrats would become capitalist millionaires.

The world of the Left that was dominated by 1917 has come to an end. Nineteen eighty-nine, the year that witnessed the collapse of the Soviet Union and the extraordinary Chinese spurt towards capitalism that structurally altered the world market, marked the end of traditional social democracy. The Washington consensus imploded in 2008, but those who challenged it during its prime were not traditional workers' organizations, but the social movements in South America: in Venezuela, Bolivia, Ecuador, Argentina, Peru and Paraguay. These movements produced political parties and leaders of a new type who triumphed electorally and began to implement social programmes that defied the norms of the new world order. Mandel would have had a great deal to write about all this were he alive, but even he would have found it difficult to link all this to the certainties of the previous epoch, characterized as one of 'wars and revolutions'. Soon after the Partido dos Trabahaldores (PT) was formed in Brazil, he was asked to write its programme. 'Not easy,' he told me. 'Difficult to find the key transitional demands.' I don't know whether he produced a draft but it was certainly the first time I heard him speaking about difficulties. However, he often held back from writing material that might 'demoralize the movement'. This was a great pity, because critical analysis was desperately needed and might have helped the movement survive. It would have been worth a try.

Jan Willem Stutje does not offer us a hagiography: he writes of Mandel's frequent 'unwillingness – if not incapacity – to defend the integrity of his convictions, his tendency to compromise at crucial moments.' In my opinion this was more the case when Mandel was participating in the interminable polemics that marked the Trotskyist movement. On one occasion he told me, 'I wish I had the time to write a history of the Jesuits. Very similar to our movement in many ways.' He knew. Yet so strong were his convictions that in their service he persisted in a daily routine that was often arid and unrewarding. 'Your generation doesn't have the stamina of our generation,' he said when I told him in 1980 that it had become impossible for me to remain a member of his organization in Britain. 'We survived fascism and Stalinism and it was worth the wait. You've just been put off by some sectarian idiots.' This was not exactly so, but he thought that anyone who left must begin a move rightwards. (I am glad to say he was wrong in more than a few cases, including mine.)

Despite our disagreements, we remained friends and he always maintained a strong collaboration with the *New Left Review*, even though 'you people are centrists [i.e., vacillating between reform and revolution] but I'm pleased that the quality of the magazine remains high. That's important. It reminds me of *Die Neue Zeit* under Kautsky's editorship.' I laughed – the Berlin Wall had come down a few weeks previously – and told him that given what was happening in the world, very few of my *NLR* colleagues would regard this comparison as an insult. Ironically, the few who did soon moved on to other pastures.

Ernest Mandel was a Trotskyist, but one able to think independently and to engage with many whose views were far removed from his own. Some of his finest essays were written for audiences that needed convincing. I miss him greatly. He had a profound influence on me that will never completely disappear.

Yeats wrote that 'The intellect of man is forced to choose / Perfection of the life, or of the work.'

For Mandel it was always the latter.

Tariq Ali
December 2008

Preface

This book is an exercise in critical admiration: an attempt to explore frankly and freely the life and work of Ernest Mandel, a Flemish revolutionary Marxist with whose ideas I feel a close affinity. My approach is both open and critical; Mandel deserves no less.

Ernest Mandel was an undogmatic radical theoretician, who exerted considerable influence internationally on the 'generation of '68'. He is also the most translated Belgian author after Georges Simenon. Around the globe, his writings have appeared in hundreds of thousands of editions in more than forty languages. In 2006 the international journal *Post-Autistic Economics Review* named him one of the thirty greatest economists of the twentieth century.[1]

Mandel's connection with Belgium was strong. Among the varied evidence of that bond are his editorships (1954–85) of the Liège periodical *La Wallonie* and *Le Peuple*, the Brussels daily of the Belgian Socialist Party; his activity in the ABVV (General Belgian Trade Union Federation); and his participation in the great strike in the winter of 1960–61. Mandel played a key role in establishing two weeklies – *La Gauche* and *Links*, its Flemish counterpart – which attracted the attention of a broad trade union and left intellectual public in the second half of the 1950s. In addition he was a highly valued and frequently invited debating partner in liberal, Catholic and social democratic circles.

Mandel was a gifted speaker and polyglot, who opened new perspectives for many audiences in half a dozen languages. He was also a prominent scholar, who delivered the prestigious Alfred Marshall lectures at Cambridge University in 1978. He wrote both *Delightful Murder*, a history of the crime novel, and the scholarly introductions Penguin's English edition of the three volumes of Marx's *Capital*. At his death the *Frankfurter Allgemeine Zeitung* wrote, 'More than anyone, this Belgian political scientist endured the anathemas of both the right and the orthodox left . . . but for the generation of 1968 Mandel's name was an inspiration and an example.'[2] Along with renowned progressive intellectuals such as Herbert Marcuse, Ernst Bloch, and Jean-Paul Sartre, Mandel celebrated the Prague Spring, just as he embraced the rebellions in Western Europe and America that promoted an anti-authoritarian and utopian revolutionary spirit against the bourgeois conformism of modern consumer society.

Mandel was a breed of socialist rare in the second half of the twentieth century: a theoretician who situated his scholarly work in the broader endeavour of his revolutionary aspirations. From his early youth, the focus and outlet for his activism was the Fourth International, founded and inspired by Leon Trotsky.

The reader of this biography will encounter Mandel and his comrades in their own words, as well as the biographer's. Where the Marxist idiom does not predominate, their language adds colour and expresses the authentic voice of their period and milieux. Countless meetings and happenings wind through this story. His life was formed of a complex fabric, incorporating the threads of various disciplines – economics, philosophy, sociology, psychology and history – but interweaving these academic interests with literature and love. It was not always easy to select the most representative continuities; this work is not intended to be a study of the Fourth International. Moreover, I had to choose carefully the historical contexts that would best represent Mandel's life and work without restricting his ideas to confines too narrow to hold them. His thought – at once social and conceptual – is explored under three headings: 1) the history of international capital; 2) the nature of the so-called socialist countries; and 3) the role of the subjective: self-activity, the revolutionary party and the democracy of workers' councils. This biography offers an opportunity to meet Mandel in guises other than those of intellectual, ideologue or party member. He was also an active participant in the Resistance, as well as a scholar and teacher.

Mandel came to maturity years before feminism broke down the barrier between the personal and the political. Like many socialists of the time, he sequestered his private life and protected it from intrusion. For him, the personal was irrelevant to the struggle for emancipation. Today we are more likely to believe that the sometimes complex, intimate details of private lives are often essential to understanding a person's history and need not remain hidden. In each case I have tried to determine whether the personal and emotional experiences of my subject's life are historically relevant or, to put it another way, if knowledge of Mandel's intimate world enhances the understanding of his public actions.

★   ★   ★

After the relatively wide recognition of Mandel's thought in the 1970s and
'80s, above all in France and Germany but also in the United States and Latin
America, there was a shift in the reception of his ideas in the 1990s. This was
linked to the decline of the European workers' movement and the collapse
of the Soviet Union, which ended any hope that its authoritarian bureaucratic regime would give way to a democratic and humanistic socialism.
Mandel's books ceased to sell as they once had, and his work was no longer
translated and reprinted. That fate befell other socialist political writers, such
as Paul Baran and Paul Sweezy in the United States, Herbert Marcuse and
Ernst Bloch in Germany, and Louis Althusser and Henri Lefebvre in France.
New liberal and postmodern theories triumphed, filling the void left by the
sudden eclipse of Marxism. This break stimulated me to re-evaluate
Mandel's work, to discover what is worth retaining and what has been
superseded and should be discarded. When the generation of '68 began to
study capitalism, they rediscovered the creative Marxist tradition of the
1920s and such authors as Gramsci, Lukács, Lenin, Trotsky and Luxemburg.
Novice Marxists were struck by their contemporaneity. The next generation of capitalism's critics should encounter the thinkers who enriched and
broadened the horizons of materialist thought in the 1970s and 1980s.
Mandel's positive and utopian spirit will be remembered, and his masterwork, *Late Capitalism*, and his theory of the long waves of capitalism will
once again be studied. Until now there has been no comprehensive
biography that reconstructs the landscape of Mandel's life and thought
and gives access to his work. This study aims to fill that gap.

I am greatly indebted to the Vlaams Fonds voor Wetenschappelijk Onderzoek (FWO, Flemish Fund for Scholarly Research), which gave generous support, under the sponsorship of Professor Els Witte of the Free
University of Brussels, allowing me to work uninterruptedly on this
biography for four years. Plans for the biography arose in conversations
with Dr Joost Kircz and with Professor Marcel van der Linden. I appreciate
their confidence enormously. I have Els Witte to thank for convincing the
Flemish academic world of the importance of my research. It was an honour
to work with her. Reaal Insurance subsidized my initial work, enabling me
to start on the book. The International Institute of Social History in
Amsterdam gave me a most hospitable base over four years, as well as
providing a stimulating and learned environment. In Marcel van der Linden
I had an erudite and reliable interlocutor. I am greatly indebted to him, as
well as to Anne Mandel-Sprimont and the Ernest Mandel Foundation,
which gave me permission to consult their Mandel collection. Although the
book is not a collective product – historical judgements are too fluid for that

– many others contributed their encouragement, ideas and criticism. I thank Hans Blom, Hans Boot, Willem Bos, Wilfried Dubois, Bruno Coppieters, Peter Drucker, Lex Heerma van Voss, Karin Hofmeester, Joost Kircz, Marcel van der Linden, Michel Mandel, Tom van der Meer, Klaas Stutje, Fritjof Tichelman, François Vercammen and Els Witte for their valuable comments. Without Wilfried Dubois's assistance the bibliography and footnotes would surely have been inadequate.

Finally I owe the most thanks to those who were willing to share their recollections of Mandel with me, whether orally or in writing, and the depth of their feelings. This book is dedicated to them: Gilbert Achcar, Elmar Altvater, Daniel Bensaïd, Bruno Coppieters, Helmut Dahmer, Guy Desolre, Jan Debrouwere, Georges Dobbeleer, Ernst Federn, Hilde Federn, Maurice Ferares, Maurice Fischer, Adolfo Gilly, Janette Habel, Willy van der Helst, Joost Kircz, Victor Klapholz, Gretchen Klotz-Dutschke, Leszek Kolakowski, Zbigniew Kowalewski, Hubert Krivine, Jean Van Lierde, Livio Maitan, Jan Malewski, Anne Mandel-Sprimont, Michel Mandel, Karl Manfred,[3] Klaus Meschkat, Wilbert van Miert, Jakob Moneta, Sigi Moneta, Bodo Morawe, Herman Pieterson, Max Plekker, Catherine Samary, Rudi Segall, Fritjof Tichelman, Charles-André Udry, François Vercammen and Robert Went.

Jan Willem Stutje

Translators' Note

One complication in translating the biography of a Belgian is the fact that towns, organizations and even streets sometimes have both Dutch (Flemish) and French names. We have used the French names for places and organizations in Wallonia and Brussels, and otherwise used the Dutch (Ernest Mandel was after all Flemish). We have followed this rule even when English readers might be more familiar with the French name. For example, we use Leuven instead of Louvain. However, we use distinctive English names (Brussels, Ghent) where they exist. In the List of Abbreviations, French acronyms are indicated in parentheses after the Dutch acronyms and English translations.

We would like to thank Charlie Post for his help in locating English-language sources.

Christopher Beck and Peter Drucker

List of Abbreviations

ABVV	General Belgian Trade Union Federation (post-World War II) (French: FGTB)
AJB	Belgian Jewish Society (World War II)
AMSAB	Institute for Social History (Ghent)
BAVI	Archives of the Belgian section of the Fourth International, Institute for Social History (Ghent)
BSP	Belgian Socialist Party (post-World War II) (French: PSB)
BWP	Belgian Workers Party (social-democratic, pre-World War II)
CCL	Confederation of Committees in Struggle (Belgium) (World War II)
CDU	Christian Democratic Union (post-World War II) (Germany)
CGT	General Confederation of Labour (French trade union federation, CP-led from 1940s to 1980s)
CRISP	Centre for Socio-Political Research and Information (Brussels)
DGB	German Trade Union Federation (post-World War II)
EEC	European Economic Community
ERP	Revolutionary People's Army (1970s) (Argentina)
FDP	Free Democratic Party (post-World War II) (Germany)
FI	Fourth International (since 1938)
FLN	National Liberation Front (since 1950s) (Algeria)
FO	Workers' Force (French trade union federation, since 1947)
FRG	Federal Republic of Germany (until 1990, West Germany)
FSSB	Socialist Students Federation of Belgium
FWO	Fund for Scholarly Research (Flanders)
GDR	German Democratic Republic (until 1990, East Germany)
GIM	International Marxist Group (German section of the Fourth International, 1970s)

GPU	Soviet secret service (1930s)
IC	International Committee (Fourth International)
IIRE	International Institute for Research and Education (Amsterdam)
IKD	International Communists of Germany (Trotskyists) (1930s and '40s)
IMG	International Marxist Group (British section of the Fourth International, 1970s)
IS	International Secretariat of the Fourth International
JCR	Revolutionary Communist Youth (since 1960s) (France)
KOR	Workers Defence Committee (1970s and '80s) (Poland)
KPB	Communist Party of Belgium (French: PCB)
LC	Communist League (French section of the Fourth International, 1969–73)
LCR	Revolutionary Communist League (French section of the Fourth International since 1973)
LCR-ETAVI	Revolutionary Communist League-Euskadi and Freedom VI (Spanish section of the Fourth International, 1970s)
MIR	Revolutionary Left Movement (1960s and '70s) (Chile)
MPW	Walloon Popular Movement (1960s)
MSU	United Union Movement (Belgium)
OCI	International Communist Organization (1950s and '60s) (France, 'Lambertiste')
OKDE	Organization of Internationalist Communists of Greece (section of the Fourth International)
OLAS	Latin American Solidarity Organization (1960s)
OSP	Independent Socialist Party (early 1930s) (Netherlands)
PCF	French Communist Party
PCI	Internationalist Communist Party (French section of the Fourth International, 1940s–60s)
POI	Internationalist Workers Party (French section of the Fourth International, late 1930s)
POR	Revolutionary Workers Party (Bolivian section of the Fourth International, since 1950s)
POR-S	Coordinating Committee of the Workers' Opposition (1980s) (Poland)
POUM	Workers Party of Marxist Unification (1930s) (Spain)
PRT	Revolutionary Workers Party (Argentinian section of the Fourth International, 1970s; Mexican section, since 1970s)
PSIUP	Socialist Party of Proletarian Unity (1960s–80s) (Italy)

PSU	United Socialist Party (1960s and '70s) (France)
PT	Workers Party (since 1980s) (Brazil)
PWT	Walloon Workers Party
RAL	Revolutionary Workers League (Belgian section of the Fourth International, 1970s) (French: LRT)
RCP	Revolutionary Communist Party (Belgian section of Fourth International, 1940s) (French: PCR)
RDR	Revolutionary Democratic Alliance (1940s) (France)
RSAP	Revolutionary Socialist Workers Party (1930s) (Netherlands)
RSP	Revolutionary Socialist Party (Belgian section of the Fourth International, 1930s) (French: PSR)
SAP	Socialist Workers Party (Germany, 1930s; Belgian section of the Fourth International since 1980s) (French: POS)
SBV	Socialist Movement of Flanders (1960s)
SD	(German) security service (1930s and '40s)
SDS	German Socialist Student Union (1960s)
SECTa	Service, Technical and Managers Union (Belgium)
SED	Socialist Unity Party of Germany (East German ruling party)
SFIO	Socialist Party (until 1971) (France)
Sipo	(German) security police (1930s and '40s)
SJV	Young Socialist League (Germany, pre-World War II)
SJW	Socialist Young Guard (Belgian Socialist and later Trotskyist youth) (French: JGS)
SOMA	Centre for Historical Research and Documentation on War and Contemporary Society (Brussels)
SPD	Social Democratic Party of Germany
SWP	Socialist Workers Party (since 1938) (US)
TKK	Provisional Coordinating Committee (of Polish Solidarity, 1980s)
UAW	United Auto Workers (US)
UGS	Union of the Socialist Left (Brussels left-wing socialists, 1960s)
VNV	Flemish National League (extreme right, 1930s and '40s)
VONS	Committee to Protect the Unjustly Persecuted (1970s and '80s) (Czechoslovakia)

Youth: 'My politics were determined then for the rest of my life'

Ernest Mandel would rarely place much emphasis on his Jewish background. Neither did his parents. No Yiddish was spoken in the family home; he did not read Hebrew; he received no religious instruction. In later life, he would later devote only a few articles to the question of Jewish identity. Like Leon Trotsky, the Ukrainian Jew who became a Russian revolutionary, Mandel's loyalties were above all to the working class, and he saw the question of Jewish oppression and liberation in the context of a world revolution.[1] He did not abandon his roots, but considered himself 'a Flemish internationalist of Jewish origin'. He was the non-Jewish Jew, a freethinker whose thoughts crossed the borders of different cultures and national identities, whose thought ranged beyond the limits of the society in which he was born, yet remained connected to it.[2] He preserved, however partially, ethnic and cultural ties that Trotsky cut.[3] He was able to join seamlessly his identities as internationalist, Jew and Flemish rebel.

From Krakow to Antwerp

Ernest Mandel owed his broad outlook and culture to his father, who raised him in an assimilated, cosmopolitan milieu. Henri (Henoch) Mandel was born on 12 May 1896, in Wieliczka, a Polish village in a rolling landscape known for its 700-year-old salt mines. The village lay just 15 kilometres south-east of Krakow, in the part of Poland then under Austrian rule. When Henri was ten, his parents bought a house in Krakow so that their children – Henri, his older brother, Simon, and his three younger sisters, Manya, Gina, and Bertha – could receive a better education. Krakow's large Jewish community was still mostly crowded into the Kazimierz ghetto, where for several hundred years Jews had been confined by law. In the early nineteenth century, the ban was lifted, and the more affluent and assimilated families moved into neighbouring districts, leaving behind Orthodox believers and the poor, who clung to the ghetto's narrow streets, baroque synagogues and Jewish cemetery, whose oldest headstones dated from the sixteenth century.[4]

The Mandel family was well off.[5] Henri's father owned a textile store, run mostly by his wife, with the help of Manya, her oldest daughter. As was customary among Orthodox Jews, the men of the family worked only at their studies. Henri, too, was set to studying the Bible, and acquired the necessary command of Hebrew and a thorough knowledge of Torah and Talmud, but had no interest in pursuing a religious education. Like his younger sister Gina, he felt drawn to the socialist–Zionist organization Poale Zion (Workers of Zion), and he refused to live by the strict rules of the Orthodox community. In July 1913, after completing secondary school, he left Krakow for Antwerp, hoping to continue his studies in the more secular atmosphere of the city on the Schelde, where he also had family connections.[6] He maintained little contact afterwards with his family in Poland. Only on the death of his father, in October 1932, would he visit his homeland again.

In Antwerp, he quickly learned French and Dutch, Belgium's two languages, but his plans for further study were interrupted by the outbreak of the First World War, in August 1914. That summer, as Antwerp prepared for a siege, ominous rumours made the rounds: the forts of Liège had fallen; Leuven had been burned to the ground – according to enemy high command, it was destroyed in reprisal after its citizens attacked German troops. Without warning, zeppelins had appeared above the city and dropped their bombs. While buildings went up in flames, the Belgian army withdrew westward towards the coast and Belgian civilians headed north in an endless procession, hoping to find refuge in the Netherlands.

Henri Mandel was one of these refugees. Because he held an Austrian passport, he was in danger of being conscripted into the Austrian army, and he wanted to avoid that at all costs.[7] He settled with an uncle and aunt in Scheveningen, then a seaside village near The Hague known as Little Warsaw because of the many affluent Jews of East European, German or Austrian origin who sought refuge there.[8] In Scheveningen, he found a job in a pharmacy and passed his free time in solitary study, concentrating on chemistry but also pursuing an interest in politics that he had begun to develop while still in Poland.

In The Hague he came into contact with young Communists and through them with fugitives from Germany. The party published a paper, *Der Kampf* (The Struggle); one of the contributors was Wilhelm Pieck (1876–1960), who succeeded Ernst Thälmann as leader of the German Communist Party in 1935 and after the war became the first president of the German Democratic

Republic. He had fled to the Netherlands to avoid conscription into the German imperial army, and for a while earned a living as a furniture maker in Amsterdam.[9] Later, when the revolutionary wind that was sweeping Europe blew full-strength into Germany, Mandel and Pieck hurried to Berlin to offer their services.[10] In Berlin, Mandel helped establish the Russian telegraph agency Rosta and the first Soviet Russian press bureau, the direct predecessor to Tass.[11] He moved in left-wing intellectual and journalistic circles and got to know revolutionaries such as Karl Radek, another Polish Jew with cultural roots in Germany, who had been sent as an envoy by Lenin and Trotsky to aid the German revolutionaries.

In January 1919, Rosa Luxemburg and Karl Liebknecht, leaders of the Spartacus League, were arrested and then murdered. Deeply shocked, Mandel returned at once to Antwerp,[12] and for the time being his direct participation in politics came to an end, though his interest in it did not.

In 1920 Henri established himself as a diamond merchant on Lange Kievitstraat, in the heart of Antwerp's Jewish neighbourhood.[13] Shortly afterwards he fell in love with Rosa Mateles, a distant connection of his mother's, who was living in Antwerp with her father, also a diamond merchant, and her brother Motek, or Markus. Like Henri, she was from Krakow, where her parents had run an art and antiques firm. In 1905 her father had begun travelling regularly to Antwerp, where he developed a relatively successful diamond business. The whole family moved there, from Krakow, in 1911 after the death of Rosa's mother. Father and son were observant Jews and highly respected in the Orthodox community – so much so that rabbis regularly came to the father for advice.[14]

As citizens of the Austrian Empire, Rosa, her brother and their parents were deported to Germany at the beginning of the First World War. They spent the war years in Frankfurt on Main, and by 1921, Rosa had returned to Antwerp,[15] where she met Henri Mandel. They were very close in age – she was just six months older than he – and had much in common. Henri Mandel was highly intelligent, expressing himself as easily in Polish, Hebrew, Yiddish and German as in French and Dutch. Rosa, too, had broad interests and from childhood spoke fluent German and Polish; in Antwerp, she had also learned Dutch and French, though she attended a private school that used German as its language of instruction. Unlike her brother and father, she was a freethinker, which suited Henri, who was opposed to any form of organized religion. She was also a beautiful woman, with a gentle yet dignified appearance, who seldom raised her voice. Her composed temperament contrasted with that of her husband, who was a dynamo, perpetually absorbed in some endeavour.[16] Rosa adored him.

They were married on 17 May 1921 and received the permits required for permanent residency, though this did not make them Belgian nationals. A year later, Rosa became pregnant. It proved to be a difficult pregnancy, and on her doctors' advice she checked in to a clinic in Frankfurt,[17] where Ezra (Ernest) Mandel was born on 5 April 1923.[18] After ten days in the hospital, she and the baby returned with Henri to Antwerp.

A cosmopolitan childhood

Henri Mandel had a dominant personality, was tall of stature, and appeared to emanate a natural authority.[19] He proved a successful diamond merchant, trading in Belgium and abroad, and was able to buy a luxurious house on Waterloostraat,[20] in Zurenborg, a fashionable neighbourhood of palatial villas and mansions with big gardens and imposing façades in a bizarre mix of styles – neo-classical, neo-Gothic and, here and there, art nouveau. Before 1914 the district had been home to a stylish upper middle class, prominent bankers, merchants and industrialists who had made their fortunes during a period of spectacular growth that began in 1863 with the lifting of Antwerp harbour's protectionist Schelde tolls, which had been levied on incoming ships since 1574.

Between the wars, a Jewish colony settled there. The new tenants of Zurenborg's apartments and rooms en suite were mostly diamond merchants and traders. Ernest and his younger brother, Michel, born in 1926, spent their youth in this neighbourhood.[21] They horsed around in the streets and became familiar with the mostly French-speaking local bourgeoisie, whose doings they observed daily. At home, they played to their hearts' content with friends and cousins.

Ernest and Michel Mandel were raised and educated by both parents, and from them gained an early love of literature, music and painting. They attended performances and exhibitions, and their home had one of the first electric phonographs and a large collection of recordings. They also enjoyed the use of a valuable library. *Die Neue Zeit* (Modern Times), the German social democratic weekly, and the works of Marx, Lenin, Gorter and Trotsky in Dutch and German were ready to hand, as well as literary classics in Russian, German, and French. At twelve or thirteen Ernest read Charles De Coster's *Thyl Ulenspiegel*, *De Leeuw van Vlaanderen* by Hendrik Conscience and Victor Hugo's *Les Misérables*. He later recalled that it was the ethical ideals embodied by the characters of Hugo's masterwork and the author's depiction of the Paris insurrection of June 1832 that made him a socialist: 'My politics were determined then, for good, for the rest of my life.'[22] He also read Dickens and Jack London, *Het gezin van Paemel* by Cyriel

Buysse, *Op hoop van Zegen* by Herman Heyermans, and, somewhat later, *Een mens van goede wil* by Gerard Walschap.

His taste in reading reflected his character. Ernest was a high-spirited child yet also serious and caring. Though he could laugh heartily, he was anything but light-hearted. In appearance he was most like his mother – he had her face, her soft, regular features and her smile – but in energy and tenacity he resembled his father. He had a powerful imagination, learned fast and excelled in all subjects at school. His brother took things more easily. For Michel, it was enough to reach the finish line with ease; he didn't need to reach it first. But Ernest wanted to win. Because of these differences they occasionally clashed. Then Ernest's mother would urge her older son to be sensible and behave,[23] but his father would sometimes explode, taking Michel's part, especially if the younger boy was being shut out of a game or only allowed to watch. This happened at times with 'Geheim Spelen' (the Secret Game), the favourite recreation of Ernest and Maurice Fischer, an older cousin and Ernest's best friend in those days. The youngsters had all sorts of adventures in an imaginary country, using various props to uncover a secret known only to one of them. Fischer recalled later that as the years passed, these fantasies became steadily more complex – farther journeys, a shipwreck à la Robinson Crusoe – and more realistic. When such topics as Nazi propaganda, anti-Semitism or the boycott of German products became subjects of their fantasy, the game evolved from exciting adventures to stirring debates. Ernest then proved particularly resourceful, discovering and indulging his love of oratory.[24]

The brothers attended Municipal Educational Institution for Boys No. 3, housed in the former residence of Baron Dhanis, colonizer of the Congo. The building lay on the Belgelei, one of the boulevards that adorned Antwerp from the mid-nineteenth century, after the city broke through its constricting ring of Spanish fortifications. The school had a good reputation. Reports on pupils were given every fortnight. In addition to instruction in their native Dutch, the pupils received extensive lessons in French.[25] Judging by his instructors' comments – 'a first-rate student', 'excellent', 'very good' – Ernest had little difficulty with this curriculum.[26] It was his habit while studying to skip through the room playing with a tennis ball; that was his manner of concentrating while learning a text by rote.[27] The method was successful: he was admitted to the Royal Athenaeum in 1936. That same year, he saw himself in print for the first time, when the Dutch weekly *Haagsche Post* ran a letter in which he complained about the indifference the Dutch showed to their own language.[28] It was also during this period that an incident at school made him fully aware of the existence of social inequalities and his own developing resistance to injustice. An instructor humiliated two of his classmates, working-class youngsters from the Rupel area, because of their head lice. 'It made my blood boil,' he recalled.[29]

The Royal Athenaeum had been built in 1818, when Holland and Belgium were still united, and stood proudly classical on Victorieplein (now Franklin Rooseveltplein), popularly known as the Geusenhofkes, a stone's throw from Central Station and the Antwerp Zoo.[30] The school was crowded, with 1,100 students, and, just as at Ernest's lower school, among them were a fair number of Jewish boys. There were even boys from Orthodox families, dressed not in their distinctive clothing but in the garb of students, trading their yarmulkes for the dark blue school cap, with its visor, red and white piping, and stars that indicated seniority, not race. In fact, the boys experienced little direct anti-Semitism: good-natured teasing, yes, but also solidarity. Michel, two classes behind Ernest, had classmates who at the start of the war suddenly appeared in the uniform of the Flemish National League (VNV), but this did not immediately lead to problems. When wearing the Star of David became mandatory, one of the other boys offered to accompany him in public.[31]

The Athenaeum was known as freethinking with Flemish leanings, but, as befitted an elite institution, it never lapsed into extremism. The library had thousands of titles, amply representing not only Flemish but also other literatures. The students were introduced to the great Flemish epic, Conscience's *De Leeuw van Vlaanderen* (The Lion of Flanders), and also to contemporary linguistic and cultural conflicts and the socioeconomic situation. Few of them could help noticing the social implications of the Flemish-language movement. The French-speaking Antwerp bourgeois spoke Flemish only to workers and servants. Championship of the Flemish tongue fitted well with the kind of local patriotism that Henri Mandel sometimes expressed;[32] he was not the only Jew with Flemish sympathies.

Ernest pursued the old-fashioned humanities, the Greek and Latin classics, with verve. He studied hard and was pleased when he was first in his year, something that did not always happen. During one term, a chronic middle ear infection caused him to fall behind; he was furious and only his mother was able to console him. He took his final examination in the summer of 1941, heading the entire school with 90 per cent of the available points, and received the coveted government medal inscribed 'summa cum laude'.[33] His history teacher, Leo Michielsen, who watched him develop into a Trotskyist, remembered his student as 'extraordinarily intelligent'.[34] 'Good in everything', acknowledged his classmate Jan Craeybeckx, who became a professor of history. 'Even in scoring handball goals! He was one of few who dared oppose the arbitrariness of some teachers.'[35]

Though he had also excelled in physics and chemistry Ernest was not inclined towards the exact sciences. Unlike his brother, who did pursue chemistry, he disliked anything mechanical. He was too romantic; technical subjects were not for him; music and literature were everything. Since his boyhood Mozart and Bach had been his favourite composers and the home library his goldmine. He devoured the novels of Marnix Gijsen. He loved his mother tongue, read poetry and tried to write it. When he was well past the age of fifty, he wrote to a publisher friend, 'I'll tell you a secret: in my youth I was "guilty" of some Flemish poetry, which I have carefully hidden but could never bring myself to destroy.'[36]

Since his return to Antwerp in 1919 Henri Mandel had been a successful independent businessman. But diamonds are a luxury business, traditional and small-scale, sensitive to economic ups and downs, and the trade was badly hit by the worldwide economic crisis that began in 1929. Mandel suffered heavy losses, exacerbated by the dishonesty of an associate who, unable to distinguish between 'mine' and 'thine', absconded with a supply of stones. Though the family was not impoverished – part of Henri's capital remained – their well-to-do life came to an end.[37] There were no more vacations at the coast, and the family had to look for more modest living quarters. Henri Mandel left the diamond business and accepted a job as director of Lemonime, a cooperative producer of spring water and soft drinks, while he cautiously explored opportunities as an insurance and mortgage agent.[38] Lemonime was based in Borgerhout; the factory was on Lanteernhofstraat, across from the Antwerp airport, and had a residence attached. The firm employed few workers, and Henri not only managed them but also laboured beside them in the factory.[39] Wages were not high, and after a few years' struggle he decided to devote himself entirely to insurance and bookkeeping. The family found a new five-room apartment in Deurne, on the Cruyslei, a pleasant street that connected Te Boelaer and Boekenberg parks, formerly private grounds. The boys walked in both parks and swam regularly in Boekenberg, which had an Olympic-size swimming pool, unusual in those times.

Hitler and Stalin

The world was changing, and soon the muses and his studies were no longer the only pursuits Ernest Mandel found worthy of his devotion. After Hitler seized power in Germany, political refugees flooded the neighbouring countries. In Antwerp, the Mandel house played a notable role in their reception. Henri Mandel recognized what Hitler's accession meant for the world. Ernest recalled that when he was nine, at the time of the so-called

Papen Putsch[40] in 1932, he heard his father speak prophetic, even apocalyptic words: 'This is going to turn out badly . . . This is the beginning of the end.'[41]

Ernest's social and political interests grew with the arrival of the refugees. They were so poor that often they ate only one meal a day, a soup made from half-spoiled leftovers that the greengrocers let them take as their shops closed. He listened eagerly to the conversations, began to read deeply and soon joined in the debates that took place in his family's home evening after evening. His sympathies – not surprisingly, considering the mostly Trotskyist background of the refugees – were with Trotsky and his followers, who were repressed by both Stalin and Hitler.[42] Surrounded by this living drama, Ernest, though still in his teens, felt more excitement than fear thanks to the intense political activity in which the family had always engaged.[43] New experiences with anti-Semitism also developed his political consciousness. One day, as he was returning from school, a snarling figure shoved him against some barbed wire, ripping a large hole in his only winter coat. Ernest hit him back. 'From my earliest youth, my father always impressed upon me that I should boldly and confidently defend myself, and never yield to anger or villains.'[44]

In helping to hide refugees, Henri Mandel did not act alone. A sizeable organization was involved and Jewish refugees especially were aided by generous donations from rich diamond merchants. These were stirring times and the rescuers did their work with spirit. The Austrian Trotskyist Georg Scheuer recalled, 'Comrade Henri Mandel sheltered us for several days. He was hospitable, witty and sparkling with humour and German-Yiddish puns.'[45] Scheuer, nicknamed Roter Hanzl (Red Hans) because of his red hair and the political beliefs that had repeatedly seen him jailed, was a founder of the Revolutionary Communists of Austria and had been on the run since 1938.[46] The refugees attempted to soothe their sufferings with humour. Scheuer told a typical story: 'Comrade Nissenbaum [Nut Tree] lived by chance on Nootenboomstraat [Nut Tree Street]. His dog was highly trained. On hearing the name "Schtallin" (Stalin), the poodle began to whine; for "Trotsky" he wagged his tail with joy.'[47]

But evil struck ever more frighteningly, as it did in Laren, an idyllic artists' colony 20 kilometres south-east of Amsterdam, where in 1934 the Dutch Independent Socialist Party (OSP) held an international youth conference on the movement for a Fourth International. Trotsky, who had left his Turkish exile and was staying in Barbizon, in France, attached great importance to this conference.[48] So did Stalin. The Dutch Communist Party received a telegram from Moscow, sent via the Comintern transmission service headed by Daan Goulooze, ordering them to attack the participants. 'In no circumstances can the Trotskyists be allowed to execute their criminal plans unmolested.'[49]

The conference organizers had failed to arrange adequate security.[50] The police were watching as the thirty to forty persons attending, many of them illegal aliens, assembled in the Roode Leeuw Hotel in Amsterdam to wait for the bus to Laren. At the conference, discussions had just begun when the police broke in and arrested the foreign delegates, among them Herbert Frahm, alias Willy Brandt, then not a prominent social democrat but a member of the left-wing Socialist Workers Party, or SAP. Also arrested were the Frenchman Yvan Craipeau, the American Albert Glotzer, and the Germans Fritz Besser and Walter Held. After two days in jail, they were deported to Belgium.[51] The delegates were not cowed, however; one day later the conference was resumed, in Café Maison d'Artiste in Brussels, directly opposite police headquarters.[52]

These events were extensively discussed at the Mandels'. Henri warmly welcomed the deported Fritz Besser, who arrived with identity papers in the name of Simon Schagen.[53] After Hitler's accession he had fled to the Netherlands, where his host was Henk Sneevliet, a revolutionary Marxist and cofounder of the Dutch, Indonesian and Chinese Communist parties.[54] With his childhood and school friend Heinz Epe,[55] publicly known as Walter Held, Besser was responsible for sending illegal publications, including *Unser Wort* (Our Word), to Germany via inland shipping from Rotterdam.[56]

The modest and unassuming Besser got on well with Ernest and Michel. He played the piano exceptionally well and gave both of them lessons.[57] Ernest quickly tired of scales and exercises.[58] He preferred listening to Besser's captivating speeches. Looking back, he would remember Besser as 'my best friend', and 'a teacher . . . humane, humorous and passionately socialist'.[59] 'More even than my father he moulded me into a Marxist, a militant in the Trotskyist organization. And he gave me the gift of love for classical music. Since then these have been the two bases of my existence.'[60] Henri Mandel provided Besser, who was poor as a church mouse, with a growing number of piano students and rented office space for him on Pelikaanstraat, where Besser could devote himself undisturbed to his political work in the shelter of the Utrecht Life Insurance Company.[61] Besser was always grateful to him. Long after the war he wrote to Ernest,

> You cannot imagine how lively he [Henri Mandel] still seems in my memory and how often I recall conversations with him . . . How often he kept me enthralled until the last tram had gone, leisurely telling me in his unique way some Jewish story or another, probably to the dismay of your mother, who then felt compelled yet again to make up a bed in the living room! . . . Of all the political animals I met in my life, he was one of the few human beings.[62]

Though Henri Mandel had given up practising Judaism in 1913, he never tried to hide his origins. He spoke frequently of the history of the Jewish people.[63] He took pride in his Zionist background and gladly talked about leaders of the labour movement in Palestine, like David Ben Gurion, who in 1948 would become Israel's first president, and Itzhak Ben Zvi, who later held the same office and whom Mandel had received in his home.[64] And in the 1920s Mandel himself was still devoting his energies to the League for Working Palestine, which provided moral and material assistance to the Jewish colonists of Eretz Israel.

In Antwerp, the Mandels had remained connected to the Jewish community through 'the trade' – as an insurance agent, Henri still did business with the diamond industry – and through the circle of German-Jewish political refugees. In this milieu Ernest learned early about 'the Jewish question' but still more about the wider world of revolutionary politics. He met Red Max, or Max Laufer, originally from Magdeburg, who escaped to Antwerp in 1936 with the help of refugees who had gone before him.[65] In 1937 Laufer ascended to the leadership of the German Trotskyist IKD.[66] Ernest also met Hermann Bortfeldt, another Magdeburg native, who after the war held an important position in the government of East Germany until discovery of his Trotskyist past forced him to flee to West Germany, where he became a high functionary in the Social Democratic Party.[67] Bortfeldt arrived destitute in Antwerp and was 'substantially helped throughout' by the Mandel family.[68] Beresch Nissenbaum from Odessa stopped in Antwerp on his westward journey and ended up staying as well. The soulful Nissenbaum worked as a diamond polisher, and when there was no work, he helped his wife make 'knepplechlachs' – buttonholes. He survived Auschwitz; his wife did not.[69]

For a while Else Bormann, another German refugee, helped the Mandel family with household tasks. She was a friend of Franz Meyer, a talented artist from Gelsenkirchen, in the central Ruhr region, who had immigrated to the Netherlands in 1934. Under the name Franz Holss, or the initials H, FH, SZ or BN, his woodcuts and linoleum prints appeared in the left-wing press of the day, even in the Dutch social democratic paper De Notenkraker (The Nutcracker).[70]

From late 1936 Franz Meyer and Fritz Besser oversaw publication of Unser Wort, the paper of the German Trotskyists who had organized themselves into the IKD. Meyer did the layout and illustrations;[71] the printing was done by Léon de Lee in his Antwerp printing studio and bookshop in Borgerhout, on Onderwijsstraat. A designer in Rotterdam provided the fonts.[72]

Joseph Weber was in charge of the group's political work.[73] Weber, alias Johre, was the son of a tile setter and, like Meyer, had been raised in

Gelsenkirchen. After studying philosophy for several years, he had switched to music, taking his examinations in conducting and composition.[74] Trotsky regarded him as one of the most important Marxist theoreticians of the younger generation.[75] He praised Johre's idiosyncratic view of resistance work. Johre believed opposing the Nazification of the church (Kirchenkampf) was of central importance, 'the first attempt to form a channel into which the broad democratic people's movement can flow'.[76] The working class had to 'unconditionally support every movement that would lead to a confrontation with the fascist state'.[77] These German revolutionaries stood apart from Antwerp's branch of the Revolutionary Socialist Party (RSP), a group of six or seven Trotskyist labourers led by Lode Polk, who had helped found the Belgian Communist Party in 1920. The group of German exiles was not much bigger, but unlike the Flemish RSP, consisted primarily of intellectuals.

The year 1936 was a turning point for Henri Mandel and the thirteen-year-old Ernest. Two events made a deep impression on them: the Spanish civil war and the Moscow trials.[78] The civil war evoked a flood of emotions. Perhaps ten young Belgian Trotskyists succeeded in reaching Spain.[79] Whether or not it was right to support the 'centrist' POUM (Workers Party of Marxist Unification) and whether there was or was not a Spanish section of the Fourth International were heavily debated questions.[80] Besser complained to Held about opportunism in the Belgian party and held the Brussels member Georges Vereeken, with his adulation of the POUM, primarily responsible.[81]

On May Day 1937 around 100,000 demonstrators marched through the streets in solidarity with the defenders of the Spanish Republic. Long after the war Ernest remained impressed. 'They were greeted with ovations – unforgettable!'[82] The Mandels were deeply involved with the Republican cause.[83] When thousands of anarchists and members of POUM were faced with Stalinist terror in 1937, the Mandels supported them through fundraising and other campaigns.[84]

People in Mandel's circle had no illusions about Moscow or Communists linked to the USSR. The case of Jef Last, a Dutch writer who questioned Soviet Communism, was striking. In 1936 he travelled through Russia with his friend André Gide, the future Nobel Prize winner. Gide's subsequent account, *Return From the USSR* was not flattering.[85] Last attempted to ease his own dissatisfaction by travelling to Spain to serve the Republican cause.[86] When Gide was overwhelmed with abuse from the Communists, Last defended him. Already suspect because of this, Last faced even worse after it was reported that a J. Last was appearing as a defence witness for Trotsky at the commission of inquiry in Mexico led by the American philosopher John

Dewey. The account appeared in the *Bulletin of the Committee for Justice and Truth,* a Belgian Trotskyist paper established by Henri Mandel with help from Fritz Besser and Léond de Lee, with the express purpose of spreading the truth about the trials of Trotskyists then under way in Moscow.[87] The Dutch Communist Party would not want a treacherous Trotskyist in its midst while the Moscow trials were in full swing. Last feared that he might share the fate of Ignaz Reiss, the head of the Red Army intelligence service, who had broken with Stalin and been assassinated by the GPU, the Soviet secret service, as he was preparing to join the Fourth International. He exerted himself to prove that he was not the J. Last in question. He contacted the Antwerp group[88] through the writer Harry Schulze Wilde,[89] and was soon able to inform his party bosses that there had been an error.[90] The troublesome witness was a Frenchman named Laste; the Dutch Last was assured that the final *e* had been dropped accidentally, though he was not allowed to see the original text; for security reasons, the Frenchman's identity could not be revealed.[91] Besser remembered that Last was definitely suspicious:

> He had just returned from Spain . . . In an interview that appeared in Antwerp he praised the solidarity and exemplary fighting spirit in the Republican camp. When I questioned this, he repeated the same nonsense until Harry [Schulze-Wilde] assured him that I was trustworthy. Then came a gruesome account of oppression and Stalinist death squads aimed at comrades, which even I . . . found almost unbelievable.[92]

Last's willingness to cover up Stalinist outrages was, sadly, typical of many left-wing intellectuals', and indicative of their lack of character.

Romain Rolland, Ernst Bloch and Lion Feuchtwanger all defended the January 1937 trials of the so-called opposition.[93] Feuchtwanger, a witness against Karl Radek although he spoke not a word of Russian, was the nadir for Henri Mandel.[94] Mandel had known the accused quite well and was so indignant that he formed a solidarity committee on the spot, and rebuked the cowardice of the widely honoured novelist in the publication 'Der Schutzgeist der Stalinschen Justiz' (The Tutelary Genius of Stalinist Justice).[95] Because he was not a Belgian citizen, to be on the safe side Mandel used the pseudonym Henri Almond (English for Mandel). His criticism was sharp:

> In what constitutional state anywhere, Mr. Feuchtwanger, would it go without saying that a prosecutor can, in the name of the law (!), demand the death penalty without offering the slightest proof of any crime? Or

were we perhaps all notorious idiots when we screamed blue murder in chorus at the judicial murder of . . . Van der Lubbe? You were one of us then, Mr. Feuchtwanger.[96]

Mandel had a strong sense of justice. He no longer had a good word to say about the miserable scribbler Feuchtwanger. If Feuchtwanger hoped to 'dispose of Trotskyism within and without the Soviet Union', then he had miscalculated: 'Precisely through the Moscow show trials the Stalinist cliques added many worthy supporters and fellow combatants to the Trotskyist movement.'[97]

The Fourth International

Henri Mandel was also thinking of himself. He had become closely involved in the work of the Fourth International. The committee met at his house, and he participated in the production of its pamphlets and the publication of its documents. His thirteen-year-old son became the group's most fiery supporter, putting in an appearance at all meetings.

Henri's polemic against Feuchtwanger was brought to Trotsky's attention by Fritz Besser, who pointed out that although the author was not a member of the organization, 'he has the greatest sympathy for us, as can be seen from his work; he is prepared to help us in every possible way, including financially, and above all to build our small publishing house into a big and financially healthy commercial undertaking.'[98]

In the spring of 1937 this new publishing house was established, with the goal of publishing in German the works of Trotsky and others sympathetic to the Fourth International. The initiative came from Besser and Henri Mandel, who this time chose the pseudonym H. Schaked (Hebrew for almond).[99] First, they took over the assets and liabilities of the publisher Editions De Lee. Shortly afterwards, they merged with Dynamo-Verlag, a Trotskyist publisher based in Zurich. Dynamo-Verlag became the official imprint of the new entity.[100] Its first publication was a 2,500-copy edition of Trotsky's *Verratene Revolution* (The Revolution Betrayed), at a time when no other publisher was prepared to produce a German edition of Trotsky's most important book.[101] Then on 1 December 1937, in collaboration with the International Secretariat in Paris, they began publication of *Der Einzige Weg* (The Only Way), the periodical of the Fourth International.[102]

With the crucial help of Mandel, Meyer and Besser, and watched by the eager-to-learn Ernest, the periodicals, printed on the cheapest paper available, rolled from the press of De Proletariër (The Proletarian), a small print shop on Onderwijsstraat, in the working-class neighbourhood of De

Seefhoek. The press was run by Léon de Lee, a short, black-haired, forty-year-old diamond worker. De Lee was no leader, orator or theoretician, but, according to Besser, he had an infallible class instinct, and he was quick to abandon his polishing stone on Somerstraat whenever a comrade asked for his help.[103]

Henri Mandel wrote to Trotsky's son Leon Sedov about his new involvement in the work of the organization, and proposed that the publishing effort be expanded into a profitable enterprise for the movement.[104] Its importance was growing as the war approached. There was a plan to transfer the German organization – or at least a number of its important members – to America. The connection with Europe would need to be maintained through regular German publications. This was something that Dynamo-Verlag, headquartered in Zurich and with branches in Antwerp and Prague, could do.[105]

By the end of the 1930s, premonitions of apocalyptic violence, of approaching worldwide cataclysm, were growing, and Henri Mandel felt bound to do whatever he could to halt the evil that not only Hitler but also Stalin embodied. Dismayed by the events in Moscow, he came to sympathize strongly with Trotsky. It was a defensive choice, born of his contempt for Stalinism; he did not share Trotsky's revolutionary expectations and was not prepared to justify the tragedy of Kronstadt.[106] He was not indifferent to the promise of communism, but he found the road to it too narrow to dedicate his life to its service. When darkness covered Europe, Mandel said farewell to revolutionary politics and sought other ways to defeat the forces of fascism and totalitarianism.

As his father took his leave of the movement, the young Ernest – or rather Ezra, as he was still called at the time – became actively involved in it. He was fifteen when he was admitted to the RSP, at the end of 1938. The founding conference of the Fourth International had just taken place, in September, in Périgny, a suburb of Paris.

The story of the Trotskyists' struggle to put their ideas into practice is punctuated by assassinations and disappearances, and the period immediately before the war, when Ernest joined the movement, was especially deadly. It was a hecatomb: in 1937 Ignaz Reiss and Trotsky's secretary Erwin Wolf were killed by the GPU; in February 1938 Leon Sedov died in suspicious circumstances in a Paris clinic; and in July the mutilated body of thirty-year-old Rudolf Klement, organizer of the imminent founding conference of the Fourth International, was recovered from the Seine. Ernest had known Klement, who came from Hamburg: 'He was an honest but totally overworked man, of whose qualities everyone was in awe.'[107]

Ernest got the news of Klement's death and of the conference from

Nathan (Nathie) Gould, one of three representatives from the US Socialist Workers Party (SWP) who toured Europe after the conference.[108] Gould spoke in Antwerp, at the Mandels' house on the Cruyslei. 'I think that it was after that meeting that I was formally admitted as a candidate member', recalled Mandel sixty years later in an interview with the British–Pakistani writer Tariq Ali.[109] The Antwerp group was a small one; besides German comrades such as Fritz Besser, Max Laufer and the artist Franz Meyer, there were Léon de Lee, Lode Polk, Camille Loots, who had been in Barcelona in 1937, the popular Pier Doremans and Jef van der Elst, a ship repairman, small in stature but a 'remarkable workers' leader . . . who had a mass audience' and who made an unforgettable impression on Mandel.[110] The Flemish Trotskyists were then working with the Anti-Oorlogsliga (Anti-War League), the socialist organization that had declared war on the war. But their pamphlets, written without passion as abstract propaganda, met with a tepid reception.

In 1937 the entire Belgian Trotskyist party, French and Flemish, had just 750 total members. It was strongest in French-speaking Wallonia, particularly among the miners in the Borinage, who, like their leader Walter Dauge, came originally from the social democratic Belgian Workers Party (BWP).[111] The 'old' spokesmen of the Left Opposition, Georges Vereeken from Brussels and Léon Lesoil, influential in the Charleroi basin, also played a significant role. But the group was far from stable, being given to vicious infighting. In 1938 Georges Vereeken with a few others established a new group, Contre le Courant (Against the Current). He took this step out of pessimism about the future of the world Trotskyist movement, which he felt remained too isolated. In his eyes, it was nonsense to proclaim the Fourth International on the eve of its disappearance.

Events that followed seemed to confirm Vereeken's views. When the war broke out, in September 1939, the RSP went into precipitous decline. The Borinage federation fell apart; its members, almost entirely from the working class, had been admitted without regard to their political commitment or experience – or lack of them. After the optimistic years of the struggle, they were the first to fall victim to doubt and demoralization.[112] The members in Charleroi were more seasoned. Like the Brussels and Antwerp groups, they included a high percentage of politically educated workers and could hang on to them. Nevertheless, on the eve of the German Occupation the party was a shambles. Of the 750 original members, only 80 remained. Fewer than half would prove suitable for rebuilding the party underground.

2

A Young Man in the War

There's nothing sacred now – the ties
Are burst of life's sublimest awe;
Before the vicious, virtue flies
And universal crime is law!
Man fears the lion's kingly tread;
And views the tiger's fangs with terror
And still the dreadliest of the dread,
Is man himself in error!
– Friedrich von Schiller[1]

On the morning of 10 May 1940, the forty-one-year-old Antwerp ship repairman Jef van der Elst was surprised by news of the German advance. He was astonished when the Belgian state security service entered his working man's home on Pionierstraat and asked him to accompany them. For Van der Elst, an ex-Communist who had converted to Trotskyism in 1925, the day ended in the Begijnenstraat prison.[2] Many shared his fate on that day or in the days that followed.[3] Besides such kindred spirits as the German artist Franz Meyer, who had been interned in Camp Merksplas, near Turnhout, since August 1939, many members of the Belgian Communist Party and the fascist-leaning groups VNV (Flemish National League) and Rex were arrested, along with former activists from the First World War and countless German and Austrian refugees.[4]

The 'ghost trains' left from Antwerp, Mechelen, Bruges, Brussels and Bergen, filled with prisoners, left-wing and right-wing mixed together, headed towards France. The train cars were labelled with chalked slogans – 'fifth column', 'spies', 'parachutists' – calculated to incite the curious who crowded the stations to harass the prisoners. It was a hellish journey that for men ended in the camps at Le Vernet and St-Cyprien, at the foot of the Pyrenees, and for women at Gurs.[5]

Van der Elst was spared the worst. His convoy was overtaken by the advancing German army, and its Belgian escort, no longer seeing the point of what they were doing, released the prisoners. Van der Elst returned to Antwerp on foot from northern France, a trek that lasted almost three weeks.[6]

The Mandels were in no danger from retaliation for suspected sabotage. They were Polish nationals, and unlike Van der Elst, who was known as an agitator in the Antwerp harbour, were not the subject of political rumours. Even so, in case the family should have to flee, Henri deposited a suitcase weighing 50 kilos at Denderleeuw Station, packed with linens, lace, silverware, miniatures and other personal belongings. It was never recovered after the war.[7]

The war had been under discussion for months. Unlike the Communists, Henri Mandel denounced the Molotov-Ribbentrop agreement, the mutual non-aggression pact between Germany and the Soviet Union. He reproached the Communists for refraining from criticizing Germany while not softening their criticism of England. In November 1939 the Belgian government signalled their own disapproval, banning publication of the Communist daily *La Voix du Peuple* (People's Voice). But they also banned the Trotskyist press, the papers *La Lutte Ouvrière* (Workers' Struggle) and *Contre le Courant* and also its pamphlets and brochures.[8] In those months revolutionary politics existed in a semi-illegal state.[9] Party activity gradually decreased because, as René Groslambert from Brussels put it, 'We knew that war was coming [but] did not know what to do.'[10] Meanwhile ordinary Belgians were quiet as mice, looking for guidance to a government that clung to neutrality and national unity as the only option.

Government repression and the people's tepid reaction were only partly responsible for the stagnation of the Trotskyist movement.[11] Squabbles within the Trotskyist family contributed as well. The behaviour of Walter Dauge, leader of the Borinage group, was astonishing. Under police questioning in September 1939 he betrayed Georges Vereeken by divulging his pseudonym, Give, which Vereeken had used to sign a manifesto against the threatening war. This paper had attracted the attention of the authorities.[12] They arrested Vereeken but could not prove that he was Give until Dauge helped them out.[13] Several members wanted to expel Dauge from the party, but Léon Lesoil, next in importance to Dauge in the RSP (Revolutionary Socialist Party), spoke against this, insisting that a motion of censure was sufficient.[14] According to the American Trotskyist Sherry Mangan, in a letter to the International Secretariat and the leadership of the SWP, Dauge himself argued that 'V's [Vereeken's] action was a sheer provocation, that by doing as he [Dauge] did he protected the rest of the party'.[15]

Walter Dauge (1907–44) was not a leader the party would have lightly dismissed. He was from Flénu, in the centre of the Borinage coal region, which in the 1920s and 1930s had been the very symbol of protests against exploitation.[16] He came from a family of working-class socialists; his father was a mine worker, his mother a seamstress. Dauge entered the revolutionary movement after the strikes in the summer of 1932. The struggle meant everything to him, especially the general strike. He was a gifted speaker, appearing for a time on the French-language radio broadcasting system. The miners idolized him. Beginning in the summer of 1935 he edited *L'Action socialiste révolutionnaire* (Revolutionary Socialist Action), a paper to which Paul-Henri Spaak also contributed until, in that same year, he joined the Van Zeeland cabinet, a government of national unity.[17] During his tenure the Belgian Socialist Party (BWP) anticipated a breakthrough at the national level; when it failed to materialize, Dauge's position in the party became untenable. In 1936 he and his cohorts left the socialist mainstream and joined the Trotskyists. Next to Georges Vereeken, another working-class comrade – a Brussels taxi driver – and Léon Lesoil from Charleroi, Walter Dauge became the movement's best-known leader. He exchanged letters with Trotsky during Trotsky's time in Norway. In the Flénu local council election of 1938, he received an absolute majority. The king prevented his being named mayor because Dauge had refused to swear allegiance to the crown.

Dauge personified the always visible divisions within the Trotskyist movement. The core of the party – ideologically trained, well educated and coming from the Communist Party – coexisted uneasily with the hundreds of uneducated, often illiterate mine workers from the Borinage, who came from the BWP and were under the influence of Dauge, a brilliant leader but not a Marxist and certainly not a Leninist.[18]

As soon as the war broke out, the miners' combativeness gave way to anxiety and confusion. A party member from Brussels who visited Flénu as the Occupation was beginning later recalled, 'They were seized by panic and dared not move. They even refused to distribute leaflets for fear that their leader would be arrested.'[19]

Dauge himself wanted to remain law-abiding, as the Vereeken affair showed. A report to the secretariat of the Fourth International noted, 'Since the outbreak of the war, Dauge is flouting the will of the party. He is not resisting the dictatorship . . . He will have nothing more to do with illegal activities . . . This has completely demoralized his federation.'[20] Moreover, Dauge seemed ill and subject to the darkest thoughts.

But even before the RSP went underground it had fallen apart. Of the 700 members in the Borinage, only a handful remained active after 10 May.

Dauge went his own way. He broke with politics, got involved in smuggling and entered into dubious contacts with Rexists. In 1944, he was murdered.[21] The Communist *Drapeau Rouge* (Red Flag) exulted at this 'well-deserved punishment' for 'that vile Trotskyist collaborator'.[22]

Describing that period in later years, Ernest Mandel emphasized that the RSP was unprepared morally and politically to go underground. He attributed this to the party's hybrid character. In Brussels, Antwerp and Liège it was a tight group of experienced activists but in the Borinage and Charleroi it was an 'organization with a popular following, based . . . on the mine workers who unavoidably adopted the ideas and concerns of their surroundings . . . The ranks of the RSP were thus infected with the hesitations and disappointments evoked by the war.'[23]

This malaise lasted almost a year, while the leadership, thrown off balance, focused on safeguarding and strengthening its cadres while waiting for a more favourable climate for mass agitation.[24] But even that intention came to nothing when Walter Dauge and Léon Lesoil, the strongest opponents of illegal action, were arrested on 10 May 1940, along with Van der Elst, Meyer and many other comrades.[25] The remainder sank into passivity. Even Lesoil ceased all political activity after his release. So did Lode Polk, like Lesoil, a veteran of the anti-Stalinist opposition. The organization shrank to a couple of dozen members who barely stayed in contact with one another. When the Trotskyists once again began to organize, in August 1940, younger militants, some of whom had joined after the strike actions of 1932 and some after 1938, took the lead.

The call to resist

The fighting came to an end in Belgium on 28 May 1940. The government and the leaders of the Socialist Party and trade unions fled the country and Hendrik de Man, the former minister and party chairman, called for collaboration with the German occupying forces. Trade union leaders who remained decided to suspend all actions for the duration of the Occupation. Hampered by the Soviet-German non-aggression pact, the Communists also struggled with their position. In Antwerp, they continued to publish a legal paper, *Ulenspiegel*, which focused its criticisms on the French and English.[26] The Antwerp paper proclaimed 'the purest and most complete neutrality . . . We call upon all those desiring peace firstly to behave correctly towards the occupier.'[27] The people in the streets were filled with anger at the old guard for being the first to run away and tense uncertainty about what the Occupation would bring.

These developments shocked Ernest Mandel.[28] Most in the Athenaeum

were convinced that the Germans would win the war with ease.[29] Many of
his political friends had disappeared. Fritz Besser was in London.[30] So was
Max Laufer, repatriated in the nick of time. Franz Meyer and Else Bormann
were in French prisons. To avoid being arrested again after his return from
France, Jef van der Elst had signed up with the pro-German Union of Blue-
and White-Collar Workers for voluntary labour in Germany.[31] This was a
tough decision for an activist known in the Antwerp shipyards as 'the little
Communist', because of his small stature.

Then Trotsky was assassinated. Belgian papers reported his death on 21
August 1940. The news fell like a bomb. Many of his followers sought
comfort in the house on the Cruyslei. Lode Polk showed up distraught. He
had known Trotsky personally, corresponded with him and received him in
his home when the Russian revolutionary passed through Antwerp on his
way to Norway.[32] Soon other comrades arrived. The group of seven or
eight men decided that it was long past time to resist. In the days that
followed their plan expanded to include about eleven people, all of whom
had known one another for years. At the beginning of September 1940 they
founded the 'independent, patriotic' resistance group Vrank en Vrij (Open
and Free).

Though the original goal was only to distribute leaflets, the propaganda
machine of the collaborationist right-wing Flemish National League (VNV)
persuaded them that their own plan was too modest, and they decided to
publish a monthly paper. The first issue of *Het Vrije Woord* (The Free Word)
appeared in an edition of 3,000 at the end of September, run off on an
automatic Gestettner copying machine that Henri Mandel had acquired
before the war. They had been unable to find a willing publisher.[33]

So the first underground Flemish-language paper was produced in the
Mandels' own home, and the entire family participated.[34] Eventually the
publishing group expanded to about a hundred members, divided into six
branches for greater security. Camille Loots, a twenty-nine-year-old Trotskyist and veteran of the Spanish civil war, was responsible for distribution in
Brussels. Jean Briquemont, ten years older, was responsible for the members'
safety. He arranged false identity papers and led a resistance group in the
trade school he directed in the town of St Pieters Woluwe. Other key
members were personal connections of the Mandels' who had helped found
the group. Marcel Devlieghere, as chief inspector of the Belgian General
Insurance Company, was a colleague of Henri Mandel's. Cécile Piller was a
single woman who acted as a courier until September 1943, when she was
betrayed to the Gestapo in Forest, a Brussels borough. Maurice Spiegel had a
son at the Athenaeum, who helped Michel and Ernest distribute the paper at
the school. When the deportation of Jews from Mechelen began in July

1942, this boy escaped to France and joined the Resistance. His parents tried to flee, too, but were captured and died in Auschwitz.

Het Vrije Woord was initially distributed in Antwerp and environs, usually in homes and stores during the evening, but also in post offices and railway stations, and on trams and trains. Its four (sometimes six) pages were read as far away as Mechelen and Turnhout. The average print run was a bare 5,000. After the Wehrmacht invaded the Soviet Union, in June 1941, an issue was published in German especially for the soldiers.

The paper surely owed some of its success to its inclusiveness. No overt ideological vision was articulated in *Het Vrije Woord*; it was an independent, anti-Nazi paper that found its way from hand to hand in a mixed political milieu.[35] This was remarkable, considering that a substantial part of the active group, around 15 per cent, were Trotskyists. Ernest and his father wrote the lion's share of the articles.[36] Henri could not have wished for a better platform for unity propaganda. The paper's central theme was the defence of freedom against the occupiers and their lackeys in Rex and the VNV. England's resistance gave the writers 'JUSTIFIED HOPE that NOT HITLER, BUT THE FREE PEOPLES, NOT THE THIRD REICH, BUT England, France, the United States and probably THE SOVIET UNION as well, will have the final say in this world war.'[37] When Mussolini attacked Greece, seventeen-year-old Ernest expressed his firm conviction that 'Great Britain will stand beside the courageous Greek people . . . It is not only a question of British honour and tradition to stand by her friends and allies, but in this war against the Axis powers also a means of self-defence.'[38] (Ernest had long abandoned this perspective by the time the British smothered the Greek revolution with blood five years later.)

The paper took a clear position when the first anti-Jewish regulations were announced in the *Verordnungsblatt* (Official Gazette) on 6 November 1940.[39] It was the first of the Antwerp Resistance papers to report the story, and it warned readers that the regulations were 'only the BEGINNING', that 'Nazi barbarism [knew] no bounds', and that against 'the brown and black Nazi plague true Belgians [could] give only one answer: SABOTAGE!'[40]

But not all Belgians were 'true' in that sense. Anti-Semitic riots broke out in April 1941 around Pelikaanstraat and Lange Kievitstraat after a screening of *Der Ewige Jude* (The Eternal Jew) in Cinema Rex on the Keyzerlei. Hundreds of members of People's Defence, the Black Brigade and the Flemish SS armed themselves with sticks and metal bars and attacked every Jew they encountered, shouting 'Damned Jews!' 'Death to the Jews!' and 'Down with the bastards!'[41] Synagogues and Jewish-owned stores were also targets. *Het Vrije Woord* insisted once again that 'JEWISH PERSECU-TIONS by the Nazis are not fables but bitter REALITY!' The paper also declared that the riots had filled the Antwerp population with 'horror and disgust', but the editors must have known that this was not the whole truth.[42] A pogrom had taken place unchecked and had gone unpunished, and there continued to be regular anti-Jewish disturbances in the once tolerant city on the Scheldt.

Ernest Mandel left school that summer; he had planned to study history at the Free University of Brussels, but the professors decided almost unanimously in November to suspend classes, in protest against the appointment of three teachers sympathetic to the Nazis.[43]

His family had been officially registered as Jews since December 1940, and had to be careful at all times not to offend the authorities. In June 1942 they were ordered to begin wearing the yellow star. The stars were distributed at the building on the Belgiëlei where the boys had attended primary school; a strip of three cost a franc. In their identity cards the letter *J* was stamped in black ink. Eleven days later, on Wednesday 22 July, came the first round-ups. All those who were taken by the Germans that day were sent to their deaths in Auschwitz.

Henri Mandel knew well enough that the star on his coat was the last step before deportation.[44] He had already reached the conclusion that the goal of the 'Nazi barbarians' was to destroy 'all the Jews within their power', not only to 'persecute them in the most barbaric ways' but also 'exterminate them systematically'.[45] He warned Ernest and Michel to be ready to go into hiding.[46] He sold such costly possessions as the old family jewels and three oriental carpets and stored part of his library, some paintings and other valuables with friends.[47] He also acquired false identity papers, issued to 'Nicolas Jules Robert'. Worried that fourteen-year-old Michel looked too Jewish, he ordered the boy to stay inside during the day. Ernest and Michel also sought a home for Bibi and Titi, two parakeets that flew freely around the Cruyslei house.

Many other members of Vrank en Vrij, and most workers in the diamond trade, were of Jewish background;[48] Henri Mandel encouraged all of them to go into hiding and not to report to the Dossin Barracks in Mechelen, the terminal for the trains to the East. Rosa's elderly father and her brother Motek shaved their beards and left for Switzerland. Maurice Spiegel and his family made their ill-fated attempt to reach America via Portugal.

'Don't report, don't report!' Jef van der Elst felt like screaming it out. The centre on Pelikaanstraat where Jews were ordered 'to report for work' was the departure point for transport to Mechelen. Like the Mandels, Van der Elst tried to convince people not to obey. His campaign went well until the security service (SD) descended. Van der Elst escaped, barely in time.[49] Other friends were less fortunate. Nissenbaum disappeared. As for Lode

Polk, one day he showed up at home and was ordered to accompany a German soldier, supposedly to the dentist. Before departing with his captive, the soldier, out of who knows what nostalgic impulse, set his gun against the mantelpiece and asked if he might pinch the suckers on the tomato plants in the garden. 'Why don't you grab his weapon and shoot him dead?' Polk's son asked despairingly. Polk answered the boy, 'The man has kids; you don't do that.'[50] No one ever saw Polk again.

In mid-August Cécile Piller warned the Mandels that the Gestapo was on their track.[51] Overnight the family finally decided to flee. Ernest was away; up to his ears in work. He stayed mostly with comrades, usually in or near Brussels, Liège or Charleroi. Henri, Rosa and Michel ripped the yellow stars from their clothes, grabbed their suitcases and got on the train to Brussels. There they found shelter in a furnished villa in Tervuren that the Trotskyist party had rented in order to offer comrades temporary refuge. The house was managed by twenty-five-year-old, red-haired Christiane Vanacker.[52] Frederic, her boyfriend, younger than she, Jewish, and a party member, was in hiding elsewhere. Christiane looked after the Mandels and did their shopping; Rosa and Michel, who did not yet have false identity papers, could not go outside.[53] When their papers were ready, they left for a new hiding place in the Ardennes. Henri stayed behind in Brussels, where he prepared to resume publication of *Het Vrije Woord*. A contact informed him that the Gestapo had raided the Cruyslei apartment sometime around 20 December.[54] Had they been looking for the publisher of *Het Vrije Woord*? Or simply carrying out operation Möbelaktion, the plundering of Jewish possessions?[55] Whatever their motive, the Germans had seized the part of the library that had not been moved to safety – around 1,400 volumes – and torn the rest of the apartment apart. Four entries in the SD tracking registry read: 'Disappeared; on 24/2/43 deleted from Antwerp.'[56]

East European migrants and international links

By now the Trotskyist movement had recovered from its apparent disintegration at the start of the Occupation. After Trotsky's assassination a handful of Antwerp comrades had united to breathe new life into the organization, seeking contact with like-minded friends in Brussels.[57] This re-formed group had largely escaped the arrests of May 1940; only René Groslambert and Hans Alexandrovich, a Viennese-born radio technician, had been interned. Groslambert was held in Camp Le Vernet but was back in Brussels by the end of July 1940.[58] Alexandrovich was shuttled from Camp Lalande to Drancy, and landed in Auschwitz in September 1942.[59]

The new group was led by Abraham Wajnsztock, alias Abraham Léon; Optat Henry, pseudonym Sem, a self-effacing professor at the University of Brussels and an RSP member since 1936; Camille Loots; and Philippe Szyper. Léon, a twenty-two-year-old Jew born in Warsaw, played a key role. He had moved with his parents to Brussels in 1928, where he was active in the Hashomer Hatzair (Young Guard), a socialist–Zionist youth movement that had been started around the time of the First World War. In 1939 he and some twenty kindred spirits had left that movement and joined the Trotskyists.[60] He would not survive the war, but his book, *The Jewish Question: A Marxist Interpretation*, an original perspective on the distinctiveness and continuity of Jewish history, did. The introduction to this posthumously published work, which Léon completed in 1942, was written by Ernest Mandel. Under the pseudonym E. Germain, Mandel paid tribute to his friend's accomplishments and character:

> When Léon joined international communism, the workers' movement seemed dead in Belgium . . . The situation seemed to justify only resignation and watchful waiting. Any other attitude appeared like a manifestation of desperate and impotent revolt. What was lacking was not so much courage to act as courage to think . . . Léon noted that the workers' movement in Europe had already reached the lowest point of its ebb. It was necessary not to await it passively but to prepare for it.[61]

The end of the first year of the war saw the beginning of a renaissance for the Trotskyists, and Abraham Léon was its moving force. Once the new organization had been consolidated, Léon was named its political secretary, and the group began to publish a monthly paper, *La Voie de Lénine* (Lenin's Way). The editing was done in Brussels. The galleys were then hidden in satchels with false bottoms and carried to Liège, where the paper was printed on an illegal press, which also published *Travail* (Work), the paper of André Renard's unified Trade Union Movement (MSU).[62] The Trotskyists had been in contact with the thirty-two-year-old leader of the Liège metal workers since his medical release from a German prisoner of war camp in May 1942.

Ernest Mandel met Léon for the first time in Brussels in June 1941, at a gathering of the central committee of the reawakened RSP, now called the Revolutionary Communist Party (RCP).[63] By the end of the 1930s, many children of Eastern European immigrants had found their way into the Trotskyist movement. Like Léon they had participated in the Hashomer Hatzair, which prepared pioneers for emigration to Palestine and which by 1925 had branches in Antwerp and Brussels. Second-generation immigrants like Léon, who saw their integration into non-Jewish society blocked by the economic crisis yet rejected the idea of returning to traditional Jewish ways, turned out to be impatient rebels. Emigration to Palestine seemed an insufficient solution to the majority of lives crippled by poverty and unemployment. Communism, on the other hand, offered a universal way out. In the early 1930s the radicalization of Jewish youth mostly benefited the Third International, but that began to change when it became clear that the German Communists were unable to stop Hitler, and the nationalistic politics of the Popular Front and the anti-Semitic Moscow trials closed the door for good.[64] Though the Antwerp group remained sympathetic to Stalinism, the Brussels pioneers were open to Trotskyist influences from 1936 or 1937.[65] Encouraged by Léon, they joined the RSP.

Jewish support for the party was strengthened in other ways. In 1939 Paul Widelin, pseudonym Victor, joined.[66] A promising student of mathematics, he too had been a member of Hashomer Hatzair and had lived in Poland and Berlin until the invasion.[67] With the Gestapo hot on his trail, he fled to Brussels, where Léon took him in. Ernest Mandel, who remained in Antwerp until July 1942, retained a vivid memory of his first meeting with Paul Widelin: 'I was struck by his courage . . . He was far from impressed by the Germans . . . He already had long experience of clandestine activities.'[68] In May 1943 Widelin moved to Paris, where, along with Paul Thalmann, he produced the first issue of *Arbeiter und Soldat* (Worker and Soldier). German soldiers helped with its distribution until betrayal made the work impossible. In July 1944 Widelin was killed by the Gestapo.[69]

As soon as the RSP was functioning once again, as the RCP, Léon began to renew its international connections. He failed to make contact with Henk Sneevliet's Marx-Lenin-Luxemburg Front in the Netherlands, but had better success with France. In January 1942 a French delegation made first contact in Brussels, using a safe route between Tourcoing and Mouscron. This encouraging overture was quickly followed by the founding meeting of the first European Secretariat of the Fourth International, in St-Hubert in the Ardennes.[70] In deepest secrecy, half a dozen comrades gathered at a farm owned by Optat Henry's family. Henry, Léon and probably Widelin made up the Belgian delegation. Marcel Hic, Yvan Craipeau and the twenty-two-year-old Parisian Emile Guikovaty represented France. Guikovaty, who never understood why he of all people had been asked to be a delegate, remembered the conference this way: 'There were six of us and we ate Ardennes ham in the evenings'.[71]

For the others, at least, the great point of the conference was to decide what position to take on the national question, that is, the right of the occupied countries to self-determination. This was a special concern of the Belgian revolutionaries. Many comrades were of the opinion that as long as the Nazi regime showed no signs of falling apart, struggling to rebuild a parliamentary democracy was senseless. They favoured a period of observation and preparation over open resistance. This position was defended notably by Georges Vereeken in *Contre le Courant*. But Abraham Léon wanted nothing to do with the forty-five-year-old Vereeken's short-sighted fatalism. Instead, he called for supporting every form of resistance and at the same time trying to expand that resistance into a revolutionary working-class movement.[72] Some critics of the RCP had accused the new party of chauvinistic tendencies;[73] at this clandestine congress in 1943, Léon proudly declared that the party had played a role in every social action in Belgium since 1941, including the protests surrounding the closing of the university in Brussels, the strikes in Antwerp and Liège in 1941 and the resistance to anti-Jewish measures and deportations.

Still the Trotskyists waited in vain for their great breakthrough. There had been some encouraging signs of interest in the RCP, but these were largely owed to the Trotskyists' being the only party visibly involved in fighting the Occupation, a situation that lasted until March 1941. Once the Communists reappeared on the stage – proceeding cautiously at first, then aggressively after Hitler's attack on the Soviet Union – the Trotskyists rapidly lost their advantage.[74]

In the view of Yvan Craipeau, Trotsky's former secretary, the RCP was hardly aware of how much resistance there actually was. Craipeau declared that the party still had a long way to go: 'The RCP has kept too much from the RSP – its social democratic naïveté, its provincialism, its federalism and its legalism.'[75] Ernest Mandel, too, wondered if the RCP was capable of leading the working class to victory.[76] In a document of some twenty-five closely typed pages, Mandel, himself not yet twenty years old, pleaded for propagandizing among young workers, on whom the depressing defeats of the past had left the fewest traces. He had no patience with those who sat on the sidelines waiting for the ideal moment to carry out a perfect action: 'Better to do a lot of work with errors than little work without them.' He also knew that anyone who termed resistance to deportations Germanophobic or called hungry people marching on the German commandant's office nationalistic understood nothing about working-class struggle. Of course he rejected the delusions of outright chauvinism, but he emphasized that every people – the Flemish and Walloons included – had the right to self-determination, and that militants must always support people fighting for that right. And although some groups, like the Communist-inspired Independence Front, were struggling for nationalistic ends, that should not lead anyone to the 'absurd' conclusion that 'the revolutionary struggle and every class struggle must be postponed as long as the German occupation lasts'.[77]

Mandel wrote with genuine insight into the theory of the workers' movement, drawing on a rich reservoir of historical knowledge, with almost playful ease citing Marx, Lenin, Luxemburg and Trotsky to support his arguments. He was more a teacher than a propagandist, though he did not disdain the latter role. But his often striking metaphors were backed by self-confidence and a firm grasp of reality. He sought to make the big connections and he expressed a contagious optimism. Looking back much later, he recalled, 'I was a young man, not very mature – very foolish from many points of view – but I must say that I never doubted that one day the Nazis would be defeated. Of that I was absolutely convinced. This led me into some crazy actions.'[78] He was not alone in that.

Arrest and escape

Was it inattention, or underestimation of the risks they ran, or were the comrades simply tired of hearing how dangerous their work was? Perhaps they were lulled into complacency by their belief that the security police (Sipo) had more dangerous opponents to contend with.[79] However it was, the small group of Trotskyists forgot to observe the unwritten but strict rules of illegal political action, and operation Solstice took them completely by surprise. On 22 June 1941, the morning of the German invasion of the Soviet Union, at least thirteen Trotskyist militants were arrested. Fortunately, these did not include the party's leadership. Most of the thirteen, in fact, had stopped their political activity at the start of the Occupation. Clearly the Sipo had been using out of date evidence, gathered before the war.[80] Just the same, it was frightening.

The Germans had timed the sweep carefully, well aware that defence of the Soviet Union, 'the socialist fatherland' was central to the Communists' commitment. The Communist paper *Drapeau Rouge* ran the headline 'Thousands of arrests in the country!'[81] Such exaggeration was presumably meant to strengthen the comrades' resolve, but instead heightened the general anxiety and aided the occupiers' efforts to discourage any spirit of resistance.

But gradually, nervous circumspection gave way to the reassuring acceptance of the routine. The risks of subversion (for non-Jewish comrades) were seldom life-threatening. What was there to fear from an occupier that punished the massive Liège strikes with eight days of forced labour for a few hundred strikers?[82] It was no different elsewhere. Jef van der Elst reported that managers fearful of provoking further unrest responded to worker sabotage by looking the other way. Production at the Mercantile and the Engineering, Antwerp's two largest shipyards, fell to a quarter of the pre-war level.[83]

Jef van der Elst and Ernest Mandel spoke with each other regularly. Above the introduction to the yellowing manifesto 'To all workers: we will not be silent', Van der Elst scrawled: 'Written and published with Mandel's foreknowledge' – tacit admission of a close collaboration.[84] After his return from Germany, Van der Elst was put to work in the EKLA aeroplane factory near Deurne, where planes for the Luftwaffe were repaired. Hired as an assistant pipefitter, he earned the lowest wage, but he learned from a German co-worker how to interfere with a plane's brakes so that the plane would only crash after its third or fourth landing.[85] When he got the chance, he went back to work repairing ships. His heart lay there, with the men he knew well, who greeted him as one of their leaders.

Despite the Trotskyists' courage, their carelessness and inexperience continued to take a toll on their ranks. The various cells maintained contact with one another and, more dangerously, stayed aware of each other's activities.[86] After August 1942, Ernest Mandel was forced to go under-ground, earlier than the other members of the leadership, because the Sipo was looking for the publishers of *Het Vrije Woord* and because of the round-ups. Comrades of Jewish background had special reason for caution.

The risks for Mandel were great as long as the party members with whom he kept in contact maintained their legal status. One of these members was Camille Loots. Loots was a clerk in the Central Distribution Fund of Social and Fiscal Premiums on Rue Royale in Brussels. He was arrested at his work by two plain-clothes Gestapo agents shortly after the lunch break.[87] Some office colleagues had betrayed him after overhearing him encourage another colleague to join the Resistance. Loots was taken to St-Gillis prison and interrogated a few times at Gestapo headquarters on Avenue Louise. On the day of his arrest his home in St-Agatha-Berchem, near Brussels, was searched. Mandel had been living there clandestinely since September 1942 but, fortuitously, had left the apartment just before the Germans arrived.[88] Less fortu-nately, en route it occurred to him that he had forgotten to take a bag of groceries. He went back and ran smack into the Gestapo. Who was he and what did he have in his case? Mandel showed an identity card in the name of Ernest Raes and opened the case. Out fell a bundle of flyers that he and Loots had produced the previous evening. At Gestapo head-quarters they determined that Mandel's identity card and the address he had given them were both false. They pressed him harder, and mean-while quickly discovered his real identity from letters exchanged be-tween Referat IV A, the section of the Sipo specializing in combating Communism and Marxism, and the St-Gillis Wehrmacht prison.[89] In the margin of one a Star of David was sketched in pencil. The Sipo in

Antwerp checked out the Cruyslei apartment and concluded that it had been vacant for some time; it had also been turned upside down.

A small group of comrades met in Brussels to discuss the situation. The first to speak was Albert Clement, a strapping twenty-six-year-old mechanic from cell number 3, who was responsible for various technical and financial tasks: acquiring paper and printing materials; guaranteeing the wages of party employees; and assisting comrades and their families when they were forced to go underground. Money was always scarce, but by hook or crook he got what was needed.

Clement said, 'What it comes down to is that Ernest is being held and there's a chance to free him.' Then he turned to Claire Prowizur. 'Contact needs to be made with a woman who has ties with the Gestapo and can influence his release. Will you do that?'[90] Claire Prowizur was then twenty and had just married Philippe Szyper, a tailor and member of the RCP executive committee. Both she and her husband were the children of Polish immigrants. Prowizur, born in Altona, near Hamburg, had been less than a year old when her parents moved to Brussels. Her childhood was spent in poverty. She and Szyper got to know each other in the Brussels branch of the Bund, the non-Zionist Jewish socialist movement that belonged to the Socialist (Second) International. The RSP had encouraged Szyper to join the Bund in order to make contact with what they were in the habit of calling 'interesting elements'. At seventeen, Claire had turned away from her Jewish roots and joined the RSP: 'I slid gently into Trotskyism.'[91]

Prowizur did not know Ernest Mandel personally. She had only met him once, in the woods of Waterloo, near Brussels, where the comrades were meeting – not the most comfortable location, but the safest. Claire did not need long to think over Clement's request; she was deeply flattered that the comrades would ask her to undertake such a dangerous task.

Two days later she went to the Chaussée de Vleurgat to keep an afternoon appointment with strangers, arranged by phone. 'They let me in . . . A woman – attractive, strong, curly-haired, arrogant . . . She was forty; I was twenty. We had one thing in common: we were both Jews!' Prowizur knew that she had entered the lions' den; on the floor above male voices could be heard in lively conversation – in German. She asked the woman if she could get in touch with Ernest.

'To her question I responded, "Yes, he's Jewish." To her second question I responded, "Yes, so am I." ' Then she gave her hostess a hasty description of Ernest: 'Big; dark, wavy hair; sharp, deep-set eyes; a strong mouth and a hoarse, mocking laugh that often lends weight to his words.' The woman said that she would do her best and told Claire to phone back in three days. Claire consulted Clement about what to do next. When they spoke again, he said, Claire must ask the woman how high the ransom would be.

On their second contact the woman claimed to have indeed met Ernest and said that he was being held as a political prisoner and not as a Jew. Claire asked her for a ransom figure and for proof that the person with whom the woman had spoken really was Ernest. Ernest had two parakeets. Next time, could she name them and Ernest's mother's favourite piece of music? Ernest's father, who was following the negotiations closely, had suggested these questions.

Henri Mandel put everything into the task of freeing his son. He had even sought contact with Von Falkenhausen, the military commander for Belgium and Northern France, through an intermediary.[92] That attempt had failed, but this new approach looked promising. Whenever there was chance of news, he would hasten from his secret address to the home of Claire's parents to get the latest news from the young Trotskyist. The ransom had been set: the woman had asked for 100,000 francs, a substantial sum that amounted to half the party's monthly budget. She wanted 30,000 francs in advance. Clement had silently handed the bank notes to Claire. She took them without asking their source. He would not have revealed it.

At the next meeting Claire got her answers. The parakeets? Titi and Bibi. Beethoven's *Für Elise* was the piece that Ernest's mother loved best. Claire was delighted; the answers were absolutely correct! She paid the woman her advance and left. Then began the long, anxious wait for the telephone call that would tell her where and when to hand over the rest of the money. The signal arrived, and Claire brought the money to a safe address. 'She counted it and told me, "Tomorrow Ernest will be free." '[93]

In cell 159 of the St-Gillis prison Ernest remained completely ignorant of the strange negotiations on which his future depended. He was interrogated by the Gestapo a number of times, in the prison and at their Avenue Louise headquarters. On 5 January, a month after his arrest, he was once again hauled up by the Sipo. Another session at Avenue Louise? He could not imagine anything else. He hadn't seen the document that the agents had presented: 'Ernest Mandel, held in this department, born 5.4.1923 in Frankfurt/Main, last residing in Antwerp-Deurne, at Cruyslei 83, is today discharged and handed over to the undersigned.'[94] The agents handcuffed him and placed him in the back of an auto. As he told it,

Before reaching Gestapo headquarters on Avenue Louise, the car stopped at a crossroads. I was in handcuffs . . . but the door on my side was not locked. When we stopped I suddenly pushed the door open, let myself fall out and disappeared into the crowd . . . They came after me but couldn't find me.[95]

Afterwards he always credited his escape to his own quick thinking. He never wanted to believe he was ransomed, which was Claire Prowizur's story. But his brother Michel confirmed that ransom had been paid, and documents showed that his father had provided the 100,000 francs.[96] Coincidence cannot be ruled out, but it was highly unlikely that the Gestapo, whose discipline and conscientiousness were proverbial, would have transported a prisoner in a car with unlocked doors. Mandel's daring flight may well have been staged by agents anxious to avoid being questioned about an unauthorized release. A lapse in discipline would be much more readily forgiven than corruption.

Whatever actually happened, the question of why Ernest Mandel publicly insisted on his version remains fascinating. Very likely he had difficulty admitting that his life had been saved at such cost at a time when the party was unable – financially and as an organization – to provide all of its Jewish members with shelter and false papers.[97] A number of party sympathizers and even a few members had already had to report to Mechelen, the first stage on the road to Auschwitz. Fearful, powerless, doubting that they could be saved or save themselves, they had given themselves up rather than become a burden on the others.[98] Although Mandel had played no conscious part in the ransom scheme that saved him, feelings of guilt gnawed at him continually: Why me and not them?

Above all, he felt that his father's intervention, far from liberating him, had only made him another kind of prisoner. It seemed to emphasize his dependence, and he longed for independence. After the war, he felt no need to shed light on this complex question. As late as 1977 he wrote to Rudolphe Prager, who was researching Trotskyist resistance during the war, 'Perhaps I escaped because of my father's connections . . . But please be reticent about my biography because of the delicate question of security.'[99]

His sense of guilt, at least, was shared by the RCP. At its July 1943 congress the party officially acknowledged that it had failed in its 'responsibility to guarantee an illegal existence to the Jewish comrades. A bolder leadership would have strongly resisted the deportations of our Jewish comrades.' In mitigation, the statement noted that 'hiding the leading, most indispensable comrades was a well-nigh insoluble problem. Furthermore, at that time there was in all respects a shortage of funds.' By a substantial majority, the congress rejected a more far-reaching declaration that severely censured 'the passive attitude, anti-democratic stance and favouritism of comrades in the Executive Committee in this

respect, without excusing the criminal indifference of the entire organization'.[100]

After his liberation Mandel spent two weeks recuperating in the Ardennes, in the village where his mother and brother lay in hiding.[101] As soon
as he had recovered, he returned to Brussels, preferring the anonymity of the
city to the relative quiet of the country. In Brussels, he found shelter with the
steadfast René Groslambert in Auderghem.[102]

The city offered protection, and the rules for living illegally were now
being more strictly observed. The party had formed a technical and financial
commission that gave them more flexibility.[103] The leadership – Abraham
Léon, Optat Henry, Philippe Szyper, Charles Szatan and Paul Widelin – was
based in Brussels. And eventually Ernest's family was reunited there, and he
was able to visit them.

In May 1943, Henri and Rosa Mandel, after living for several months in
the 'small space' belonging to Cécile Piller in Forest, moved into a mansion
on Rue Charles-Quint. This was done with help from Marcel Devlieghere,
who as chief inspector of the Belgian General Insurance Company was able
to disguise the residence as an agency of this prominent company.[104] While
Henri Mandel received and advised clients upstairs, in the cellar the stencil
machine was being prepared for night-time and weekend production of the
German paper *Das Freie Wort* (The Free Word) and the Dutch-language
Vrank en Vrij (Open and Free).[105] These papers continued to appear until
September 1944. *Das Freie Wort*, subtitled 'Special Edition for German
Soldiers and Those Belonging to the Military', was so compelling that two
Wehrmacht soldiers, convinced that the paper was produced by fellow
soldiers, made contact and offered to work on distribution.[106] One of them,
Joseph, a social democrat who worked in the army mail service, successfully
managed to enclose 'these damned inflammatory pamphlets' in already
censored letters from and to German soldiers for four months.[107] With an
eye to the risks of distribution – copies were thrown into German trucks,
and others were left in barracks and in cafés and restaurants where soldiers
gathered – the paper was kept to two pages. Looking back, the whole
undertaking seems unbelievable, even absurd.

Henri's wife and younger son now had false identity papers, but they were
under a different name than his. To satisfy the curious it was said that Henri
Mandel was unmarried and that Rosa was his sister and Michel his nephew.
They only let themselves be seen on the weekends, supposedly visiting to
take care of Henri. The rest of the week they stayed in the basement,
stepping outside for a breath of fresh air at nightfall. From 1943 on Rosa's
father and her brother Motek, still unmarried, also shared the basement with
them. The two men had failed to reach Switzerland; their well-paid guide

had let them down. In a panic they returned to Brussels, where Henri took them in. Once hidden, they were able to let their beards grow again and throughout the war they refused to eat any meat that was not kosher.[108]

Illegal in France

Though Ernest had no patriotic sentiment and did not support the Allied war effort, he contributed regularly to *Das Freie Wort*. He produced a column, 'Deutsche Dichter sprechen zu euch' (German Poets Speak to You), in which rebellious lines from Schiller, Herwegh and Goethe were cited to discourage Hitler's troops. He also criticized the Wehrmacht's military theatrics in such articles as 'Es ist aus mit dem Rommel-Rummel' (The Rommel Hullabaloo Is Over): 'Do not wait until it is TOO LATE! You have the weapons in your hands: STOP them!'[109] He also reported on the Polish death camps, in terms both alarming and inflammatory:

> The Nazi criminal assassins are destroying hundreds of thousands of innocent and helpless men, women and children, considering these naked Poles, Russians and Jews to be 'subhumans'! . . . Civilized humanity can and will NOT tolerate this! Each of you German soldiers is complicit if you do not protest against these crimes and instead keep silent. None of you can shelter under such concepts as 'obeying orders' or 'soldierly duty'. There, too, are boundaries that no soldier dare cross. Your duty is to put a stop to the Nazi beasts: Mad dogs must be chained![110]

Mandel's circle was convinced early on of the reality of the death camps. In October 1942 a French comrade who had been forced to work as a prisoner in the Silesian salt mines arrived in Brussels, and told them that he had seen the death factories with his own eyes.[111]

While writing commentary and articles for the Vrank en Vrij group and for the Trotskyist *La Voie de Lénine* and its Flemish edition *Klassenstrijd* (Class Struggle), Ernest Mandel also became involved in international work.[112] After Stalingrad in November 1942 and Mussolini's downfall in July 1943, the winds of revolution blew stronger and the Brussels group began seeking closer contact with their French comrades. In the summer of 1943 a temporary European Secretariat was formed and a new conference proposed, for February 1944, which would be open to all organizations in agreement with the principles of the Fourth International.[113] In November 1943 Mandel and Paul Widelin travelled to Paris together – a dangerous step, as Widelin was a wanted man in France.[114] He had remained in Paris from May till October that year, supporting the publication of *Arbeiter und*

Soldat that had some influence, especially on German soldiers stationed in Brest, in Brittany. About fifteen of these even helped with its distribution. But in October, the group was betrayed and its members arrested. At the same time, the Gestapo struck the leadership of the French section; the journalist David Rousset and the up-and-coming man Marcel Hic were arrested. Widelin escaped and fled back to Belgium. Now, one month later, he was again in Paris with Ernest Mandel.

While in Paris, Mandel met Michel Raptis (pseudonym Pablo), the Greek revolutionary, who had been living in France since 1938. It was thanks to Raptis's initiative that the conference had been organized. For decades afterwards, his and Mandel's paths would continually cross.

The conference took place at the beginning of February 1944 on a remote farm in St-Germain-La-Poterie, near Beauvais in the department of Seine-et-Oise. It was the broadest international gathering since Trotsky's death in August 1940. Mandel and Abraham Léon travelled by train from Paris to Beauvais and then rode the last 20 kilometres hidden under the canvas of a delivery van. The delegates met for six days and nights, with breaks for only short periods of sleep on the floor of the shed where the conference was being held. This venue had been provided by Louis Dalmas, head of a small resistance group, an aristocrat who had become a Trotskyist only a few months earlier. At the age of sixteen, Marquis Louis Dalmas de Polignac had broken with his noble family and left for Paris.[115] Now he used this small farm building on the 10-hectare (about 25-acre) family estate as a site for meetings.[116] The open hearth barely warmed half the space, so the delegates from five countries took turns near the fire. Young militants from the French section, armed with revolvers and machine pistols, stood guard.[117] Their food was mostly kohlrabi.

The conference focused on the approaching European revolution: everyone was convinced that the German workers would play a key role.[118] What had happened in Italy between July and September 1943 was child's play, they said, compared with what was to come. If the German working class would only get into step, the long-awaited European revolution would come and it would be unstoppable. (The Trotskyists' analysis was actually shared by Roosevelt, Churchill and Stalin – a common conclusion reached from very different philosophical standpoints.) The delegates laid out an extensive campaign of fraternization with the 'German workers in uniform'.

They could not count on support from the Soviet Union. In 1944 Trotsky's prediction that the Soviet bureaucracy would collapse, whether under pressure from imperialism or the world revolution, seemed as relevant as ever.[119] A tidal wave of rebellion would push the Stalinist parties into leadership of the masses, but when they showed themselves to be Judases they would be quickly cast aside. (This, certainly, was an optimistic forecast.) Few doubted that there would be ample opportunity to build revolutionary parties. Only Mandel and Léon urged caution. They noted a structural crisis in the workers' movement that was expressed in the workers' weak commitment and reformist consciousness.[120] Un-Marxist! responded the French comrades.[121] Mandel was wrong, they said, to draw a direct connection between class, party and party leadership, so that 'if the leadership degenerates, it's the working class that degenerates'. On the contrary, defeats were caused not by any crisis among the members of the workers' movement but only by failures within the leadership. This was a position very close to that laid out by the Trotskyist transitional programme of 1938 – and who dared question that?[122]

Yet it was also the Achilles heel of the argument that a revolution was imminent. What would happen if the mass movements in Europe did not follow the Italian pattern? What if the tempo and scope of radicalization in Germany or France lagged behind? What if no new revolutionary mass parties developed? Was that not plausible after twenty-five years of defeats? Fascism and Stalinism were the consequences of such defeats, not their cause. Wasn't it somewhat facile to compare the end of the Second World War with that of the First? Even if the analogy were sound, shouldn't some attention be paid to the tragic outcome of the German workers' movement as well as to the success of the Russian Revolution? In 1918, the German revolutionaries were completely cut off from the masses, just as the young Trotskyists were. Isolated and besieged, if they were not as sectarian as the early German Communists, they were at least as weak. Could they prevail where Rosa Luxemburg and Karl Liebknecht had failed?

Mandel felt that if there was any chance of revolution it was only because 'stagnation gives the young revolutionaries of Europe the urgent task of rebuilding and renewing the workers' movement as a whole and creating the subjective conditions for victory after a period of terrible defeats.'[123] In other words, he did not assign responsibility for creating the necessary conditions for success to the party or the party leadership alone. What was needed was the restructuring of the entire workers' movement. Could a handful of members of the Fourth International contribute to this? According to Mandel, only if they relinquished their sectarianism. 'Without a true revolutionary organization bound to the populace, even the most refined tactics and the best programme are incapable of changing the course of developments.'[124]

In all, a wide range of ideas was aired at the conference. Afterwards, the theses of the provisional secretariat were discussed in national meetings. In Belgium, Mandel and Léon once again spoke against those afraid of engagement and nervous about the so-called nationalist sympathies of the populace, Léon going so far as to mock such sectarianism and suspiciousness as an 'infantile disorder of Trotskyism'.[125]

Deportation to Germany

The Belgian party's real heart had been in Brussels. The group was barely active in the industrial areas of Liège, Antwerp and Charleroi. By the start of the Occupation its influence had also largely disappeared from the centre of the country and in the Borinage. Now, however, the factories and mines in Liège and Charleroi began to play a central role in the Trotskyists' strategy. Mandel was made responsible for organizing the proletariat in Liège, while Abraham Léon went to work recruiting the Charleroi miners. Led by Jules Davister, Emile de Donder and Pierre Wouwermans, mine workers themselves, around two dozen party activists had already formed an illegal organization of mine workers' delegates, the Confederation of Committees in Struggle (CCL), which had influence in about fifteen mines.[126] As the autonomous Workers' Front they opposed the 'political chauvinism of the sacred union', that is, the Communist-dominated Independence Front. To maintain daily contact with the CCL, Léon and his wife, Tsica Silberstein, moved to Charleroi.

As early as the May 1941 Liège strike, held to mark the first anniversary of the Occupation, *La Voie de Lénine* had been distributed at the gates of Cockerill, the giant steel company, which employed 20,000 workers. The Trotskyists considered the steel workers' organization the prototype for the coming struggle. Under the leadership of André Renard the factory committees were combined into a single entity, the united Trade Union Movement (MSU), which was independent of both the Socialist and Communist parties. Up to 1942 the metal industry in Liège had been a Communist stronghold. Fearful of losing influence, the Communists attacked Renard and the MSU paper *Travail* (Work). The fact that the first issues of *Travail* were printed on the press of the Trotskyist paper *La Voie de Lénine* fuelled Communist suspicions. Mandel remembered their reaction as 'filthy tricks': 'Their hostility knew no bounds. They dragged us through the mud and treated us as Nazis, fascists and collaborators.'[127] In a pointed reference to the murder of Walter Dauge, he added, 'They didn't stop at political disputes but took action.'

Whatever the Communists feared, however, the RCP's influence in Liège was not great; they had only a handful of activists there. Mandel and Optat Henry worked to change that, making contacts and distributing materials.[128]

And gaining information to disseminate wasn't easy. Up to the end of

1943 their sources were very limited: the streets, of course; the collaborationist press and German media; BBC Radio; Radio Moscow; and, after the
landing in North Africa, Radio Algiers. Once European connections had
been restored, news also trickled in through the better-informed French
Resistance. One sensational item came in: in Portugal there had been
contacts between German and American chemical corporations. *La Voie de
Lénine* reported the story, and a bilingual pamphlet was prepared for
distribution to German soldiers: 'You are being sacrificed as cannon fodder
while your masters negotiate to save their possessions.'[129]

The group leafleted in Rue Jean in Seraing for some time before the
Gestapo surprised them, on 28 March 1944. Only Optat Henry got away;
Mandel was arrested. Less than two months after the European conference
he found himself in prison for the second time, in the St-Léonard facility
near the citadel of Liège. His trial took place a month and a half later. It was
his paradoxical good fortune to be charged with undermining the Wehrmacht, which put him under military jurisdiction and saved him from the
SS. On Friday morning, 12 May 1944, in the military court of the Liège high
command, he was sentenced to two and a half years of forced labour. As he
was led back to his cell Mandel had the pleasure of hearing his German
guards talking about the leaflet that had been used as evidence: 'That was
extremely interesting. Do you think it's true?'[130] It was some consolation to
have led at least a few Germans to have doubts.

Through intermediaries Mandel wrote to the family at Rue Charles
Quint that he was

> full of good spirits and healthy . . . But I naturally suffer at the thought of
> my poor parents . . . If only I knew where my dearest mother can be
> found – but alas, I am totally in the dark! – then I would beg her to remain
> strong and healthy.[131]

Thus he made it clear that he had not revealed the real identities of his
'relatives' at that address. Evidently the Germans were concerned with the
Vrank en Vrij group and not with the Fourth International. In the last message
he sent before leaving for the camp, Mandel warned his parents in a
deliberately silly sounding passage that they had figured significantly in his
interrogations: 'Fourteen days ago an SS high company commander told me
that [you] were together in Auschwitz in Upper Silesia and that my father was
doubtless practising his profession there. That gave me much pleasure.'[132]

Once he had been sentenced he was treated more leniently. He could
receive packages and write letters and he was even allowed to have visitors.
'But I naturally do not expect that,' he wrote meaningfully. He became

absorbed in studying the seventeenth-century Catholic theologian Bossuet and also read Verlaine, Rimbaud and Melville. The evening before his deportation he was full of self-confidence and only a bit sad: 'My heart may be heavy and my mind distracted; my unquenchable will is at rest and says, "Patience. Everything comes to an end." And I will wait.'[133]

Abraham Léon had been living underground for two years, in St-Gillis, Forest and St-Joost-ten-Node. On 18 June 1944, two weeks after Ernest Mandel's deportation, Léon and his wife set off for Charleroi, sped on by news of the Normandy landing and their fear that contact between the regions might be lost.[134] That evening they reported to the safehouse of twenty-eight-year-old Oliva Ruland in the Charleroi Chaussée. Gradually more comrades dropped in. There were two former mine workers, Florent Gallois and the striking-looking Jules Henin, small, blonde, over fifty, with the head of a patriarch. There was an escaped Russian prisoner of war who had found work in the mines and a hiding place with Ruland. Unfortunately, the house was also full of political contraband – money, a radio transmitter, propaganda materials and printing materials – a carelessness that was typical of the underground, even in 1944.

'Open up! Open up!' Before Ruland had the door fully open, the military police forced their way inside. It was past midnight, and the soldiers were doing a blackout inspection. They had been alerted by a streak of light visible through one of the windows. Henin, Gallois and Léon's wife, Tsica, escaped, probably through the back door. But Léon and the Russian escapee were trapped in the upstairs bedrooms. The Germans found suspicious materials everywhere, and they immediately called for reinforcements. A four-hour search of the house followed and its remaining occupants were arrested. At his first interrogation Léon admitted to being Jewish and in hiding. Ruland, Léon and the Russian were sent to prison.

Long days of physical and psychological torture followed. After his initial confession, Léon denied being politically active.[135] He managed to win the friendship of one of his guards, who helped him smuggle letters to party comrades. Without bitterness, he urged them to take warning from the Ruland disaster and exercise greater caution, 'Because it is not you but others who bear the physical consequences of your carelessness.'[136] The comrades made plans to free him, and as speedily as possible: Léon had warned them that Ruland could no longer withstand the torture, and the SS had threatened to beat him to death 'if I remain silent'. He added, 'They keep their promises. Do everything you can to organize an escape.'[137] He also asked for a fast-working poison.

On Tuesday, 20 July, suspecting that he'd soon be transferred to Mechelen, he wrote them these final words:

> I hope that you will do all you can so the cause does not suffer from my departure . . . I don't know what fate awaits me but know that when it arrives my last cry will be: Long live the Fourth International![138]

Via Mechelen Léon was shipped to Auschwitz.

Ernest Mandel and Abraham Léon had worked together intensively for several years. Both were still young men, both had left the Jewish community without renouncing their Jewish background. History had left them no choice. It wasn't their ideas that had made a 'normal' existence impossible, but life itself: the savage divisions of modern society – between poor and rich, between the powerful and the powerless – and the apparently unbridgeable gulf between the Jews and the outside world. The force that drove their souls to rebellion also shaped their intellect. They strove to understand the world in terms of class struggle, which they saw in their contacts with German political refugees as well as in the left-Zionist youth movement. Their understanding helped them free themselves from family bonds and unquestioning respect for authority. As Mandel put it, their characters allowed them to liberate their minds and dedicate themselves to the struggle for socialism. They submitted their wills to that ideal, and the more they were tested in the war, the stronger their resistance became.

They shared an aversion to all forms of chauvinism, including left-wing Zionism.[139] Léon had freed himself from such ideals through his study of Jewish history. Yet both were far from indifferent to the national question. Their very internationalism directed them to participate in the struggle of any people oppressed by an occupying power.

Now both had become casualties of that struggle, and neither knew the fate of the other. In his last letter smuggled from prison Léon wrote to Mandel in a postscript, 'I count on your publishing my work on the Jewish question as soon as circumstances permit; I'm very attached to this.'[140] Right after the war *La conception matérialiste de la question juive* (The Materialist Conception of the Jewish Question) was published posthumously by Edition Pionniers in Paris. Mandel wrote for it a moving introductory sketch of the fighter whom he regarded as one of his teachers.[141]

The Liberation approaches

In the spring of 1944 Mandel was deported to Germany in the company of nine other prisoners. It was the start of a journey that would take him through half a dozen prisons and work camps.[142] That he survived it all is a miracle. As a Resistance fighter, a Jew and a Trotskyist, despised by Stalinist fellow prisoners, his chances of staying alive were minimal. About his survival he said,

> I shouldn't exaggerate because there was just luck in it too. But through political behaviour and I think a correct approach to a certain number of basic problems, I could immediately establish good relations with some of the guards. I did not behave like most of the Belgian and the French prisoners who were very anti-German. I deliberately looked for politically sympathetic warders. That was the intelligent thing to do even from the point of view of self-preservation.[143]

In Camp Hürth-Wesseling near Cologne the guards were not SS members, as they had been in the concentration camp; in fact, some of them had worked there since the 1920s. Mandel found quite a few with social democratic backgrounds. He also found kindred spirits among the German prisoners. He won the trust of the son of a socialist railway worker from Cologne; this man gave Mandel addresses for his father and friends, who would help him if he could manage to escape. And so an escape plan began to take shape.

Mandel was assigned to work for IG-Farben, one of the German chemicals giants, for which some 60,000 workers – Russian and western prisoners of war, political prisoners, forced labourers from concentration camps and even ordinary Germans – were busy producing synthetic fuel for the war machine. It was a microcosm of European society under Nazi rule. In an earlier camp he had worked as a nurse's aide; now the work was harder.[144] He had never before done hard physical labour. He also had to watch his step. Some Polish prisoners discovered that he was Jewish; a priest's intervention saved him from being killed.[145] He wrote home, 'The prison is one great school of stoicism and patience, and God knows I need good lessons in them.' Much that previously seemed important now seemed trivial. He believed that he had overcome many of the faults in his character and was convinced that he would leave the camp stronger for the experience.[146]

But he didn't mean to wait for an official discharge. With help from Belgian fellow prisoners he managed to get hold of some gloves and to replace his jail clothes with a civilian outfit. He had noticed that during the changing of the guard the current in the fence around the camp was turned off. The interval was dangerously brief, but one day he decided to risk it. In an instant he scaled the fence, cleared the barbed wire and vanished into the woods.[147] It was an insane undertaking, and if he had failed he'd have been shot dead. Instead, he enjoyed a day of freedom, 'which was very exhilarating, very intoxicating'.[148] The next morning he was pulled in on the way to Aachen, in the woods near Eschweiler on the Belgian border.[149] Because he was without papers and refused to name the camp from which he had escaped, he was taken to Siegburg prison. There he spent two weeks handcuffed in a cell with only a few slices of bread to eat.[150] Finally he revealed the camp's name, was returned to it and taken to the camp commander. Forty-five years later, Mandel still remembered the commander's confusion: ' "You're an odd bird. Do you realize that if you'd been brought directly back you could have been immediately hanged?" I nodded. He looked at me with amazement.'[151]

The tensions of camp life did not leave Mandel unscathed. Since the beginning of the Occupation he had suffered from eczema on his legs. Now he became emaciated, had intestinal complaints and suffered heart arrhythmia. As he was transferred from camp to camp his condition deteriorated. He spent the winter of 1944–5 in the camps at Eberstadt and Eich: the work was cutting reeds on frozen lakes. He ended up in the Eich field hospital with hunger oedema. On 25 March 1945, he was liberated from Camp Niederroden by the Americans.

3

The Power of the Will

The Liberation filled Mandel with happiness, but also with doubt. Would he see his family again? And what of the long-awaited German revolution? His hope for that had kept him going: 'The German revolution is the world revolution.'[1] He later said, 'I was happy to be deported to Germany because I would be in the centre of the German revolution', an expectation doomed to disappointment.[2]

His parents on Rue Charles-Quint in Brussels were also living in uncertainty. Was Ernest still alive, and if so, where? No one knew. On 26 April the Office of Repatriation reported that it had been unable to trace him. That same afternoon, Henri and Rosa were dumbstruck to find Ernest at their door.[3] He had come by train from Darmstadt, wearing sturdy American soldier's shoes but gaunt and in tattered clothes, without underwear or a jacket. He had been working almost four weeks for his liberators, helping with the repatriation of political prisoners. He was raring to go, as shown in a letter that reached his home only after he did:

> My head is full, I want to write, to write . . . Everything I saw, heard and went through strengthened my convictions. I long to get back to work – be so kind as to find out if students in my circumstances can take the university exams.[4]

His family had survived the war intact. Rosa's father and brother Motek were also alive. But his happiness at this was overshadowed by the evil that had been inflicted on Henri's mother, sister and brother and their families in Auschwitz. Until May 1940, Henri had been sending them packages with tea, coffee, soap and even clothing.[5] Then all contact had been lost.

The Mandels helped others where they could. They took in Jan Spiegel, back from France. He had heard nothing from his own parents since June 1942.[6] Henek and Victor Klapholz, sons of Henri's oldest sister, Manya, who had survived Auschwitz, also found refuge in the Rue Charles-Quint.[7] In August Henri had news of his youngest sister, Bertha. Her name had appeared on Schindler's list, though she had nonetheless been deported.[8] She had lost her eight-year-old daughter, Amalia, and endured Bergen Belsen bereft and alone. She wrote movingly to Henri: 'When your letter came, I laughed and cried at the same time and people thought I was mad.'[9] Henri Mandel also tried to adopt the daughter of his brother Simon, killed in Auschwitz. The authorities refused to grant her an entry visa. He concluded bitterly, 'I maintain that this is definite proof that the Hitler barbarism has left clear traces . . . When forced to yield, the Nazis slammed the door so hard behind them that now the whole world is going through a moral and humanitarian crisis.'[10] Henri advised his niece, 'Just . . . come. I'll bear all the costs. We ardently await you.'[11]

Life gets back on track

Those who returned from the camps or who had lived underground for years and evaded the sweeps of the security police had little interest in looking back. Ernest, too, preferred to leave memories of the war behind. He made an exception in a letter to his father's sister Gina, who had emigrated to Palestine in 1926. On the day that Nazi Germany surrendered he wrote her a description of his experiences:

> Worst were the mental ordeals: being forced to assume a false identity, to find a hiding place, to stay inside unless it was absolutely necessary to go out, and to break every contact with the free world and free thought. The radio was the only luxury we permitted ourselves. We listened to it from early morning till late at night.
>
> I was never hit or mishandled in the German prison camps. But circumstances there were quite bad. The food was inadequate; the work was hard, especially for a student unused to manual labour; and life there included innumerable moral humiliations – our heads were shaved; we could not read or write; for four months long we were not allowed to wash; we did the dirtiest work; and we were ordered about by criminals. I spent fourteen months in these conditions.[12]

And that was all he cared to say. For Ernest, this short, sober account was enough. His eyes were on the future.

Life quickly got back on track. The paintings and books that had been safely stored were back in place, and every hour of the day 78 rpm records played Bach or Mozart. There wasn't time to clear the basement, which was filled with stacks of papers, old and new and from everywhere – hundreds of kilos of them. Now and then the young people went to the Savoy Cinema on the Chaussée de Louvain, where Ernest often attracted attention with his roaring laugh. Occasionally they attended football matches, going with Victor Klapholz to Anderlecht and to Heizel Stadium for the match between Belgium and England – though the Belgians weren't much competition for Stanley Matthews and his team, who won 5–3.[13]

At the same time, their father wrote to a friend, 'We all worked hard and tirelessly.' Michel took the entrance exams for the French-language Royal Athenaeum in Ixelles, a Brussels borough. This school was no sinecure for a boy who had previously been educated in Flemish in Antwerp but, like his brother, he would graduate with the highest honours and the government prize. Ernest, meanwhile, resumed his history studies at the reopened university. In addition, as his father remarked jokingly, he was busy 'with issues that could be of use in making humanity happy.'[14] He quickly made a name for himself in the Socialist Students, a group of some 200 left-wing scholars at the Free University whose approach to socialism was far from traditional. Among those he met there were Louis Van Geyt, chosen in 1972 as the last chair of the Belgian Communist Party, and Wim Geldolf, later an Antwerp alderman, member of Parliament and, in the 1980s, senator representing the Belgian Socialist Party.[15] There were fierce debates about Stalinism, Eastern Europe and the Prague coup in the spring of 1948, which were eventually won by members who favoured working with the Communists.[16]

Henri Mandel was thinking of an academic career for Ernest. He proudly announced to a family friend,

> I am happy to be able to inform you that Ezra is already reviving, gradually but surely . . . I mean, of course, physically. Because the Nazi barbarians were never able to damage, much less break, his mental capacities. His mental abilities – above all visible in an immense intellect, in his studies and in his talent for writing and commentary – not only remained intact but even went through a certain ripening process in that Nazi mess. He will thus easily recoup his lost four years of study without much difficulty and without needing to perform any mental tricks.[17]

But his high expectations for his adored oldest son turned into disappointment as Ernest sank deeper into politics.[18] Differences of opinion about Stalin and the Soviet Union drove father and son even further apart.

Ernest also clashed with Fritz Besser, the friend and teacher who had spent the war in exile in London.[19] Besser encouraged him to complete his studies before making a strong political commitment; he wanted Ernest to become acquainted with a broader milieu than the closed little circle of Trotskyists. The twenty-two-year-old Ernest wouldn't hear of it, not because he wanted to receive star treatment – Besser's reproach – but because the times left him no choice. The International had emerged from the war decimated. The party needed him, particularly now on the eve of a great upheaval in Germany, one even more cataclysmic than the revolt that followed the First World War.[20] Even thinkers outside the Fourth International expected a revolution.[21] So, after his comprehensive examinations, which he completed with distinction in April 1946, Mandel interrupted his studies to look for work as a journalist. The American Trotskyist Sherry Mangan helped him obtain assignments from the Paris bureau of *Time-Life-Fortune*.[22] He was also hired as a correspondent for the Amsterdam daily *Het Parool*; a fellow camp inmate recommended him to this former Dutch resistance paper.[23]

Ernest was up to his ears in work. With only sixty to seventy-five members, the Belgian section of the Fourth International was always short of manpower.[24] From a vacation spot on the coast in Wenduine he wrote to his friend Ernst Federn, 'I am indeed on vacation, having just finished off forty typewritten pages with still yet another enormous mass of work to round off.'[25] He was composing an update of what he termed dialectical materialism:

> The decline of capitalism is also apparent in the disappearance . . . of interest in Marxism. Only eccentrics seem to be involved. This naturally results from the objective situation – but only in the final analysis. Marxists themselves bear the heaviest responsibility. They are simply not able to understand society today, much less overthrow it.[26]

Interrupted by innumerable political activities, Mandel would work fifteen years on his *Marxist Economic Theory*, the study that was finally published in Paris in 1962 as *Traité d'économie marxiste*, and that brought him international recognition.[27]

The Shoah

Ernst Federn, nine years older than Ernest Mandel, was the son of an influential doctor who had been a member of the famous Vienna Psychoanalytic Institute and a former confidant of Sigmund Freud.[28] He and Mandel spoke not only about politics but also about their emotional lives.

Federn encouraged him to learn more about psychology. Their conversations around the table in Rue Charles-Quint generated great excitement, with the Freudian Federn jumping about defending the role of the unconscious while Mandel appealed to the 'power of the will'.[29]

Mandel had first met Federn at the home of Lazare Liebman, a respected member of the Brussels Jewish community. Liebman's parents and his youngest son had been killed in Auschwitz.[30] When Federn arrived destitute with the first group of Belgian political prisoners from Buchenwald on 1 May 1945, Liebman had offered him warm hospitality. Their connection had been made through Florent Gallois, the mine worker deported to Buchenwald after his arrest with Abraham Léon in Charleroi in June 1944.[31]

In Buchenwald, Gallois and Federn had been part of a Trotskyist cell that also included Federn's compatriot Karl Fischer and the Frenchman Marcel Baufrère. Shortly after the Liberation, while still in the camp, they had produced a manifesto celebrating the imminent European revolution.[32] They rejected the idea that the German people bore collective guilt, and opposed the Communists, who were ready to disband their own party to further the peace and order required for postwar reconstruction.[33] Such chauvinistic thinking could never inspire the proletariat.

Mandel heard that Liebman was hosting a Trotskyist from Buchenwald and immediately sought him out. He found a shaven-headed, skin-and-bones thirty-year-old, clad in a scruffy uniform, always hungry and with only one subject, the camps and the prisoners, which he talked about in too loud a voice.[34] 'I was as wild as a savage', recalled Federn years later. He had been interned since March 1938, first in Dachau and then in Buchenwald. As a 'political Jew', with the red and yellow star on his left breast, he had suffered terrible torture. Being set to work as a mason saved his life. When Buchenwald was made *Judenrein* (free of Jews) in the fall of 1942, an exception was made for those who were working. Still, his life remained in danger, not only from the Nazis but also from Communist Party members,[35] whose violent attacks on the Trotskyists continued even in the camps.[36] The hounded Federn found protection among the Belgian political prisoners and managed to join them as they boarded the British plane that flew them to Brussels. In Vienna, his fiancée who had not seem him for seven years heard the news from a Communist: he told her that the 'pig' had escaped to Belgium.[37]

Mandel and Federn worked together intensively during those first postwar years. Outside the Fourth International, Federn was the better known of the two. Being the one Jew who had survived Buchenwald gave him authority. He opposed the concept of collective German guilt, an idea spread by the Communists, and insisted that there had been Germans who had resisted the terror.[38] He did not hide the fact that life among the political prisoners had sometimes been quite nasty, that petty party conflicts, jealousies, racism and sexism had been daily realities. Oscar de Swaef from the Socialist daily *Vooruit* (Forward) encouraged Federn to put his account on paper.[39] The resulting pamphlet, titled *De terreur als systeem* (Systematic Terror), was never distributed. After discussing it with Communist ex-prisoners, De Swaef did not dare. Even the left-wing British publisher Victor Gollancz, one of Federn's fellow prisoners in Buchenwald, considered it too inflammatory.[40]

In fact, directly after the war what had happened in the camps, even in Auschwitz, was barely spoken of.[41] Only a few survivors dared to break the silence – writers and poets such as Jean Améry, Paul Celan and Primo Levi, who had been deported as Jews, and those who had been persecuted for their political convictions, such as Robert Antelme, Eugen Kogon and the preacher's son David Rousset.[42] Ernst Federn belonged to this small group. In *Les jours de notre mort* (The Days of Our Death) Rousset, who like Federn had been involved in Trotskyist activities in Buchenwald, devoted several flawless paragraphs to his companion in adversity. These portrayed Federn not only as a political analyst but also as a victim.[43]

Federn influenced Mandel's thinking about the Shoah. Federn's experiences with German guards reminded Mandel of the German soldiers – ex-Communists and Social Democrats – who had saved his life by helping him to escape. Germany was not only a land of tyranny but also the cradle of the socialist movement, the country of Rosa Luxemburg and the heart of the European revolution.[44] Mandel's pseudonym, Ernest Germain, acknowledged that debt.

In his postscript to Abraham Léon's *The Jewish Question: A Marxist Interpretation*, Mandel examined the genocide, 'a balance sheet frightful in its clarity: five million dead out of six million European Jews'.[45] It was grotesque, beyond comprehension. Yet he warned of the tendency to view the destruction as a 'unique catastrophe'. 'The fate of the Jews' is no more than 'a symbol of the fate of humanity'; in addition to 6 million Jews, 50 million non-Jews had died. For Mandel, the genocide was

> only an extreme expression of the barbarism of the general methods of imperialism in our period . . . Far from being a phenomenon isolated from the destiny of humanity, the tragedy of the Jews is only the herald to other peoples of their coming fate.[46]

He referred whoever was unconvinced to the atomic bombings of Hiroshima and Nagasaki, proof that Hitler had no monopoly on barbarism.

Mandel considered the Holocaust a crime of imperialism; according to him, there were no watertight divisions between the Jewish genocide, colonial massacres and the customary violence of capitalism. The Shoah was the 'Satanizing' of capitalism in its 'imperialistic phase'. He insisted on a rational explanation for it, unlike Jean Améry, who spoke of 'a dark puzzle', or Primo Levi, for whom Auschwitz had been 'a black hole' (*un buco nero*). He did not always do justice to the questions raised by victims of the genocide. For eyewitnesses like Primo Levi, blaming the material needs of capital for the Shoah was one-dimensional, too reductionist to be convincing.[47] For him all attempts at explanation left a residue of disbelief.

Forty years after the publication of Léon's *The Jewish Question*, Mandel reconsidered his position.[48] He refined his interpretation of the Shoah without relinquishing its essential framework: the mass murder of the Jews could be explained rationally as a result of imperialism and was comparable to other barbarities. On one point, however, his ideas had changed substantially.[49] By the 1980s he had come to see biological racism and industrial modernization as additional causes of the genocide, equal to the capitalist crisis. He distanced himself from his 1946 analysis, in which he had assigned racism only a secondary role. In fact racism could only play a secondary role in that analysis, because in 1946 his Marxism allowed no independent role to ideology or politics. This was pure party dogma, inherited by the Trotskyist movement from the Second and Third Internationals.[50]

Visions of collapse

That Marxist legacy led Mandel astray in another area. Like Trotsky, Mandel believed that capitalism had reached its final phase. In the orthodox party view, fascism and world war were manifestations of capitalism's death agony and would be resolved by the coming of a new revolutionary period.[51] All too soon, facts on the ground refuted this theory. In March 1946 Mandel rather conservatively explained,

> Though the war in Europe has not directly led to a revolution, it has certainly disrupted the capitalist equilibrium and ushered in a long revolutionary period. Our self-criticism . . . therefore relates only to an incorrect evaluation of the tempo of events but not of the nature of the period.[52]

Though allowing for a postponement, Mandel – and with him many in the Fourth International – clung stubbornly to Trotsky's apocalyptic vision and insisted that an economic revival was impossible. Whoever pointed to the start of a boom, for example in England, was told that 'in the period of capitalist decadence British industry can no longer overgrow [sic] the stage of revival and attain one of real boom'.[53] Was Mandel afraid that admitting even the possibility of a new expansion might demoralize the party? The idea that capitalism was in its death throes, which should have been no more than a working hypothesis, achieved almost the status of a dogma.

Visions of economic catastrophe were not confined to left-wing circles. Pessimism about the future was also widespread in the bourgeois camp. In 1943 Joseph Schumpeter, a critic of Marx, noted, 'It is a commonplace that capitalist society is, and for some time has been, in a state of decay.'[54] Ten years later some still expected the sudden collapse of the American economy. John Kenneth Galbraith researched the crash of 1929, hoping to find useful insights.[55] Only after 1955 would the 'golden years of capitalism', two decades of continuous economic growth, put an end to the doomsaying. By then the West had become, in Galbraith's words, 'the affluent society'.[56]

But the first conference of the Fourth International in Europe was held in March 1946, and Mandel had no trouble sticking to his guns:

> Only a superficial, petty bourgeois defeatist sees in the fact that the war did not result in a European revolution a negation of our revolutionary perspective. That the German revolution did not take place, that . . . Stalinist parties are experiencing a new period of growth, must never make the Fourth International forget that the death crisis of capitalism and the destruction of its equilibrium . . . are the most important facts.[57]

Such exaggerated optimism did not draw many followers. Even so, Mandel refused to stray from what he considered a correct analysis of the period.

A disrupted conference

Certainly he heard his position extensively criticized during that 1946 conference in Paris. The Germans wanted to abandon all revolutionary slogans, saying that fascism had destroyed the European workers' movement and there was nothing to hope for now beyond the restoration of democracy.[58] Participants' ideas about the Soviet Union also diverged radically, but the outside world had no eye for these fine political distinctions. Its attention was caught not by the impassioned debates at the conference but by the spectacular police raid that put an end to them. The thirty or so participants from twelve countries who had gathered from 3 to 6 March on the first floor of a café in the Porte St-Denis neighbourhood had avoided publicity,

because the PCI, the French Trotskyists, were still working underground
and also feared harassment from the Communists. Around 11:00 a.m. on the
penultimate day a small army of pistol-brandishing police suddenly stormed
up the stairs and arrested all of those present. The conference participants
were initially afraid these were Stalinists, but it quickly appeared that they
were only security police. In the confusion Michel Raptis and Sherry
Mangan grabbed all the papers from the table and crammed them into a bag,
which Mangan, a true journalist, had no intention of relinquishing.[59]

Those arrested were taken to the Hall of Justice in police vans. In transit
Mangan lit one cigarette after another; as he explained later, this was to
disguise how he was discarding his pistol and ammunition. A bullet went out
the window of the vehicle with each cigarette butt, and finally the weapon
went too. Mangan had not dared discard the pistol at once, afraid that,
lacking a safety catch, it would go off as soon as it hit the pavement. At the
Hall of Justice, Mangan was ordered to open the bag. Calmly he informed
the officer that he was a journalist and demanded to speak immediately with
the American ambassador. The man cleared off and not another word was
said about the bag.

As for Mandel, he wore different glasses and had a head of brown hair
instead of a shaven skull, but in general he was hardly altered – the same
broad forehead, the friendly, somewhat mocking eyes and the tapering face
with its pointed chin. The prefect of police knew well enough that the man
before him was the fellow inmate from Camp Niederroden who had been
responsible for the repatriation of political prisoners. The prefect had been
thankful when Mandel had given his case priority. Now, one year later, he
dared not return the favour: 'But me, I can do nothing for you . . .'[60]

So, resigned, Mandel joined the others who were being guarded by
armed gendarmes. In the small hours of that night they continued their
conference in whispers, and ended it as always by singing 'The Internationale'. Next morning, papers such as *Franc-Tireur* and *Combat* blazed with
outrage: 'What has become of freedom of assembly? And the right to
sanctuary? And individual freedom? Are we back to the worst days of
Vichy?'[61] A week later, when the incarcerated delegates were freed, there
was a well-attended protest in the Horticultural Hall.

With friends

Mandel first met Sherry Mangan, then over forty, in Paris. Mangan, a
Harvard-educated classicist, belonged to the generation of American writers
and poets who became involved in revolutionary politics in the period
between the wars. He had gone to Europe as a pilgrim would to the source

of his inspiration. Only a handful of writers had held fast to their convictions throughout the war; Mangan was one of them.[62] In 1938 he became closely involved with the Fourth International. As a correspondent for *Time* magazine, he was able to settle in Paris, a 'place where I always feel completely at home, and either naturally happy, or, if sad, sad in so agreeable a form of gentle *tristesse* that it is as good as being happy.'[63] Using the pseudonym Sean Niall, he wrote a much praised column for *Partisan Review*.[64] His circle of friends included the surrealists André Breton and Maurice Nadeau, the poets Benjamin Péret and Georges Hugnet and the journalist David Rousset. He was tough and colourful; he resembled Hemingway, a drinker and gambler, burly and charming.

In August 1940, two months after the start of the Occupation, Mangan was ordered to leave France. Up to then, he had been the only American journalist able to keep working. Afterwards, he assisted David Rousset in helping the French Trotskyists go underground.[65] During the war years he travelled for the Fourth International using the pseudonym Terence Phelan, making trips to South America, India and the United States. From the fall of 1943 he lived in London, where he was European manager for *Life* magazine and stayed in the fashionable Dorchester hotel. In September 1944 he returned to Paris, joined the European Secretariat and became the financial expert of the Fourth International in Europe. Through him, the American press indirectly helped to consolidate the International.

Mangan and Mandel shared a passion for politics and culture and also a love of good food, though Mandel always remained a moderate drinker. Mangan called his friend 'the Lenin of our time', though he once said sardonically, 'We hope that he will be the Lenin of our day.'[66] The dissipated-looking Mangan had a certain attraction, above all for young party members, to whom he sent long, elegantly handwritten letters of advice. Yet his often witty conversation could not hide the fact that politics took a big toll on him emotionally.[67] Literary imagination and party discipline did not coexist peacefully in him, and his ambition to 'see everything, do everything, live everything'[68] undermined his mental equilibrium. Shortly after a visit to Nice, in February 1948, Mangan suffered a breakdown, which Mandel witnessed.

When he was in Paris Mandel stayed with Mangan on the Left Bank near Boulevard Saint-Germain on Rue de l'Université, where Mangan had a roomy apartment on the second floor. It was notable for an attention-grabbing erotic picture by Salvador Dalí, which Mangan had pointedly hung next to his grand piano.[69] Mandel received mail there under the name A. de Jonckheere (a Dutch title of nobility). He was staying in this apartment when Mangan returned from Nice, and saw his previously robust friend crumble.

Mangan could not sleep, refused to eat and showed symptoms of a persecution complex. In one month he lost 37 pounds.[70] He entered the American Hospital for a four-day rest cure, but was convinced that only psychoanalysis could save him from ruin. Mandel consulted Ernst Federn, who had been living in New York since January 1948. Mangan possessed sensitive party information, so Mandel asked Federn if he or his father would undertake his case: 'An analysis by a bourgeois or politically untrustworthy analyst [is] out of the question.'[71] Federn thought an accurate diagnosis the first necessity and advised that Mangan be taken to see the Amsterdam psychiatrist and sexologist Coen van Emde Boas.[72] Van Emde Boas was known in Trotskyist circles and had treated Sal Santen, a friend of Federn's and son-in-law of the revolutionary Henk Sneevliet, who had been executed by firing squad in 1942. Mangan went to Amsterdam, and reported, 'I got a diagnosis from a Viennese medicine man. After some reflection he concluded that the vehicle did not have to be completely disassembled but that I could do with a patch-up job.'[73] In other words, Van Emde Boas considered a short-term, intensive therapy sufficient: four and a half hours a day for nine days would be enough to get the patient back on his feet.[74]

Mangan's wretched experience was not unique. In the same weeks Mandel had to stand by helpless as Optat Henry also fell apart. Mandel's wartime companion had just lost his wife to a young artist and was in despair. Alarmed, Mandel consulted Federn once more:

> it was difficult to advise [Henry] in this situation because he said nothing to anyone, not even his wife. Above all I cannot presume too much because I am much younger than he. He has turned to my father . . . We have to wait and see how the case develops.[75]

Not long afterward Mandel wrote to his friend in New York that Henry had taken his own life.[76]

Mandel was deeply shocked by Henry's death. Optat Henry had been dear to him; he considered him one of the most valuable Belgian comrades. He had led the organization in Brussels since 1938. In a farewell letter Henry apologized for his suicide. He stressed that his whole life had been burdened with depression, hoping to spare his wife. Her feelings of guilt were not eased in the least. Mandel too was filled with self-reproach and felt obligated to help her and the two children. For months he had seen his friend sliding into the abyss and had often spoken to him, but without offering any effective help. He confided to Federn, 'I believe that we should have been able to save him.' About the deeper causes, Henry's depressions and the impossible marriage, Mandel acknowledged,

[Henry's] tragic fate has made clear to me for the first time that we must never make light of these issues even when they are still in their beginning stages; just as in politics, the smallest deviation can have the worst consequences decades later.[77]

As he had after the Holocaust, Mandel used his intellect to cope with tragedy. However, his attempt to understand his friend's emotions did not help him overcome a congenital reluctance to express his own. Mandel's reticence irritated Ernst Federn, who saw his friend growing more reserved as his political and academic ambitions increased. As a psychotherapist, he knew the importance of emotions and his own emotional life was a full one. In Brussels he had finally been reunited with Hilde Paar, the woman he had wanted to marry since 1938. After the war she had taken the first possible plane from Vienna and flown via Prague to Brussels, where they had finally been married, in February 1947; Mandel had been one of their witnesses.[78]

Federn was also beginning to distance himself from the Fourth International. In New York he did not know what to do with the traditions of the European workers' movement: 'America was so very different!' Mandel was concerned and encouraged Federn to look up comrades,

> precisely because contact with the unbelievably dull average American must be deadly boring. Also . . . when personal contact with the movement is broken for years, political contacts are also lost . . . No one is strong enough to withstand the pressure of bourgeois surroundings for long. Naturally you are old and sensible enough, but I wanted in any case to have warned you.[79]

This was typical. Throughout his life, Mandel would caution those friends who gave their doubts free rein to keep in mind the importance of collective support and their own vulnerability as individuals.

In turn, Federn warned Mandel to beware of naïve optimism, to open his eyes to the impasse in which the workers' movement had landed. Mandel could not let that pass. He replied,

> What you call my 'optimism' is nothing more than trust in the historical destiny of the world proletariat and of civilization, to which a few years or a few decades more or less do not matter at all. In that sense Marx, Engels, Lenin and 'the Old Man' [Trotsky] were also optimists, who consciously distanced themselves from the permanent malaise of the despicable petty-bourgeois rabble – above all the pseudo-intellectuals . . . I find myself, that is to say, in good company, but I will not repeat their mistakes.[80]

Federn knew that Mandel was temperamental, but felt that was no excuse
for Mandel's rudeness. After six months Mandel complained at having still
received no answer to his letter.[81] He got it by return post; Federn had
broken with politics. This must have saddened Mandel, but it also relieved
him. Now there would be room to discuss the issues that separated them. It
often happened that a political break-up gave Mandel the opportunity to
repair a personal friendship. He had no truck with rancour.

The Russian question

Mandel's remark that 'a few years or a few decades more or less don't matter'
was a reference to the 'Russian question', the debate over the true political
and social nature of the Soviet Union and the new East European buffer
states. In these years this debate took place chiefly in the Fourth International
and its surroundings.[82] Outside this sphere and in social democratic circles,
Russia and its allies were considered simply totalitarian. The theory of
totalitarianism, developed in the 1930s, emphasized the similarities between
dictatorial regimes. Or, as Truman put it in 1947, 'There isn't any difference
in totalitarian states. I don't care what you call them, nazi, communist or
fascist.'[83]

The Trotskyist critics who took part in this debate did not all subscribe
absolutely to Trotsky's theory that the Soviet Union was a degenerated
workers' state.[84] On the contrary, internal controversies were legion.
Some members concluded from the Russian experience that something
was amiss with scientific socialism, that revolutionary class struggle could
no longer be seen as the engine leading to a socialist society. Other
theorists, like Mandel, ascribed the degeneration of the Russian Revolution to the bureaucratic leadership of the Soviet Union: 'Marxism cannot
be renewed without creating a leadership that truly assimilates Marxism.'[85] This belief in a subjective factor was based on Trotsky's conviction that there was no historical place for a stable bureaucratic mode
of production. Workers' democracy was so intimately bound up with a
planned economy that optimal production was impossible without the
greatest possible participation by the producers.[86] Therefore, according
to Trotsky, bureaucratic degeneration could last only for a short time.[87]
It was like a cancerous tumour that must be cut away – but with what
sort of surgery? Trotsky never found the time to develop his views fully
on the subject of the 'political' (anti-bureaucratic) revolution.[88] He had
concentrated on the international situation, saying that the approaching
war and the revolutions that must follow it would put an end to both
capitalism and Stalinism. If that did not happen, the world would sink

into barbarism.[89] He ruled out any middle way that would leave the social structures of East and West intact.[90]

But despite Trotsky's prediction, the Soviet Union had emerged from the war stronger than ever. How could this be? And how were the new regimes in Eastern Europe to be characterized? Wasn't a workers' state supposed to result only from a revolution led by a revolutionary mass party? What did it mean if such a state were established from above, led by the bureaucracy? Trotsky himself had declared shortly before his death, 'If there has been no change in the Soviet Union within five years, the question must be reviewed anew.' Five years had passed and now some critics in the party were saying that it was high time to discard Trotsky's original prognosis, which no longer appeared justified.[91]

Mandel strongly opposed this view and spent his August vacation composing a forty-page rebuttal, which he presented[92] in September 1946 at the congress of the Internationalist Communist Party (PCI), the French section of the Fourth International.[93] In the first paragraph of this report he said once again, 'The fundamental dilemma for the Soviet Union remains unchanged; this degenerated workers' state stands . . . at a crossroads: either forward to socialism or back to capitalism.' He went on to respond to the question of why the regime had not fallen. The consolidation of Stalinism was relative and temporary and had nothing to do with 'the transition to a "new phase", a "new exploiter state" or a new "class society"'. He ascribed this stability to favourable but temporary circumstances that were on the verge of disappearing. Trotsky's prognosis had not been disproved: Trotsky had correctly described a tendency and erred only in predicting when it would manifest itself; his timing was off but his analysis was sound. Mandel did not explain why history had lagged behind Trotsky's prediction.[94]

Mandel characterized the new states in Eastern Europe as capitalist states in the process of structural assimilation, of political and economic adaptation to the Soviet Union.[95] He completely rejected the idea of revolutions from above. Proponents of that theory misunderstood Marx's thesis that only the workers could liberate themselves, that capitalism could only be overthrown by the active intervention of the labouring class.

At the congress at least five other perspectives on the Soviet Union, Eastern Europe and Stalinism were presented.[96] Pierre Frank successfully defended Mandel's report.[97] At forty, Frank was a compelling figure, with a stocky build, large head, and eyes as grey as his bristling hair. He had been born in Montmartre, where his parents, Jewish tailors from Vilna in Lithuania, had found refuge at the beginning of the century.[98] He had spent most of the war in prison in Britain. After his return to Paris he had been elected to the International's leadership, in March 1946, along with Ernest Mandel.[99]

Despite Frank's championship, Mandel's analysis could not lay the debate to rest.[100] From other sections of the International came further calls to revise Trotsky's theory of the degenerated workers' state.[101] The controversy reached its climax during the Second World Congress, which took place in Paris from 2 to 21 April 1948. This event had been in preparation for almost two years, a process that involved publication of twenty internal bulletins totalling hundreds of pages, many of them contributed by Ernest Mandel.[102] During the three weeks of the congress Mandel defended his thesis 'The USSR and Stalinism'.[103] His opponents were so divided among themselves that Mandel had little difficulty in holding his own against them. He argued that the proponents of the state capitalism theory made only superficial comparisons between the Soviet Union and the capitalist world. Of course the nationalization and long-term planning in the West bore some resemblance to what was being done in the Soviet Union, but that did not prove that the USSR was capitalist.[104] He accused theoreticians who termed the USSR bureaucratic-collectivist of calling historical materialism into question. If the bureaucracy was a social class, then from a historical perspective it had little in common with other classes, for it had no roots in production and no ideology of its own.

Mandel was very pleased with the outcome of the congress. He wrote to Ernst Federn that there had been no conflicts worth mentioning. He described ten days of plenary sessions in various halls, and around a hundred commission meetings in private homes. Everything had proceeded smoothly, and their security measures had been successful. This was a near miracle, as many delegates went in fear for their lives in their own countries. In Paris, they had been able to lodge with local comrades. His only concern had been over Sherry Mangan. Staying in the journalist's apartment, he could see how the exhausted Mangan was letting his work slip from his hands. As the congress proceeded he worried about what he considered a 'terrible responsibility', the well-being of his American friend.[105]

His glowing general report to Federn was not entirely true.[106] On the opening day of the congress, La Vérité, the biweekly paper of the French section, ran a story about the expulsion of six Executive Committee members because of their support for the Revolutionary Democratic Alliance (RDR). This party, formed around Jean-Paul Sartre, David Rousset and Gérard Rosenthal, Trotsky's former lawyer, had been announced with great fanfare in February 1948. An estimated 45 per cent of International Communist Party members had left the PCI for the RDR.[107]

Calling this no conflict was sheer arrogance. More blow-ups would follow, nationally and internationally. The workers' states, and Yugoslavia in particular, would provide the detonators.

Yugoslavia

Mandel had always maintained that the states of Eastern Europe were capitalist. He continued to do so even when the Soviet Union had Yugoslavia thrown out of the Cominform, the organization of Europe's most important Communist parties, in June 1948. The conflict between Moscow and Belgrade seemed to him a superficial disagreement that in no way disproved the capitalist nature of Yugoslavia.[108] As long as Tito did not return to 'a world strategy of class struggle', Mandel saw no cause for celebration.[109] He may have overestimated Stalin's ability to force every dissident Communist party to submit to him, or perhaps he considered it unthinkable that a bureaucratic leadership like that of the Yugoslav party would adopt a revolutionary course, though Trotsky had speculated that such a leadership might do so in a crisis.[110] Whatever his reasons, Mandel's reaction to Tito's revolt was cautious rather than exuberant.

Michel Raptis, who had been general secretary of the Fourth International since 1946, disagreed with Mandel about the nature of Yugoslavia.[111] He pointed out that Tito's regime rested on a system of people's committees; therefore, Tito's Communists were not Stalinists but 'the bureaucratic distortion of an anti-capitalist, revolutionary, plebeian current'.[112] Less than a year later Raptis, writing under his pseudonym, Pablo, recognized without qualification 'the "proletarian" nature of the resulting state, however bureaucratically deformed it was to begin with'.[113]

Mandel was not convinced.[114] He did not deny that Tito's partisans had destroyed the old order, but noted that they had stopped short of reaching the ultimate goal: 'And this stagnation was the price the Yugoslav Communist Party paid for recognition by imperialism and the monarchy.'[115] Yugoslavia was the result of reconciliation with capitalism, not of a proletarian revolution, and therefore could not be termed a workers' state, not even a degenerated one. Mandel did acknowledge that the conflict with Moscow was a genuine revolt against the Soviet bureaucracy. But how successful was it? Mandel would say only that everything was in motion, an analysis that even he admitted was 'a little vague'.[116]

A year later, he finally acknowledged that Yugoslavia had become a post-capitalist state, but, he emphasized, that did not discredit his earlier judgements.[117] His re-evaluation was based on facts that had only emerged since 1948. He wrote to Federn that the Yugoslavs 'feel compelled by their own experience to reiterate point for point our twenty-five-year-old criticisms of Stalinism . . . What a shame "the Old Man" did not live to see this! . . . In the present situation he could have decisively influenced Yugoslav developments.'[118] That same year the Fourth International organized the first youth brigades to help rebuild the impoverished country.

Mandel saw Yugoslavia as the exception that proved his general analysis of Eastern Europe; he continued to describe the other buffer countries as bourgeois states in the process of structural assimilation to the Soviet Union. Only in 1951 would he accept reality and admit that these countries too were post-capitalist. Still, he would not use the adjective 'degenerated', as he did when describing the Soviet Union; instead, these regimes were 'deformed', because they had been the products of bureaucracy from the beginning. No mass action, annexation or federation had played a role in their creation. Instead, the exceptional circumstances of the Cold War had forced the bureaucracy to complete the assimilation.

Mandel had underestimated the Soviet Union. It had seemed to him impossible that the Kremlin could eliminate a bourgeois regime without losing its control over the masses, yet Moscow had done just that.[119] The question of Yugoslavia was also more complex than he had admitted. He had not been able to reconcile the reality of a Stalinist-led revolution with his own party's accepted ideas. He had failed to recognize the possibilities for bureaucratic reform. He clearly found it very difficult to abandon his conviction that the Fourth International would lead the world revolution.

In the end, he was forced to recognize Michel Raptis as his superior in political intuition. Pablo could move more quickly beyond superficial facts and found it easier to distance himself from orthodoxy. He was more of a politician than Mandel, who had difficulty putting aside key Marxist concepts and who held on to his facts with the tenacity of a positivist. Only when it was clear to him that the facts had changed was he prepared to revise his views and follow Pablo.[120]

There was something objectivist in Mandel's wary analysis of Tito's break with the Soviet Union. Even if the Kremlin was exercising power, he said, the working class was objectively stronger and more conscious when it was organized over a broader area. This interpretation was skewed in that it failed to take into account Stalinist repression of the achievements of the Yugoslav masses. Perhaps his lack of first-hand knowledge also him astray; he did not visit Yugoslavia himself until 1948.

Mandel learned something from the debates over Yugoslavia and later was able to understand the Chinese and Cuban revolutions – here too the question arose as to how a societal transformation could occur without a revolutionary socialist mass organization. The debates also gave him better insight into the aftermath of the Second World War. Though neither capitalism nor Stalinism had collapsed, new workers' states had emerged and workers' resistance had increased. The alliance against fascism had consolidated both the democratic and the Stalinist regimes, but under working-class pressure. This insight would be crucial to Mandel's understanding of late capitalism and of post-Stalin transitional societies.

4

La Gauche and the Social Democrats

It took Belgian scholars a long time to begin researching the social history of the months that followed the Liberation.[1] Even journalists were mostly silent on the subject. The country's mood was too complex to be easily analysed and clearly described. Joy over the Liberation, panic about the fate of family and friends, unexpressed shame over acts of collaboration and anger at the abuses of power – any one of these feelings would have been difficult to absorb and analyse, let alone all of them together, and few authors or even journalists made an attempt.

One remarkable witness who did was the Flemish writer Louis-Paul Boon, who sketched his impressions of the labour exchange and the life of the poor in the Communist daily *De Roode Vaan* (The Red Banner). In 'The Brussels Jungle', a series of articles published in February 1946, he painted a vivid picture of the hopelessness of the working man's condition.

> There are frosted-glass windows chock full of notices . . . Inside a little stove is burning and everyone is clustered around a table behind which a young woman hands out work assignments as if she is re-creating the world. A couple of young men are smoking cigarettes and leaning against the mantel or the window. When questioned, the man checking the want ads calls out, 'Another kid with two heads.' . . . An old man leaves, and a woman says that you were better off before with 40 francs than you are now with 200; one shopping stop and you're out of money. Someone asks when the goddamn revolution is coming and goes on to quarrel about the price of candy.[2]

The old powers recover

There were countless complaints: was there absolutely nothing new to be written in the epic of the people's struggle? Of course there was, but there were no triumphs recorded for the working class. In Brussels, just as in Paris and Rome, after the Liberation the old guard returned and resumed control of the political and economic stage once more. This was enough to lower people's spirits. A veteran Trotskyist sighed, 'The workers have achieved nothing. As in the old days, they are still exploited and have let a historic opportunity pass them by.'[3]

Belgium's Trotskyists, numbering only eighty-five, were not up to the task. They had no influence among the workers – even their Charleroi following had crumbled[4] – and they fell into decline.[5] This was a bitter pill to swallow, since the first five years after the war saw a record number of militant actions, measured by the number of strikes and strikers and of work days lost.[6]

Meanwhile, the Communists of the KPB benefited from the situation. In the first postwar election, in 1946, they got an unprecedented total of 12.5 per cent of the vote – in Wallonia, more than 20 per cent.[7] They owed this unprecedented success to their resistance during the war. Their role in coordinating the Independence Front, the loss of life they suffered and the fame of the triumphant Red Army all contributed to their prestige.[8]

The Socialists' unified trade unions also won a following. This was particularly true in Wallonia, where the Liège metal workers enthusiastically supported them. During the Occupation, under the leadership of André Renard, they had already begun to fill the vacuum created by the dissolution of the traditional trade unions.[9] In April 1945 they forced the Socialists to replace the old trade union federation with the General Belgian Trade Union Federation (ABVV), which was both more independent and further to the left.[10]

The Communists, on the other hand, were not out to make a revolution. *Le Drapeau Rouge* trumpeted, 'We are for law and order', and *Clarté*, the paper of the Communist Brussels federation, warned, 'This is not the time for experiments or adventures.'[11] The Belgian Communist Party was reconciled to the monarchy that Leopold III had so discredited by his collaboration with the German occupiers. The Communists lived entirely in the spirit of the Popular Front, and their moderate politics gave the Socialists every opportunity to recapture their pre-war ascendancy over non-Catholic workers.[12] By 1950 the tightly knit Socialist block had been largely restored.[13] Like the other nations of Western Europe, Belgium regained stability without any spectacular crisis.

In *Revolutionary Marxism Today*, a collection of interviews published in 1979, Mandel once more considered the question of why the revolution predicted by Trotsky had failed to materialize in Western Europe.[14] At that distance, a critical look back was not too difficult. He concluded that Trotsky had underestimated the severity of the setbacks the working class had suffered in that period. Twenty years of Stalinism and fascism had left the masses demoralized and easy to control, even though the class struggle after the Second World War was just as lively as the one that took place between 1918 and 1923. Moreover, the collaboration between the traditional workers' parties was no four-year aberration, as it had been in 1914–18. Instead, it was the outcome of developments of more than two decades, 'taking 1927, the year the Left Opposition was expelled from the Soviet Communist Party, as the beginning of the extirpation of internationalism.' Incidental factors also played a role, notably the absence of an uprising in Germany and the unanticipated appeal of the Communists, thanks to their part in vanquishing Hitler. In these circumstances, Mandel noted, revolutionaries had been unable to strengthen their own position.[15]

The British historian Perry Anderson, editor of *New Left Review*, was elated by the Mandel interviews, but he did not think they resolved all the big questions they touched upon. Hadn't the working class had more reason for disappointment after the First World War than after the Second? And hadn't the Second World War produced an active resistance movement 'of an infinitely more combative and popular character than any produced by the First World War?' Was it not obvious that 'the combativeness of the European proletariat in 1945 was not less but more than in 1918?' Hadn't Mandel underestimated 'the new expansion of bourgeois democracy in Western Europe after 1945, something at least as important as the post-war boom in guaranteeing stability on the continent?'[16] These were stimulating questions from an author whose own works on European absolutism and the transition to feudalism were widely praised.[17]

This exchange of ideas took place at the end of the 1970s. Immediately after the liberation no one in Mandel's circle doubted that Trotsky's prognosis would be proved correct.[18] When this expectation was disappointed, they stood powerless on the sidelines, while the Social Democrats profited from the discrediting of the Communists. This was very different from the situation in 1920–21, when workers were breaking away from the Social Democratic parties. Mandel concluded sourly, 'Objective conditions were never so favourable, but we were also never so weak.'[19] Despite his disillusionment, he found the year 1945 an exciting one.[20] In the year of the Liberation, he began his scholarly career and fell in love for the first time.

Love and sorrow

Micky Traks was one of the thirty or so young Jewish people who had joined the Trotskyists after the liberation.[21] She was slender and petite – standing shoulder height to Ernest – with mid-length wavy hair, and she was something of a beauty. Everyone could see that Ernest was entranced by her, but no one knew the details. He was typically reticent about his feelings, and this turn of events must have taken him by surprise. He confided only in Ernst Federn, and he was sworn to silence.[22] There were complications; Micky was already involved in a relationship with another party member.

Ernest Mandel had plenty of charm. His tall stature, twinkling eyes and unfailing curiosity made him attractive to women. But despite the harsh experiences of the war he retained a certain innocence, at least regarding love, which had thus far revealed few of its secrets to him. Usually Ernest was responsive to people only when politics was involved. With Micky it was different.[23] She was studying psychology at the French-language Free University of Brussels and was active in the radical organization of socialist students. She was also on the editorial board of *L'Avant-Garde*, a monthly publication on revolutionary politics that was distributed at the university and to which Mandel contributed articles under a variety of pseudonyms.[24]

But Micky's political activities exhausted her, and eventually she gave them up in order to have sufficient time for her studies.[25] She was plagued by gloomy moods that destroyed her sense of self-worth: 'What have I done with my life? Nothing. Nothing and again nothing.'[26] At such times she preferred to shut herself away. She asked Ernest not to talk to her about politics any more: 'Why do you want to remind me of sad things? You know that I do better when I'm carefree . . . It's enough for me to know that you are working to make the world better.'[27]

She could also be euphoric. Then the world lay at her feet. 'I am experiencing a very happy time; I hadn't known that just the feeling of being alive – simply to live – could be so beautiful . . . I don't know what's come over me; is this the beginning of a new era?'[28]

Micky's mood swings had a big impact on Ernest. She was unstable and unpredictable, but sadder still was her inability to respond fully to Ernest's love. It was a complicated situation, not helped by Mandel's staying alternately in Brussels and Paris and Micky's regular, sometimes unannounced, trips abroad. She was thoroughly aware of her unbalanced nature and took guilty responsibility for the situation, attempting to ease the burden on Ernest.[29] 'And whenever I fail to appear, you always put up with it without complaint . . . Forgive me that I sometimes think so little about you. I wouldn't hurt you for all the world.'[30] Pain could not dull his love:

My dearest, I haven't the heart to write any philosophical or political thoughts today, the most beautiful and the saddest day of the year. I am so filled with you – in my being, my heart and head, my thoughts and body. Passion has me by the throat, and my love for you makes my heart beat faster.[31]

For a long time Ernest hoped that Micky's life would become less turbulent as her relationship with her other lover ended. Micky begged him to let go of that hope: she was unworthy of his love and was not the woman he imagined. She did not want to see him any more, fearing that he would take the slightest sign from her as an encouragement to hope: 'Ernest, you must give me up because I can never be yours.'[32]

They did not stop to writing to each other. After some time she explained again that she only meant to do what was best for them both:

I am unfaithful, selfish, capricious. Even with great love you couldn't stand all this together . . . I am not what you need, not even what you want – I should distort you in your work and don't think you would change me. Don't worry; you can't imagine what a terrible life you escape . . .[33]

This letter in English was sent from Switzerland, where Micky was taking an English course in Arosa.

Her letter wounded Ernest and he tried to turn away from her. He sought comfort for his soul from the French poet Louis Aragon.

Ô mon amour ô mon amour toi seule existe
À cette heure pour moi du crépuscule triste
Où je perds à la fois le fil de mon poème
Et celui de ma vie et la joie et la voix
Parce que j'ai voulu te redire Je t'aime
Et que ce mot fait mal quand il est dit sans toi.

Mon bel amour mon bel amour ma déchirure
Je te porte dans moi comme un oiseau blessé
Et ceux-là sans savoir tous regardent passer
Répétant après moi les mots que j'ai tressés
Et qui pour tes grands yeux tout aussi tôt moururent
Il n'y a pas d'amour heureux.[34]

'There is no happy love.' Micky was his first passion, and he did not understand why his longings remained unrequited. He seldom spoke about it, but he trusted Ernst Federn enough to write, 'It is so hard . . . to say anything about it or to write.'[35] He only later admitted that the pain was sometimes unbearable; the situation had 'messed up his life'; he had suffered deeply from grief.[36]

When Micky insisted that their relationship be only a friendship, Mandel tried to avoid all contact.[37] Was this self-protection? The separation, however, was never complete. Even in the 1970s when he was getting to know the German student Gisela Scholtz, his meetings with Micky did not end.

The difficulty Mandel experienced in trying to find emotional balance in his life was manifested yet again when his father died. Henri Mandel suffered a heart attack in the fall of 1952, yet recovered so quickly that by the spring of next year the doctors pronounced him completely recovered. The following winter, on the evening of 15 December, he was back at work when he suffered a second attack. He died the same night of an embolism, aged fifty-seven.[38]

No burial instructions were found in his will. At the insistence of his sister Bertha and his devout brother-in-law Markus, he was buried in the Jewish cemetery in Kraainem, near Brussels. There was no religious service.[39] On his gravestone are the following words:

To the memory of Henri Mandel
12 May 1896 – 16 December 1953
A brave spirit and profound mind
A generous heart
All who came near became his friends.

The night he died marked the end of Ernest's youth. 'I will never again feel the ease and happiness of life that I enjoyed under my father's protection, that I unconsciously experienced everywhere, even in the camp, and to which I owe my carefree youth', he wrote to Federn. He expressed something of his despair when he noted, 'Reason allows us to comprehend that everyone dies. But when it happens to someone so close, it is incomprehensible and unbelievable . . . For Michel and me it's a terrible experience.'[40] Then he turned to his old help, reason, and continued, 'Some day I'll witness humanity spending as much energy and money developing medicine as weaponry. Then there will be hardly any illness that can't be fought with success.'[41] For a long time afterwards he clung for comfort to this rather naïve and sorrowful illusion.[42]

Ernst Federn, who had lost his own parents a few years earlier, was concerned about what he called Mandel's self-pity.

> You're no longer a child left helpless by his father. Death is historically inevitable; you've pointed this out often. Now that death has touched you nearly, you must not cry . . . The death of your father is very, very tragic, but cry for him, not for yourself.

Mandel's despairing protest against the backwardness of medical science found Federn unresponsive: 'You know full well that there is but one answer to death, the thought of eternal life in the hereafter. For us, who find that naïve, the only consolation is in unending intellectual life, not in science or medicine.'[43]

Federn was right: Mandel had cast himself as the main victim in his father's death, just as he had in the break with Micky. He had been abandoned; that was the dominant feeling that he attempted to escape by looking for explanations for his loss. He had responded in the same way to the suicide of Optat Henry, his comrade in the Resistance. Just as he always found it difficult to open himself to someone else, he also found it difficult to imagine himself in someone else's place. His relationships were always somewhat one-sided, whether in sunny times or sad.

Though Federn's words did not hide his irritation, they were nevertheless an expression of sympathy. Federn had personally witnessed Ernest's struggle for independence and had also felt a deep affection for Henri Mandel. His closing lines must have heartened Ernest:

> You seem to reproach yourself for the many things you said and did to your father. You know this is foolish. A son must rebel against his father; only thus can humanity progress. A father in his turn must recognize that his son is making the same mistakes that he himself made in order to progress a bit. Above all keep hold of the thought that you are closely following your father's ideals and talents and not that he worried about you so much.[44]

Inside social democracy

Mandel had never experienced financial distress. He had lived with his parents and effortlessly earned what he needed for his personal expenses from a lively career in journalism. From 1946 to 1947 he had been Brussels correspondent for the Amsterdam daily *Het Parool* and from 1947 to 1949 worked in the Paris office of the American magazine *Fortune*. After 1950 he wrote for the Cologne daily *Rheinische Zeitung*. Using the pseudonym Pierre Gousset, he contributed articles on Western Europe and particularly Germany. In the fall of 1953, he had travelled for three months in East Asia, including India, Malaysia and Indonesia, for the independent new Paris weekly *L'Observateur*, which paid all his expenses. Thanks to these resources, he had had the luxury of being indifferent to money, but that changed with his father's death: now he had his mother to support.

In 1948 he had applied for naturalization.[45] The security police had a file that identified him as a Communist, and ruled out the possibility of his getting citizenship.[46] Meanwhile, his passport declared him 'a UN refugee of Polish origin'. However awkward this designation, it allowed him to claim compensation from Germany for the period he spent underground and in the camps.[47] In February 1954, he applied to be editor of the socialist daily *Le Peuple* and was hired.[48] In the same month, he published some articles in the *Frankfurter Rundschau*. He was such a success at *Le Peuple* that he was made permanent after six months' probation instead of the customary two years.[49] In 1957, however, the paper decided that their editor's involvement with the weekly paper *La Gauche* was incompatible with his work for *Le Peuple*, and forced him to resign.[50] He began to work for the Liège daily *La Wallonie*. Under the leadership of the charismatic André Renard from 1951 onwards, *La Wallonie* had become the voice of the left wing of the union movement. Mandel also wrote regularly for *Metall*, the paper of the German IG Metall, using the pseudonym Peter Kipp. His good friend Jakob Moneta was the editor-in-chief of *Metall* from October 1962 until his retirement in March 1978. Finally, Mandel made a connection with the Essen-based *Westdeutscher Pressedienst* (West German Press Service), which gave him an additional source of income and an association that lasted the rest of his life. Until the 1980s he contributed articles and commentary on current events.

Through his editorship at *Le Peuple* Mandel got to know the social democrats, and, more importantly, they became acquainted with him. Shortly before the Third World Congress of the Fourth International, in August 1951 in Paris, he became a member of the Belgian Socialist Party (BSP) in St-Joose-ten-Node, a borough of Brussels.[51]

Since their hoped-for breakthrough had not occurred, the Trotskyists had decided to join the most broadly based workers' party in each European country. In France and Italy this meant joining the Communist Party; in Britain, Germany, Belgium and the Netherlands, the Social Democrats.[52] A new world war was anticipated, and the Trotskyists expected the confrontation between East and West to radicalize these parties first.[53] The Trotskyists had to take root in them now and begin to stimulate critical

tendencies in them, awakening and developing new revolutionary workers'
parties from within.

For some years Mandel had toyed with the idea of entering the Social
Democratic party. The Trotskyists were a dull bunch with a few notable
exceptions, like the teacher Pierre Le Grève and the devoted though
temperamental René Groslambert.[54] In November 1948 Mandel wrote
to Federn,

> It would take a year of hard work and assembling a core of resolute
> militants to be ready to join the BSP, within which a left wing is
> developing. There will be a good opportunity when the BSP is forced
> into opposition, which will most likely occur in the coming year.[55]

The Social Democrats did indeed leave the government in 1949, in the
final act of the struggle over the 'royal question' that had convulsed
Belgium for well over five years. Leopold III was the very symbol of
collaboration. For revolutionaries, his abdication was not enough – they
wanted an end to the system that had produced him: 'Down with the
monarchy / Long live the republic!'[56] But the Catholic People's Party
(CVP), which set the tone in parliament, favoured the king, and Leopold's
return seemed only a matter of time[57] – good reason for the BSP to go
into opposition. A wave of strikes that began on 6 July 1950 washed
through the industrial heart of Wallonia and crippled transport.[58] There
were prospects of a general strike in the steel industry and a march on
Brussels before the beginning of August. Liège threatened to declare a
Walloon republic.[59] The drama reached its climax when four people were
killed in Grâce-Berleur not far from Liège.[60] André Renard, now national
secretary of the ABVV, declared, 'This strike is and will be general. It is
unlimited . . . This strike is total . . . From today the words "revolution"
and "insurrection" will have a political meaning for us.'[61]

These were exciting events that recalled struggles at the century's turn,
when Rosa Luxemburg had urged the European proletariat to 'speak
Belgian'.[62] But no revolution ensued. At the first signs of insurrection,
Leopold decided to abdicate in favour of his son Baudouin. The masses went
home, and the workers went back to work. The bourgeois state, the
monarchy, even the Saxe-Coburg dynasty had been saved.

Ernest Mandel had welcomed the strike with jubilation: 'Men, women
and children are competing in revolutionary enthusiasm . . . The hours of
bourgeois power in Belgium seem to be limited.' But spontaneous activity
by itself proved insufficient. A compromise had been reached even before
the regime was genuinely endangered. Mandel concluded that what was

lacking was 'a revolutionary leadership capable of leading the masses into a battle for the conquest of power'. Nevertheless, he anticipated a coming divergence of opinion in the Socialist Party and called on revolutionaries to side with 'socialist workers who have shown in action an immense revolutionary capacity'.[63] In other words, joining the BSP was his response to a new objective situation.[64] The fact that the Trotskyist organization was in a terrible state made no difference to Mandel's argument. It did, however, mean that they could enter the Socialist Party as, at best, a minimal force.[65]

Besides Mandel, Jules Henin and Emile van Ceulen were the main advocates for this strategy. Van Ceulen, a Brussels resident and leather worker in a small Anderlecht shop, had been a Trotskyist since the 1930s and a member of the political bureau since 1947. Henin, a former mine worker and also a member of the political bureau, had been part of the first generation of Communists in 1919. Better than most, they understood that workers long not only for bread alone but also for roses. Such realism allowed them to fight for democratic demands during the Occupation, even in movements that, according to critics, were not politically pure. They appreciated the importance of defending democratic rights during the debate on the fate of the monarchy, and unlike many Trotskyists they had no qualms about working with Social Democrats. In the 1950s and 1960s Mandel would distinguish himself in the movement for social democracy, strengthening his prestige.[66]

Structural reform and *La Gauche*

André Renard had played a prominent role in the opposition to Leopold III. He told the workers of Liège, 'The fate of democracy is at stake, as is the fate of our organizations and of the social rights we have won.'[67] Renard, originally from Valenciennes in northern France, stood for direct action and workers' unity, the inheritance of an anarcho-syndicalist past.[68] He was not happy about the resolution of the royal question; he felt the Socialist Party had not thrown its whole weight into the battle.[69]

As a labour leader, Renard was concerned with more than local, bread-and-butter issues. He supported economic democracy and structural reforms like nationalization of the banks and the energy sector. Inspired by prominent pre-war Socialists like Hendrik de Man and Louis de Brouckère, he also supported worker-controlled industry.[70] He was deeply concerned about the Walloon economy, particularly the decline of mining and the Liège steel industry, sectors in which his current had great influence.

At the end of 1951 the ABVV formed a study commission of trusted associates to lay out in detail these necessary reforms, naming Jacques Yerna, a Liège native, as its secretary. Three years later they presented what Yerna called a mostly well-thought-out programme, 'without Marxist character or doctrinaire formulations, avoiding any problems that might divide the workers'.[71] But the Socialists were not interested. They were afraid of a negative reaction from their Liberal coalition partners in the anticlerical cabinet of Achille van Acker (1954–8). The moderate wing of the ABVV, under the aegis of general secretary Louis Major and influential in Flanders, was equally unenthusiastic.

Looking for supporters to help elaborate the plan, Yerna made contact with Mandel in the spring of 1954. Mandel was then attracting attention with his column 'The Economic Week in Belgium', which appeared in Le Peuple. Mandel and Yerna got along well. Yerna recalled, 'He quickly came to play a very important part in my own political education.'[72]

Mandel also played a key role in the development of 'Cartels and Economic Democracy', the revised plan for economic structural reform, which was accepted in October 1956. The new plan included an analysis of the major financial groups in Belgium. It provided for control of the cartels and nationalization of the energy sector.[73] The cartels were held responsible for the decline of industry and its inability to adapt to rapid technological developments.[74] The plan was enthusiastically received particularly in Wallonia, where industries were antiquated. It inspired the strike against the closing of the coalmines in 1959 and the famous strike in the winter of 1960–61 against the austerity measures of the Liberal–Christian Democratic Eyskens cabinet.

The idea of workers' control was not new. Together with unity and combative unionism it formed the core of André Renard's politics. What was new was connecting the idea with a strategy, tacitly directed toward the transition to socialism.[75] At times Renard was not afraid to make the tacit explicit. In La Gauche he wrote,

> This is no longer about partial reforms . . . By tackling the cartels the ABVV is mounting a struggle against Belgian capital in its entirety . . . Disbanding the 'financial groups' . . . aims at dismantling capitalism itself. In this sense the struggle against the cartels is nothing other than the form the struggle for socialism is taking today.[76]

He also made his dedication to socialism unmistakable in the pamphlet 'Vers le socialisme par l'action'[77] (Socialism through Action) and emphatically dismissed any interpretation of it that reduced workers' control to simple co-management.[78] The sixty-page pamphlet had been ghostwritten by Mandel, but Renard was willing to put his name to it.

Mandel's hand was clearly visible in the commission's new report.[79] Its analysis of the Belgian cartels was largely based on his study of monopoly capitalism.[80] Though it was not generally known, he was also the author of *Qui contrôle la Société Générale?* (Who Controls the Société Générale?), published at about the same time.[81] His exposé of the 'grand old lady', the biggest of Belgium's many financial groups, demonstrated clearly that the country's economic decline was caused by the conservative investment policy of the cartels.

When Yerna asked him to join the study commission, Mandel was ready to do much more:

> People are sick of bureaucracy in the Socialist Party. Wouldn't it be possible to organize a tendency? And there should be a paper, *La Gauche* (The Left), with André Renard as patron for the French speakers. If that happens, I'll try to get Camille Huysmans . . . for the Flemings.[82]

Since November 1955 party members had been discussing producing a weekly. Interest was especially high in the city hall of St-Joose-ten-Node, where the mayor was Guy Cudell, a friend of Mandel's and a supporter of his initiative.[83] Yerna joined the group in the spring of 1956.[84] Mandel had convinced him that a left-wing publication would be viable if party discipline were respected. The paper would work towards an absolute parliamentary majority, realization of the ABVV structural reform plan and a foreign policy that was neither nationalist nor aligned with either of the Cold War blocs.

The first issue of *La Gauche*, subtitled *Organe de Combat Socialiste* (Journal of Socialist Struggle), appeared in December 1956. The advisory board, which consisted of Senator Henri Rolin, André Renard and the eighty-five-year-old Camille Huysmans, probably did not agree with all of its editors' ideas, but they defended its right to exist. Renard had arranged for the paper's eight pages to be printed on the presses of *La Wallonie*. Also thanks to him, the new weekly could count on around 1,500 subscriptions.[85] Three months later it had 1,800 subscriptions; these combined with single issues sold accounted for 2,000 to 2,500 copies each week.[86]

The editorial committee consisted of ten or so journalists, who also wrote for such papers as *Le Peuple, Journal de Charleroi* and *Volksgazet*.[87] In addition *La Gauche* employed various specialists and correspondents.[88] It was a heterogeneous group that included union men like Jacques Yerna and Robert Lambion; Trotskyists like Emile van Ceulen and Georges Dobbeleer of the Socialist Young Guard (SJW); independent intellectuals like Gabriel

Thoveron and Marcel Liebman and scholars like René Evalenko, Jacques Defay and André Cools, who were connected to the left wing of the Socialist Party or the ABVV.[89] A few were genuine radicals – some out of concern for the party and some influenced by anti-colonialism or pacifism, like Ernest Glinne and Jean van Lierde.

Thanks to their heterogeneity they were able to publish a paper with an independent identity, secured by Mandel's authority. He guarded the paper's pluralism and ensured that there were no personal attacks or provocations within the ranks.[90] He rebuked the impatience of one of the comrades: 'You have to understand that *La Gauche* is not a Trotskyist mouthpiece but a paper that we produce together with centrists, union leaders from the Renard tendency and even with left-wing reformists like Huysmans. We cannot dictate its line.'[91]

Mandel was the driving force behind the paper in the areas of politics, journalism and organization. He also recruited the international correspondents, left-wing socialists like Wolfgang Abendroth in Germany, Oreste Rosenfeld and Pierre Naville in France, Michael Foot and Ralph Miliband in England and Giorgio Galli and Lelio Basso in Italy.[92] He asked the surrealist and ex-Trotskyist Maurice Nadeau and the writer Ignazio Silone to produce cultural and literary columns.

In conflict with party and union

The paper caused much controversy. The dailies criticized it in lengthy opinion pieces. The Communist *Drapeau Rouge* even devoted two editorials to it. The right-wing *Libre Belgique* and the Catholic daily *De Standaard* hammered away at the differences between *La Gauche* and the Socialist Party. Nonetheless, the party generally took a friendly view of it until April 1957, when *La Gauche* was accused of taking a malicious tone towards the Socialist ministers.[93] Mandel and three other editors were charged with disloyalty.[94] Mandel promised not to make denigrating remarks about individuals in the future but demanded the right to criticize government functionaries or ministers as long as no party principles were involved.[95] He asked how he could shut his eyes to the gulf between the government's pro-market economic policies and the ABVV's proposals for structural reform. How much longer, he asked, would the party and union wait before resisting?

He asked that the announced sanctions be reconsidered. If not, 'then I will feel obliged to resign as editor of *Le Peuple* . . . because the alternative is to be fired for political reasons, which risks a public scandal damaging to the party'.[96]

And Mandel wanted to remain a party member. By giving up his position at *Le Peuple* in favour of *La Gauche* he had avoided expulsion, while making it clear that he would not submit to political censorship.[97] Fellow party members offered help, but he wanted no overt action. He was not surprised by the attacks and saw no reason to panic, 'or to have a "pessimistic" opinion of our chances of success'.[98] Financially he was secure enough: he was writing a daily column for *La Wallonie*, called 'Target', and Renard had asked him to begin writing a socioeconomic chronicle as well.[99]

Mandel felt that the questioning of his loyalty was hypocritical.[100] *La Gauche* had been created to push for the structural reform programme, and that was something many in Van Acker's Socialist-Liberal government disliked intensely. Mandel warned that no one should be under the illusion that *La Gauche* would stop publication; that would not happen. He continued wholeheartedly to support Renard's strategy of structural reform and direct action, to the annoyance of the editorial board of *Le Peuple*, who finally pushed him out in the summer of 1957.[101]

The weekly *Links*

The influence of *La Gauche* spread steadily, and demand grew for a Flemish equivalent. Mandel let Marcel Deneckere, a thirty-five-year-old teacher and scholar of Romance languages in Aalst, know that he very much wanted to help establish one.[102] Deneckere was head of the Aalst Socialist cultural committee, and he invited Mandel to come and speak about *La Gauche* in the native city of the radical priest Adolf Daens. Deneckere assured him that 'the ideas you support are beginning to ferment among such varied groups as trade unionists, young socialists, intellectuals, etc.'[103] Mandel also encountered this enthusiasm (or, as he put it, 'unusually positive atmosphere')[104] in Antwerp. There he was in contact with the writer and filmmaker Frans Buyens and with Willy 'The Beard' Caluwaerts. Since 1956 these two, previously active in the Communist Party, had been producing the satirical left-wing periodical *De Satan* (Satan). The title had been suggested by Camille Huysmans.[105] Mandel saw this paper as the forerunner of a Flemish version of *La Gauche* and considered that in Buyens, a born rebel, he had found the ideal editor-in-chief.[106] Mandel confided in him, 'If we can set about it well, we can crystallize something lasting, in Flanders as well as in Wallonia, and then there will be a solid core for a new vanguard.'[107]

Mandel concluded that a fermentation process was taking place in Flanders, comparable to what had already been under way for some years in Wallonia, and he wanted to strike while the iron was hot. Caluwaerts and

Buyens were also ready to take the chance.[108] They sought support from prominent figures to strengthen themselves against intimidation.[109] While this was happening, a Communist leader told Deneckere over a drink that he was going to accuse Mandel of Trotskyism in order to get him expelled from the Socialist Party.[110] Mandel assured Deneckere that this was nothing to be nervous about: 'In Liège I accidentally heard that their party leadership . . . said that *La Gauche* is costing the Communists votes because it got leftists to vote for the Socialist Party. In any case, thanks for your warning.'[111]

The new Flemish weekly first appeared in November 1958, under the title *Links* (Left) and the subtitle 'For a Fighting Socialism'; sadly, Buyens and Caluwaerts were no longer a part of it. At the last minute they had got cold feet.[112] They had written to him describing their doubts and Mandel wrote back that for six months he had been 'taken for an idiot'.[113] He had no more time to waste. With an eight-member editorial board under the leadership of Lievin de Pauw and the circumspect Deneckere, and with twenty-six signatures to the paper's statement of principles, he felt there was sufficient support to begin.[114] The editorial board was composed primarily of intellectuals, with more connection to the party than to the unions. It was thus understandable that *Links* centred its attention on the party, unlike *La Gauche*, which was oriented towards the Walloon ABVV.[115]

The paper's highest priority was to get the Socialist Party to accept the structural reform proposals. *Links* aimed at a socialist breakthrough in Flanders. The Belgian economy was headed into a recession, and the paper emphasized Flemish suffering, unemployment, migrant labour and low wages. Both Mandel and Deneckere insisted that the paper take a pro-Flemish position. Mandel also pushed for Flemish demands in *La Gauche*.[116] Walloons and Flemings were called upon to fight together for anti-capitalist structural reforms. Only that could ensure cultural advancement and a solution to the language question that perennially pitted French and Flemish speakers against each other.[117] Walloons and Flemings needed each other! Mandel continued to sound this theme even when the low participation of Flemish workers in the general strike of winter 1960–61 led a disenchanted Renard to propose a federal solution. He urged Renard,

> [Don't] put the cart before the horse . . . The campaign for federalism is no substitute for a socialist solution to economic suffering. As long as the cartels and 'high finance' remain untouched federalism is deceptive make-believe . . . To realize a federal reform of the state requires first that the power of the cartels be broken. Neither the Walloon nor the Flemish workers can complete this difficult task as long as they act separately. Unity in action is essential.[118]

Friction with André Renard

By the time Mandel issued this warning, his relations with Renard had already cooled. A year earlier he had praised Renard as a people's tribune, 'cast in a very exceptional mould . . . without any parliamentary cretinism, who thinks as we do about the bourgeois state and democracy'. Even if Renard sometimes showed signs of opportunism, Mandel was convinced that he responded in a revolutionary manner to revolutionary situations.[119] Yet a month later the two quarrelled. The occasion was the February 1959 coalminers' strike in the Borinage. Mandel called for a national strike.[120] Renard went along with this idea in *L'Action*, but then, just before *La Gauche* went to press, he changed his position and followed the ABVV into negotiations, thanks partly to a telephone call from Prime Minister Gaston Eyskens, who promised to introduce laws on social control and co-management similar to those in Germany.[121] Renard gave orders to stop the distribution of *La Gauche*. 'If the paper gets out, the general strike will be a fact!' he told an astonished Mandel.[122] Mandel decided that 'he is and remains at base a left-centrist'.[123] For Jacques Yerna, formerly Renard's secretary, this incident meant a parting of the ways. He came from an unyielding trade union family, and could not forgive Renard's demoralizing surrender to the ABVV.

The general strike of 1960–61

In the Borinage, Socialist and Christian workers were marching under banners calling for nationalization of the mines and the energy sector, an indication that the programme of structural reform was popular. After losing the election of June 1958 the Socialist Party finally endorsed the idea.[124] That was 'a great and beautiful congress',[125] but Mandel realized full well that the party leadership hardly cared about the reforms:

> What they really want is a new coalition government in two years. A little verbal radicalism to put pressure on the bourgeois parties will not come amiss; but a too radical programme that would make a coalition impossible without cynical betrayal of the newly adopted platform . . . must be avoided at all cost.[126]

Along with Yerna and Renard, Mandel had addressed the congress. He warned against an implementation of structural reforms that would include a few nationalizations but leave property relationships essentially unchanged. André Genot, Renard's right-hand man in the ABVV, smelled 'a shrimp salad' with a great deal of mayonnaise and not many shrimp. The hall cheered this sally and sang the *Internationale* as he left the platform and returned to his seat.[127] During the anthem the party leaders got to their feet with very obvious reluctance; former Prime Minister Achille van Acker did not rise at all, which earned him a chorus of catcalls. When Mandel shouted something in his direction, Louis Major snapped at him, 'Shut up, Mandel, you're just an anti-party element!'[128]

In fact, Mandel advocated a labour government that would enact socialist policies and be based on the trade unions, Socialist and Christian.[129] 'That's why all participation in government must be ruled out unless the . . . structural reforms are part of the government programme.'[130] Coalitions with bourgeois parties were out of the question. 'Get to Work!' rang the headline in *La Gauche* above Mandel's editorial the day after the congress.[131]

The party needed a battle plan; that became clear in the winter of 1960–61 when the Christian-Liberal Eyskens government introduced a so-called Unity Law that would raise taxes and cut social spending.[132] The protests this law provoked grew into one of the sharpest conflicts in Belgian social history. The philosopher Cornelius Castoriadis spoke of a strike wave 'that, after the events in Poland and Hungary in 1956, is the most important event in the workers' movement since the war'.[133] 'The strike of the century', as it remains engraved in many memories, earned its moniker in full. In the freezing cold of winter 700,000 workers struck for five weeks.

It was actually two strikes in one: a strike against the Unity Law, called by the public sector unions that were most directly affected by the spending cuts, and a strike against conditions caused by the crisis in the Walloon coal and steel industries. Hundreds of thousands of supporters joined in spontaneously.[134] 'No one had predicted anything quite like this', Mandel noted in the Paris weekly *France Observateur*.[135]

La Gauche and *Links* called for actions on the street, the correct place to join battle. The conflict was fierce and the outcome uncertain. 'But the workers are fighting in a truly remarkable way . . . setting an example for all Europe.' Mandel wrote to an American sympathizer,

> Despite their limited strength our friends are playing a huge role . . . they're pointing the way, fostering unity and in various places standing at the head of the struggle. Our papers are a resounding success. Our Flemish paper that first called for a general strike sold 18,000 copies. So far we've published three special editions of the French paper, of 18,500, 22,500 and 27,500 copies respectively . . . A success that we could only dream of before.[136]

Playing the part of guide and stimulus, Mandel did not conceal his excitement. The proposed march on Brussels, designed to stop regionalization of the strike, was gathering impetus.[137] Mandel told the readers of *France Observateur* that it was the equal of the great French strike wave of June 1936.[138] Yet he had to admit that *La Gauche* and *Links* and the fifty to sixty Trotskyists were having no decisive influence on the movement.

He had little contact with Renard.[139] The union leader was enthusiastically received everywhere, not only in Liège and Wallonia but also in Brussels and Flanders. Renard was opposed to a march on Brussels. He feared it would empty the Walloon strongholds of their forces, and that it was futile to expect any comparable turnout from Flanders or Brussels. Mandel thought this an underestimation. He detected behind Renard's opposition a decision to use the strike to push for a federalist solution that would give priority to the socioeconomic well-being of Wallonia.[140] Mandel was confirmed in his opinion when in January Renard launched *Combat*, a new weekly mouthpiece for a projected Walloon social movement, and asked *La Gauche* to look for another printer.[141]

Mandel told his sympathizers, 'We have succeeded in developing a tremendous pressure in favour of a March on Brussels, but it may come too late.'[142] He ridiculed Renard's 'stupid Walloonism' and reported that chanting in favour of the march on Brussels had prevented Renard from speaking for minutes at a stretch, even in Liège. Mandel feared that Renard's tactics increased the danger that the strike would simply crumble, a danger already great because of the moderate position of the ABVV in Flanders and repression by the army and police. Choosing this moment to fight for Walloon rights was no way of getting discouraged Flemings to join the battle. In writing off the march on Brussels and opting for a purely Walloon programme, Renard was squandering the workers' best chance of a real confrontation with the state.[143]

He was right: The movement was caught in an impasse. Deprived of clear goals, impatient protesters resorted to violence and sabotage.[144] The initiative gradually shifted from the workers to parliament, where the conflict was finally 'solved' by new elections. A new government of Catholics and Socialists passed the Unity Law piecemeal, and at a high price to the movement: an additional law on public order that was intended to prevent further revolutionary turbulence.

The strike had been an angry outburst against the Unity Law and the employers and also against the conservative wings of the ABVV and the Christian unions. It rarely happened that the leadership so completely lost control, and Mandel blamed Renard for not having seized such an opportunity. By entrenching himself in Wallonia he had let slide any chance of gaining a majority in the ABVV.

By 1960 the 'golden years of capitalism' had arrived in Belgium. 'The European economies seemed to have learned the secret of eternal growth and prosperity', noted the American David S. Landes.[145] The working class was supposedly on the verge of disappearing, and optimism about a society free from crises was omnipresent. Anyone who doubted this was either a stiff-necked intellectual or a utopian – in any case a conservative holding fast to a nineteenth-century ideology. Two months after the strike there appeared an issue of *Les Temps Modernes*, the journal founded in 1945 and edited by Jean-Paul Sartre, with Mandel's analysis of the events. According to the established political and academic elite, the short-lived revolt should not have occurred at all.[146] Was it just a historical accident? Or the swan song of class struggle? Or had the strike held the promise of a revival of the European proletariat?

Mandel wanted to avoid any misunderstanding. He rejected the idea that there was a direct connection between the degree of prosperity and the degree of political consciousness, or as he put it, 'between level of living and level of combativeness'. The standard of living in Belgium was one of the highest in Europe, and its best-paid workers were the most combative.

> Neither the social nor the economic consequences of stagnation can explain the strike. What does explain it is the conviction which had penetrated the masses that capitalism could not solve the burning questions, the insight that the economic regime required fundamental change.[147]

The Belgian proletariat had a rich tradition of struggle, Mandel said, from strikes for universal suffrage to hunger riots. This tradition had been given new life: the recent strike was the first general strike in the history of the European workers' movement '*whose fundamental objective was neither material gains nor democratic political demands, but rather the reorganization of the economy on a socialist basis*'.[148] This was what the structural reforms meant to those hundreds of thousands of strikers. It was for this that they had struck for thirty-two days, and had called on other workers around the world to take their fate into their own hands. This call for freedom could not be silenced, particularly not in Belgium, 'the land of good living and of funfairs, of the insolent rich and the arrogant elite'.[149] The strike had not been the swan song of nineteenth-century tradition; it had been anything but a rearguard action. On the contrary, it was the impressive herald of a working-class radicalization that would shake Western Europe to its foundations.

It heralded the radicalization of another class, too. In photos from those days small contingents of demonstrators can be seen carrying simple banners declaring them to be students in solidarity with the workers. This was the beginning of a student movement converging with the labour movement.

Mandel's prognosis was daring at a time when everyone else was convinced that uninterrupted economic growth alone would put an end to poverty, unemployment and inequality.[150] In 1961, whoever kept a critical distance instead of believing unquestioningly in abundance faced at best pity. Ten years later, the edifice of a socially conscious and wrinkle-free capitalism would be pulverized. The strike of the century had been an initial sign.

The death of André Renard

The Socialist Party leadership did not appreciate anyone's questioning its agreement with the Christian Democrats. When *La Gauche* ran the headline 'NO' above the programme for participating in the government, there was great indignation.[151] Party chair Collard said he did not want to interfere with Mandel's right to be critical but that criticisms must be 'justified, not offensive; objective, fraternal and disciplined'.[152] The party leadership was extremely irritated. It already felt threatened by Renard and Genot, who had resigned as secretaries of the ABVV and launched the Walloon Popular Movement (MPW). *La Gauche* too was seen as a threat. Mandel had expected even stronger opposition after the election, but wrote to a Dutch friend, 'we do not believe that under the current balance of power . . . serious measures can be taken against us'.[153] That turned out to be a miscalculation.

Mandel's position received little support. Three cofounders of *La Gauche*, among them Guy Cudell, advocated participation in the government and broke with the paper. Tensions mounted at *Links* as well.[154] People complained about the anti-Flemish tenor of the Walloon Popular Movement. Mandel, however, viewed the MPW as 'a space for political encounters and discussion'. He believed the left had to work with it and encouraged Walloons in his party to join it: 'The MPW includes most of Wallonia's most militant unionists and working masses.'[155] The readers of *La Gauche* were also urged to join.[156]

Shortly before, Renard had told Mandel that his services were no longer wanted at *La Wallonie* – he had wandered too far from its course.[157] Mandel was caught by surprise and was also surprised at receiving a mere twenty days' notice. But just as he had with *Le Peuple*, he left without a murmur.[158] According to Renard there were no hard feelings, but 'you also know that we have just formed the Walloon Popular Movement . . . You're not for federalism, so you can't support this initiative.' But, he said, Mandel should not be disappointed. 'I fully recognize the value of the support you've always given us, and I regret having to do without your support.' He invited Mandel to remain at *La Wallonie* as long as he had no other work and ended tellingly, 'If I am mistaken about your basic position, then the problem would take on a different aspect.'[159] By return mail, Mandel wrote that he was no opponent of federalism, 'but it would be difficult for me as a Fleming to join the Walloon Popular Movement'.[160] He wanted to discuss these issues with Renard. Gladly, replied Renard, but Mandel was unable to persuade the Frenchman to keep him on.[161] This was the second time in four years that Mandel had had to give up an editorial position because of *La Gauche*.[162] Yet he was careful not to burn his bridges with Renard. When he was invited to join a new ABVV study commission, he asked Renard's advice: 'I do not want to undertake anything that can be seen . . . as out of solidarity with your movement, which I consider the most left-wing in our union movement.'[163]

Mandel continued to do all he could to strengthen that left wing.[164] On 13 May 1961 he wrote in *La Gauche*: 'Do not be discouraged! . . . Strengthen the BSP left wing, which is demanding a renewed struggle for socialist structural reforms.' The call could not have been clearer, and it was coming not in the name of Spaak or Collard but from *La Gauche* and *Links*. Party leaders were alarmed: the Walloon Popular Movement was becoming a competitor, with around 180,000 members. Some wanted to outlaw the MPW by declaring membership in it incompatible with membership in the Socialist Party. *La Gauche* responded with an unequivocal defence of the right to form tendencies within the party, the lifeblood of 'our movement'.[165]

In 1962–3 the party's leadership and its left wing headed gradually towards direct confrontation, over the new law on public order, which *La Gauche* consistently called the anti-strike law. Sadly, the left had just lost one soldier who should have been a captain in the charge: André Renard had suffered a cerebral haemorrhage. Two weeks later, on 23 July 1962, *La Wallonie* ran his picture on its front page, framed in black, and the headline 'ANDRÉ RENARD IS NO MORE. An unyielding fighter is gone.' Radio Luxemburg had already prematurely reported his death at the time of the stroke, understandably, as his condition was hopeless.[166] *La Gauche* also published a photograph, showing a strong yet tranquil face with soft, dark eyes, and thick silver hair swept back, accompanied by the headline, 'A Class Mourns'.[167]

In his memorial article Mandel compared Renard with Hendrik de Man; both had been searching for new directions, both had been in thrall to the pre-war ideology of planning and both had been averse to the parliamentary circus. But the likeness ended there: 'De Man . . . lost his trust in the working class and was overcome with anxiety and confusion when the Borinage greeted him in 1935 with the battle cry of "General strike!" ' By contrast, Renard had felt himself at one with the working class and was the embodiment of its hopes and boldest dreams: 'That's why his belief in planning pushed him to the left.' Mandel affirmed that Renard would be remembered as the tribune of the great strikes of 1947 and 1950, of 1957 and 1960. 'On these occasions all the reactionary and conservative powers ranged themselves in struggle against this so-called anarchist, this Trotskyist, this "revolutionary and organizer of insurrection." ' But, Mandel concluded, the more hatred was poured on his head, the more profoundly this restless fighter had felt bound to the countless workers who owed him their faith in a socialist future.[168]

Thousands came to pay their last respects to their leader at his burial in Seraing. His opponents were present too – Socialist Party chair Leo Collard, minister Edmond Leburton and ABVV general secretary Louis Major. *La Gauche* asked bitterly if they had come to bury 'the iron brigade' of Belgian socialism along with Renard.[169] A few days later *La Wallonie* was headlined 'ANDRE RENARD'S WATCHWORD: continue tomorrow what was interrupted yesterday . . .'[170]

Towards a split

Agitation against the anti-strike law was high on the left wing's agenda. The right wing of the Socialist Party wanted to avoid any repetition of what had happened in the winter of 1960–61, and party officials airily described the law as merely an updated version of what already existed – nothing more! But the Walloon Popular Movement, the Communists and the left-wing Socialists associated with *La Gauche* and *Links* were sounding the alarm.

When Jacques Yerna was chosen as secretary of the Liège trade unions, Mandel thought that *La Gauche* could truly take the lead. He told American friends, 'We have managed to bring off a very broad mobilization of workers and unions that may provoke the fall of the government.'[171] *La Gauche* published an edition against the anti-strike law with a print run of 130,000 copies. The reaction was predictable; Yerna was accused of being a Trotskyist. Not an easy charge to ignore, the more so as it came from the Service, Technical and Managers Union (SETCa). Until now Mandel had always kept quiet about his membership in the Fourth International. Now it was time to break the silence. He went to Yerna's office and confessed to his bewildered friend, 'I need to tell you the truth. I am a member of the Fourth International.'[172] Yerna was disappointed that his comrade had not trusted him sooner; it wouldn't have changed their relationship, he said. This sounded like a reproach and was meant as one. 'Perhaps I might have joined you', Yerna added. 'In any case I wouldn't have turned my back on everything that we had done together.'[173] He backed up this statement by indignantly rejecting the party's demand that he resign as managing editor of *La Gauche*.[174] The attack had been repulsed.

There were various calls for a new party. Mandel saw little value in them, particularly in light of the uneven developments in Wallonia, Brussels and Flanders, but he wouldn't rule anything out. The left wing must limit the concessions it would make; otherwise, the Walloon vanguard, which Mandel said 'best understood the treacherous nature of the leadership', would become discouraged. The best policy was 'not to provoke a split but not to shrink from it if "the rightists" decide on one'.[175]

At a special Socialist Party congress held 2–3 March 1963, Mandel bore the brunt of the members' attacks when he called for opposing the anti-strike law regardless of the positions of the Socialist ministers and members of parliament. He was accused of putting himself above the party and refusing to accept party discipline.[176] Leo Collard and Paul-Henri Spaak threatened to expel him, but Yerna hastened to his defence. If party members were to be forbidden to agitate against the government, Yerna pointed out, Collard could reckon on opposition from 'hundreds of trade union activists, undoubtedly including the majority of the Walloon militants in the ABVV'.[177] The day after the congress Mandel received encouragement from thirty or so rail workers: 'If those bureaucratic curs yelp at your heels, pay the dirty dogs no mind.'[178] A month later the laws were passed, albeit with substantial amendments. The Walloon Socialist MPs voted against, them, the Flemish and Brussels Socialist MPs for them. The members of parliament from Liège abstained. Yerna called this an 'error of exceptional gravity' and promised to do all he could to get the decision reversed.[179] Collard responded in *Le Peuple*: 'I consider the existence of two kinds of rules or two disciplines within one party an impossibility . . . Then congresses would no longer be possible or necessary for the simple reason that there would be no party left.'[180]

The time for sanctions had arrived. Ernest Glinne (pseudonym Ernest-the-Rebel)[181] and the teacher Pierre Le Grève, who had once received a mail bomb because of his support for the Algerian independence struggle, faced the threat of disciplinary measures.[182] The party began an investigation of Ernest Mandel, and the dissident members of parliament were suspended for two months.[183] This was child's play compared with the party's assault on the Walloon Popular Movement. Calls for a new party resounded more strongly than ever.

Mandel still wanted to avoid a split. A Walloon party would be a poor alternative, because the Flemish and Brussels workers, including the vanguard influenced by *La Gauche* and *Links*, would remain in the BSP. He faced a dilemma. Leaving a new formation in the hands of Walloon regionalists was not an attractive prospect, but quarrelling with the Walloon and Liège vanguard was even less so. The only way out would be to threaten a walkout by a majority, or at least a strong minority, and this was no longer possible. It might have been in the first half of 1961, but Renard, the only one with the authority to bring it off, would not hear of it. By entrenching himself in the MPW, he had let slide his opportunity to take over the ABVV and unify the Belgian workers' movement, which had such divergent social, political and cultural dynamics. Now Renard's premature death had complicated the debate and given the right wing the chance to discipline the opposition.

Collard was ready for a split; the only question was when. In the fall of 1964 the party paper *La Voix Socialiste* (The Socialist Voice) accused the opposition of existing only for the contemptible purpose of 'Trotskyist infiltration'.[184] Nor was this all. At the demonstration in honour of the hundredth anniversary of the First International, the BSP marshals of the demonstration wanted to remove the Socialist Young Guard (SJW).[185] When the police helped them confiscate anti-NATO banners, fierce fighting broke out.[186] *La Gauche* called the incident 'shameful for the whole socialist movement'.[187] Next, party leaders called for the expulsion of Jacques Yerna, who had rather foolishly supported a friend, a worker at Cockerill and a member of the MPW, in the municipal council elections on a list in opposition to the Socialist Party list. Yerna survived by one vote.

These skirmishes merely foreshadowed the decisive battle, which became unavoidable when the party leadership asked participants at a congress held 12–13 December 1964 to declare both MWP membership and association with *La Gauche* or *Links* incompatible with membership in the Socialist Party. Forty-four years after their break with the Communists, in December 1920, the socialist movement faced another split.

Mandel was surprised by the sudden acceleration of the conflict. He abruptly cancelled a scheduled tour of Germany, along with the talks planned for a number of cities there.[188] He was uneasy about how things would turn out: 'We've won more delegates than last time . . . but whether this will be sufficient . . .'[189] For the first time the congress had gathered not in the legendary nineteenth-century Maison du Peuple but in the Palais des Congrès, a mastodon of a building that had been opened during the 1958 Expo. The usual red flags and banners were missing from the big hall; only the faded red carpet was reminiscent of the old days. Almost a thousand delegates listened to Chairman Collard indict the opposition for 'rebellion', 'treason' and 'subversion': 'If the party accepts this, it accepts the disappearance of the party . . . It would mean anarchy.'[190] In his response Mandel cogently summed up Collard's aims: 'He is striking out at the left in order to turn to the right.'[191] There were calls for reconciliation, including from members of *Links*. Collard's right-hand man, Jos van Eynde, ridiculed them: spoken *mea culpa*'s were not enough. He demanded Mandel's signed surrender but couldn't get it. He challenged him scornfully: 'Where are the men of *La Gauche* now? Come to the podium!'[192]

That Saturday Ernest Mandel was the last to speak. Contrary to his usual habit he read some of his remarks from notes, partly to be careful but also fearing for his performance under such pressure. He defended the right to form tendencies and a minority's right to defend its ideas in a publication of its own. That was the only way it had a chance of convincing the majority. Banning tendency publications would only be defensible, Mandel said, if party leaders were perfect, 'if our comrades Collard, Van Eynde and Spaak were as infallible as Pope Pius XII or Joseph Stalin'.[193] At these words, the hall erupted, with curses flying back and forth.[194] Mandel was rudely interrupted several times, sometimes spontaneously but more often by design. Louis Major and Antoine Spinoy were audibly hissing from the front row: 'Traitor!' 'Trotskyist!' 'Idiot!'[195] It was far from elevating.

Yet Mandel's defence was to the point. Structural reforms were being sacrificed on the altar of participation in government. The fact that *La Gauche* proudly championed the reforms had nothing to do with 'archeo-Marxism', as was sneeringly asserted. Workers' control and workers' management were in keeping 'with the reality of our age'. Mandel called on the workers to unite in a single party without regard for ethnicity or philosophical or religious belief. Such a party would only have the right to exist if it guaranteed freedom of opinion and tendency formation. He emphatically rejected Collard's proposal to vote on 'incompatibility' first and attempt reconciliation afterwards: 'For us the situation is clear. We will neither bend nor keep silent. We will not put down our pens. *La Gauche* will continue to appear.'[196]

When the motion declaring incompatibility between the Socialist Party and the opposition passed that evening, Mandel's activity in social democracy came to an end. A week later a new party began to take shape and in February 1965 was born in Brussels and christened the Union of the Socialist Left (UGS). The Socialist Movement of Flanders (SBV) and the Walloon Workers Party (PWT) were founded shortly afterwards as its Flemish and Walloon counterparts, but struggled from the beginning and ended up as mere refuges for the homeless left-wingers. It wasn't until 1971 that the

Trotskyists of the SJW managed to form their own independent organization, the Revolutionary Workers League (RAL), which became the Belgian
section of the Fourth International.

For Mandel, the outcome of the conflict had been unavoidable. Even if he
had given up *La Gauche*, he told a British comrade, 'which would confuse
and demoralize a large part of our working class followers . . . they would
have found another pretext for pushing us out immediately after the
elections.'[197] A left wing had been built in the Socialist Party from 1951
on, accompanied by an autonomous, clandestine Trotskyist core group. In
1953 it had won a majority in the SJW and the Socialist Students Federation
(FSSB). *La Gauche* and to a lesser extent *Links* had had a tremendous
influence. Together with Renard's current, they had struck fear into the
Socialist Party leadership. The question of when, where and how to leave
the SP was clearly on the agenda from the early 1960s. Mandel had only
wanted to make sure they left with a substantial group – and by that he
meant thousands. His goal was optimistic, but he had counted on leaving
with Renard. When Renard retreated to his Walloon fortress in 1961 and
died soon afterwards, and the rapid resurgence of class struggle that Mandel
had expected failed to occur, he was left empty-handed. The fear of
discouraging his allies inhibited him from admitting that the left wing
was in bad shape and that a split was a question of now or never. The longer
he hesitated, the more inevitable expulsion became. He showed the same
hesitation in 1964–5 in the PWT, which had 700 Walloon workers in its
ranks when it was founded but saw its influence evaporate rapidly as
Wallonia's industry was dismantled. Leaving a party was clearly harder
for him than joining it.

   More than twenty years later Mandel admitted that his assessment of the
social and political conjunction in 1961 had been too positive, though he
justifiably added that 'the situation was not immediately clear in 1962–3'.
But he defended himself, asking whether a different analysis would have led
to a better outcome. He pointed out that party formation and class struggle
are not completely parallel processes: 'The strength of the party is not an
expression of what it does (achieves or fails to achieve) in a particular phase of
the class struggle; essentially it is a function of what it has achieved in the
previous period.' He called this idea 'the law of entry and exit', or,
sardonically, 'the Mandel coefficient'. He realized that his and his allies'
most important mistake had been to set too ambitious a goal in leaving the
Socialist Party: they had hoped 'to break off entire layers from social
democracy'.[198] Precisely because a group of ten or a hundred cannot recruit
thousands of workers, they should have decided in the early 1950s that their

main goal was to create an organization of five hundred. This would have allowed them to make more realistic preparations for leaving the party. Expressed more crudely, the amount of fish you can catch depends on the size of your net.

Following this debacle Mandel turned his attention to international work. A new generation joined him. Youngsters like Eric Corijn, Guido Totté, Freddy de Pauw, Jan Calewaert, Frank Maerten, Paul Verbraeken and François Vercammen took up the fight. They represented what would come to be known as the generation of the 1960s. Of them all, Vercammen stood closest to Mandel. With him, Mandel discussed the trajectory of the SJW and its development into the nationwide organization that became the core of the new Belgian section of the Fourth International in 1971.

At the time he joined the group Vercammen was twenty-two, with an athletic figure and a thick thatch of hair. Born in Antwerp, he grew up in the Luchtbal neighbourhood on the city's edge, a neighbourhood built just before the war by Onze Woning (Our House), the social democratic housing authority. His father was a dockworker, and before the birth of her children, his mother had worked in a sweet factory. Though not militants, they were anticlerical and trusted in rational thought. Before beginning to study moral philosophy in Ghent, Vercammen had trained to be a teacher, the career that epitomized upward mobility in a working-class community. He loved jazz, and learned about intolerance from the furious conservative reactions to the rebellious sounds of Elvis Presley and later the Beatles. He saw the social face of this conservatism in the repression of the strikers' demonstrations of 1960–61, which brought him into contact with *Links*. From then on politics would never let him go. He first read Ernest Mandel's *Marxist Economic Theory* in 1962. He had his copy specially bound – this treasure of a book, as he called it, a revelation, just like Deutscher's biography of Trotsky.[199] In 1964 he joined the International.

5

Marxist Economic Theory:
A Book about the World

Mandel had been overloaded with work for years. Obligations ranging from *La Gauche* to the Fourth International and responses to the crises in Eastern Europe, the Belgian Congo and Algeria demanded all his time. He wrote Federn, 'I roam around in world history continuously. Sometimes I feel myself the last European.'[1] His correspondence fell weeks behind. When Marcel Deneckere complained about his own workload, Mandel responded that he fared no better and cited a sample week with a dizzying schedule of meetings, lectures and editorial work, plus a weekend course he taught to young metal workers in West Germany. 'And so it goes, week after week', he concluded. On top of that he had his professional work, and he was more than a month late in correcting the proofs of his book.[2] This book was the long-awaited *Traité d'économie marxiste*, which would finally appear in 1962. Its English translation, *Marxist Economic Theory*, published in 1967, made Mandel an internationally recognized economist.[3]

Marxist Economic Theory was a daring experiment in updating Marx while adhering to Marx's method, which Mandel considered the only acceptable orthodoxy: 'Marxist economic theory ought not to be regarded as a completed outcome of past investigation but rather as a summation of a method, of the results obtained by using this method, and of results which are continually subject to re-examination.'[4] For this reason, he noted, 'The scientifically correct position is obviously that which *endeavours to start from the empirical data of the science of today in order to examine whether or not the essence of Marx's economic propositions remains valid.*'[5]

Mandel argued for a 'genetico-evolutionary' method of exposition, a dialectic that placed all social phenomena in a historical context. *Marxist Economic Theory* was an attempt, rare in its time, to integrate that theory with history. Mandel made use of the insights of modern anthropology, history, sociology and psychology and avoided a one-dimensional economic account of capitalism. He deliberately refrained from citing the usual sources.

He tried to base his criticisms of capitalism on the work of capitalist writers and its criticisms of the Soviet economy on Soviet ones. His bibliography ran to some fifty pages.

The first four chapters of the book were devoted to the history of pre-capitalist economies. Readers who had questioned the official Stalinist-inspired texts experienced the novel sensation of reading a history that moved from Neolithic to modern times and was not limited to Western countries but took the whole world as its subject. Mandel exerted himself to offer a counterweight to the view that every society must follow the same development in the same order. He intended to satisfy the growing interest in Marxism in the non-Western world.

He sought to answer the question of why capitalism had developed in Europe and not in China, India or the Arabic countries, societies that had been superior for centuries.[6] According to Jairus Banaji, an expert in early modern history, he succeeded in writing 'one of the best short histories of early capitalism'.[7]

He also dealt comprehensively with the contradictions of late modern capitalism. In lively descriptions of historical events and trends he analysed the development of production and distribution, the mechanism of exploitation, the periodic crises of overproduction, the role of money, credit and land ownership, and the functions of the state, guarantor of the profits of the monopolies.

In the concluding section he turned to an analysis of the economy of the transitional period and a critique of the Soviet economy. He described the consequences of '*the contradiction between the non-capitalist mode of production and the bourgeois norms of distribution*', in his judgement '*the basic contradiction of every society transitional between capitalism and socialism*'.[8] Bureaucratic control of the state and the economy would ensure that the contradiction would not lessen but rather grow. Mandel moved into a field in which there was as yet no viable theory in the Marxist tradition.[9] This made *Marxist Economic Theory* challenging as well as widely discussed.

Trotskyism was founded in part as a critique of Stalinism, dedicated to defending the true Marx, the true Lenin and the true Trotsky from Stalinist falsifications. With *Marxist Economic Theory* Mandel attempted to move beyond merely defensive critiques. Though experts questioned some of his formulations, his bold attempt to analyse society as a whole in Marxist terms contributed to the book's success. Moreover Mandel appealed to a critical way of thinking that gained ground among the younger generation, slowly at first and then with gathering speed. Mandel articulated the idea that reality could be changed and that humanity was not condemned forever to be enslaved by money and the market economy, inequality and tyranny. His book marked the start of the Marxist renaissance of the second half of the twentieth century.[10]

The history of Mandel's book had its own dialectic. Its ideas had come into existence in dialogue with other, sometimes contradictory visions that its author had encountered in the political and intellectual milieu of the 1940s and '50s.

Mentors and friends

Mandel had worked on *Marxist Economic Theory* for ten years. Shortly before completing it, he asked a friend, 'If you see G[eorge] No[vack] . . . remind him that this work is the result of a suggestion he once made. A suggestion that found its eventual form in around 900 pages.'[11]

Originally from Boston, George Novack (1905–92), born Yasef Mendel Novograbelski, belonged to the pre-war group known as the 'New York intellectuals'. This was a mostly Jewish group of literati who expressed their anti-Stalinist views in periodicals such as *Partisan Review, Politics* and *Dissent*.[12] In January 1937 Novack was the first to welcome Trotsky on his arrival in Mexico.[13] In 1953 Novak was living in Paris and got to know Ernest Mandel, with whom he shared a passion for politics and learning.[14] Novack inspired Mandel to seek an explanation for the period of expansion that seemed to have arrived in the 1950s and that had apparently disproved the traditional Marxist view of economic stagnation. Novack also urged Mandel to use Trotsky's law of uneven and combined development as a guideline in his analysis of the capitalist world and the so-called transitional societies.[15] Though Mandel made no explicit mention of Trotsky's law in his book, he used it in his analyses, as many passages in *Marxist Economic Theory* attest.[16]

Novack was not the only one to whom Mandel was indebted. In 1948, through Ernst Federn, he got to know and began corresponding with Roman Rosdolsky, and learned much from him. Even before the war Rosdolsky, the son of a noted Ukrainian ethnologist, had made his name as a sociologist and historian.[17] Born in Lviv in 1898, he had studied in Prague and Vienna, where he earned his doctorate in 1929.[18] He became a correspondent for the Moscow-based Marx-Engels Institute with the assignment of collecting all materials available in Vienna about Marx, Engels and the early socialist movement. After the defeat of the Socialist uprising against the clerical dictatorship in February 1934, Rosdolsky returned to Lviv, where until the beginning of the war he worked at the university. There he met Isaac Deutscher, the later biographer of Stalin and Trotsky.[19] Arrested by the Gestapo in Krakow in 1942, Rosdolsky was sent to

Auschwitz, then Ravensbrück, and finally to Oranienburg, from which he was liberated in 1945. While many political refugees prepared to leave the United States and return to Germany and Austria, Rosdolsky and his Austrian wife, Emily, headed in the opposite direction. As a Trotskyist, his life was in danger in Soviet-occupied Vienna.

In Detroit Rosdolsky worked as an independent scholar, without an official academic position. His 'university' was a circle of friends, including the philosopher Karl Korsch, the East Prussian Council Communist Paul Mattick, the Swiss Marxist Otto Morf, Ernst Federn, Rosa Luxemburg's biographer Paul Frölich, Isaac Deutscher and, from 1948, Ernest Mandel. The Rosdolskys survived on Emily's salary as an economic researcher for the United Auto Workers (UAW). The connection with Mandel developed into a friendship that lasted until Rosdolsky's death in September 1967.[20] Federn's address became their mailbox, as the McCarthy witch-hunt had made Rosdolsky cautious.[21] He signed letters with the pseudonym S (emper) T(iro), a tribute to the eponymous collection of poems by the rebellious Ukrainian poet Ivan Franko.[22]

The leitmotif of *Marxist Economic Theory*, Mandel confided to Rosdolsky, was 'to present the core of Marx's economic thought not as incontestable but as a synthesis, as the summation of all the empirical data from official science'.[23] It was not a matter of deciding what Marx had or had not written but of examining to what degree Marxist economics could be confirmed by historical and empirical research. Considering Rosdolsky the most knowledgeable Marxist of the time, Mandel did not hesitate to consult him about various complex theoretical problems, such as Marx's theory of wages, the so-called Hilferding revision of Marx's theory of money, Otto Bauer's theory of crisis and the meaning of the concept of productive work in a transitional society. Rosdolsky provided him with commentary on the conceptual sections and praised his friend's accomplishment: 'One rarely encounters such good work.'[24]

Mandel had written his first draft in the 1950s out of dissatisfaction with the untenable position then current among Marxists that capitalism was doomed to permanent stagnation. At that point titled *The History and Concepts of Political Economy*, the book had been scheduled for publication by a London firm in the autumn of 1952.[25] Various postponements, however, led to its cancellation. At the time, Mandel was afflicted with depression and insomnia, the psychological and physical after-effects of the Occupation years. This slowed him down considerably, as did time-consuming problems with the book's content. These particularly concerned the method and conceptual structure of Marx's thought. In

December 1954 he wrote to Federn, 'The manuscript is half typed; I'm revising the second half for the umpteenth time.'[26] Two years later Mandel had made little progress. *La Gauche* and *Links* had been devouring him. Federn wrote to hearten him, 'Good things take time. We have no use for mediocrity, at any rate you and I don't.'[27]

Shortly after arriving in New York, in 1947, Rosdolsky had managed to acquire one of the three or four copies of Marx's *Grundrisse* that were available in the West.[28] Rosdolsky considered it his task to analyse this work, the foundation for *Capital* but still unknown even to specialists, and make it available to a wider public.[29] This project resulted in his magnum opus, *The Making of Marx's 'Capital'*, a detailed account of the development of Marx's thought in the 1850s.[30] In 1955 he sent Mandel one of the first copies and Mandel wrote to him that he hoped 'to learn much from it'.[31] Before that time little attention had been paid to the origins of Marx's economic theories, let alone their methodological aspects. Rosdolsky's book convinced Mandel of the correctness of Marx's historical method. He realized that any work that was not founded on a 'genetic evolutionary' basis was doomed to recapitulate received wisdom. The book also convinced him that Rosdolsky's approach to the debate over Marx's reproduction schemes was correct. In accord with Rosdolsky, Mandel concluded that Marx had meant these schemes to show the possibility of a temporary economic equilibrium despite the anarchy of production. Crises could not be explained by these schemes, and this had caused misunderstandings in one form or another in earlier Marxist writings, like those of Rosa Luxemburg, Rudolf Hilferding and Nikolai Bukharin.

Mandel repeatedly asked Rosdolsky's advice and requested him to read each draft chapter attentively and critically. For example, he consulted Rosdolsky about a section in which he sought to answer the question of why the simple production of goods, usury capital and merchant capital had only led to modern capitalism in Western and Central Europe and not elsewhere.[32] Rosdolsky found this an interesting question, handled in a challenging manner. Mandel urged him to make his sometimes rather laconic commentary more specific, 'In general nothing really good can come from a single solitary head; more thick skulls have to crash together, then the sparks can fly.'[33]

Despite their intellectual kinship, differences of opinion arose between them. On the occasion of the Polish and Hungarian insurrections of 1956–7 Rosdolsky was infuriated at the 'childish' optimism of Mandel's comrades.[34]

> I hope you don't take this frank criticism amiss. I know that you have the best intentions. But that does not give you free rein to get carried away by

leftist 'infantile disorders' out of revolutionary impatience . . . But now 'an end to it'; I promise not to speak of it any more. I am old and lonely enough; why should I gamble with our friendship?[35]

Two years later Rosdolsky was less resigned. After a critique with the tone of an indictment and the advice to stop 'playing at an International', he ended with:

> You will surely be very angry, but I have 'spoken and saved my soul'. Because just as the Trotskyist movement in the 'historical sense' is so important to me, I have to distance myself emphatically from what you are getting up to in the name of Trotskyism. In a certain sense you can take this as a farewell letter.[36]

Rosdolsky left Mandel's extensive reply unanswered.[37]

Some months later, in July 1960, their correspondence was resumed, and would remain uninterrupted for a longer time. Rosdolsky was close to Isaac Deutscher, whose dismissal of Trotsky's plea for a Fourth International remained a thorn in Mandel's side. Mandel confided to a mutual friend,

> Rosdolsky is a good friend, but for several years the friendship has been cooler (I think for political reasons). I value him highly and regard him as one of the best living Marxist economists. On political issues . . . he inclines toward Deutscher's views, which naturally often put us at odds.[38]

Just like Deutscher, Rosdolsky saw the Stalinist development of the Soviet Union as historically inevitable.[39] For him too the terms 'workers' state' and 'degenerated workers' state' were empty formulae as long as the working class exercised no political power.

Critics

The publication of Mandel's book was fraught with difficulties. In 1959, in search of a new publisher, Mandel had approached the sociologist Edgar Morin, ex-Communist and cofounder of the periodical *Arguments*. The manuscript, over 1,000 pages long, was offered to the Presses Universitaires de France and to ex-Trotskyist Pierre Naville, who edited a series for the Paris publishing house Marcel Rivière.[40] Mandel guaranteed Naville sales of 1,000 copies in Belgium, the Belgian Congo and North Africa. The publisher, however, dared not accept the book, an indication of the marginal position of independent Marxist thought at the time.[41]

Only in 1961 was Mandel's book definitely accepted, by the large Paris firm René Julliard, publisher of such books as Natalie Sagan's best-selling *Bonjour tristesse*.[42] Encouraged by Claude Bourdet, editor-in-chief of *France Observateur* ('This is an absolutely remarkable young man'),[43] Julliard was prepared to publish an edition of 3,500 copies, subject to an assurance of advance sales by subscription of 1,000 copies in order to make the financial risk acceptable. Mandel got *La Gauche* to deposit 20,000 French francs as a guarantee.[44] With subscription sales of 760 in Belgium and 613 in France, the goal was reached without difficulty.[45]

The book actually appeared in April 1962. Elated, Mandel wrote to Federn, 'The shipment of the subscribed copies to Belgium will weigh more than a ton; imagine: a ton of explosives carried by train . . .'[46] Mandel dedicated his brainchild to his father, who had wanted a scholarly career for him instead of the political life he had chosen. In *Marxist Economic Theory* the father's ambition and the son's had finally been reconciled. The following words appeared on the flyleaf:

> To the memory of my father,
> Henri Mandel,
> Brave in spirit, generous in heart,
> Who introduced me to Marxism
> And taught me to combat exploitation and oppression in all their forms
> So that all men can become brothers.[47]

Marxist Economic Theory received a mixed reception in political and intellectual circles. It was highly praised – Belgian radio spoke with great respect of a sequel to Marx's *Capital* – but there was a deafening silence from official Social Democratic sources. Mandel complained to André Renard of feeling himself victim of 'a conspiracy of silence on the part of the "big press" '.[48] The Belgian historian Marcel Liebman wrote to Isaac Deutscher about the book, calling it 'an important contribution to Marxist thinking', only regretting that the chapter on the Soviet economy '[is] so strikingly biased and so poorly documents present developments in Russia'.[49] Deutscher shared this opinion, which seemed to be inspired by their expectations of the self-reform of the bureaucracy.[50] That was an illusion, as Mandel did not fail to point out. Yet Deutscher's appreciation for the book was undiminished. He praised the 'great intellectual merit' of the work, for which, as he wrote Rosdolsky, 'we have been waiting since [sic] many, many years'.[51] At their first meeting in May 1962 in London,

Deutscher promised Mandel that he would review it in *The Economist*. Since the war Deutscher, who was just finishing his own trilogy on Trotsky, had been writing for the City of London's house organ.[52]

Deutscher's review appeared under the title 'Marxist Heretic', which was an undeniable tribute from the pen of the author of *Heretics and Renegades*. Deutscher praised Mandel as

> an independent thinker, combining an exceptionally wide erudition with a remarkable lucidity and fluency of expression. His treatise is by far the best popularisation of Marx's economic theory that has appeared for forty or fifty years. And it is far more than that – an ambitious, and largely successful, attempt to bring the doctrine up to date.

There were weaknesses, of course, but 'no student can afford to ignore this very important work'.[53] Deutscher's encomiums surprised Mandel: 'I'm sure I don't deserve half your praise, and there are certainly much [sic] more weaknesses in the book than those you mention.'[54]

More flattering responses followed, in such journals as *New Left Review*, the Italian *Critica marxista*, *Survey*, the Belgian *Socialistische Standpunten*, *La Nouvelle Revue Marxiste*, *L'Express* and *Combat* – the last three all from Paris. André Barjonet, the economic specialist of the French General Confederation of Labour (CGT); the Austrian-born French Marxist Lucien Laurat; the French historian Maximilien Rubel; the Yugoslav Rudi Supek; and the British Communist Maurice Dobb devoted essays to it.[55] André Renard wrote, 'Weighing my words carefully, I have to call your book remarkable and even fantastic.'[56] The dissident Polish economist Oskar Lange praised Mandel directly: 'The book has made a strong impression on me. It is definitely an original attempt to handle Marxist economics in the spirit of our times.'[57] The British *Observer* called it the best Marxist creation of the last fifty years. The book would be reprinted countless times and be translated into languages ranging from Spanish to Japanese and Hindi to Hebrew.

When the English edition was published, a review by Robert L. Heilbroner appeared in the *New York Review of Books*. A professor at the New School for Social Research in New York, Heilbroner acclaimed the publication as 'an event of great importance' and a 'masterful representation of Marxism'. It would be an inducement to become a Marxist were it not that 'in reading so free a work as Mandel's the limitations of Marxism and Marxian economics also stand forth, at least in my eyes', limitations that, Heilbroner said, made it impossible for him to join the Marxist camp. Among these Heilbroner included 'the belief in dialectics and class struggle' as basic to human history. For him, this was a theoretical bed of Procrustes that would not naturally fit every historical experience.[58]

Mandel was curious to know how Rosdolsky would judge the book. He sent him a copy, but got no reaction. Rosdolsky told the young Swiss Marxist and Hegel specialist Otto Morf that he found the book 'weak'.[59] The study would have benefited from being discussed in broader circles.[60] Mandel remained ignorant of these judgements. Rosdolsky recoiled from giving such criticism outright, particularly if it concerned work by friends he considered serious scholars. Deutscher complained that Rosdolsky too often pulled his punches.[61] Finally in 1964 after much urging from Mandel ('Why haven't you sent me more criticism of my book? I would be very grateful for a thorough critique'), Rosdolsky confessed that he felt driven into a corner.[62] Too often he had experienced authors who could not bear criticism: 'Thus Isaac [Deutscher] *broke with me* because of my critique of his third volume; since then I mostly hold myself back.'[63] Now, however, Mandel was pressing him.

Rosdolsky summarized his concerns in three points. To begin with, Mandel had sacrificed Marx's economic methodology in his wish to reach a broad public. He had gone too deeply into 'mere facts' and had thereby abandoned Marx's specific dialectical method, the heart of his economic theory. He had also been unclear about what Rosdolsky considered the core of Marxism, the theory of collapse, the final collapse of the capitalist order. This concept distinguished revolutionary Marxism from Austro-Marxism and its equilibrium theorists, such as Hilferding and Otto Bauer. Finally, Mandel had been too vague about the question of the falling rate of profit and crisis theory.[64]

Mandel had to understand that he, Rosdolsky – as long as the situation remained as it was – did not want to write publicly about the book. For the sake of the movement, publicity as favourable as possible was essential: 'But you have forced me to tell you my opinion, and I hope now that you will react differently from the way Isaac did.'[65] Mandel replied that if he reproached Rosdolsky for anything, it was that his criticisms were too brief. He subscribed to the remarks about the collapse theory and asked Rosdolsky to amplify his critique of the treatment of crisis theory.[66] He made it obvious that he took seriously the remarks on what he had titled 'The Epoch of Capitalist Decline'. He would gain new insights from this criticism for his later work on the long waves of capitalist development.

Debate with Jean-Paul Sartre

Marx's economic theory was not the first subject into which Mandel had sunk his teeth. At the end of the 1940s he had gone deeply into 'an extensive history of the rise and fall of the Communist International'. Federn understood that this would be a 'tremendous work', one in which Mandel had been engaged 'for years already', and from which he hoped his first book would emerge.[67] This indicates that Mandel's thought at that time was dominated by the debate over Stalinism, the nature of the Soviet Union and the question of workers' states.

During this period Mandel published '*Die Wissenschaft der Entschleierung*' (The Science of Revelation). This was a response to Professor Carlo Schmid, the leader of the Social Democratic Party (SPD) in the German parliament, who had attempted to 'reveal' the nature of historical materialism at a party congress.[68] In addition Mandel wrote articles on political theory for the Berlin periodical *Pro und contra: Diskussionsblätter für demokratischen Sozialismus* (For and Against: Discussion Papers for Democratic Socialism), using the pseudonym Wilhelm Sprenger. Finally, in the early 1950s he contributed to the debate on 'The Communists and Peace' that Jean-Paul Sartre had launched in *Les Temps Modernes*.[69]

Although Sartre was not a member of the French Communist Party (PCF), he argued that it was indispensable. The working class did not exist until it was organized in a vanguard party, and the PCF seemed to be such a party.[70] This view was criticized from various sides. In *Adventures of the Dialectic* Maurice Merleau-Ponty called Sartre's position 'ultra-Bolshevism',[71] and Claude Lefort, a member of the group 'Socialisme ou Barbarie', blamed Sartre for considering the working class only in the context of the party and having no eye for its separate existence.[72] As for Ernest Mandel, he accused the existentialist philosopher of an un-Marxist fatalism.[73]

In an extended argument Sartre replied that Mandel was cursed with 'a probabilistic idealism' and that he dealt not with realities but possibilities, 'which are based most often on simple extrapolations'.[74] Mandel had argued that the PCF had missed the opportunity to take power in 1944–45.[75] He did not agree with Sartre that the PCF's politics of restraint was the only possible strategy at the time, or, in Sartre's words: 'it reveals itself as existence only manifesting itself as *praxis*'.[76] According to Mandel this was the same argument that Hegel had used 'to declare the absolutist state holy, a position that Marx had mercilessly mocked'.[77] If success were to be the only criterion for realism and effectiveness, then Sartre had to admit that in Belgium or Britain, where social democrats set the tone, the Communists were tarred with the same 'idealism of possibilities' as the Trotskyists were in France.

Mandel considered the idea that reality could only develop in one direction to be fatalistic and in conflict with Marxism. In the years 1944–5 the revolutionary situation in France had allowed two diametrically opposed prospects, victory or defeat. Sartre considered the role of the

Communists in the defeat that ensued to be accidental, while Mandel considered it decisive.[78]

> We don't say that they could have taken power on 27 August 1944 . . .
> We do say that in 1944–5 there were hundreds of opportunities to build
> oppositional power for which the seeds had been formed by the masses
> themselves (liberation committees, factory committees, militias). A true
> communist leadership . . . would have seen its duty as taking the greatest
> possible advantage of these achievements. What the results might have
> been would have depended on developments in the relationship of forces
> that no one could have predicted exactly.[79]

Mandel, revolutionary and anti-determinist that he was, concerned himself
with what was possible, with 'thinking that did not yet exist', in the words of
the German philosopher Ernst Bloch,[80] not with what was realistic or
necessary, the excuse made by every conformist current.[81]

Mandel offered his critique to *Les Temps Modernes*, but Sartre did not
publish it. Following the events of May 1968 Sartre would revise his
perspective:

> After 1945 Stalinism made it impossible for Western Communist parties,
> and particularly the French Communist Party, to take power . . . Anyone
> who attempted to take advantage of the Communists' admirable position
> during the war, anyone who attempted to push through revolutionary
> reforms or encouraged the workers to be more combative, was called to
> order by the party, silenced or expelled. The party simply did not aim to
> make a revolution.[82]

One can easily see this judgement as a late echo of Mandel's 1952 critique.

6

In the Fourth International

Michalis (Michel) Raptis went through life under the pseudonym Michel Pablo. When Ernest Mandel met him he was thirty-three, tall and already balding, with a soft yet clear voice and a round face undercut by a receding chin. He was a native of Alexandria born in 1911to a Greek father and an Egyptian mother.[1]

He had originally studied to be an architect, and there was something of the artist in his dress – in the hat he wore, in the cut of his collar. Distinguished and stylish, he was well matched with his aristocratic life partner Hélène, with her coal black eyes and electric hair. He adored her. Born Ellie Diovoniotis in 1907, she came from an influential Greek family and had grown up in Athens and studied law. Her inheritance was sufficient to free them from having to earn a living. She and Pablo were able to devote themselves entirely to the revolution.

As a student at the polytechnic institute in Athens in the late 1920s, Pablo joined a quasi-illegal revolutionary group that had split from the Communist Party. In 1934 he and Pantelis Pouliopoulos, the ex–general secretary of the CP, helped form the first Greek Trotskyist group, the Organization of Internationalist Communists of Greece (OKDE).[2] This was two years before the coup d'état of General Metaxas, which sent Pablo to a prison on the island Folegandros and then to Acronauplion, an eighteenth-century Venetian fort that towered above the Peloponnesian coast. Above its entry gate was the inscription 'Concentration Camp for Communists'.[3]

He and Hélène were given the choice of submission or exile. They chose to emigrate. In 1937, after a short stay in Switzerland, they arrived in Paris. There they became acquainted with Pierre Naville, an influential Trotskyist who had made his name in the Surrealist movement of the 1920s. They enrolled as students at the Sorbonne and were often to be found at the famous café Les Deux Magots in company with such kindred spirits as Jacques Prévert and the actor Jean-Louis Barrault. Using a second pseudonym, Speros, Pablo took part in founding the Fourth International at Périgny in September 1938.

Shortly after the founding conference he contracted tuberculosis. He was nursed at a sanatorium in St-Hilaire-du-Touvet near Grenoble, where he stayed until 1943. He was also able to obtain travel documents in order to receive regular medical treatment in Geneva. His stay in St-Hilaire proved a great stroke of luck, because the parents of Marcel Hic, the leader of the French section of the Fourth International (POI), had a bookshop there. By way of this village in the Isère, the European Secretariat led by Hic in Paris was able to remain in contact with the rest of the Fourth International.

When Hic was arrested in October 1943, Pablo, then relatively unknown but very knowledgeable, replaced him as secretary. He returned to Paris, where for a while he was able to keep Paul Widelin out of the hands of the Gestapo[4] – Pablo's room on the Boulevard St-Michel was next to that of the intrepid publisher of *Arbeiter und Soldat*.[5] Pablo also managed to unite the three French Trotskyist groups into a single party, the International Communist Party (PCI). Mandel witnessed this success when he and Abraham Léon attended the underground European conference of the International, held at St-Germain-la-Poterie in February 1944. Mandel admired Pablo's courage and skill. On his visits to Paris he stayed with Pablo and enjoyed his fatherly sympathy. The charming young Greek with his fluent French bore no resemblance then to the authoritarian figure with whom Mandel would one day clash.

A third world war

In the early 1950s, Pablo (by then known in the International by a third pseudonym, Gabriel or Gabe), became convinced that history was taking an apocalyptic turn. The Korean War had broken out in April 1950. Was it the beginning of a new world war? Not only the communists but even De Gaulle considered this a possibility. In *Où allons-nous?* (Where Are We Going?) Pablo argued that the approaching world cataclysm would take the form of a world 'War-Revolution' that would pit two great blocs – the 'Stalinist world' and the capitalist – against each other. Like it or not, 'the overwhelming majority of the forces opposing capitalism are right now to be found under the leadership or influence of the Soviet bureaucracy'.[6]

A Stalinist world objectively opposed to the capitalist regime – this idea marked the complete disappearance of the idea of a counterrevolutionary bureaucracy. This was ominous, because Marxist thinkers predicted that the transition from capitalism to communism, the condition in which classes and state would be abandoned, would take several centuries.[7] Pablo was reproached with judging the Soviet bureaucracy too mildly. He had replaced a class analysis with a campist theory in which the world was divided into two power blocs, using terms such as class, nation and state all jumbled up together.[8] Pablo's analysis had touched sensitive nerves. Hatred for Stalinism was often based on personal trauma. The idea of backing Stalinist-led revolutions was too much for Trotskyists to swallow. Comrades asked indignantly whether they were supposed to turn the other cheek when the Stalinists lynched them in the streets. Pablo also considered the changes in Yugoslavia and China to be authentic revolutions. But if a revolution could occur when a Stalinist party broke completely with the bourgeoisie independently of the Kremlin[9] – in other words, if Stalinists had the power to lead revolutions – why struggle to build new revolutionary parties? Pablo's opponents were horrified by the very idea. As the later Trotsky biographer Pierre Broué put it, 'A cold shiver runs down my spine.'[10]

In his *Ten Theses*, an essay on Stalinism, Ernest Mandel proposed a limited acceptance of Pablo's analysis and somewhat dimmed the rather rosy light Pablo had shone on the Soviet bureaucracy.[11] Members of the French section, particularly its leaders Marcel Bleibtreu, Michel Lequenne and Pierre Lambert, were far from reassured.[12] Bleibtreu had been raised in a cultured and political family. His father was one of France's biggest textile manufacturers, a collector of modern art and also an 'important, militant partisan of Dreyfus'.[13] Bleibtreu resisted what Pablo considered the logical outcome of his analysis: the necessity for entry into the mass parties, which in France meant the Communist Party. The PCF was a closed fortress, to which every revolutionary sentiment was alien. Critics saw in what soon came to be called Pabloism a betrayal of the anti-bureaucratic revolution and in Pablo a pro-Stalinist liquidator who had to be thwarted.

Mandel also had his doubts. Pablo's generalizations, the ambiguous concept of the 'Stalinist world' and the idea that the transition to socialism would take centuries – these required clarification. But his doubts did not prevent him from supporting Pablo.[14] The threat of a third world war was decisive. Mandel pointed out that 'rearmament knows its own logic . . . and almost inexorably leads to war'.[15] There was just too little time to build independent organizations. Only through entry into existing ones could the way to the workers be found.

No one in the leadership of the Fourth International doubted the threat of war.[16] They even began preparing to go underground. Pablo sounded out the Dutchman Sal Santen about a mission to South America to look for an alternative location for the International Secretariat.[17] Though short of funds, Santen left willingly enough, in 1952, taking a boat from Marseilles to

Montevideo. Santen, the thirty-six-year-old newspaper stenographer and son-in-law of the revolutionary Henk Sneevliet, who had been killed by the Nazis, would stay in South America for a year.

Criticism of Pablo continued. Six months after the World Congress of August 1951, the French section was no closer to entry.[18] Driven by the conviction that he was right, Pablo pushed for the suspension of dissidents in the French Central Committee, who were relieved of their positions. Hesitatingly, Mandel accepted the assignment to carry out the entry policy in the name of the Secretariat and 'with majority support'.[19] This was an absurd manoeuvre considering that two-thirds of the members were actually opposed. The debaters did not confine themselves to reasoned arguments for or against the merits of the policy. There was name-calling as well ('Deserters!' 'Unmasked petty-bourgeois moralists!') and in the old theatre building on Rue l'Arbre-Sec that was the section's headquarters there were nocturnal battles over possession of the stencil machines, the offices and the files. Mandel was punched when he tried to attend a meeting of the opposition. The section, which had numbered 250 members in 1951, fell apart.[20] Bleibtreu and Lambert went their own way.[21] So did Pierre Frank, taking with him the remnants of the PCI, perhaps a hundred members.

These were painful months, during which lifelong friends fought with each other as if they were deadly enemies. According to a stunned contemporary, 'There was an element of love turned sour in this violence.'[22] Why had there been such haste to push through this policy? Such excessive centralism? It was legitimate to want to belong to a larger movement, but why concoct an adventurist theory about a 'war-revolution' to which Stalinist parties would react in a revolutionary way? Why the coercion? The Fourth International found itself at a low point everywhere. The one exception was the section in Ceylon (Sri Lanka) the Lanka Sama Samaya Party, which had developed into the strongest workers' party on the island. But in most countries section membership could be counted in the tens, with a worldwide total of only a few hundred. And the French PCI and the US SWP, the biggest sections, turned inward under pressure from McCarthyism and the Cold War.[23]

Anticipated breakthroughs failed to materialize, and demoralization spread. Collective entry into large workers' parties was an attempt to find a way out and stave off complete dissolution. This strategy had worked in Belgium, but as Mandel realized, the Social Democrats simply offered more scope than the Communists. But was there any alternative to the Communists in a country like France? The theory of entry, however abstract, aided discipline. But the triumphant claim that with entry the International was making the most progress since its founding, because the logic of the international situation was Trotskyist, simply had no basis in reality.

Strong personalities in the sections, like Pablo, the American James P. Cannon, Pierre Frank, Pierre Lambert, the Argentinean Homero Cristali (pseudonym Juan Posadas) and the Briton Gerry Healy (pseudonyms Tom Burns, Mason, Paddy O'Reagan, G. Preston and Philip Williams), exercised a dominant influence. These leading figures were often the focus of devotion and imitation, yet they lived in mutual jealousy. They were the products of organizations that were tight moralistic communities, not only because of their idealistic aims but also because of the threats they faced, some of which were real but just as many of which were imagined. The tight bonds among their members gave the organizations an appearance of strength but the resulting incestuous conflicts weakened them. Doubts were not tolerated; only loyalty counted. This was a recipe for disaster in small, isolated organizations.

Split in the Fourth International

In 1952 and 1953 the rupture in France spread to Britain, the United States and other countries.[24] Initially there was no difference in perspective between the SWP and the International Secretariat led by Pablo. James P. Cannon, leader of the SWP and founder of the left opposition in the US Communist Party in 1928, defended Pablo's vision as 'completely Trotskyist'. Their personal connection also seemed problem-free. For Cannon's sixtieth birthday the sum of 400 dollars had been collected, which he wanted to donate to the International, but not if it would simply disappear into the organization's general funds. As he informed Mandel and his friends, 'With this strict limitation, I don't care what you do with the money . . . If you are thirsty, you can spend it all on cognac as far as I am concerned', preferably with a toast to 'the old son-of-a-bitch who believes that money was made to be spent and shared with friends'.[25]

But this friendship turned sour when Cannon became the butt of criticism from the circle around the SWP weekly *The Militant*. Dissidents, among them Harry Braverman,[26] turned to Pablo's analyses to support their position and Pablo did not discourage them.[27] Some even used Pablo's ideas as a pretext to begin discussing the continued existence of the SWP. Cannon accused them of being agents of Pablo, capitulating to Stalinism.[28] As Lambert had done in France, Cannon decided to break with the International and form a rival organization. The SWP, Gerry Healy's group in Britain and the group led by Argentinean Hugo Bressano (pseudonym Nahuel Moreno) came together as the International Committee (IC).

Mandel was dismayed. The International was of supreme importance to him. He accused Cannon of bad faith, and asked George Breitman, the editor of *The Militant*,

> Do you really believe that we are 'capitulating before Stalinism'? . . .
> More concretely: do you believe that I, who have predicted perhaps alone
> in the world what would happen in Russia and the rest of the Stalinist
> sphere of influence . . . have 'capitulated before Stalinism'?[29]

Breitman, a thin, silent man originally from New Jersey was one of the founders of the SWP. He had got to know Mandel in 1946 at the first postwar conference of the International in Paris. By the end of 1953 their exchange of letters was the only remaining dialogue between the International Secretariat and the SWP.[30]

Mandel told Breitman that he did not think what he termed a tragi-comedy of error and misunderstanding was worth a split.[31] But in that case, Breitman wanted to know, why had Pablo not distanced himself from dissidents like Braverman?[32] Cannon thought Pablo was misusing Mandel.[33] Breitman warned his friend,

> I hope you won't serve as Pablo's advocate . . . I urge you: reconsider
> what has happened . . . I earnestly hope that you will take your place . . .
> against those whose . . . disorientation is driving them to conciliation with
> Stalinism and other alien forces.[34]

But Mandel refused to separate himself from Pablo. Cannon suggested that Breitman end the correspondence, and he did so.[35]

A secret contact

Though their dialogue had been ended, Mandel kept himself informed on the SWP. He was amazed at the Americans' habit of elevating their own orthodoxy to the status of absolute truth. 'Trotsky or Deutscher?', the title of Cannon's commentary on *The Prophet Armed*, the first volume of the Polish–British historian Isaac Deutscher's monumental biography of Trotsky, was telling.[36] According to Cannon, Deutscher's belief in the possibility of reforming Stalinism was heresy. Mandel's review was more respectful, though he did not think much of the book's characterization of Trotsky as a classic tragic hero who unwillingly paved the way for Stalinism.[37] Deutscher thanked him for 'the objective and open-minded manner in which [he] has treated [the] writings.'[38]

Mandel was in confidential contact with Karl Manfred, another editor of *The Militant*. Using the pseudonym James Parkner, Manfred contributed items to *La Gauche*. Manfred was originally from Frankfurt on Main, where he was raised in a rich, liberal Jewish family. His father was a prominent urologist; his mother came from Sephardic aristocracy.[39] After Kristallnacht, in November 1938, the Manfred family moved to Brussels.[40] Before the deportation of Jews from Belgium began in 1942, the twenty-two-year-old Manfred escaped to Switzerland. After the war he returned to Brussels, where he became friends with Ernest Mandel, who recruited him to Trotskyism.[41] By 1954 Manfred had been living in New York for five years. Destitute after the war, he thought he could most quickly become self-supporting as a journalist in the US, where it was easier to obtain citizenship. Manfred was not the only German immigrant who wound up in or around the SWP. Despite the struggle that had broken out between its factions, he assured Mandel, 'I continue to have a most favourable impression of the American organization.'[42]

Manfred was certainly no factionalist, and he had the highest respect for Mandel. Their continued and extensive exchange of views was an open secret.[43] Mandel thought it important to gauge the political barometer in the US, and he wanted an audience for his calls for reunification. In 1956 he wrote to Manfred that on all questions – including Hungary, Poland, Suez and China – 'our respective papers say exactly the same things'. If any profit were to be made from the Stalinist crisis, then it was essential to join together what had been put asunder: 'The mere fact of this division prevents many ex-Stalinists from joining our ranks'.[44]

Poland and Hungary (1956)

In the spring of 1956 Mandel was absorbed by events in Eastern Europe. In the Poznan revolt that broke out on 27 June he detected signs of an incipient revolution.[45] Deutscher's comment that 'the demonstrations . . . began with singing "The International" but ended with the slogans "Down with the Jews!" and "Away with the Russians!" ' made no impression on Mandel.[46] He was concerned with the underlying tenor of the revolt, which opposed the country's bureaucracy but did not question its social structure. He enthusiastically cited the weekly *Po Prostu*, mouthpiece of the Warsaw dissidents. Its editor-in-chief, Eligiuz Lasota, had been imprisoned for Trotskyism in 1949 and only released a few months earlier. The censors were giving *Po Prostu* a free hand. 'So events seem to be even more important than we had thought. I'm putting everything into getting there as soon as possible.'[47] Mandel asked Deutscher and Rosdolsky for the addresses of old friends in Poland.[48]

There was no Trotskyist group in Poland, though there were a few pre-war Trotskyists without much postwar connection. One of them was Kazimierz Badowski, a teacher from Kozienice who had stayed in Antwerp in the 1930s. Once back in Poland, he had been deported first by Hitler and then by Stalin. Badowski lived in Krakow and was in contact with kindred spirits in France.[49] Another was the historian Ludwik Hass, who in September 1939 had been deported to forced labour in the Vorkuta mines in northern Russia. He returned to Warsaw in 1957 after seventeen years' imprisonment. His family had been killed in Auschwitz.[50] In these months Badowski and Hass assembled a group of around twenty activists.[51] This was a modest number, yet more than were in Hungary, where things looked less rosy.

There too an anti-bureaucratic revolution was beginning, but Mandel recognized the real possibility of a restoration of capitalism in Hungary because of the strength of its conservative parties and the Catholic Church. He asked Austrian comrades to translate into Hungarian the appeal 'LONG LIVE THE INDEPENDENT, DEMOCRATIC HUNGARIAN RE-PUBLIC OF WORKERS' COUNCILS!'[52] and to smuggle it over the border. Money was no object: 'This is today the first priority of the entire movement . . . At revolutionary moments a dozen militants with clear ideas can influence thousands of people.'[53] Mandel warned that without revolutionary leadership 'a positive outcome . . . is certainly not assured'.[54] On 4 November 1956, Russian tanks raged through Budapest to crush the insurrection. Mandel rushed headlong to Vienna as a correspondent for *Le Peuple*. He stayed for less than a week, from 5–9 November. For a while still he hoped that the Kremlin could be brought to its knees by a general strike.[55] Despite the Soviet occupation, the workers' committees remained vocal in support of the socialist economy. Could the socialist consciousness of the Hungarian working class be more convincingly proven? Mandel phoned his reports through from the Hungarian border, travelling around the country for as long as he could.[56]

Once back in Belgium, he concentrated his energies on *La Gauche*. The first issue was supposed to appear on 15 December, but he felt unable to stay for the paper's inauguration. On 10 December he returned again to Eastern Europe, this time taking a plane to Warsaw, where he would remain for over two weeks at the invitation of *Zycie Warszawy*, which had arranged an exchange of journalists with *Le Peuple*.[57] Mandel expected a lot from the trip; he considered that the circumstances 'seem propitious for an intervention on our part'.[58] His travel journal, a densely written notebook, gives an impression of frenzied activity, not only in Warsaw but also in Lodz, Poznan, Krakow and Nowa Huta.[59] Mandel spoke with Eligiuz Lasota of *Po Prostu* and the economists Michal Kalecki, Edward Lipinski and Oskar

Lange, who, as Mandel reported to Rosdolsky, 'had developed in a good direction'.[60] He also spoke with Stanislaw Brodski, chair of the journalists' union; Jerzy Tepicht, a specialist in agricultural questions; the young philosopher Jerzy Wiatr; the literary critic, poet and ex-Trotskyist Edward Janus, only recently released from prison; Tatarkowna, the first party secretary of Lodz; and Leszek Kolakowski, a promising philosopher at the University of Warsaw.[61] In addition, he met many students and young workers. To his surprise, despite their 'dreadful education' they were by no means lost causes.[62]

Mandel sensed a deep-rooted fear of the Kremlin, which considered Poland, like Hungary, a source of revolutionary infection. Mandel knew that a Stalinist party faction was being nurtured from the Russian Embassy, made up of party members who would be trustworthy accomplices 'just in case. In any event I urge you to be discreet . . . because few foreigners know about this and I do not want to make it too easy for the source to be discovered.'[63] When he raised the idea of publishing Trotsky's writings, he was given to understand that Moscow would regard this as a *casus belli*. Mandel presented himself in Poland as a 'left-wing socialist sympathetic to Trotsky'.[64] This left him free, as he said, to meet with whomever he wished, and at the same time able to talk to Communist Party people. This was important, because he expected new divisions in the Polish CP; everyone's position was shifting.

Mandel recounted his impressions in *Le Peuple* and *La Gauche* and also in the German *Sozialistische Politik* and in *France Observateur*. He gave lectures on Eastern European developments at the Maison du Peuple in Brussels and La Populaire in Liège.[65] Poland was a sensitive but promising arena for work. Later, in the 1970s, he discussed it with the historian Theo van Tijn, a professor at the University of Utrecht.[66] Van Tijn had become friends with Leszek Kolakowski in Poland. When Kolakowski went to Amsterdam in 1958 to study seventeenth-century Dutch religions, he lived for six months with Van Tijn's mother.[67] Eventually he became a renowned philosopher. He said later, 'I had a personal affection for Mandel and for Theo [van Tijn]; they were sincere and had a realistic perspective on the socialist world.' But he wanted nothing to do with a secret gathering in Brussels: 'I was ready to go to prison in Poland but please not for Trotskyism; all friends would laugh at me.'[68]

In 1957, the Belgian Socialist Young Guard (SJW) established contact with the Polish Union of Socialist Youth.[69] A few of the Poles visited Brussels and Antwerp in the summer and were hosted by the Socialist Party and the ABVV. Mandel had high expectations for one of them, Ludwik Mikrut, a steel worker from Nowa Huta and vice-chair of the Socialist

Youth. He stayed with Georges Dobbeleer in Liège, read Trotsky's *The Revolution Betrayed* in one night and converted to Trotskyism.[70] When Communist Party General Secretary Wadysaw Gomulka gradually reassumed control, Mikrut was expelled from the party and fired. He communicated with Trotskyist friends in a roundabout manner:

> I ask you to observe silence about me because people from our embassy are also concerned in the affair. They have assembled a nasty report about my 'anti-communist' social-democratic activities in Belgium. At this moment I am slaving away like a beast of burden and praising our god and Holy Father Gomulka.[71]

In 1959 Mandel asked Dobbeleer to renew the lapsed connection with Poland. Georges Dobbeleer, then almost thirty, was from a Liège family that had earned its spurs in the struggle against the Nazis, and in 1953, after a brief flirtation with Communism, he had turned to the Fourth International.[72] On his first trip to Poland he had visited Badowski in Krakow. Badowski was distributing an illegal paper, and Dobbeleer's financial help was very welcome.[73] In Warsaw Dobbeleer tried to make contact with Karol Modzelewski, a student of medieval history and the son of a member of the Politburo and former foreign minister. He had played a key role in the events of 1956, but now he seemed disillusioned. He told Dobbeleer, 'No, I'm not going to get involved with politics. It's over now. People aren't interested in all that any more.' But in the summer of 1963, in collaboration with Jacek Kuron, Modzelewski wrote an 'Open Letter to the Party', containing a heretical view of the bureaucracy and the single-party system, stating that 'a monopoly of power went hand-in-hand with the destruction of freedom'.[74] Originally this manifesto had no title, nor was it signed. It was to be duplicated and distributed clandestinely, and Dobbeleer offered to help.[75]

At the invitation of the Polish Communist youth group, Dobbeleer had gone to Warsaw that July. In his baggage he had 1,000 copies of 'Stalinism in Crisis', a resolution written by Mandel for the Sixth World Congress of the Fourth International in 1961, translated into Polish.[76] Shortly before, a West German comrade had smuggled a stencil machine over the Polish border.[77] The copies of the resolution and the stencil machine were intended for Ludwik Hass, who made no secret of his sympathies and showed the resolution to Kuron and Modzelewski. Kuron told Hass that he had little interest in it. It looked disreputable, having been typed by Mandel's elderly aunt on an ancient typewriter in an old-fashioned spelling no longer current in Poland. Though the resolution was scorned, the stencil machine was avidly received: it gave Kuron and Modzelewski a chance to reproduce the

'Open Letter'. Sixteen copies were made and circulated in March 1965. In his memoir *Belief and Guilt*, Jacek Kuron wrote, 'I handed two to Ludwik Hass, remarking, "These are for the West."'[78] The next morning Kuron and Modzelewski were arrested. A few days later a postcard picturing a fountain appeared in Dobbeleer's mailbox in Liège – the pre-arranged signal that there had been arrests.[79]

Kuron was sentenced to three years in prison, Modzelewski to three and a half. Hass and Badowski were also sentenced to three years, as was Dobbeleer *in absentia*.[80] The 'Open Letter' reached Paris in April 1966.[81] Mandel wrote of it, 'The analysis is not only Marxist. It is also profoundly revolutionary . . . profoundly internationalist.'[82]

Sherry Mangan, writer and revolutionary

There was much to criticize in the work that the International had done in Eastern Europe in the 1950s, but at least it was clear that Mandel and Pablo had not yielded to Stalinism. The Americans could not fail to notice that everything they had done expressed the desire to build a new revolutionary movement. With satisfaction, Mandel recorded that 'our assessment today of Russian developments, as well as the Polish and Hungarian revolutions and the entire international situation, no longer separates [us] from the SWP'.[83] And in 1957 the SWP gave Sherry Mangan the task of looking into the prospects for reunification.[84]

Mangan had spent the early 1950s in Cochabamba in Bolivia ('the nicest place to live'[85]), where he was writing *The Mountain of Death*, a novel about workers in the tin mines. Since his psychiatric treatment in Amsterdam, he had been preparing a literary comeback. But the sickness and death of his life partner Marguerite Landin upset him deeply, and he was unable to complete his novel. Mandel read the manuscript and praised it as having 'fine language' and 'living characters'.[86] After a visit to New York, where he spent time with the ex-Trotskyists Mary McCarthy and Saul Bellow, and a brief Spanish adventure, Mangan wound up again in Paris, where he translated Paul Valéry's poetry.[87] He returned to New York in March 1957, with the addresses of Manfred and Breitman in his pocket, and rented a modest room in the Chelsea Hotel. When he spoke with the SWP, he sensed a sympathetic stance toward Mandel and Pablo's group, but a meeting with James P. Cannon, the only one who could actually move a reunification forward, deteriorated into an exchange of abuse.[88] After two months he returned to Paris empty-handed. A little while later he turned his attention to aiding the Algerian National Liberation Front (FLN), then fighting for Algerian independence from France.

Supporting the Algerian independence struggle

In 1953, the Korean War ended and Stalin died, and the threat of a third world war receded. With its rapid growth, the Western European economy was bringing about radical changes.[89] Washing machines, transistor radios, the first televisions, motorbikes and automobiles opened unprecedented possibilities for a better standard of living. The radios were broadcasting not only rock-and-roll and the songs of Charles Aznavour and Jacques Brel but also ever more frequent reports about the French colony of Algeria. It was 1956, and the Algerians' fight for independence was growing fiercer.

Though Mandel and Pablo had been mistaken about a third world war, their intuitions about the onrushing colonial revolution had not let them down; India, Ceylon, Pakistan, Indochina, Indonesia, Iran and now North Africa had all risen against the imperialist powers in a strike for self-determination.

Little support for them could be expected from the social democrats or Communists.[90] It was forthcoming from progressive Catholics, anarchists, a small faction of the Socialist SFIO, the cream of French intellectuals from Sartre to Signoret, and the Trotskyists.[91] They were at the forefront, not only in France but elsewhere in Europe. Pablo, Mandel and their bare hundred French comrades were among the very first to support the still-mysterious FLN. It was deed as well as words that counted. Pablo said that 'a new chapter has opened in the struggle for freedom in this country, a liberation that it will be impossible to stop'.[92]

The FLN was leading the Algerian revolution, but its influence in France – the famous Seventh Wilaya[93] – was as yet limited. This was an opportunity for the International to help the FLN grow by enabling it to collect a revolutionary tax from the tens of thousands of Algerians who were working in France. The Trotskyists were backed by what was taking shape as the New Left, a loosely structured milieu containing 'old Trotskyists for life' like Craipeau, Naville and the mathematician Laurent Schwartz, and radical socialists, ex-Communists, academics like Edgar Morin and journalists like Claude Bourdet and Gilles Martinet. The International was entrusted with the production and distribution of *Résistance algérienne* (Algerian Resistance), the FLN's first illegal paper in France.[94] Pierre Avot-Meyers was given the task of coordinating production and distribution. The connecting links with the FLN were Hadj M'hammed Cherchalli and Mohammed Harbi, a twenty-year-old student and one of the few Marxists in the Front. After the revolution Harbi became a noted historian.[95]

As repression against the movement grew, security became an ever greater concern. Mangan left his beloved Paris for the village of Orne, in the

Norman countryside. No one suspected that the American journalist living in such seclusion spent his evenings running a Gestetner duplicating machine on behalf of the Algerian rebels. Halfway to Paris he had a weekly rendezvous to exchange materials.[96] Eventually the printing was switched to Belgium, which lessened the risks. The many Algerians working in the Liège steel industry and in the mines formed a screen behind which the illegal work was easily masked.[97] Mandel took chief responsibility for this operation too. Others who were prominently involved were Adolphine 'Doudou' and Jean Neyens, journalists with Belgian television; the jurist Mathé Lambert; Malou Roriv; and Pierre Le Grève, the actual leader, assisted by Jean Godin as publisher. The papers were produced in Brussels, in Neyens's cellar.[98]

The Belgian Trotskyists, like their French counterparts, were active in wide-ranging milieux. The Belgian Committee for Peace in Algeria, founded in April 1958, soon had around 300 members.[99] 'It's incredible; you all know each other!' an FLN representative said to Pierre Le Grève, who nodded approvingly.[100] However, the representative showed concern as well as admiration. Didn't this large and intimate community endanger the secrecy necessary to protect such a project? Le Grève assured him that on Mandel's orders he took *Résistance algérienne* to Paris personally and regularly accompanied FLN leaders across the border.[101] The Algerians suggested that he replace his little Citroën with a faster car. Incidents such as assassinations and attacks occurred regularly – the work of The Red Hand, an offshoot of the French security police.

On a Friday in March 1960 Le Grève was teaching at his school. At his home in Uccle, a borough of Brussels, his wife opened a package that had arrived in the mail, with a legitimate sender identified on the wrapping, which was stamped 'special edition' and claiming to be a book titled *The Pacification*, an indictment of French torture. She opened the package and discovered a bomb, which miraculously did not explode. Such good fortune did not befall Georges Laperche, a history teacher in Liège. A similar device exploded in his hands, and caused his gruesome death. The same day Mandel warned Sal Santen in the Netherlands and Georg Jungclas in Germany to be careful: 'I have the feeling that the bandits are on our trail internationally . . . Particular safety measures that I already spoke about at the last meeting [of the International Secretariat] have now become *extremely urgent*.'[102] Le Grève began carrying a pistol.

Georg Jungclas, a lifelong Trotskyist, now almost sixty, was up to his neck in the Algerian work.[103] The Trotskyists published *Freies Algerien* (Free Algeria) in Cologne, sometimes in an edition of 6,000 copies. Hans-Jürgen Wischnewski, later a minister and vice-chair for the Social Democratic Party

(SPD), was persuaded to act as publisher.[104] The contact had been made through Mohammed Harbi. A drunken yet cool-headed Sherry Mangan had helped him cross the border.[105] Harbi had met beforehand with Pablo and Mandel in a Paris station restaurant, where they assured him that the Germans would painstakingly abide by the rules of underground work.[106]

Jungclas, who had conspiracy in his blood, coordinated the movement of money and the production of weapons. French and Belgian soldiers serving in occupied Germany were used as porters across the border, which they could cross inconspicuously.[107] Bags filled with the money that had been collected were handed over at the German embassy in Paris.[108] Since November 1953 Galician-born Jakob Moneta had been there as the accredited representative of the German Trade Union Federation (DGB). With his diplomatic passport he could cross the border unhindered, carrying documents for the FLN, and he could deposit money in an account at the Deutsche Bank in Frankfurt. In 1961, Moneta would be named an officer of the Legion of Honour by De Gaulle.[109] His illegal activities had gone unnoticed. A year later he became the editor-in-chief of both *Der Gewerkschafter*, a monthly for trade union administrators, and *Metall*, the paper of the metal workers' union IG Metall.[110] Mandel wrote articles for him under the pseudonym Peter Kipp; Moneta's daughter Dalia called him Uncle Kipp.

Jungclas, Santen and Pablo recruited an international group of skilled craftsmen who helped the Algerians make weapons at various locations in Morocco. They came from Argentina, Venezuela, England, France, Germany, Greece and the Netherlands, and worked non-stop to produce machine pistols and small mortars.[111] The work was done in orange groves and abandoned factories and even in the centre of Rabat, a stone's throw from the American embassy.[112] For weeks, sometimes months, the members of this international brigade did not see the light of day.[113] A Dutch engraver helped equip the factories and supplied the FLN with perfect French identity papers, work permits, factory passes and payroll lists seemingly from the largest French auto manufacturers.[114]

Conflict with Michel Pablo

Because of the bombings, the Secretariat of the International decided to leave Paris in May 1958, as did the FLN, which transferred its leadership to Germany. De Gaulle had taken power without the slightest opposition, a turn to the right that Pablo thought involved the danger of dictatorship.[115] Pablo and Hélène left for Amsterdam, where they stayed with Maurice Ferares, a violinist and trade union leader. Ferares was from a dirt-poor

family and he had seen every one of them taken away in the war. He had
joined the International soon after the Occupation ended. The entire third
floor and attic of a house on the Nieuwe Prinsengracht, on the border of a
Jewish neighbourhood decimated by the Germans, was made available to
Pablo. His secretary took up residence on the mezzanine floor, where the
original Jewish inhabitants had been accustomed to celebrate Sukkoth, the
Feast of the Tabernacles.

Only Pablo had expressed a preference for Amsterdam; the others
considered Rome a more suitable location.[116] They had gone along with
Pablo to keep him happy. Sal Santen was there: he and Santen were thick as
thieves, and Santen was unwilling after his South American adventure of
1952–3 to be separated again from his family. Moreover Pablo needed
Santen to back him in the sharp differences of opinion about developments
in Europe that were coming to light. In Paris Hélène Raptis had called
Pierre Frank an idiot because he failed to recognize the historic defeat of the
working class. Frank objected to Hélène's presence at leadership meetings,
and Mandel and the Italian Livio Maitan supported him in this. The
grumbling trio gave in when Pablo offered them the choice of accepting
Amsterdam and Hélène or his resignation.[117]

Ernest Mandel and Livio Maitan had known each other since 1947.
Maitan, originally from Venice, had studied classical languages in Padua and
joined the Resistance during the war.[118] In the last year of the war he went
to Switzerland, where he came into contact with Trotskyism. After the
Liberation Maitan was chosen to be the national secretary of the Italian
Socialist youth organization, which had some 30,000 members. In April
1947 he attended the congress of its French counterpart, where he first met
Mandel. Soon afterward Mandel looked him up in Milan; Maitan never
forgot how Mandel, seeing chalked on walls everywhere the slogan 'Viva
Internazionale!', delightedly exclaimed, 'Absolutely incredible! So many
internationalists in Italy in spite of the Stalinists and the reformists.' Mandel
hadn't realized that 'Internazionale' was simply the name of a big Milan
football team.[119] With Pierre Frank, Maitan and Mandel formed a trio in
whom Pablo and Santen would meet their match.

Pablo was a complex figure. He was friendly and generous, but not when
faced with differences of opinion. Then he became suspicious and convinced that plots were being hatched against him. This led to regular clashes
in the course of 1958. Mangan and Maitan threatened to leave the
International's leadership.[120] Mandel convinced them to reconsider, though
he was at least as troubled as they were by Pablo's high-handed behaviour.
Too often Pablo took positions that had not – or not yet – been collectively
discussed. Furthermore, Mandel realized that Pablo lacked a sense of

proportion; everything was all or nothing, now or never. This was an exaggerated style of activism that would exhaust a small organization like the Fourth International. Lenin's motto, 'Better fewer but better!' was not for Pablo.[121] Mandel thought it was time to break with this frenzied way of working: 'Wouldn't it have been better if I had been able to finish writing my book and had written somewhat fewer articles for periodicals?'[122] In Belgian social democratic circles he had learned to value a more balanced rhythm, to give and take rather than seeing everything sharply as black or white.

Instead of an administrative office that bickered about priorities, Mandel longed for a collective leadership, working with patience instead of pressure: 'It's only human that it makes me boil to hear that I'm not doing enough (I work an average eight hours a day on politics in addition to a full-time job).'[123]

He couldn't change his own position without affecting Pablo's. But by 1959 the situation had become untenable. Pablo's imperiousness was unbearable. Apart from Santen no one saw the organization's correspondence or knew what was going on with contacts or finances. This had to end. As Mandel said,

> I had to listen to all these heated stories about the necessity of immediate, sharp changes of course – supposedly 'the only way to avoid crises' – about France in 1950 and about the [US] SWP in 1953, with the tragic results we all know.

He feared a fiasco, now that Pablo insisted the situation in Europe required a change in tactics.[124] Pablo was ready to give up on Europe. The working class was further than ever from revolution. Only liberation movements in the Third World merited support. This pronouncement elicited a sigh from Pierre Frank: 'M[ichel Pablo] doesn't lead, he brutalizes.'[125]

In dismay Mandel saw the 'paralyzed' European proletariat thrown on the scrapheap, with Pablo proposing the most exotic solidarity initiatives as the alternative. Mandel was not inclined to abandon entry work now that it finally appeared to be bearing fruit, with *La Gauche* and *Links* gaining readers in Belgium, membership doubling in Germany and Italy, and influence growing among the Communist youth in France.[126] In November 1959 in Amsterdam he and Pablo had a blazing row. During a break, Hélène disdainfully referred to Mandel as a 'so-called Trotskyist'. Mandel snapped back, 'If you can say that, my response is that you're either stupid or crazy.'[127] The scene became more grotesque when Pablo ordered him to leave the meeting and Santen, known for his gentleness, threatened him with violence. Mandel felt deeply humiliated.[128] Pierre Frank avoided a

break by convincing the Secretariat to refrain from making a choice between
Pablo and Mandel.[129] The incident was seen as a clash of temperaments, and
'even if one thinks there are political divergences, that does not justify
eliminating a comrade'.[130]

Though tempers cooled, nothing changed in the organization's operation. As before, Pablo and Santen controlled daily affairs. Once a month
they were assisted by Mandel, Frank, Mangan (now living in Rome),
Jungclas, Maitan and the Argentinian Adolfo Gilly, who spent the spring of
1960 in Amsterdam.[131] There was still no open accounting of the finances,
which remained in Pablo's hands. The same was true for contacts and
correspondence.[132] The dissatisfaction of others made little difference to
Pablo. He and no one else had made the International into what it was. He
was convinced that without his participation, everything would fall to
pieces.

Should Mandel have gone into battle against him? There wasn't enough
time. In addition to *La Wallonie* and his work for *La Gauche* and *Links*, he
was trying to finish *Marxist Economic Theory* and find a publisher for it. He
told Mangan, 'I really have no time to breathe . . .' and pleaded with him,

> Please don't start overworking. *It isn't worth it.* The most precious thing
> we have . . . are capable, trained and reliable leaders of the movement. To
> get their health in danger for *any* current job is what the Italians call *contra-*
> *producente* [counter-productive].[133]

Mangan was just recovering from a heart ailment.[134]

Arrests, weapons and counterfeiting

On Friday 10 June 1960, a small army of Dutch national police stormed into
Nieuwe Prinsengracht 47 to arrest Pablo and his wife Hélène. It was her
birthday. Sal Santen was being held elsewhere in Amsterdam. The Dutch
and West German security police were rounding up a band of counterfeiters
that was about to produce millions of French banknotes. Raiding a printer in
Osnabrück, the authorities had found Ab Oeldrich, the Dutch engraver and
master counterfeiter who had been producing money and documents for
the Algerian cause. The newspapers reported that they were now looking
for the printer Joop Zwart, an old friend of Oeldrich's from his youth and
student days.[135]

On his way home from work Maurice Ferares ran into his oldest
daughter. She had been waiting for him by the canal and in tears told
him what had happened. Ferares went immediately to the main post office

and telephoned Mandel to let him know. He made an appointment to go to Brussels the next day to report in person. Back at home – Hélène had been released – Feroues learned for the first time about the production of false papers and counterfeit money and was completely stunned.[136] The next day in Brussels he was met at the North Station and driven by a roundabout route to an empty apartment in the city centre. The Secretariat – consisting of Mandel, Frank, Jungclas and Maitan – was meeting there. Ferares gave his account. Ferares recalled later that the reactions were unequivocal: 'But those are criminal activities! We can't defend something like that!' Something clicked for Ferares: 'If that's the vanguard of the revolution . . .' Bewildered, he headed homeward. Forty years later he said that 'Mandel had known about it anyway' – Hélène had sworn it.[137] Maitan also thought that Mandel and Pierre Frank had known about it, but 'only in outline, not in detail'. It had never been discussed; he and Jungclas knew nothing.[138] Mandel, however, denied that he had known anything about the counterfeiting. Because of the risks, he would never have supported such an activity. That was different from preparing false papers, which was defensible when it allowed underground activists to survive.[139]

The counterfeiting seemed to have been Pablo's solo effort; only Hélène and Santen had been taken into his confidence. 'Didn't we have to help the Algerians? Who else could or would?' Pablo's conscience had been gnawed at by such questions.[140] Omar Boudaoud had made the request on behalf of the FLN. Pablo had hesitated and consulted Mohammed Harbi in Frankfurt, who advised against the adventure.[141] Nonetheless Pablo had gone ahead with it. Santen asked assistance from Oeldrich, a Haarlem resident. In his turn Oeldrich took on two colleagues, one of whom was a pawn of Oeldrich's friend Joop Zwart. Once a student at the Lenin School in Moscow, since 1948 Zwart had been active in secret service circles. He called himself a printer-publicist and, unknown to Santen, had previously helped Oeldrich produce false identity papers. Thanks to Zwart, the Dutch security police were following the group's preparations step by step. The authorities struck just before the first printing.[142]

Pablo and Santen's arrests did not improve their relations with the Secretariat. They felt abandoned if not betrayed.[143] Pablo was afraid of being sentenced to at least four years and being deported to France or Greece. Hélène added to the tensions. Partial and self-willed, she refused to make funds available for the work of the Secretariat.[144] This did not stop Mandel, Frank and Maitan from getting a campaign under way to defend the act of supporting the Algerian revolution by providing identity papers and weapons. They said the counterfeit bank notes were a provocation planted by the French Red Hand.[145]

Even from prison Pablo tried to keep the International's leadership in his own hands. Bypassing the Secretariat, he appealed 'to you all, comrades of the International . . . I have the most complete trust in your proletarian and revolutionary morality. You will know how to defend the International.'[146] His alarming tone gave the impression that the International was threatened from within. Filled with suspicion, Hélène was convinced that their lives were endangered.[147] Money problems made the atmosphere even worse.[148] The Sixth World Congress was approaching, and travel costs for the hundred delegates would draw heavily on the International's funds. Delegates would be travelling from the far corners of the world to Schwerte, a small place south of Dortmund. The extra money that Hélène demanded for Santen, Pablo and herself was hard to justify.

Mandel attended only part of the congress, held in December 1960. In Belgium the strike against the Unity Law was being fought, and he could not miss this high point in the class struggle. He heard from Emile van Ceulen that the congress had ended in chaos. Election of the leadership bodies took place only after many delegates had left. That allowed Juan Posadas, supported by Adolfo Gilly and the Uruguayan Albert Sendic, to get a majority. Posadas, born in Argentina to poor Italian immigrants, had been recruited by Sherry Mangan in 1941–2.[149] He supported Pablo in the struggle against the Western Europeans. Pablo praised his dynamism: 'I declare to all the world that you're the best.'[150] Posadas was authoritarian, but also and above all charismatic.[151] Between twenty-five and thirty people had followed him to Europe by boat and idolized him. One after another they declared, 'I agree with comrade Posadas', and 'I fully agree with comrade Posadas.' Never before had a world congress echoed with such repetitive testimony from disciples.[152] Encouraged by Hélène, Posadas presented himself as Pablo's substitute. He felt himself to be the soul of the colonial revolution. He wanted nothing to do with Mandel and took pleasure in belittling him, remarking that he should stop reading detective stories.[153]

The death of Sherry Mangan

The conflict with Pablo and Posadas stimulated Mandel to resume his attempts at reconciliation with the US SWP. 'Very tactful, very sensitive, very nuanced . . . but please keep it under your hat, for the time being', he confided to Mangan in Rome.[154] On the eve of Santen and Pablo's trial Mangan sent him a brief letter: 'I am a bit breathless about the trial . . . I am relatively optimistic. Still.'[155] A few days later Mangan was dead. For three days he had lain sick in bed in his minuscule apartment, eating nothing. Beset by money worries, he refused to call a doctor. Disquieted friends alerted the police, who found him dead on Saturday 24 June 1961. The authorities were fascinated by the various papers spread around his apartment: 'Had they found a poet or a dangerous subversive?'[156]

Mangan had enclosed a poem in one of his last letters to Mandel. 'A new poem on a somewhat political subject – "Beethoven and the Bomb" – conceived many years ago in New York at an outdoor Stadium concert' was written in the margin:[157]

> Smack in the middle of the 'Emperor' under the stars
> that plane shrieked over, deafening, and you grimaced,
> you and three thousand others, till it passed,
> and then forgot it utterly. While I,
> my head rolled back, watched it rejoin far squadrons
> (whose gibbering, colored lights, in night manoeuvres,
> mocked searchlights' fingers groping after them),
> and pictured radars' sweeps and nukes following points,
> H-bombs air-borne each hour of the day and night,
> and others sheathed in lethal penciled length
> on earth, below the sea, at any madman's mercy;
> and turned my gaze again to watch you – rapt,
> unheeding, as if the world were only music.
>
> Or on that other evening when you'd grown
> impatient with me for the time I'd spent
> in working on the protest, and in fear of talk
> that might again grow bitter, we had fled
> the issue, and we were recapturing
> our menaced sense of love by listening
> together, sprawled on a couch, with just
> our fingers touching, to the one-eleventh,
> while through them love flowed back, under the spell,
> and outside there was passingly sirens
> (this time, just fire-sirens, but sirens still
> sufficient to recall the final ones to come)
> and passingly also my thought: there is
> so little time to head them off, to save
> all time for love and music; but when I rolled
> my head upon the pillow toward you, you
> were listening as if there were forever.
> > If we would still hear music, we
> > must also listen to the knell

tolling for music and for love.
Will it be only when I see your loved flesh turn
from red to black, and my already black
flesh is crackling, and we realize
that we had missed the epicenter, so we were not
blissfully vaporized, but must go on,
and, it being of course the moment for
the supreme kiss, will it only be when
our four lips fall together to the floor
that we shall wonder: did we always,
always in every way, with all our strength,
fight to prevent this moment, or,
were we, like all your clever friends,
just listening to Beethoven?

Art and politics were blended together in this synthesis of Mangan's hybrid personality. That pattern was repeated in his choice of the Emperor Concerto, Beethoven's ode to Napoleon, the aestheticization of his political convictions.

Mandel must have understood the essence. His Marxism was more than a critical research method, more than an indictment and an analysis. Just as with Mangan, it expressed a longing to change the world. Sherry Mangan and his alter ego Terence Phelan, poet and Bolshevik; Ernest Mandel and his alter ego Ernest Germain, intellectual and revolutionary – the personalities could not be separated.

Mandel was depressed by Mangan's death. He reproached himself for the impoverished circumstances in which Mangan had died. In a memorial he called attention to Mangan as a poet and novelist: 'Above all, mention that he wrote a remarkable novel about the Bolivian mineworkers – still unpublished – and that he lived among them for three years in order to write it.'[158] Mangan was buried in the Protestant cemetery in Rome, near the ruins. Nearby lay Shelley, Keats and Antonio Gramsci.[159] It was actually a misunderstanding on the part of the friends who organized it without knowing of Mangan's wish to be cremated.[160] Mandel was not present at the ceremony.

In Amsterdam the court case against Pablo and Santen was dragging on. To spare them, the Secretariat temporarily withheld the news of Mangan's death.[161] They were given fifteen months, a milder sentence than the prosecution's demand for three years for Pablo and two for Santen. They were saved by a secret box that Ab Oeldrich had kept as a sort of insurance in case the illegal work went awry. It contained documents that compromised high-ranking civil servants and authorities – even Prince Bernhard, husband of the Dutch queen, was mentioned. The documents came from the archives of the Dutch Political Investigation Service, where Oeldrich had worked in 1945. The box had been given in a roundabout way to a trustworthy Leiden anarchist for safekeeping.[162] The defence negotiated secretly with the minister of justice about a limited sentence, approximating the pre-trial time served, in exchange for return of the compromising documents.

Mandel coordinated Pablo's safe departure for North Africa, an act of loyalty hardly appreciated by Hélène, who complained of Pablo's being let down.[163] She blamed Mandel for starting a witchhunt: 'The man is completely out of his mind; he has no decency. He makes it seem as if he is turning against me, while his attacks are actually aimed against [Pablo] and our tendency.'[164] This was the same indecent Mandel who shortly afterward arranged her departure too, writing that 'we have every reason to believe that the application will be favourably considered and approved'.[165] The last details of Pablo's passport were settled in Belgrade in consultation with Ben Khedda, the minister for social affairs in the provisional Algerian government.[166]

The liberated Pablo left for Morocco. In 1962 he moved on to Algiers, where he became an advisor to the new Algerian president, Ahmed Ben Bella.[167] Santen was unable to follow him, even if he had wanted to.[168] He was paying for his newfound freedom with serious psychological problems; he had already been haunted by the loss of his family in the war. On his psychiatrist's advice he withdrew from political activity.[169] Pablo also advised him against coming to Algiers.[170]

Reconciliation with the US SWP

After Pablo's arrest, Posadas took over leadership of the struggle in the International against the 'Europeans', who refused to give the colonial revolution first priority. A former soccer player, Posadas would not give up the team captaincy even when Pablo was once again free. The Argentinian turned against his former ally with slanderous imputations, a more than bizarre state of affairs.[171] Using one pseudonym he would praise articles he himself had written using another. He called on the Soviet Union to launch a preventive nuclear war – a war he considered unavoidable – in order to support the colonial revolution. He denounced Fidel Castro as a petty-bourgeois adventurer. He expelled Ismael Frias, the leader of the Peruvian section, for his homosexuality and condemned

Hugo Blanco, the Peruvian farmers' leader, as a provocateur in the service of American imperialism.[172] His followers hailed Posadas as a modern Trotsky. Mandel considered his ideas the incoherent thoughts of a man drunk with power and called Posadas one of the nastiest schismatics the movement had ever known.[173] In 1962 the fifty-year-old Posadas broke with the International.

Following Posadas's departure and with Pablo in Rabat, Mandel was free to push for reunification with the SWP, which now had between 500 and 600 members.[174] Karl Manfred, Mandel's trusted ally in the US organization, supported him but did not understand why he ruled out a reunification 'on the basis of equality': 'Wouldn't it be a shame if this question stands in the way of reunification?'[175] Mandel said he was open to any solution and acknowledged that the International did not represent all Trotskyist currents. But he drew the line at a parity settlement that denied the International and its continuity: 'To be a realist is one thing, to abandon principles is another.'[176] By return post Manfred let him know that his American friends had given up on negotiations.[177]

These friends were Trotsky's former secretary, Joseph Hansen; Farrell Dobbs, leader of the legendary Teamster rebels in the 1930s, maligned by some for his bureaucratic attitude; and Tom Kerry, the fifty-year-old SWP organizing secretary. In the background as always was James P. Cannon, the movement veteran who had been living retired in California since 1954. They preferred to negotiate from strength. Because of opposition from their European allies Lambert and Healy, who refused any solidarity with the Algerian FLN or Cuba, they warned that negotiations would be long-term. Nevertheless, Mandel was pleased that space had been opened for a more realistic political view. Little psychological blows were hitting home,[178] such as his protest when Lambert revealed in a pamphlet on the Belgian general strike that Mandel was the author of the unsigned *La Gauche* editorials – a revelation that Mandel denounced as a betrayal 'both to the police and the leaders of the Belgian Socialist Party'.[179]

In the summer of 1961 Manfred wrote to Mandel that 'the door toward reunification is opening!' But he warned against going too fast 'because our friends still think differently about the so-called "center" and its way of working.'[180] He would gladly help create a favourable climate for a New York visit.[181] Mandel finally had the time, as *Marxist Economic Theory* was finished at last. His only concern was getting a visa. The New Left journalist Claude Bourdet was asked if his friend, the famous journalist I.F. Stone, could arrange for an invitation.[182] It was a touchy question, because if the US immigration service rejected this first invitation it would continue to prevent Mandel's entry. Murry Weiss, the rangy editor-in-chief of *The*

Militant, who had participated in the movement defending Sacco and Vanzetti when he was only eleven, advised Mandel to visit Cannon in California before proceeding to New York. Cannon's authority counted for a great deal.[183] Mandel ventured on the crossing in mid-March, travelling in an old Icelandic Airlines DC6 to save money.[184] Before going on to California he spent three days with Karl Manfred in New York, a stopover that no one else knew about. It gave Mandel the opportunity to renew their friendship and to get acquainted with the city and root around in the numerous big and small bookstores, new and second-hand. Manfred paid for his hotel.

The meeting with Cannon was a success. The seventy-year-old patriarch of American Trotskyism appreciated Mandel's diplomatic approach. George Novack also took part in the meeting, and his report convinced Mandel that 'it's all arranged, if there are no last-minute hitches on our side'.[185] Mandel's visit did not go unnoticed by outsiders.[186] A headline in the *Columbus Dispatch*, a conservative daily in Columbus, Ohio, read, 'Fourth International Revival Being Watched.' The accompanying article continued, 'An emissary of one faction of the Trotskyite movement in Belgium recently visited the United States to discuss with SWP leaders efforts to reunite the Fourth International.'[187] The FBI had substantial information about the SWP. Its special agents continuously observed SWP headquarters, a four-storey red-brown brick building overlooking Union Square in New York.[188]

As anticipated, Lambert and Healy stayed out of the reunification, which was confirmed the day after the Seventh World Congress in 1963. They could not agree with the idea that Cuba was a new workers' state. Pablo also had objections. He regarded depriving the Secretariat of the right to interfere with national leaderships and their tactical decisions as an unacceptable concession to the SWP. He also disagreed with the assessment of Khrushchev's reforms in the Soviet Union as Stalinist, which he regarded as incorrect. In addition he rejected support for the Maoists in the Sino-Soviet conflict.[189] Never before had Pablo expressed such a strong belief in the capacity of the Soviet bureaucracy for self-reform. He characterized de-Stalinization as an irreversible process 'with an unavoidable revolutionary effect on the foreign policy of the Soviet Union'.[190] He carried on an intensive exchange of views with Isaac Deutscher, who confirmed him in his optimism.[191] In the reunified International, Pablo's followers made up 10 per cent, active in the Dutch, Danish, Austrian and Australian sections and in part of the French section.[192] Until they split in 1965, they worked ever more openly as a public faction.

★   ★   ★

More strongly than Pablo, Mandel held to such key concepts of Marxism as the working class, the bureaucracy and the political revolution. Pablo was more impressionistic intellectually, an instinctive politician who if necessary would throw overboard every structure, dogma or scientific fact in order to focus on the realities of a situation. Sometimes this had remarkable results, as with his analysis of the Yugoslav revolution. But often the results were more doubtful, leading to his scepticism about the European working class, his naïve Third Worldism and his belief in de-Stalinization.

For the first fifteen years after the war the Greek was the leader. Mandel valued Pablo's accomplishments and practised modesty and patience. When they differed Mandel chose unity above his own opinions, as he had in the conflicts with the French section in 1951–2 and with the SWP in 1953. To avoid isolation he had stood with Pablo in trying to put down roots in the actually existing movements of the colonial revolution and among the communist and social democratic masses. But their bond gradually eroded during the late 1950s and the early 1960s.

For Mandel Belgian politics and the Fourth International became separate worlds. While the International was locked in sterile discussions about the coming world war, the role of the Soviet Union, entry into the French and Italian Communist parties and the issue of the colonial revolution – a debate in which his and Pablo's positions increasingly diverged – Mandel was struggling with the intractability of daily politics in Belgium. There it was all about questions of social welfare, democratic rights, opposition to the monarchy and support for a republic. A little later, focus shifted to *La Gauche*, opposition within the Socialist Party and the general strike of 1960–61. Mandel became involved with practical issues and, more importantly, with people influential in the working class, such as left-wing Social Democrats like André Renard.

Though the general strike of 1960–61 was overshadowed by the revolution in Algeria, it helped Mandel to defend his belief in the working class of the industrial world, and defend it, not least against Pablo. By the end of the 1950s Pablo had lost faith in the European proletariat and come to idealize the colonial revolution, above all the Algerian, and demanded a change in the sections' work that would reflect the change in his own ideas. Pablo's and Mandel's personalities clashed more and more often. Mandel found Pablo's methods, his individualism, his faits accomplis, his instability and tyranny ever more offensive. With irritation he observed how Pablo, with his plea for unlimited support for the colonial revolution, disparaged the entry work in Belgian social democracy. Pablo's descriptions of *La Gauche* as 'reformist', 'opportunistic', and 'pro-Western' also threw a spanner in the works, and his characterization of Renard's tendency as 'reactionary' sowed suspicion.[193] Pablo saw Mandel as shut into 'his little Belgium' and as displaying 'dangerously right-wing political tendencies' in his failure to do justice to the colonial revolution.[194] This exhausting discussion lasted almost ten years. Mandel told Pierre Frank that he had finally had enough of Pablo's pernicious wilfulness.[195]

But the conflict with Pablo gave Mandel's scholarly work, like *Marxist Economic Theory*, an unanticipated political significance. In breaking with Eurocentrism in his book, Mandel indicated the importance of the Third World and the Soviet world while keeping the place of the working class and imperialism central in his analysis of capitalism. In addition he gave new reality to the possibilities of revolution in the developed capitalist countries. In May 1965 he noted,

> I have shown . . . that with neo-capitalism there has been no end to the causes for workers' dissatisfaction and that it remains possible to wage powerful campaigns – perhaps unavoidable. The question is: can the campaigns assume a revolutionary dynamic in the context of the welfare state? Or will they necessarily remain limited to reforms so long as there's an atmosphere of more or less general prosperity.[196]

Mandel agreed with critics who saw no possibility of replicating such revolutions as the German one of 1918 or the Yugoslav one of 1947. But he denied that revolution was only possible following an economic or military catastrophe. 'There is a different historic model which we can refer to: that of the general strike of June 1936 in France (and to a lesser extent, the Belgian general strike of 1960–1961 . . .).'[197]

His classic view of the colonial and political revolutions formed the theoretical basis of his conflict with Pablo. Finally, fed up with pandering to his former mentor, he prepared a comprehensive critique in which he did not limit himself to objections to this or that aspect but made the entirety of Pablo's analysis his target. In the key document for the Seventh World Congress (1963), he investigated the interaction of what he considered the three sectors of the world revolution: the capitalist, industrial world (Belgium in 1960–61); the poor, dependent countries (Algeria and Cuba); and the transitional societies (Poland and Hungary in 1956). He saw in this dialectic, rather than in Pablo's one-sided focus on the colonial revolution, the possibility for a fundamental change in the international political framework.

7

The Worlds of Politics and Scholarship: An Odyssey

In the introduction to the Italian translation of *Marxist Economic Theory*, which appeared in 1965, three years after the French edition, Ernest Mandel observed that the debate about the contradictions within capitalism was booming. Leaving aside the question of how great a role *Marxist Economic Theory* had played,[1] he announced a new book, on the subject of what he called neo-capitalism and neo-colonialism. In it, he hoped to focus on the connections between economic growth and social structure and what they revealed about prevailing economic theory.[2]

In April 1964 Mandel had published a short article titled 'The Economics of Neo-Capitalism' in *The Socialist Register*, an annual publication from London edited by Ralph Miliband and John Saville and also in Sartre's *Les Temps Modernes*.[3] The projected book was intended as an expansion of this article. The plan looked promising: 300 pages in eight chapters, to be completed in six months.[4] It would be almost ten years before the greatly expanded manuscript, titled *Late Capitalism*, was delivered to the German publisher Suhrkamp.[5]

In 'The Economics of Neo-Capitalism' Mandel expressed his conviction that following the periods of open competition and imperialism, capitalism had entered a new, third period, neo-capitalism, or capitalism in decline, or, as he finally termed it, late capitalism[6]. He had expressed his thoughts about its anatomy earlier, in the spring of 1963, in a number of lectures for a weekend leadership gathering of the Unified Socialist Party (PSU) in Paris. These were published as *Introduction to the Theory of Marxist Economics*.[7]

Mandel held that the postwar expansion in the industrialized world was not primarily a result of reconstruction but of what he called a third industrial – or technological – revolution in a changed climate, marked by an uninterrupted arms race, growing state intervention in economic life, government planning and permanent inflation.[8] Mandel emphasized that despite capitalism's new ways of functioning, the general laws of capitalist development, as initially revealed by Marx, had in no way been suspended. The new period was both a prolongation and a partial negation of the imperialist period, just as the imperialist period had been a continuation and a partial negation of unrestrained capitalist competition.

Mandel had not yet reached a detailed analysis of this phase, but was constructing the beginnings of a framework that would allow him to connect economic, political, technological and social factors and variables. Still following Marx in *Marxist Economic Theory*, he had analyzed the cyclical course of capitalist development as short-term fluctuations determined by recurrent industrial crises.[9] He had not considered other time spans, but he broadened his perspective in the article for *The Socialist Register*. He situated the postwar expansion within the theory of long waves of capitalist development. The foundations for this theory had been laid by Parvus[10] and Van Gelderen[11] early in the century, then by Kondratieff[12] and Trotsky[13] in the 1920s and Schumpeter[14] in the 1930s.[15] Using their approach, Mandel declared that the end of the 'golden days of world capitalism' was near.[16]

Mandel's article was a response to Rosdolsky's criticism of his handling of crisis theory in *Marxist Economic Theory*. Though Mandel had emphasized the unavoidability of crises and recessions,[17] he had not offered a systematic treatment of the theory of collapse, which Rosdolsky considered the heart of Marxism.[18] Moreover, Rosdolsky considered Mandel's synthesis of the theories of underconsumption and disproportionality[19] – two influential explanatory models of economic cycles – incorrect: 'Marx opposed both of these theories; how can they be "reconciled" from a Marxist standpoint?'[20]

Mandel felt that in his latest article he had overcome the weaknesses that Rosdolsky found in *Marxist Economic Theory*, particularly those in the overly descriptive fourteenth chapter, 'The Epoch of Capitalist Decline'. Now his new insights needed to be integrated into a more extensive synthesis of the third period of capitalism. In 1969, although his analysis remained incomplete Mandel decided to include it as a supplement to the second French edition of *Marxist Economic Theory*.

Opposing Eurocentrism

Though Mandel had not yet achieved a finished synthesis of late capitalism for his book, he took opportunities in less extensive writings to systematize his analysis and iron out theoretical wrinkles.[21] Soon after the appearance of *Marxist Economic Theory* he was given one such opportunity by Lucien Goldmann, a philosopher and literary critic from south-eastern Galicia and a disciple of the Hungarian Marxist Georg Lukács. Goldmann taught at the

Sorbonne in Paris and was editing *A History of Marxist Thought* in six volumes. He asked Mandel for a contribution on the theme 'Marx's Economic Thought Prior to *Capital*'.[22] But when Mandel delivered his article of more than seventy pages in August 1965, Goldmann was so taken up with his own studies that the project was abandoned.[23] Mandel decided to rework his contribution, and it was published by Maspero in 1967 under the title *La Formation de la pensée économique de Karl Marx, de 1843 jusqu'à la rédaction du Capital: Etude génétique* (The Formation of the Economic Thought of Karl Marx: 1843 to *Capital*). It appeared exactly 100 years after the publication of the first volume of *Capital*.[24]

In this study Mandel followed the development of Marx's thought in detail. He showed how Marx came to accept David Ricardo's labour theory of value and then to improve it.[25] He also discussed the most important discoveries Marx made before conceiving *Capital*. He analyzed in detail the place of the idea of alienation in the various phases of Marx's intellectual development and the importance of this concept to his theory in general. Finally, in a fascinating chapter on the so-called Asiatic mode of production, Mandel joined the debate opened in 1964 in *La Pensée*, a theoretical journal close to the French Communist Party, on the non-unilinear character of the succession of modes of production.[26]

There was a tendency at the time to characterize all social formations that did not fit the unilinear schema[27] as having an 'Asiatic' mode of production, which deprived the concept of its analytical specificity.[28] But what was Asian about a mode of production that, as Maurice Godelier demonstrated, could be found in Africa, America and even in Mediterranean Europe (in the Creto-Mycenean civilization)?[29] Mandel recalled that Marx and Engels had not developed the concept with a primitive society in mind.[30] It was intended to describe Indian and Chinese societies at the moment when they came into contact with European industrial capital in the eighteenth century. In short, to answer the question why India, China, Egypt and the Islamic world, which for thousands of years had formed the centres of ritual and material culture, had followed a different developmental path than had Western and Southern Europe.[31] Mandel wrote, 'Marx only spends time on the "pre-capitalist forms of production" in order to show up, *negatively,* the factors which in Europe have led, positively, to the flowering of capital and capitalism'.[32]

Mandel was committed to de-Westernizing the explanation of the development of capitalism as a world system, and this non-Eurocentrism required independent attention to pre-colonial Asia, Africa, the Islamic world and pre-Columbian America. This explains the importance he attributed to slave-based, semi-feudal and Asian modes of production.[33]

The unilinearists had sown confusion with their theory of successive stages that every society in the world had to pass through. They took no account of diversity and the coexistence of capitalist, semi-capitalist and pre-capitalist worlds. To Mandel this variety was characteristic of the world economy and not a temporary situation that eventually would be abolished by a supposed general law of capitalist development. The capitalist mode of production was not tending to become universal, contrary to what Rosa Luxemburg had attempted to demonstrate.[34] There had been no industrial revolution in cultural areas other than Europe between the sixteenth and nineteenth centuries. For just this reason, under the influence of international processes of concentration, the world market was preventing any successful leap by the Third World from primitive accumulation of money capital to primitive accumulation of industrial capital. Mandel noted, 'Capitalism itself produces underdevelopment . . . Capitalism is the dialectical unity of development and underdevelopment; the one necessarily determines the other.'[35] Marx's classic dictum that underdeveloped countries could see their future reflected in the developed countries had lost its general validity during the imperialist period. In place of a general law of capitalist development, Mandel posited unequal and combined development: a capitalism that, in order to expand, produced and maintained pre- or non-capitalist countries, sectors and regions.[36]

Against Louis Althusser

The Formation of the Economic Thought of Karl Marx provoked discussion not only about the Asiatic mode of production but even more about Mandel's ideas concerning the meaning of Marx's early works, the *Economic–Philosophical Manuscripts* of 1844 and *The German Ideology* of 1845.[37] In his chapter 'From the *Economic and Philosophic Manuscripts* to the *Grundrisse*: From an Anthropological to a Historical Concept of Alienation', Mandel took a definite position in a dispute that was raging in Europe and to a lesser extent in the United States, fuelled by the 1965 publication of *For Marx* and *Reading Capital*, both by the influential French Communist and philosopher Louis Althusser.[38]

What was the relationship of Marx's earlier work to the *Grundrisse* and *Capital*? Did Marx continue to hold Hegel's anthropologically based notion of alienation, alienation conceived as characteristic of human nature?[39] Or was there a discontinuity that required conceptualizing different phases in Marx's thinking? And, if so, what were these phases?

Mandel distinguished three currents in the controversy, each of which responded differently to these questions.[40] The first denied that there was a

difference between early and late Marx and saw the heart of *Capital* –
alienated labour – as implicitly present in the *Economic-Philosophical Manuscripts*.[41]

A second current held that the Marx of the *Manuscripts* had handled the
problem of alienated labour more fully than the Marx of *Capital*, that this
younger Marx had given the concept an ethical, anthropological and
philosophical dimension.[42] Some of these theorists pitted the two Marxes
against each other, while others reinterpreted *Capital* in the light of the
Manuscripts.

Mandel, along with the German philosopher Jürgen Habermas, thought
that both of these currents had failed to take into account the difference
between an anthropological and a historical concept of labour[43] and that
they did not recognize that the Marx of *Capital* had abandoned the
metaphysical concept of the Marx of 1844.

The final current, represented by Louis Althusser,[44] held that the alienated
labour concept of the young Marx contradicted that of *Capital* and that this
concept had originally hindered acceptance of the labour theory of value. In
Althusser's eyes alienation was a pre-Marxist idea that Marx had to discard
before he could begin his scientific work.[45]

Mandel did not agree with any of these currents. On the one hand he
recognized the discontinuity in Marx's thinking; on the other, he denied
that Marx had discarded the concept of alienation. Mandel thought that the
concept had undergone a qualitative change, analogous to the transformation of Marx's anthropologically-based thinking into thinking based on
historical-materialist categories. This transformation found a cautious first
expression in the *Economic-Philosophical Manuscripts* of 1844, where Marx no
longer founded his critique of political economy on a Feuerbachian or
Hegelian construct of alienated labour but on '*his practical observation of the
misery of the workers*'. Marx was no longer interested in a 'philosophical
solution on the plane of thoughts, ideas', but rather in an abolition of private
property through '*actual* communist action'. Here, Mandel concluded, 'The
call to revolutionary action, to be carried out by the proletariat, is already
substituted for the resignation of the "philosophy of labour".'[46] He hastened
to add that Marx's thought at the time was still far from mature, because he
went back and forth between the two conceptions, sometimes seeking the
source of worker alienation in the specific form of the society, its division
into classes and private property, and at other times viewing alienation as an
expression of the human as 'species being' – with its source in human nature,
if not in the Hegelian sense, then as a negation of the so-called ideal man.

Marx gradually overcame these contradictions, Mandel said. He reached
an important turning point in *The German Ideology*, when he abandoned the

idea of man as 'species being' and situated the roots of exploitation in the division of labour and commodity production, in private property and competition. It was to Marx's credit that he placed the concept of alienated labour in the domain of history and transformed the Feuerbachian-Hegelian anthropological understanding that preceded the *Manuscripts* into a historical concept in *The German Ideology*, the *Grundrisse* and *Capital*.[47]

The Formation of the Economic Thought of Karl Marx was Ernest Mandel's most philosophical book, an ode to Marx's insight and revolutionary passion.[48] It was a polemic against conservative and social democratic circles that attempted to enlist Marx's authority by only recognizing his humanistic, Hegelian form – a young, ethical Marx in opposition to a communist movement mired in so-called economic problems. Mandel also wrote against Marxists like Wolfgang Jahn, Auguste Cornu and Louis Althusser who rejected the term 'alienation' as romantic, unscientific and pre-Marxist, and against Soviet apologists who would have liked to see the term disappear entirely from public usage: 'In Soviet society, *alienation could not and must no longer be an issue*. By order from above, for reasons of State, the concept had to disappear.'[49]

The heart of Mandel's critique was directed at Althusser, who refused to integrate history into his methodology. Mandel wrote to Perry Anderson that the author of *For Marx* and *Reading Capital* had declared war

> on everything which is historical, i.e. dialectical in Marxism, and trans-formed it into a kind of metaphysical neo-positivism (static structuralism, without built-in contradictions, without motion, without understanding that the basis of Marxism – as Marx himself said – was the understanding of the historically perishable nature of all 'structures', and the logic of their evolution-revolution).[50]

Althusser was a central figure in the French debates about Marxism. This was enough incentive for Mandel to speak out wherever he could against Althusserian structuralism – what Anderson termed 'brilliant neo-dogmatism'.[51] He did so in his 1969 essay 'Althusser Corrects Marx'[52] and during the much-discussed three-day Marx colloquium at the Goethe University in Frankfurt in September 1967,[53] where an impressive array of scholars from East and West had gathered to rehabilitate Marxism as a critique of political economy.

The death of Roman Rosdolsky

During the 1930s Marxism had withdrawn into the universities, where attention had shifted from political economy to philosophy and sociology,

with research into cultural and ideological phenomena.[54] Under the
dominance of Soviet Marxism, Marxist economics had degenerated into
a dogmatism within which there was no place for new development.[55]
There were a few exceptional writers on the subject, including Gramsci,
Moskowska, Meek, Dobb and Sweezy. In general, however, the 1930s,
1940s and 1950s were a lost time. The tide turned in the following decade.
Mandel, Baran, Sweezy, Gunder Frank, and Gorz and economists like
Heilbroner, Barrat Brown and Rosdolsky contributed to this renaissance.
The *Grundrisse* was also important; after its initial publication before the war
it was reprinted in 1953, and its influence gradually spread.[56] Coming in the
wake of a revived anti-capitalist movement inspired by decolonization, anti-
racism, anti-Stalinism and the struggle against the war in Vietnam, the 1967
Frankfurt colloquium marked a renewal of the role of political economy in
creative Marxism.

Both Mandel and Rosdolsky were invited to speak at the colloquium,
Rosdolsky on the method of Marx's *Capital*, Mandel on post-Keynesian
growth theory. Mandel looked forward to the reunion and told Rosdolsky
to go deeply into Marx in order to put Althusser in his place.[57] Althusser was
supposed to respond to Rosdolsky on *Capital* but at the last moment decided
not to participate, to Rosdolsky's disappointment. He complained, 'Isn't the
occasion important enough for him, or did all those Stalinists . . . oppose his
participation?'[58] He meant the five East German experts at the conference,
among them the secret dissident Fritz Behrens, director of the Institute for
Economic Affairs in Berlin.

Nicos Poulantzas replaced Althusser, but then Rosdolsky fell ill and had to
miss the debate himself. He was in no condition to travel to Europe. Both
his heart and kidneys were diseased, and the doctors would make no
prognosis, as Rosdolsky's wife informed Mandel: 'I mean well in sharing
this with you. Though I've never had the opportunity to become acquainted with you personally, I know that my husband regards you as one of
his closest co-thinkers.'[59] Mandel wrote back by return post to let his friend
know what had transpired in Frankfurt, emphasizing the value accorded
Rosdolsky's written contribution.[60]

> Poulantzas's short response and his longer paper (we had to do without
> Althusser) seemed thin by comparison . . . I tried to defend you as well as
> possible against Poulantzas, which wasn't very difficult. When the
> Althusser school claims that *Capital* is ahistorical and anti-historical and
> has nothing to do with Hegel's dialectic, which means that Marx had no
> clarity about his own methodology – just as little as Lenin – then there's
> no lack of arguments to put them in their place.[61]

At the end of October Mandel received the sad message from Detroit that Rosdolsky had died.[62] In a moving letter his wife wrote,

> Because Roman never felt at home in this country, I'm flying with his ashes next week to Vienna, the city where I was born and where he spent a few good years of his youth. I can't take him any closer to his birthplace, and his wish to be buried on the banks of the Dnieper will always remain unfulfilled. He experienced great support from you and hoped that you would continue to be important for the 'party in the historical sense', to which he felt committed.[63]

Rosdolsky's death shocked Mandel. He had lost more than a kindred spirit and a mentor; he had also lost a modest and affectionate friend. Of all the thinkers of his time, Rosdolsky was possibly the most knowledgeable about Marx's writings and represented best the living Marxism of the pre-war years.[64] A few months earlier in the summer of 1967, at news of the sudden death of Isaac Deutscher, also a survivor of fascism and Stalinism, Rosdolsky had bitterly exclaimed, 'O death, you cruel thief! . . . Why do you rob us of the best and most gifted?'[65] Mandel felt himself just as abandoned now as Rosdolsky had then:

> In a brief time I've lost two close friends, who, however differently, both embodied in their own ways two essential aspects of the great tradition: Roman and 'Che' [Guevara].[66] It was a blessing to have gotten to know them and to have been friends with them both; it is hard to comprehend that they are no longer here.[67]

Mandel could offer Rosdolsky's widow no more than a helping hand. He inquired about the financial circumstances in which Emmy and her son, still at university, had been left. He emphatically requested her to 'write without reserve how my friends and I can help you so that Roman can at least receive the recognition he deserved with post-humous publication of his work.'[68] In a remembrance Mandel praised *Engels and the 'Nonhistoric' Peoples* as Rosdolsky's most brilliant work. In this book Rosdolsky had made a plausible case that Marx and Engels's opposition to the aspirations of national minorities – like the Czechs, Slovaks, Croats and Ukrainians – was based on an inadequate analysis of the social forces in the revolution of 1848.[69]

A multiplicity of factors

At the Frankfurt colloquium Mandel had scrutinized economic growth in
the industrialized countries.[70] Did the idea of growth without crises reflect
reality or was it wishful thinking? Mandel argued that in the long run a
growth in productive investment was incompatible with a falling rate of
profit or the underuse of productive capacity. Neither the creation of money
and credit, nor planning, could affect this. In a given economic cycle, rising
rates of profit only temporarily coincided with an expansion of markets,
never permanently. Therefore investments also came in waves, no matter
what countercyclical measures were taken.

But why then didn't employers periodically engage in feverish investing?
Why didn't they try to avoid overheating the economy? The question
seemed all the more pressing because employers had ways to direct the
economy nationally, even internationally through the EEC (Common
Market). Mandel followed in Marx's footsteps with his answer: what
prevented them was 'competition between capitalists on the one hand,
and between capitalists and the working class on the other.'[71]

Mandel conceived the latter competition as inherent in neo-capitalism.
Late capitalism could not permit severe economic crises, given the complex
international relationship of forces. A policy of countercyclical and anti-
recessionary measures, however, would lead to a reduction of unemployment and therefore to such sharp wage increases that a rapid decline in the
rates of surplus value and profit would be unavoidable. Because trade unions
could only be forced to limit their freedom of movement by dictatorial
measures, Mandel thought, competition would force individual employers
to replace workers rapidly with machines in order to avoid a lasting increase
in the wage portion of added value: 'Technological progress and innovation
are thus not exogenous factors in the growth processes of a capitalist
economy. They are an unavoidable result of the inner logic and inherent
contradictions of this mode of production.'[72]

Severe crises could only be stopped at the cost of growing overcapacity
and a creeping, uninterrupted currency devaluation, with obvious consequences for economic growth. The downside of intermittent bursts of
investment activity introducing new technology was a slowing, if not
stagnation, in economic growth, due to an ever greater number of monopolies and sectors where price competition was eliminated and markets were
divided. Only the arms industry and the service sector still provided
opportunities for converting an increasing part of surplus value into capital.
The ordinary capitalization of the bulk of surplus value would have
endangered the valorization of the total capital in sectors with a socially

average rate of profit threatened by overcapacity. Mandel reproached the pragmatic, post-Keynesian growth theorists for paying no attention to overcapacity, which is a characteristic of late capitalism. Faced with a fresh rise in unemployment, the Keynesian school would immediately begin swinging between deficit spending and combating inflation with credit limits, because it was unequipped to recognize structural problems, let alone solve them.

Mandel thought that Marx's economic theory led to structural, and therefore much better, solutions. According to Marx, the rhythm and extent of economic growth were determined by five strategic factors: the rate of surplus value, the rate of accumulation, the organic composition of capital, the turnover time of fixed capital and the extent of the expenditure of non-accumulated surplus value as revenue, that is, as private consumption by capitalists. The interplay of these factors could explain how, as monopolization and market control increased, a growing surplus of capital emerged, whose unproductive consumption revealed an overcapacity that led to a long-term decline in growth rates. Were these dependent, half-dependent or independent variables? Mandel did not show exactly how the interplay of these factors transpired or their relationship to one another.[73] For the first time he was presenting a theory of late capitalism in which the dynamic of the system was not deduced from one factor alone but from an array of factors.[74] Here his approach differed from the traditional Marxist mono-causal analysis.[75] For example, Henryk Grossmann[76] proposed over-accumulation as the motor of development; Rosa Luxemburg and Paul Sweezy assigned the leading role to the problematic realization of surplus value;[77] Rudolf Hilferding[78] highlighted competition; and Michael Kidron[79] emphasized unproductive consumption of surplus value. Mandel, on the other hand, thought the complexity of modern capitalism permitted no reductionism. He followed Roman Rosdolsky, who had clearly polemicized fruitfully against the neglect of Marx's economic methodology. As shown earlier, in his critique of Mandel's *Marxist Economic Theory* Rosdolsky emphatically demanded attention for the dialectic totality in Marx's work, beyond the 'tangible' and the 'mere facts'.[80]

In later works as well, Mandel insisted that only the development and correlation of all variables could account for the dynamic of the mode of production. He seemed less sure about the question of which variables were most basic. In his contribution to the Frankfurt colloquium he selected five; in his main work *Late Capitalism* (1972), six; in his study *Long Waves of Capitalist Development* (1980), again five;[81] and in a 1984 essay he raised the number to ten.[82] Sociopolitical conditions, like the struggle between capital and labour, did not count as basic factors in his formula in either 1967 or

1972. Only in 1984 would he add 'the law of class struggle determination of wages' as a 'partially independent' variable.[83] In the 1960s and 1970s Mandel discussed only variables that were endogenous from an economic perspective, that seemed to flow naturally from the structure of the system, factors that determined the speed and direction of developments but that did not essentially change the system itself.

Wary of mechanistic determinism, Mandel considered class struggle as an independent, exogenous factor of equal value that was to be placed alongside the endogenous logic, the logic of the extraction of surplus value.

Dissatisfied with analytical indeterminacy, Mandel reached a more specific formulation in 1984: 'Besides the inner logic of the system, exogenous factors are at work, which partially co-determine the system's development, at least at short- and medium-term ranges.'[84] He added that the possibilities for change are circumscribed by the nature of the system itself: '*Inside* the system you can boost or undermine profits, deliberately or inadvertently. But you cannot suppress profits'. That could be done only by eliminating the system; that is, by abolishing capitalism. 'Hence any interaction between endogenous and exogenous forces is always limited by these parameters . . .' Mandel gave as an example class struggle in the form of the basic conflict over wages and working conditions. The struggle would reach 'its limit when it threatens to eliminate basic mechanisms of the system'.[85]

Class struggle was thus to some extent determined by the logic of the system, through fluctuations in the labour market and in the rate of accumulation, but not mechanistically and not exclusively. The variables were therefore 'partially independent', bound to the system by an umbilical cord, though not directly born of it.[86] Averse to economism, Mandel pleaded for an integrated analysis of the total societal reality. In an autobiographical entry written for the *Biographical Dictionary of Dissenting Economists*, Mandel counted among his merits in the last part of his life that he had developed an economic, historical theory based on the dialectical, parametric concept of determinism.[87] Unlike a mechanistic, deterministic, unilinear Marxism, his theory took into account the possibility, 'nay the inevitability'[88] of choices in economic and social processes – but choices within the parameters of the system, determined by conflicting social interests. It described the playing field on which the struggle for power takes place.

Lectures in Berlin

One of the participants chosen to discuss Mandel's contribution to the Frankfurt colloquium was Elmar Altvater. Mandel confided to Rosdolsky that Altvater was 'a very gifted young Marxist economist'.[89] Altvater, not yet thirty years old, had grown up in a mine worker's family in the Ruhr valley and had studied in Munich. In the 1960s he worked at the universities of Nuremburg and Erlangen.[90] From a young age he had been a member of the German Social Democratic Party (SPD), but he left the party along with the Social Democratic student organization (SDS) when the SPD adopted the anti-Marxist Godesberg programme in 1959. Opposed to the governing Grand Coalition[91] and influenced by the movement against the Vietnam War, the SDS grew into an extra-parliamentary movement with influence beyond the universities.

Altvater developed into a Marxist economist on his own initiative – within the portals of academia it was unthinkable to study Marx's *Capital*. Then came the recession of 1966-7, which marked the end of Germany's 'economic miracle', and the myth of crisis-free economic development without over-production or unemployment collapsed. Seeking an explanation for the re-emergence of the business cycle, Altvater discovered Mandel, who had first attracted attention with the publication of *Marxist Economic Theory*[92] and now again with *The German Economic Crisis*.[93] The latter work argued that this first postwar recession in the Federal Republic was no anomaly; on the contrary, it was symptomatic of late capitalism, which was heading for a general crisis that would break out simultaneously in the most important Western industrialized countries.[94] Mandel had proposed this perspective hesitantly in 1964 but more and more emphatically by the end of the decade.[95]

Altvater found in Mandel a Marxist who besides offering his own analysis of contemporary capitalism also had insights that provided keys to Marx's works. This was what Altvater and his rebellious generation had been seeking.

Even in the early 1960s Mandel had been much in demand as a speaker in Germany, where his opinions were taken seriously.[96] The evening before the Frankfurt Marx colloquium in 1967, student leaders Rudi Dutschke and Hans Jürgen Krahl met with Mandel in the back room of a café. While Krahl, a graduate student of Theodor Adorno's, presented his own theory of capital, Dutschke snared Mandel for a course in economics for the Berlin comrades.[97] Altvater stressed that without Mandel's theoretical contribu-tion, the New Left and the German student movement would have had difficulty emerging.[98]

Unlike France, with its uninterrupted tradition of a heterodox left, Germany had seen its Marxist continuity broken. Between 1933 and 1945 the left-wing milieu had been completely destroyed, to be replaced only by an orthodox party doctrine that derived its inspiration chiefly from East Germany and the Soviet Union.

Mandel could fill the gap because his personal history had frequently intersected that of the German workers' movement. He had been born in Frankfurt and raised in a family that spoke German with the political refugees who enjoyed their hospitality in the 1930s. The family library had exuded the atmosphere of the German workers' movement, with bound volumes of the Social Democratic theoretical journal *Neue Zeit* and the works of Bebel, Kautsky and Luxemburg standing shoulder to shoulder on its shelves. More than the Russian Revolution, the German revolt of November 1918 was the critical harbinger of the classless world to come. Mandel's personal experience of fascism and Nazism in the camps had not impaired his trust in the German working class, which he continued to see as the driving force of the European revolution. Finally, his marriage in the summer of 1966 to the thirty-year-old SDS activist Gisela Scholtz gave special imprimatur to his role as ideologue and theoretician in Germany. Through her, he easily gained access to the radical milieu where Marxism was gaining fresh impetus. When he was deported from Germany, in 1972, he was devastated and unable to speak for days.[99] Germany had felt like a second fatherland.

Mandel had great expectations of the German student movement. His theories on Marx met a real response there. The hall overflowed when he debated about the Chinese Cultural Revolution with Rudi Dutschke[100] or the Soviet Union with Richard Löwenthal, a confidant of Willy Brandt and chair of the conservative Council for Scientific Freedom at the Berlin Otto Suhr Institute.[101]

Famous as a scholar and popular with students, Ernest Mandel was more than ready to assume the academic mantle his father had dreamed of for him. He had not only his financial security in mind, but political and legal considerations as well: a university position would make him less vulnerable. He also hoped that an academic position would aid him in his scholarly work. He began to seek one seriously.

In 1970 he received an invitation from the leading Institute for Political Science to give four months of guest lectures. He proposed as his subject theories of late capitalism, 'or would you find the theme "Market and Plan in Eastern European Economic Theory" more interesting?'[102] The Institute was happy to make use of Mandel's expertise in both areas.[103]

A Brussels appointment was much harder to land. Since 1970-71 he had given a course on 'Principles and Application of Marxist Economics' at the Dutch-language Free University of Brussels, originally as a substitute for Professor Van der Eycken. Marcel Liebman and other researchers counted on Mandel's appointment to give greater scholarly prestige to left-wing ideas and to their own Faculty of Economic, Social and Political Sciences. But some faculty members tried to block the appointment, citing Mandel's lack of a PhD.[104] Mandel asked Lucien Goldmann to confirm that under Goldmann's supervision he was preparing a thesis titled 'Plan and Market in Marxist Theory'.[105] But he complained to Liebman that the affair was costing him sympathy and was all the more distasteful to him now that he was being forced to collect testimonials on his own behalf to stop petty-minded opponents from making a fool of him.[106] Robert Heilbroner, Maurice Dobb, Maximilien Rubel, Wolfgang Abendroth, Ekkehart Krippendorff and other celebrities rushed to Mandel's aid. When his scholarly qualifications were questioned in discussion, Piet Vermeylen, a Flemish Socialist and former government minister, threw a pile of Mandel's books down on the table and asked who still dared cast doubt on Mandel's reputation as a writer.

In February 1971 his appointment was finally confirmed.[107] His course load was soon expanded to a full roster, including a variety of subjects in political science.[108] In July 1986 he was made a full professor, with his area the study of Marxist theory.

Mandel enjoyed lecturing. As he entered the classroom, unpacked his bag and hung his jacket over the chair with a smile, the hum of voices stilled. Leaving his notes untouched, he presented clear arguments, sprinkling them with spirited anecdotes of the bourgeoisie's doings. In his V-neck sleeveless pullover, light blue shirt and dark red tie, he hardly looked like an enemy of the state. He kept his post at the Free University of Brussels until the beginning of the 1990s.

University politics were not the only stumbling block in Mandel's academic career. State politics, too, stood in his way. In 1970, France, the United States and Australia all closed their borders to him. For some time his scholarly work in these countries came to an end. He could still travel to Germany unhindered, and his appointment as visiting professor in Berlin for the winter semester of 1970-71 filled him with pride. As he let slip to his American publisher, 'For the first time in my life I have gotten "academic recognition".'[109] Mandel spent two days a week in West Berlin. Every Wednesday for sixteen weeks, between 3:00 and 5:00 in the afternoon, around a thousand students filled the Great Auditorium to listen to his exposition of the theory of late capitalism. His two seminars on transitional societies and organizational questions also attracted overwhelming interest. There were 2,500 people present at a Hamburg lecture. The theologian Helmut Gollwitzer greeted him as 'your grateful reader and auditor'.[110] As Mandel wrote to the famous philosopher Ernst Bloch and his wife Karola, 'It is all very strenuous.'[111]

Bloch and Mandel together had become close to Rudi Dutschke, who was staying in England for a little while after surviving an assassination attempt in April 1968. From there he wrote to Mandel ironically, 'Ernest, can a Free University department become a revolutionary cadre school?'[112] Until Dutschke's death Mandel would remain good friends with the 'expert of the youth rebellion', as Bloch had called him admiringly.[113] Bloch and Mandel had met each other for the first time in the summer of 1970 on the Croatian island Korcula, during a seminar on the timeliness of Hegel organized by the critical philosophical journal *Praxis*.[114] Since 1963 the island had been a meeting ground for intellectuals from East and West, an unusual place for free debate.

Mandel was able to complete his theory of late capitalism during his tenure at the Otto Suhr Institute in Berlin. Staying in the leafy Dahlem neighbourhood, he was immersed in an intellectual milieu in which a good range of critical theories were in fashion. Just as capitalism's renewal at the turn of the twentieth century had fostered a revisionist tendency, its unprecedented renaissance after 1945 stimulated reformulations of Marx's theories.[115] Mandel thought that all of the current ideas denied a role to the Western proletariat in the struggle against imperialism and capitalism, and that their proponents cited a supposed change in the classic workings of capitalism to rationalize their stance. This way of thinking was popular above all in non-dogmatic left-wing circles. It coexisted with the theory of state monopoly capitalism, common among communists, which embraced the idea that the power of the monopolies could be restrained with the help of the state and that a transition to socialism could be accomplished without having to destroy capitalism. Mandel believed that the question of whether the state could eliminate fundamental contradictions or at least neutralize them depended on whether the law of value was still valid under late capitalism. He counterposed his own unambiguous 'yes' to a 'yes' so qualified that in his opinion it amounted to 'a miserable "yes/no"'.

The anatomy of late capitalism

Mandel constructed his lecture cycle 'Theory of Late Capitalism: Laws of Motion and Stages of the Capitalist Mode of Production' around seventeen themes that roughly corresponded to the chapters in his book *Late Capitalism*, which was published two years later.[116] As early as his first lecture Mandel emphasized the need for a historical explanation, essential according to his concept of the partially independent variables[117] that represented 'all the basic proportions of the capitalist mode of produc-tion'.[118] By placing the interplay of these variables in a historical framework, one could analyze successive stages in the history of capitalism. Mandel thought that the fluctuation of the rate of profit was expressed in the interplay of variables, and registered economic cycles and waves like a historical seismograph.

Late capitalism thus constituted a new phase in the epoch of decline of the capitalist mode of production which began with the First World War. Following the defeats of the international workers' movement – by fascism and in the Second World War – the substantial increase in the rate of surplus value brought about a sudden and prolonged increase in the rate of profit[119] and therefore in the accumulation of capital and faster economic growth. In time, however, the laws of the motion of capital would make a falling tendency in the rate of profit inescapable and initiate a new period of slow growth.

With his reconciliation of theory and history – here many doctrinaire Marxists would use the terms 'theory' and 'praxis' – Mandel established himself as an intellectual free spirit, outside mainstream Marxism, outside doctrinaire Althusserianism and outside what Perry Anderson called 'Western Marxism', which had turned its back on economic research.[120] He had also moved beyond the disciples' tradition represented by figures like Luxemburg, Hilferding, Bukharin, Grossmann and Sternberg, all of whom had based their attempts to explain the specific stages of the capitalist mode of production on Marx's reproduction schemes.

In *Marxist Economic Theory* Mandel had explained that these schemes were unsuitable instruments for analyzing disequilibria; now he began asking if it were possible to establish other, modified schemes, consisting of not two but three or four departments.[121] These would take into account the tendency to uneven development, with the reproduction schemes forming only a special case, just as economic equilibrium is a borderline case of the capitalist tendency to uneven development between sectors, departments and elements.[122] It was necessary to analyze the way partially independent variables developed under differing conditions, as well as such questions as why disequilibria are unavoidable, how a new equilibrium arises, why new disruptions occur and when and under what conditions these lead to a crisis of overproduction. Mandel was not successful in designing such dynamic schemes. Harry Chester, an American statistician, commented to him,

> The great difficulty is not the large number of independent variables – in these days of the computer this is a minor technicality. The greatest difficulty is rather the dialectical aspect of the system, the fact that the same variable under some circumstances has one effect and at other times, under different circumstances has the opposite effect. How do I build a model . . . ?[123]

Mandel emphasized time after time that the history of capitalism 'can only be explained and understood as a function of the interplay of these . . . variables'.[124] The interplay – that was what it was all about. But now he could not manage to use dynamic reproduction schemes to create a framework for investigating the development and interrelationships of the basic variables – the six fundamental laws of development. This meant that not only the analytical tools (the reproduction schemes) but also the analytical method (the interplay of all the variables) seemed unusable.[125]

Could this be why Mandel's book is not always adequately structured or coherent, despite its far-reaching analysis of the separate variables in successive chapters? Is this why its historical portrait of a complex and integrated reality does not add up to a convincing synthesis?[126] After reading the text critically, Elmar Altvater told Mandel, 'It's as if the chapters, at least for the most part, are separate essays pasted together about separate manifestations of late capitalism. Most of them could have been published as separate essays with a short foreword.'[127]

Chapter 17, 'Late Capitalism as a Whole', which promises a synthesis of the book, devotes so much attention to criticizing other economists' theories – there are lengthy polemics against Baran and Sweezy, Galbraith, Mattick and Altvater – that once Mandel has given a general theoretical foundation for the persistence of the law of value, he has little space left to present the new and specific combination of competition, monopoly and state that is typical of this phase of capitalism.[128] He makes clear that late capitalism is only a phase of monopoly capitalism; but what distinguishes it from other phases, such as classical imperialism (1890–1940), he leaves less clear.[129] A formulation like 'monopoly capitalism, and especially late capitalism' suggests continuity rather than change, and that the difference is only one of degree.

Or perhaps the transition to late capitalism is an overdetermination of the postwar long expansive wave. By contrast, the preceding, interwar phase was characterized by a long recessive wave. This had many consequences in terms of state regulation and for the relationship between the monopolized and non-monopolized sectors and the related divergence in rates of profit.

Marxists often take refuge in reductionism, the search for a universal answer. Mandel resisted this temptation. Yet *Late Capitalism* lends itself to interpretations that reduce the synthesis to long waves, determined by what his critics called the one dominant variable: the rate of profit.[130] Were his critics merely reading poorly, as some have said?[131] In fact, even Mandel does not manage to do justice to the complexity of his subject. The book sparkles but, despite his best intentions, does not yield the promised synthesis.

Long waves

The history of capitalism appears as a cyclical movement of capital accumulation, a succession of expansion and contraction, prosperity and crisis. During the postwar boom, mainstream academics and even some Marxists thought that crises were a problem of the past. Mandel, however, insisted that the business cycle still existed. He tried to refine business cycle theory, taking Chapter 11 of *Marxist Economic Theory* as his starting point.[132] In *Late Capitalism* he devoted extensive attention to the role of credit expansion and permanent inflation in postponing crisis in the short run but also making it more explosive in the long run.[133]

Mandel argued that the history of international capitalism is not just a succession of five-, seven- or ten-year cyclical movements, but also a succession of longer periods of about fifty years. These constitute a third type of cycle between the short industrial cycle and the long cycle constituted by the rise and fall of the capitalist system itself.[134]

In Mandel's theory, these long waves do not have any fixed rhythm or duration. There is an asymmetry between the transition from a long expansive wave to a depression and the transition from a long recessive wave to expansion. Mandel admitted that an empirical verification of long waves was not the statistical proof that his critics demanded: 'We . . . regard the main problem *not* as one of statistical verification, but of theoretical explanation.'[135] An immense field had gone unexplored because the debate had fallen silent since the 1930s. Despite Mandel's rehabilitation of long-wave theory, it was only in the second half of the 1970s that interest in it revived in broader circles.[136] The 1974-45 recession provoked an explosion of articles and debates.

Unlike Parvus and Van Gelderen, Mandel did not seek to explain long waves in terms of market expansion or expanding production.[137] Nor did he endorse Kondratiev's explanation, which relied on the long lifespan of major investments,[138] or Schumpeter's,[139] which derived long waves from entrepreneurs' innovative activities.[140] Mandel said that 'the fluctuations of the rate of profit' were missing from all these analyses. As early as 1964 Mandel had argued that any theory of long waves that neglected the rate of profit would be inadequate.[141] The rise and fall of the rate of profit depends not on one but on several factors, and each new takeoff requires a historical investigation of its mechanism. Writing long before the recession of 1974-5, Mandel concluded that 'we should today have entered into the second phase of the "long wave" which began with the Second World War, characterized by decelerated capital accumulation.'[142]

Although Mandel characterized the transition from rapid to slow growth

as inevitable, he did not believe that the transition in the other direction was
brought about by endogenous factors rooted in the economic process itself.
External 'system shocks' – an image used earlier by Trotsky to refer to a
range of non-economic factors such as wars, revolutions and
counterrevolutions – were deciding factors.[143] Only these kinds of external
shocks could explain the sudden jump in the long-term average rate of
profit – a paradox for Marxists – without which economic growth was ruled
out.[144] There had been such shocks after 1848, 1893 and 1940 (USA)/1948
(Western Europe).[145] These transitions could be integrated into Marxist
economic analysis because – as Mandel argued at the 1967 Frankfurt
colloquium – different key variables are partially autonomous. Historical
research is necessary to show their non-mechanical correlations. 'This
vindicates again the incorporation of history into real life economics', he
wrote the Portuguese economist Francisco Louçã.[146] Economics and history
are inextricably linked in Mandel's conclusion: 'We can therefore accept the
idea that the long waves are much more than just rhythmic ups and downs in
the rate of growth of the capitalist economy. They are distinct historical
periods in a real sense.'[147]

    If late capitalism is a 'distinct historical period' and coincides with the long
wave that began in 1940/1948, however, then shouldn't its continuity with
the preceding phase be qualified? In the Introduction to *Late Capitalism*,
Mandel in passing called postwar capitalism merely a further development of
the imperialist, monopoly-capitalist epoch.[148] The long wave – with its
unique combination of contradictions – he seems to have considered as a
secondary mechanism and not as a new regime of accumulation.[149] Did
Mandel's aversion to the popular notion of 'organized capitalism', with its
implication of harmonious development, lead him to emphasize this continuity? Did his Leninism prompt this line of reasoning? Mandel seemed
unable to choose between seeing late capitalism as a mere continuation and
recognizing it as something new; his discontent with the term late
capitalism – a chronological rather than synthetic concept – betrayed this
difficulty.[150] It is as if late capitalism could not be analyzed solely as an older
phase after all.[151]

There was no interest in long-wave theory during the boom after the
Second World War. Mandel was an exception: he predicted in the mid-
1960s that the period of expansion would give way to a depression, and that
the turning point would come at the end of the 1960s or the beginning of
the 1970s.

    Following in Marx's footsteps, Mandel placed history back at the heart of
economic theory. This represented, as did his anti-Eurocentrism, a major

contribution. He set about analyzing late capitalism as soon as he had a clear picture of its historical dynamic, when he realized that a new expansive phase had taken off after the war. He set himself the task of explaining its fundamental causes. The theory of long waves helped him to understand the alternation of ebb and flow in investments, production, growth, employment and income. He succeeded in defining a new sub-phase of the history of capitalism, which in his words maintained 'the main characteristics of monopoly capitalism [imperialism, according to Lenin's vocabulary]' while adding 'significant new features'.[152] He considered the internationalization of the productive forces and of capital, made possible by the third technological revolution, as the main trend in postwar capitalism. In *Late Capitalism* and 'The EEC and European-US Competition' he predicted the decline of absolute US hegemony and the decreasing capacity of the nation-state for economic intervention. Structural transformations and adjustments were indispensable to the resolution of these problems. This was a remarkable anticipation of the debate on globalization that would occur in the 1990s.

Several important elements of *Late Capitalism* were already present in *Marxist Economic Theory* – such as the theory of uneven exchange, the existence of two average rates of profit under monopoly capitalism and the theory of crisis – but the earlier book had no coherent analysis of capitalism after 1945. Although Mandel was critical of other thinkers who let the flourishing postwar economy convince them that the inherent contradictions of capitalism had been weakened, his criticism applied to a certain extent to his own *Marxist Economic Theory* as well. In it, he had not sufficiently distanced himself from the new theorists of economic harmony.[153] In the course of the 1960s he tried to overcome the book's weaknesses. By rehabilitating long-wave theory in 1964; elaborating on the concept of alienation and his critique of Althusser's structuralism in *The Formation of the Economic Thought of Karl Marx* in 1967; and finally developing a dialectical (parametric) concept of determination, also in 1967, he laid the foundation for an analysis of late capitalism based on 'the immanent laws of motion of capital'.[154]

Yet Mandel's work provoked much criticism, even in his own circle. As we have seen, Rosdolsky, whom Mandel regarded as his mentor, considered *Marxist Economic Theory* weak. Some had serious reservations about *Late Capitalism* as well. Elmar Altvater said the book lacked coherence, and rejected several of its theses. Mandel had not succeeded sufficiently in investigating the development and correlation of the fundamental laws of capitalist development. In the final analysis, he did not make sufficiently clear what distinguishes late capitalism from monopoly capitalism or imperialism. If Mandel had sketched the relationship between the long waves and the various epochs of capitalist accumulation (regimes of accumulation), his periodization might have gained in clarity. Beginning with the production of surplus value and the development of the rate of surplus value, a reference to Taylorism and Fordism as new regimes of surplus extraction after the First World War would have been useful. Mandel could have analyzed the expansive period of the third technological revolution – the 'thirty glorious years' after the world war – as a special phase of Fordism largely continuous with it. This would have made the term 'late capitalism', with its inevitably fatalistic connotations, unnecessary.

A doctoral defence in Brussels

Although Mandel's book had a mixed reception, his lectures on late capitalism were widely praised. During a lecture cycle in early 1971, Mandel resolved to use this material to obtain his doctorate. Altvater, who had recently become a professor at the Otto Suhr Institute, joined Mandel's doctoral dissertation committee 'with pleasure'. Meanwhile Mandel, still only forty-nine years old, had been offered a regular professorship in social economy in the faculty of economics at the Free University of Berlin. Paul Sweezy told Hajo Riese, another economist there, that he was fortunate to be present at the arrival of 'one of the world's foremost Marxist economists'.[155] But those who offered Mandel their congratulations forgot to take the Berlin Senate into account. On the authority of the Social Democratic senator for science and culture, the appointment was blocked, not because of Mandel's lack of a PhD but because Mandel did not agree with the 'fundamental free, democratic order'. As an official declaration put it, 'Mandel calls for pushing aside parliamentary democracy and replacing it with a republic of councils . . . Mandel wants to create the republic of councils by illegal means, that is illegally and violently.'[156]

This opposition scarcely came as a surprise. Altvater had already told Mandel that 'in any case we are ready here [at the Otto Suhr Institute] to wage a campaign to guarantee your appointment'.[157] A few days after the Berlin Senate's decision, Mandel went to West Berlin to defend himself at a press conference and to take part in a protest teach-in. At Frankfurt, where he was changing planes, he was informed that he was now persona non grata in West Germany and Berlin. The decisive consideration, according to Hans Dietrich Genscher, the Liberal minister for foreign affairs, was that 'Professor Mandel not only upholds the doctrine of permanent revolution in his teaching but also actively works for it.'[158]

Protests quickly followed. Indignant students occupied the building that housed the faculty of economics. The Austrian philosopher Jean Améry wrote with exasperation in the *Frankfurter Rundschau*, 'Why, in god's name, does anyone want to deny the democratic right to freedom of movement to this theoretician and writer, this advocate of a cause that has not yet historically compromised itself?'[159] The historian Wolfgang Abendroth agreed: 'Unconditional solidarity with Ernest Mandel . . . is a prerequisite of our own freedom.'[160] Mandel, the scholar, teacher, activist and agitator, was defended by a committee that included Ernst Bloch, Hans Magnus Enzenberger, Ossip Flechtheim, Helmut Gollwitzer, Jakob Moneta, Oskar Negt, Peter Weiss and many others from the worlds of scholarship and culture, trade unions and politics.[161] From 24–26 April, around 4,000 students held a congress in Berlin against political repression. A strike paralyzed the university, a protest not only against Mandel's entry ban and the law banning radicals from all civil service jobs but also against attacks on the left in the wake of the hunt for the Baader-Meinhof group. While the police were on the lookout to prevent Mandel's announced arrival, a full auditorium heard him declare:

> When we protest the entry ban, we are not only in solidarity with one person or with a representative of a particular revolutionary socialist group; we are defending the elementary interests of all wage earners in the Federal Republic and in Europe.[162]

Mandel's voice had been tape-recorded in Brussels.

The protest was unsuccessful, despite the international response. A letter of support for Mandel was sent to Chancellor Willy Brandt. Among those signing were Sicco Mansholt, Edith Russell, Tom Bottomore, Noam Chomsky, Michael Foot, Christopher Hill, Joan Robinson, Ken Coates, André Gorz, Meghnad Desai and the American microbiologist and Nobel Prize–winner Salvador E. Luria, who announced that he would not set foot in West Germany as long as the restriction remained in force.[163] Even so, Mandel's entry ban was only lifted in 1978.

Conservatives at the Otto Suhr Institute now went on the offensive. Altvater was told to resign from Mandel's doctoral committee. He complied, saying 'It's not sensible to make a fuss about it because that would only interfere with his getting the degree.'[164] Mandel's supporters were careful not to give right-wingers cause for refusing Mandel his doctorate. On Friday 25 August 1972, the doctoral committee travelled to Brussels for Mandel's oral defence. His defence and the thesis *Late Capitalism: In Search of a Marxist Explanation* earned Mandel his PhD summa cum laude.[165] Mandel's committee – consisting of the historian Reinhard Rürup, the economist

Hajo Riese and the political scientist Gilbert Ziebura, who chaired it – was unanimous in its praise.

Before submitting his manuscript to the committee, Mandel had circulated it among friends. These included Jakob Moneta,[166] the Cremona economist Michele Salvati,[167] Elmar Altvater,[168] Perry Anderson, Robin Blackburn and Bob Sutcliffe. Wherever possible, Mandel had incorporated their criticisms. The book had to be completed without the late Roman Rosdolsky's judgement, though Rosdolsky had been the political and scholarly theorist with whom Mandel had had the closest affinity. Mandel dedicated *Late Capitalism* to him.

Ernst and Karola Bloch, who knew the pain of exile, tried to comfort Mandel: 'You are one of the few men entirely faithful to the revolution.'[169] Bloch's poor health did not permit him to visit Mandel in Brussels; they stayed in touch by exchanging letters. He also corresponded with Rudi Dutschke, now living in Aarhus in Denmark after being deported from England in the spring of 1971. Dutschke demanded that Werner Maihöfer, Hans Dietrich Genscher's successor as German minister for foreign affairs and once Dutschke's interlocutor in Bad Boll, lift Mandel's entry ban.[170] The Blochs also urged Maihöfer to reconsider. There was no response. Karola Bloch did not hide her disenchantment: 'The hell with him.'[171] A year later she wrote to Dutschke excitedly, 'Ernest Mandel has been admitted to PEN [the writers' association]. We can hope that he'll soon be able to visit.'[172] This couldn't have happened without old Ernst Bloch;[173] a majority of the presidium of the writers' organization had come out against Mandel's joining. The alarmed Bloch had written,

> This is how it is at present in West Germany. Despite laws banning political discrimination, an important scholar, superb writer and irreproachable man has been refused admittance to PEN, only because his political ideas do not please the presidium. Ernest Mandel was born in Frankfurt/Main, was held in German prisons and concentration camps, and is a sincere, combative anti-fascist – German PEN should consider it an honour to welcome him as a member. I request that this letter be read publicly.[174]

In protest against Mandel's admission, nineteen members left the organization, whose charter upheld freedom of opinion. These included Werner Maihöfer, the Hitler biographer Joachim Fest and the Adenauer biographer Arnulf Baring. Rudi Dutschke commented, 'Good riddance to bad rubbish.'[175] Six and a half years after his entry ban, Mandel was again able to enter West Germany in the summer of 1978, in order to plead in Berlin for liberation of the East German dissident Rudolf Bahro.

8

Love and Revolution

It is more pleasant and useful to go through the 'experience of the revolution' than to write about it.
— V.I. Lenin, *The State and Revolution*[1]

The progressive revival of the 1960s, which in Belgium began with the general strike of 1960–61, brought with it a renewal of the connection between struggle and theoretical debate, a connection that had been lost during the interwar 'darkness at noon' of Stalinism.

Although Marxist critical thought had not been entirely silenced, as shown by the works of Cornelius Castoriadis and Paul Sweezy, Gramsci's *Prison Notebooks* and Karl Korsch's later work, in academia it had been marginalized, confined to the domains of aesthetics and philosophy.[2] In the 1960s such publishers as Maspero in France and Feltrinelli in Italy rediscovered the heterodox political literature that had long been on Stalin's index. Creative Marxist thought emerged from the shadow of the universities and stimulated – in addition to the debates about neo-capitalism and the role of the proletariat – thinking about decolonization, revolution and post-capitalist society, the Soviet Union and China, Algeria and Cuba.

In *Marxist Economic Theory* Mandel had examined the economics of transitional societies.[3] The sociologist Pierre Naville encouraged him to pursue the subject further. Naville was preparing to republish *New Economics* (first published in 1923), an analysis of the Soviet economy by Yevgeni Preobrazhensky, who had been killed by Stalin in 1937.[4] He asked Mandel to write a foreword.[5] Central to the book was the question of what dynamic would arise in an agricultural society in transition from capitalism to socialism and what sources of socialist accumulation would be available. Mandel wrote that Preobrazhensky had made possible an economic policy free of pragmatism and empiricism.[6] This book's publication contributed to the economic debate in Cuba.

In Cuba with Che Guevara and Fidel Castro

Ernesto 'Che' Guevara, who with Fidel Castro was the face of the Cuban revolution, took a leading role in this debate. In 1958–59 guerrillas had ended the oppressive, US-backed Batista regime. In doing so they broke with the prevailing understanding of revolution that had held sway since 1935. The dominant conception dated back to the stages theory held by Stalin's Comintern, which had limited revolutionary ambitions to formation of a national democratic government with the task of achieving agricultural reform, industrialization and democratic renewal. The struggle between the proletariat and the bourgeoisie would only take place in a more-or-less distant future phase of socialist revolution. The Cuban revolutionaries discovered that in practice such a revolution was impossible and looked for a model that would put a definitive end to capitalism in Cuba. In the process they risked an American invasion, a threat made clear during the Bay of Pigs (Playa Giron) incident and the October 1962 missile crisis. They also earned anathemas from Moscow, which saw Cuba's support for revolutionary movements in Latin America, Asia and Africa as undermining a foreign policy aimed at peaceful coexistence with the West.

From 1962 to 1964 Che Guevara headed the Cuban ministry of industry. He opposed the growing influence of Moscow-oriented Communists and the state's increasing bureaucratic tendencies. His ideas about the economy were formed in the debates of 1963–4, which were not only about economic development but also about the essence of socialism: a central budget structure versus financial independence of companies, moral versus material incentives, the law of value versus planning, and the role of consciousness.

Che considered an economy without a humanistic perspective, without communist ethics, unthinkable.[7] 'We fight against poverty but also against alienation . . . If Communism were to bypass consciousness . . . then the spirit of the revolution would die.'[8] In a famous 1965 essay, 'Socialism and Man in Cuba', Che warned against 'the pipe dream that socialism can be achieved with the help of the dull instruments left to us by capitalism', like making value and profitability the absolute economic measure or using material incentives. Che held that fully realized communism would require changing not only the economic structure but also human beings.[9]

Impressed by the wave of nationalizations there, Mandel concluded in the fall of 1960 that Cuba had developed into a post-capitalist state.[10] 'Reality has shown that to consolidate power the revolutionary leaders have unconsciously resorted to Trotskyism.'[11] Shortly after the publication of *Marxist Economic Theory* Mandel had a copy sent to Che and Castro via their embassy in Brussels.[12] He had informal contacts with the Cuban regime through Nelson Zayas Pazos,[13] a Cuban Trotskyist and French teacher working in the foreign ministry, and Hilde Gadea, Che's ex-wife, a Peruvian economist of Indian and Chinese descent who lived in Havana.[14] Gadea was sympathetic to Trotskyist ideas, and through her and Zayas documents of the Fourth International were regularly forwarded to Che.[15]

In October 1963 Zayas told Mandel about the debate raging between what he called the Stalino-Khrushchevists and the circle around Che.[16] While the former were arguing for financial independence for companies and for material incentives to increase productivity,[17] Che called for centralizing finances and strengthening moral incentives.[18] Zayas encouraged Mandel to intervene in the debate: 'It seems to me that the entire Castro leadership would welcome such a contribution . . . Fidel, Che, Aragonés, Hart, Faure Chomón and many others are favourably disposed to us.'[19] A month later Zayas distributed a stencilled contribution from Mandel to those taking part in the debate.[20] Mandel supported Che's resistance to financial autonomy, not because he was opposed to decentralization but because centralized financing for small–scale industry seemed at that time the optimal solution. He shared Che's fears of the growth of bureaucracy, all the more so because Che's opponents wanted to make decentralized financial administration efficient by using material incentives. Mandel was not against material incentives as such, on two conditions: that they were not individual but collective incentives in order to ensure solidarity, and that their use was restrained in order to curb the selfishness that a system of enrichment produces.

To combat bureaucratization Mandel argued for democratic and centralized self-management, 'a management by the workers at the workplace, subject to strict discipline on the part of a central authority that is directly chosen by workers' councils'.[21] Mandel and Che differed on this last point. Che did support management of the enterprises by the trade unions, but only if they were representative and not controlled by Communists, who, he said, were very unpopular. The results of decentralized self-management in Yugoslavia, where companies acted like slaves of the market, had also made Che cautious. Mandel warned him against throwing the baby out with the bath water. Self-management by workers was entirely compatible with a central plan democratically decided by the direct producers.[22]

In early 1964 Mandel was invited to visit Havana. There were prospects of meetings with Che and Castro.[23] Che had read *Marxist Economic Theory* enthusiastically and had large parts of it translated.[24] Mandel confided to Livio Maitan: 'I think that I can raise many issues openly and frankly',[25] and wrote again a few days later, 'And in any case I can resolve the question of training our Bolivian friends.'[26]

Maitan had visited South America for the first time in 1962. He had made contact with insurrectionary movements in Bolivia, Chile, Peru, Venezuela, Uruguay and Argentina and had urged them to work with the Cubans.[27] In Buenos Aires he met such left-wing Peronistas as the poet Alicia Eguren and her partner John William Cooke, who had been in contact with Che since 1959.[28] In Peru Maitan's contacts were with the United Left and its peasant leader Hugo Blanco. In Bolivia he met with the mine workers in Huanuni, Catavi and Siglo XX. Trotskyists had strong influence there and hoped to be trained in Cuba for armed struggle.

Mandel stayed in Havana for almost seven weeks. It was a visit without official duties, an occasion for exchanging ideas, and these exchanges convinced him completely that Cuba 'constitutes . . . the most advanced bastion in the liberation of labour and of humanity'.[29] The Marxist classics were widely studied in cadre schools, in ministries and beyond. Mandel wrote a friend, 'The class I took part in had just finished volume one of *Capital*, with a minister and three deputy ministers present . . . And it was serious study, even Talmudic, studying page by page . . .'[30] Mandel's own works, including *Marxist Economic Theory*, were discussed; translated, stencilled excerpts circulated among the leadership.[31] He addressed hundreds of auditors at the University of Havana, speaking in Spanish – with a sprinkling of Italian when a word escaped him. There was even an announcement of his visit in *Hoy*, the paper of the Communist Blas Roca. *Revolución*, the largest and most influential daily paper, published an interview.

'I was literally kidnapped by the finance ministry and the ministry of industry [Che's ministry] to write a long article about the problem of the law of value in the economy of a transitional society.'[32] Speaking French, Mandel met for four hours with Che, who received him dressed in olive green fatigues, his famous black beret with its red star within reach. Totally enchanted, Mandel wrote a friend, 'Confidentially, he is extremely close to your friend Germain [the pseudonym Mandel used most], whom you know well.'[33]

Mandel and Che worked together on a response to the French economist Charles Bettelheim. In April 1964 Bettelheim had published an article in the monthly *Cuba Socialista*[34] that held that the central planning that Che advocated was unwise policy, considering the limited development of the forces of production. The Marxist Bettelheim had become Che's most profound critic. Other opponents included Alberto Mora, the minister of foreign trade, and Carlos Rafael Rodríguez, the minister of agriculture. Years later Bettelheim commented,

Cuba's level of development meant that the various units of production needed a sufficient measure of autonomy, that they be integrated into the market so that they could buy and sell their products at prices reflecting the costs of production. I also found that the low level of productive forces required the principle: to each according to his work. The more one worked, the higher the pay. This was the core of our divergence, because Che found differences acceptable only when they arose from what each contributed to the best of his ability.[35]

The research director of the Paris Ecole des Hautes Etudes en Sciences Sociales still did not agree with Che's thinking.

Mandel thought that Bettelheim was making the mistake of looking for pure forms in historical reality. For example, according to the French economist, there could be no collective ownership of the means of production as long as legally there was no completely collective ownership. Mandel found Bettelheim's insistence on such complete ownership – 'to the last nail' – a bit technocratic. Complete ownership was not necessary as long as there was possession sufficient to suspend capital's laws of motion and initiate planned development.[36] Mandel pointed out that the withering away of the commodity form was determined not only by the development of the forces of production but also by changes in human behaviour. It was a commonplace to say that the law of value also played a role in a post-capitalist economy without saying what parts of the economy it would govern. The key question was whether or not the law of value determined investment in the socialist sector. If that was necessarily the case, Mandel said, then all underdeveloped countries – including all of the post-capitalist countries except Czechoslovakia and East Germany – were doomed to eternal underdevelopment. He pointed out that in these countries agriculture was more profitable than industry, light and small-scale industry more profitable than heavy and large-scale industry, and above all obtaining industrial products on the world market more profitable than domestic manufacturing. 'To permit investment to be governed by the law of value would actually be to preserve the imbalance of the economic structure handed down from capitalism.'[37] With his criticism Mandel was not denying the law of value but opposing what he termed Bettelheim's fatalism, which denied that a long and hard struggle was necessary *between the principle of conscious planning and the blind operation of the law of value*.[38]

Luis Alvarez Rom, Cuba's finance minister, spent ten hours correcting the Spanish translation of Mandel's article. It appeared in June 1964 under the title 'Las categorias mercantiles en el periodo de transición' (Mercantile Categories in the Period of Transition); 20,000 copies were published in

periodicals of the ministries of industry and of finance.[39] It included a
flattering biography of the author.[40] Mandel wondered if this was 'to
neutralize in advance certain ill-intentioned criticisms of my spiritual family
[the Fourth International]?'[41] He treasured in his wallet a banknote personally signed by Che: more than a currency note, it was a proof of trust.
Mandel admired Che's courage in inviting him to Cuba for a debate that the
Soviets and orthodox Communists had to accept, however grudgingly. He
praised Che as a theoretician, a leader in the tradition of Marx, Lenin and
Trotsky.[42]

Looking back in 1977, Mandel considered Cuba's open debate on the
economy 'the big turning point' in the Cuban revolution.[43] Behind that
debate had raged another, not held in public. This debate concerned the
revolution's sociopolitical orientation, the role of the workers and the issue
of power. That is, along with the question of the law of value came the issue
of how much freedom the proletariat would have to make its own decisions.
As Mandel saw it, though Che triumphed in the public debate, he was
defeated in the hidden one. Guaranteeing freedom was a political problem:
it required the creation of workers' councils and popular assemblies. Such
organs were never developed.

When Che left Cuba in 1965, he was the most popular leader on the
island. If the voice of the people had been heard, Che would have won the
political as well as the economic round. But, as Mandel said, 'Che did not
want to appeal to the people. He did not want to split the party openly. This
is why he left after his defeat.'[44] In his 1964 correspondence Mandel had
acknowledged that he did not dare put some of his impressions on paper.[45]
Did he already suspect that the debate would have a tragic outcome?

On Mandel's departure Luis Alvarez Rom assured him that he was always
welcome; a request would be sufficient to assure an invitation.[46] There was a
rumour that within a few months Castro would officially invite him 'so I can
deal a bit with his affairs'.[47] He returned to Brussels in a hopeful mood:

> The influence of the Stalinist 'sectarians' (that's what they're called there)
> continues to decline . . . Slowly a new vanguard is forming, one that is
> close to our ideas . . . The revolution is still bursting with life, and on that
> basis democracy [can] bloom.[48]

He had also been assured that 'the group around Che was noticeably
stronger' and that 'workers' assemblies would soon be started'.[49] Was this the
beginning of workers' self-management, however modest? The promise did
not amount to much, but Mandel closed his eyes to its limits. He reacted
negatively to Nelson Zayas's advice to pressure Che 'and to convince him

that he'll lose the battle if it's only fought in the government and bureaucratic arena'.[50] The people's support for the government must not be underestimated.[51] The die was not yet cast: 'Nothing was definitely decided yet in the economic discussion.'[52] Mandel did not want to hamper Che and Fidel in their conflicts with the pro-Soviet currents. This would not have been appreciated, either, by the swelling multitude of radical youth in France and elsewhere, for whom Che was nearing the status of hero. Mandel's reaction disappointed Zayas and hastened his decision to turn his back on Cuba and complete his study of French in Paris. He asked Mandel to use his influence with Che to secure the necessary exit visa.[53]

Mandel's thoughts about Cuba changed only slowly. The Latin American revolution came to a halt: Salvador Allende lost the Chilean election in September 1964, there were military coups in Brazil and Bolivia, and leftist guerrillas in Peru and Venezuela were defeated. Cuba paid for these failures with its growing dependence on the Soviet Union. This was an arid climate in which social democracy could not thrive. As Mandel frankly admitted to ex-Trotskyist Jesus Vazquez Mendez,

> I subscribe to your opinion that participation by the people is essential . . . I had heard that management of the enterprises would come into the hands of the trade unions after their leadership was replaced; but the latest news is that nothing has happened. I'm sorry about it, and like you I'm afraid that if things are left to take their course, the result will be an economic impasse. Maybe I'll go to Cuba again in 1965 and can give the debate new impetus.[54]

But he didn't visit in 1965, and he never saw Che again, not even when Che was in Algiers to address an Afro-Asian conference at the end of a trip through Africa in February that year. Never before had Che come out so strongly against the Soviet Union. He declared that 'the socialist countries are, in a way, accomplices of imperialist exploitation'. Before all else oppressed peoples had to be helped with weapons, 'without any charge at all, and in quantities determined by the need'.[55] Che's words took root in the fertile soil of Latin American campuses and the radical milieu in Paris, where his speech was duplicated and distributed,[56] and the Union of Communist Students (UEC) invited Che to Paris for a debate on Stalinism.[57] The initiative came from the UEC left wing, in which Mandel's fellow-thinkers played a prominent role. Six months earlier they had been received by a deputy minister of industry, a close colleague of Che's.[58] One of the group's spokespeople, twenty-seven-year-old Janette Pienkny (Janette Habel after 1966), travelled regularly between Paris and Havana. She contacted the Cuban ambassador, who relayed the invitation to Che by phone. Meanwhile Mandel was attempting to get a visa for Algeria. After Che's speech, Mandel had phoned him his congratulations. Che had immediately agreed to a meeting but it had to be the following day, a Monday, because he was about to leave.[59] But that Sunday Mandel sought vainly to make contact – at home and at the embassy – with the ambassador and the consul. Without a visa, 'they wouldn't even have let me telephone from the airport . . . I finally decided, heartbroken, to miss the meeting that meant so much to me.'[60]

The debate in Paris never took place. The Communist Party put a stop to it.[61] Che was now viewed as a heretic, not only in Moscow but also within the Communist parties. Algiers was his last public appearance. He went to the Congo and Bolivia to help break the isolation of their revolutions, a solidarity that he summed up in his testamentary message with the call: 'Make two, three, many Vietnams!'[62] That slogan became the catchphrase for the generation of '68.

Love

Mandel's letters were always filled with facts, judgements and fragmentary analyses; he seldom let his emotions show. As he wrote to an Argentinian friend, the Peronista Alicia Eguren:

> Don't give way to discomfort for too long . . . I'm working on two . . . books, but I'm so wrapped up in ongoing affairs that I can't find the time for writing. This irritates me hugely . . . But luckily there are rewards that ordinary 'writers' or 'scholars' will never know.[63]

Did those rewards compensate him for the absence of a love life? He was not looking for love; he could not forget his relationship with Micky Traks. As he confided to Ernest Federn, 'Like Papageno I still say "I'll stay single" until I find Papagena.'[64]

Mandel was forty-two when he met Gisela Scholtz. In the spring of 1965 he took part in a London conference with African Trotskyists. As usual he was run ragged in the days immediately preceding and following this event. He gave lectures at the London School of Economics, met with the editorial boards of *New Left Review* and the *Socialist Register*, and lectured to a group of Ceylonese students. It was there he met the mercurial thirty-year-old student. She was in the British capital studying Hindi and preparing for a stay in India and Ceylon.

Gisela Scholtz was slender and energetic, with short dark hair and engaging eyes. She was a bit shorter than Mandel. She came originally

from Hirschberg in Lower Silesia, in a part of Germany transferred to Poland
after the war; Hirschberg was renamed Jelena Gora. After 1945 her family
emigrated to Mühlacker in Baden-Württemberg.[65] Gisela was raised in a
Protestant milieu, one in which people cared deeply for music and art. Her
father taught chemistry at the local high school. He was from a conservative
Prussian background and had disdained the uncultured Nazis. Gisela was
creative, loved German literature and painted throughout her life, without
wanting to make art her profession. Her favourite writers included Bertold
Brecht and the expressionist poet Gottfried Benn.[66] Robert Musil's *Man
Without Qualities* made a profound impression on her.[67]

In the late 1950s Gisela attended the Europa College in Hamburg. This
was a school open to all European students, with a curriculum designed to
counteract narrow nationalistic thinking. She formed part of a circle of
intellectuals and artists and was friends with the daughter of the novelist
Hans Henny Jahnn. After studying sociology at Europa, she went to work as
a researcher in the Berlin bureau of *Der Spiegel*.

In 1962 Gisela married Klaus Meschkat. Like her, he was born in 1935. A
Berlin native, he was now an assistant at the city's East European Institute,
where he wrote a dissertation about the view of the Paris Commune in
Soviet historiography.[68] A freethinking Marxist, Meschkat had already been
a member of the SDS for a decade. He was president of the West Berlin
General Students Council and since 1959 had been chair of the national
student union. He got to know Rudi Dutschke, five years his junior, at the
Institute some time before Dutschke united the SDS with the situationist
group Subversive Action in 1965.[69] Meschkat felt drawn to Dutschke and
his ideas.

Eventually Gisela found her work for *Der Spiegel* so unsatisfying that she
handed in her resignation directly to the publisher, Rudolf Augstein. She
applied for a scholarship to study Hindi, which was easy to get because of
Germany's interest in the Third World. At the same time she got her
scholarship, Meschkat finished his dissertation. Nothing seemed to stand in
the way of their starting a new life together, but in October 1964 Gisela
travelled to London, where she moved into student housing that lacked
most creature comforts.

She had more serious reasons than that to feel unhappy. For some time
her relationship with Meschkat had left something to be desired. What had
begun as passionate love had gradually dwindled, until there was no glimmer
of happiness left in it for her. Her longing had been replaced by apprehen-
sion about the future, her hope by depression. Meeting Ernest Mandel was a
liberation, though she could not immediately shake off all her doubts about
starting a new relationship with a man his age. She worried too much about

her appearance and awkwardness and was afraid they gave the impression that she was only eighteen.

She seemed to be flirting with the ideas of Freud, embracing in her own state of mind his division of the personality into three parts: ego, hypercritical super-ego and emotional id.[70] At the same time, she felt she was not in control of her own body. She wrote to Mandel that she couldn't stand it:

> My super-ego is incredibly hateful and nasty . . . It makes me continually ridiculous and afflicts me. Often the Id really makes me cry with rage with no reason . . . It [the Id] sounds very logical . . . It also often sounds sensible and gets rid of the worst thing, the vileness.[71]

This 'vileness' led her to feel that she had avoided the crisis of becoming an adult and had not been tough enough to be free. She reproached herself for remaining dependent on authority. She was overcome by the fear that

> the id triumphs: Ernest, the great man . . . He! . . . This is but another new authority, a new governor, a new master! . . . I know precisely why I love you, Great One. I love you because you already know everything . . . because you know what life is.[72]

These were thoughts from a shadowy world that undermined her self-confidence. Though she felt awakened to life, she begged Ernest not to love her if he could not or would rather not.

Ernest's feelings for her were beyond question; he was possessed by love. He asked her to travel to Spain with him. Gisela wanted nothing better. She told Meschkat about it, and he recommended accepting: 'a wonderful chance to really get to know the thinking of comrade Mandel'.[73] Meschkat was kept ignorant of the love relationship. Gisela wrote Ernest, 'I have not written him that I love you, not because I'm afraid . . . but because I still can't and don't want to say the words. First I have to process the feelings a bit for myself.'[74] It did not take long. When she told him, Meschkat showed little patience with her naïveté:

> Of course I agree that you should travel to Spain with Mandel . . . The personal aspect, I'm sorry to say, I can't judge; I don't know Mandel well enough for that. But it doesn't matter to me if he is interested in more than a connection between comrades and if the fortnight's vacation turns out differently from what you now imagine . . . You have to take account of these possibilities, but that is exclusively your

business . . . Go with him, but don't be disappointed when it takes a turn you haven't anticipated.[75]

The imminent separation depressed Meschkat. It was the failure of his marriage that caused him pain, not that Gisela and Ernest would be together.[76] He did think that Mandel must have guessed what his invitation would lead to. As he wrote Gisela, 'Even if this were the case, Mandel has been resolute and rational and right, but this resoluteness and rationality are alien to me, even if they're necessary to make life conscious.'[77]

Their farewell seemed tragic, and Gisela felt helpless and guilty about Klaus: 'Ernest, Ernest . . . It doesn't seem to me possible to build a new life on the ruins of the old and at the expense of another.' She wrote despairingly, 'My God, why must this all happen and what have I done? . . . O Ernest, please, please help me.'[78]

Was Gisela recoiling from her decision? Did she feel herself too weak for a new start? Her dejection worried Mandel. Their stay in Spain lasted three weeks. She could have easily been mistaken in him and be looking for a way out. He had been devastated by Micky's indecision and did not want to go through that again. A few days later Gisela found the words to reassure him.

> I know what I'm saying when I write you, now I belong to you for all time . . . I am . . . made very conscious by today's letter how you suffered then from the indecision of your lover and that this must not happen again. My dearest, believe me . . . And please do not ever again be afraid of letters. They will always contain the same words: that I love you . . . It's final – and these are no empty words.[79]

In addition to her literary and artistic interests, Gisela was also curious about politics, though without being an activist. However, she was a member of the SPD, and Meschkat had initiated her into the Berlin SDS in 1960. There she had first seen Mandel speak. Once she was in his company, her life, at least the political side of it, took wing. She read Marx and Trotsky and pamphlets from the International, though she found the jargon of the pamphlets not always easy to understand. Back in Berlin she became the oracle for everyone interested in Mandel's work. Rudi Dutschke was not easy to satisfy. A member of the Attack Group, he knew Mandel's work thoroughly but was curious, as Gisela told Mandel, about 'who you are "as a person"'. Dutschke also wondered if their conversations together were as interesting as Mandel's work and lectures.[80]

Gisela joined the Fourth International before she left for India in September. Passionate as she was, the image of revolutionary will appealed to her. Her conscience was eased now that her accursed dependency served a higher goal. Love and revolution were inextricably bound together.

She would remain in India until February 1966, staying in Bombay, New Delhi, Calcutta, Madras and Kerala. She had a tough time of it, afflicted with homesickness and longing for Mandel. She was worried about her love life and the complications that stood in the way of their happiness.[81] She had been looking forward to her journey for ten years, originally from a longing to discover the world, later also from a desire to understand its history. Also, travel was always a way to escape reality, a kind of substitute suicide, as she confessed. It was something she had to do. 'And now I'm sailing on a ship to India, and now I don't want to any more. I simply don't want to any more.'[82] When she realized this she collapsed into a depression.[83] She continued the trip with feelings of guilt and a shattered self-image, yet gradually felt better in India. The comrades there considered her 'a little Mandel'.[84] Playing this role kept her out of the mire of dark thoughts.

Her experiences in India overwhelmed her yet stimulated her combative spirit and sense of humour. She started to learn Dutch and considered living together with Ernest in Brussels. Ernest enthusiastically sent a plan of the Rue Josse Impens house, arranged as if she already lived there. He wanted to get married as soon as possible.[85] He was looking forward to February and the moment when he could take her in his arms on the Marseilles dock – perhaps a sign that a more peaceful time was ahead for Gisela. There was certainly hope, and she would not even rule out having children.[86] In any case, her divorce from Meschkat was already being handled by Horst Mahler, a Berlin lawyer and friend.[87]

Ernest and Gisela's plan to live together failed to take account of his mother, who ruled the roost at home. Gisela came from Germany, and there could well have been anti-Semitic feelings in her family. Even worse, Rosa's devoutly Orthodox brother might use Ernest's marriage with a non-Jew to break with his sister. Gisela was distraught. Rosa had to know that her family had never distinguished between Jew and non-Jew, whether positively or negatively. Not wanting to hurt unmarried Uncle Motek, Gisela suggested, 'Since we wouldn't see him often, couldn't we simply tell him that I at least had a Jewish mother?'[88] But for the time being, she decided to resume her life in Berlin, not Brussels.

In her last letter, sent from the *Laos,* the ship carrying her from Bombay to Marseilles, Gisela divulged a closely held secret. She recalled that her grandmother had been manic-depressive and that this had ruined her life. Gisela said that she too had suffered terrible depressions between the ages of sixteen and eighteen. She had overcome them by rationalizing her emotions – a sad thing, to be sure, because this also dampened feelings of happiness. She acknowledged,

> It's also like that for me with you . . . In moments when I want to merge entirely into you, my mind automatically butts in and I can no longer lose myself in you . . . A bit dismal, but hardly comparable to the positive effect that these automatic rationalizations have when I'm depressed. These depressions often feel very real.

She sketched for example how she was overcome with a severe anxiety attack at Bombay dockside shortly before departure: 'Without cause or warning I was completely convinced . . . that I had to take my life . . . It was best to die in the face of happiness because anticipation was always more beautiful than everyday reality.' The thought was so overwhelming that 'I had to draw on all my energy and reason and afterwards was completely empty and exhausted for hours'.[89] Gisela thought that rationalizing in such circumstances was a matter of life and death. In exchange she was prepared to put up with less than euphoric feelings in happier situations.

Gisela had never before spoken with anyone about all this. She laid her happiness in Ernest's hands: 'You must shelter me from everything and . . . hold me really tight . . . I want to be happy and can only be so when you are wholly so.'[90] Mandel saw himself faced with an impossible task. He did not give happiness the same importance Gisela did. After his hopeless, un-requited love for Micky Traks, he could no longer plumb the depths of his feelings. He maintained a certain reserve that was sometimes perceived as a rather cool, egocentric outlook. Eduard Mörike's line applied to him: 'Do not overwhelm me with happiness or suffering.'[91] In the end this would do his relationship with Gisela no good.

Before Gisela returned to Berlin, the loving couple spent a week in Nice, staying half-board at the Pavillon de Rivoli Hotel near the Promenade des Anglais. Mandel lived modestly but now and then enjoyed a little nineteenth-century grandeur. In their correspondence such questions as whether or not to live together and whether or not to have children had remained unresolved. Now, at the Mediterranean shore, it was time to consider them. Mandel had little interest in fathering children; if Gisela wanted a child, she would have to assume all the caretaking responsibilities. Young children unnerved him because of their boisterousness and because one could not talk to them. This attitude reflected clearly his difficulty with taking direct responsibility for another person. Politics came first. He did not talk about emotions and did not know how to cope with them. Mandel lived at a remove from daily life, and this grew with his increasing involvement in the work of the Fourth International. He was seldom disappointed in politics; if they went badly in one area, possibilities were rosier elsewhere; for every ebb there was a flow. He easily lost sight of individuals and their longings. His commitment – intellectual leader of an international revolutionary movement with universal ambitions – was laden with such responsibilities that he neither could nor would reveal his private self fully. He lacked the energy, and Micky Traks had revealed to him his vulnerability.

Mandel was a complex figure. He spoke with feeling and was attentive and considerate. He was never moody. As long as his work would not suffer, he agreed to anything. Comrades walking in and out of the house, or his mother's showering him with attention day and night, did not bother him. But he went out of his way to avoid the demands of intimacy and children. Rosa, now seventy, was the archetypal Jewish mother, overprotective and intent on keeping women away from him. Her husband's death and the absence of Ernest's brother Michel made her all the more possessive of him, and Ernest put up with her. He was wrapped up in scholarship and politics and seemed not to bother about women. But in truth he was prey to mixed emotions about them.

Gisela forced him for the first time to abandon his reservations and to stand up to his mother. They lived only a short while in the family's three-storey mansion in the Schaerbeek borough of Brussels, although with its ground floor and attic the house had ample room for their library and for them; they might all have remained together without inconvenience. Ernest's mother wanted their relationship legitimized by marriage. He agreed, and Gisela followed reluctantly: 'I couldn't bear to think constantly that someone was living with me in the same house who saw my life as "immoral" or something.'[92]

From Berlin Gisela had regularly kept Ernest informed about the people around her. These included Meschkat; the philosopher Helmut Fleischer; Michael Mauke, a family friend who died young;[93] and Rudi Dutschke. After his flight from East Germany to West Berlin in 1961 Dutschke had come to represent the radical anti-authoritarian current in the SDS. This movement against the emergency laws and the Vietnam War had grown into a mass extra-parliamentary opposition. Dutschke and Meschkat were friends. Gisela found Dutschke an 'absolute and pure anarchist' but also 'loving' and 'ironic'.[94] 'I like him very, very much.'[95] Mandel was interested in working with Dutschke, anarchist or not. Internationalism was Dutschke's credo, and that was not the only similarity between them. They lived in the same sober manner, and Dutschke's parents did not hesitate to scold or correct him, the terror of the bourgeoisie.[96] The excitements of the 1960s – promiscuity, rock-and-roll and beat music – had passed them both by.

Dutschke and Mandel sharpened their rhetorical teeth on each other for the first time in December 1966 in a debate on 'The Proletarian Cultural Revolution in China', held in Berlin-Tempelhof.[97] The Springer newspaper *Berliner Zeitung* headlined Dutschke as 'ringleader, Red-Guardist and star agitator' who 'runs the whole crazy business . . . Wherever he shows his face, there's uproar . . . He wants revolution in entirely new forms.' According to the *Berliner Zeitung*, a witches' sabbath was performed in the packed auditorium of the Askanische School, with Mandel and Dutschke taking turns in the part of the devil:

> Early on Dutschke threw his pullover into a corner. As he boxed his Trotskyite opponent in, he rolled up his sleeves. He's never at a loss for an answer. He kneads his arguments into the multitude like a baker raisins in the dough.[98]

Dutschke's diary gave a different picture. Mandel's critique of his admiration for Mao had not missed its mark. 'Mao does not permit real self-organization by the people, a damned crucial remark', according to Dutschke, who recognized Mandel as his superior. 'I have a lot to learn from him.'[99] Dutschke showed himself to be thoughtful and self-critical, far from impervious to argument. He wasn't a man who had to win every debate.

In December 1966 Gisela and Ernest were united at last. Her divorce from Meschkat had been finalized in June 1966, but her marriage to Mandel was not performed until 10 December, in Schaerbeek.[100] Had they delayed the ceremony any longer, their intended January departure for Asia would have been in jeopardy. Now the two-month trip to India, Ceylon, Singapore, Hong Kong and Japan could go forward unhindered. The trip was paid for by Mandel's sale of a series of seven articles to the *Nouvel Observateur*, the Milan daily *Il Giorno* and Stockholm's *Dagens Nyheter*.

The death of Che Guevara

Though a trip to Cuba had proved impossible in 1965–6, Mandel's thinking about the Latin American revolution continued to develop. He praised the young philosopher Régis Debray, a student of Althusser's. In a January 1965 essay in *Les Temps Modernes* Debray had characterized Castroism as the Latin American version of Leninism.[101] Mandel described it as 'an excellent piece', though he dismissed out of hand Debray's ideas about spontaneous party formation.[102] Mandel expressed himself more cautiously about Cuba's relationship with Moscow: 'politically they continue to have their own line . . . What is bad, however, is that [Castro] made a series of unprincipled moves to satisfy the Russians (like his attacks against the Chinese and against the "counter-revolutionary trotskyists").'[103] At the final sitting of the Tricontinental Conference in Havana's Chaplin Theatre, Castro had spoken of 'the stupidities, the discredit, and the repugnant thing which Trotskyism today is in the field of politics'.[104]

Mandel thought that must be a genuflection towards Moscow, camouflage for the call to armed struggle that Moscow might interpret as a concession to Trotskyism. In a confidential meeting with Victor Rico Galan, Castro's representative in Mexico, Mandel later learned that Castro regretted his statement. Galan had pointed out to Castro that the attack on Trotskyism was unfounded. Admitting his mistake, Castro had asked Galan to give him 'a month or two to make public corrections of this at the proper time'.[105] At the end of May Mandel unexpectedly got an invitation to visit Havana. The Cuban ambassador spoke of a personal invitation from Castro and promised a meeting with President Osvaldo Dorticós.[106]

In June 1967 Ernest and Gisela arrived at the former Havana Hilton, re-christened the Free Havana but with its former splendour carefully preserved. At the hotel's bar, replacing the Americans of earlier times, were Russians and a few East German technicians. Politics was never far away, even at the hairdresser's, as Gisela discovered: 'The girl sitting beside me was reading Lenin, and on the other side a woman was reading Mills's *The Marxists*.'[107]

A beautiful English-speaking guide took care of all the formalities, including credit cards and a shabby Cadillac with chauffeur. Gisela immediately fell in love with the impoverished country. She sent Meschkat enthusiastic reports about their wanderings and the encounters in tobacco and sugar factories, on plantations and in prisons and schools. 'Everything is exquisite and for us so encouraging and hopeful.'[108]

Their programme was overloaded. Ernest often returned only at 1:00 or 2:00 in the morning from a debate or lecture at the university or a party school. The atmosphere was frank and candid, as were the meetings with the host of Latin Americans attending the first conference of the Organization in Solidarity with Latin America (OLAS), held in Havana at the beginning of August.[109] Ernest and Gisela were furious when the Czechoslovakian paper *Rudé Právo* published three pages slandering Che on the day that Soviet premier Kosygin arrived. Gisela wrote, 'You should just hear how they talk about the Russians in all circles here, from the highest to the lowest. I've never heard such talk, from socialists yet.'[110] Typically, Castro charged the

Venezuelan Communists with failing the guerrilla movement.[111] Though Cuba was dependent on the Russians, Castro continued to provoke them.[112]

Mandel spoke with functionaries high and low, but Castro and Dorticós avoided him. Every time he announced his departure, he received overnight a request to stay 'because the President and the Prime Minister both wanted to see me'.[113] Fed up with waiting, he finally left, three weeks later than planned and without meeting them. Perhaps a meeting would have seemed too clear a provocation to the Russians. Castro had nothing to gain, as he had demonstrated his independence sufficiently at the OLAS conference.

On 9 October 1967, the world learned of the murder of Ernesto Che Guevara. Convinced that guerrilla warfare was the only way to victory, he had gone to join the Bolivian struggle. His body was found mutilated in a remote village. This was the death of a revolutionary, a modern-day warrior chief. The left was in mourning; poets wrote elegies, laments that ended with calls to rebellion. In an interview with Gerhard Horst (pseudonym André Gorz), an editor of *Les Temps Modernes*, Mandel spoke of 'a severe shock, all the more as I regarded him as a personal friend'.[114] In *La Gauche* he mourned 'a great friend, an exemplary comrade, a heroic militant'.[115] On the Boulevard St-Michel in Paris and Berlin's Kurfürstendamm, in London and Milan people shouted: 'Che, Che, Gue-va-ra!' The chopped syllables formed a battle cry against the established order. Neither Moscow nor Beijing had expressed even the most grudging sympathy.[116] In openly showing their regret the Italian and French Communist parties proved they still possessed a little autonomy.

Mandel's sympathizers in the French Revolutionary Communist Youth (JCR), a radical group founded in 1966 in a split from the Union of Communist Students, refused to accept his death. 'Che was our best antidote to the Maoist mystique', Daniel Bensaïd recalled.[117] In the Latin Quarter of Paris, the Mutualité, temple of the French workers' movement, was full to overflowing. Mandel spoke alongside Maurice Nadeau, just back from Havana, and Janette 'The Cuban' Habel. He portrayed Che as he had come to know him in 1964.[118] Emotion crested as those present softly hummed 'The Song of the Martyrs', the mourning march from the 1905 Russian Revolution, before launching into, 'You have fallen for all those who hunger' and belting out the chorus, 'But the hour will sound, and the people conquer . . .'[119]

In Berlin too people were deeply moved. The SDS called for intensifying actions. Che had been Dutschke's inspiration. With Gaston Salvatore, a Chilean comrade and friend in the SDS,[120] Dutschke had translated Che's last public statement, with its famous appeal for 'two, three, many Vietnams', from Spanish into German. Like Che, Dutschke lived the conviction that there 'is no life outside the revolution'.[121] He named his recently born son Hosea Che. Latin America would not let Dutschke go. In 1968 he wrote a foreword to *The Long March: The Course of the Revolution in Latin America*, a collection of articles by such figures as Régis Debray, Castro and K.S. Karol.[122] Meschkat was surprised to see letters from Gisela, which she had sent him from Havana in the summer of 1967, printed in the book. As far as he had known, Dutschke had asked only for permission to read them.[123]

Berlin 1968: with Rudi Dutschke

In the summer of 1967 Mandel and Dutschke grew closer. Dutschke noted in his diary: 'Discussion with Gisela and Ernest, [Adorno's student Hans-Jürgen] Krahl, etc. about organizational questions and preliminary theoretical discussions for a conference in Berlin.'[124] Shortly before, Dutschke and Krahl had presented a so-called organization report to an SDS conference in the old refectory of the University of Frankfurt.[125] Krahl was for Frankfurt what Dutschke was for Berlin – the undisputed chief ideologue. The SDS was growing dramatically, with 2,000 members and easily several times that many sympathizers, including not only university students but also high school students and young workers. They were for reform of the universities and against the Vietnam War, against the Greek dictatorship, against the emergency decrees and against the 'emperor of torture', Shah Reza Pahlevi of Iran. Participating in their actions cost Benno Ohnesorg, a twenty-six-year-old student, his life. On 2 June 1967 he was shot dead by the police in Berlin, setting off a month-long rebellion.

Once the students' slogan had been 'No theory without praxis.' Suddenly that time seemed long past. Now the question was what strategy the SDS should choose and what type of organization was suited to it. Mandel discussed this in the summer of 1967 with Dutschke, Krahl, Meschkat, Altvater, Semler, Rabehl and other student leaders.[126] Their task was to 'select the best comrades to create an organization within the SDS . . . to form a cadre . . . and to build a vanguard from inside the social-democratic union'.[127]

Dutschke held on to his position because of his flexibility. As Meschkat confided to Mandel, this 'is surely a big danger for continuity but also an opportunity to reach agreement step-by-step after thorough discussion'.[128] Mandel set out to persuade Dutschke to transform the Marxist wing of the SDS into a revolutionary socialist youth organization,[129] following the example of the French JCR. The JCR was a hybrid formation of Guevarists and Trotskyists, anti-Stalinists with considerable influence among rebellious youth.[130] The two or at most three hundred dissidents included Catherine

Samary, Janette Habel, Henri Weber, Daniel Bensaïd, Pierre Rousset and Alain Krivine. These were all spokespeople who felt the winds of change at their backs and who would make their mark on the world in May 1968. Mandel had been present at the foundation of the JCR, at a meeting high in the Alps near Briançon in the winter of 1965. Among the last drivers to get police permission to cross the mountain pass was Krivine with his passenger, Ernest Mandel. Snow flurries and fog hindered visibility. In his suit and elegant shoes Mandel had to walk in front of the car for an hour through knee-high snow in order to show Krivine the way. They both arrived soaked through.[131]

In December 1967 there was a meeting between Dutschke and Krivine, whom Mandel described as 'one of the most intelligent and revolutionary of our young cadre'. A few days previously Dutschke had met, as Mandel expressed it, 'some specialists . . . with interest in the specific matter about which we have confidentially spoken'.[132] He meant the decision to sabotage the Vietnam War with blockades of weapon and troop transports and possibly by blowing up ships that were carrying military goods to Vietnam from German ports. The Milan publisher Giangiacomo Feltrinelli provided the explosives.[133] The group involved had nothing at all in common with the Red Army Faction (Bader-Meinhof Gang), Dutschke declared ten years later. Their planned action was 'violence against things, not against people', and when they decided the risks were too great, they had the dynamite quietly dropped into the sea.[134]

Mandel had the highest expectations of German events.[135] In November he spoke on Cuba and Latin America to an audience of 1,500 students in Berlin. Two days later he spoke to 4,000, all of them waving red flags in honour of the fiftieth anniversary of the October Revolution. The high point was the Vietnam congress held on 17 and 18 February 1968 in the central auditorium of the Technical University of Berlin, where Mandel was one of the most important speakers besides Dutschke.[136] For those two days West Berlin was the centre of the international Left Opposition, drawing 5,000 participants from Germany and neighbouring countries.[137]

Even earlier, in October 1966, opponents of the war had demonstrated in Liège, in a protest initiated officially by the Socialist Young Guard but in fact by the Fourth International. There too there were thousands of sympathizers from different countries demonstrating in the streets – Maoists, Trotskyists, young Communists and provos.[138] Berlin 1967 was a follow-up to that, with the additional support of intellectual and cultural notables.[139] Over the auditorium hung a gigantic flag, the banner of the South Vietnamese National Liberation Front, and beneath it Che's summons: 'The duty of

every revolutionary is to make the revolution.' They made a fitting background for two days of impassioned speeches.

Tariq Ali, born in Lahore but living in Oxford since 1963, a student leader
and Trotskyist, was one speaker. He was continually interrupted with
applause and shouted slogans. On the platform he sat next to Mandel,
who translated for him.[140] In his own speech Mandel assured his listeners
that the US could expect a defeat:

> You all know Karl Marx's clear vision that capital came into the world
> dripping from head to toe, from every pore, with blood and dirt . . .
> Today we are witnessing the fall of capitalism . . . dripping from head to
> toe, from every pore, with blood and dirt . . . Capital is sentenced to
> death. Our duty is not to look on passively . . . but actively to engage in
> the struggle.[141]

His listeners knew he was supporting them when he condemned the
violence of the authorities and the stream of slander from the Springer
press. 'A few technical points', said Mandel, building up the suspense:

> I don't know if you know the photos of the Zengakuren students[142]
> where you see them marching against the American aircraft carrier
> *Enterprise,* armed with helmets and clubs . . . I can only tell you that
> their example was followed last week by radical youth in Paris, and I
> suggest that the West Berlin students consider doing the same.[143]

Dutschke, sitting next to the chairman, and Mandel, at the far end of the
table, had been making eye contact throughout; nods of approval showed
their agreement.[144]

The organizers had planned to follow the congress with a demonstration
and march to the American military base in Berlin-Dahlem. The hall was
buzzing with rumours about anticipated violence by the army and
police.[145] The audience alternated between taking part in the debates
and carrying on heated conversations about how to cope with tear gas and
how to pad clothing for protection against police clubs: 'And don't forget
your helmets!'

Alain Krivine, founder and leader of the JCR, stepped up to the
microphone to describe the French student movement and the role of
radical Paris youth. With his dreamy gaze, student's glasses and necktie – an
object of anarchist mockery – Krivine seemed to have something of the
romantic about him. In fact, he was a 'hyperactive pragmatist' with a definite
vocation for politics.[146]

Krivine spent the nights of the congress at Dutschke's.[147] They had held a discussion with the 300 or so French participants the evening before the congress began. There the French delegates got to know Dutschke, the Berlin 'Terror of the Bourgeoisie', a short, athletic figure in a leather jacket, with lank hair falling into his eyes. He spoke so fast the translator had trouble keeping up. Dutschke drew the route of the demonstration on a blackboard, outlining danger zones, security measures and tactics.[148] Because of their experience, the JCR's specialists were charged with providing security for the demonstrators.

On the afternoon of Sunday 18 February, around 15,000 mostly young protesters assembled for an exceptionally militant march through the city. Above a sea of red flags rose huge portraits of Rosa Luxemburg, Karl Liebknecht, Che Guevara and Ho Chi Minh. From time to time a section would pause, then rush forward shouting slogans in cadence. Berlin had not witnessed a spectacle like this since the 1930s.

At 5:23 on the evening of 11 April 1968, the German Press Agency in Berlin distributed the following report: 'On Thursday afternoon the SDS ideologue Rudi Dutschke was shot by an as yet unidentified perpetrator.' Dutschke had received a potentially fatal wound in his face. The gunman, Josef Erwin Bachmann, was an unskilled house painter from Munich. He had waited for his victim some 50 metres outside SDS headquarters on the Kurfürstendamm. Pulling the trigger, he screamed in rage, 'You dirty Communist pig!'[149]

For some time right-wing circles had entertained violent fantasies. Encouraged by the Springer press, right-wing hostility had taken personal forms. The twenty-eight-year-old Dutschke had been labelled 'Public Enemy Number 1'. Short work had to be made of him: 'Gas Dutschke!' 'Away with this gang!' 'Political enemy to the concentration camp!'[150] Asked that very day if he ever feared an attack, Dutschke had responded: 'Not fear. It could happen, but friends are on the lookout. Usually I don't travel alone. Of course some neurotic or lunatic can attack in a panic reaction.'[151] A few hours later the shots had rung out.

Dutschke lay on the operating table for seven hours. Students took to the streets to prevent the witch-hunting Springer papers from appearing. From Paris Mandel phoned Tariq Ali. The next day 2,000 people demonstrated in front of the German embassy in London and at the British Springer office.[152] In Brussels young people shouted their solidarity with the slogan 'Create two, three, many Berlins!' There was a similar scene in Paris, where three or four hundred JCR members lay siege to the German embassy. There was a clash with the police on the Boulevard St-Michel.[153] By Easter Saturday Dutschke was out of danger, but the bullets in his head had left him with a severe speech impediment. His recovery was slow, and he had to learn to live with periodic epileptic seizures.

Dutschke's last diary entry before the attack was: 'I'm very happy about . . . Paris. The comrades . . . have done it: getting the French left tendencies to one table. On 1 May I'll make a speech there . . .'[154] May 1968 went down in history as the largest strike and protest ever in France,[155] but the struggle began without Dutschke.

He wanted to get out of Germany and away from the scene of the disaster. First he stayed briefly in Switzerland, working on his recovery with the psychologist Thomas Ehleiter. Then he went on to Italy, to Marino, south of Rome, at the invitation of the composer Hans-Werner Henze. Politics came calling sooner than he wished. There were bad tidings from Berlin: 'Christian [Semler] phoned, telling me the Russians' filthy tricks – Czechoslovakia is occupied. In Prague I'd have thought this impossible, but the students were much more realistic.'[156] 'What dogs, what barbarians, what traitors.'[157]

Dutschke's stay at Henze's villa could not be concealed from the press – and once they knew, he had no more peace. In August his wife Gretchen flew to the United States to arrange a visa for him. Meanwhile Dutschke travelled unobserved to Brussels, where he stayed at the Mandels' home on Rue Josse Impens, a restful haven that he had to himself, since Gisela and Ernest were travelling in Canada and the US from September through November.[158] Ernest was lecturing at something like twenty-five universities. Gisela was speaking about the European student protests at the SWP's invitation.[159] Ernest heard from his mother that Dutschke was going through a crisis. Berlin friends had informed him that Canada had refused him a visa. Ignoring the possibility that the authorities might be eavesdropping, Dutschke had tried from the Rue Josse Impens house to contact Gretchen in the United States. The next day the police came to the door with a deportation order.[160] In the stress of the moment Dutschke had suffered an epileptic seizure. Friends decided to send him to Berlin for tests. As Mandel heard from his mother, 'He tried to convince me not to tell his wife that his friends had accompanied him to the doctor; instead to tell her that he had decided to drive himself there. Please keep to that story!!'[161] To convey her concern to Ernest, Rosa continued,

> I've done everything to make his being alone easier . . . Only I was a bit afraid that he'd get sick. It's obvious that friends have to help! Dear Ernest, from your earliest years at home, you've seen that we always helped friends![162]

In his posthumously published *Aufrecht Gehen: Eine fragmentarische Autobiographie* (Going Upright: A Fragmentary Autobiography), Dutschke noted that after staying two weeks at the Mandels' he had been declared persona non grata by the authorities.[163]

Paris 1968: on the barricades

In October 1967 *Les Temps Modernes* asked Mandel to write an article on 'the nature and development of the socialist revolution in the developed countries of Europe and America'.[164] Mandel rather liked the idea. Questions about how the social, political and psychological climate could be transformed lay close to his heart. He sought to discover how the workers could turn against the neo-capitalist regime that they had accepted in practice and move into a pre-revolutionary situation, continuing on to a revolutionary one. He wryly commented, 'I suppose there's not much competition for this kind of subject.' Mandel was not unrealistic.[165]

No one would have dared claim that a revolution was on the agenda in Western Europe. Certainly not in France, where there was no chronic economic crisis, no involvement in a hopeless war and no student movement comparable to that in West Germany or Japan. And yet in May 1968 a volcano erupted, giving the lie to all theories about the co-optation of the working class. There was still a note of disbelief in the commentary of *Les Temps Modernes* as late as June 1968 even as they reported: 'Now we know that a socialist revolution is not impossible in a Western European country, and perhaps in two or three.'[166]

Mandel never wrote his own article for the paper; there was simply no time amid the turmoil. Lenin's declaration, 'It is more pleasant and useful to go through the "experience of the revolution" than to write about it',[167] certainly held true for Mandel. Nonetheless, he was not theoretically unequipped for the subject.

The Belgian general strike of 1960–61 had led Mandel to a new theory of Western European revolutions. He developed a revolutionary typology based not on the German revolution of 1918 or on the Yugoslav revolution of 1941–5[168] but on 'the French general strike of June 1936', when the arrival of the leftist Popular Front government was accompanied by a wave of factory occupations, 'and to a lesser extent on the model of the Belgian general strike of 1960–1961'.[169] As he wrote in June 1965, workers in welfare states also radicalize in reaction to social, political, economic and military crises; and

> once they are radicalised, they will launch more and more far-reaching campaigns during the course of which they will begin to link their

immediate demands with a programme of anti-capitalist structural reforms, until eventually the struggle concludes with a general strike which
either overthrows the regime or creates a duality of powers.[170]

Mandel's theory was not completely developed in May 1968 but did
provide sufficient material to comprehend what happened then. The
particular moment was a surprise, but the event itself was not.[171]

In this rebellion of youth and workers, Mandel served not only as a
theoretician and political analyst but also as an agitator directly involved in
the debates – as in Berlin – and a participant in combat during the Paris
'night of the barricades'. The rebellion's aims can be traced back in earlier
form to the colonial war in Algeria and the workers' unrest of the mid-
1960s. Its goals were simple and drastic: 'Down with American imperialism,
down with Gaullism!' On 3 May troops entered the Sorbonne and arrested
students who were demonstrating against the closure of the University of
Nanterre, a centre of protest against the Vietnam War and against un-
democratic educational reforms. The University of Nanterre was also where
the unity of students and workers had first been manifested. Sending troops
into the Sorbonne led to weeks of confrontations in the Latin Quarter,
which in turn led to strikes in almost every industry and every region of the
country, with around 10 million workers involved.[172]

On the evening of Thursday 9 May, the JCR organized a rally in the
Mutualité, with, among others, Daniel Bensaïd, Henri Weber and Ernest
Mandel. Bensaïd and Daniel Cohn-Bendit had been the driving force
behind the 22 March Movement, founded in Nanterre. Weber was a
sociologist and at this time Alain Krivine's right-hand man. In the hall were
delegations from Germany, Italy and Belgium. Hundreds of students had
been occupying the square in front of the Sorbonne all afternoon. This was
the famous sit-in at which Cohn-Bendit called the onlooker Louis Aragon
to account for the CP's *L'Humanité*, the 'Stalinist piece of shit' that wouldn't
stop smearing what it called ultra-leftists. On the spot, the JCR decided to
make their rally into a broad show of unity. They removed their emblems
and invited Cohn-Bendit to take a place on the stage under a banner
reading, 'Youth: from Revolt to Revolution'. Inside and out, on the stairs
and in the aisles, the place was packed.

Mandel took the floor. Now past forty-five, his wavy hair greying and his
friendly eyes glancing from behind serious glasses, dressed in a suit and tie, he
seemed to have wandered into the rebellion by mistake. Once behind the
lectern the image changed instantly; he sparkled and shone with fervour and
excitement. Land occupations in Bolivia, factory occupations in Switzerland, demonstrations in Prague – he gave the French student protests their

place in a whirlwind trip around the world. In closing he declared,

> When this universal struggle succeeds in enlisting the adult workers, then
> we can remake today's vanguard into a powerful revolutionary party that
> can take its place at the forefront of the masses . . . Only together are we
> unconquerable. Only together will we be able to complete the great work
> that began fifty years ago with the October revolution, the victory of the
> socialist world revolution![173]

Enthusiastically Cohn-Bendit and Bensaïd called for unity, before giving the
elated audience the orders to 'gather tomorrow evening at the foot of the
Belfort Lion', the monument to French resistance in the Franco-Prussian
War on Place Denfert-Rochereau.

In the afternoon of 10 May the procession of around 35,000 students,
flanked by an army of police, started off from the Lion. It was quiet as they
marched via Boulevard St-Michel past the closed-down Sorbonne and by
the Luxembourg gardens.[174] The bridges over the Seine were closed, and
the Latin Quarter was surrounded by riot police. The crowd continuously
chanted slogans like 'Nous irons jusqu'au bout!' (We will go all the way!); no
one thought of leaving. Suddenly there were muffled thuds, signalling that
demonstrators had begun to break up the pavement. Shouts rang out: 'The
Quarter is ours!' From that moment the days of the Paris Commune were
lived again. Behind the Panthéon, from Rue Gay Lussac to Rue d'Ulm,
metres-high barricades arose, though it was not clear who was laying siege to
whom. The more troops and police turned out, the higher the barricades
grew. As night fell, the crowd's spirits rose higher. Trees were cut down and
cars overturned. As though in a competition, the cobblestone barricades
were decorated with pots of blooming flowers, red and black flags, banners
and sundry bric-a-brac. That night Ernest and Gisela helped build barricades
on Rue Gay Lussac in the heart of the Latin Quarter. Doing the same work
nearby were Alain Krivine, Pierre Rousset, Daniel Bensaïd, Henri Weber
and Janette Habel. At Janette's side was Roberto Santucho, leader of the
Argentinian Revolutionary Workers Party (PRT), who was en route to
Cuba via Paris with a group of Latin American guerrillas.[175] By 11:00 p.m.
the JCR had set up headquarters in the besieged neighbourhood. In Rue
Gay Lussac, where a sympathizer ran a travel bureau, they gathered on the
bureau's ground floor behind lowered blinds, at least when they were not
standing on the barricades. Messengers came and went. Loudspeakers on the
shop front kept the barricade-builders informed about the negotiations with
the university authorities.[176]'It's the night of the comrades.' Acquaintances
and strangers embraced. 'You're here too?' 'I couldn't possibly miss this –

it's been so long!' Mandel and Nicos Poulantzas had last spoken to each other at the three-day Marx colloquium at Frankfurt's Goethe University in September 1967. In debate they had not spared one another. It was different on the barricades. 'After theoretical philosophy, practical philosophy and after controversy, united front. It's nice, isn't it?'[177] Perry Anderson agreed absolutely.

In the small hours of the night a handful of comrades who had evaded the police ran into one another at the Ecole Normale Supérieure on Rue d'Ulm, red-eyed from the clouds of tear gas that had been unleashed. Among them were Bensaïd, Weber, Rousset and Krivine.[178] Ernest and Gisela had also escaped when the police opened their attack at 2:30 that morning. From one of the barricades Mandel had witnessed the play of fire and the destruction. A reporter from the *Observer* heard him shout, 'Oh! How beautiful! It's the revolution!'[179] Gisela's car had gone up in flames like a torch and they had continued on foot. Exhausted, they finally reached their apartment in Rue Vincennes, near the Bastille.[180]

May '68 had begun. Two days later, on 13 May, 10 million workers went on strike; factories were occupied; a million Parisians took to the streets. 'Together we will be invincible.' Not only politically but also materially, the Fourth International was at full combat strength. Because of the strike, they were without fuel. Belgian and German comrades arrived every other day, their cars packed with jerrycans of petrol. Those who had to flee France were welcomed hospitably in Brussels, Cologne and Frankfurt.

Mandel's 9 May speech had attracted attention from other quarters besides the Latin. Returning from a trip to Spain in early July, Ernest and Gisela were hauled from their hotel beds in Narbonne at an early hour. Mandel had been forbidden to enter France by an order dated 10 June, without his ever being informed.[181] Gisela got permission to continue the trip, but Ernest was held for more than twelve hours at the police station. He was given a pickled pig's foot to eat, with only a spoon – a knife and fork would have made him too dangerous.[182] Accompanied by two officers from the security service, he was taken across the border into Belgium by train – first class.[183] His status as persona non grata in France was only lifted in 1981.[184]

Paris had not become St Petersburg, nor had May '68 become October '17; the revolt did not become a revolution. Nonetheless the European left was suddenly seeing what revolution looked with its own eyes after so many years of reports from abroad. The struggle in Vietnam, Cuba and Algeria was still 'our struggle', but this was no longer only symbolic but actual, with direct influence back and forth recognized and acknowledged.[185]

Where had this transformation in the political culture come from? Why the change from resignation to rebellion, from obedience to mutiny? And, once more, what prevented a definitive breakthrough? Why had the revolt remained incomplete? Just back from Spain, Mandel posed these questions in 'The Lessons of May 1968', an article published in *Les Temps Modernes* and *New Left Review*.[186] He said that May '68 had been a consequence of the contradictions of neo-capitalism. The standard of living had risen, but demands had risen even more, particularly for democracy and an end to alienation. Though the West had experienced no catastrophe like that of 1929, it was hardly free from recessions. The crisis in university education that led to the explosion of May '68 was heightened by a system that, absorbed by the interests of planning long-term labour costs, left no room for normal trade union action. That made resistance explosive and violent.

In his analysis of the objective socioeconomic factors, Mandel was elaborating on earlier work.[187] What was new was his thinking on the model of revolution that became visible in May '68. The revolt showed resemblances to the general strikes in France in 1936 and Belgium in 1960-61. May '68 helped Mandel refine his model in four aspects.

First, he noted the explosive character of the actions, a combination of strikes, sit-ins, factory occupations, demonstrations and confrontations with the repressive forces. He considered all of these to be forms of resistance that arose spontaneously. They had nothing to do with the middle-class origins of students, with political immaturity or with provocateurs, contrary to the claims of their opponents and the Communists of the CP and the CGT. Second, he noted that once active, the proletariat spontaneously became aware of its power. It came to realize that the existing order was bourgeois, and every assault against it was in vain as long as the opponents' rules of play were respected. Third, he observed that the younger workers in particular defended radical forms of action. This was confirmed by every revolution: experiments are first made by minorities.[188] Finally, Mandel said that May '68 showed that the idea of a gradual, institutionalized establishment of workers' control or other anti-capitalist structural change was an illusion.

Despite the massiveness of the May explosion, the Gaullist system had consolidated its power. The vanguard, the most conscious and active group, had not bonded sufficiently with the broader movement. Nonetheless, the workers had been concerned with more than direct economic demands. For example, in Paris print shops the workers demanded correction of inaccurate headlines in *Le Figaro* and refused to print articles in *La Nation* that harmed the strike. Still, Mandel emphasized to Perry Anderson, there had been limits:

They rejected instinctively 'pure' trade-union goals, but generally didn't know by what to complement them. Propaganda and education (incl. agitation and action) for transitional demands (anti-capitalist structural reforms) *prior* to the crisis would have been necessary in order to assure that 'conscious leap' from wage demand to workers control or workers power.[189]

Faithful to Leninist orthodoxy, Mandel pointed to the absence of a vanguard with influence in key factories comparable to its influence in the universities. Even had there been such, he added, he did not think that France would have been a mere twenty-four hours away from socialism, nor that a French 'October' would have been just around the corner. But he did think there might have been a French 'February', a breakthrough to a situation of dual power. Had this taken place, Mandel considered that a decisive page in French and European history would have been turned.

9

Hope and Despair

... so easy to understand and yet, as Brecht said ... so hard to do. You
are in the front ranks of those who are fighting against the most unnatural
thing that exists: the master–slave relationship.
            – Ernst Bloch to Ernest Mandel (1974)[1]

Every revolutionary success was felt around the world – and every defeat.
The Warsaw Pact troops that overran Czechoslovakia in August 1968
proved this once again. Deploying their own tanks, the Kremlin helped
legitimate the misdeeds of imperialist countries in Vietnam, Latin America,
Africa and the Middle East and hindered any attempts by Cuba or Vietnam
to take an independent path.

'Not "capitalist restoration" but socialist democracy was the [Kremlin's]
enemy,' Mandel said.[2] Moscow was afraid of the influence of the Prague
Spring, in the first place on the Soviet people but also on Poland, Hungary
and the other countries within its sphere of influence.

Cuba acquiesced in the invasion of Czechoslovakia. Hanging over an
economic abyss, Castro saw Russia as his only hope. At least 98 per cent of
Cuba's oil came from the Soviet Union. Not long before, Castro had
boasted that he did not fear at all that the Soviets would decrease their
support as punishment for his independent course.[3]

La Gauche reacted hesitantly: 'Castro confuses day with night ...
He is sowing confusion among a great many young people who have
always regarded Cuba as an anti-Stalinist alternative.'[4] At first it was all
seen as a mistake;[5] disillusionment came later.[6] Mandel looked for rays
of hope, but there was no comment even from Hilda Gadea, Che's
first life partner. Ralph Schoenman, an observer of Régis Debray's
1967 Bolivia trial,[7] wrote to Mandel, 'She has no opportunity to fight
from the left. She is tolerated as a necessary nuisance by the
authorities.'[8]

The Trotskyist Schoenman was the director of the Bertrand Russell Peace Foundation[9] and had contacts with Prague reformers like the economist Ota Šik and the writer Antonin Liehm. He organized a conference on Czechoslovakia in Stockholm in February 1969, along with Sartre, the Yugoslav Vladimir Dedijer and the French mathematician Laurent Schwartz, 'a one-time lifelong Trotskyist'.[10] A few days after the Soviet invasion, Sartre had declared to the Italian Communist daily *Paese Sera*: 'The Soviet example is no longer relevant these days, smothered as it is by the bureaucracy.'[11] This recognition came rather late, as the Communists were already being spoon-fed by Moscow in 1945.[12] Sartre had opposed this anti-Stalinist perspective in every possible way in his 1952 debate with Mandel in *Les Temps Modernes*.[13] Now Sartre asked Schoenman to ask Mandel to analyze the Czechoslovakian economy and to judge if the reforms had a 'socialist' slant.[14]

Mandel did not make an appearance in Stockholm.[15] His trip with Gisela to the US in the fall of 1968 had lasted for two months and left him exhausted on his return to Brussels. His doctor advised him against undertaking any new duties.[16] Moreover, his last remaining energy was needed for the International's Ninth World Congress in Rimini and the April 1969 founding of the Communist League (LC), the new French section.

Nonetheless, Mandel did not lose sight of Czechoslovakia; above all he was concerned with Petr Uhl's fate. In October 1968 people sympathetic to the International had formed a loose group around Uhl, a teacher at a Prague technical school.[17] The group consisted of between fifty and a hundred young people, among them Sybille Plogstedt, a twenty-four-year-old student and member of the SDS in West Berlin. She was captivated not only by the struggle against the Russian occupation but also by Uhl. In 1965 and 1967 Uhl had visited Paris, where he had got to know Alain Krivine at the Sorbonne, where Krivine was studying history. Krivine had familiarized him with Trotskyism.[18] Uhl and his comrades unleashed a storm of activity, including organizing the massive turnout for Jan Palach's Prague funeral in January 1969. Palach was the student who had immolated himself in Wenceslas Square in protest against the Russians and died from his burns. Plogstedt requested Mandel to send a stencil machine quickly: 'Even though the situation in this pathetic country has not really improved, the borders still aren't hermetically sealed.'[19] With Jakob Moneta's help, Mandel arranged to have the machine shipped to Prague.[20]

Uhl and Mandel met a few times in Berlin and discussed the challenges facing the Czech anti-Stalinist opposition. In Prague as in the West, Trotsky's closest competitor was Mao. To many, China appeared attractive materially and ideologically. When Maoist groups paraded under portraits of Stalin and his notorious police chief Lavrenti Beria, Mandel worried that this cast the entire radical left in a bad light. Naturally he wanted nothing to do with anarchism or dogmatic insistence on spontaneity.[21] The challenge was to create an alternative pole of attraction, to promote the idea of an International and to show that in its own national interest Beijing would sacrifice the revolutions of other nations, like Indonesia and Pakistan, just as cynically as Moscow.

Uhl's group did not go unnoticed by Prague's secret service. *Rudé Právo*, the Communist Party paper, discovered a so-called Trotskyist plot and devoted a page to the 'anti-socialist scum'.[22] Mandel warned Plogstedt, 'The surveillance is intense, and the watchers know an awful lot.'[23] In early December Plogstedt was arrested at the Czech–East German border while en route to Berlin; soon afterwards Uhl and three other comrades were also arrested. Books and papers were confiscated and houses sealed. There followed home searches and the arrest of an additional 118 people, all accused of 'Trotskyism'.[24]

A year later, nineteen of the accused appeared before the court. Sybille Plogstedt was sentenced to two and a half years in jail.[25] Petr Uhl was given a four-year sentence. Radio Prague accused them of being linked to the 'notorious Trotskyist sectarian Ernest Mandel' and of being financed by the CIA and the FBI.[26] 'In Foreign Service', read the *Rudé Právo* headline.[27]

Mandel considered the trial a test case 'in which the Stalinists hoped that there would be less public outcry than if they were to convict "liberal Communists" or prominent members of the Dubèek regime'.[28] If that was what they hoped, they were disappointed. From Germany and France came demands for Uhl's release from Ernst Bloch, Jean-Paul Sartre and Roger Garaudy.[29] Demonstrations were held in Berlin, Stockholm, New York and Tokyo. Once freed, Uhl was one of the first signers of Charter 77. A year later, along with Václav Havel and Jiøi Dienstbier, he was present at the birth of the Committee to Protect the Unjustly Persecuted (VONS). In no time he was jailed again. When Czech CP Secretary Husák visited Vienna, Mandel asked his friend Ernst Federn to induce Austrian president Bruno Kreisky to bring up Uhl's fate: 'at least to procure an end to the sadistic bullying and to urge treatment equal to that of all other political prisoners in Czechoslovakia'.[30] Federn had access to the highest levels of the Austrian government. Two years later he finally received a message from the chancellor's office that Uhl had been released from prison.[31]

The Prague Spring had been inspiring, and events in Poland and East Germany were equally promising. In addition to his Trotskyist observation post in West Berlin,[32] Mandel had a trustworthy informant in Werner Tzschoppe, an East Berlin historian and economist. In the 1950s he had studied at the University of Moscow and at the CP school.[33] Back in Berlin,

Tzschoppe was head of the party organization at Humboldt University. In February 1964, after allowing lectures there by the dissident theoretician Robert Havemann, he was summarily dismissed.[34] Tzschoppe was charged with a lack of vigilance. He was interrogated for months: 'Are you now for Havemann or for our Party?' Tzschoppe had regularly attended gatherings in living rooms where Havemann, Heise, Biermann and other dissidents took part and where Ernest Mandel's ideas were eagerly discussed. Through Tzschoppe, Mandel heard that Polish strike committees remained active even after the 1970 insurrection, that the strikers had brought Russian families to safety so as not to give the Kremlin any pretext for intervention, and that strike pickets had protected stores against plunderers.[35] The strike committees had negotiated with the regime in public; everything could be followed by radio in the factories. Mandel could not believe his ears: during the struggle sailors from stranded Soviet ships shared their food with the people of Gdansk and Szczecin. There were sympathy strikes in East Germany on the Rostock piers and in Riga in Latvia.[36] Mandel did everything he could to protect his informant Tzschoppe, who maintained contact with dissidents elsewhere in Eastern Europe. Only a few other people knew about their connection.[37]

Revolutionary party and council democracy

The wave of strikes strengthened Mandel's conviction that since Stalin's death the monolithic immobility of Eastern Europe had come to an end. Nonetheless the collapse of the system was far from immediately at hand. Just as in the developed capitalist countries, what was missing was a proletariat that would take on the organization of society. Formation of a revolutionary leadership and international coordination had yet to begin. Hence the acuteness of the question that Mandel called 'the *Marxist science of the subjective factor*':[38] the problem of the revolutionary party and council democracy.

Why had the Communist Party and the trade union organizations absented themselves from the '68 Paris rebellion? Why had Moscow crushed the Prague Spring and Cuba failed to help the opposition? Did the working class require its own party in order to take power? Was the degeneration of such a party unavoidable, and what did this have to do with the Leninist form of organization? Mandel was occupied with such knotty questions throughout the 1960s.

Mandel focused attention on the bureaucracy, particularly in the workers' movement, in his book *On Bureaucracy*, which was based on lectures he gave in 1965 and 1967 and has since been translated into many languages.[39] He developed his thought further in the years following, a process that culminated in the publication of *Power and Money: A Marxist Theory of Bureaucracy*. This work probed the historical and social roots of bureaucracy in the capitalist world as well as in workers' organizations and post-capitalist societies.[40]

Unlike such thinkers as Robert Michels, Mandel considered bureaucratization, the autonomy and reification of organizations, to be avoidable.[41] Every organization in society tends to prioritize and defend its own interests. Whether this leads to bureaucratic degeneration depends on the strength of the society's counter-tendencies. The key question for Mandel was under what circumstances these could best be encouraged. Without a party that consciously engaged in the leadership of liberation movements, the concrete utopia of a humane society would remain unattainable.

Yet Mandel never developed a theory of the revolutionary party. In his 1970 essay 'The Leninist Theory of Organization', one of his few attempts to concentrate on this theme, he aligned himself with the young Marx, with Trotsky and with Rosa Luxemburg, who emphasized the revolutionary creativity of the workers' movement in action. Mandel subscribed to Lenin's thesis that in revolutionary and pre-revolutionary situations the working class develops a 'naturally anti-capitalist' consciousness.[42] Thus Mandel did not put the party and its relative autonomy in the foreground, but rather focused on revolutionary class-consciousness. In the 1960s, the theories of such thinkers as Marcuse and Horkheimer about the *embourgeoisement* of the working class began to gain acceptance; at the same time, the Stalinist bureaucracy was spreading the deepest mistrust of spontaneous mass actions. Mandel was not about to highlight the limitations of mass movements while their very legitimacy was being denied.

In addition, the intense though brief resurgence in resistance after the Second World War had been followed by a period of demoralization and passivity. For the Trotskyists, this was a time of hibernation within the dominant Social Democratic and Communist parties – not a suitable environment for testing the classic theory of the party through new experiences.[43] It was no consolation that the revolution had detoured to the colonial and semi-colonial world. There the influence of the proletariat was limited in proportion to that of other social groups, like farmers, rural labourers and semi-proletarians; moreover, there was no Marxist tradition there. Only in the second half of the 1960s, with a new generation of young people, did a tendency towards change reappear, with May 1968 as its most striking expression. But although now and then the movement escaped the control of the French Communist Party and its CGT trade union federation, the majority of the 10 million strikers of May '68 remained under the

influence of the traditional workers' parties. Developments were uneven
and contradictory, which also hindered Mandel's working out a theory of
the party.

Though Mandel, like Trotsky, was unable to achieve a general theory of
the party,[44] he attempted to update the theory of the Leninist party in
numerous partial studies.[45] He called for the broadest possible inclusion of
grassroots democracy in the form of workers' councils in combination with
parties. Central to his thought was the idea that in a revolutionary process
two levels of organization develop, that of the masses and that of a separate
vanguard organization that unites with the most conscious groups, those
active in the developing organs of workers' power.[46] Mandel's historical
examples were the Paris Commune of 1871, the Russian revolutions of
1905 and 1917 and Germany between 1918 and 1923. He thought that the
appearance of workers' councils in the Austrian, Hungarian and Spanish
revolutions made it plausible that they would also play a role in future
upheavals.[47] Therefore, it was obviously important to research the phenomenon of bureaucratic degeneration. Was there a connection between
council democracy and Stalinist dictatorship? And had the Bolshevik Party
contributed to the degeneration? Why had the opposition – including that
of Trotsky – not succeeded in stopping these developments?

In 1918 Rosa Luxemburg had warned, 'Without general elections,
without unrestricted freedom of press and assembly, without a free struggle
of opinion, life dies out in every public institution, becomes a mere
semblance of life in which only the bureaucracy remains as the active
element.'[48] This diagnosis of potential developments, which became particularly visible after 1920 and 1921, was astounding because of its emphasis
on general elections and unrestricted freedom of press and assembly, an
unrestricted freedom intended also for peasants, the middle class and the
bourgeoisie. Had Luxemburg considered council democracy insufficient?
Mandel never entertained the possibility. He acknowledged that workers'
councils in non-revolutionary situations could lose strength with declining
mass activity. But working together with a stable vanguard organization,
they could withstand an unfavourable relationship of class forces. Self-
organization and vanguard parties were not mutually exclusive but rather
mutually reinforcing. In 1989 Mandel wrote, 'The years 1918 and 1919
were high points of autonomous self-organization in the Russian working
class, even more than in 1917.'[49]

But was this because of, or in spite of, the Bolsheviks' policies? And was
this assessment an adequate response to Luxemburg's scepticism? She had
been less interested in the state of affairs than in their development, in the
dynamic that came into play with the decrees against freedom of the press

and against formation of a constituent assembly through general elections. Her fears of a bureaucratic degeneration had proved well founded.

The problem of bureaucratic degeneration was also central to a 1967 *New Left Review* debate between Mandel and Nicolas Krassó, a Hungarian Marxist on the review's editorial board.[50] Krassó had been the organizer of the central workers' council in Budapest in 1956 and had been forced to flee to England when the Russian tanks restored order.[51] Mandel's debate with Krassó attracted attention even in Cuba.[52] Krassó said that neither Stalin nor Trotsky could be considered Lenin's heir. He rejected the theory of permanent revolution and called it a falsification of Lenin's thought, even worse than Stalin's theory of 'socialism in one country'. Furthermore he criticized Trotsky's actions in the party following the revolution; in the conflict with Stalin he had grossly underestimated the autonomous power of political institutions. Krassó reproached Trotsky with voluntarism and sociologism, the idea that social forces can make history without any political mediation. He contended that this weakness ran like a red thread through Trotsky's life, from his break with Bolshevism in 1904 through his defeat in the party struggles of 1923–7. Krassó's article was edited by Perry Anderson. According to his biographer, Anderson 'introduced Althusserian and Maoist motifs into the critique of Trotskyism by Lukács' former pupil'.[53]

In Trotsky's defence, Mandel argued that Krassó, with his emphasis on the autonomy of political institutions, failed to understand that parties represent social interests. Autonomy can thus only be relative. Only this perspective made it possible to understand that the struggle between Trotsky and Stalin was not over personalities but was a social conflict. Stalinism was more than a dangerous theory; it was the ideology of a bureaucracy. Mandel wrote that it was essential to understand, as Marx had in *The Eighteenth Brumaire of Louis Bonaparte*, 'how the class struggle . . . created circumstances and relationships that made it possible for a grotesque mediocrity to play a hero's part'.[54]

Mandel thought Krassó had been blind to the connection between the party's 1920–21 internal struggle and social developments in which the apathy of the working class grew in proportion to the growth of the bureaucracy. That the old Bolshevik leaders discovered the danger late, and only one after the other, explained the ease with which Stalin had taken power. Mandel did not ignore Lenin's and Trotsky's responsibilities. The ban on parties and the ban on factions within the Communist Party during the grim years of 1920–21 had blocked the way to political self-activity. The repression of the Mensheviks and the anarchists – of their press and organizations – had been a grave mistake.[55] But this had nothing to do with sociologism, but rather far more with the illusion that a single party could defend the proletariat. The substitution of the party for the class – which Trotsky later regretted[56] – showed how far Krassó missed the boat in saying that Trotsky underestimated the autonomous strength of political institutions.

New Left Review

Krassó represented Trotsky and Stalin as false prophets and dwarves compared with Lenin, 'the one great Marxist of that epoch'.[57] This perspective was then current in *New Left Review* circles, but Mandel's critique of it had a surprising consequence. Appreciation for Trotsky began to grow,[58] and *New Left Review* gradually became a periodical that gave Mandel free rein.[59] New Left Books, the publisher connected with the magazine, eventually published at least seven titles by Mandel.[60] Perry Anderson said that the Trotskyists 'alone had proved capable of an adult view of socialism on a world scale'.[61] Elsewhere he wrote that 'this political-theoretical heritage provides one of the central elements for any renaissance of revolutionary Marxism on an international scale'.[62] Not everyone connected with *New Left Review* shared this perspective. Tom Nairn and Gareth Stedman Jones questioned it, as did the Communist historian Eric Hobsbawm, who did not consider Trotskyism able 'to transcend the historical framework of the communist discussions in the USSR of the 1920s'.[63] Doubts increased during the second half of the 1970s, when Greece, Portugal and Spain were transformed peacefully into parliamentary democracies and the mass movements in France and Italy were in full retreat. These were signs that the future of socialism was not so bright. Trotskyism no longer seemed the viable alternative some of the editorial board had thought it was: 'The reserves of the Trotskyist tradition have proved far less than might have been expected: certainly insufficient to outweigh the default within Western Marxism'.[64]

Despite their mutual scepticism, Anderson and Mandel maintained intense political and scholarly contact. Anderson, a historical sociologist and a student of Isaac Deutscher's, understood the art of thinking in terms of epochs and continents. He felt a natural affinity with Mandel, who had shown himself a master in the art of waiting, as Sartre had remarked in 1952.[65] In turn, Mandel considered Anderson 'among the handful of Marxists in the world who have made and are making constructive contributions to the development of theory'.[66] Anderson came from an Anglo-Irish aristocratic family and had spent his youth in England, China, the United States and Ireland. Like Mandel he was a child of diverse cultures.[67] They were both erudite and had broad historical interests, exceptional among people who devote their lives to politics. Anderson, in his forties and even-tempered, was, as editor of *New Left Review*, the right man in the right place to stage debates within the non-Stalinist left in England and beyond.[68]

Their collaboration reached its high point with Mandel's 1979 book *Revolutionary Marxism Today*, which was dedicated to the 'world class struggle'. Mandel had come to the conclusion that with the changed political climate in Portugal and Italy, the prospect of a sudden revolutionary crisis was less credible than it had been in 1975–6. Nevertheless, he held fast to the possibility of a revolution in the medium term. As he informed Anderson, this prompted him to adapt the structure of the book 'to show that throughout the twentieth century, the concrete practice of the working class has not been simply "reformist", but has combined day-to-day struggles for immediate (economic and political) demands . . . with periodical huge explosions . . .'[69] Anderson was elated by the preliminary studies that Mandel published in *New Left Review* and *Critique Communiste*,[70] the theoretical journal of the French section of the Fourth International. He wrote to Mandel that 'this is certainly going to be your most important book, together with *Late Capitalism*'.[71] He was just as lyrical about Mandel's other works. He placed *Trotsky: A Study in the Dynamic of His Thought* on an equally high level with Lukács's essay about Lenin; they shared the same 'clarity and coherence of the synthesis . . . It should help – and win – many militants to the cause of revolutionary socialism.'[72]

Mandel also got the opportunity to distinguish himself as an economist in *New Left Review* circles. Anderson asked him to write the introductions to the three newly translated volumes of Marx's *Capital*, which were to be published by Sphere Books in an eight-part Marx collection edited by Eric Hobsbawm.[73] This was an honour that had been assigned to Isaac Deutscher, but which Deutscher's unexpected death prevented him from fulfilling. Mandel had not as yet published much about Marx's magnum opus, which he had first read when he was eighteen – only two articles on partial aspects.[74] It was true that his study of Marx's economic thought was about to be published by Maspero in French.[75] In addition he was working on three essays, one on methodology (a critique of Althusser), one on the modern proletariat (a critique of Marcuse) and one on the law of value in the so-called socialist countries (a critique of Bettelheim). He wrote to Anderson: 'As you see, these subjects do not really conflict with a general introduction to the three volumes.'[76] It was agreed that Mandel would deliver the completed introduction in March 1969 and that he would try to 'deal with historical, political and sociological aspects' as well, because 'not all the readers will be scientific economists'.[77]

But the edition of *Capital* with Mandel's introductions was published not in 1969 but in 1976, and then not by Sphere Books but by Penguin; Volume III did not come out until 1981. The edition was a paperback, accessible to a broad public.[78] Perry Anderson, the communist economist Ben Fine and the political scientist Ian Gough commented on Mandel's introductions. They were written with elegance and erudition and emphasized the various theories that formed the heart of Marx's doctrine. Mandel handled capital's laws of motion and the tendencies of long-term development revealed by Marx with bravura. His introductions considered not only classic problems but also such controversies as the survival of commodity production in the Soviet Union,[79] the misuse of the reproduction schemes,[80] the problem of the transformation of value into production prices,[81] the controversial law of the falling tendency of the rate of profit,[82] and the definition of productive and unproductive labour.[83] Mandel made short work of theories wrongly attributed to Marx. He showed that a long-term increase in real wages was compatible with Marx's thought, and also that the tendency to relative impoverishment of a section of society, defended by Marx, was not so nonsensical. Finally, he explained what the famous falling tendency of the rate of profit did and, above all, did not mean: it was not a theory of crisis or collapse. Numerous theorists, Marxist and non-Marxist alike, were subjected to Mandel's scrutiny. These ranged from Bernstein to Oskar Lange, from Böhm-Bawerk to Schumpeter, Sraffa and so-called Keynesians like Robinson and Samuelson. Mandel's introductions to Marx were a history of Marxist economics and its reception in Keynesian and neoclassical circles.

These introductions and his book *Late Capitalism* solidly established Mandel's name in the English-speaking world. His reputation gained yet more lustre when he was invited to give the prestigious Alfred Marshall lectures at the University of Cambridge in September and October 1978. Mandel gave his Cambridge audience an account of the economic long waves, a theme that had occupied him since the mid–1960s. The lectures appeared in book form in 1980, published by Cambridge University Press under the title *Long Waves of Capitalist Development: The Marxist Interpretation*.[84]

Persona non grata

A day before the Marshall lectures were to begin in Cambridge, Mandel went to Germany to participate in a debate about Europe. This was his first public appearance in the country since the revocation of the travel ban that Genscher had issued in 1972.[85] According to the security service report, German Trotskyism was past its high-water mark and Mandel was no longer a danger to public order.[86] The authorities thought otherwise in France and the US; there Mandel remained persona non grata.

Banned or not, Mandel did not let himself be stopped, as was seen at the centenary of the Paris Commune in 1971. Twenty thousand demonstrators from every corner of Western Europe – and not just Trotskyists – flooded Père Lachaise cemetery, heading for the Mur des Fédérés, the wall where the Commune martyrs were shot. It was a splendid day, coloured red from all the banners. Towards the end of the demonstration a motor scooter with a sputtering exhaust pipe wormed its way through the crowd. Alain Krivine's brother Hubert was driving, with a broadly smiling Mandel perched behind like a processing pope. Though lightly disguised, he was hailed from all sides.[87] He climbed onto a railing and quickly had the crowd hanging on his words. According to an eyewitness, 'He gave a magnificent speech' exceptionally lyrical, for he knew 'how to give his socialist ecstasies a universal appeal'.[88]

A year later Mandel and the British student leader Tariq Ali held a clandestine press conference in the centre of Paris to protest official restrictions on their movements.[89] Journalists were told its time and location only at the last minute. Protests in his favour did not put an end to Mandel's various expulsions. In 1979, he was seized by the police at Roissy airport, where his flight from South America had just landed. He was held in a hotel room near the airport, from which he phoned Gisela in Paris. She alerted Alain Krivine. Half an hour later, tipped-off journalists surrounded the bewildered police in the hotel lobby. After a short period of hesitation, they put Mandel on the first plane for Belgium. A Brussels comrade prepared to drive him back over the border and to Paris that same day, via a secret route. At ten in the evening Mandel arrived at Porte de la Chapelle station, where he took the metro to the Rue de Charonne.[90] He'd been expelled that morning but was back the same night. Mandel's ban from France remained in force until February 1981.[91]

The reaction to him in Washington was at least as overwrought as that in Paris. In the autumn of 1969 Stanford University invited Mandel to engage John Kenneth Galbraith in a debate over 'Technology and the Third World'. Galbraith was a Harvard economist, former US ambassador to India and the author of *The Affluent Society* (1958) and *The New Industrial State* (1967).[92] Mandel was informed by telegram, 'We are pursuing your visa through the highest channels and expect positive results.'[93] The US State Department, however, refused, reportedly because Mandel had collected money for jailed French students on an earlier visit.[94] Mandel proposed to Galbraith that their meeting proceed via taped contributions to a discussion, followed by a public telephone debate.[95] Penguin Books was ready to publish the results. Galbraith gladly cooperated in the debate, although he eventually blocked its publication.[96]

The New York Times editorial page called the ban on Mandel an 'idiotic decision' and 'a vestige of the restrictive era of the nineteen-fifties'.[97] A committee that included Arno Mayer, Gabriel Kolko, Noam Chomsky, Susan Sontag, Robert Paul Wolff, Robert Heilbroner and the microbiologist Salvador Luria recorded their protest.[98] *The New York Review of Books* and *Partisan Review* joined in. The Nixon administration had not anticipated so much opposition. US Attorney General John N. Mitchell was grilled about it on *Meet the Press*. Even the *Wall Street Journal* questioned the decision: 'Legal, but was it wise?'[99]

News media in Europe also paid attention to the issue, and soon a new incident threw fuel on the fire. At Zaventem, the Brussels airport, in April 1970, Gisela was stopped from boarding her flight to New York. Sabena Airlines refused her access because the US consulate had revoked her visa.[100] The papers were full of it.[101] In the Belgian parliament written questions were submitted to the government.[102] Was it a matter of an abhorrent 'guilt by association and by family bonds'?

Mandel was worried. He was now banned from entering five countries: the US, France, Switzerland, Australia and Germany. He was afraid that Britain and Italy would be next. The *Sunday Telegraph* in England had speculated over whether he was connected with the IRA. Like *Newsweek*, the Belgian paper *La Libre Belgique* ha associated Mandel with terrorism.[103] Kindred spirits received the same treatment, as in the incident with Gisela and the travel bans affecting Alain Krivine, Tariq Ali, Bernadette Devlin, the Swiss Charles-André Udry and the Peruvian Hugo Blanco. In July 1975 the US Senate Subcommittee for Internal Security branded Mandel 'the major theoretician of terrorism for the Fourth International.' A highly placed security official expressed amazement that Mandel had been refused entry into the US only because in a previous visa request he had violated visa conditions: 'No one has raised the question of Mandel being a major advocate of worldwide terrorism.'[104] Only under President Carter was Mandel again – though barely – allowed to tread US soil, under limited conditions and only for a specific time. This indicated that the McCarthy-inspired McCarran-Walter Act of 1952 was up for discussion, but when Ronald Reagan became president the door was once more locked tight.[105]

Armed struggle, a 'basic human duty'

Mandel was labelled a terrorist because he considered the armed struggles in Latin America a defensible strategy. He was not alone in this view, as shown by the Ninth World Congress of the Fourth International, held in April 1969 in Rimini in Italy. Tariq Ali said, 'The gathering was a strange mix of old and new in every sense.'[106] He saw Mandel as building bridges across the different generations, between the sceptical old veterans who had guided the Fourth International through the Occupation and the Cold War and the fresh, passionate recruits from the '68 generation. The one hundred or so representatives from thirty countries were euphoric. The French delegation was received with great acclaim. The thirty-one-year-old Janette Habel let it be known immediately that the new generation was not to be trifled with, that the time of smoke-filled, endless debates was past and that the guerrillas in Latin America deserved all possible help.[107] Habel, Bensaïd, Krivine and others in the French leadership were burning with impatience to turn the International into a fighting organization.[108]

The question was whether so optimistic a perspective was justified. Didn't the debacle of Che Guevara warrant caution? Surely the fact that so many pioneers of the armed struggle had fallen in battle in Peru, Colombia and Central America was cause for second thoughts. But most of the French representatives and the like-minded Latin American comrades refused to entertain any doubts. They felt bound to their peers who, like Che, had taken up arms – young militants in the Chilean Revolutionary Left Movement (MIR), the Tupamaros in Uruguay, the Bolivian Revolutionary Workers Party (POR) of Hugo Gonzales Moscoso, the Peruvians around Hugo Blanco, and the Argentinian Revolutionary Workers Party-Armed Struggle (PRT-Combatiente) led by Mario Roberto Santucho.

Those who were too sober for such romantic allies could always appeal to Mandel's authority. He thought the national bourgeoisies of Latin America had only one political function: to serve imperialism by keeping mass movements in check at all cost. This would exclude the possibility of legal self-organization for a long time to come. 'The thing is to avoid any illusion that constitutional regimes and classic bourgeois parliamentary democracy can be restored', he said. Only through a 'strategy of armed struggle' could a revolutionary leadership be formed.[109] It remains questionable whether Mandel, despite his insistence, was a fully convinced supporter of the armed struggle position. He must have recognized the error, as his was a classical way of thinking: an armed mass insurgency was capable of defending itself against its enemies, but a guerrilla struggle isolated from the mass movements was tantamount to Blanquism and individual terrorism, which had to be rejected. Yet had Mandel followed this line, he would have alienated the young radicals, particularly the French. Their Communist League (LC), the crown jewel of the International with its hundreds of new members, would have slipped from his hands. He wanted to avoid that, if necessary by defending a position that took no account of reality. Was his decision to do so a failure of leadership?

The American Joseph Hansen, an old comrade of Trotsky's, thought Mandel had yielded to French ultra-leftism in order to win the allegiance of European youth. The Argentinian Nahuel Moreno, who had broken with Santucho's PRT-Combatiente to found the rival PRT-La Verdad (PRT-The Truth), subscribed to Hansen's criticism. Mandel waved away their objections.[110] A resolution was passed to send funds to the hard-pressed Bolivian section for the purchase of new weapons.[111]

Setbacks soon followed. In 1971, thirty-five to forty comrades were killed in Bolivia.[112] There were more deaths in Peru and among the Tupamaros in Uruguay. Some sections of the International fell apart, while others lost influence.[113] There were tragic developments in Argentina, where the PRT-Combatiente had got international press attention in 1969 through its part in uprisings in Cordoba and Rosario and at least 150 members had been taken prisoner.

In that same year Santucho's PRT-Combatiente tried to make the northern province of Tucumán – where Argentina, Peru, Brazil, Bolivia and Chile all meet – into a centre of resistance, using its Revolutionary People's Army (ERP). Hubert Krivine and Jean-Pierre Beauvais helped comrades from the French LC, the young movement.[114] Then came the Salustro affair, which dominated the March 1972 LC congress in Rouen. Salustro, the director of Fiat Argentina, had been kidnapped by the ERP, who in return for his release demanded freedom for fifty jailed comrades, the reinstatement of 500 fired workers and 1 million dollars in assistance to the poor.[115] As though this were a strike at Renault or the French railways, the delegates rose from their seats to applaud the guerrillas as each new telegram was read.[116] But they were shaken when they heard that the guerrillas had executed Salustro just before the police stormed the place where he was held.[117]

At this time Mandel was in Berlin giving his lectures on late capitalism and preparing for his doctoral exams. He was called on to condemn the execution. Michael Tolksdorf, a prominent economist of the liberal Free Democratic Party (FDP), declared that his support for Mandel's appointment as professor depended on it.[118] Mandel responded that armed resistance in South America was 'an elementary human right'. 'One must regret the death of Salustro, but it must be seen as a consequence of the armed resistance.' Where basic democratic rights have been abrogated, he argued, the right to armed self-defence is beyond dispute. 'Whether an armed struggle is indeed expedient must be determined in each specific case and judged by those concerned.' Therefore he wanted no part in presuming to judge his Argentinian comrades. He did condemn the hypocrisy of the media, silent about kidnapped and murdered revolutionaries but flocking together when it concerned the fate of 'a big capitalist'. 'Do you understand that I am disgusted by such hypocrisy and that I am therefore not prepared to criticize the Argentinian revolutionaries openly?' He then added,

> You cannot expect that I would equate the violence of the oppressed with that of the oppressors, that I would declare the murderer of [the Nazi official] Heydrich just as bad as Heydrich or that Count Stauffenberg [a German army officer who tried to kill Hitler] was as much a monster as Adolf Hitler.

Resistance was a right – in fact a duty. As long as they can expect to remain unpunished, 'criminals are only encouraged to commit ever more terrible crimes'.[119]

Mandel refused to be intimidated, even when Tolksdorf labelled his perspective 'a manifestation of a prettified fascism'.[120] In Mandel's words: 'After the awful experience of the Nazi regime, no right-minded person can in principle reject the right [to self-defence] in whatever form, even in direct armed struggle', an honourable argument from a man who had personally experienced terror.[121] Yet criticism of his position did not come only from outside the International. The Canadian section and the US SWP spoke out against the kidnapping and the execution.[122] Santucho condemned their statements as betrayal and collaboration with the enemy.[123] Mandel feared 'a dangerous course of escalating public polemics between leading bodies of many sections'.[124] In that same year, at the initiative of the SWP and the PRT-La Verdad, a minority tendency was formed with the aim of convincing the International to abandon the guerrilla strategy.[125]

In December 1972 a lengthy meeting took place on the top floor of the Mandel home in Brussels. Those present in addition to Mandel were Daniel Bensaïd, Hubert Krivine, 'Marcos' and Santucho. Bensaïd, the son of a Jewish amateur boxer from Oran in Algeria and a rebellious milliner from Blois, had been involved in underground work in Spain and Latin America. The physicist Hubert Krivine had won the trust of Santucho during a stay in Argentina. He had also won the trust of the mysterious Joe Baxter (pseudonym El Gordo), co-organizer of the PRT-ERP and one of the founders of the Tupamaros.[126] 'Marcos' was an Argentinian who had made weapons for the Algerian FLN in Morocco in the late 1950s. Santucho, the thirty-six-year-old leader of the PRT-ERP, was on the point of returning to Argentina after escaping four months earlier from Rawson prison in the Patagonian desert. Around 120 political prisoners had been involved in the escape, but for most it went awry because they lacked sufficient transport.[127]

Ten or so guerrillas, among them Santucho, who had already escaped twice before, managed to reach the Trelew airfield, hijack a plane and fly to Havana via Chile. A second group reached the airfield but waited in vain for another plane that never landed. Sixteen of these men and women were killed by the army, including Ana María 'Sayo' Villareal, Santucho's wife and the mother of their three children.[128]

The meeting was tense, 'seized with a strange malaise', as Bensaïd recounted in his memoirs. The refined Bruges lace and heavy furniture of the Mandel library formed an ambience that jarred with the angry tone of the discussion. The meeting was also too late in coming. The Argentinians would have preferred to resume their guerrilla struggle long before with aid from the Cubans and, if need be, from China or North Korea: 'That's just the way it's done!' 'You do what you have to!'[129] The others did all they could to dissuade Santucho from resuming the armed struggle. They told him that Kim Il-sung and Mao were false prophets and pointed out the lies Castro had spread about the Prague Spring and May '68. They implored him to abandon his short-sighted campism, but Santucho would hear none of it. Ten thousand kilometres from Buenos Aires, sitting over a languid cup of tea, such pleas remained abstract. Back in Argentina the PRT-ERP was intensifying the armed struggle. Instead of profiting from the return of Perón and the short interval of democratic restoration, the ERP had lost around a third of its fighters in two years. Finally Santucho broke with the International, and in July 1976 he and his new partner, Liliana Delfino, were killed in a gunfight with the army.

Persuaded by the death throes of the Franco dictatorship in Spain, the powder-keg situation in Italy, a wave of strikes in Britain and radicalization in France and West Germany, Mandel anticipated revolutionary explosions in at least several European countries.[130] He spoke of pre-revolutionary situations, and was not content with mere analysis: the world had to be changed! 'Only the one who makes the revolution is revolutionary': this summed up Mandel's thinking, à la Che. There would be decisive battles within five years.[131] This prognosis could be defended as long as a revolutionary fire burned somewhere in Europe and its sparks might spread. But with the defeat of the Portuguese and Spanish revolutions in 1975, the cycle came to an end. Mandel collided with a reality that he accepted only late and very slowly.

Mandel's rhetoric in the 1970s was fuelled by success and fit the ultra-leftism that had taken root in the ranks of the International, an assimilation of Europe to Latin America. Bensaïd, at that time a member of the LC Political Committee, spoke of using urban guerrilla warfare to forestall a Pinochet-style scenario following a left-wing election victory in France. 'The issue was not purely theoretical', he wrote later.[132] The LC was battling not only the fascists but also the police. As a result, in 1973 it was banned. Bensaïd reasoned that if the question of taking power arose before the working class was ready to act, then the vanguard could not keep aloof: 'History is breathing down our necks'. His reasoning was a combination of Blanquism and belief in armed struggle. 'This perspective on history put an over-whelming responsibility on our frail shoulders . . . Each one of us felt personally responsible for the fate of humanity. It was an unbearable burden.'[133] Although the ultra-leftists had been reined in, the comrades' hearts still beat for the revolution. Revolutionary sentiment frequently interfered with tedious work in the trade unions and other popular organizations.

Impatient activism also suited the temperament of Gisela Scholtz, who now used the pseudonym Martine Knoeller. The CIA did not know who Knoeller was, only that she was 'one of the leaders of the pro-terrorist faction'.[134] Gisela was undoubtedly a compelling advocate of resistance activities.[135] In secret she was involved in preparations to kidnap the Greek ambassador in Brussels and turn him over to the resistance that was putting up a fight against the Colonels' Regime. 'The package' would be delivered via France and Italy.[136] The operation was called off because collection could not be assured. But Gisela did not depend on conspir-atorial operations alone. In March 1969 she and Bernd Rabehl, an influential SDS activist, thought up a campaign for raising money for the guerrillas from the well-to-do community of 'coffeehouse Marxists' in Berlin.[137] At the same time she was doing all she could to transform the traditional, annual Brussels anti-atom bomb march, which had sunk into a comfortable routine, into an unparalleled happening, 'a demon-stration beyond legal bounds'. The programme was to include laying siege to the stock exchange, the symbol of capitalism, and storming NATO headquarters in the Brussels borough Evere. The planners gathered in smoky, noisy cafés, where outsiders could not follow their discussions. The march numbered 10,000 demonstrators, with the Bel-gian Socialist Young Guard in the lead. Gisela was an active eyewitness: 'Then the horses, the tanks and whatever came into action.' The police turned out in full battle array.

> We fought as hard as we could and were proud that we counted only a few wounded among us. At the most 40 lightly wounded and only one severely wounded . . . I was thrown over an auto by two soldiers, but luckily I was able to break my fall in time.[138]

The fight was well prepared, like the rally that preceded it, at which Tariq
Ali, Bensaïd, Rabehl, François Vercammen and Mandel all spoke. Around
300 foreign comrades were there to swell the ranks.[139] The Danish
comrades in particular stood their ground. Had the goal of 'recruitment
amongst the radical youth'[140] been reached? *La Gauche* defended the action
against sceptics who 'speak of romanticism'.[141]

New wings for Gisela

In 1968 Gisela became closely involved with the work of the International.
No meeting of the United Secretariat occurred without her giving a report,
at first about youth work, then on finances.[142] With her activities for the
Belgian section added to her job with West German television in Brussels,
her workload began to rival Ernest's. Meschkat, who was in Colombia,
urged her to be careful, considering 'a sixteen-hour workday . . . unreason-
able and alarming . . . When do you get any reading done?' The movement
had no shortage of rank-and-file supporters but rather of 'politically
educated Marxists'.[143]

Meschkat touched a sensitive nerve. Gisela longed for independence, but
no matter how much work she took on she still felt dependent. The aloofness
of the comrades with whom she came into contact at the International's Paris
headquarters heightened her uncertainty and discouragement. They completely failed to appreciate her. The more she tried to measure up to Ernest,
the more she felt their barely concealed disdain. Independence seemed as
hopeless as Mandel's attempt to encourage Gisela by indulging her rivalry. He
had her co-sign articles, and they planned a joint study of the student
rebellions.[144] Few took their partnership seriously, but they resigned themselves to the situation because they did not want to quarrel about something
that seemed personal, not political. Gisela wrote to Karola Bloch that she was
'almost at the point of collapse' so that 'every little criticism by comrades
quickly reduces me to tears, which is very unpleasant'.[145]

In 1971 Gisela accepted an invitation from Meschkat to spend some
weeks on vacation in Colombia 'if your broadcasting company and the
engineers of world revolution would be so kind'.[146] Ernest preferred to stay
at home to concentrate quietly on completing *Late Capitalism*.[147] His
lectures in Berlin had caused him to fall behind in his writing. Every
Tuesday morning he left Brussels at six in the morning, returning late
Wednesday night. Concerned, Gisela wrote to Karola Bloch that her
husband was 'absolutely exhausting himself'.[148]

Their friendship with Ernst Bloch and his wife was important to Ernest
and Gisela. Since meeting them on Korcula in the summer of 1970, both

had been corresponding regularly with them. The frail ninety-year-old philosopher could now only move with difficulty and was no longer able to read, yet his mind was still creative and agile.[149] He was putting the final touch to his *Experimentum Mundi*, the doctrine of categories that he'd been working on since before the First World War, when he and Georg Lukács were close friends.[150] Bloch and Ernest Mandel wrote to each other candidly; both were concerned about Rudi Dutschke, who had been ordered to leave England.[151] Mandel regarded their friendship highly. To his surprise – 'in my circle birthdays, even 50th birthdays, were no longer celebrated'[152] – Bloch sent him as a fiftieth birthday present a facsimile edition of the *Westphälische Dampfboot*, the rebellious periodical that Friedrich Engels had enthusiastically praised in 1847.[153] Mandel read and re-read Bloch's works, just as he studied Marx and Hegel. He carried *Experimentum Mundi* around for weeks. Gisela wondered 'what will he have to read (other than the classics) when Bloch is no longer writing?'[154] Particularly because of this friendship, Mandel felt his ban from Germany as a stab to the heart. There was no greater pain than missing the creator of *The Principle of Hope* and being alone in responding to 'the call to the upright course'.

The trip to Colombia did Gisela good, giving her some peace, yet her letters showed a continued need to make herself important. She noted one encounter with pleasure: 'Yesterday we talked for a long time about the general political situation.'[155] She imagined herself a quartermaster whose opinions mattered: 'Today I wrote Livio [Maitan] a long letter . . . I wanted to show him again that I take his leadership role seriously.'[156] What she did not say was how much she hoped he reciprocated her respect. She wrote to Ernest that 'it's doing me theoretical and political good to stand on my own two feet' and not have him there to always back her up. With pride she added, 'Every day Klaus [Meschkat] is surprised at my development and says that I'm an outstanding theoretical cadre.' She wanted Ernest to know that she had been abused by the arrogant French comrades, 'which really offended me very much, more than I realized'.[157] She had had enough of being seen only as an appendage, as nothing more than Ernest's woman.

Gisela was never able to live free of anxiety; her too-loud, agitated laugh betrayed her insecurity. A deep depression came over her in the spring of 1975. She was unable even to speak, and sudden dizzy spells, particularly in the evenings, made being alone a hell for her. Mandel didn't dare to make any more journeys.[158] The situation gradually worsened. Gisela felt exhausted and complained of unbearable headaches. In a fit of pessimism, she commented to Ernest about a colleague who was playing with thoughts of suicide: 'And that she turned to me is also interesting. She said she was sure that I understand her and that I also would not rule out suicide if it were not for your being here. A clever woman, isn't she?'[159] Mandel was disquieted by these hints, but Gisela refused his help. As she told a friend, she wanted to 'deal with the illness myself . . . and spare [Ernest] completely'.[160] Despite Ernest's urging, she stubbornly refused to name the doctors treating her and left him in the dark as to whether her illness was a psychological disorder or had a physical cause.[161] For a while she gave him the impression that she was suffering from cancer. Fantasy and reality readily mixed in her mind. In a quieter moment she acknowledged, 'I often felt extremely lonely and wanted for once in my life to be the focus of attention, which had never happened. This was another reason why I invented the "tumour".'[162] Mandel tried to stay at home as much as possible and to humour her. If he had to leave the house, he made sure there was company for Gisela, who had become quite gaunt.

Ernst and Karola Bloch were among the few people with whom Mandel spoke about Gisela. When her depression subsided at summer's end, business as usual had already been ruled out. Gisela decided to leave the Rue Josse Impens house in the rather starchy Schaerbeek district of Brussels. She had never felt so alone anywhere: she was often bullied by Ernest's mother, she was always playing second fiddle and waiting for him to come home. Though she regretted having to leave her television job, she wanted to make a new start as a photographer and to live in Paris, or rather in Rueil Malmaison, a suburb about 8 kilometres west of Paris. She moved in with comrades there,[163] not far from Le Vésinet, the chic town where some friends of hers, the Morawes, lived; she regularly dropped in on them. In the late 1950s, when they both attended the Europa College in Hamburg, she had become friends with Bodo Morawe, a German TV correspondent in Paris.[164] She wrote to the Blochs, 'After a severe illness in the summer, with Ernest's help, I have radically changed course and can now finally do what gives me pleasure: examining the environment through pictures.' Through photography she hoped to organize her life and make full use of her creativity. 'Though photographs do not make a revolution, they can compel thought.'[165]

Every couple of weeks she visited Ernest in Brussels. As she confided to the Blochs, 'That's nicer than always having to wait here for him.'[166] She added:

I have to try to free myself from many things, also more from him, in order to find myself again. I'm making progress, and Ernest is happy about that . . . All the trouble to find myself again, to get closer to myself – I'm doing it for love of him and only for him . . .[167]

Though residence in Paris was forbidden him, Mandel visited her there a few days a week whenever he could, and he asked friends to keep an eye on her when he was travelling.[168]

Gisela and Ernest hoped soon to visit the Blochs in Tübingen. Mandel's admission to the writers' organization PEN seemed to herald a lifting of his banishment from Germany.[169] He was deeply disappointed when he was refused a visa yet again. Karola Bloch encouraged him:

> You should actually be proud; you must really be a giant if they're so afraid of you! You're the ruling class's enemy number one. Ah, and I really thought that we'd see each other this year. What joy it would have given us![170]

In August 1977 Mandel heard that his beloved Ernst Bloch had died. Neither Ernest nor Gisela was able to attend the funeral in Tübingen. At a memorial colloquium at Ghent University in April 1978, Mandel spoke about hope and anticipation as categories of historical materialism.[171] With this lecture he honoured the compelling philosopher whose Marxism of hope he so admired.

Daydreams

In this period Mandel's own hopes, daydreams and anticipation were particularly connected to Southern Europe. In 1971–72 an influential Spanish section of the International had emerged thanks to the students' struggles and the mobilizations against the death sentences of a half dozen Basque nationalists. In Euskadi, the Basque region itself, the leadership of the organization Euskadi and Freedom (ETA), elected in September 1970 at their sixth assembly – hence their new name, ETA VI – fused with the Revolutionary Communist League (LCR) in 1973 to become the International's new Spanish section (LCR-ETA VI). A majority of their members in jail also joined.[172] 'Euskadi, the Cuba of Europe!' crowed one of their manifestos.

Expectations were no less high in Portugal. In 1974–75 a revolutionary spectacle unfolded there complete with factory and land occupations and the development of alternative power even in the barracks: in the summer of 1975 tanks rolled and demonstrators marched side by side through the streets of Lisbon. The headline in Le Monde read, 'It's Cuba at the other end of the

motorway south.'[173] Three days after the overthrow of Portugal's dictatorship, Mandel addressed a mass demonstration in Lisbon, speaking in Spanish.
Filled with emotion, he cited the French revolutionary Saint-Just, who had
warned, 'One does not make revolutions by halves.'[174] Mandel was not
unknown in the country's universities. Some of his works, such as his
Introduction to Marxist Economic Theory, had circulated even during the
dictatorship.[175] He was hailed as an inspired orator.[176]

Mandel was proud of what had been achieved on the Iberian Peninsula
since the beginning of the 1970s. Just as in Argentina, here too the French
comrades were nurturing the new sections – politically, materially and
technically.[177] Mandel said, 'What is happening now in southern Europe
[is] the most promising development since 1917–21, above all because it
isn't limited to one or two countries but is spread over four or five
countries.'[178]

Despite the continued repression in Spain, Mandel spoke there to tens of
thousands of demonstrators and received 'approval and enthusiasm . . . as
never before, not even in France'.[179] After Franco's death in November
1975, Mandel was continually on the peninsula, holding educational
sessions, speaking at rallies and assisting the underground leadership of
the LCR-ETA VI. He took the risk of deportation in his stride. At other
times his emotions ran unusually high. He told Gisela that he was 'close to
tears' when he met comrades who had been suddenly set free after surviving
five to ten years in prison.[180]

The Spanish and Portuguese dictatorships collapsed, but no revolution
occurred. Mandel's promise in 1974 at the Tenth World Congress of the
International that the next congress would take place in a liberated
Barcelona had written a bad cheque on the future. The French and Belgian
printers who had been preparing to produce a Trotskyist daily paper in the
Catalan capital packed their bags.[181] What disillusionment, what disappointment! In 1975 the revolutionary tide receded, beginning with the Portuguese *coup d'état* in the fall. In Spain the transition to representative
democracy was completed more quietly than either friends or enemies
had anticipated.

The 1974–75 recession marked an economic change as well, an end to the
long postwar expansion.[182] Fast-growing unemployment, the dismantling
of some key industries – such as coal and steel in France and Britain – and the
conciliatory position of the trade unions prevented the social explosion that
had been so fervently anticipated. In the same period there were setbacks in
Latin America, following successive *coups d'état* in Bolivia (1971), Uruguay
(1973), Chile (1973) and Argentina (1976). When Indochina's revolution
was disfigured by the war between China and Vietnam and Pol Pot's regime

in Cambodia, the moment had come, as Daniel Bensaïd put it, to don the armour of 'slow impatience'[183] and to give the revolution more time. In 1979 the Eleventh World Congress was held not in Barcelona but, much less triumphantly, back in Rimini.

Pain and bitterness

Because of these political disappointments and his personal circumstances, the turn of this decade was a sad time for Mandel. During the 1979 Christmas holidays Rudi Dutschke suffered a fatal epileptic attack. Only thirty-nine, he died from the consequences of the assault on him eleven years earlier.

'We communists are all dead men on leave.'[184] Dutschke was quoting Eugen Leviné, the leader of the Bavarian Soviet Republic, in a speech he gave in 1977 in memory of Elisabeth Käsemann, a friend of his killed in Argentina. Dutschke continued, 'but that does not soften either the sorrow and pain of the survivors or the bitterness of those who know how great our loss is'.[185] The emptiness that he himself left behind two years later was inexpressible. The radical singer-songwriter Wolf Biermann wrote, 'My friend is dead and I am too sad/ To paint a big painting/ He was gentle, gentle, perhaps a bit too gentle/ Like all true radicals.'[186]

Mandel had been very fond of Dutschke; the younger man's decision to join the Greens in 1976 had not diminished his affection.[187] Mandel had helped Dutschke with his dissertation.[188] For his part, the former student leader had regarded Mandel with a mixture of admiration and affection. As he told Tariq Ali not long before his death, 'He continues to surprise and yet remains the same.'[189] Like Ernst and Karola Bloch, Dutschke supported Mandel in the struggle against his exclusion from Germany. He wrote to Werner Maihofer, the German Minister of the Interior, 'Ernest Mandel, a long-time friend of mine, is a socialist and convinced communist, who, in my opinion, cleaves more closely to the constitution than many in the CDU-CSU [Christian Democratic parties] or in other parties.'[190] Mandel saw this as a sign of Dutschke's fondness for him.[191] As he recalled, 'Whenever it was necessary, we could be sure of his solidarity.'[192] Even sharp political or scholarly differences could do their friendship no harm.[193] As Ernst Bloch had put it, the cold waters of criticism and the warm waters of solidarity flowed in a single current.

Mandel's pain was increased by his life with Gisela, which was never problem-free. In Paris too, she hit low points, though for a while they alternated with happier times. But after 1978 things declined precipitously.

That summer Gisela broke four ribs in a car accident. She spent ten days in hospital, followed by a period of considerable physical discomfort,[194] which added to her emotional distress. She anticipated little benefit from psychotherapy, but at Ernest's insistence she sought analysis, finding a woman analyst originally from Berlin who had lived in France since the 1930s.[195] She wrote to Karola Bloch, 'She says correctly that I need no analysis at all in connection with all the blows I've endured. Once a week we spend an hour together and are in complete agreement.'[196]

When she could no longer bear her melancholy, she resorted to antidepressants. Increasingly, whenever Ernest was away, she had accidents. Were these mere chance or cries for attention? Mandel became irritated, took her situation less seriously and disregarded advice from concerned friends.[197] Shortly after his departure for Mexico and Peru in July 1980, Gisela fell in the bath and broke her ankle and fibula. She was taken to hospital and underwent several operations. Her recovery took a long time, hindered by insomnia and anxiety. She complained of feeling abandoned in heartless Paris and of being neglected by Ernest. Only the psychologist Nicole Geneste, who like Gisela was now over forty, was looking out for her. Nicole worked in the office of the International where she was responsible for the monthly journal *Inprecor*. Gisela was eating less and less, though she knew 'that it [is] important for my stomach because of all the medicines. But I have absolutely no appetite and yet am afraid of losing weight and strength.' There was something self-destructive in her behaviour. Absolute quiet was prescribed to control her insecurity. Sleeping pills and painkillers kept her going, yet the anxieties they aroused made her panic. Desperately she asked Ernest, 'Maybe you can find something similar in Peru. Otherwise it will be a catastrophe.'[198] Ernest returned from Peru with yet more pills.

Back from his journey, Mandel took care to be home more often, however difficult it was for him. In 1980 he and Gisela had moved into a small two-room apartment on the fifth floor on the Rue de Charonne near the Place de la Bastille. He cancelled a trip to Brazil and only left Paris for his lectures in Brussels. Although the ban on his entering France would only be officially lifted in 1981, since March he had been routinely granted permission to visit.

Gisela recovered somewhat, but life continued to be difficult for her. She seldom went outside anymore. The elevator was often broken, and she preferred to study amidst her towering piles of books. She rediscovered her interest in politics, closely following events in Poland, Nicaragua and El Salvador, though she was far from optimistic about them. Her correspondence with Karola Bloch also revealed some recovery; she no longer demanded such complete attention. Gisela was looking forward to a visit from Karola in the middle of January 1982. She was sorely disappointed when Karola had to cancel because of illness.[199]

Never before had Gisela been so depressed. She wrote: 'Our best wishes for a good new year 1982 – for you personally and for Poland – though it has begun so miserably for them and so many other countries.' She said that her pains had all returned and that the medicines no longer helped. She couldn't take the bleak weather and the pressures around her. 'Of course it's nothing in comparison with Poland, Turkey, Chile, Nicaragua, Afghanistan, etc., etc. But everything together is just too much and simply no longer bearable.' Ernest could not help her. 'Ernest drags himself through rallies all over the place, analyses, etc.; I've never seen him so demoralized.' She closed resignedly, 'Now, Karola, you know about all this and follow it all, and I'm sure you feel it as deeply as we do.'[200] In those days she was no longer accessible to comfort from anyone.

On 14 February 1982, Gisela Scholtz died, aged forty-seven. The pills had wrecked her; she was used up, all her strength and energy exhausted. A few days later a brief announcement in *Le Soir* reported that she'd been cremated at Père Lachaise cemetery.[201] Ernest wrote to Karola Bloch, 'Gisela died suddenly last week. It's a very heavy blow for me; she was such a dear, talented, valiant, kind-hearted person, besides being my dear wife.'[202]

Gisela had found in her older husband someone who offered her an anchor amidst the turbulence of existence. But this hadn't diminished the pressure of her emotions. On the contrary, thousands of interests were added to her life, which became richer and more intense. In fighting for the revolution, Gisela gave not only her heart in spontaneous solidarity with the suffering and oppressed but if necessary her last penny as well. Too often, extremes of feeling had dominated her: she would be delirious with happiness, then weighed down with sorrow. The alternation of excitement and quiet was intrinsic to her nature. She was a Brechtian Mother Courage, bound to life, honest and realistic. But she was also, as a friend of her youth characterized her, a Rahel Varnhagen, whom Heinrich Heine had described as the most gifted woman in the universe, sensitive, discerning and vulnerable.[203]

If her longing for a strong figure to lead her represented one side of her character, her search for a passionate and independent existence reflected the other. It had been hard for her to make her mark in the competitive and disciplined climate of the Fourth International. There her ambition was not enough, even if she put everything else aside. Her total devotion to the cause was a sacrifice to the spirit of the times; she thought that changing the world depended on her as much as on Ernest. For the sake of her liberation as a woman, too, she had to play an equally important role or otherwise regard herself as incomplete. Gisela lost herself in the struggle, which had to be ever more intense, ever more radical. The pain that consumed her was inherent in the illusion that she could conquer her dependence.

Henry and Rosa Mandel and their sons (Antwerp, September 1937)

On the eve of the Second World Congress of the Fourth International, theatre on Rue de l'Arbre Sec, the French Trotskyist HQ (Paris, April 1948). From left to right: Marcel Favre-Bleibtreu (France), Sal Santen (Netherlands), Pierre Frank (France), Jock Haston (Britain), Colvin de Silva (Ceylon), Grandizo Munis (Spanish group in Mexico), Nora Saxe (secretary); foreground: Sylvia Coper (interpreter).

Somewhere in Germany, April 4th

Dearest Father, Mother and Brother,

I am very very happy to inform you now after so long a time about my liberation. I have been liberated by the US Army. I am in good health, and the time being, I am working for the US Military Government of Germany. I hope I will be back very soon and kiss you a thousand times.

Your son who loves you for ever,

Ernesto

P.S. I promised to a friend of mine who stayed together with me in a German prisoners camp for nearly 1 year to do all my possible to inform his family of his being liberated and in good health. Please have the kindness to write this to

Mme Martin,
80 rue Royaumont 30,
Nogent sur Oise, Oise, France

Won't you forget to mark your address on this letter?

Ernesto

Ernest Mandel
Civilian Employee of dep. F.B.
APO 658   2. E.A. Regt
US Army

Mr.
Nicolas Jules Robert,
67 rue Charles Quint,
Brussels
Belgium.

W. a. Od,

A sign of life: a letter from Ernest Mandel after his release ('somewhere in Germany', April 1945).

Ernest Mandel and Pierre Le Grève selling *La Gauche* (early 1960s).

Sherry Mangan (ca. 1950).

Ernest Mandel and Pierre Le Grève (with pipe) at the founding conference of the Union de la Gauche Socialiste (1964).

Ernest Mandel at work on *Late Capitalism* (1970).

Ernest Mandel the professor.

Rudi Dutschke, 'specialist of the youth revolt'.

Clandestine press conference with Tariq Ali, Alain Krivine and Ernest Mandel on official travel restrictions.

Ernest Bloch (mid 1970s).

Gisela Scholtz (late 1970s).

Verso dinner celebrating the publication of Mandel's *The Meaning of the Second World War* (1986). From left to right: South African Trotskyist Charlie van Gelderen, Ernest Mandel, Tariq Ali, Robin Blackburn.

Ernest Mandel and Anne Sprimont in Rio de Janeiro on their way to a conference on economic policy (August 1984).

At the Fifteenth World Congress of the Fourth International (Belgian coast, February 2003). From left to right: Jan Malewski, Michael Löwy, Zbigniew Kowalewski.

10

Revolution Deferred

Dozens of people came to Gisela's cremation at the Père Lachaise cemetery in Paris. Some were old friends and comrades from Germany; except for a few Americans, Swiss and Belgians, most of the others were French. The different groups did not mingle; their recollections of Gisela differed too widely for that. After the speeches, music by Wolf Biermann was played. Gisela had been quite fond of him.

Mandel asked others to do the speaking; he was too distraught. His decision not to speak was an expression of how overwhelmed he had been by anxieties and a tacit admission that he had failed to truly connect with Gisela. In an hours-long conversation the day before, he had told his friend Charles-André Udry how hard it had been – that she would phone him in Brussels at two or three in the morning, that she injured herself deliberately, used drugs and had been contemplating suicide. In tears he told Udry how he had tried to talk some sense into her and had dropped everything to rush to Paris.[1] His account was filled with self-pity yet acknowledged his inability to bear her problems; at his wits' end, he had finally fled.

Mandel was of a generation that divided life into public and private spheres. These worlds were carefully kept separate, and in Mandel's case naturally ranked so that the political always took priority over the personal. He found the need to change society ample justification for remaining blind to the soul, whether this concerned the emotions of his loved ones or his own. He was thus inclined to exclude or deny whatever was emotional or, especially, irrational. When that failed, he saw himself as being able to bring the irrational and emotional under rational control. Mandel resembled Françoise, the character in Proust's *Remembrance of Things Past*; like her, he showed more concern for humanity as a whole than for himself or those around him.[2]

Mandel always showed a certain naïveté in his daily life, and was full of illusions concerning women, particularly his mother and Gisela. He was unable to make these relationships adult. In correspondence as well as in daily contact, he was in the habit of using all sorts of pet names and adolescent formulae. Vacations with his wife – a fantasy life of three or four weeks a year in a fairytale setting in Italy or far-away Mexico – could not compensate for their lack of intimacy.

What was the source of this imbalance in Mandel – an adult as politician and scholar, a child in emotional life? He wanted to live on a large and compelling scale, helping to change the world. Politics dominated history; nothing was predetermined. When in 1948 he returned from a Yugoslavia then at odds with Stalin, he announced that the following world congress of the Fourth International would be held in Belgrade.[3] Time after time he made such predictions. Hungary and Poland in 1956, Portugal and Spain in 1975 – every insurrectionary event proved the correctness of his perspective. If things fell apart, he seldom wrote that into his balance sheet. He walled himself off from self-criticism and preferred to move on to the next item on the agenda. This impatient, adolescent attitude helped him keep aloof from key problems – from realities – that were too unruly for analysis and prognosis. Yet it also helped him delude himself that he could protect his sympathizers from demoralization and avert the danger of losing them. In a 1992 essay 'Trotsky the Man,' Mandel argued that for Trotsky, 'Only the long-term results of our political actions will allow us to pass judgement on their rationality, effectiveness or historical justification. This was why, throughout his life, he was politically not as self-confident as Lenin.'[4] Couldn't that also be said of Mandel? He found it difficult to fight unhesitatingly, if need be alone, for what he believed was right. Anxiety about losing supporters kept him from telling the full truth. Trotsky was called to account for this by Adolf Joffe, a friend and fellow leader of the Soviet Left Opposition, shortly before Joffe killed himself in November 1927. His judgement contained an observation that would be no less telling applied to Mandel: 'You have always been right politically . . . But you have often renounced your right position in favour of an agreement, a compromise, whose value you overestimated. That was wrong.'[5]

Self-deception and pragmatism were also present in Mandel's personal life. His relationships were seldom equal, and most were dominated by scholarship or politics. Intimate problems remained unstated. Mandel's development had stalled on the way to adulthood. When he opted for the revolution in his youth, his father stood in the way. In the following years, Pablo dominated him; once again, only with difficulty was Mandel able to liberate himself from an elder's tutelage. Each time he paid dearly for his independence, losing friends to whom he owed his intellectual and political education. In love he also attempted to throw off the chains of dependency; his yearning for equality went unrealized. Micky Traks, the young woman he had so ardently loved, remained unreachable. Each successive conflict with her roused his anxiety and fear of loss. This was a price he no longer wished to pay. He avoided close friendships and in his love relationships shut himself off from intimacy and emotion. A real personal life was therefore only partially accessible to him. This did not protect him from disappointments, but it did save him from total emotional paralysis.

Growing tensions and fading prestige

Mandel spoke with no one else about Gisela's death; only with Udry, that once, did he open his heart. He considered the indifference with which Gisela was treated once she fell ill to be 'scandalous'. He even blamed comrades' heartlessness for the fatal fall that confined her to bed for months in 1980 and from which she never recovered: 'I'm sure that if I'd been at the apartment, the accident would never have happened.' He criticized the 'pseudo-egalitarian formalism' that passed for comradeship in the International.[6] It was a lament filled with disappointment. The members of the International's Bureau did not take his criticisms to heart. Shouldn't he have accused himself in the first place? Only a few Bureau members responded. Udry recalled that Nicole Geneste, the office coordinator at the Rue Godefroy-Cavaignac where the monthly *Inprecor* was edited, had taken Gisela's condition seriously. 'My friendship with Nicole and the discussions we had about the situation oblige me to say that.' But he admitted that she was an exception. Udry confessed his own failure: 'I did not have the psychological insight to support Gisela in her depressive condition. That is in no way an excuse, only an explanation.'[7]

It was not that the younger leaders lacked compassion, but they found compassion difficult to express. Their idea of privacy was different from Ernest's or Gisela's, in which life was part of the private sphere and others were to keep away. Among themselves the younger generation were more spontaneous.

The sphinx-like Charles-André Udry was closer to Mandel than anyone. They had met in 1967. He was Swiss, and had studied economics and history in Lausanne.[8] He admired Mandel's theoretical coherence, his universalism and his ability to embody the continuity with the past without dogmatism. Like Mandel, he was a cultural hybrid, French-speaking yet formed in the classical tradition of the German workers' movement. Their thought and work required a framework that was broader than that offered by their native countries. From 1973 onwards Udry worked full-time in the Brussels

office and moved with it to Paris. He used the pseudonym Duret, a play on
the name of the 'soft' Swiss Communist leader Muret; Udry by contrast was
a 'hard man' (*dur*). Udry could be quite crude at times; he had no patience
with doubters. In Paris he was known as the Bulldog, but sensitivity and a
generous solidarity were hidden behind this façade. He was a skilful, untiring
organizer, and intellectually a match for Mandel. With Udry to push it, the
International grew into an effective, centralized organization.

As the 1980s dawned, Mandel and Udry spoke almost daily, often
about the nature of the times and the tempo of the revolution – was it
rising or stagnating? Did Reagan's neo-liberal offensive mark a break
with the previous decade? Was the workers' movement on the defensive?
If so, how could one interpret the formation of the Brazilian Workers
Party (PT) in 1979, Mitterrand's accession to the French presidency in
1981 or Solidarity's struggle in Poland? Was this a new blossoming, a
proof that such prophets as André Gorz in his *Farewell to the Working
Class* and Lucio Colletti were wrong to see Marxism as having come to a
dead end?[9]

Only in the 1980s – and then still doubting – did Mandel realize that the
upturn that had begun in May 1968 had petered out. In 1979 he still
considered all possibilities open, despite long discussions with Udry and
Charles Michaloux, held in the latter's Paris apartment.[10] The resolution on
Europe he presented at the Eleventh World Congress of the Fourth
International bore witness to Mandel's own irresolution. Anyone could
find in it whatever he wanted: upsurge or decline; it was neither fish nor
fowl.[11] Mandel recoiled from taking a definite stand, fearing demoralization.
The generation of '68 had few bonds with the working class; France, Italy
and to a certain extent Spain were exceptions. Unlike the generation of the
1920s and '30s, the youth of most European sections of the International had
never stood face-to-face with revolution, war or fascism, confrontations that
required clear choices. Now that their revolutionary fervour was ebbing,
Mandel feared a weakening of the sections and urged caution.

It was not the first time that he had closed his eyes when he should have
forced himself to look.[12] A decade before, in 1969, he had gone along with
the idea of armed struggle, particularly in fear of losing the rebellious French
youth. He had counted on their later political maturation. Hubert Krivine,
author of a critical report on the Argentinian PRT-Combatiente, said that
Mandel's silence helped fuel the militants' romantic illusions.[13] Bensaïd,
who had lived for some time in Argentina in 1973, also considered that the
International had succumbed to myths.[14] It came as no surprise that Mandel
avoided the debate at the Tenth World Congress in 1974.[15] This was not
because of his mistakes; these mattered little to him. He was afraid that for

some the revolutionary dream would disappear forever beyond the horizon, an anxiety that clearly still gripped him in the 1980s.

It was not only the complex debate about the political conjuncture that created this tension, but also events in Nicaragua and the Soviet occupation of Afghanistan. Only a minority of the International leadership clearly rejected the occupation of Afghanistan, fearing that it would benefit religious and nationalistic forces. The International finally condemned the occupation in 1982. At first Mandel did not speak out clearly against the occupation either.[16] Afghanistan, Poland, Pol Pot in Cambodia and the war between Cambodia, China and Vietnam – never before had so many situations invited debate about the crisis of socialism. But Mandel let the opportunities slip away.

He preferred to cross swords with Alec Nove, author of an economic history of the Soviet Union,[17] over the possibility of socialist planning.[18] Why was Mandel so reserved in the discussions about anti-bureaucratic revolution – once again, the fear of losing comrades? Mandel was aware of what he termed the 'monstrous waste and imbalances' of the Soviet system.[19] In 1984 he compared its decline with the fate of the Asiatic mode of production.[20] Sections of the bureaucracy were visibly transforming themselves into 'the old well-known class of capitalist and private owners'. Mandel considered this process irreversible, although the 'historical defeat of the Soviet working class' was not yet final.[21] Few comrades contradicted his conclusion.[22] Mandel ignored the fact that since 1980 conditions in the USSR had been ripening for a capitalist restoration. The world revolution had been steadily losing ground. Mandel must have realized this, but it was hard for him to accept.

Mandel's slowly dawning awareness of the changing political conjuncture was more apparent in his cautious reaction to the Sandinista revolution in July 1979. He pointed out its limited social weight: at most there were 40,000 Nicaraguan workers, half of them in Managua – too few to reverse the Latin American relapse after the *coups d'état* in Bolivia, Uruguay and Chile in 1973 and in Argentina in 1975. We support the revolution, but it will not bring about any new upturn: this was Mandel's perspective in a nutshell.[23] His cool, objective attitude irritated the Nicaragua solidarity movement.

It was a while before Mandel first went to Nicaragua, which he finally did in December 1984, invited by Jaime Wheelock, the minister of land reform. He had declined earlier invitations. Nonetheless, the Sandinista leaders had great respect for him. In his memoirs Omar Cabezas recounted how Henry Ruiz, one of the nine commanders of the Sandinista Liberation Front, had carried Mandel's economic works with him into the mountains, taking up the little room in his knapsack not taken up by necessary provisions.[24] Nicaragua confirmed Mandel's opinion that the colonial revolution was in decline. After a long detour, the world revolution's centre of gravity again lay in the industrialized countries. Europe, the US and Brazil were key; Mandel thought the revolution would regain its classic proletarian form there. He had not yet realized that here too its wings had been clipped. To broaden support for the new challenge, Mandel favoured calling the Trotskyist diaspora together and carrying out a radical proletarianization of the International's sections. This 'turn to industry', in the American comrades' jargon, meant that the majority of the members were expected to find industrial work. This roused little enthusiasm. Convincing comrades to adopt such a programme meant abandoning realistic analysis and arguing that the project would open up glorious prospects.[25] Moreover, its execution required maintaining the illusion that all organizational problems could be solved by strict discipline.

Revolutionary breakthroughs had failed to materialize in Spain, Portugal and Central America, and complications involving Afghanistan and the turn to industry caused conflicts within the International. This led the younger generation that had dominated the International since May '68 to examine the organization's failings. They understood better than Mandel the difficulties of building a party and saw more clearly than he the turnaround in the industrialized world.

The team in the International's Rue Godefroy-Cavaignac headquarters, a stone's throw from Mandel's apartment, came from every continent. It included the Briton John Ross, until recently one of Ken Livingstone's advisors at London City Hall; Livio Maitan, the short, cocky Italian who lived in Paris; the Swedish biologist Tom Gustafsson; Jean-Pierre Beauvais, a journalist and later a leader of the French global justice movement; the Mexican cineaste Manuel Aguilar Mora; and Daniel Bensaïd, a born Guevarist and a passionate philosopher with a great talent for teaching, who felt more respect than affection for Mandel. Others were the Irish-American Gerry Foley, for many years the editor-in-chief of the International's English-language journal *Inprecor* (later *International Viewpoint*); the Valencian Miguel Romero, called El Moro because he had been born in North Africa; and the American Barry Sheppard. For some time Janette Habel was the only woman in the group. She was married to a doctor from the Grimaldi family and had close ties with Cuba. Habel, like Mandel a Polish-German Jew, shared a warm and special bond with him because of their common roots. Rounding out the group were the Japanese Sakaï, who expressed himself in halting English, and the occasional visitor from Australia or New Zealand. They met twice a week, with Mandel and Udry presiding, debating the latest economic outlook, with *The Financial Times*, *Le Monde* and the *Neue Zürcher Zeitung* before them on the table. It was a mini-Babel, a picturesque scene, filled with competitive body language. Leaving aside the participants' megalomaniacal ambition, as Bensaïd put it, to grab the world revolution by the scruff of its neck, the meetings were an excellent training ground for 'languages, methods, writing and collective work'.[26]

Divisions began to appear in the team at Paris headquarters at the beginning of the 1980s. The full-timers experienced growing doubts. One exhausted worker went home to recuperate, another to rescue his own national section from disaster, and a third, who was already past forty, to seize his last opportunity for a personal career. This centrifugal tendency was counterbalanced in 1981 by the establishment of the International Institute for Research and Education (IIRE) in Amsterdam, housed in four adjoining houses near Vondel Park. The IIRE was a permanent cadre-training school where around twenty students drawn from various continents could attend three-month courses, given alternately in Spanish, French and English.

This costly project had been made possible by Jan Philipp Reemtsma, the Hamburg heir to the huge Rothmann tobacco fortune and from his youth a member of the Fourth International.[27] In 1978 Reemtsma had spoken with Mandel in Oostende in Belgium about the future of his cigarette imperium. Winfried Wolf, an economist and full-time worker for the German section, was also present, along with a friendly Berlin lawyer.[28] Mandel urged Reemtsma to sell and use the funds to establish an international airline that would allow comrades to fly gratis, a happy fantasy that did not stand in the way of other suggestions, such as setting up a publishing house and reprinting Marxist classics. The plan to found a school where internationalism could take a solid, tangible form came from Udry.[29] The Antwerp political scientist François Vercammen came in as cofounder. The school, headed by Pierre Rousset, a French specialist on Southeast Asia, developed into a nexus for study and collective reflection. Mandel was a regular and passionate lecturer there. His lessons on economics, the Russian Revolution and the Italian factory council movement were eagerly anticipated and yielded memorable gatherings, some of them extraordinarily good.

The IIRE was a hothouse of ideas and a breeding ground for critique. Mandel's optimism and his propagandistic idea of party-building had already been subject to discussion. And the truth cloaked in ambiguous formulations in 1979 was clearly stated in 1983: the cycle that had begun in May 1968 was over. Udry, Rousset, Habel, Vercammen, Bensaïd and Romero, who regularly met at the Institute in Amsterdam, along with Claude Jacquin and Jacqueline Heinen − all of them had lost any illusions. The younger generation's heresy culminated in the summer of 1983 at a leadership gathering of the European sections, held in a beautiful setting outside Toulouse. There a balance sheet was made of the catastrophic fate of the Italian section and the stagnation of the Spanish and French sections, and Udry sketched the consequences of the disintegrating fabric of the International.

Mandel arrived by car, but too late. The sixty or so European leaders had already spent half a day in conclave. In a lengthy contribution Mandel expressed his concern about the criticisms that had been offered. He was worried that the idea that a revolutionary perspective was no longer realistic for Europe[30] would not only take hold among the rank and file but also persuade such prominent figures as Perry Anderson and Tariq Ali. Not long afterwards Mandel declared to Anderson and Ali that the ongoing Italian strikes were 'the strongest movement of self-organisation of the Western European working class since [sic] decades'. He did not want to be perceived as overly optimistic, he said, but insisted, 'It is the strength of the [Fourth International] to understand that. The fact alone . . . more than justifies our existence.'[31] Mandel was having trouble coming to terms with reality. Was he afraid of losing old political friends? After the clashes in Toulouse, Udry found him shocked and depressed.[32]

New love

Mandel had not been on his own in Toulouse. Scarcely anyone had previously met the young woman who waited for him at the conference location every evening in an old BMW. She was Anne Sprimont, blonde, delicate, bold and thirty years younger than Ernest, an English teacher at the high school in Lier in Belgium and a gifted pianist. The Fourth International was a closed book to her; politics had never particularly fascinated her. Nonetheless, Mandel presented her as a militant from the Belgian section, an exaggerated gesture. Anne was hardly given a glance; unlike Gisela, she hardly cared.[33] But the chilly atmosphere indicated the gradual erosion Mandel's prestige had suffered.

Ernest had met Anne Sprimont at the Free University of Brussels in the summer of 1982.[34] She was studying German. She knew Mandel only by name and immediately found his electrifying aura both inspiring and stimulating. They fell into an interminable conversation. A few days later Mandel invited her out to dinner. During the meal, Anne could not overcome her agitation. She fixed her eyes on his tie pin, and dared not look up. Ernest, off his usual guard, spoke frankly to her, and asked questions that he answered himself. Anyone seeing the two of them could not have failed to notice their love. More dinners followed, and at their meetings they became ever more trusting. Then Mandel asked her to go to Mexico with him on holiday.

They spent a couple of weeks in Mexico City, with a side trip to Acapulco to escape the bustle. They saw the magnificent Diego Rivera frescoes; visited the anthropological museum in Chapultepec Park several times, finding it superior to ethnological collections elsewhere in the world; and browsed the markets in the poorer neighbourhoods. Mandel was full of information about Aztec culture and the artisans who had built the Plaza de Zócalo cathedral. Amidst these diversions he wrote a long essay about detective stories, sitting by the hotel swimming pool and dipping his pen into a leaky inkwell. He had been hooked on the genre all his life, the way someone else might be on alcohol or tobacco.[35] This essay was his only work to be translated into Russian before the fall of the Soviet Union.

A few months later, in November 1982, Mandel was again in Mexico, this time in the company of Charles-André Udry. On the aeroplane home he told Udry he was in love and said he was concerned about people's reactions. He admitted that unlike Gisela, his new love had no political background, but he implied that she was no less dedicated 'and what's more with a firmer character, more independence from me and more authority over me to make up for my weaknesses and extravagances'.[36]

After a long drought, Ernest once again tasted happiness in love. He felt he'd come home. For the first time since he had turned seventeen he could relax and speak Dutch. In the evenings they played recordings of Bach's Goldberg Variations two or three times over, and Ernest thoroughly enjoyed it when Anne played the music of his favourite composer on her piano, suddenly breaking into an uncontrollable Buddha laugh from deep in his belly. What a blessing after the sombre years with Gisela, when he had always just wanted to get away. Anne quietly accepted that Ernest took too little time for intimate conversation and neglected his friends. The laughter in his eyes moved her, and when in her company he was attentive and always concerned. Whenever she had to leave, she would turn back and wave again and again. She remained herself and did not become entangled in rivalry, as Gisela had.

They married in October 1983, and Anne moved from Antwerp into the Rue Josse Impens house in Brussels. Mandel's mother was dead set against her coming. Anne asked only to bring her grand piano with her but even that was too much. Mandel won her permission through a fierce argument. Another drama occurred one evening when despite Anne's repeated rings the front door remained closed. When it was finally opened, she was told that she only had to let Rosa know whether she was coming home and how late.[37] Anne learned to retort in kind – no second Gisela she! After two years

Rosa was found an apartment in a retirement home. At ninety, she finally let herself be persuaded to leave Rue Josse Impens, the fortress where she had so often stayed alone.

Monday through Thursday Anne taught at the Athenaeum, the same high school she herself had attended. She came from a freethinking and music-loving family; her father, an English teacher at a teacher training college and the driving force behind the concert society Pro Musica, loved piano music, as did his wife. Their home had no fewer than four pianos once Anne's older sister had decided to pursue her studies at the conservatory. Anne chose to study Germanic languages at the Free University of Brussels.

Teaching was not Anne's natural calling, and she was often ill. She spent the weekends with Ernest in Paris, where he had exchanged his Rue de Charonne apartment for a two-room mezzanine flat on the quiet Rue des Meuniers, on the border between Vincennes and Montreuil. Tom Gustafsson and his partner had lived there before returning to Sweden. Though this apartment seemed larger than the previous one, its rooms, too, were crowded with books, but a communal courtyard garden gave him a sense of space.

History and crime

For a while Mandel considered writing a book about philately. He was an ardent stamp collector and had a large collection, 'Jewish life insurance', partly inherited from his father.[38] The British publisher Pluto Press was planning a series about Marxists and their hobbies. Mandel decided that he did not want to write about stamps but about his other hobby, crime fiction. He found the 'fairy tales of crime' (as Dutch author Simon Vestdijk called them) to be truly relaxing reading, because 'while you're reading you don't think about anything else' and 'when you're finished . . . you don't think about it any more'.[39] The crime novel as a reflection of society was a surprising theme, more offbeat than generally expected from a Marxist, yet broader than any a crime specialist would provide.[40]

Where did the mass popularity of this kind of trivial literature come from? Mandel considered such writers as Arthur Conan Doyle, Agatha Christie, Dorothy Sayers, Raymond Chandler, Dashiel Hammett, Georges Simenon, Friedrich Dürrenmatt, Graham Greene and others. He argued that the demand is decisive, not the supply. He particularly wanted to write a history of two centuries of social evolution reflected in the evolution of crime and crime stories. Portraits of the writers were secondary.[41] He focused on the development of the hero in the genre from adventurer to private detective to policeman. This paralleled the phases of bourgeois development, from rebellion to triumph and consolidation, initially taking a distrustful stance towards feudal law and order but eventually finding it an ally. The literary shift to organized crime as villain reflected the expansion of capitalism. With the strengthening of the nation-state – first in reality, then in thrillers – state crime appeared that became interwoven with Mafia practices and the deceptions of multinationals.

Mandel confided in crime writer Jef Geeraerts that he read *romans noirs*, spy stories, psychological thrillers and tales of psychopathic crime: 'preferably I read . . . authors who write believable stories . . . it mustn't have really happened, just be believable'. He liked Ross McDonald, John Le Carré, Eric Ambler, Graham Greene, Morris West and the Italian duo Futtero and Lucentini. Their social realism was often more convincing than what socialists wrote – this was how Mandel explained his preference.[42]

Delightful Murder was a first. As literary and social history, it was Mandel's first publication outside the fields of politics and economics. Critical reactions were not slow in coming: not serious enough,[43] sloppy, one-dimensional. 'Mandel always sees the crime novel only as sociological illustration, not as a work of literature or even art.'[44] This evaluation showed that some were put off by Mandel's Marxism.[45] But most reviewers were well-disposed, praising an original analysis that gave a fresh impetus to literary studies.[46]

History and the Second World War

Mandel stood in the tradition of the Enlightenment. He was a classically educated thinker, not limited to Marxist culture but with his sights on a broader historical, literary and philosophical universe. His work broke disciplinary borders; he was at one and the same time an economist, sociologist and historian. Like Marx, he was heir to Hegel's contemplation of the totality. Nonetheless, he made his reputation especially as an economist, challenged to do so by Michel Pablo, who gave the highest priority in the struggle against Stalinism to a renewal of the critique of political economy. Mandel was prepared to devote himself to this, and his *Marxist Economic Theory* and *Late Capitalism* were monuments of Marxist economics.

Yet Mandel had not intended to become an economist. His passion was history, the course of study he had begun in the Occupation years 1941–2.[47] The possibility of reaching explanations from a historical perspective fascinated him. When he distanced himself more from day-to-day politics in the 1980s, he began to focus on the writing of history. He had never completely abandoned the field, as shown by the pieces on pre-capitalist society and imperialism in *Marxist Economic Theory*, the sections on the internationalization of capital in *Late Capitalism*, his essay on the rising fourth estate of the revolutions in the southern Netherlands[48] and his contributions to the debate on the Asiatic mode of production. He even gave his theory of long waves a historical context.

But only with his 1986 study of the Second World War did he present himself as a true historian.[49] Yet he remained a maverick, certainly in Belgium, where historiography was very empirically oriented. Mandel stood out with his more theoretical synthesis. In *The Meaning of the Second World War* he returned to a concept he first expressed in *Revolutionary Marxism Today*, the collection of interviews published by New Left Books in 1979. He characterized the world conflagration as 'five wars in one'[50]: an inter-imperialist competition for world hegemony, which the United States had won; a struggle by the Soviet Union to safeguard the 1917 revolution; a defensive war by semi-colonial China against imperialist Japan that developed into a revolution; a liberation struggle by colonized Asian peoples for national independence, which in the single instance of Indochina turned into a social revolution; and finally a war of liberation in Europe against the Occupation and Nazi oppression.[51] Mandel considered the four last conflicts to have been just wars.

Mandel avoided the usual portrayal of good guys against bad ones, the anti-fascist (bourgeois democratic) forces versus the fascist Axis. According to him such a dichotomy failed to lay bare the roots of the conflict: 'The American and British ruling classes fought the war not in order to defeat fascism, but to break the resistance of the German and Japanese bourgeoisies to the maintenance or extension of their own particular interests.'[52] This was certainly a heretical analysis that contained provocative positions on a wide range of topics, from armaments and logistics to scholarship and ideology.[53] About this attempt to analyze the war in its totality Perry Anderson wrote: 'Powerful and original. I was constantly . . . obliged to think about contemporary history anew.'[54]

In the 1980s powerful memories of the war had forced themselves on Mandel. He was mesmerized by the genocide and other Nazi crimes.[55] He let slip to Udry that he was amazed that so few Jews had resisted because 'without fighting there was no escaping the shoah!'[56] The Holocaust was emphatically present in his book.[57]

Auschwitz had put an end to the pre-war Marxist debate over the so-called Jewish question,[58] not because everything had been elucidated but because the principals were no longer alive.[59] There had been silence about Auschwitz, and – leaving aside a few unorthodox analyses – the tragedy of the Jews had been interpreted as being at most a subsidiary aspect of the European catastrophe that was too marginal to be debated.

The silence was broken from two directions: first, from the Frankfurt School, Horkheimer and Adorno, who were soon followed by Herbert Marcuse, Günther Anders and his ex-wife Hannah Arendt, who were all philosophers who took Auschwitz as the starting point for their cultural critiques; and second, from Mandel, who first analyzed the genocide in 1946 in his afterword to Abraham Léon's *The Jewish Question: A Marxist Interpretation.*[60]

Mandel and the members of the Frankfurt School took separate paths, without ever meeting each other, a consequence of the Frankfurt thinkers' break with the organized workers' movement.[61] They sought support in a paradigm that the Italian political scientist Enzo Traverso called – echoing Ernst Bloch's Principle of Hope – the Principle of Despair, a critique filled with scepticism.[62] This was quite different from Mandel, who radiated hope and was always seeking a revolutionary breakthrough, an attitude that had saved him from deportation to Auschwitz. When imprisoned, he had seen that even the guards could be persuaded by argument. At age twenty-one, Mandel had experienced the august power of language. His affinity with the Enlightenment clearly had a personal dimension – and included its delusions, as when he wrongly imagined that he had succeeded in convincing people of something. Silence – no sign of agreement – was too often the response to his deafening flood of arguments.

With his typical self-confidence Mandel maintained in 1946 that the Jewish genocide could be rationally explained in Marxist terms. While Isaac Deutscher called the Shoah the mystery of 'the degeneration of the human character',[63] Mandel held it to be a product of capitalism and warned against viewing the destruction as a unique catastrophe. He said the Final Solution was essentially no different from the colonial massacres or the nuclear destruction of Hiroshima and Nagasaki. Nazism was far from having a monopoly on genocide and mass destruction.

Forty years later Mandel finally returned to this subject, in his study *The Meaning of the Second World War*. In the intervening decades he had written about fascism but said nothing about anti-Semitism or genocide.[64] His afterword to Léon's *The Jewish Question*, originally published in 1946, had not been included in the book's 1968 edition.[65]

German Nazism, with which anti-Semitism had already become identified in the 1930s,[66] no longer posed an acute danger after the war. There was more interest in the right-wing dictatorships in Latin America, Greece and Turkey, in Pinochet, Papadopoulos and the Grey Wolves. Moreover,

because of the genocide and resulting guilt feelings among non-Jewish
Europeans and Americans, anti-Semitism had become a marginal phenom-
enon. In the 1980s that changed: the return of poverty and insecurity, the
Arab–Israeli conflict and the social consequences of the collapse of Eastern
European Stalinism reawakened anti-Semitism and activated a debate about
Auschwitz. The world heard about it from *Shoah*, Claude Lanzmann's heart-
rending film; the sharp controversy among German historians and the West
German television film *Holocaust*;[67] and David Irving's malignant denial of
the genocide.

Mandel felt himself challenged to rethink the Jewish tragedy.[68] As he had
not in 1946, he stressed the uniqueness of the Final Solution. However, he
also stressed that it was unique neither because of the Nazis' inhumanity nor
because of their ideology and fanaticism.[69] The deliberate dehumanizing of
slaves and those destined for slavery did not of itself lead to Auschwitz. The
uniqueness lay in the combination of dehumanization with a half dozen
other factors typical of the modern industrial system: 'this precise combination occurred up to now only once', he explained to Perry Anderson, 'The
advantage of the analysis is that it is able to add the ominous words: "up to
now" . . . given the nature of decadent late capitalism and racism . . . My
analysis implies: this can repeat itself, if we don't watch out!'[70]

Also unlike his 1946 essay, his new book included more than material
circumstances in its compilation of explanatory factors. Mandel now
sought a wider connection between ideology and the rationality of the
industrial system. Only in part flowing from semi-feudal, petty bourgeois
fear of Jews – 'This type of anti-Semitism led to pogroms, which were to
the Nazi murderers what knives are to the atom bomb' – the genocide was
rooted in a non-Christian, biological racism.[71] It was an extreme form of
Social Darwinism that stamped Jews as subhuman and deprived them not
only of the right to freedom but the right to life itself, simultaneously
freeing perpetrators and their accessories from any guilt feelings. The
ideology was related to the culture of colonialism and imperialism, of
which the African slave traffickers and the Caribbean and Latin American
conquistadores were the earliest personifications. Auschwitz was the
product of Western civilization, of its culture and social relations, not
of an uncontrolled technology,[72] Hitler's evil spirit or 'the evil empire in all
of us'.[73]

Mandel emphasized, however, that this racist ideology was not a sufficient
cause. Auschwitz was unthinkable without the modern industrial system,
without its material and technological possibilities. In the Holocaust anti-
Semitism was amalgamated with what Mandel analyzed in *Late Capitalism* as
the characteristic moments of industrial capitalism: a global irrationality

growing to absurd proportions (the decision to exterminate all Jews) and a
no less pronounced partial rationality (the perfect industrial planning and
execution of the decision).[74] The fact that Germany had been the locale for
this fusion of racism and industry Mandel ascribed to a series of accompanying economic, political, cultural and psychological circumstances.[75]

Though a shift had taken place in Mandel's thinking – he did call the
Shoah a unique occurrence – he still held fast to the possibility of rationally
explaining the genocide, as convinced as he had been in 1946 that the
destruction resulted from the crisis of capitalism. This showed that he
remained pre-eminently an Enlightenment thinker. Yet something has
to be added: he was not especially alert to the tragic side of history, to
those features that defy rational explanation, what Primo Levi termed the
'black hole' or Isaac Deutscher called the 'degeneration of the human
character'. Mandel made no allowance for this,[76] and that was the trouble,
according to the British philosopher Norman Geras. He suggested carefully
that in all Mandel's attempts to explain the Holocaust he did not succeed in
completely eliminating an inexplicable residue, for example employing the
term 'barbaric' as a generic, 'essentially anthropological' category.[77] Geras
held that phenomena such as servility, obsessive hatred, indifference and
sadism were not specifically capitalist – and that Mandel's explanation fell
short in yet another respect. The Jews were but the first of the inferior races
to be destroyed, according to Mandel, partly because of 'the demented faith
of Hitler and some of his lieutenants in the "world Jewish conspiracy"'.[78]
But what did the spiritual sickness of the Nazis, who persevered with their
own logic, have to do with the crisis of capitalism, apart from the social
forces that had brought them to power?[79]

Mandel also found Nazism as a mass phenomenon unthinkable without
the First World War.[80] This catastrophe of destruction and cruelty, which
promoted the worship and exaltation of violence, was 'the first, distinctive
step towards barbarism. Without it, there would have been no Hitler.'[81]
This was a staggering suggestion from Mandel: that the scars and traumas of
1914–17 laid the decisive moral foundations for the Nazi genocide. Finally,
Mandel argued that the Holocaust could not have happened without the
passive complicity of millions, in Germany and beyond. In the first place
there were the executors, a minority of psychopaths and fanatics. In
addition, however, there was a majority of fellow-travellers, who from
cowardice, calculation or obedience, set aside their moral code – 'Thou shalt
not kill' – for a state authority under whose motto 'Orders are orders', they
were called upon to kill for that state's greater glory. After all, 2,500 years
before the Holocaust, Sophocles's tragedy *Antigone* had portrayed the refusal
of an individual to capitulate to group pressure or state interests. Why look

for the source of this archetypal drama in the crisis of capitalism? Wasn't this a reductio ad absurdum?

Treating such concepts as servility, cowardice and obsessive bloodthirstiness, wasn't Mandel, despite himself, running up against 'the sub-soil of the human psyche'?[82] Against what Deutscher termed the 'mystery of the degeneration of the human character that will forever baffle and terrify mankind'?[83] Mandel was too strong a rationalist to give in to such obscurantism; he was not prepared to accept the incomprehensible.

Similarly, he opposed thinkers who ascribed to the Nazis a primarily ideological and political motivation, leaving out economic considerations. One such was Perry Anderson, who denied the Shoah any economic rationality in an otherwise passionate critique. He told Mandel, 'The whole specificity of the Holocaust was its lack of any economic purpose. There was no class rationality to it whatsoever.'[84] In his response Mandel denied that all great political events had to have a direct, intrinsic economic rationale.[85] An economic advantage can manifest itself after ten, twenty or thirty years. The Nazis had intended to make Eastern Europe into a 'settlers' colony'. Jews were considered unable to be settled there in the role of 'illiterate manual unskilled slaves'. (Mandel thought this a compliment.) If the Germans could have made short work of it, after twenty years they could have realized a substantial economic profit, like the Spanish colonists in some American countries where the indigenous peoples were completely annihilated.[86] Besides that, Mandel considered the Holocaust economically rational in a direct sense. It was the logic of overabundant slave labour carried to the extreme. Otto Thierack, the Nazi minister of justice, was not just out to kill; his slogan was 'Death through [i.e., after] work.' Mandel said that as soon as the supply of slave labourers began to dry up, the camp administrators began 'to weed out skilled labourers and technicians, including among the (surviving) Jews (not many alas)'. Fanatics like Goebbels were a minority, even in the SS. Mandel found that the struggle to create a slave state 'had an (inhuman) economic logic of its own'.[87]

He was certain that there was a connection between destructive capitalism with its exploitation and barbarism with its extermination. The Holocaust was not an end in itself, nor were its motives purely ideological and non-economic. Making this claim would require redefining the extermination as an isolated, one-time, unrepeatable phenomenon. Like Rosa Luxemburg, who felt 'at home wherever in the world there are clouds, birds and human tears', Mandel cherished no special feelings for the sufferings of the Jewish people.[88] He resisted admitting that the Shoah conflicted with the interests of German capital. This would have demanded an explanation of the so-called autonomy of the German state in 1943–5. As early as 1969, criticizing the historian Tim Mason in his introduction to *The Struggle Against Fascism in Germany*, Mandel had rejected the primacy of politics in the history of the Third Reich. He found untenable the proposition that the Nazis' internal and external policies had increasingly broken free from the demands of Germany's economic ruling class.[89]

Theory as history

Mandel defended the role of economic analysis without lapsing into economic determinism. How freely he approached historical reality was shown once more in an essay dedicated to the role of the individual in history in the light of the Second World War. He had written it for a Festschrift for the Communist and forensic psychiatrist Jean Pierre de Waele, a colleague at the Free University of Brussels. His contribution quickly found its way into *New Left Review*.[90]

The Marxist perspective on the role of the individual had been set forth by the Russian theorist Georgii Plekhanov in a classic text of 1898.[91] Plekhanov polemicized against the subjectivist sociology that elevated the hero to the driving force of history, irrespective of the relationships between classes and their most important fractions. Plekhanov's subtlety saved him from the opposite misunderstanding, a reductionism in which 'the personal element is of no significance whatever in history, and . . . everything can be reduced to the operation of general causes, to the general laws of historical progress'.[92]

The debate had received fresh impetus in the 1960s with publication of *The Prophet Outcast*, the third and final volume of Isaac Deutscher's biography of Trotsky.[93] Deutscher posed, as had Trotsky, the question whether the 1917 revolution could have occurred without Lenin.[94] Trotsky's idea of the unique, irreplaceable role of Lenin found no favour with his biographer: 'The trend worked not through a single individual but through a team.'[95]

Necessity or chance? What is the individual subject's relation to the broader framework of society? These were the historical-philosophical questions being discussed in England at the time by such historians and philosophers as Hugh Trevor-Roper, A.J.P. Taylor, Karl Popper, Isaiah Berlin, E.H. Carr and others – questions, as Carr put it, about 'the wickedness of Hegel' or 'Cleopatra's nose'.[96] In *What Is History?* Carr, also the author of a multi-volume study of the Soviet Union, accused Marx as well as Trotsky of a determinism that allowed only a marginal place for chance in history.[97] Carr's diatribe so irritated Roman Rosdolsky – 'I'm just itching . . . to write a little something'[98] – that he decided to come to Marx's and Trotsky's defence against Carr and Deutscher.[99]

Rosdolsky wrote that for Marx chance in human history was far from a historical stepchild.[100] Accident and the lawfulness abstracted from it were 'both equally real and important'.[101] They were also mutually interpenetrating, so that, as Engels put it, 'what is maintained to be necessary is composed of sheer accidents and . . . the so-called accidental is the form behind which necessity hides itself'.[102] This perspective had been borrowed from Hegel and was paraphrased by Trotsky in a Darwinian analogy: 'The historical law is realized through the natural selection of accidents.'[103]

The key, Rosdolsky maintained, was to distinguish between long-range tendencies, like the collapse of capitalism, and particular historical events, like revolutions or wars. The first are not influenced by chance – chance occurrences being always compensated for by other random occurrences – but singular events in contrast are so influenced.[104]

If the element of chance is visible, it is visible above all in the role of so-called great figures in history. If Lenin had been absent from St. Petersburg in 1917, would the October Revolution have occurred? Without Hitler, would the Second World War have broken out? And if Churchill had not lived, would Hitler have won?[105] In their subjectivity, such questions seem in conflict with the Marxist tradition. Nevertheless, they formed the core of Mandel's study 'The Role of the Individual in History: The Case of World War Two'. He must have had Rosdolsky's polemic of twenty years earlier in mind as he wrote.

He concisely put the sceptics in their place: 'When historical materialism posits the primacy of social forces over individual actions in determining the course of history, it does not deny that certain individuals play exceptional roles.' But, he warned, the individuals' room for manoeuvre is limited. Hitler's failed project for a slave economy proved that even 'the most powerful tyrant in the world cannot escape the implacable demands of capital accumulation'. Yet within these social and material limitations some figures can influence history 'either by possessing a clearer perception than others of the historical needs of their class, or by retarding the recognition of these objective needs'.[106]

It's questionable whether Mandel's chosen examples always hit the mark, but in any case his essay was a remarkable contribution to the theory of history. Fellow historians, however, paid little attention. The tendency to propose the individual as the decisive factor in the historical process had incidentally been the hallmark of the primitive phase of historical consciousness. Besides the relationship of individual to social class, Mandel also examined the role of collective mental constructs and the processes of selecting leaders. His argument culminated in a synthesis of Hitler's rise.

The gangster mentality that found its expression in Hitler was already visible in November 1918; there were literally hundreds of potential Hitlers and Himmlers walking around:

> [The] way in which the Third Reich actually emerged from the collapse of the Weimar Republic, and paved the road to another world war, was only to a limited extent determined by the particular gifts and weaknesses of Hitler as an individual politician. Incomparably more significant was the broader social crisis of which the Hitler-type was only an epiphenom-enon.[107]

Hitler perfected his merciless, opportunistic and deceitful modus operandi in a process taking around ten years, in which he developed into the undisputed leader of a host of would-be Führers. One had to conclude that anyone seeking the origin of Hitler's gangster mentality in his early biography, rather than in the social milieu of right-wing Germany after Versailles, had misunderstood the actual historical dynamic.

In his contribution Mandel showed his aversion to interpreting Hitler's rise as the organic unfolding of an inherently diabolical character. This would have meant accepting the thesis that the Führer had made history independently of social conditions and conflicts. But he also recoiled from the opposite, from a sociological determinism in which Hitler had no independent role, in which action was only the expression of the social constellation and in which there was no place for the margins where idiosyncrasies played a certain role. With his analysis Mandel tried to balance structure and agency, the dialectic between psychological infrastructure and social superstructure in the context of the war.

A self-destructive way of life

War, torture, fascism and racism were themes that kept Mandel fully occupied in the mid-1980s. He spoke on their socioeconomic backgrounds to an investigating committee of the European parliament and at symposia held by the Belgian Auschwitz Committee.[108] He investigated the history of torture for the Hamburg Institute for Social Research, the first research project of the institute established by Jan Philipp Reemtsma in 1984 following the model of the Frankfurt School.[109] Mandel also sat on the institute's scholarly advisory board.[110] To the end of his life he continued discussing the destructiveness of the twentieth century with Reemtsma.[111]

Mandel also continued to occupy himself with the war, which fascinated him ever more irresistibly as the years went by, and he used it as an excuse for other obsessive behaviour. From his youth he had had a hearty appetite, which gradually became a dangerous habit of overeating. He paid no attention to his health, parrying criticism with a rationalizing account of the war years and the hunger he had known. Anyway, he reassured himself, he had always been strong. But as early as the 1960s he had begun to have heart problems; after two months' travel through America, he was advised in November 1968 to take some rest. Franz Breth, a doctor friend, a Czech living in Austria who had treated Trotsky in France in the 1930s,[112] prescribed movement therapy for his arteriosclerosis, probably an inherited complaint.[113] Mandel replied, 'I don't know if I can manage to find the time. Would a more or less useful alternative be an exercise bicycle in the bathroom and at least a ten minutes' walk each morning? The suggestion comes from my wife.'[114] But he did not take his physical condition seriously. Mandel belonged to a generation that easily separated the mind from the body. He seldom went for a walk and mostly used taxis to get around, unhealthy habits that became addictions in the course of the 1980s when a herniated disc and bad circulation made movement more difficult for him. Only on vacation did he take any physical exercise – some swimming – and only in small doses.

Mandel's way of life had devastating results. A physician he consulted in Lausanne in the 1980s found that his body was ten years older than would be expected at his age. By then he was barely moving at all, and more than three or four hours' sleep a night was exceptional for him. His health was fast being undermined by his custom of eating too much and by the diet pills that he was taking too generously. Ironically, all of his habits had been formed for the sake of the work that always awaited him. He had wanted to gain hours, but had lost ten years.

Much of Mandel's work in the 1980s was lifted from his shoulders by Paul Verbraeken, a sociologist in his thirties, born in Mortsel in Flanders. Verbraeken had landed in the socialist opposition around *Links* and *La Gauche* via his anti-militarism in the early 1960s, and he was a member of the Belgian section of the International from its establishment in 1971. He had left the Trotskyist movement in 1980, but this was no impediment to Mandel's collaborating intensively with this creative Marxist,[115] 'one of the least public great intellectuals of this little country'.[116] Verbraeken translated Mandel's *Marxist Economic Theory* into Dutch.[117] In 1983 he helped organize an international colloquium marking the hundredth anniversary of Marx's death. The colloquium brought Mandel much renewed prestige. Numerous scholars debated a wide range of subjects under the rubric 'The Relationship Between Politics and Economics in Marx'. The event was a sensation because it was the first time not only social democrats and Trotskyists but also representatives from Eastern and Western Communist parties participated together.[118]

Despite his efforts, Verbraeken could not prevent Mandel's remaining overburdened with work.[119] Like eating, work seemed to be a necessary outlet for him; a fourteen-hour day was no exception. It was a vicious circle – eating more in order to work harder.

Criticizing Eurocommunism

In his *Marxist Economic Theory* Mandel had already attempted to break through the Eurocentrism in Marxist theory formation, pleading for the internationalization of data collection, for freeing problem formulation from a Western corset and for broadening collaboration in all directions.[120] In the mid-1980s Mandel was the central figure in an international project to defend Marx's labour theory of value against such economists as Michio Morishima and Ian Steedman, who were using the work of Piero Sraffa as the basis for a fundamental critique.[121] A close friend of Antonio Gramsci's, Sraffa had been brought to Cambridge by John Maynard Keynes in the 1920s.

The controversy concerned Marx's handling of the 'transformation problem' in the third volume of *Capital*, the transformation of value into production prices and of surplus value into profit.[122] In 1907 the Prussian statistician Von Bortkiewicz had provoked a long and detailed debate over the problem that only ended with Sraffa's contribution in 1961.[123] His findings were the point of departure for a current that became known as the neo-Ricardians. Against them, the defenders of Marx's labour theory of value mounted dogmatic arguments (X is true, because, as Marx said) and political-ideological arguments (the neo-Ricardians are wrong because they undermine the proletariat), but they failed to come up with any scientific response.

Mandel assembled a choice group of economists and mathematicians to defend Marx's theory against the Cambridge school's revisions. His team included the Pakistani Anwar Shaikh, a professor at the New School for Social Research in New York; the Frenchman Pierre Salama; Alan Freeman of Great Britain; and Emmanuel Farjoun, a mathematician at the Hebrew University in Jerusalem. The project was funded with a gift from the widow of Robert H. Langston, a member of the US SWP who had died in 1977.[124] In 1984 the results of their studies were published in London by Verso under the title *Ricardo, Marx, Sraffa*.[125]

However refined, this debate was for Mandel more than an academic exercise. The neo-Ricardians had influence on European social democracy, the trade unions and Eurocommunist circles in England and Italy. The Communists were justifying their support for austerity policies with the neo-Ricardian hypothesis that raising wages stimulated inflation, which was the chief obsession of mainstream economists in those years.[126] For these reasons Langston's widow allowed Mandel to convince her that a 'conclusive scientific refutation of the Von Bortkiewicz-Sraffa challenge to Marx . . . represents the most important theoretical task for Marxists today'.[127]

Not every specialist reader was impressed with the results. M. Desai called them 'a very uneven collection of papers'; B. Fine complained of a 'lack of sophistication and rigour'; and G.M. Hodgson evaluated them as having 'a very low quality'.[128] Theoreticians of the labour theory of value did not regard them highly and found Mandel's mathematics lacking in subtlety. Some Marxist-inspired economists considered the intellectual exercises on price determination in particular as pompous distractions from liberation struggles.[129] Nonetheless, after five years of research, Mandel wanted the results published, 'be it after some severe editing'. What he considered the politically dangerous implications of Sraffianism cried out for a response 'without self-restraint or concessions to the dominant ideology'.[130] On a more mundane level, he would have found it heartless to scrap contributions or disappoint Langston's heirs by giving up on publication.

Mandel's concern about the perspective of some neo-Ricardians reflected his involvement in the Eurocommunist debate about different models of communism and the doctrine of the dictatorship of the proletariat. Marx's theory of the state was at issue here, a theory to which Mandel adhered absolutely. The twentieth century, from Germany in 1918 to Chile in 1973, had shown that a revolution in which the bourgeois state apparatus remained intact would be crushed by that same apparatus. The repressive state was a key question that Mandel thought the Eurocommunists ignored 'at the price of loss of liberty and life'.[131] He collected his thoughts on the subject in *From Stalinism to Eurocommunism*, first published by Maspero in French in 1978.[132] In this book, despite the title's implication, Mandel also analyzed Communist parties outside Europe.[133] He sketched the gradual development of the parties from dependence on the Soviet bureaucracy to loyalty to bourgeois parliamentary democracy, from Bolshevism to national communism. This was a return to Bernstein, Kautsky, Bauer and Hilferding, a process of 'social democratization' very comparable to what classic German and Austrian social democracy had undergone at the time of the First World War. Mandel thought it a new stage in the crisis of Stalinism.

In Eastern Europe and the Soviet Union these developments had evoked both irritation and expectation. Reform-minded Communists found support in the criticism of the so-called excesses of the dictatorships. The convergence between the Communist opposition in the East and Euro-communism did not escape Mandel. He argued hopefully that the debates about socialism and democracy 'inevitably get transported into Eastern Europe and the Soviet Union . . . They deal hammer blows against bureaucratic monolithism. They are motors . . . of the coming political antibureaucratic revolution.'[134]

Mandel made an emphatic distinction between Eurocommunism's adaptation to social democracy and imperialism on the one hand and its criticism of bureaucratic dictatorships on the other. 'It is perfectly . . . consistent to support . . . anticapitalist struggle, and at the same time to support every struggle of the oppressed masses in the workers' states.' Criticizing the bureaucracy only strengthened socialism. Mandel strongly opposed the revision of Marx's theory of the state that was taking place within Euro-communism.[135] He considered electoralism, gradualism and reformism to be the ingredients of a strategy doomed to defeat, as he told Roger Garaudy.[136] Garaudy had been a Eurocommunist from the beginning and had been expelled from the French Communist Party for his criticisms. Yet many in left-wing circles were wondering if there was an alternative to class collaboration, the modern version of Kautsky's 'strategy of attrition' that had taken the guise of 'historic compromise' in Italy and of 'anti-monopoly alliance' or 'advanced democracy' in France. In 1980 Mandel had to admit that the idea of a revolutionary response was evoking no enthusiasm at all among Western European workers.[137]

Mandel's position in *From Stalinism to Eurocommunism* was a particularly defensive one. He polemicized against social democratization, class collaboration and theoretical revisionism. The text quickly lost its relevance. It would have been otherwise had Mandel concentrated less on the ideology and strategy of the Eurocommunist parties and instead explained why they had changed sociologically and to what extent this reflected a more profound restructuring of the working class. Such a study would have been less time-bound. Only when he realized that the time of political upturn was past did Mandel come to study these questions.

He worked on a sequel to *Late Capitalism* that was to be a synthesis of capitalism in its period of downturn. This had to be more than an update of his original dissertation. He aspired to anticipate the new evolution in its entirety by investigating the dialectic of the long recessive wave and the sociological, ideological and political structures of the working class. What were the possibilities for revolutionary change? What new elements characterized the subjective factor? What was the relationship between the breaks in the continuity of the labour movement and the continuity of the working class? What was the role of the new social movements? And after a century of nation-centred organization, was an internationalization of resistance ahead?

But Mandel was no longer in his prime. In December 1993 he had a heart attack, after which two hours of work a day was prescribed as his limit. The projected book, to be titled *A General Theory of Waged Work, the Workers' Movement and Socialism*, was never completed.[138]

Revolution in Poland

Though by the early 1980s hope for a breakthrough in Western Europe was waning, the disintegration of Stalinism caused some excitement. Only the location and the players had changed: the charismatic Walesa and his opponents Gierek, Jaruzelski and Brezhnev had driven Marchais, Berlinguer and Carrillo from the stage. In August 1980 strikes at the Lenin shipyard in Gdansk led to the birth of the independent trade union Solidarity, which, with its 10 million members, shook the foundations of the bureaucratic world in Poland and beyond. The headline in *Inprecor*, the International's fortnightly news magazine, read 'The Start of a New Era' and continued: 'The ongoing confrontation has placed political revolution on the agenda.' The regime's concessions were overwhelming, but Charles-André Udry issued an editorial warning:

> If [the bureaucracy] is now agreeing to everything, it is only to achieve a quick normalization so as to be better able to organize a counter-offensive and, as in the past, buy off, divide and violently suppress the irreconcilable portion of the movement.[139]

The bureaucracy had not yet lost, Udry said, nor had a new Poland yet been born — a warning that was borne out by General Jaruzelski's coup on 13 December 1981. All too soon, Udry saw his intuition proven right. Solidarity was banned, the mine workers of Upper Silesia were fired upon and 40,000 union members imprisoned.

Udry was closely connected with the issue of Poland. Others in the International were similarly concerned, such as the twenty-three-year-old Jan Malewski, originally from Warsaw, where his parents worked at the university and had been part of the dissident intelligentsia in the 1950s and '60s.[140] Not a party member, Malewski's father wrote for the critical weekly *Po Prostu* in 1956, publishing a study of class-consciousness among Warsaw factory workers. He committed suicide in 1963. In 1970 young Malewski moved to Paris with his mother, a psychologist involved with an international investigation into human intelligence. Three years later, at the age of sixteen, he joined the French section of the International, following a strike at his high school. His membership was kept secret so that he could continue travelling freely to and from Poland, where he was taken into the clandestine Polish cell. He attended the regular meetings of the Eastern European Commission of the International, whose members included Hubert Krivine, Catherine Samary, Charles-André Udry, Bogdan Krawchenko and Peter Gowan. Krawchenko was a Ukrainian from Canada; Gowan was a British political scientist, a leader of the British section (IMG) and associated with *New Left Review*.

In 1975 Malewski and Mandel had met for the first time, in London, where Mandel was speaking about the Czechoslovak revolution after 1968. Malewski maintained that after 1956 in Hungary and Poland and 1968 in Czechoslovakia, the role of intellectuals was played out. Mandel disagreed, impressing Malewski, who knew Mandel's writings through and through.

Malewski travelled to Poland three or four times a year and while there he helped distribute bulletins produced in Paris. Swedish comrades would smuggle a hundred or so copies across the border in a camper. Malewski provided envelopes and addresses, and the Swedes would mail them. It was not a terribly professional operation. The comrades in Czechoslovakia, also few in number, had at least had enough structure to distribute material themselves.

With its eight or so members, men and women, the Eastern European Commission was little more than a discussion club, and their influence in Poland was limited to contacts with a few intellectuals and activists. Among these were the historian Jan Jozef Lipski, one of the founders of the Workers Defence Committee (KOR) in 1976; Jerzy Jasinski, a progressive Catholic who taught at the University of Warsaw and kept his clandestine archives hidden in a forest; and KOR member Jan Lytinski, who, along with Adam Michnik and others, was considered by the university's CP leadership to be part of the 'airborne troupes' because they unexpectedly appeared every-where. Others were Alexander and Barbara Labuda, both in their thirties, Romance language scholars and members of the International who had returned to Poland from France in 1973. They had connections with the KOR but gradually withdrew from Trotskyism. In 1989 Barbara Labuda was elected to the Polish parliament for Solidarity, and in 1996 she became a minister in the Kwasniewski government.

For years Malewski consulted on the phone with Jacek Kuron and Adam Michnik in connection with his work for *Rouge*, the daily paper of the French section. Jacqueline Heinen, now a sociologist and professor at the University of Versailles, but then an actress in the circle around filmmaker Andrzej Wajda, director of such movies as *Man of Marble* (1977) and *Man of*

Iron (1981), was present at the founding of the KOR. Heinen spoke fluent Polish and knew all the attendees. The KOR founding statement, received via telex, appeared the next day in *Rouge*.[141]

The group also maintained ties with veteran activists like Badowski in Krakow, who was too ill to play an active part, and Ludwik Hass, an impoverished and unemployed historian. The colourful but inflexible Hass knew jails inside and out, in both the Soviet Union and Poland; there was no moving him. He spoke disapprovingly of a Khomeinization of the working class, a Polish sickness that was transforming Solidarity into a Catholic, anti-communist organization. Hass was a critic whom Mandel preferred to bypass. Through its involvement with Kuron and Modzelewski in the 1960s, the International enjoyed some authority in Poland, and Mandel did not want to waste its prestige, though just then Kuron was trying to wash himself clean of all Trotskyist stain. Walesa was anything but a Trotskyist, but as Mandel confided to a comrade, 'What does it matter, if millions of workers are in motion; then we mustn't busy ourselves seeking out small, pure groups but simply support the revolutionary dynamic of the whole.'[142] But how? In Poland the International had no members, let alone an organization.

Yet the contacts they had made were useful. The strikes in the summer of 1980 did not come as a surprise. As early as February *Rouge* had published an interview with Andrzej Gwiazda, a leader at the Gdansk shipyards.[143] And in the months of June, July and August Malewski was reciting the list of strikes with growing admiration and enthusiasm.[144] Even Radio Free Europe relayed his well-informed reporting.[145]

There was great excitement in the International. Eastern Europe and anti-Stalinism formed part of the Trotskyist identity, and the 'Polish test' gave a concrete turn to the debate over Eurocommunism. True to character, the Communist *L'Humanité* mainly saw in the strikes the hand of anti-socialist forces.[146] The Trotskyists, despite their enthusiasm, had only limited insight into what was taking place on the Baltic coast and in the Silesian minefields. How was consciousness developing? How quickly and in what directions? And what part did socialist tradition play? Provisionally, Mandel concluded that the course of the struggle would be determined by international relationships of forces and that practical solidarity was the highest priority.[147]

The continuing mobilizations strengthened Mandel's optimism and fed his belief that political differences were bound to emerge in Poland. An Eastern European section of the International finally seemed close at hand. Was this mere wishful thinking? His longing for it was so strong that Mandel readily succumbed to overenthusiasm. Malewski recalled conflicts centred on this in 1981. He proposed that they do a first-hand investigation in

Poland, but Mandel refused the invitation. He would never be able to get a visa, he said, which Malewski considered a dubious excuse.[148] In any event, Malewski's comments caused Mandel little concern. Both were convinced that a breakthrough was imminent and no sacrifice too great to accelerate the process. Poland was the greatest material effort ever for the International. From August 1981 they published a Polish edition of *Inprecor*, which was miniaturized on Bible-thin paper after Jaruzelski's coup. Between 1,500 and 2,000 copies of each issue were printed and packed into 1-kilo cans labelled 'duck fat' or 'orange juice', or stuffed into boxes of Nesquick or freeze-dried soup, fifteen to twenty-five copies per container, depending on the number of pages. These were passed on by the Swedish comrades. After some of these were arrested, German comrades were used, which was more complicated because of the additional border crossing. Soon there were pirated printings for distribution in editions of thousands of copies.[149] The main editors were the energetic Jan Malewski and Zbigniew Marcin Kowalewski.

Malewski had come in contact with the forty-year-old Kowalewski – or rather with his ideas – in June 1981 while in Poland for a month.[150] Kowalewski was part of the Solidarity leadership in the large industrial city of Lodz. He argued for the formation of workers' power in the workplace and for active strikes in which the workers kept working but took control of the production process.[151] The comrades sought contact with him through Gerry Foley and then through Jacqueline Heinen. Kowalewski was prepared to write for *Inprecor*, and the first number was distributed at Solidarity's national congress in Gdansk in September 1981.[152] Five hundred copies had been photocopied in A4 format. Malewski, Heinen and Kowalewski were soon the key figures in the International's Polish work.

The three shared Mandel's optimism, but other members of the Eastern European Commission found that optimism impossible to swallow. One of these was the thirty-five-year-old Catherine Samary, an economist and Yugoslavia specialist. Alain Krivine had recruited her to the International in 1963 when she was eighteen and studying in Paris at the Sorbonne. There she had been part of the Communist Party opposition, having joined the party three years previously in her birthplace Cannes. Travelling with the Communist youth organization in East Germany, she had been put off by the Stalinist symbolism she saw; those songs and statues made the first dent in her communist faith, which was finally broken beyond repair when she looked for debate in the party and observed its lack of openness and democracy. Samary wanted to know if the International had a section in the Soviet Union. From her youth she'd been fascinated by the Russian Revolution; Krivine had just explained its degeneration to her. Though he admitted there was no Soviet section, his eloquence in the car outside her Latin Quarter apartment was effective; she unhesitatingly joined the organization. An alternative to Stalinism that also opposed capitalism – that became her life's motto. In this, her heart and head were united.[153]

In the 1970s Samary specialized in Yugoslavia with Mandel at her side. She was impressed by his undogmatic thinking about societies in transition: they were no longer capitalist but not yet socialist. Any one-sided concept was unacceptable because it oversimplified contradictory and unclear situations. Yet in Poland her mentor now seemed to be violating this methodological golden rule. Weren't contradictory features being hidden behind his one-sided and overoptimistic presentation of the facts?

Samary attended the September 1981 Solidarity congress. When she returned not only singing its praises but also mentioning the great influence of the Catholic Church and in general the contradictory nature of workers' consciousness within Solidarity, she was reproached with a lack of confidence in the Polish working class.[154] This critique was provoked by fear of demoralization and above all supported by a conception in which the workers' consciousness was first and foremost determined by the objective situation and not by religious or Stalinist traditions.

This sort of thing sounded all too familiar to Samary, who had in Hubert Krivine not only a life partner but also an ally. He too had been accused of pessimism when he produced a critical report on the Argentinean PRT-Combatiente at the beginning of the 1970s. Hadn't it also been said then that not everything should be revealed because that could cause despondency? The group's positions on the issue gradually diverged, making a doubting and questioning minority of Krivine, Samary and Peter Gowan, who sensed that the Polish reforms could have contradictory outcomes. Mandel was on the other side, with Malewski, Heinen and Kowalewski in his camp. The impatient Polish comrades claimed to have the only truly close connection to the real situation because they knew the language. They were full of optimism about the anti-bureaucratic revolution and full of hope that they would finally have an Eastern European section.

Mandel and his allies exerted their authority with great fervour, as Winfried Wolf discovered. Wolf, a thirty-two-year-old German who in 1977 had co-authored with Mandel a study on the 1974–75 recession,[155] wrote a two-volume analysis of the 'long Polish summer' brought down on Wolf the charge that he was an unqualified outsider who had no right to address the question. Wolf suspected his critics of a 'spirit of petty competition'. He felt himself completely abandoned by Mandel and wounded at being compared to 'an Australian comrade writing about a demonstration in

Bonn'. He responded pointedly that in Poland there was neither a section nor a sympathizing organization on hand to ask for an opinion.[156]

When General Jaruzelski, in collaboration with the Kremlin, declared war on the Polish working class during the night of 12–13 December 1981, Kowalewski was in Paris. He had come at the invitation of the French trade union movement and had met with Mandel the day before at a safe address somewhere in the city. After the Czech Petr Uhl, Kowalewski was the second leading dissident from the Soviet world to have been won over to the Fourth International.

No Trotskyist had doubted that a confrontation was looming in Poland. In February Mandel had let a friend in East Germany know that he feared that 'it will not end well because of the [Soviet] Big Brother'.[157] In the late summer *Inprecor* wrote, 'It would be an illusion to imagine that . . . bureaucratic power in decline can be reconciled with the workers' power that is spreading more and more . . . In the long run they're irreconcilable; the one cannot survive without eliminating the other.'[158] Conservatives had also speculated openly about a bloodbath if Solidarity continued to demand power.[159] But what weight did the contending forces actually have? Who would attack – and when and where? No one knew, and few were worrying about it. Weren't the state and the Party powerless? Furthermore, Polish soldiers would not fire on Polish citizens! This was a concept that doomed the Solidarity leadership to passive waiting during the weekend of the coup. Zbigniew Bujak, Solidarity chair in Warsaw, told *The New York Times*: 'It was becoming clear that the authorities were planning a sizeable operation . . . But we never thought it would be as serious as this.'[160] Kowalewski explained in Paris that he had anticipated a confrontation only later in the winter. He acknowledged his naïveté. Here and there technical preparations had been made, such as an emergency plan in case of arrests and an underground printing press, for example in Lodz. But although the active strike had grown in popularity, even the most revolutionary current had 'nothing to propose on "the struggle to win over the army"'.[161] With so strong a movement, the Poles had thought that the army stood no chance. Kowalewski, a newly minted Trotskyist, said that had been an illusion. Now considered an enemy of the state and a counterrevolutionary in his own country, he was permitted to remain in France.

During those weeks Mandel dragged himself back and forth, from speaking engagements to rallies. Gisela's health had worsened dramatically, which did not stop him writing day and night.[162] Three weeks before her death, Gisela wrote to Karola Bloch that she had never before seen her husband so discouraged 'about the fact that we are so feeble and can do so little'. Ernest had taken account of a possible Russian invasion but 'without support from the Warsaw Pact countries which had already massively drawn their own lesson'. He had hoped that 'the proud people and their good army would have mounted resistance in order to throw the Russians out. That Pole would shoot against Pole however – at a moment's notice, whoever gave the command – came as a surprise and a shock.'[163]

During those days the political and human dramas in Mandel's life drew closer together than ever before. While he continued to count on a revolutionary breakthrough in Eastern Europe, focusing and increasing his literary and propaganda efforts to this end, Gisela was left in an increasingly oppressive isolation that ultimately proved fatal. His aloofness from Gisela's suffering and his denial of raw political reality coincided cruelly.

11

Socialism or Death

Immediately after the 13 December 1981 coup, Charles-André Udry and Hubert Krivine began the debate over the defeat of the Polish reformers. Krivine pointed to ideological weaknesses, while Udry – following Mandel, Heinen and Kowalewski – drew consolation from the might of the 10 million Solidarity members. Though the movement had suffered a defeat, it was not yet crushed; its strength and experience still made resistance on a massive scale possible.[1] 'For the working class, the loss of self-confidence would be the greatest defeat', Mandel said, but Jaruzelski and Brezhnev had been unable to inflict that decisive blow.[2] He ascribed the coup to a lack of revolutionary leadership.[3]

Early in 1984, a resolution on Poland was proposed, intended for the International's world congress the following year.[4] Mandel had asked Kowalewski to write it, admiring his level-headedness and considering no one better informed.[5] Since December 1981 Kowalewski had been the key figure in the Solidarity Coordinating Committee, which aided victims of repression and sent assistance to the underground resistance. He had the status of Solidarity's unofficial spokesman and maintained contacts with the underground leadership. They included Jan Pomorski, active in the radical Lublin group and a university lecturer there; Stefan Priekarczyk, who distributed the Polish *Inprekor* and was connected with Sigma, a critical group at the University of Warsaw; Wladyslaw Frasyniuk; and Jozef Pinior, who represented Lower Silesia in the Provisional Coordinating Committee (TKK), the clandestine national Solidarity leadership.

In December 1982 a rumour surfaced in the TKK that Kowalewski was an agent of the secret service, which led the five-member TKK to break contact with him. Was the rumour a provocation by the Polish and American intelligence services? At a subsequent meeting, Jozef Pinior, who had not taken part in the TKK's decision, convinced the leadership of Kowalewski's integrity and laid the issue of his trustworthiness to rest.[6]

The Poland resolution was an extensive document; its thrust was that the fighting strength of the working class was still intact. This optimism conflicted with the views of Krivine, Samary and Gowan. Udry, too, was more and more dubious about the idealization of Polish workers, whose radicalism was too readily interpreted as anti-bureaucratic, socialist consciousness.[7] Krivine summed up the criticisms: 'The movement is not everything; the goal also counts.'[8] Mandel reluctantly concurred, against the wishes of Kowalewski, who refused to accept a critical amendment to the resolution from Krivine and Samary. Upset at so much intransigence, Mandel left, slamming the door of the meeting room in Paris's Gare du Nord station.[9]

Yet Mandel still rejected Krivine's position, which was that the issue of taking power in Poland had never been brought up. Mandel considered this view incorrect, one that would inevitably result in a self-imposed limitation, like the one Jacek Kuron imposed on Solidarity. Krivine denied that he was genuflecting to the conciliators of the Workers Defence Committee (KOR) who had held back from revolution for fear of a Soviet invasion.[10] He recognized that a crisis had developed prior to December 1981 and that there should have been some consideration of the possibility of taking power. But that alone would not have made victory a certainty. It would have required a situation of dual power and the arming of the workers, which the Soviet Union would not have tolerated. It was unrealistic, therefore, to keep silent for fear of discouraging the workers. The Soviet threat would always haunt them. Mandel had done well to bear the possibility of an intervention in mind and to prepare for it. All the more since the events in Poland had had no influence at all on the Soviet proletariat, let alone led to divisions within the Red Army or the CP. Only in such circumstances could Mandel rightly have argued 'that one could not fool the masses into imagining that Soviet intervention could be avoided'.[11] But even the Polish army showed no symptoms of disintegration. That would have required a revolutionary leadership supported by the majority of the people. 'But what could be done if there was no such leadership?'[12] Krivine thought exaggerated optimism a bad counsellor and saw no evidence of a new revolutionary upturn.[13]

A phantom section in Poland

In 1981 there was no sign of a revolutionary leadership, acknowledged and ready for its task. Solidarity would not form such a leadership, if only because of the disproportionate influence of their economic experts, who embraced a market orientation. Naturally Mandel would have nothing to do with self-proclaimed leaderships lacking mass support. But could he resist the temptation to imagine that a genuine leadership was emerging? He yearned for a Polish section of the International and considered it plausible to begin with a modest group, which could multiply many times over in a subsequent upsurge.[14] The wide distribution of the Polish *Inprekor* testified to the opportunities for revolutionary Marxism. Krivine and Udry had grave doubts about a Trotskyist group in Poland; it was impossible that such a group would develop spontaneously.[15] If it emerged at all, it could only be a product of Western Trotskyist sects offering their aid along with their ready-made formulae. In exchange for money there were Poles prepared to pay lip service to the movement, but this would always be a form of corruption.

It was a great surprise to the International's leadership in the spring of 1985 when Kowalewski and Malewski passed on an announcement from Poland of the formation of the POR-S (Coordinating Committee of the Workers' Opposition).[16] In the same year, from what had originally been an editorial collaboration among four papers,[17] a political-labour group emerged. It had around a hundred members and a national centre.[18] Nine months later, in September 1986, Paris received the first issue of *Zryw* (Our Way), billed as the official publication of the Polish section of the Fourth International, linked to the POR-S.[19] The group had grown to a thousand members, the most prominent being Stefan Piekarczyk, born in Scotland where his father had served as a soldier in the Second World War but living in Poland since 1978, and Eugeniusz Kundruciuk, originally from Gliwice.

Kundruciuk had visited Paris in June. His trip had been fully subsidized, but – mysteriously – he did not appear at the appointed time and place. He only checked in two days later. He was lodged in a safehouse in the heart of Paris, where he could discuss the new section undisturbed for several days with Kowalewski, Malewski and Heinen. On the last day of his visit, Kundruciuk spoke at Mandel's home on Rue des Meuniers with the leaders of the International Bureau and pressed for their support. Mandel gave him a reproduction of Diego Rivera's mural painting of Trotsky and Lenin from the presidential palace in Mexico City. Only the pseudonymous Simon, who knew all the ins and outs of underground political work, and the Spaniard El Moro cast doubt on Kundruciuk's credibility.[20] Simon had spoken with him for ten hours.[21] Mandel was deaf to their suspicions. He did consider, because of Krivine and Udry's advice, that it was best not to move too fast on the question of public recognition of the section but to keep it under consideration.[22] Charles-André Udry was notably absent, and he did not believe any of Kundruciuk's extravagant promises. Convinced that the leadership was being taken in, Udry accused the Paris Polish team of triumphalism and promoting a self-proclaimed leadership. Krivine agreed.[23]

He wrote to Mandel, 'Naturally I'm mistrustful, extremely mistrustful. I'll say it again, the only things that you and I can check are the links of our friends here – and they don't amount to anything – and especially the political documents. *These documents do not in any way prove the existence of an organization that amounts to anything.*'[24]

Tensions mounted. 'Sectarian!' 'Crypto-Stalinist!' 'Ultra-revolutionary!' were just a few of the epithets slung about to add force to the arguments. Jacqueline Heinen considered withdrawing from the work altogether: 'I didn't feel capable any more of helping bridge the tensions and oppositions', she said. She was especially concerned about the discord because she was having a relationship with Kowalewski.[25]

Udry was extremely irritated by the fact that the POR-S presented itself as a direct adversary of Solidarity and that Kuron was a constant target of its criticism.[26] Krivine called on Mandel 'to play for time as long as possible'.[27] Kowalewski apologized: 'You have to understand that we have little political experience.'[28]

Udry did not believe that the Poles' sectarianism was merely a youthful error. He had too high an opinion of Kowalewski's capacity and experience for that. Kowalewski, an ethnologist born in Lodz in 1943 and from an intellectual background, had specialized in Latin American social history at the Polish Academy of Sciences between 1969 and 1975. He then worked until 1980 for the Cuban Ministry of Education, where he developed in-depth knowledge of Latin American guerrilla movements.[29] In the 1970s he had been recruited to the Argentinian PRT-ERP by Roberto Guevara, Che's brother, and Julio Santucho, Mario Roberto's brother. This was a crucial period for the hard-line Guevarist Kowalewski, during which he learned to orient himself to the working class as a revolutionary subject instead of to the peasantry. In Poland and later in Cuba he had become familiar with works of Trotsky and of Mandel, with *Marxist Economic Theory* and *Late Capitalism* being 'very important for the formation of my political ideas'.[30] On his return to Poland in 1980 he joined Solidarity and became a member of the executive for the Lodz region, with 470,000 members. He was the initiator of the radical movement for workers' self-management. At the first Solidarity congress in the fall of 1981 in Gdansk, he was recruited to the International by Heinen and Samary. Udry could not imagine that such a heavyweight could stray so far from reality and be so gullible.[31]

The phantom stalks Paris

In December Kowalewski was again confronted with a rumour that he was a secret agent. Udry was the supposed source. For the second time in four years doubts were cast on his integrity. On his own initiative Udry began an investigation.[32] He used a courier to gather information about the POR-S and sent him off with a list of questions to ask Polish insiders.[33] Udry was not the only one with doubts about Kowalewski's trustworthiness, but no one would express them openly. Mandel tried to prevent Udry from going ahead; on a visit to Geneva he warned that no scandal should be created. Udry responded by saying that he was only saying openly what others were spreading as rumours. He wanted an investigation of the POR-S. But because this would have been perceived as an attack on Kowalewski in any case, the only way to do it was to target Kowalewski directly, with an investigation of the group as the obvious next step.[34]

The situation was absurd. At a mid-December meeting Heinen brought up the rumours: 'Come on, out with it!' She called on those present to express their suspicions.[35] Only Mandel reacted. Aware of the explosive situation, he said she had no right to denounce comrades' unspoken thoughts without any proof of what those thoughts were.[36] A ghostly rumour was making the rounds, against which Kowalewski could not defend himself. Ten days later the accusation was out in the open. Kowalewski saw a letter in which Udry asked a former comrade to send writings by Kowalewski from his Latin American stay: 'This will make it possible to better understand some aspects of [Kowaleski's] thought. His views are fairly unusual among independent Polish trade union activists!'[37] This was an astonishing letter, with its scarcely veiled invitation to supply damaging information. The recipient informed Kowalewski,[38] and he presented the letter directly to the Bureau of the United Secretariat, along with commentary expressing his surprise: 'A strange affair, I'd like to hear your reaction as soon as possible.'[39]

Kowalewski felt that Udry was becoming obsessed with his professional knowledge of armed struggle,[40] that he conjectured a relationship between Kowalewski and a 'specialized state apparatus' that could only exist in Cuba. When pressed, Udry admitted that he took Kowalewski to be a Cuban agent and considered it possible that he had gone to Poland as a provocateur. An investigation got under way, and rapidly gained momentum once the message reached Paris that the POR-S had disintegrated – and the supposed section of the International with it. As Piekarczyk reported from Warsaw, that was because Kundruciuk and his cohorts had apparently made off with all the funds, and their stories had been lies and deceits. 'I don't know what the ex-comrade [Kundruciuk] has told you, but don't be fooled by his megalomania and mythologizing . . . The affair is extremely serious.'[41] Jan Malewski immediately left Paris for Silesia, on his own initiative because the Bureau would not agree to send anyone due to the danger of arrests.[42] He travelled by car to Gliwice with Serge, a French sympathizer who worked at Renault. There they found a comrade who had previously met Malewski in Liège. They saw all sorts of materials, from which Malewski deduced that the whole business stank. The office looked like a brothel, and the section and its paper – a bizarre combination of contradictory ideas – were the concoctions of a set of swindlers out for money.[43] It was certainly a tragedy, but it was at least a consolation that Kowalewski's name had been cleared. The investigation, which included sources as far away as Cuba, absolved him of all blame. There were no grounds to connect Kowalewski with the swindle, but the Polish debacle made the political question – why comrades who had so little knowledge of reality were taken seriously for so long – all the more pressing. Hubert Krivine was quick to draw conclusions: 'The foundation of the [imaginary] Polish section may not have followed necessarily from the line of the last World Congress, but it was made possible by it.'[44] Hadn't he warned that, apart from the fantasies of the Paris team, the climate in Poland had been anything but fruitful?[45] 'If we continue to follow this logic, then in the best case we'll gain nothing and in the worst only sectarians and swindlers.'[46] Mandel had to admit that Krivine had been reasonably realistic.[47]

Human tragedy

The imaginary Polish section, the imputations against Kowalewski, the hurtful conflicts – not everyone could live with the outcome without bitterness. Personal relationships had been put to the severest test. Everyone in the Bureau had been aware of Udry's suspicions except Jacqueline Heinen. Was this because she was a woman in a relationship with Kowalewski? Was she therefore considered unable to form her own opinion? Her disappointment over what she perceived as manipulation was so deep that she broke all ties with the International.

In the beginning Mandel and Kowalewski had enjoyed a good relationship. Mandel was usually conscientious and averse to paternalism, but in the debacle around the Polish section his attitude had changed. Kowalewski was disappointed that Mandel had considered him implicated in the Kundruciuk affair.[48] In subsequent years as well, their relationship was troubled by differences of opinion on such topics as the national question in the Soviet Union and Gorbachev's role.[49] Even so, shortly before his death in 1995 Mandel proposed to the World Congress of the International that it name Kowalewski as a permanent member of the International Executive Committee. As Kowalewski put it, 'It was obvious that from his point of view . . . former disputes with me were over.'[50] Kowalewski had returned to live in Poland in 1989.

Mandel had always maintained close ties with Hubert Krivine. In addition to politics, they shared the same scholarly and philosophical interests; their bond was a warm one. But the controversy left its mark on Krivine. He had seen his critique rejected as pessimism and pomposity on the part of someone who knew nothing, spoke no Polish and was a 'liquidationist'. Yet he had gone to the trouble of staying up for many nights studying all the documents of the Polish section.[51] He said that 'Mandel wanted too much to hear what he hoped for.'[52] When Krivine expressed his mistrust at the sudden birth of the Polish section, Mandel had commented laconically, 'It's not all that surprising considering the dimensions and the engagement of the movement during the recent past. It's normal that under these circumstances political differences arise and that part of the movement radicalizes in our direction.' He added that the same thing had occurred in Italy in 1945–48, in Portugal and Spain in the 1970s and in Brazil in the early 1980s.[53] There was something rather objectivist in his belief that a section was bound to emerge out of the Polish mass movement. His belief did not change in 1986 when the group turned out not to exist. Krivine found objectivism and predictability anything but synonymous, and by the time of the Thirteenth World Congress in 1991 he had broken with Mandel. Unlike Udry, Krivine had always kept the debate about Poland separate from the question of whether Kowalewski was trustworthy. Nevertheless, Malewski and Kowalewski worked to block his re-election to the Control [Appeals] Commission of the International. They saw Krivine, even more than Udry, as the evil genius of the affair.[54] Mandel knew better, yet he did not feel moved to defend Krivine – a member for thirty-five years, twenty of them in the leadership – against the slander. This was unacceptable to someone like Janette Habel, who, in a rage, called Mandel a coward.[55] Mandel's subsequent praise for Krivine had a bitter taste: 'Your personal probity and honesty are for me above any suspicion of factionalism.'[56] Krivine rejected the proposal at a subsequent congress to nominate him to the International Executive Committee: 'I urgently request you not to begin any election campaign on my behalf.'[57] He never returned to the Eastern European Commission.[58]

Though the empty shell of the POR-S and the phantom section justified Udry post-facto, he had to acknowledge having treated Kowalewski impermissibly. As he admitted twenty years later, 'Not only because the accusation was incorrect; the approach itself was wrong!'[59] He should have immediately voiced his suspicion in the fall of 1986 and not first have tried to collect evidence on his own in order to back up an accusation. Then he would not have had to remain silent in December 1986 when Heinen called for openness about the situation: 'I harmed comrade [Kowalewski] without giving him the chance to defend himself. The same with [Heinen] and

[Malewski]. The atmosphere was dire.'[60] Udry considered himself obliged to leave the leadership of the International. It was painful to conclude that he had 'failed so miserably, and done the comrades wrong'.[61]

Thus began a period of depression for Udry. First Latin America and then Poland and the Kowalewski question had been extremely stressful. He left Paris and returned to Lausanne.

In the early 1980s the International reached its organizational high point with more than 10,000 active members.[62] Several times as many who had been members for a shorter or longer time still maintained a connection with the International, even at a distance. The leadership in Paris decided to organize a strong political centre with about twenty full-timers. As it would turn out, this was swimming against the current, though that was hard to recognize in the early 1980s. The Sandinista victory in Nicaragua, the fall of the Shah in Iran, the unprecedented struggle against the cruise missiles in Europe, and the deep economic recession of 1979–81 – all these promised exciting times. But after 1983 Reagan and Thatcher were sounding a neoliberal awakening in the industrialized world, while the defeat of Solidarity in retrospect meant the end of any prospect of anti-bureaucratic revolution in Eastern Europe. The largest trade union in history had turned to the right, politically and ideologically.

Though the climate in the International's Paris office was open and intense, life there was debilitating. Disappointments, the shift into a defensive phase, conflicts, members' advancing age, and social marginality – all these took their toll. The Swede Tom Gustafsson died in 1987, at the age of thirty-nine.[63] Udry returned to Switzerland; Daniel Bensaïd and Miguel Romero left the International staff in order to deal with the setbacks of the French and Spanish sections.[64] These departures signalled the fading of the ambitions that the International had cherished at the decade's beginning. At the same time they showed that no centre could be created without the participants' maintaining organic connections with their own social milieu.

Apart from the revolution itself, the Fourth International was Mandel's greatest love.[65] It came first for him and meant far more to him than an academic career. Understandably he viewed centrifugal tendencies with anxiety, and he gradually began to feel as though the current generation lacked sufficient discipline. He was looking for continuity, and there was little of it, because of the nature of the period. Lack of continuity made dialogue difficult. Mandel became less open to discussion and preferred to focus on his own concerns. He was more often in Brussels than Paris and participated less and less in the Amsterdam educational institute. The new life that he began with Anne Sprimont in 1982 fitted into this pattern. Nor was he unduly concerned with Charles-André Udry's departure, though their bond was close and Mandel considered him his spiritual son and political heir.

The last battle

Mandel's prestige had been damaged by the Polish complications. It did not recover when he made it clear that he viewed the disintegration of the Eastern Europe and Soviet regimes with undiminished optimism. Mikhail Gorbachev's becoming general secretary of the Soviet CP in March 1985 filled him with hope: 'I'm completely convinced that the developments in the USSR are the most important since May '68.'[66] The politics of perestroika, an attempt to modernize the economy, were accompanied by economic decline and growing social inequality. At the same time glasnost, the new openness that gave Gorbachev so positive an image in the West, facilitated the expression of social and ethnic tensions. These paradoxes brought Mandel to the conclusion that after almost a half-century, anti-bureaucratic revolution was once again on the agenda for the Soviet Union. Was the USSR on the brink of a renewal of the debate between Trotsky and Bukharin and a reassessment of Rosa Luxemburg? These lyrical recollections of the past had little to do with reality. But could Mandel go on without these delusions? His marginal position forced him to trust in the spontaneity of the masses and their will to free themselves from the Stalinist yoke. This gave him an overly optimistic picture, at once the product of hope and fear. He hoped that he, at sixty-eight and with all sorts of physical ailments, might still be witness to the revolution; he feared that a restoration to capitalism was still one of the possible outcomes.

As early as 1933 Trotsky had warned that the unbridled growth of bureaucracy 'must lead inevitably to the cessation of economic and cultural growth, to a terrible social crisis and to the downward plunge of the entire society'.[67] Mandel thought this prediction had been confirmed by what happened between 1989 and 1991, despite the unorthodox delay of several decades.[68] In his analysis of the Soviet economy, stagnation and waste played a prominent role; not dynamism but immobility had become its hallmark.[69] The economy had been trapped in such bureaucratic disorder that the Soviet Union had to watch the third technological revolution and the transition from extensive to intensive growth pass it by.[70] Mandel thought the pragmatic wing of the bureaucracy was trying to save its privileges by restoring capitalism, but that could only happen after a crushing defeat of the working class. If Mandel were to be believed, 'This defeat [had] not yet taken place'[71] and was not about to.

In his 1989 book *Beyond Perestroika: The Future of Gorbachev's USSR*, a study of glasnost and perestroika published simultaneously in London and Paris, Mandel sketched four possible scenarios for what Gorbachev had set in motion.[72] He did not devote a single word to the possible restoration of capitalism. Ten years earlier, in *Revolutionary Marxism Today*, he had considered a restoration extremely unlikely and even called a gradual reintroduction impossible: 'To believe otherwise is, to use an apt phrase of Trotsky's, "to unwind the reformist film in reverse".'[73] Now he investigated as the most probable variant a combination of a lagging standard of living with growing dissatisfaction leading to mass actions and self-organization. 'The slogan "All power to the Soviets" will be revived in its classic form . . . A new communist leadership will emerge from the working class . . . The political revolution, in the classical Marxist sense of the term, will triumph.'[74] He ended his book with a citation from Trotsky's *The Revolution Betrayed*, in which Trotsky predicted the replacement of the bureaucracy with a democracy of soviets:

> 'Ranks will be immediately abolished. The tinsel of decorations will go into the melting pot. The youth will receive the opportunity to breathe freely, criticize, make mistakes and grow up. Science and art will be freed of their chains. And, finally, foreign policy will return to the traditions of revolutionary internationalism.'[75] That is how it will be.[76]

This was a romantic final chord to a work that not everyone considered Mandel's most convincing synthesis. For two days in Paris Udry tried to convince him not to publish it, but Mandel it was adamant. He told a Dutch sympathizer that he believed

> the number of intellectuals and youth in the Soviet Union who identify with Marx and Lenin is greater than in any Western European country . . . Did you know that the official [youth organization] Komsomol of Lomonosov University has published *The Revolution Betrayed*? The circle has now turned 360 degrees and returned to its starting place: it was there that the Left Opposition was born in 1923 . . .[77]

Mandel imagined that he could have some influence on Gorbachev, and even discerned a radical anti-bureaucrat in his opponent Boris Yeltsin.[78] Gorbachev, however, was not open to 'socialist' ideas. He did not respond to the international campaign for rehabilitation of those who, like Leon Trotsky, had been condemned at the 1936–38 Moscow trials.[79] Trotsky remained persona non grata even for the liberal wing of Soviet bureaucracy.

But what did that matter? Rebellions were also emerging outside the Soviet Union, in East Germany, Czechoslovakia and Romania. In the fall of 1989 millions of demonstrators were proving that in East Germany the anti-bureaucratic revolution was at the point of breaking out.

In the summer of that same year Mandel was turned away at the border checkpoint from West into East Berlin as an undesirable alien. The Stasi, East Germany's secret service, had classified him as a 'neo-Trotskyist' and an 'enemy of the Soviet Union'. He was also on record as a 'soberly calculating person whose responses show a certain sensitivity'.[80] Otherwise, the report said, no 'specific hostile acts against the GDR are to be expected' from him[81] – not a description to provoke anxiety.

Soon afterwards the Stasi's organization fell apart. A few days before the fall of the Berlin Wall on 9 November, Anne and Ernest received a warm welcome in East Berlin. They arrived at West Berlin's Tegel airport, taking a taxi from there to the East Berlin border. Their visit was the product of a partnership between the Free University of Brussels and Humboldt University in East Berlin. There had been an earlier exchange of scholars, but only that autumn was the time ripe for convincing the Humboldt group working on Marxism-Leninism to invite Mandel.[82] He gave two lectures on long waves at the Academy of Sciences and Humboldt University to hundreds of students who overflowed into the aisles; Anne was glad to find a place on the floor.[83] Every innovation got attention, and Mandel's name was not unknown among East German Marxists even though his books, hidden away in the forbidden sections of libraries, had only been available to a few specialists. A few days later he attended a debate at the university between the ruling Socialist Unity Party's (SED) reformers working at the university and Gregor Gysi, a brave defender of dissidents as yet unknown as a politician. With his nose for talent, Mandel asked curiously who this Gysi was.[84]

In a meeting with fifteen to twenty East German dissidents, Mandel enquired intensively about conditions in Berlin and elsewhere. Bruno Coppieters, a political scientist from Brussels and Mandel's assistant at the Free University, was his companion during these days. He was struck by the groping, improvisational way Mandel and his interlocutors explored East Germany's future. They asked him about everything. What did a democratic planned economy mean? What were the prospects for the weak East German economy? What should be done about the non-convertible East German mark? Mandel spoke about the possibilities of barter trade, for example with left-wing communities in Southern Europe. East German workers could build social housing in Rimini or other left-wing coastal resorts and holiday there in exchange. Mandel was assuming East Germans' clear desire to maintain the GDR as an independent country. Apart from the

question of whether the workers really wanted to holiday with colleagues in
Rimini or other left-wing resorts – weren't they longing for opportunities to
travel on their own? – the country's problems could scarcely be solved in
this manner. But who did have a blueprint?

Activity in the streets became more and more exciting, with the thrilling
series of demonstrations in Berlin, Dresden and Leipzig that preceded the fall
of the Wall. Mandel was an eyewitness and walked in the processions,
carrying a folding stool in case his fatigue exceeded his enthusiasm. As he
wrote for *International Viewpoint*, 'The upsurge of the mass movement
rocking the GDR has assumed the dimensions of a real revolution. This
movement exceeds anything that has been seen in Europe since 1968, if not
since the Spanish revolution.'[85]

On 4 November, one million people demonstrated in East Berlin alone.
The fact that the overwhelming majority were workers and youth, with all
their combativeness and creativity, was a 'hallmark of every true revolution',
as Mandel wrote. He had counted more than 7,000 posters, 'and not one
urged German reunification . . . Rosa Luxemburg's descendents proved
themselves worthy of her. Today history has proclaimed that she did not
fight in vain; that she did not die in vain.'[86] Mandel listened intently to the
speeches that afternoon but paid even more attention to the demonstrators.
He considered the catcalls that greeted Markus Wolf, ex-chief of the secret
service and a reform-minded follower of Gorbachev, a sign of radicalization.

Memories of Rosa Luxemburg inevitably coloured Mandel's hopes,
conjuring up a continuity with the struggle that had begun with the
German revolution of 1918. He declared to a surprised public in the Paris
Mutualité that the workers had taken up the thread that had been broken by
Luxemburg's killing: 'The citizens' committees in Berlin and Dresden are
continuing the tradition of the council movement in Bavaria and
Saxony . . .'[87] He recounted that he had not seen a single slogan for
German national unity. But his listeners wondered if this was because of
people's conviction or their caution, possibly even fear. Wasn't Mandel
exaggerating? He could not have encountered more than the embryos of
real self-organization. Modesty was not his strongest point in those days. He
was certain that the movement would respond to a classic dialectic: 'An
initial movement from below in the USSR would evoke radical reforms
from above, which in their turn would lead to a broader autonomous mass
movement in the USSR and help to unleash a genuine revolution from
below in the GDR and Czechoslovakia.'[88] Poland was missing from this
sunny picture. Since the dreadful results of the process of economic
liberalization under way there were already visible, shouldn't he have taken
Poland into consideration?

Mandel did visit Poland in December 1989 for the first time since 1956, flying into Wroclaw from Berlin. Jan Malewski was waiting for him and together they crisscrossed the country, with Malewski acting as chauffeur, secretary and translator in one.[89] Mandel spoke at rallies at the universities in Katowice, Warsaw and Wroclaw and in Upper Silesia, every time to an audience of 600 to 700 people; they also met with members of the Communist Party and Solidarity. The East German revolution dominated the discussions. Mandel held that, more than anyone else, the German working class – the heirs of Marx, Engels and Luxemburg – deserved the Left's confidence. He was deaf to criticism, including that of Jozef Pinior, who had recently joined the International. With the best will in the world, Pinior could not discern in East Germany any self-organization worthy of the name. He objected that as far as experience went, the Polish workers had proved themselves and hugely overshadowed the German working class, who had been quiet as mice since 1953. Pinior was disappointed in Mandel, whom he had valued for his independence and creativity. Now he saw an old man who took no time to listen and – even worse – had succumbed to an idealization of a people for whom the slogan 'We are the people' had in November already been superseded by the slogans 'Germany, the only fatherland' and 'We are one people.'[90] Still, in late December, Mandel – admittedly ever less hopefully – spoke of

a chance for a world historical turning point; what had been missed in 1918–1921/33 with tragic consequences for all humanity: Hitler, Stalin, Hiroshima – could now be realized . . . Even if there were only one chance in a hundred, we would have to devote everything to the effort to reach it: so much depends on it.[91]

One chance in a hundred? Countless people expressed their disbelief at the Paris Mutualité a few days later. Possessed by hope and without hesitation or doubt, Mandel had chosen a path that few could follow. A staggered Daniel Bensaïd called it 'a pathetic rally [which] in hindsight seems like a harbinger of death'.[92] Yet Mandel's emotion was understandable. For him the revolution had always been based on the objective interest of the working class in the broadest sense. When that perspective was lost, he appealed, following Marx, to the ethical duty to struggle against every form of exploitation, humiliation and oppression – an inescapable duty, founded on the axiom that '*man is the highest essence for man*':[93] 'To struggle against inhuman conditions is a right and a human duty, independently of any scientific knowledge or future expectation.'[94] That principle resounded in

Mandel's words, though these burst like soap bubbles above the heads of his bemused audience.

From the end of the 1980s Mandel regularly appealed to moral commitment to justify solidarity with the oppressed. He did not shrink from painting such human tragedies as nuclear war, genocide and ecological destruction in the darkest colours. In Mandel's rhetoric this angry messianism replaced the classic dichotomy between socialism and barbarism with an apocalyptic choice between socialism and death – socialism or the destruction of humanity.[95]

If socialism still had a future, it was in any event not in East Germany. In the beginning, his need to encourage others had prevented Mandel from seeing the reality, but the facts spoke for themselves. In March 1990 the International plainly admitted,

> For the time being the overwhelming political tendency is towards a rapid unification of Germany via the absorption of the GDR by the FRG. The masses tend to give priority to the unification of Germany regardless of its social and economic content . . . A capitalist unification of Germany would represent a serious defeat for the working class in the GDR, the FRG and the whole of Europe . . .[96]

A few weeks later in an East Berlin debate with Gregor Gysi, today a leader of Die Linke (the Left), Mandel confronted an audience of over 1,000 with the fact that imperialism was on the offensive and that the left had a long way to go in a tough struggle against the current. The audience showed disbelief when he held social democracy responsible for the rise of Stalinism; the hall reverberated with catcalls. It was a gloomy report that appeared on the front page of *Neues Deutschland* the following day. This was the daily paper that just a year earlier, as the organ of the Central Committee of the ruling SED, had been in the habit of treating Trotskyists as medieval popes did heretics.[97]

In defence of Marxism

The real situation made Mandel depressed and anxious. In 1990 he probed the depth of the crisis in an essay on the future of socialism:

> The crisis of socialism is above all a crisis in the credibility of the socialist project. Five generations of socialists and three generations of workers were convinced that socialism is possible and necessary. Today's generation is not convinced that it's possible.[98]

Mandel considered it an unparalleled crisis, the horsemen of the Apocalypse running amok, threatening wars, ecological disasters, hunger and poverty. Yet he remained an optimist; in his eyes, striving for freedom was what made humans human.[99] But his optimism did not lead him to trust blindly in the future. If in Marxism, following the words of Antonio Gramsci, there had to be optimism of the will together with pessimism of the intellect, then Mandel had never lacked for rational pessimism.[100] This was even more the case after 1990, when the crisis of the socialist project made a pessimistic outlook more credible. Mandel warned in his 1992 book *Power and Money: A Marxist Theory of Bureaucracy*, 'If irrationality continues to prevail', for instance in the areas of nuclear weapons and the environment, then 'humankind is doomed to extinction'. Who could call a halt to self-destruction? Where was the shining future? Mandel felt no more than a moderate optimism in posing as 'the fundamental argument in favour of socialism' the fact that 'humankind can no longer endure the costs of aggregate irrationality'. A more defensive justification of the socialist dream hardly seems possible. Mandel was feeling the growing army of 'pessimists-cum-misanthropes' – they considered themselves realists – breathing down his neck.[101] He predicted that 'those fools who really believe that socialism is finished and that we are witnessing "the end of history" will get their comeuppance'.[102] He could not deny that the initiative lay in the enemy's hands. The socialist workers' movement had not been in so bad a state since the 1930s.[103]

The East European thaw had awakened intense hope in Mandel; its reactionary turn made him bitter. He feared the theoretical implications of the restoration of capitalism. Did the collapse of the Soviet model mean the historical bankruptcy of Marxism? Were new developments proving Marxism out-of-date? Was the Marxist model of society unrealizable and the hope for it unrealistic? A positive answer to any one of these questions would make Marxism irrelevant.

In *Power and Money*, the study of bureaucratic degeneration on which he had long been resolved, Mandel applied himself to a heartfelt defence of Marxism.[104] The failure of bureaucratic socialism was the failure of the bureaucracy, not of socialism. In a broad approach, Mandel investigated the social and historical roots of bureaucracy in the capitalist state and in the mass organizations.[105] He refined his analysis, not only to comprehend the debacle in Eastern Europe and the Soviet Union but also to avoid any possible repetition. He did not cover up his own past mistakes, such as having underestimated the disastrous effects of Stalinism on working-class consciousness.[106] He did deny the socialist character of the Soviet Union, but he recognized clearly that Marxism would lose its meaning if every struggle to create a society in Marxist form was bound to degenerate following the pattern of the Russian Revolution. Mandel defended the revolution against the swelling ranks of its critics, who said it had not been a mass action but rather a totalitarian seizure of power.[107] In the spirit of Rosa Luxemburg, whom he so admired, he commented on what he saw as the revolution's shortcomings, particularly in 1917–21.[108] This critique was broadened in his book *Trotsky As Alternative*, first published in 1992 in Germany – to his delight, by Dietz Verlag, the former publisher of the East German ruling party. Those who were inclined to idolize 'the Old Man', as they lovingly called Trotsky still, were surprised by Mandel's razor-sharp analysis of 'the dark years 1920–1921',[109] the years in which Trotsky, too, had been unable to withstand the siren song of substitutionism, replacing working-class power with the rule of the party.

The Fourth International at risk

Mandel did not try to fill the ideological and moral vacuum left by Stalinism's collapse with his writing alone. He considered it his duty to ensure the political and organizational continuity of the Fourth International, his life's great passion. Given his age and health, this commitment became ever more strenuous. In addition to finances, Mandel was concerned about the selection and integration of new leadership. When Charles-André Udry and others left Paris, there remained only five or six comrades of the twenty who had constituted the full-time leadership, too few to guarantee even a minimum of activity. Mandel tried everything to overcome the climate of scepticism and attract new leaders to Paris, an aspiration that he realized by doubling the number of full-timers in 1990. He waved off the objection of critics that the organization's finances were too shaky for this.[110] In large measure the crisis of socialism had bypassed the International, 'a miracle when you see what's happening with the far left internationally, not to mention the "respectable left"'.[111]

Wasn't Mandel reacting too casually and underestimating the crisis in the credibility of socialism and its consequences, even for the International? He swore that in the forty-five years that he'd been part of its leadership, the International had always 'met its responsibilities to the comrades who had served it over a longer term'. Moreover, according to Mandel, the International had withstood worse crises: its isolation had been greater in the years 1939–42 and even greater in the period 1948–55. He displayed shock at the scepticism and confusion he found even in his own circle.[112]

'But François [Vercammen], you too, you who are so sensible!' The Belgian Vercammen was speechless in the face of Mandel's theatricality, but

Mandel shrank from nothing when putting across his ideas: he used threatening body language, paternalistic bullying, and more.[113] 'Who still believed in the future of socialism in 1940? . . . Were we wrong not to yield, even though our forces were much smaller than they are now?' But Mandel's dramatic pleas could not ease the organization's financial crisis.[114] For many this was cause enough to rethink the future, that of the International and their own. In the early 1990s Vercammen looked for work outside the International; the grinding job of a party full-timer had 'dried him out'.[115] Mandel moved heaven and earth to get him to change his mind:

> You are an exceptionally skilled . . . leader . . . I think it a total waste of talent . . . to lose your time with a bourgeois job, even half-time. We guarantee you . . . an income and pension for the rest of your life.

Mandel was honest enough to leave open the question whether the International would have the required financial means in ten or fifteen years. 'That is a question of political judgement . . . Your own judgement, since it's about your future. My advice: do not doubt it for a moment.'[116]

Mandel's lines were theatrical, but they were not feigned; they were the expression of a genuine and deep regard. But they were also spoken in the service of a cause that was his whole life. Vercammen, a full-timer since 1966, yielded to them; others did not.

The end

Mandel paid a heavy price for his exertions, psychologically and physically. He appeared exhausted, a sad contrast to the lively, dynamic man of earlier times. Wherever he went, he took a folding stool so he could rest his back when necessary. His trips to Latin America[117] and South Africa in 1992 wore him out despite their quiet pace; he avoided sightseeing and visited only a few comrades.[118] Udry was concerned about his gloominess.[119] Optimism had been ingrained in Mandel; it was an infectious part of his thinking and combativeness. Now it seemed to be eroded by fear for the future, over-shadowed by the dark thoughts of an intellect that was sinking into the depths because of the crisis in the credibility of socialism. That crisis was marking the end of his life, and he was aware of it.

On the afternoon of 6 December 1993, the seventy-year-old Mandel collapsed a few metres away from the Willemsparkweg entrance to the IIRE, where the United Secretariat, the executive leadership of the International, had just completed their deliberations on finances and Russia. Back inside the Institute, Mandel made light of what had happened to him; he did not need a doctor. But an ambulance was called and rushed him to the Free University Hospital, where the doctors diagnosed a severe heart attack.[120] That same evening Anne came to Amsterdam, and the deathly ill Mandel was transferred to a hospital in Haarlem. He remained in intensive care for over three weeks.

Back in Brussels, Mandel needed time for recuperation, time that passed too slowly to suit him. Whenever he had a cardiological examination, he interpreted the result as better than it was. To prove that nothing serious had happened to him, he wanted to travel again soon after getting out of the hospital.[121] He remarked jokingly that Anne would serve as his life insurance. She accompanied him on each trip, made sure he rested and encouraged him to adopt a different, healthier diet. But there was a continual tension between the will and the deed. He confessed to Jan Philipp Reemstma that he looked forward to visiting Hamburg, where 'the crispest Peking duck was served'.[122] He was scarcely able to return to political or scholarly activity.[123] He avoided meetings, afraid of getting carried away by his temperament.[124] On invitations to colloquia, for contributions to scholarly publications or to take part in advisory committees he steadfastly scribbled: 'Refuse – health.' He was reserving his precious time for 'writing key books and documents'.[125]

In May 1994 he told Udry that the cardiologist said he could do five hours' work a day and again take planes.[126] This was a new opportunity to complete his long-planned *General Theory of Waged Work, the Workers' Movement and Socialism*, a book he said would be a theoretical tour de force comparable to *Late Capitalism* or *Power and Money*. As he told Vercammen, 'If God spares my life, after that I'll prepare a book with the general (provisional) title "Marx and Marxism at the Turn of the 21st Century".'[127] Meanwhile he proposed to Udry and the French economist Michel Husson that they investigate the new finance capital that was developing along with economic globalization: 'I think that the material is on hand and I am presumptuous enough to think that I know the theory . . . With you I can go further than alone.'[128]

But there was no doubt that the study on wage labour took priority. It was an ambitious project that remained uncompleted and failed to achieve the quality of Mandel's earlier work, hampered as its author was by age and illness.

Before his heart attack, Mandel had agreed to a debate with representatives of the US Spartacist League, an obscure group keen on attacking the Fourth International. Mandel's New York friends were not undividedly enthusiastic,[129] and the Paris comrades heartily disapproved.[130] But Mandel said he had no intention of debating; he was preparing a trick for the Spartacists. In addressing their meeting he would take revenge for their abuse of the International and their disruptions of its gatherings. He promised fireworks.[131]

As *New York Newsday* ironically put it the day after the meeting, 'Keep waiting for lefty.' Held in Greenwich Village, the debate had been attended by 500 people. The newspaper continued, 'One of the most endearing truths about our city is that no matter how obscure the subject, you can fill an auditorium with New Yorkers ready to argue about it.' Mandel spoke for thirty minutes, seated in front of a red banner, too weak to stand. According to the reporter he was 'reading in a mumbling monotone . . . without lifting his eyes from the text'.[132]

Back in Brussels, Mandel worked conscientiously to articulate his political credo in defence of revolutionary Marxism against what he termed 'Trotskyist sectarianism'. The resulting brochure contained a remarkable appendix, a bibliography of around a hundred titles written by members of the International and distributed in over 3 million copies, a measure of the intellectual strength of the movement. He did not neglect – 'in all modesty' – to include his own works as well but did omit mentioning that many of the listed authors had left the ranks of the International.[133] Comrades seemed slightly embarrassed by Mandel's engagement with the Spartacists – so much attention to so insignificant a sect. Michael Löwy warned, 'This obscure American sect will only remain in the memory of the workers' movement thanks to your polemic.'[134] Mandel wanted to stick to his guns. The document was too important 'for the self-awareness of our movement and its public image'.[135] Above all, he was in a hurry; this concerned the International, the keystone of his life. Unlike Trotsky, he had led no revolution, but at the core of his being was the drive 'to create the necessary organizational conditions for it'.[136] This was the greatest and also the most difficult challenge of his life.

The Fourteenth World Congress of the Fourth International took place at the beginning of June 1995. Held in Belgium, in Wépion near Namur, this was the congress that frankly confronted the crisis of socialism. Mandel attended, though he could only move with difficulty. He scarcely participated in the deliberations. Hastily and almost unprepared, he paid tribute to deceased comrades, a traditional beginning to every congress. He made only one other contribution, emotional and ominous. For the rest, he kept to himself in hopeless silence. He was staying in a hotel several kilometres from the meetings, and when Udry brought him back in the evenings he was exhausted. It was obvious to Udry that this would be Ernest's last World Congress,[137] a sad thought formed in desolate surroundings.

In April 1995, a few weeks earlier, at his Brussels home, Mandel had lured Vercammen upstairs. In half darkness, dimly lit by two low-watt bulbs, he launched into his plea for sympathy: 'I won't live much longer.' Then he made Vercammen swear to remain faithful to the International.[138] In those days he called Udry and Vercammen his very best friends, in an expression of affection free from rivalry.[139]

Mandel could no longer read for any length of time, and his handwriting had become shaky. He cancelled papers and journals, and in the remaining few that he read, like *The Times* of London, his attention went to the obituaries. It was warm and sultry on 20 July 1995. On Thursday afternoons Mandel usually went out to buy *Die Zeit*, but that day his wife suggested that he stay inside and said she would go buy it. When she got home Anne did not hear the usual welcoming call from upstairs. It was totally still. She felt something had happened, ran into the conservatory and found Ernest lying on the floor by the open doors, breathing heavily. He was unconscious, and the ambulance personnel could not revive him. He died without waking again.

The morning of 21 July, in an Aegean Greek harbour town named Horefte, Michel Raptis reminisced to Adolfo Gilly about his first meeting the youthful Mandel in Paris during the Occupation. Gilly had met Mandel often but knew little about the European Trotskyist underground – he had spent the war in his native Buenos Aires. Raptis told Gilly that he had left the International in 1965 after an intense conflict, but almost thirty years later had returned to the fold. The maestro and his former pupil Mandel had embraced each other at their reunion: 'There are a fair number of things for us to discuss.'[140]

At 2:30 that afternoon Gilly answered the phone and heard a shaken Raptis on the line: 'I have to give you sad news: Ernest has died.'[141]

On 30 September 1995, under a warm autumn sun, around 1,200 comrades accompanied the urn with Mandel's ashes to the fighter's final resting place in the old Père Lachaise cemetery in Paris.[142] The ashes were buried at the foot of the Mur des Fédérés, where the last combatants of the Paris Commune had been executed in 1871. The urn with Gisela's ashes, transferred from the Columbarium, was placed next to Ernest's, as he had requested.[143] The funeral was a militant demonstration carried out in his spirit, without grief or mourning. Key figures from Mandel's life were present: Michel Raptis, Petr Uhl from Prague, Bala Tampoe from Sri Lanka, Mohammed Harbi, Perry Anderson, Robin Blackburn, Winfried Wolf, Hubert Krivine, Jakob Moneta, Charles-André Udry, João Machado and François Vercammen. Gregor Gysi, Rosario Ibarra and Fausto Bertinotti sent remembrances; Alain Krivine and Livio Maitan spoke; red banners waved in the wind; the 'Song of the Martyrs' and 'The Internationale' resounded. It was a farewell to a life dedicated to the revolution, a farewell to a prophet dedicated to faith in humanity.[144]

12

Conclusion

Nobody wins – but I want to be there at Trotsky's victory celebration in the summer when the tables and chairs are out in the sun.

— Finnish poet Heimo Saarikoski

Self-confident, convinced of his historical mission, hard on himself and others, averse to material privileges and indifferent to the trivial sorrows and pleasures of life – these are some characteristics of Trotsky's personality as described by Ernest Mandel at the end of his own life.[1] It is not difficult to discern a self-portrait in these words, expressing the strengths and weaknesses of a life dedicated to the revolution.[2] Yet it is little more than a rough impression. It doesn't do justice to the fully rounded person, scholar and revolutionary Ernest Mandel was.

Too few of the man's qualities are visible, such as his rhetorical talent and his exceptional power to convince. This was a man who, to a small circle, could expound memorably, lucidly and charismatically on the Russian Revolution or the Italian factory council movement. At the same time he was a gifted orator who spoke easily to stadium crowds of 20,000 during the Portuguese Carnation Revolution. Nor does this portrait reveal the man who continued to express his historical optimism despite the greatest personal and political disappointments, who kept his belief in the human urge to resist and who never stopped praising the beauty of civilization, his only homeland. Here was a man who, though part of a small minority, considered it his task to bring Marxism to life. He wanted to transmit not dogma but culture; his aim was not to preserve doctrine but to develop theory. Finally, that incomplete picture does not shade in the tragic shortcoming that frustrated Mandel's endeavours at key moments: his need to conciliate, to reach a compromise rather than risk losing all.

In gauging the sources of Mandel's life, three mainsprings seem central. First, he was moved by an instinctive defiance of injustice and oppression.

His father's open-hearted solidarity and the example of the German refugees he met in the 1930s inspired him to live his life for the working class and its emancipation. Second, he was stimulated by an equally instinctive need to investigate reality as a prerequisite to changing it. His rationalism fit in easily with the classical Marxist tradition, in which no distinction in principle is made between science and ideology: both are seen as tools the working class must use for its liberation. Third, he learned at a young age to comprehend the world from the perspective of class struggle, to view the world and its history as a contradictory process, in which evolution and revolution, revolution and counterrevolution compete for dominance with results that cannot be predicted with certainty.

After the collapse of the Soviet Union in 1990, Mandel noted, 'Five generations of socialists and three generations of workers were convinced that socialism is possible and necessary. Today's generation is not convinced that it's possible.'[3] This bitterness apart, Mandel's devotion to the five generations of socialists and three generations of workers remained unshakeable. He wanted to be the theoretician, the ideologist, the historian and the organizer for these generations. And for a significant part of the generation of '68 he achieved that ambition. He embodied a bond with the creative, pre-Stalinist Marxism that had existed until the 1920s, and was thereby able to contribute greatly to the cognitive framework of the activists of May '68.[4] His was a far-reaching influence, thanks to his broad network of contacts and his world-encompassing vision. The period from 1965 to the 1980s formed the high-water mark of his creative thought and political influence.

Mandel possessed exceptional intellectual and literary talent. He remained creative to the end of his life and made efforts to fathom both late capitalism in its downturn phase from the 1970s onwards and the restoration of capitalism in the Soviet Union and Eastern Europe after 1990. He wrote prolifically throughout his life, yet he never responded to those who urged him to write his memoirs or an autobiography. Was this a sign of modesty? In any case, it reflected his insight into the limited role the individual played against the background of historical patterns, an insight that was neither fatalism nor a surrender to historical determinism.

Like Rousseau, Mandel believed in the goodness of humankind. He was an optimist, a dreamer of the revolution. Like Ernst Bloch, he typified *homo sperans*, aspiring humanity, inspired by 'the principle of hope', the prophesy of possibilities.[5] His belief in human creativity and solidarity had no bounds. As early as 1952 he wrote, 'Trotskyism is above all the belief, the unshakeable trust, in the capacity of the proletariat to take its fate into its own hands.'[6] This thought made Mandel into a revolutionary Marxist, who, like Trotsky, gave the subjective factor a leading role in overcoming what he considered the tragedy of the twentieth century: the antithesis between 'the ripeness of the objective revolutionary conditions and the unripeness of the proletariat and its vanguard'.[7]

Mandel was often accused of dogmatism, unjustly insofar as he gave theory the status of hypothesis requiring verification or falsification by empirical reality. This position – following Marx's motto 'Doubt everything' – was no dead letter for Mandel. This is evident from his willingness to re-evaluate the revolution in Tito's Yugoslavia and from his study of late capitalism, which broke with the prevailing Marxist theory that an increase in productive forces was impossible under imperialism. The picture of economic stagnation, more or less correct for the period 1914–45, was belied by the postwar boom, and since 1948 Mandel had devoted himself to analyzing this situation.[8] His efforts were not without faults, sometimes serious ones. But he found himself in good company with Marx, Engels, Lenin, Trotsky, Luxemburg and lesser lights, all of whom had tasted the bitterness of even worse defeats. It is not faults that determine the failure of a scholarly method but the inability to correct them. To exorcise political wishful thinking, he avoided a direct connection between more pragmatic political-theoretical efforts, directed towards problems of the here and now, and scholarly-theoretical work. For the latter, he felt, theories should be formulated on a much broader scale of time and space. Mandel emphasized that anyone who neglected the difference would make mistakes in formulating theories 'even if he is politically correct (or almost correct)'.[9]

Mandel was an economist with a strong ideological commitment. In this respect he was no exception. Even such conservatives as Joseph Schumpeter, Friedrich Hayek and Milton Friedman were motivated by the desire to improve human well-being. As Gunnar Myrdal stressed, 'Useful economics can never be free of ideology and value judgements. The problem is to keep them in harness.'[10]

Mandel worked above all towards synthesis. His area of research was not empirical; he seldom consulted archives or delved into sources, nor did he test economic models. He was not mathematically educated. His was the talent to erect original historical syntheses based on the detailed analyses of others. A thinker formed in an almost classical nineteenth-century mould and an heir to the Enlightenment, Mandel felt at home in many disciplines and was familiar with a literary and philosophical world broader than Marxist culture alone. Yet there was also a weakness hidden in that remarkable talent. Apart from the field of politics, where he contributed to the development of countless people, many of whom considered themselves his heirs, Mandel had scarcely any following in scholarly circles. With a few exceptions, such as his plan to organize an international project on the conjuncture, or his coordination of the defence of Marx's labour theory of value against Sraffa and the neo-Ricardians, he was not interested in leading research projects. Perhaps this was because his theoretical work was too much a vehicle for his political thought, or perhaps because the academic world was not his priority, though he yearned for recognition there. Or it could have been because it is hard to learn to synthesize a group's work cogently for publication. It is clear that he did not train anyone as a historical economist or economic historian.[11] He collaborated with only a very few others, like Winfried Wolf.

Mandel's wide knowledge and agile rhetoric were always highly convincing, yet he sometimes avoided analyzing the situations that were most complex and difficult to explain, taking flight instead in historical examples and analogies.[12] He silenced many critics with hyperbole and apocalyptic metaphors. His partners in dialogue were paralyzed or lost their critical sense because they were mesmerized by his paradigms in spite of themselves. If necessary he cut the ground from under his critics' feet by criticizing himself. Mandel took up the cudgels for an 'open' Marxism, yet the coherence of Marxist theory was so essential to him that his openness consisted of no more than a willingness for dialogue.[13] He seldom collaborated on theoretical issues with representatives from other left-wing currents, with the possible exception of Che Guevara in Cuba. Though sharp in polemics and a master of irony, Mandel showed regard for his opponents; he judged their ideas without resorting to personal attacks. He was not arrogant. Though capable of epic outbursts of anger, he remained always tolerant and inclined towards reconciliation. His old teacher Fritz Besser evaluated him early as sometimes 'irrepressible', but his impatience or cheek was usually of short duration.[14] 'He had the ability to disagree with you . . . and still let you know how much he valued you.'[15] Mandel's empathy helped the young leadership of the International to keep its independence and allowed it to contradict him despite his authority.

Charming and warm in his circle of family and friends, Mandel demanded of himself a strict discipline, which was necessary if he were to have space for any private life where he could live out his passion for literature, music and painting. Rembrandt, Goya, Monet and Chagall were his favourite painters, and he admired Käthe Kollwitz's graphics and sculpture. He also felt at home with architecture and could go into raptures over it. His beaming eyes and bellowing laugh were childlike; he kept such youthful qualities throughout his life. Robin Blackburn, a sociologist and editor of New Left Review, found Mandel unusually exciting when he first met him at a conference in 1963:

Mandel insisted that we take time out from the Conference to visit Canterbury Cathedral; my school-induced reluctance to enter an Anglican place of worship soon evaporated as Mandel discoursed on the fine points of Gothic architecture and the achievement of the artisans who had built the Cathedral – we paused for a moment at the grave of the Archbishop martyred during the Peasants' Revolt, a plaque inviting us to pray for industrial peace. Subsequently I had the pleasure and instruction of accompanying Mandel on a trip to Tenochtitlan – and to canals on the outskirts of Mexico City, which had only recently, Mandel explained, recovered the levels of agricultural productivity achieved in Aztec times.[16]

The Flemish writer Jef Geeraerts said, 'His interests were so comprehensive that he was one of those rare individuals born with a spiritual x-ray vision.'[17] But too often his vision was distracted. Before the fall of the Berlin Wall, Ernest and Anne had visited the Thomas Church in Leipzig, where Bach, the composer he most adored, had been cantor until he died. Ernest would spend scarcely any time looking at it. As Anne put it, 'He would not admit to his feelings, though he was an emotional man. How did that come about? Probably you don't write twenty books if you indulge your feelings.'[18]

Mandel began his theoretical work in the 1950s. He focused most intensely, though far from exclusively, on investigating the history and contemporary development of international capitalism, analyzing the so-called socialist countries and looking into the subjective factor – council democracy, bureaucracy and the revolutionary party. No matter how powerfully he defended the independence of scholarship and approved of the demand that falsifiability be the standard of scholarship, Mandel performed his dual role as intellectual and politician with a 'certain ambivalence', according to the Dutch sociologist Marcel van der Linden, an expert on Western Marxist theories of the Soviet Union, and a sometime member of the International.[19] He said,

> In the mid-1980s, a while after I had broken with the Fourth International, I got a letter from Mandel requesting a private discussion on his next visit to Amsterdam. He wanted to know more precisely why I no longer believed in the concept of the 'degenerated workers' state'. A few weeks later we engaged in a lively and friendly conversation that became increasingly difficult for Mandel . . . He closed the discussion with the words 'If you'll think about it again, I'll do the same.' Since then he never again raised that subject in our conversations or correspondence. It was clear to me that for political reasons Mandel could not revise his ideas: if he had considered doing so it would have led to severe conflicts within the Fourth International.[20]

In his defence Mandel might have suggested that even if he was ambivalent, Van der Linden's conclusion was not logically justified. Why should someone who accepts that in history there exist empirically verifiable – and empirically verified – regularities suddenly become unwilling to test their validity against new, empirically relevant evidence? Mandel had earlier posed this question to the French philosopher Maurice Merleau-Ponty in response to his criticism of the so-called subjectivism of Marxists: 'For someone who thinks he knows the future, individual events have no meaning or importance; the future unfolds, come what may.'[21] Mandel held that behind the criticism was incomprehension of the duality of Marxism, which combines a strict scientific attitude with the moral imperative to fight all relationships and to combat all institutions in which man is a subordinate, servile, mutilated creature. Mandel considered this 'a categorical imperative', which he was never willing to abandon, any more than he was willing to abandon the fundamental value of scientific objectivity.[22] He approvingly cited Trotsky, who, at the start of the Second World War, offered a pregnant summary of the duality in a possible outcome:

> if the world proletariat should actually prove incapable of fulfilling the mission placed upon it by the course of development, nothing else would remain except only to recognize that the socialist program, based on the internal contradictions of capitalist society, ended as a Utopia. It is self-evident that a new 'minimum' program would be required – for the defence of the interests of the slaves of the totalitarian bureaucratic society.[23]

One may assume that Mandel, no less than Trotsky, had been prepared to relinquish a fundamental thesis if he were convinced as a scholar that the thesis was no longer valid in the light of new empirical data. 'As a scholar' must be emphasized: it cannot be denied that there was more than mere ambivalence in Mandel's double role as political thinker-analyst and activist-organizer, between his pragmatic political analyses and his concern for the unity of the International and the quest for the broadest possible resistance. In this study I have frequently mentioned Mandel's hesitations, and sought an explanation of his unwillingness – if not incapacity – to defend the integrity of his convictions, his tendency to compromise at crucial moments. Because of it he made detours into unfounded optimism, as he did in 1989 after the fall of the Berlin Wall.

Michael Löwy has argued convincingly that this reckless optimism was not a product of the optimistic view of humanity on which Mandel's revolutionary humanism was based. It was an optimism, independent of any historical considerations, grounded in the conviction that resisting injustice and striving for freedom are profoundly human.[24] Mandel's anthropological optimism – or optimism of the will, to use Gramsci's term – was counterbalanced by the intellectual pessimism that gave his work such enviable urgency. Löwy correctly characterized optimism as the quintessence of Mandel's being as thinker and activist. 'Without it one can hardly understand such incredible episodes in his life as his two escapes . . . during the Second World War.'[25] But then the following questions must be asked: What was the source of his recklessness if it did not spring from optimism of the will? Can his bold predictions actually be understood in terms of optimism versus pessimism?[26] Mandel made undeniable – even legendary – mistakes, but he was no intellectual adventurer; he was too aware of the destructive power of an economy founded on universal commodification and hunger for profit. He never expressed this more strongly than at the end of the 1980s:

> Capitalism is fast approaching the limit of its adaptability. The periodical transformations of the productive forces into destructive forces are becoming ever more permanent . . . Today's generation is no longer convinced that socialism is possible. Some of them are even sceptical and wonder if it is necessary or sensible.[27]

For Mandel the crisis of socialism was a fact; not a position that an intellectual optimist could easily assimilate.

Any explanation of Mandel's sometimes exuberant optimism must take into account the historical period of which Mandel and the Fourth International were the expression, the century that began with the Second International in the 1880s and ended in the 1980s. This was the century in which the working class grew, developed socially and culturally and gave rise to vast, nationally organized unions and parties. The Fourth International identified with the left wing of this movement and searched for cracks in the hegemony of the traditional leaderships. Its aspiration derived from the conviction that the working class was the only force with the objective power to overthrow capitalism.

Mandel rightly considered that the capacity for resistance could not be mechanically derived from what took place here and now, but that class-consciousness was a function of the experiences of longer historical periods.[28] The question is whether the 1980s constituted such a break in this historical period that the decade disappointed some of Mandel's expectations. In his account of the working class – its composition, growth and consciousness – Mandel pointed, for example, to its enormous growth in numbers and homogeneity since the beginning of industrial capitalism and particularly since the Second World War. He spoke of the growing homogeneity of trade union organization. He also explained, with striking objectivism: 'That is certainly no purely formal development. Whenever we speak of a growing unionization, then at the same time we are speaking of a growing readiness to struggle.'[29]

Two critical comments are called for. One is expressed in a study of the German working class, written in the 1980s, that emphasized that 'the workers as a social class' were indeed more homogeneous but that

> the social significance of class affiliation has sharply declined. The old form of the 'proletariat' is disappearing, due on the one hand to the extension of socio-political insurance against market risks and increasing living standards, and on the other hand to the generalization of market-dependent, alienated wage labour, which in the past almost exclusively characterized the workers.[30]

Secondly, Mandel, by limiting his concept of the proletariat to those performing modern waged work, seems to have ignored unfree and informal labour in Asia, Africa and Latin America, as well as what Marx termed the impoverished 'lazarus-layers' of the unemployed, ill and disabled. Though globalization of the working class was beginning, unfree and informal labour and self-employment remained its most prevalent forms worldwide.[31] This blind spot of Mandel's was the source of errors, when what had been defined in the capitalist metropoles as 'the residue of the old society' grew explosively in numbers during the 1970s and '80s. With mass unemployment, spectacular growth in marginal, informal and precarious work, and the transformation from Fordist-Keynesian relations of production into neoliberal and flexible ones, the trend towards homogenization and strengthening of the working class was reversed. The working class was divided and weakened.[32] Real wages declined while intensification of work increased, and work shifted from the formal into the informal sector. For the second time in the history of capitalism, after the first regression in the economic crisis of 1929–32, the relative growth of the working class slowed. In Europe and North America as well, deregulated labour relations have become normal.[33]

In conclusion, we cannot avoid asking whether Mandel took sufficient account of these changes in the socioeconomic structure. Did his repeatedly expressed belief in the unshaken objective strength of the working class lie at the root of his recklessness? His exaggerated optimism assumed an undeniable urgency, partly through his poignantly formulated catastrophic prophecy: socialism or death. Mandel did not succeed in grasping the nature of the world in which he'd reached old age; his optimism gave way in the face of the peaceful restoration of capitalism in the Soviet Union and the reunification of Germany. As the long historical period that had begun in the 1880s approached its end, he highlighted the ethical dimension of the struggle more emphatically. To the last he tolerated neither fatalism nor resignation; his will to resist continued to rest on his conviction that the class of wage workers would some day free itself from domination. After his death Mandel was critically remembered but also missed. Although his optimism was not always comprehensible in light of the facts, the more the world becomes buried under those facts, the more longingly we recall his optimism and humanism and miss his analyses, his hopes of finding a way out.

Notes

Preface

1 'Greatest Twentieth-Century Economists Poll', in *Post-Autistic Economics Review*, no. 36, 24 February 2006.
2 'Der Trotzkist: Zum Tod von Ernest Mandel', *Frankfurter Allgemeine Zeitung*, 22 July 1995.
3 The informant who used this pseudonym prefers to remain anonymous.

Youth: 'My politics were determined then for the rest of my life'

1 The expression 'the Jewish question' was long used in debates in the Marxist workers' movement to mean Jewish oppression. It was taken to fall under the much broader rubric 'the national question', which refers to people struggling for their national freedom. In this sense Marxists referred to 'the Irish question', 'the Polish question' and, in the nineteenth century, even 'the German question' or 'the Italian question'.
2 I. Deutscher, *The Non-Jewish Jew and Other Essays*, Cambridge, 1968, p. 25.
3 E. Traverso, 'Lev Davidovich Bronstein (Trotsky): The Itinerary of a Non-Jewish Jew', in: H. Mayer, *Außenseiter*, Frankfurt on Main, 1975, p. 428.
4 During the German Occupation, Krakow's 70,000 Jews were forced to live in Kazimierz – their first step on the way to Auschwitz, where almost all of them were exterminated, including Henri's mother, Manya, Simon and many of their loved ones.
5 Author's interviews with M. Mandel, 27 June 2000 and 29 September 2001.
6 H. Mandel, 'Biografische notitie' (Biographical Notes), H. Mandel Archives. An aunt who was married to the diamond worker Piller lived in Antwerp.
7 Krakow, where Henri Mandel came from, had been annexed by Austria in 1846. After the First World War the city became Polish again.
8 C.A. van der Velde, *De ANDB, een overzicht van zijn ontstaan: ontwikkeling en betekenis*, Amsterdam, 1925, p. 551.
9 R. Prager interview with E. Mandel, 12 November 1977, R. Prager Archives, folder 270. 'The Luck of a Crazy Youth, Ernest Mandel Interviewed by Tariq

Ali', in: G. Achcar, ed., *The Legacy of Ernest Mandel*, London, 1999, p. 218.

10 T. Ali interview with E. Mandel (complete text), 1995, E. Mandel Archives, folder 680.

11 Interview with E. Mandel, Jours de Guerre Collection, Centre for Historical Research and Documentation on War and Contemporary Society (SOMA), Brussels, AA 1450.

12 R. Prager interview with E. Mandel, 12 November 1977, R. Prager Archives, folder 270.

13 According to the Antwerp Population Registry, his previous addresses were Van Den Perenboomstraat 3 in Borgerhout; then, as of 23 March 1920, Groote Beer 15. He registered at Lange Kievitstraat 42 on 18 August 1920. He moved later to Waterloostraat 32, where he registered on 23 September 1924.

14 Author's interview with M. Mandel, 29 September 2001. M. Fischer to J.W. Stutje, 30 April 2003.

15 On 5 April 1921, Rosa was again registered in Antwerp, as coming from Frankfurt on Main in Germany. She lived at Marialei 38. Information from the Antwerp Population Registry.

16 M. Fischer, 'Ernest Mandel, tel que je l'ai connu' (Ernest Mandel as I Knew Him), unpublished note, n.d., 7 pp., E. Mandel Archives.

17 E. Mandel, Biographical Note, 26 June 1953, E. Mandel Archives, folder 184. H. Mandel, Biographical Note, 2 July 1945, H. Mandel Archives, folder 27.

18 According to extracts from the registry office, it was at 4:00 p.m. on 7 April 1923 in the Liesenras Hospital, Nibelungenallee 37/41. E. Mandel to C. Rühlig, 19 June 1983, E. Mandel Archives, folder 71.

19 Author's interviews with M. Mandel, 27 June 2000 and 29 September 2001.

20 Waterloostraat 32. The façade was designed by E. Geefs, who also created the neighbourhood Old Antwerp for the World Exhibition of 1894. Houses on the Waterloostraat had no front gardens, nor were they freestanding.

21 Mishee (Michel) Mandel was born in Antwerp on 24 January 1926.

22 E. Mandel statement in *De Internationale*, vol. 39, no. 55, fall 1995, p. 21. Papers from the 1988 Utrecht conference: *Meesters van de westerse filosofie*, pp. 38–40.

23 Author's interview with M. Mandel, 29 September 2001.

24 M. Fischer, 'Ernest Mandel, tel que je l'ai connu', unpublished note, n.d., 7 pp., E Mandel Archives.

25 Before the Second World War the number of French-speakers in Antwerp – particularly in the city centre – was considerable, between 5 and 10 per cent of the adult population. At the start of the 1960s there were still three French daily papers in Antwerp.

26 See reports of Stedelijk Onderwijsgesticht (local educational foundation) No. 3, 1931–32, 1932–33, 1933–34, 1934–35. E. Mandel Archives, folders 184–6.

27 M. Fischer, 'Mandel, tel que je l'ai connu'.

28 *Haagsche Post*, 14 March 1936. J. Jansen van Galen interview with E. Mandel, *Haagsche Post*, 22 February 1969.

29 E. Mandel, Memoir fragment, E. Mandel Archives.

30 Author's interview with the former student J. Debrouwere, 9 April 2002.

31 Author's interview with M. Mandel, 27 June 2000.

32 M. Fischer to J.W. Stutje, 30 April 2003.

33 Honours received by the students of the Royal Athenaeum (Antwerp) in

competitions and daily work for the school year 1940–41, Antwerp, 1941, E. Mandel Archives, folders 184–6.

34 L. Michielsen, 'Admiration et divergences', *La Gauche*, no. 15/16, 1 September 1995. L. Michielsen to A. de Smet, 23 August 1995, A. de Smet Archives. Leo Michielsen taught at the Royal Athenaeum and was later a professor at the Free University of Brussels. At the start of the war in 1940 he joined the Belgian Communist Party. He published regularly on the Belgian workers' movement. J. Debrouwere, ed., *Stappen naar de Verte: Leo Michielsen, leraar, marxist*, Leuven, 1997. In a memoir Mandel wrote about Michielsen: 'One of the best teachers I ever met. His lessons in history permanently imparted to me the basic principles of historical materialism.' E. Mandel, Memoir fragment.

35 J. Craeybeckx to A. Mandel-Sprimont, 2 August 1995.

36 E. Mandel to R. Coeckelbergh, 6 October 1975, E. Mandel Archives, folder 55.

37 A sign of the poverty of the Jewish people of Antwerp is that between 1929 and 1933 the number of families receiving financial assistance for Passover grew from 400 to 1,100. M. Frey, *Een joodse solidariteitsbeweging te Antwerpen: de Centrale, 1920–1940*, Ghent, 1975, p. 41. Other Jewish businesses, such as clothing and leather work, were not spared.

38 H. Mandel, Biographical Note, H. Mandel Archives.

39 M. Fischer, 'Mandel, tel que je l'ai connu'.

40 Papen Putsch: July 1932 coup by Von Papen against the social democratic government of Prussia because of its supposed tolerance of the Communists.

41 'The Luck of a Crazy Youth, Ernest Mandel Interviewed by Tariq Ali', p. 218.

42 Before Hitler seized power there were around 500 Trotskyists. Between fifty and seventy fled from Germany to other countries. There were groups in Prague, Paris, Amsterdam, Antwerp, Basel, Vienna, Liberec (Reichenberg), Copenhagen and London. In 1934–35 the Internationale Kommunisten Deutschlands (IKD), as the German Left Opposition was known from October/November 1933, still had around 200 members. After 1936 the Gestapo struck hard. At the start of 1937 only two groups remained active, one in Berlin-Charlottenburg and one in Dresden. In 1940 there were an estimated 150 German Trotskyists in prisons and concentration camps. W. Alles, *Zur Politik und Geschichte der deutschen Trotzkisten ab 1930*, Frankfurt on Main, 1987, pp. 155, 221, 342.

43 'The Luck of a Crazy Youth, Ernest Mandel Interviewed by Tariq Ali', p. 217.

44 E. Mandel, Memoir fragment, E. Mandel Archives.

45 G. Scheuer, *Nur Narren fürchten nichts, Szenen aus dem dreiszigjährigen Krieg 1915–1945*, Vienna, 1991, p. 120.

46 F. Keller and K. Lhotzky, 'In Memoriam Georg Scheuer', *Archiv für die Geschichte des Widerstandes und der Arbeit*, no. 15, 1998, p. 475. F. Keller, *In den Gulag von Ost und West: Karl Fischer, Arbeiter und Revolutionär*, Frankfurt on Main, 1980, p. 12.

47 G. Scheuer, *Nur Narren fürchten nichts*, p. 120.

48 A. Glotzer, *Trotsky: Memoir and Critique*, New York, 1989, p. 176.

49 Mels to D. Goulooze, 26 November 1933, CPN Archives, folder 1,741.

50 W. Held to L. Trotsky, 1 February 1934, R. Prager Archives, folder 187.

51 F. Besser, *Meine Überlebnisse*, London, n.d., p. 85. E. Lorenz, *Willy Brandt in Norwegen: Die Jahre des Exils 1933 bis 1940*, Kiel, 1989, pp. 151–2. Y. Craipeau, *Mémoires d'un dinosaure trotskyste: Secrétaire de Trotsky en 1933*, Paris, 1999, pp.

116–7. W. Brandt, *Hitler ist nicht Deutschland: Jugend in Lübeck – Exil in Norwegen, 1928–1940*, Bonn, 2002, p. 499. Four German exiles whose passports were not in order were handed over to the Gestapo. These were Franz Bobzien (1906), Heinz Hoose (1909), Kurt Liebermann (1903), all members of the Sozialistische Jugendverband (SJV, Young Socialist League), and Hans Goldstein, member of no party. P. Schneiders, *Het Larense geval: een vluchtelingen affaire*, Amsterdam, n.d. Willy Brandt's deportation to Germany was prevented (cf. E. Lorenz, Introduction, in W. Brandt, *Hitler ist nicht Deutschland*, p. 36).

52   A. Glotzer, *Trotsky*, p. 195.
53   G. Block, officier-commissaris bij de rechterlijke opdrachten (public prosecutor), Confidential report, 20 November 1944. (With thanks to Rudi van Doorslaer.)
54   F. Besser to H. Epe, 12 September 1933, R. Prager Archives, folder 188. Besser was staying with Ms Müller van der Berg, Nieuwe Keizersgracht 18 in Amsterdam.
55   Heinz Epe (pseudonym Walter Held): 1910(Remscheid)–1942 (Saratov). P. Broué, 'Quelques prôches collaborateurs de Trotsky', *Cahiers Léon Trotsky*, no. 1, January 1979. E. Lorenz, *Willy Brandt in Norwegen*. E. Lorenz, 'Heinz Epe – Mitarbeiter von Willy Brandt und Leo Trotzki', in *Widerstand und Verfolgung in Remscheid*, vol. 2, Wuppertal, 1986, pp. 16–26.
56   W. Held to L. Trotsky, 31 October 1933, R. Prager Archives, folder 178. W. Held to E. Ackerknecht, 10 November 1933, R. Prager Archives, folder 187.
57   M. Fischer to J.W. Stutje, 30 April 2003.
58   Author's interview with M. Mandel, 29 September 2001.
59   E. Mandel to W. Besser, 30 January 1992, E. Mandel Archives, folder 81.
60   E. Mandel to W. Besser, 9 December 1991, E. Mandel Archives, folder 81. F. Besser, *Meine Überlebnisse*, p. 70.
61   F. Besser to E. Mandel, 1 March 1969, E. Mandel Archives, folder 43.
62   Ibid. Fritz Besser died in London on 21 October 1977.
63   M. Fischer to J.W. Stutje, 30 April 2003.
64   M. Fischer, to J.W. Stutje, 30 April 2003, V. Klapholz, 'Herinnering' (Recollections), n.d., E. Mandel Archives. Itzhak Ben Zvi was president from 1952 to 1963.
65   Max Laufer had various pseudonyms: Fred Lohenbill, NN, Marcel, Fritz. J. Foitzik, *Zwischen den Fronten: Zur Politik, Organisation und Funktion linker politischer Kleinorganisationen im Widerstand 1933 bis 1939/40*, Bonn, 1986, p. 295.
66   IKD: Internationale Kommunisten Deutschlands (International Communists of Germany), founded in October/November 1933.
67   H. Bortfeldt to E. Mandel, 9 September 1977, E. Mandel Archives, folder 60.
68   H. Bortfeldt to Sehr Geehrter Herr (Most Honoured Sir), 23 May 1977, E. Mandel Archives, folder 60.
69   F. Besser, *Meine Überlebnisse*, p. 2. I. Nissenbaum to Cher Lucien [Sania Gontarbert], 13 August 1945, S. Gontarbert Archives.
70   D. de Winter, *Franz Holz: Kunstenaar op de vlucht voor Hitler*, Breda, 2001. F. Meyer, *Flucht aus Deutschland: Bilder aus dem Exil*, Frankfurt on Main, 1984. S. Goch, 'Widerstand gegen den Nationalsozialismus aus einer Gelsenkirchener Gruppe der "Links-Opposition/Trotzki-Gruppe" mit Verbindung zur SAP', 27 April 1993. Meyer published in *Ruhrecho*, the paper of the KPD; *Lutte Ouvrière*, the paper of the Belgian RSP; *de Nieuwe Fakkel*, *de Rode October* and *de Arbeid*, papers of the Dutch RSAP and the NAS; and *Unser Wort*, the paper of the IKD.

71 D. de Winter, *Franz Holz*, p. 29.

72 G. Block, officier-commissaris.

73 Weber's pseudonyms were Johre, Ernst Zander, Erik Erikson, Wilhelm Lunen, Jo, Joe, Rosch and Dewey.

74 'Joseph Weber: Leben, Literatur, Politik: Eine Einführung', in J. Weber, *'Dinge der Zeit': Kritische Beiträge zur Kultur und Politik*, Hamburg, 1995, pp.16–28. M. van der Linden, 'The Prehistory of Post-Scarcity Anarchism: Josef Weber and the Movement for a Democracy of Content (1947–64)', *Anarchist Studies* 9, 2001, pp. 127–45.

75 L. Trotsky, *Oeuvres*, vol. 15, pp. 46–7. M. Stobnicer, 'Des Émigrés dans le grand vent: Les IKD et la construction de la IVe Internationale', *Cahiers Léon Trotzky*, no. 22, June 1985, pp. 41–55. Walter Held also regarded Johre as 'one of the most talented and most able of the entire International, a man who can perform theoretical tasks extraordinarily well.' W. Held to 'Dear Comrade Trotsky', 4 September 1937, R. Prager Archives, folder 190.

76 L. Adorno, 'Der Kirchenkampf und die Politik der Arbeiterklasse', *Unser Wort*, vol. 3, no. 6 (58), June 1935.

77 Ibid.

78 'The Luck of a Crazy Youth, Ernest Mandel Interviewed by Tariq Ali', p. 218.

79 N. De Beule, 'Met de loupe op zoek naar de Belgische trotskisten in de Spaanse Arena', *Belgisch Tijdschrift voor Nieuwste Geschiedenis,* vol. XVIII, no. 1/2, 1987. The RSP, the Belgian section of the Fourth International, numbered around 700 members between 1932 and 1937.

80 The POUM (Partido Obrero de Unificación Marxista) was founded in 1935 by Andrés Nin and Joaquin Maurin.

81 F. Besser to Dear Heinz, 2 March 1937, R. Prager Archives, folder 151d.

82 'The Luck of a Crazy Youth, Ernest Mandel Interviewed by Tariq Ali', p. 218.

83 M. Fischer to J.W. Stutje, 30 April 2003.

84 N. De Beule, 'Belgische trotskisten', p. 113.

85 J. Last, *Mijn vriend André Gide*, Amsterdam, 1966, pp. 50–6. A. Gide, *Return From the USSR*, London, 1937.

86 J.W. Stutje, 'Tussen hoop en angst: De communistische jaren van Jef Last', *Maatstaf*, no. 10, 1994, pp. 58–71. J.W. Stutje, *De man die de weg wees*, pp. 132–4.

87 J. Last, 'Welche Beweise gibt es?', *Informatie- en persdienst*, no. 4/5, August/September 1937. Reprinted from the Russian *Bulletin de l'opposition*, no. 54/55, March 1937.

88 H. Schulze Wilde, *Buch der Freunde: Komitee zum 70. Geburtstag von Harry Schulze Wilde*, ed. L. Kolawski, n.p., n.d.

89 F. Besser, *Meine Überlebnisse* , p. 73.

90 F. Besser to Gil [Leon Sedov], 19 November 1937, Hoover Institution, B. Nicolaevsky Collection 357/55.

91 L. Sedov to Brink [Fritz Besser], 22 November 1937, Hoover Institution, B. Nicolaevsky Collection 357/56.

92 F. Besser, *Meine Überlebnisse*, p. 75.

93 In justification of the trials the philosopher Ernst Bloch wrote, 'This is what has called forth the united energies of the Nazi beast, the Japanese pirate state and the hate-filled Trotskyists. To make light of, to expose to ridicule and even

traduce the trial against these machinations testifies to an inconceivable mindset whose like must be sought in vain in the entire history of political emigration. The final result of these Trotskyist activities obviously could not be the world revolution . . . The outcome could only be in spite of everything the introduction of capitalism in Russia.' E. Bloch, *Vom Hasard zur Katastrophe: Politische Aufsätze (1934–1939)*, Frankfurt on Main, 1972, p. 179. A. Münster, *L'Utopie concrète d'Ernst Bloch: Une biographie*, Paris, 2001, pp. 207–15.

94 'Lion Feuchtwanger über den Prozesz', *Rundschau*, 30 January 1937. This contains the passage: 'There is no question that the guilt of the accused is clearly proven. Beyond that whoever is not in bad faith must admit that Trotsky was the intellectual and in part real author of their crimes.'

95 H. Almond, 'Der Schutzgeist der Stalinschen Justiz: Eine Abrechnung mit Lion Feuchtwanger', February 1937, The Houghton Library, bMs 13.1 (17,185) Trotsky Collection.

96 Ibid., p. 5.

97 Ibid., p. 29.

98 Brink to Trotsky, 4 May 1937, Houghton Library, bMs Russ. 13.1 373 Trotsky Collection.

99 H. Schaked to Werter Genosse, 1 May 1937, Houghton Library, bMs Russ. 13.1 (13,808) Trotsky Collection.

100 Circulaire Genossenschaft Dynamo Verlag (Zürich), G. Scheuer Archives, folder 934.

101 Braun [Erwin Wolf] to Lieber Brink, 2 April 1937, R. Prager Archives, folder 151d. Trotsky completed the original Russian manuscript, *Tsjto takoe SSR i kuda on idiot?*, in 1936.

102 Only three issues appeared before the war. Publication ceased in 1938 due to the events in Austria and Czechoslovakia and Stalinist persecution (the murders of Erwin Wolf and Rudolf Klement and the death of Leon Sedov). *Der Einzige Weg*, 9 June 1946.

103 Brink, 'Léon de Lee', *Revolutionary History*, vol. 7, no. 1, 1998.

104 H. Almond to Lieber Genosse Gil, 1 September 1937, Hoover Institution, B. Nicolaevsky Collection 360/24; H. Almond to Lieber Genosse Gil, 5 November 1937, Houghton Library, BMS Russ. 13.1 (12,596) Trotsky Collection.

105 W. Held to L. Trotsky, 19 December 1938, R. Prager Archives, folder 190.

106 Using the pseudonym H. Schaked, Mandel wrote a polemic against Josef Weber (Johre). Neither it nor Johre's reply can be found. Johre to Lieber Otto, 3 May 1939, R. Prager Archives, folder 151.

107 E. Poretsky, *Our Own People: A Memoir of 'Ignaz Reiss' and His Friends*, London, 1969. P. Naville, 'Sur l'assasinat de Rudolf Klement', *Cahiers Léon Trotsky*, no. 2, April/June 1979. Otto to Lieber Genosse LD [Trotsky], 19 July 1938, R. Prager Archives, folder 151e. E. Mandel to R. Alexander, 10 March 1983, E. Mandel Archives, folder 74.

108 The other SWP representatives were Max Shachtman and James Cannon.

109 'The Luck of a Crazy Youth, Ernest Mandel Interviewed by Tariq Ali', p. 219.

110 G. Vereeken to T. van Driesten, 27 February 1937, G. Vereeken Archives, folder 5. Loots (Cami) assisted the Dutch Theo van Driesten, who represented the RSAP (Dutch Revolutionary Socialist Workers Party) in the POUM. R.

Prager interview with E. Mandel, 12 November 1977, R. Prager Archives, folder 290.

111 N. de Beule, *Het Belgisch trotskisme 1925–1940*, Ghent, 1980, p. 227.

112 Joseph to Stuart, 1 May 1940. Joseph was the pseudonym of O. Henry; Stuart the pseudonym of the American Sam Gordon.

A Young Man in the War

1 'The Lay of the Bell'; excerpt published in *Das Freie Wort*, February 1943.

2 Author's interview with W. van der Elst, 28 May 2002.

3 Jules Gerard-Libois and José Gotovitch estimate the number arrested at 2,000 to 3,000 Belgians and a comparable number of foreigners. J. Gerard-Libois and J. Gotovitch, *L'An 40: La Belgique occupée*, Brussels, 1971, p. 142.

4 D. de Winter, *Franz Holß: Kunstenaar op de vlucht voor Hitler*, Breda, 2001, p. 33. Note on René Groslambert, R. Prager Archives, folder 270. Rex: followers of Léon Degrelle, whose group sympathized with Italian fascism in the 1930s. The VNV was a party led by Staf de Clercq, who offered his services to Hitler in 1940. *De Nieuwe Gazet*, cited in: D. Martin, 'De Duitse "Vijfde Kolonne" in België 1936–1940', *Belgisch Tijdschrift voor Nieuwste Geschiedenis*, vol. 11, no. 1/2, 1980, p. 85. G. Deneckere, 'Het rode gevaar tijdens het interbellum', *Brood en Rozen: Tijdschrift voor de geschiedenis van sociale bewegingen*, no. 4, 1997. J. Gerard-Libois and J. Gotovitch, *L'An 40*, p. 105.

5 Ibid., p. 114.

6 Author's interview with W. van der Elst, 28 May 2002.

7 'Proces verbaal der opzoekingen, identificeerings- en vereffeningsambt van Belgische goederen' (Report on searches, identifications and settlements for Belgian goods), 27 May 1962, E. Mandel Archives, folder 190.

8 J. Gerard-Libois and J. Gotovitch, *L'An 40*, p. 73.

9 C. Prowizur-Szyper, *Conte à rebours: Une résistante juive sous l'Occupation*, Brussels, 1979, p. 29. Joseph to 'Chers camarades', 2 April 1940, R. Prager Archives, folder 143. Joseph's letter mentions the arrest of three foreigners.

10 M. Lorneau, *Contribution à l'Histoire du mouvement trotskyste Belge, 1939–1960*, vol. 3, Liège, 1983, p. 273.

11 E. Witte, J. Craeybeckx and A. Meynen, *Politieke geschiedenis van België*, Antwerp, 2005, pp. 199–206.

12 The manifesto appeared in the first number of *Correspondance Internationaliste*, a publication of the group around Vereeken, the group *La Verité* (PCI) around Raymond Molinier, Rudolphe Prager and Pierre Frank, and a few Spanish and English Trotskyists. They stood outside the official Fourth International and were attempting to use their publication for regroupment purposes. R. Prager, 'Georges Vereeken, un pionnier du mouvement trotskyste', R. Prager Archives, folder 225.

13 G. Vereeken, *The GPU in the Trotskyist Movement*, New York, 1976, p. 370. Vereeken spent a month in jail.

14 R. Prager to E. Mandel, 6 February 1979; R. Prager to J. Puissant, 15 June 1979, R. Prager Archives, folder 290. TP to IS and SWP PC.

15 TP [T. Phelan] to IS [International Secretariat] and SWP PC [Political Committee of the US SWP], 31 October 1939, R. Prager Archives, folder 227.

16 R. Lefèbvre, 'Dauge et le daugisme: un page de l'histoire du mouvement ouvrier dans le Borinage', Brussels, 1979 (unpublished dissertation).

17 M. Liebman, 'P.-H. Spaak ou la politique du cynisme: Cent ans de socialisme belge', *Contradictions*, no. 44, 1985, pp. 35–44.

18 Before the war in the 'maisons du peuple' (community centres) in the Borinage, in Brussels and elsewhere, newspapers were read aloud because many militants could not themselves read. For more on Dauge's political sensibilities, see R. Lefèbvre, 'Dauge et le daugisme', p. 88.

19 Interview with R. Groslambert, cited in M. Lorneau, *Contribution à l'Histoire du mouvement*, p. 330.

20 Joseph to 'Mon cher Stuart [S. Gordon]', 1 May 1940, R. Prager Archives, folder 143.

21 R. Lefèbvre, 'Dauge et le daugisme', p. 83.

22 *Le Drapeau Rouge*, 31 July 1944, cited in A. Colignon, 'W. Dauge', *Nouvelle Biographie Nationale, Académie Royale de Belgique*, 1999, vol. 5. Mandel was strongly opposed to the idea that Dauge was a collaborator: 'It's true that he betrayed us politically and organizationally, but he never had anything to do with the fascists.' E. Mandel to R. Prager, 8 February 1980, E. Mandel Archives, folder 122. And in an earlier letter: 'We condemn him for desertion, black marketeering (he was terribly ill and needed very expensive medicines), etc., but never for collaboration.' E. Mandel to R. Prager, 1 February 1979, E. Mandel Archives, folder 122.

23 Interview with E. Mandel, cited in: M. Lorneau, *Contribution à l'Histoire du mouvement*, pp. 281, 301. Though sociologically there were great similarities, according to Mandel, the Charleroi group was more stable than the Borinage group in its origins, experience and political formation.

24 Joseph to mon cher Stuart (S. Gordon), 1 May 1940, R. Prager Archives, folder 143.

25 M. Lorneau concludes that the rules were only systematically and collectively applied from 1941. M. Lorneau, *Contribution à l'Histoire du mouvement*, p. 296.

26 R. van Doorslaer, *De Kommunistische Partij van België en het Sovjet-Duits niet-aanvalspakt* Brussels, 1975, p. 121. J. Gotovitch, *Du Rouge au tricolore: Résistance et parti communiste*, Brussels, 1992, p. 97.

27 *Ulenspiegel*, 18 June 1940, cited in: R. van Doorslaer, *De Kommunistische Partij*, p. 125.

28 'The Luck of a Crazy Youth: Ernest Mandel Interviewed by Tariq Ali', *The Legacy of Ernest Mandel*, London, G. Achcar, ed., 1999, p. 220.

29 Interview with E. Mandel, Jours de Guerre Collection, Centre for Historical Research and Documentation on War and Contemporary Society (SOMA), Brussels, AA 1,450.

30 His departure from Antwerp had already been decided in March 1939. Johre to Lieber Fritz, 22 March 1939, R. Prager Archives, folder 151E.

31 Until the fall of 1941 the KPB also formed an opposition in the trade organizations that were part of the Union of Blue- and White-Collar Workers. R. Hemmerijckx, 'De Belgische communisten en het syndicaal verzet: de actie der syndicale strijdkomitees', *La Résistance et les Européens du Nord:*

communications présentées lors du colloque de Bruxelles, 23–25 novembre 1994, p. 209. On the Union, see W. Steenhaut, *De Unie van hand- en geestesarbeiders: Een onderzoek naar het optreden van de vakbonden in de bezettingsjaren*, Ghent 1982–3.

32 P. Broué, *Trotsky*, Paris, 1988, p. 808.

33 'Beknopt overzicht van de activiteit der onafhankelijke groep "Vrank en Vrij" tijdens de bezetting 1940–1944' (Summary overview of the activities of the independent group Vrank en Vrij during the Occupation 1940–44); Excerpt from a report to the Verbond der Journalisten der periodieke pers (League of Journalists of the Periodical Press), December 1944, H. Mandel Archives, folders 33–4. L. Lejeune Archives, SOMA, AA 756.

34 The patriotic group 'Vrank en Vrij', 20 November 1950, L. Lejeune Archives, SOMA, AA 756. H. Mandel to A. Vasann, 8 July 1950, H. Mandel Archives, folder 56.

35 Lieven Saerens incorrectly characterized *Het Vrije Woord* as a paper of Trotskyist cast. L. Saerens, *Vreemdelingen in een wereldstad: Een geschiedenis van Antwerpen en zijn joodse bevolking (1880–1944)*, Tielt, 2000, p. 670.

36 Of the approximately sixty articles published between October 1940 and August 1942, Henri Mandel was responsible for thirty-six and Ernest for eighteen. Note, H. Mandel Archives, folder 60.

37 H. Mandel, 'Hun taak en de onze'(Their Task and Ours), *Het Vrije Woord*, no. 1, October 1940.

38 E. Mandel, 'De sluipmordenaar van Mateotti delft zijn eigen graf' (Van Mateotti's Assassin Is Digging His Own Grave), *Het Vrije Woord*, no. 2, November 1940.

39 L. Saerens, *Vreemdelingen in een wereldstad*, p. 658.

40 *Het Vrije Woord*, no. 2, November 1940.

41 L. Saerens, *Vreemdelingen in een wereldstad*, p. 571. M. Steinberg, *L'Etoile et le fusil: La question juive 1940–1942*, Brussels, 1983, p. 155.

42 *Het Vrije Woord*, no. 14, September 1941. A month earlier in Amsterdam anti-Jewish disturbances had led to a strong popular reaction, culminating in a two-day general strike. In Antwerp there was nothing of the kind. A report from the military administration stated, 'A strong anti-Jewish mood has been widely felt recently in Antwerp.' L. Saerens, *Vreemdelingen in een wereldstad*, p. 575. M. Steinberg, *L'Etoile et le fusil*, p. 159.

43 Ibid., p. 117. A. Uyttenbrouck and A. Despy-Meyer, *Les Cent-cinquante ans de l'université libre de Bruxelles (1834–1984)*, Brussels, 1984, pp. 38–47.

44 *Het Vrije Woord*, no. 17, December 1941. Henri Mandel's was the only illegal paper immediately and forcefully to oppose the Belgian Jewish Society (AJB). The AJB had only one goal: furthering the deportation of Belgian Jews.

45 *Het Vrije Woord*, no. 17, December 1941.

46 Author's interview with M. Mandel, 2 October 2001.

47 H. Mandel to 'de heer Minister van Financiën', 11 December 1944, H. Mandel Archives, folder 6.

48 I estimate that of the hundred associates a quarter were from Jewish backgrounds. This estimate is based on the number of Jewish-sounding names.

49 Author's interview with W. van der Elst, 28 May 2002.

50 Interview with P. Polk, *Zeno*, 16 March 2002.

51 For a summary overview of the activities of the independent patriotic group

Vrank en Vrij during the Occupation, 1940–1944, see H. Mandel Archives. L. Lejeune Archives, SOMA, AA 756. N. Robert to G. Luchie, 12 December 1944, H. Mandel Archives, folder 11.

52 F. Vanacker to E. Mandel, 22 March 1994, E. Mandel Archives, folder 82.

53 C. Prowizur-Szyper, *Une Résistante juive*, p. 160.

54 H. Mandel to Romer, 22 December 1950; Report signed by Henri Mandel, 5 December 1951, H. Mandel Archives, folder 24.

55 J. Pezechkian, 'La Möbelaktion en Belgique', *Bijdragen tot de Eigentijdse Geschiedenis*, no. 10, 2002.

56 SD (German Security Service) files, Dienst voor de oorlogsslachtoffers (Office for War Victims).

57 'The Luck of a Crazy Youth: Ernest Mandel Interviewed by Tariq Ali', pp. 220–1.

58 Note, R. Prager Archives, folder 290.

59 Note, R. Prager Archives, folder 233.

60 *Quatrième Internationale*, no. 5/7, July 1953. S. Ashriel to 'Chers amis', 4 January 1969, E. Mandel Archives, folder 283.

61 E. Germain [E. Mandel], 'Introduction', in A. Leon, *The Jewish Question: A Marxist Interpretation*, Mexico City, 1950; also E. Germain, 'A. Leon', *Fourth International*, vol. 8, no. 6, June 1947, pp. 172–6.

62 Interview with E. Mandel, Jours de Guerre Collection, SOMA, AA 1,450. R. Hemmerijckx, 'De KPB, haar syndicale strategie en haar verhouding tot het renardistisch syndicalisme (1940–1944)', *Vlaams Marxistisch Tijdschrijft*, vol. 21, no. 1, March 1987, p. 36. R. Hemmerijckx, *Van verzet tot koude oorlog, 1940–1949: machtsstrijd om het ABVV*, Brussels, 2003, p. 98.

63 According to Ernest Mandel the party had been called the Revolutionary Communist Party since March 1941.

64 R. van Doorslaer, 'Israel Akkerman, de diamantzager (1913–1937): Een joodse militant van de Derde Internationale in Antwerpen', *Belgisch Tijdschrift voor Nieuwste Geschiedenis*, vol. 22, 1991, pp. 721–82. According to his widow Tsika Silberstern, Léon made his decision in favour of Trotskyism during the Moscow trials. M. Lorneau, *Contribution à l'Histoire du mouvement*, p. 342.

65 C. Prowizur-Szyper, *Une Résistante juive*, pp. 26–7.

66 His real name was Martin Monat (1913–44). He was born in Berlin. His mother's maiden name was Witlin, from which he adopted the name Widelin. He lived under that name in Nazi Germany, using the pseudonym Victor for illegal activities during the war.

67 The recollections of Rudolf Segall (1911–2006), friend and comrade of Martin Monat, can be found in two interviews: R. Segall, 'Die Gestapo hat mich erschossen. Leben und Tod eines deutsch-jüdischen Widerstandskämpfers', *La Bresche*, vol. 19, no. 351, November 1989, pp. 31–4; 'Cyrano von Bergerac und die Geduld des Revolutionärs, Ein Gespräch mit Rudolf Segaal', *Inprekorr*, no. 414/415, May/June 2006, pp. 23–9 and no. 416/417, July/August 2006, pp. 23–9.

68 R. Prager interview with E. Mandel, 12 November 1977, R. Prager Archives, folder 290.

69 C. Thalmann, *Revolution für die Freiheit: Stationen eines politischen Kampfes*, Grafenau-Döffingen, 1987, p. 334.

70 R. Prager, *Les Congrès de la Quatrième Internationale, 2: L'Internationale dans la Guerre (1940–1946)*, Paris, 1981, p. 113. Y. Craipeau, *Mémoires d'un dinosaure trotskyste: Secrétaire de Trotsky en 1933*, Paris, 1999, p. 164.

71 Interview with Swann [Guikovaty], 28 January 1977, R. Prager Archives, folder 322.

72 A. Léon, 'Les Tâches de la 4ème Internationale en Europe', 1942, AMSAB-Institute for Social History, Archives of the Belgian section of the Fourth International (BAVI); 'Manifestes et résolutions du IVe Congrès (première partie)'; A. Léon, 'Rapport sur la question nationale' (1943) AMSAB, BAVI, no. 1. In July 1942 the Belgian section also supported the 'Thèses sur la Question Nationale' drafted by Marcel Hic, which gave great weight to the national movement. It also supported the rights of national minorities – Bretons, Basques, Flemings, Walloons, Albanians – to their own languages and administrations. R. Prager, *Les Congrès de la Quatrième Internationale*, pp. 119–45. D. Bensaïd, *Les Trotskysmes*, Paris, 2002, p. 52.

73 H. Ratner, 'Report on the PCR, Belgian section of the Fourth International', 18 January 1945, *Revolutionary History*, vol. 7, no. 1, 1998.

74 According to Hemmerijckx, the growing activity of Communist cells was already visible during the Liège strikes of January 1941. R. Hemmerijckx, 'Le Mouvement syndicale unifié et la naissance du renardisme', Centre for Socio-Political Research and Information, *Courrier Hebdomadaire*, no. 1119/1120, May 1986, p. 18.

75 Y. Craipeau, 'Lettre aux militants du PCR de Belgique', August 1943, R. Prager Archives, folder 146.

76 E.R. [E. Mandel], 'Les Tâches du parti et la montée révolutionnaire' in: *Intern bulletin Cuisinez a l'électricité, propreté! Confort! Economie!* (stenciled internal bulletin), April 1943, R. Prager Archives, folder 146.

77 'The programme of the Fourth International, which is the programme of the RCP, is the most powerful synthesis of the entire theoretical activity of the workers movement,' ibid., p. 15.

78 'The Luck of a Crazy Youth, Ernest Mandel Interviewed by Tariq Ali', p. 221.

79 E.R., 'Les Tâches du parti et la montée révolutionnaire', p. 15.

80 M. Lorneau, *Contribution à l'Histoire du mouvement*, pp. 350–51. J. Gotovitch, *L'An 40*, p. 138.

81 *Le Drapeau Rouge*, July 1941, cited in: J. Gotovitch, *L'An 40*, p. 138.

82 Ibid., p. 141. After 1942 the German repression of trade union activity increased sharply. R. Hemmerijckx, 'De Belgische communisten en het syndicaal verzet', *De actie der Syndicale Strijdkomitees*, in *La Résistance et les Européens du Nord: Communications présentées lors du colloque de Bruxelles, 23–25 November 1994*, p. 212.

83 J. van der Elst, 'Rapport over de industriële kontra resultaten voor de Nazi-Duitse oorlogseconomie op het werkhuis The Engineering in de jaren 1940–1944', n.d., SOMA, AA 902.

84 K. Marx, 'Open brief, Aan Alle Arbeiders. Wij zwijgen niet' (Open Letter to All Workers. We will not keep silent), n.d. [1943], SOMA, AA 902.

85 Author's interview with W. van der Elst, 28 May 2002.

86 Comité regional SYSTEME D'ORGANISATION, Doc. 3 (RCP internal document), 1944. M. Lorneau, op. cit., p. 383.

87 Ibid.

88 Report drawn up by H. Mandel, 5 December 1951, H. Mandel Archives.

89 Der Militärbefehlshaber für Belgien und Nordfrankreich M V CH. Der Beauftragte des Chefs der Sicherheitspolizei und des SD. Für Belgien und Frankreich an das Wehrmachtsuntersuchungsgefängnis St Gillis, 8 December 1942. Dossier Ernest Mandel, SWG-DOD-Dossiers E 15,032/517/483.

90 C. Prowizur-Szyper, *Une Résistante juive*, p. 65. Interview with C. Prowizur-Szyper, Jours de Guerre Collection, SOMA, AA 1,450.

91 C. Prowizur-Szyper, *Une Résistante juive*, p. 27.

92 Author's interview with M. Mandel, 2 October 2001. Perhaps contact was made via Betsie Hollants. From 1936 she was part of the Antwerp Catholic Office for Israel that was active in the fight against anti–Semitism. Hollants joined the Resistance and kept in touch with a resistance group of the Belgian nobility. During the Occupation she was not so active in Antwerp as in Brussels. (cf. L. Saerens, op. cit., p. 689.) Contact could have been made with Von Falkenhausen through the Belgian nobility.

93 C. Prowizur-Szyper, *Une Résistante juive*, p. 71.

94 An das Kriegswehrmachtsgefängnis St-Gillis, 5 January 1943, SWG-DOS-Dossier SDR-DDO 33,446.

95 Interview with E. Mandel, Jours de Guerre Collection, SOMA, AA 1,450.

96 Author's interview with M. Mandel, 2 October 2001. In a report dated 5 December 1951 (H. Mandel Archives, folder 24), Henri Mandel noted, 'The ransom demanded by a member of the Gestapo to facilitate the release of my son Ernest . . . was 100,000 francs, paid by me to Mme Malvine Hofstaedter, functioning as an intermediary. She affirmed this during her trial before the Belgian military court, that she in fact transmitted this ransom to the Gestapo. But according to the trial report published in the press, she claimed to have received only 80,000 francs, which is contrary to the truth.'

97 False papers were produced by Henri Bridoux (born 1909, pseudonym Charles), an excellent graphic artist, originally from Anderlecht. He was arrested on 11 April 1942, and died in Mauthausen on 14 March 1943.

98 C. Prowizur-Szyper, *Une Résistante juive*, pp. 48, 56. Interview with A. Clement, cited in: M. Lorneau, *Contribution à l'Histoire du mouvement*, p. 389.

99 E. Mandel to R. Prager, 2 October 1977; R. Prager interview with E. Mandel, 12 November 1977, R. Prager Archives, folder 290.

100 Resolution of the Fourth Congress of the RCP, part 2, R. Prager Archives, folder 146.

101 Author's interview with M. Mandel, 13 August 2002.

102 R. Groslambert, 'Attestation' (affidavit), 8 April 1959, E. Mandel Archives.

103 The lion's share of the income was made by producing false identity papers and selling them on the black market, illegally printing food coupons and stealing money through embezzlement and robbery. In one instance, comrades carrying weapons raided a jewellery store owned by a follower of Léon Degrelle's Rex movement. Cf. M. Lorneau, *Contribution à l'Histoire du mouvement*, p. 395. F. Charpier, *Histoire de l'extrême gauche, de 1929 à nos jours*, Paris, 2002, p. 143.

104 'Beknopt overzicht van de activiteit der onafhankelijke groep "Vrank en Vrij"'.

105 There were seventeen issues of *Vrank en Vrij*, with an average printing of 4,300
    copies. The paper was distributed in Brussels, Antwerp, Mechelen, Liège and
    Turnhout, Ghent and Oostende. It was transported to local depositaries by
    means of leather cases with false backs. Report on *Vrank en Vrij*, H. Mandel
    Archives, folders 33–4.
106 Report on *Das Freie Wort*, L. Lejeune Archives, SOMA, AA 756.
107 There were twenty-one issues of *Das Freie Wort* with an average print run of
    4,000 copies. Report on *Das Freie Wort*, L. Lejeune Archives.
108 Author's interview with M. Mandel, 2 October 2001.
109 *Das Freie Wort*, May 1943. Ernest Mandel published twelve contributions in
    Das Freie Wort and ten in *Vrank en Vrij*. Survey of articles by E. Mandel, H.
    Mandel Archives, folder 60.
110 *Das Freie Wort*, September 1943.
111 C. Prowizur-Szyper, *Une Résistante juive*, p. 63.
112 The first number of *Klassenstrijd*, bulletin of the RCP, appeared in November
    1943.
113 Summons, 22 September 1943, R. Prager Archives, folder 30. R. Prager, *Les
    Congrès de la Quatrième Internationale*, p. 115.
114 R. Prager interview with E. Mandel, 12 November 1977, R. Prager Archives,
    folder 290. The members of the provisional secretariat were Marcel Hic and
    Marcoux (Spoulber) for the Internationalist Workers Party (POI), Abraham
    Léon (Wajnsztock) for the RCP and Monat (Widelin) for the German section.
    R. Prager, *Les Congrès de la Quatrième Internationale*, pp. 116–7.
115 C. Nick, *Les Trotskistes*, Paris, 2002, pp. 30, 332.
116 F. Charpier, *Histoire de l'extrême gauche*, p. 137.
117 R. Prager, *Les Congrès de la Quatrième Internationale*, p. 183. Y. Craipeau, *Contre
    Vents et Marées: Les révolutionnaires pendant la deuxième guerre mondiale*, Paris,
    1977, p. 247. J. Pluet-Despatin, *Les Trotskistes et la guerre 1940–1944*, Paris,
    1980, p. 154. S. Minguet, *Mes Années Caudron: une usine autogérée à la libération*,
    Paris, 1997, pp. 14–15.
118 'Thèses sur la liquidation de la seconde guerre mondiale impérialiste et la
    montée révolutionnaire' (Theses on the Liquidation of the Second World War
    and the Revolutionary Upturn), *Quatrième Internationale*, no. 4/5, February/
    March 1944.
119 L. Trotsky, 'The USSR in War', *The New International*, vol. 5, 1939, pp. 8–9.
120 E.R. [E. Mandel], 'La Crise mondiale du mouvement ouvrier et le rôle de la
    IVe Internationale', *Quatrième Internationale*, no. 3, January 1944.
121 A.J. [R. Prager and M. Bonnet], 'La Crise de la direction révolutionnaire,
    unique cause des défaites de la Révolution Mondiale', *Quatrième Internationale*,
    no. 6/7, no. 8/9, April/May, June/August 1944.
122 Trotsky wrote the transitional programme for the establishment of the Fourth
    International in 1938. This document was titled *The Death Throes of Capitalism
    and the Tasks of the Fourth International*. On the basis of the long recessive wave
    of capitalism, Trotsky concluded that its productive capacities could no longer
    grow. The system was stagnating and manifesting more and more primitive
    and barbaric features. However, the social democratic and Stalinist leadership
    of the workers' movement was blocking the abolition of capitalism. Revo-
    lutionaries had the task of solving this key problem.

123 E.R. 'La Crise mondiale du mouvement ouvrier'.

124 'Thèses sur la liquidation de la seconde guerre mondiale impérialiste'.

125 'It is obvious, comrades, that if we let ourselves be influenced by the sterile sectarians who want to transform our party into a club of scribblers, of hair-splitting debaters, of those who would chop the horse into quarters, then WE ARE DOOMED IN ADVANCE.' A. Léon, 'Le Sectarisme stérile et fataliste, maladie infantile du trotskisme', RCP, *Bulletin Intérieur*, no. 1, R. Prager Archives, folder 146.

126 E. Germain, 'Introduction', in A. Leon, *The Jewish Question*, p. 12. From October 1943 *Le Réveil des Mineurs* (Miners' Reawakening) was published in the Charleroi area as the paper of the Miners' Struggle Federation; from September 1944 it was the paper of the Charleroi Valley miners' shop stewards.

127 Interview with E. Mandel, Jours de Guerre Collection, SOMA, AA 1,450.

128 R. Hemmerijckx, 'Le Mouvement syndical unifié et la naissance du renardisme', Centre for Socio-Political Research and Information, *Courrier Hebdomadaire*, no. 1119/1120, May 1986, p. 36.

129 Interview with E. Mandel, Jours de Guerre Collection, SOMA, AA 1,450.

130 Ibid. J. Jansen van Galen, 'Trotzkist als Thrillerkenner', *NRC Handelsblad*, 2 March 1985.

131 E. Mandel, 14 May 1944, H. Mandel Archives, folder 26.

132 E. Mandel, 2 June 1944, H. Mandel Archives, folder 26.

133 Ibid.

134 E. Germain, 'Introduction', in A. Leon, *The Jewish Question*, p. 12. C. Prowizur-Szyper, pp. 175–6. 'Conclusions de la commission d'enquête internationale sur l'arrestation de Léon' (Conclusions of the international commission of inquiry into the arrest of Léon), R. Prager Archives, folder 146. Ministerie voor Gezondheid, Dossier A. Wajnzstock, SWG-DOS-Dossier SDR-DDO 64592. T. Wajnsztock, née Silberstein to Président de la commission des pensions de Réparation, n.d., H. Mandel Archives, folder 43.

135 A. Léon, Letters, 24 June–20 July 1944, E. Mandel Archives, folder 77, Letter 2.

136 Ibid., Letter 3.

137 Ibid., Letter 6.

138 Ibid., Letter 7.

139 Hashomer Hatzair argued that Jewish workers and revolutionary socialists could only struggle for a socialist revolution in Palestine.

140 A. Léon, Letters, Letter 7.

141 E. Germain, 'Introduction', in: A. Leon, *The Jewish Question*.

142 From 3–15 June 1944, Mandel was held in a series of facilities: from the Aix-la-Chapelle prison he was transported first to a camp near Cologne and then a location near Rheinbach/Bonn; from 15 Jun–15 July, he was in the Siegburg prison; from 15 July–1 September, in the Hürth-Wesseling camp; from 1 September–15 October, in the Eberstadt camp; from 15 October 1944–1 March 1945, in the Eich camp; from 1 March–19 April 1945, in the Niederroden camp. Source: Dienst van de oorlogsslachtoffers SWG-DOS-Dossiers statuten E 15,032/517/483; SWG-DOS-Dossier SDR-DDO 33,446. NB: The dates are approximate.

143　'The Luck of a Crazy Youth, Ernest Mandel Interviewed by Tariq Ali', p. 222.

144　E. Mandel to 'Mes très très chers', 16 June 1944, H. Mandel Archives, folder 426. E. Mandel to Rechtsanwalt, 6 August 1944, H. Mandel Archives, folder 426.

145　Author's interview with M. Mandel, 27 June 2000.

146　E. Mandel to Rechtsanwalt.

147　The escape took place on 10 August 1944. Dienst voor de oorlogsslachtoffers, SWG-DOS-Dossiers Statuten E 15,032/517/483; SWG-DOS-Dossier SDR-DDO 33,446.

148　'The Luck of a Crazy Youth, Ernest Mandel Interviewed by Tariq Ali', p. 223.

149　'Gezondheidsverklaring' (Health declaration), n.d., E. Mandel Archives, folder 19.

150　A. Le Roye, Deposition, 20 January 1949, Dienst voor de oorlogsslachtoffers.

151　'The Luck of a Crazy Youth, Ernest Mandel Interviewed by Tariq Ali', p. 223.

The Power of the Will

1　*Arbeiter und Soldat*, no. 1, July 1943, *Fac-similé de La Vérité clandestine (1940–1944)*, Paris, 1978.

2　R. Prager interview with E. Mandel, 12 November 1977. 'The Luck of a Crazy Youth, Ernest Mandel Interviewed by Tariq Ali', in: G. Achcar, ed., *The Legacy of Ernest Mandel*, London, 1999, pp. 221–2.

3　H. Mandel to Lieber Eddy [Grünberg], 5 July 1945, H. Mandel Archives, folder 7.

4　Ernest to 'Dearest mother, and father and brother', 18 April 1945, H. Mandel Archives, folder 26.

5　V. Klapholz, 'Herinnering' (Recollections), n.d., E. Mandel Archives.

6　H. Mandel to Leon and Lola Leslau, 1 September 1945, H. Mandel Archives, folder 11.

7　Author's interview with M. Mandel, 2 October 2001.

8　Oskar Schindler succeeded in saving around a thousand Jews by putting them to work in his factory.

9　'Bertha' to 'My dearest Rosa, Henri and boys', Bergen Belsen, 7 August 1945, H. Mandel Archives, folder 11.

10　H. Mandel to I. Mandel, 4 August 1947, H. Mandel Archives, folder 12.

11　Ibid.

12　E. Mandel to G. Triffon, 8 May 1945, H. Mandel Archives, folder 16.

13　V. Klapholz, 'Herinnering'.

14　H. Mandel to M. Piller, 26 June 1946, H. Mandel Archives, folder 14.

15　A. Meynen, *Van Praag 1948 tot Vilvoorde 1954: politieke biografische gesprekken met Louis Van Geyt*, Brussels, 2001, p. 25.

16　Ibid., p. 40.

17　H. Mandel to M. Piller, 9 July 1945, H. Mandel Archives, folder 14.

18　V. Klapholz to J.W. Stutje, 8 May 2003.

19　With Joseph Weber (pseudonym Johre), Fritz Besser founded *Dinge der Zeit* (Contemporary Events), the publication of a group, mostly of former German political prisoners, which broke with the Fourth International in 1946. The breaking point was Weber's theory of 'retrogression', which held that capitalism was past its high point and that because the workers' movement was unable to change the system, events would pass through a retrogression to industrial backwardness, dependency and slavery. M. van der Linden. 'The Prehistory of Post-Scarcity Anarchism: Josef Weber and the Movement for a Democracy of Content (1947–1964)', *Anarchist Studies*, no. 9, 2001, pp. 127–45.

20 E. Mandel to W. Besser, 9 December 1991, E. Mandel Archives, folder 81.

21 According to Isaac Deutscher, German correspondent for *The Economist* and the *Observer* in 1945, 'I must admit I did not for a minute imagine that Nazism could be defeated otherwise than by a German revolution.' I. Deutscher, 'Germany and Marxism', *New Left Review*, no. 47, January/February 1968, p. 63.

22 E. Mandel, 'Sherry Mangan' (biographical note), 26 June 1953, E. Mandel Archives.

23 B. van Wijk to E. Mandel, 5 September 1945, E. Mandel Archives, folder 1. Mandel had met the Rotterdamer Van Wijk in Camp Eberstadt. Van Wijk had been arrested in March 1944 as part of the Parool resistance group and sentenced that summer to three years in the house of correction. M. de Keizer, *Het Parool 1940–1945: Verzetsblad in Oorlogstijd*, Amsterdam, 1991, pp. 361–7.

24 M. Lorneau, 'Le Mouvement trotskyste Belge: septembre 1939 – décembre 1964', Centre for Socio-Political Research and Information, *Courrier Hebdomadaire*, 21 December 1984.

25 E. Mandel to E. Federn, 12 August 1946, E. Mandel Archives, folder 677. It concerned a report on the nature of the postwar Soviet Union for a congress of the French section of the Fourth International.

26 E. Mandel to E. Federn, 17 August 1946, E. Mandel Archives, folder 677.

27 E. Mandel, 'Ein Mirakel', *Das Jahr 1945: Brüche und Kontinuitäten*, Berlin, 1995, p. 48.

28 Paul Federn (1871–1950). E. Federn, *Witnessing Psychoanalysis: From Vienna Back to Vienna Via Buchenwald and the USA*, London, 1990. P. Gay, *Freud: A Life for Our Time*, New York, 1988, p. 208.

29 Author's interview with K. Manfred , 21 May 2002.

30 M. Liebman, *Né juif: une famille juive pendant la guerre*, Paris, 1977.

31 Author's interview with H. and E. Federn, 13 November 2001. E. Federn, 'War memories' typescript, E. Federn Collection.

32 'Erklärung der internationalistischen Kommunisten Buchenwalds' (Declaration of the Buchenwald International Communists) (Fourth International). F. Keller, *In den Gulag von Ost und West: Karl Fischer, Arbeiter und Revolutionär*, Frankfurt on Main, 1980, pp. 149–51.

33 A memorandum with this import was signed by Dutch Communists. J.W. Stutje, *De man die de weg wees: Leven en werk van Paul de Groot*, Amsterdam, 2000, p. 256. The French Communists proudly declared, 'It's because I love my country that I belong to the PCF [French Communist Party].' *L'Humanité de Buchenwald*, 22 April 1945. See also P. Robrieux, *Histoire interieure du parti communiste*, vol. 1, Paris, 1980.

34 E. Federn, 'Memoires', R. Prager Archives.

35 Pensé [E. Federn] to 'Werte Genossen' (Dear Comrades), 19 June 1945, G. Scheuer Archives, folder 5991.

36 R. Dazy, *Fussilez ces chiens enragés . . . : Le génocide des trotskistes*, Paris, 1981, p. 237.

37 Author's interview with H. and E. Federn, 13 November 2001. Federn's kindred spirit Karl Fischer returned to Austria. Because of his Trotskyist convictions he was arrested in 1947 by the Russian occupation forces and sent to the camps of Kolyma for eight years. For him the war only ended in June 1955. F. Keller, *In den Gulag*.

38 Karl Jaspers's famous book on the question of war guilt was published in 1946. Articles on the same theme by Hannah Arendt appeared in the German periodical *Aufbau* and in *Partisan Review*.

39 E. Federn, *De terreur als systeem: Het concentratiekamp. Achter de schermen van de propaganda: Buchenwald in zijn ware gedaante*, Antwerp, 1945.

40 Author's interview with H. and E. Federn, 13 November 2001. Primo Levi also had difficulties in publishing his recollections *Se questo è un uomo* (*If This is a Man*). The book was as good as ignored when it was published in 1947. E. Ferrero, ed., *Primo Levi: Un antologia della critica*, Turin, 1997.

41 E. Traverso, *Understanding the Nazi Genocide: Marxism after Auschwitz*, London, 1999. For an example of the postwar silence about the Shoah, see Jean-Paul Sartre's *Réflexions sur la question juive*, published in Paris in 1946 (*Anti-Semite and Jew*, New York, 1970), which mentions the genocide only in passing. For a discussion of initial disbelief in it, see Y. Bauer, *The Holocaust in Historical Perspective*, Seattle, 1978; W. Laqueur, *The Terrible Secret*, London 1980; M. Marrus, *The Holocaust in History*, London, 1987. The particular importance of Auschwitz was only recognized from the 1970s. E. Traverso, *L'Histoire déchiré: Essai sur Auschwitz et les intellectuels*, Paris, 1997.

42 There was also a small group of German Jewish emigrés who had already made Auschwitz central to their thinking during the war years, like Hannah Arendt, Günther Anders, Theodor Adorno, Max Horkheimer and Herbert Marcuse. And there was a group of non-Jews in America and Europe who similarly called attention to the concentration camps like Thomas Mann, Dwight Macdonald, Karl Jaspers and Georges Bataille. E. Traverso, *L'Histoire déchiré*, p. 15.

43 David Rousset wrote *L'Univers concentrationnaire*, Paris, 1946, which was published in English as *The Other Kingdom*, New York, 1947, about his experiences in the camps. It first appeared in instalments in *La Revue Internationale* edited by C. Bettelheim, P. Naville and G. Martinet. He later wrote about the camps in his novel *Les Jours de notre mort*, Paris, 1947.

44 E. Traverso, *Understanding the Nazi Genocide*, p. 50.

45 Published in English as Ernest Germain, 'The Jewish Question Since World War II', *Fourth International*, vol. 8, no. 4, April, 1947, pp. 109–13.

46 Ibid.

47 A 1947 text that Mandel presented to the International Secretariat of the Fourth International – E. Germain [E. Mandel], 'Draft Theses on the Jewish Question Today', *Fourth International*, vol. 9, no. 1, January/February 1948, pp. 18–24 – refers to this factor without any qualification: 'In this sense it is decaying capitalism, which deliberately placed power in the hands of a band of

bloody criminals, that bears full responsibility for the horrible fate of the Jewish European masses during the war.' E. Mandel and N. Weinstock, *Zur jüdischen Frage: Beiträge zu Abraham Léons 'Judenfrage und Kapitalismus'*, Frankfurt on Main, 1977.

48 E. Mandel, *The Meaning of the Second World War*, London, 1986.

49 N. Geras, 'Marxists before the Holocaust: Trotsky, Deutscher, Mandel', G. Achcar, ed., *The Legacy of Ernest Mandel*, London, 1999, p. 191.

50 G. Hodgson, *Trotsky and Fatalistic Marxism*, Nottingham, 1975, p. 26; J. Callaghan, *British Trotskyism: Theory and Practice*, Oxford, 1984, p. 18.

51 'Le Mûrissant de la situation révolutionnaire en Europe et les tâches immédiates de la IVe Internationale', *Quatrième Internationale*, January/February 1945. Also in R. Prager, *Les Congrès de la quatrième internationale, 2: L'Internationale dans la guerre (1940–1946)*, Paris, 1981. The following passage is noteworthy: 'The revolutionary upsurge is taking place in Europe in a general context of ongoing imperialist war and the occupation of different countries by Allied or German armies.'

52 'La nouvelle paix impérialiste et la construction des partis de la IVe Internationale', *L'Internationale dans la guerre*, R. Prager, p. 405; E. Germain, 'The First Phase of the European Revolution', *Fourth International*, August 1946.

53 E. Germain, *From the ABC to Current Reading: Boom, Revival or Crisis?*, September 1947. On behalf of the RCP majority, Tony Cliff attacked Mandel's perspective in *All that Glitters Is Not Gold*, RCP Internal Document, September 1947. T. Cliff, *Neither Washington nor Moscow: Essays on Revolutionary Socialism*, London, 1982.

54 D. Cannadine, 'The Past and the Present in the English Industrial Revolution 1880–1980', *Past & Present: A Journal of Historical Studies*, no. 103, May 1984, p. 142.

55 J.K. Galbraith, *The Great Crash: 1929*, Boston, 1955.

56 J.K. Galbraith, *The Affluent Society*, London, 1962.

57 'La Nouvelle paix impérialiste et la construction des partis de la IVe Internationale', in R. Prager, *L'Internationale dans la guerre*, p. 405.

58 'Die nationale Frage: Drei Thesen der Genossen der IKD', October 1941. Johre [Joseph Weber], 'Capitalist Barbarism or Socialism', October 1944; 'Probleme der europäischen Revolution', *Quatrième Internationale*, December 1945/January 1946. R. Prager, *L'Internationale dans la guerre*; W. Alles, *Zur Politik und Geschichte der deutschen Trotzkisten ab 1930*, Frankfurt on Main, 1987.

59 A. Wald, *The Revolutionary Imagination: The Poetry and Politics of John Wheelwright and Sherry Mangan*, London, 1983, pp. 195–6. M. Pablo [M. Raptis], 'Notre ami Sherry, notre camarade Patrice (l'homme et le militant)', *Quatrième Internationale*, no. 16, July 1962.

60 E. Mandel, 'Quelques anecdotes', E. Mandel Archives, folder 346.

61 *Franc-Tireur*, 7 March 1946.

62 A. Wald, *The New York Intellectuals: The Rise and Decline of the Anti-Stalinist Left from the 1930s to the 1980s*, Chapel Hill, 1987; A. Wald, *Writing from the Left: New Essays on Radical Culture and Politics*, London-New York, 1994; C. Nelson, *Repression and Recovery: Modern American Poetry and the Politics of Cultural Memory, 1910–1945*, New York, 1989; D. Aaron, *Writers on the Left: Episodes in American Literary Communism*, New York, 1992.

63 S. Mangan to V. Thomson, 15 October 1933, cited in A. Wald, *The Revolutionary Imagination*, p. 154.

64 A. Wald, *The New York Intellectuals*, p. 146.

65 D. Rousset to S. Mangan, 10 July 1940; 18 July 1940; 24 July 1940; 4 August 1940, R. Prager Archives, folder 291. Mangan arranged papers for a number of Trotskyists and sympathizers that falsely identified them as *Time* employees. Among the recipients were Marcel Hic, the actor George Vitsoris and the writers Victor Serge and David Rousset. A. Wald, *The New York Intellectuals*, p. 184.

66 K. Steinfeld [P. Pasamonte] to A. Wald, 18 March 1979; E. Mandel to A. Wald, 26 September 1979, Ernest Mandel Archives, folder 410.

67 A. Wald, *The Revolutionary Imagination*, p. 74.

68 Author's interview with M. Mandel, 29 September 2001.

69 E. Mandel to E. and H. Federn, 31 March 1948, E. Mandel Archives, folder 677.

70 Ibid.

71 E. Mandel to E. and H. Federn, 13 April 1948, E. Mandel Archives, folder 677. Federn also recommended the Swiss analyst Heinrich Meng, a pupil of both Sigmund Freud and his own father, Paul Federn.

72 S. Mangan to C. Haywood, 13 May 1948, cited in A. Wald, *The Revolutionary Imagination*, p. 198.

73 E. Mandel to E. and H. Federn, 31 May 1948, E. Mandel Archives, folder 677.

74 E. Mandel to E. and H. Federn, 30 November 1948, E. Mandel Archives, folder 677.

75 E. Mandel to E. and H. Federn, 17 January 1949, E. Mandel Archives, folder 677.

76 Ibid.

77 Author's interview with E. and H. Federn, 13 November 2001.

78 E. Mandel to E. and H. Federn, 30 July 1948, Ernest Mandel Archives, folder 677.

79 E. Mandel to E. and H. Federn, 17 January 1949, E. Mandel Archives, folder 677.

80 E. Mandel to E. and H. Federn, 15 June 1949, E. Mandel Archives, folder 677.

81 M. van der Linden, *Het westers marxisme en de Sovjetunie*, p. 88. Periodicals that paid particular attention to the question of the Soviet Union between 1945 and 1950 included *Left* (London), *La Revue internationale* (Paris), *Funken* (Stuttgart) and *Pro und contra* (Berlin).

82 L. Adler and T. Paterson, 'Red Fascism: The Merger of Nazi Germany and Soviet Russia in the American Image of Totalitarianism, 1930s–1950s', *The American Historical Review*, vol. 75, no. 4, April 1970, p. 1046. On the concept of totalitarianism, Mandel wrote in 1947, 'The emotional power of the word "totalitarian" is curiously linked to the fact that no one can define it exactly; it works primarily by suggestion . . . The political regime in Russia is certainly quite as "totalitarian" as Hitler's. No serious Trotskyist has ever questioned this; the only thing which Trotsky questioned, entirely justifiably, was whether the totalitarian nature of the political regime sufficed to define either the social nature of the Russian state or the attitude the Fourth International should take toward it.' *Fourth International*, vol. 8, no. 5, May 1947, pp. 136–44.

83 That is, that it had been established by a genuine proletarian revolution and had created new property relationships before being usurped by a privileged bureaucracy.

84 E. Mandel to E. and H. Federn, 15 July 1949, E. Mandel Archives, folder 677.

85 L. Trotsky, 'Does the Soviet Government Still Follow the Principles Adopted Twenty Years Ago?', *Writings of Leon Trotsky, 1937–1938*, New York, 1976, p. 127.

86 Marcel van der Linden points out that this temporal perspective is virtually always ignored in commentaries on Trotsky. M. van der Linden, *Het westers marxisme en de Sovjetunie*, p. 63. C. Samary, 'Mandel's Views on the Transition to Socialism', in G. Achcar, ed., *The Legacy of Ernest Mandel*, London, 1999, p. 156.

87 P. Bellis, *Marxism and the USSR: The Theory of Proletarian Dictatorship and the Marxist Analysis of Soviet Society*, New Jersey, 1979, p. 88.

88 L. Trotsky, 'The USSR in War', *New International*, vol. 5, no. 11, November 1939; reprinted in L. Trotsky, *In Defence of Marxism*, London, 1966, pp. 3–26.

89 Trotsky noted that 'The fears of the ultralefts that the victory of the USSR may lead to the further consolidation of the positions of the Bonapartist bureaucracy, arise out of a false conception of the international relationships as well as the internal development of the USSR. The imperialists . . . will not reconcile themselves with the Soviet Union until private property in the means of production has been re-established . . . The USSR will be able to emerge from a war without a defeat only under one condition, and that is, if it is assisted by the revolution in the West or in the East. But the international revolution, the only way of saving the USSR, will at the same time signify the death blow for the Soviet bureaucracy.' L. Trotsky, 'On the Eve of World War Two', *Writings of Leon Trotsky, 1938–1939*, New York, 1969, pp. 33–7.

90 R. Guérin, 'La Question russe doit être révisée', *Bulletin Intérieur du PCI*, July 1946. Guérin said that he was making his call on behalf of the German, Greek, Mexican, Spanish and Bulgarian sections. In August 1946 they received support from Cornelius Castoriadis, a Greek economist, and Claude Lefort, a philosopher in the circle around Merleau-Ponty. They were known after their respective party names as the Chaulieu-Montal group. P. Chaulieu and C. Montal, 'Sur le régime et contre la défense de l'URSS', *Bulletin Intérieur du PCI*, 31 August 1946. C. Castoriadis, *Political and Social Writings*, vol. I: *1946–1955*, pp. 37–43, pp. 44–55; P. Chaulieu, 'Le Problème de l'URSS et la possibilité d'une 3e solution historique', *Bulletin Intérieur du Secrétariat International*, February 1947.

91 Ibid.

92 E. Mandel to E. Federn, 17 August 1946, E. Mandel Archives, folder 677. 'Projet de Thèses sur L'URSS au lendemain de la guerre', *Bulletin Intérieur du Secrétariat International*, vol. 1, no. 6, September 1946.

93 Mandel would only examine this problem at length in *Revolutionary Marxism Today*, London, 1979, pp. 170–80.

94 Mandel distinguished three groups of countries. Assimilation was complete in the group consisting of the Baltics, eastern Poland, part of East Prussia, the Ukraine south of the Carpathians and Bessarabia. The start of assimilation was in sight in the second group – Poland, East Germany, Yugoslavia and Czechoslovakia – though these states and their economies were still capitalist.

The third group – Finland, Austria, Hungary, Romania and Bulgaria – remained thoroughly capitalist.

95 Theses were submitted by the majority of the Central Committee (E. Germain, 'The USSR After the War'); by L. Schwartz ('The USSR and Stalinism'); by Marcoux, Mestre, Renan, Dural, Houdon and Lime ('The Bureaucratic Defence of the USSR'); by Chaulieu and Montal ('On the Regime and Against the Defence of the USSR'); and by Guérin, Magneux and Pennetier ('There Is Nothing to Defend in the USSR'). The first three argued from almost the same position. Only the Chaulieu-Montal and Guérin groups insisted that there was a variety of state capitalism in the Soviet Union. Y. Craipeau, *Mémoires d'un dinosaure trotskyste: secrétaire de Trotsky en 1933*, Paris, 1999, pp. 187–90. Cf. P. Frank, ' "Novateurs" et "conservateurs" dans la question de l'URSS' (29 May 1947), *Le Stalinisme*, Paris, 1968, pp. 171–219.

96 Fragment from the minutes of the Third Congress of the PCI, September 1946.

97 *Pour un portrait de Pierre Frank: Ecrits et témoignages*, Paris, 1985, p. 19.

98 Ibid.

99 F. Zeller, *Trois points c'est tout*, Paris, 1976, p. 250.

100 One example was the American SWP, where from 1947 the Johnson-Forest tendency appeared (Johnson and Forest were pseudonyms of C.L.R. James and Raya Dunayevskaya respectively). They defended their own version of the state capitalism theory and maintained contact with the Chaulieu-Montal tendency in France. From 1947 on, Ygaël Gluckstein (pseudonym Tony Cliff) was the most important exponent of the idea that the Soviet Union was a state capitalist society. In the Mexican section there was a state-capitalist opposition led by Benjamin Péret (pseudonym Peralta) and Manuel Fernandez Grandizo (pseudonym G. Munis). M. van der Linden, *Het westers marxisme en de Sovjetunie*. J. Callaghan, *British Trotskyism*. P. Drucker, *Max Shachtman and His Left: A Socialist's Odyssey Through the 'American Century'*, Atlantic Highlands, New Jersey, 1994.

101 Ibid. E. Germain, 'De L'Abstentionnisme à l'intervention active: dans le camp de l'ennemi de classe! I, II', *Quatrième Internationale*, December 1946, January 1947 (an analysis of Poland). E. Germain, 'L'Économie soviétique en 1946, I, II', *Quatrième Internationale*, March/April 1947, May/June 1947. E. Germain, 'Le Stalinisme, comment le comprendre et comment le combattre', *Quatrième Internationale*, May/June 1947.

102 'Projet de thèses: La IVe Internationale et le stalinisme', November 1947, R. Prager, *Les Congrès de la Quatrième Internationale, 3: Bouleversements et crises de l'après-guerre (1946–1950)*, Paris 1988.

103 E. Mandel, 'La IVe Internationale et le stalinisme', draft thesis, November 1947, E. Mandel Archives.

104 E. Mandel to E. Federn, 31 March 1948, E. Mandel Archives, folder 677.

105 Ibid.

106 R. Prager, *Les Congrès de la Quatrième Internationale, 3*, p. 28.

107 This interpretation was shared by the majority of the French section, the British section and the majority of the SWP. R. Prager, *Les Congrès de la Quatrième Internationale, 3*, p. 359. Statement by the Political Committee of the

Socialist Workers Party, 'Yugoslav Events and the World Crisis of Stalinism', *Fourth International*, August 1948.

108 'An Open Letter to the Congress, Central Committee and Members of the Yugoslav Communist Party', *Fourth International*, August 1948.

109 L. Trotsky, *The Transitional Program: The Death Agony of Capitalism and the Tasks of the Fourth International*, New York, 1970.

110 S. Pattieu, 'Le Camarade Pablo, la IVe Internationale, et la guerre d'Algérie', *Revue Historique*, vol. 125, no. 619, July/September 2001, pp. 695–729.

111 M. Pablo, 'The Yugoslav Affair, August 1948', *Fourth International*, December 1948.

112 M. Pablo, 'L'Évolution du PC yougoslave', 15 October 1949, *Quatrième Internationale*, October/November 1949. M. Pablo, 'Sur la nature de classe de la Yougoslavie', *Bulletin Intérieur du Secrétariat International de la IVe Internationale*, October 1949.

113 E. Germain, 'L'Évolution économique de l'Europe orientale', II, III, (10 March 1949), *Quatrième Internationale*, March/June 1949, July/August 1949; E. Germain, 'La Auestion Yougoslave, la question du glacis sovietique, et leur implication sur la theorie marxiste', *Bulletin Intérieur du Secrétariat Internationale de la IVe Internationale*, November 1949.

114 Mandel wrote, 'Unless you succumb to a grotesque interpretation of history and believe that Tito "fooled" not only London and Washington but even the Kremlin about his intentions, only one conclusion is possible: THE STATE APPARATUS BUILT IN 1944–5 IN THE BIG LIBERATED CITIES . . . CANNOT BE CHARACTERIZED AS THE APPARATUS OF A WORKERS' STATE.' E. Germain, 'La Question Yougoslave'.

115 Ibid.

116 'Résolution sur le caractère de classe de l'Etat yougoslave', présentée par Germain, VII plenum du CEI, 26–30 April 1950, *Les Congrès de la Quatrième Internationale, 3,* R. Prager, pp. 455–9.

117 E. Mandel to E. Federn, 14 November 1949, E. Mandel Archives, folder 677.

118 E. Germain, 'What Should Be Modified and What Should Be Maintained in the Theses of the Second World Congress of the Fourth International on the Question of Stalinism? (Ten Theses)', in Socialist Workers Party (USA) *International Information Bulletin*, April 1951; also in *Towards a History of the Fourth International*, New York, 1973, part 4, vol. 1, pp. 16–24.

119 S. Santen, *Adiós compañeros! Politieke herinneringen*, Amsterdam, 1974, p. 49.

La Gauche and the Social Democrats

1 Only in the 1990s did a few studies on the direct aftermath of the Occupation appear: P. Lagrou, *The Legacy of Nazi Occupation: Patriotic Memory and National Recovery in Western Europe, 1945–1965*, Cambridge, 2000; E. Witte, J.C. Burgelman and P. Stouthuysen, eds, *Tussen restauratie en vernieuwing: Aspecten van de Belgische na-oorlogse politiek (1944–1950)*, Brussels, 1990.

2 L. P. Boon, 'Brussel, een oerwoud, De werkbeurs, open van 8 tot 17 uur', *De Roode Vaan*, 26 February 1946.

3 C. Prowizur-Szyper, *Conte à rebours: Une résistante juive sous l'Occupation*, Brussels, 1979, p. 197.

4 K. Manfred, 'Mémoires d'un militant des années quarante', *Brood en Rozen: Tijdschrift voor de Geschiedenis van Sociale Bewegingen*, Ghent, 2000/3.

5 This did not prevent the Belgian security police from closely following the Trotskyist Revolutionary Communist Party (RCP). A confidential report dated 20 November 1944, prepared by George Block, commissioner of the Antwerp police, and forwarded to the Antwerp prosecutor, found its way to the Supreme Headquarters of the Allied Expeditionary Force Mission in Belgium.

6 J.-L. Degee, *L'Évolution des luttes ouvrières en Belgique*, Liège, 1980, p. 11.

7 P. Delwit, 'Des Golden sixties électorales pour le parti communiste de Belgique?', *Cahiers Marxistes*, June/July 2002.

8 E. Witte, J. Craeybeckx and A. Meynen, *Politieke geschiedenis van België: van 1830 tot heden*, Antwerp, 1990, p. 227.

9 R. Hemmerijckx, 'Le Mouvement syndicale unifié et la naissance du renardisme', Centre for Socio-Political Research and Information, *Courrier Hebdomadaire*, no. 1119/1120, 23 May 1986, p. 46.

10 R. Hemmerijkckx, *Van verzet tot koude oorlog, 1940–1949: machtsstrijd om het ABVV*, Brussels, 2003, p. 379.

11 *Le Drapeau Rouge*, 6 September 1944; *Clarté*, special issue, 4 September 1944, cited in J. Gotovitch, *Du Rouge au tricolore: Résistance et parti communiste*, Brussels 1992, p. 422.

12 Following their success in the 1946 election, the KPB saw increasingly poor results in the subsequent elections of 1949, 1950, 1954 and 1958. Their membership declined from 100,000 in 1945 to 10,000 in 1955. P. Delwit, 'Des Golden sixties électorales'.

13 E. Witte, J. Craeybeckx and A. Meynen, *Politieke geschiedenis van België*, p. 246. R. Hemmerijckx, *Van Verzet tot koude oorlog*, p. 379.

14 E. Mandel, *Revolutionary Marxism Today*, London, 1979.

15 Ibid., p. 176.

16 P. Anderson to E. Mandel, 5 February 1978, E. Mandel Archives, folder 59. After the Mandel interviews were published, Perry Anderson wrote that the Trotskyist tradition 'alone has proved capable of an adult view of socialism on a *world* scale, as anyone who reads Mandel's recent *Revolutionary Marxism Today* may see for themselves'. P. Anderson, *Arguments within English Marxism*, London, 1980, p. 156. G. Elliott, *Perry Anderson: The Merciless Laboratory of History*, Minneapolis, 1998, p. 90.

17 P. Anderson, *Passages from Antiquity to Feudalism*, London, 1975. P. Anderson, *Lineages of the Absolutist State*, London, 1974.

18 In September 1945 at the fifth congress of the RCP Mandel defended the thesis: 'The prospects of a revolutionary upsurge, which seemed illusory in the wake of the Anglo-American liberation of Europe, are more real and deeper today than ever.' E. Germain, 'Les Progrès de la barbarie et les perspectives de révolution prolétarienne', September 1945, AMSAB (Institute for Social History, Ghent), BAVI (Archives of the Belgian section of the Fourth International), 1113/2.

19 'Procès Verbal du Comité Central', 8 July 1945, AMSAB, BAVI, 1113/289.

20 'I came home with great political hopes and illusions. I was fully convinced, for example, that the international workers' movement would experience a greater upsurge than after the First World War and that the extreme left would have great opportunities for growth.' E. Mandel, 'Ein Mirakel', C. Krauss and D. Küchenmeister, eds, *Das Jahr 1945: Brüche und Kontinuitäten*, Berlin, 1995.

21 Micky Traks was not prepared to discuss this episode in her life with the author. Regarding the new young Trotskyists, see M. Lorneau, *Contribution à l'histoire du mouvement trotskyste belge, 1939–1960*, vol. III, Liège, 1983, p. 514.

22 E. Mandel to E. Federn, 17 August [no year], E. Mandel Archives, folder 677.

23 Author's interview with M. Mandel, 2 October 2001.

24 *L'Avant-Garde: organe mensuel du marxisme révolutionnaire*, no. 1, December 1945; no. 2, January 1946, no. 3, February/March 1946.

25 RCP Regional Committee minutes, 18 February 1946, BAVI, 1113/289. Micky [Traks] to E. Mandel, n.d., E. Mandel Archives, folder 1.

26 Ibid.

27 Micky to E. Mandel, Tuesday, n.d., E. Mandel Archives, folder 1.

28 Micky to E. Mandel, 11 May 1950, E. Mandel Archives, folder 1.

29 Micky to E. Mandel, n.d. [1952], E. Mandel Archives, folder 1.

30 Micky to E. Mandel, n.d., E. Mandel Archives, folder 1.

31 Fragment, E. Mandel Archives, folder 1.

32 Micky to E. Mandel, n.d., E. Mandel Archives, folder 1.

33 Micky to E. Mandel, 5 May 1954, E. Mandel Archives, folder 1.

34 Fragment, E. Mandel Archives, folder 1. Translation: 'Oh my love, oh my love, only you exist / At the moment of my twilight sadness / When I lose both the thread of my poem / And the thread of my life, and my joy, and my voice, / Because I wanted to tell you once more, I love you, / And it hurts me to say it when you are not there.
　'My beautiful love, my dear love, my torn heart, / I carry you in me like a wounded bird. /
　Those who unknowingly watch us walk by / Repeat after me my words and sigh – / They have already died in your bright eyes – / There is no happy love.' The second stanza is taken from L. Aragon, *Il n'y a pas d'amour heureux*, included in the collection *La Diane française*, Paris, 1962. It was originally published clandestinely in 1944.

35 E. Mandel to E. Federn, 16 May 1950, E. Mandel Archives, folder 1.

36 A. Mandel-Sprimont to J.W. Stutje, 30 June 2003.

37 Micky to E. Mandel, 10 January 1965, E. Mandel Archives, folder 32.

38 E. Mandel to E. Federn, 3 January 1954, E. Mandel Archives, folder 1.

39 V. Klapholz to J.W. Stutje, 8 May 2003.

40 E. Mandel to E. Federn, 3 January 1954.

41 Ibid.

42 In 1968 he wrote, 'But who can speak of limitations that man will *never* be able to break through, man who is stretching out his arms towards the stars, who is on the brink of producing life in test-tubes, and who tomorrow will embrace the entire family of mankind in a spirit of universal brotherhood?' E. Mandel, *Marxist Economic Theory*, New York, 1968, vol. 2, p. 686. M. Kellner,

Kapitalismusanalyse, Bürokratiekritik und sozialistische Strategie bei Ernest Mandel, Marburg, 2005, p. 64.

43 E. Federn to E. Mandel, 6 January 1954, E. Mandel Archives, folder 1.

44 Ibid.

45 Mandel applied for naturalization on 8 July 1948, and he was granted Belgian citizenship on 12 July 1956.

46 E. Mandel to E. Federn, 31 May 1948, E. Mandel Archives, folder 677.

47 E. Mandel to L. Markowitz, 11 August 1954, E. Mandel Archives, folder 1.

48 E. Mandel to A. Housiaux, 13 February 1954, E. Mandel Archives, folder 1. Mandel worked for *Le Peuple* from 1 March 1954 to 31 July 1957.

49 Aanstellingsbrief (letter confirming permanent employment) issued to E. Mandel, 20 August 1954, E. Mandel Archives, folder 1.

50 E. Mandel to Syndicat des Journalistes FGTB (ABVV journalists' union); 'A tous les rédacteurs du (To all the editors of *Le) Peuple*,' 14 June 1957, E. Mandel Archives, folder 6.

51 R. Prager, *Les Congrès de la Quatrième Internationale, 4: Menace de la troisième guerre mondiale et tournant politique (1950–1952)*, Paris, 1989, pp. 109–32. M. Lorneau, *Contribution à l'histoire du mouvement trotskyste belge, 1939–1960*, vol. IV, p. 739, note 3.

52 In a series of countries they persisted in building independent parties. This was the case in the United States, India, Ceylon (now Sri Lanka) and the Latin American countries. R. Prager, *Les Congrès de la Quatrième Internationale*, p. 12.

53 In preparation for the 1951 World Congress of the Fourth International, Michel Pablo published a document , influenced by his view of the Korean War (June 1950), in which he predicted a world war caused not by the decisive defeat of the working class as in the 1930s, but by revolutions like the one in China in 1949. To prepare for this war and to save itself, in the short term imperialism would be impelled to crush any developing revolution. This would call forth resistance and lead to new revolutions. M. Pablo, 'Où allons-nous', *Quatrième Internationale*, February 1951.

54 Groslambert was anything but dull. He was known for occasional angry outbursts, and whenever he was displeased with the course of a discussion he was apt to turn off the lights and leave.

55 E. Mandel to E. Federn, 30 November 1948, E. Mandel Archives, folder 677.

56 E. Germain, 'Bilan de la question royale', *L'Avant-Garde*, vol. 1, no. 1, December 1945.

57 P. Theunissen, *1950: ontknoping van de Koningskwestie*, Antwerp, 1984, p. 71.

58 The strikes were organized by the Socialist trade unions with support from the Socialist Joint Action, a front of the four branches of the socialist workers' movement. The four involved were the Socialist Party (BSP), the ABVV trade union federation, the mutual societies and the cooperatives. The BSP took the initiative in forming this front after the 1949 election. As its basis the front took the 'Labour Charter', which joined three themes: the struggles for political democracy, for defence of acquired social rights and for economic democracy.

59 J. Neuville and J. Yerna, *Le Choc de l'hiver'60–61: Les grèves contra la loi unique*, Brussels, 1992, p. 32.

60 E. Witte, J. Craeybeckx and A. Meynen, *Politieke geschiedenis van België*, p. 249.

J. Gerard-Libois and J. Gotovitch, *Leopold III: De l'an 40 à l'effacement*, Brussels, 1992.

61 *Le Soir*, 28 July 1950, cited in C. Mesnil, *La Question royale: Textes et photographies*, p. 113. M. Lorneau, *Contribution*, vol. III, p. 606.

62 M. Liebman, 'La Social-démocratie belge et l'héritage réformiste', *Contradictions: Le Réformisme social-démocrate (Allemagne, Belgique, France, Italie)*, no. 7, Brussels 1975, p. 8.

63 'La Nouvelle montée ouvrière en Belgique', *Quatrième Internationale*, vol. 8, no. 8/10, August/October 1950.

64 'Résolution sur les tâches immédiates de la section belge', Bulletin Intérieur du SI, April 1950, R. Prager Archives, folder 39. The International Secretariat of the Fourth International pronounced formally for entry into the BSP in a meeting held 13–15 September 1950. 'Compte rendu sommaire de la séance du SI élargi (13–15 September 1950)', R. Prager Archives, folder 39. The *Cahiers Léon Trotsky* devoted a special issue to entryism before the war: *Cahiers Léon Trotsky*, no. 16, December 1983, including J.-P. Joubert, 'Remarques sur la politique "entriste"'; P. Broué, 'Quand Carillo était "gauchiste"': les jeunesses socialistes d'Espagne 1934–1946'; J. Archer, 'Grand-Bretagne: L'entrisme et le Labour Party'; J.-J. Ayme, 'Ces Jeunesses dont leur parti ne voulut pas: les jeunesses socialistes de France de 1944 à 1974'.

65 'Résolution sur les tâches immédiates de la section belge'.

66 On the opposition to entryism, see: R. Prager, *Les Congrès*, pp. 7–23.

67 A. Renard, 'Pour la résistance', *Volonté*, 9 July 1949, cited in N. Latteur, *La Gauche en mal de la Gauche*, Brussels, 2000, p. 14.

68 J. Neuville and J. Yerna, *Le Choc de l'hiver '60–'61*, p. 16. R. Hemmerijckx, *Van Verzet tot koude oorlog*, pp. 99, 384.

69 J. Neuville and J. Yerna, *Le Choc de l'hiver '60–'61*, p. 34.

70 R. Hemmerijckx, 'De Mouvement Syndical Unifié en het ontstaan van het renardisme', AMSAB (Institute for Social History, Ghent), *Tijdingen* IV 1985–6, no. 2. R. Hemmerijckx, *Van verzet tot koude oorlog*, pp. 99–101. J. Neuville and J. Yerna, *Le Choc de l'hiver '60–'61* p. 52.

71 J. Yerna, 'Les Réformes de structure, 10 ans après le congrès extraordinaire de la FGTB', *Les Réformes de structure: 10 ans après le Congrès extraordinaire de la FGTB*, Liège 1965: complete transcript of the reports of the study days in Roncines, 26–7 September 1964.

72 I. Ponet interview with J. Yerna, *La Gauche*, no. 3, March/April 2003.

73 ABVV, 'Holdings en Economische Democratie', n.p., 1956.

74 A. Meynen, 'De economische en sociale politiek sinds de jaren 1950', E. Witte, J. Craeybeckx and A. Meynen, *Politieke geschiedenis van België*, p. 282; A. Meynen, 'Structuurhervormingen en algemene staking, 1958–1961', *Vooruitlopen op het Vlaamse socialisme: Vijfentwintig jaar Links*, Leuven, 1984, pp. 29–39.

75 ABVV, *Holding*, p. 34. A 'politically socialist state' and a 'classless society' were formulated as conditions for reaching economic democracy.

76 A. Renard, 'La Lutte est engagée', *La Gauche*, 9 February 1957.

77 A. Renard, *Vers le socialisme par l'action*, Liège, 1958.

78 In a 1964 report Jacques Yerna pointed out the ambiguous character of the programme of structural reform, which could be interpreted in either an anti-

capitalist or a neo-capitalist sense. J. Yerna, 'Les Réformes de structure en Belgique, 10 ans après le rapport d'André Renard', *Les Reformes de structure.* Alain Meynen also noted this ambiguity. See A. Meynen, 'De economische en sociale politiek sinds de jaren 1950', E. Witte, J. Craeybeckx and A. Meynen, *Politieke geschiedenis van België,* pp. 279–325.

79 E. Mandel, 'Les Grandes batailles du socialisme belge', *La Gauche*, 15 December 1956. In an editorial in *Le Gauche* of 19 January 1957, Mandel wrote, 'Only structural reforms can guarantee full employment, better distribution of national income and progress towards that *equality of opportunity for all citizens* that remains the fundamental object of socialism.'

80 E. Mandel, 'Il faut abattre les féodalités financières!', *La Gauche*, 9 February 1957.

81 E. Mandel, 'Qui contrôle la Société Générale?', Centre for Socio-Political Research and Information, *Courrier Hebdomadaire*, no. 17, 8 May 1959; reprinted by the SJW in the series *Etudes et documents*, no. 5 September 1959. J. van Lierde, *Un Insoumis*, Brussels, 1998, pp. 167–8.

82 Huysmans, former secretary of the International Socialist Bureau, former prime minister, *enfant terrible* and 'grand old man', was active in the left wing of the Socialist Party. Quote from I. Ponet interview with J. Yerna, *La Gauche*, no. 3, March/April 2003.

83 'Guy Cudell: L'homme des causes gagnées', *Le Soir*, 27 December 1977. E. Mandel to G. Cudell, 17 November 1955, E. Mandel Archives, folder 1. Cudell became sympathetic to Trotskyist ideas during the Occupation but never joined the RCP.

84 Jacques Yerna was first present at the meeting of 2 June 1956. According to a report the others present were R. Latin, Herman, Henry, Cudell, Mandel, Stevens, Wolff, J. Wolff, Roesseau, R. Falony, P. de Swaef, Brochard, M. Slusny, R. Rifflet, E. van Ceulen, D. Leenaerts, Clajot, Perrin, Beauvois, Leleu and Peereboom. Deschamps, R. Evalenko, Gibbon, Vloebergh, Guillot, R. Leenaerts, De Ridder, G. Debunne, Genot, Harmignies and Speyer sent regrets. E. Mandel Archives, folder 406.

85 I. Ponet interview with J. Yerna, *La Gauche*, no. 3, March/April 2003.

86 Summary of subscriptions, single-issue sales and financial situation in G. Cudell, 'Rapport', 21 March 1957, E. Mandel Archives, folder 406. In September 1957 weekly sales averaged around 3,000, of which two-thirds were subscriptions. E. Mandel to S. Cauwberghs, 13 September 1957, E. Mandel Archives, folder 410. In 1958 circulation varied between 2,500 and 3,000 copies; subscriptions between 1,600 and 1,800. E. Mandel Archives, folder 413. After October 1958, the paper consisted of twelve pages instead of eight, and in 1959 subscriptions totalled 2,200 and sales of single copies averaged around 1,350. E. Mandel to G. Cudell, n.d., E. Mandel Archives, folder 426. In October 1960 there were 2,491 subscriptions. Roger to E. Mandel, 11 October 1960, E. Mandel Archives, folder 422. Every week the Liège metal workers accounted for 500 copies. E. Mandel to O. Rosenfeld, 2 June 1959, E. Mandel Archives, folder 425. In 1961 there were 2,800 subscriptions. During the strike weeks of 1960–61 sales of single copies averaged 17,600 for each issue. 'Procès-verbal de l'Assemblée Générale des coopérateurs', 24 June 1961, E. Mandel Archives, folder 433.

87 E. Mandel, 'Note d'introduction', E. Mandel Archives, folder 125. The journalists Robert Falony, Oscar de Swaef and Brochard came from *Le Peuple*.

88 In the list of 31 December 1960, there were a total of 125 names. E. Mandel Archives, folder 423.

89 N. Latteur, *La Gauche*, p. 35. Evalenko was the director of the Emile Vandervelde Institute; Defay was a party functionary and a member of the European left; Cools was a member of parliament from 1958 to 1991, mayor of Flémalle from 1964 to 1991, various times federal minister and vice-premier from 1969 to 1972 and party chair from 1973 to 1981. Cools was shot dead in July 1991.

90 E. Mandel to J. Wantiez, 6 March 1957, E. Mandel Archives, folder 408.

91 K. Manfred (pseudonym James Parkner) to E. Mandel, 13 February 1957, E. Mandel Archives, folder 407. E. Mandel to K. Manfred, 17 February 1957, E. Mandel Archives, folder 480.

92 Rosenfeld and Naville were founders of the periodical *La Nouvelle Revue Marxiste*. Other correspondents were Theo van Tijn (Netherlands), Joseph Hindels (Austria), Karl Manfred (USA) and Lasoto (Poland).

93 E. Mandel to 'Conseil d'administration de la société d'édition *Le Peuple*' (Board of the *Le Peuple* publishing company), 22 April 1957, E. Mandel Archives, folder 408. A month earlier a report from the State Security Service dated 13 March 1957 had stated that three Trotskyists (Ernest Mandel, Emile van Ceulen and Pierre Le Grève) were part of the paper's management. P. Tilly, *André Renard*, Brussels, 2005, p. 546.

94 R. Evalenko, R. Latin and A. Renard, Note to 'Membres du Bureau au sujet de *La Gauche*', n.d., E. Mandel Archives, folder 4.

95 E. Mandel to 'Syndicat des journalistes FGTB' (ABVV journalists' union); 'A tous les rédacteurs du [To all the editors of *Le Peuple*], 14 June 1957, E. Mandel Archives, folder 6.

96 E. Mandel to 'Conseil d'administration de la société d'édition *Le Peuple*'.

97 Robert Falony continued to write for *La Gauche* using the pseudonym Jean Laffont. Brochard and De Swaef yielded.

98 E. Mandel to S. Cauwberghs, 18 August 1957, E. Mandel Archives, folder 410.

99 A. Renard to E. Mandel, 5 November 1957, E. Mandel Archives, folder 6. J. Brusson to L. Nizet, 4 September 1957, E. Mandel Archives, folder 6. Mandel began working for *La Wallonie* on 1 August 1957.

100 In a memorandum Mandel wrote, 'It's true that some more acerbic notes have crept into the first issues of *La Gauche*. We can sincerely regret this. But it would be unfair to say that these notes have determined the paper's overall editorial line, tone or audience.' E. Mandel, 'Les Rédacteurs du *Peuple* et *la Gauche*', E. Mandel Archives, folder 408.

101 *La Gauche*, 13 July 1957. E. Mandel to A. Renard, 23 March 1961, E. Mandel Archives, folder 17. E. Mandel, 'Dialogue sur la grève', *La Gauche*, 6 July 1957. Louis Major, general secretary of the ABVV, considered Mandel an accomplice of Renard on the editorial board of *Le Peuple*. P. Tilly, *André Renard*, p. 557.

102 E. Mandel to M. Deneckere, 16 May 1957, E. Mandel Archives, folder 408.

103 M. Deneckere to E. Mandel, 9 September 1957, E. Mandel Archives, folder 410.

104 E. Mandel to W. Caluwaerts, 28 October 1957, E. Mandel Archives, folder 411.

105 J. Vandenbroucke, *De sportziel van de Satan*, www.brakkehond.be/67/brouc2.html. Fourteen issues of *De Satan* appeared in the years 1956–7.

106 F. Buyens to E. Mandel, 6 November 1957, E. Mandel Archives, folder 411; E. Mandel to F. Buyens, 25 November 1957, E. Mandel Archives, folder 411.

107 E. Mandel to F. Buyens, 28 October 1957, E. Mandel Archives, folder 411.

108 W. Caluwaerts to E. Mandel, 16 November 1957, E. Mandel Archives, folder 411.

109 Mandel mentioned such threats and intimidation, particularly in the Bruges federation of the Socialist Party, in a letter to J. Craeybeckx: E. Mandel to J. Craeybeckx, 26 July 1958, E. Mandel Archives, folder 413.

110 M. Deneckere to E. Mandel, 3 June 1958, E. Mandel Archives, folder 414.

111 E. Mandel to M. Deneckere, 10 June 1958, E. Mandel Archives, folder 414.

112 F. Buyens to E. Mandel, 7 September 1958, E. Mandel Archives, folder 413.

113 E. Mandel to F. Buyens and W. Caluwaerts, 29 August 1958, E. Mandel Archives, folder 413.

114 The editorial board consisted of M. Deneckere, E. Mandel, J. Wijninckx, H. de Geest, G. Michiels, L. Depauw, M. De Kock and M. van Hemeldonck.

115 K. Borms, 'Stop een vakbond in uw tank: *Links* en de vakbeweging', *Vooruitlopen op het Vlaams socialisme*, pp. 104–5. A. Meynen, 'Structuurhervormingen en algemene staking', p. 35.

116 E. Mandel and J. Yerna, 'Perspectives socialistes sur la question flamande', *La Gauche*, 19 April 1958. Mandel and Deneckere shared the same ideas about the Flemish question. In May 1958 Deneckere wrote to Mandel, 'I congratulate you on the article about the Flemish movement. As for your interpretation of the spread of French in Flanders, it agrees completely with the position I set forth in my book *Histoire de la langue française dans les Flandres (1770–1830)*.' M. Deneckere to E. Mandel, 2 May 1958, E. Mandel Archives, folder 414. Deneckere shared Mandel's perspective that 'the spread of French in Flanders is the result of a process of internal differentiation in the Flemish community'. Here Mandel opposed the idea that it was the formation of the Belgian state in 1830 and its choice of French as the unitary official language that was the primary cause of Flemish adoption of French.

117 J. Craeybeckx, 'Het flamingantisme van Marcel Deneckere: *Links* en de Vlaamse beweging', *Vooruitlopen op het Vlaamse socialisme*.

118 E. Mandel, Note, n.d. [1961], E. Mandel Archives, folder 433.

119 E. Mandel to P. von Oertzen, 25 January 1959, E. Mandel Archives, folder 413.

120 *La Gauche*, 21 February 1959.

121 Renard's statement in *L'Action*, see ibid.; other details, see author's interview with G. Dobbeleer, 11 February 2003. P. Tilly, p. 546.

122 E. Mandel to P. von Oertzen, 5 June 1959, E. Mandel Archives, folder 17.

123 Ibid.

124 E. Witte, J. Craeybeckx and A. Meynen, *Politieke geschiedenis van België*, pp. 283–4.

125 E. Mandel to O. Rosenfeld, 10 October 1959, E. Mandel Archives, folder 424.

126 E. Mandel to P. von Oertzen, 25 January 1959, E. Mandel Archives, folder 413.

127 Author's interview with G. Dobbeleer, 11 February 2003.

128 G. Dobbeleer, *Sur les traces de la révolution: Itinéraire d'un trotskiste belge*, Paris, 2006, pp. 153–4.

129 *La Gauche*, 3 October 1959. That Mandel attributed an important role to the Christian trade union movement is also clear from a 1980 interview with the German political scientist Johannes Agnoli. After stating that the movement was divided into two camps, Catholic and Socialist, Mandel continued, 'And we face this problem. If we can bring this colossal social force to bear, then a socialist breakthrough is possible. But if this social force is divided, and half of organized labour remains in thrall to a bourgeois party, then a solution is impossible, or in any event extraordinarily difficult.' E. Mandel and J. Agnoli, *Offener Marxismus: Ein Gespräch über Dogmen, Orthodoxie und die Häresie der Realität*, Frankfurt on Main, 1980, p. 106.

130 *La Gauche*, 26 September 1959.

131 Ibid.

132 J. Neuville and J. Yerna, *Le Choc de l'hiver '60–'61*, p. 69.

133 C. Castoriadis, 'La Signification des grèves belges', *Socialisme ou Barbarie*, no. 32, April 1961, reprinted in C. Castoriadis, *L'Expérience du mouvement ouvrier*, vol. 2: *Prolétariat et organisation*, Paris, 1974, p. 255.

134 J. Neuville and J. Yerna, *Le Choc de l'hiver '60–'61*. F. Buyens, L. de Haes, B. Hogenkamp and A. Meynen, *Vechten voor onze rechten, 60–61: De staking tegen de Eenheidswet*, Leuven, 1985. P. Gousset, 'Un Nouveau "juin 36," ' *France Observateur*, 29 December 1960. P. Gousset, 'L'Unité nationale en péril?', *France Observateur*, 5 January 1961.

135 P. Gousset, 'Un Nouveau "juin 36." '

136 E. Mandel to K. Manfred, 2 January 1961, E. Mandel Archives, folder 483.

137 *La Gauche,* 7 January 1961.

138 P. Gousset, 'Un Nouveau "juin 36." '

139 N. Latteur, *La Gauche*, p. 51.

140 R. Moreau, *Combat syndicale et conscience wallonne*, Liège, n.d., pp. 149–50. P. Gousset, 'L'Unité nationale en péril?'.

141 N. Latteur, *La Gauche*, p. 43; E. Mandel to A. Renard, 12 December 1960, E. Mandel Archives, folder 431.

142 E. Mandel to 'Pierre, Livio and Edward', 5 January 1961, E. Mandel Archives, folder 483.

143 A. Meynen, 'De grote staking', F. Buyens, L. De Haes, B. Hogenkamp and A. Meynen, *Vechten voor onze rechten, 60–61*, p. 21.

144 P. Gousset, 'Le Tournant de la grève', *France Observateur*, 12 January 1961.

145 D. Landes, *The Unbound Prometheus: Technological Change and Industrial Development in Western Europe from 1750 to the Present*, Cambridge, 1969, p. 498.

146 E. Mandel, 'Les Grèves belges: essai d'explication socio-économique', *Les Temps Modernes*, vol. 16, no. 180, April 1961.

147 Ibid.

148 E.M.'s italics. In the summer of 1963 *New Left Review* published an essay by Mandel about the economic development of Belgium since its industrialization, which contained the following passage about the general strike of 1960–61: 'The general strike developed into the first campaign . . . of the most conscious members of the working-class to replace the neo-capitalist solution to the crisis of the Belgian economy with a genuinely anti-capitalist solution.' E. Mandel, 'The Dialectic of Class and Religion in Belgium', *New Left Review*, no. 20, summer 1963, p. 24. Also: E. Mandel, 'La Belgique entre néo-capitalisme et socialisme', *Partisans*, no. 12, 1963, no. 13, 1963–4.

149 E. Mandel, 'Les Grèves belges: essai d'explication socio-économique'.

150 J. K. Galbraith, *The Affluent Society*, London, 1962; M. Young, *The Rise of the Meritocracy, 1870–2033*, London, 1958. C. Crosland, *The Future of Socialism*, London, 1956; V. Bogdanor and R. Skidelsky, eds., *The Age of Affluence, 1951–1964*, London, 1970.

151 *La Gauche*, 15 April 1961; E. Mandel to D. Theophor, 23 May 1961, E. Mandel Archives, folder 432.

152 L. Van der Taelen, 'Links buiten of niet? Het onverenigbaarheidscongres (1964)', *Vooruitlopen op het Vlaamse socialisme*, p. 58.

153 E. Mandel to T. van Tijn, 5 March 1961, E. Mandel Archives, folder 483.

154 '*Links*: Etude d'un organe de tendance', Centre for Socio-Political Research and Information, *Courrier Hebdomadaire*, 26 February 1965, p. 4.

155 Author's interview with G. Dobbeleer, 11 February 2003. E. Mandel to 'Cher ami', 16 April 1961, G. Dobbeleer Archives.

156 'Procès-verbal de l'assemblée générale des coopérateurs', 20 June 1961, E. Mandel Archives, folder 433.

157 A. Renard to E. Mandel, 10 March 1961, E. Mandel Archives, folder 17.

158 E. Mandel to A. Renard, 23 March 1961, E. Mandel Archives, folder 17.

159 A. Renard to E. Mandel, 27 March 1961, E. Mandel Archives, folder 17.

160 E. Mandel to A. Renard, 28 March 1961, E. Mandel Archives, folder 17.

161 A. Renard to E. Mandel, 29 March 1961, E. Mandel Archives, folder 17.

162 E. Mandel to Danis [Théophar], 23 May 1961, E. Mandel Archives, folder 432.

163 E. Mandel to A. Renard, 18 May 1961, E. Mandel Archives, folder 10.

164 E. Mandel to Roger [Forton], 16 May 1961, E. Mandel Archives, folder 432.

165 *La Gauche*, 22 December 1961.

166 M. Lambilliotte, *André Renard et son destin*, Brussels, 1971, p. 138.

167 'André Renard et l'évolution de notre mouvement ouvrier', *La Gauche*, 3 August 1962.

168 Ibid.

169 *La Gauche*, 3 August 1962.

170 *La Wallonie*, 25 July 1962.

171 E. Mandel to K. Manfred, 5 October 1962, E. Mandel Archives.

172 I. Ponet interview with J. Yerna, *La Gauche*, no. 3, March/April 2003.

173 Ibid.

174 Ibid.

175 E. Mandel to 'Cher ami', 1 December 1962, E. Mandel Archives.

176 *La Gauche*, 8 March 1963; 15 March 1963.

177 *La Gauche*, 15 March 1963.

178 Declaration signed by twenty-nine railway workers, 4 March 1963, E. Mandel Archives, folder 18.
179 *La Gauche*, 12 April 1963.
180 *Le Peuple*, 17 April 1963.
181 J. M. Roberti, *Dossier Ernest Glinne*, Chenée, March 1974.
182 P. Le Grève, *Souvenirs d'un marxiste anti-stalinien*, Paris, 1996, pp. 144–6.
183 N. Latteur, *La Gauche*, p. 68.
184 *La Voix Socialiste*, 16 September 1964; 25 September 1964. The articles were written by Michel Géoris, a former member of the Fourth International section, co-worker at *La Gauche* and member of the SJW. He was a secret service spy who later made himself very useful to the Congolese dictator Mobutu with the periodical *Spécial*. As far as can be determined, Trotskyist influence in the Socialist Party was organized as follows: Focant was secretary of the Schaarbeek branch of the Socialist Party, Tran of the Ganshoren branch, Fortin in Woluwe and Groslambert in Brussels. Le Grève was very influential in Ukkel and Falony in Schaarbeek. Furthermore, the leadership of the SJW was in the hands of such Trotskyists as Dobbeleer, Perpette and Leenaerts in Liège; Clajot and Van Ceulen in Brussels; Rombaux and Lenne in The Center; and Perez in Charleroi. In addition, Trotskyists were strong in the Education Union and the Service Union of the ABVV, in the Socialist Young Guard (SJW) and in the committee supporting Algerian independence (P. Le Grève). Yet the size of the section was rather limited, with around sixty members in 1965, according to Georges Dobbeleer (G. Dobbeleer, *Sur les traces de la révolution*, p. 300).
185 'Le Problème des incompatibilités soumis au congrès du parti socialiste belge des 12 et 13 décembre 1964 et ses consequences' part I, Centre for Socio-Political Research and Information, *Courrier Hebdomadaire*, no. 271, 29 January 1965.
186 Author's interview with G. Dobbeleer, 11 February 2003. The objectionable banner, 'Murderer Mollet' was never found.
187 *La Gauche*, 12 September 1964.
188 E. Mandel to P. von Oertzen, 18 November 1964, E. Mandel Archives, folder 447.
189 E. Mandel to P. von Oertzen, 30 November 1964, E. Mandel Archives, folder 447.
190 'Le Problème des incompatibilités soumis au congrès du parti socialiste belge des 12 et 13 décembre 1964 et ses consequences', part II, Centre for Socio-Political Research and Information, *Courrier Hebdomadaire*, no. 272, 5 February 1965.
191 *La Gauche*, 28 November 1964.
192 *Volksgazet*, 14 December 1964.
193 E. Mandel, 'Pourquoi nous ne céderons pas', *La Gauche*, 19 December 1964.
194 *Le Peuple*, 14 December 1964.
195 N. Latteur, *La Gauche*, p. 131.
196 E. Mandel, 'Pourquoi nous ne céderons pas'.
197 E. Mandel to K. Coates, 16 December 1964, E. Mandel Archives, folder 26.
198 F. Vercammen to E. Mandel, August 19, 1985; E. Mandel to F. Vercammen, September 4, 1985, F. Vercammen Archives.
199 Author's interview with F. Vercammen, 25 November 2004.

Marxists Economic Theory: A Book about the World

1 E. Mandel to E. Federn, 4 December 1951, E. Mandel Archives, folder 677.
2 E. Mandel to M. Deneckere, 12 January 1962, E. Mandel Archives, folder 12.
3 E. Mandel, *Marxist Economic Theory*, 2 vols, New York 1968.
4 E. Mandel, *Marxist Economic Theory*, vol. 1, New York 1968, p. 18.
5 Ibid., p. 17.
6 According to Mandel, no breakthrough could occur because the more developed agriculture had led to a large growth in population, which required irrigation, farming and therefore centralization of the agricultural surplus, which in turn resulted in a politically weak bourgeoisie and thus an intermittent primitive accumulation of capital. In the West, by contrast, the lower productivity of labour in agriculture combined with a smaller population made possible the fragmentation of political powers and therefore the development of a powerful bourgeoisie, which managed to end the periodic expropriations and confiscations by the aristocracy. In the West, unlike the East, a continuous process of capital accumulation took place starting in the fifteenth century.
7 J. Banaji, 'Islam, the Mediterranean and the Rise of Capitalism', *Historical Materialism*, vol. 15, no. 1, 2007, pp. 47–74.
8 E. Mandel, *Marxist Economic Theory,* vol. 2, p. 571.
9 Ibid., pp. 548–689. M. van der Linden, *Western Marxism and the Soviet Union: A Survey of Critical Theories and Debates Since 1917*, Leiden, 2007.
10 Other important initiatives were E.P. Thompson, *The Making of the English Working Class*, London, 1963, and E. Bloch, *The Principle of Hope*, Cambridge, MA, 1986. See also the contemporary debates in *New Left Review* and *Les Temps Modernes*.
11 E. Mandel to K. Manfred, 3 October 1961, E. Mandel Archives, folder 435.
12 A. Wald, 'George Novack, 1905–92: Meaning a Life', G. Breitman, P. Le Blanc and A. Wald, *Trotskyism in the United States: Historical Essays and Considerations*, Atlantic Highlands, NJ, 1996, pp. 146–58.
13 P. Broué, *Trotsky*, Paris, 1988, p. 843.
14 A. Wald, *The New York Intellectuals: The Rise and Decline of the Anti-Stalinist Left from the 1930s to the 1980s*, Chapel Hill, 1987, p. 307.
15 W. Warde [G. Novack], 'The Law of Uneven and Combined Development', *Labour Review*, January and March/April 1957, reprinted in G. Novack, *Understanding History: Marxist Essays*, New York 1972, pp. 82–129.
16 E. Mandel, *Marxist Economic Theory*, New York 1968, chapters 12, 13 and 16.
17 R. Melville, 'Roman Rosdolsky (1898–1967) als Historiker Galiziens und der Habsburgermonarchie', R. Rosdolskly, *Untertan und Staat in Galizien: Die Reformen unter Maria Theresia und Joseph II*, Mainz, 1929, pp. vii–xxv. E. Rosdolsky, 'Leben, Motive, Werk', R. Rosdolsky, *Zur nationalen Frage: Friedrich Engels und das Problem der geschichtslosen Völker*, Berlin, 1979. J. Radziejowski, 'Roman Rosdolsky: Man, Activist, and Scholar', *Science and Society* 42, 1978 no. 2.
18 R. Rosdolsky, *Zur nationalen Frage*. In this text, based on his dissertation, Rosdolsky criticized Marx and Engels for their inimical position towards the smaller Slavic nationalities, such as the Czechs, Slovaks, Croats and Ruthenians, in the *Neue Rheinische Zeitung* during the revolution of 1848. Mandel called this the first successful Marxist criticism of Marx himself.

19 D. Singer, 'Armed with a Pen: Notes for a Political Portrait of Isaac Deutscher', D. Horowitz, ed., *Isaac Deutscher: The Man and His Work*, London, 1971, p. 33. L. Syré, *Isaac Deutscher, Marxist, Publizist, Historiker: sein Leben und Werk, 190–1967*, Hamburg, 1984.

20 J. Radziejowski, 'Roman Rosdolsky: Man, Activist, and Scholar'. E. Germain [E. Mandel], 'Roman Rosdolsky', *Quatrième Internationale*, April 1978. E. Mandel, 'Roman Rosdolsky', manuscripts in English, German and French, E. Mandel Archives, folder 41.

21 E. Rosdolsky to E. Mandel, 25 March 1968, E. Mandel Archives, folder 40.

22 Mandel wrote to Federn: 'Too bad that Roman did not search out our friends [the US Trotskyists] . . . It could have been arranged so that no one would have been harmed by that.' E. Mandel to E. and H. Federn, 25 October 1950, E. Mandel Archives, folder 677.

23 E. Mandel to R. Rosdolsky, 9 February 1957, E. Mandel Archives, folder 480.

24 R. Rosdolsky to E. Mandel, 9 January 1957, E. Mandel Archives, folder 480.

25 E. Mandel to E. Federn, 11 August 1952, E. Mandel Archives, folder 677.

26 E. Mandel to E. Federn, 24 December 1954, E. Mandel Archives, folder 1.

27 E. Federn to E. Mandel, 4 February 1957, E. Mandel Archives, folder 4.

28 The first German edition of the *Grundrisse* was published in Moscow in 1939–41 in two volumes. Only a few copies of this edition reached the West. The second edition, K. Marx, *Grundrisse der Kritik der politischen Ökonomie: Rohentwurf, 1857–1858*, was published in one volume in East Berlin in 1953.

29 E. Rosdolsky to E. Mandel, 8 December 1967, E. Mandel Archives, folder 38.

30 R. Rosdolsky, *The Making of Marx's 'Capital'*, London, 1977.

31 R. Rosdolsky to E. Mandel, 12 November 1955. E. Mandel to R. Rosdolsky, 24 November 1955, E. Mandel Archives, folder 1.

32 E. Mandel to R. Rosdolsky, 5 May 1956, E. Mandel Archives, folder 480.

33 E. Mandel to R. Rosdolsky, 21 January 1957, E. Mandel Archives, folder 480.

34 R. Rosdolsky to E. Mandel, 28 January 1957, E. Mandel Archives, folder 480.

35 R. Rosdolsky to E. Mandel, 15 February 1957, E. Mandel Archives, folder 480.

36 R. Rosdolsky to E. Mandel, 6 June 1959, E. Mandel Archives, folder 481.

37 E. Mandel to R. Rosdolsky, 8 June 1959, E. Mandel Archives, folder 481. R. Rosdolsky to E. Mandel, 17 June 1959, E. Mandel Archives, folder 481.

38 E. Mandel to S. Gordon, 29 May 1963, E. Mandel Archives, folder 321.

39 Rosdolsky wrote an essay on the 'workers' states' in 1959. It was only published after his death in 1978. R. Rosdolsky, 'Zur Analyse der russischen Revolution' (1959), *Die Sozialismusdebatte: Historische und aktuelle Fragen des Sozialismus*, U. Wolter, ed., West Berlin 1978, pp. 203–36. In his book *Russia after Stalin*, Deutscher developed the thesis that the Stalinist dictatorship had been historically necessary to accomplish industrialization and free Russia from its socioeconomic backwardness. Once the forced industrialization was accomplished, Deutscher saw a real chance of democratization of the political regime. It would be a gradual process, directed from above. I. Deutscher, *Russia After Stalin*, London, 1953. M. van der Linden, *Western Marxism and the Soviet Union*.

40 E. Mandel to P. Naville, 25 July 1960, E. Mandel Archives, folder 318.

41 P. Naville to E. Mandel, 17 September 1960, E. Mandel Archives, folder 318.

42 E. Mandel to D. Guérin, 27 July 1962, E. Mandel Archives, folder 16.

43 C. Bourdet to R. Julliard, 31 October 1960, E. Mandel Archives, folder 11.

44 R. Julliard, 'Contrat Traité d'économie marxiste', 12 May 1961, E. Mandel Archives, folder 318.

45 E. Mandel to W. Abendroth, 4 November 1961, W. Abendroth Archives, folder 66. E. Mandel to C. Bourgois, 9 May 1962; 1 July 1961, E. Mandel Archives, folder 318. The campaign was carried out in Belgium by La Gauche and such trade union papers as La Tribune, L'Employé, La Wallonie, Socialisme and Education et Socialisme. In France it was done through France Observateur and La Tribune Socialiste. The books were also sold in Switzerland by subscription through Socialisme Démocratique.

46 E. Mandel to E. and H. Federn, 18 February 1962, E. Mandel Archives, folder 13.

47 E. Mandel, Traité d'économie marxiste, vol. 1, Paris, 1962.

48 E. Mandel to A. Renard, 7 June 1962, E. Mandel Archives, folder 319.

49 M. Liebman to I. Deutscher, 3 May 1962, I. Deutscher Archives, folder 42.

50 I. Deutscher to M. Liebman, 20 May 1962, I. Deutscher Archives, folder 42.

51 I. Deutscher to R. Rosdolsky, 30 April 1962, R. Rosdolsky Archives, folder 46.

52 D. Singer, 'Notes for a Political Portrait of Isaac Deutscher'.

53 I. Deutscher, 'Marxist Heretic: Traité d'économie marxiste', The Economist, 22 September 1962, p. 1118.

54 E. Mandel to I. Deutscher, 23 September 1962, I. Deutscher Archives, folder 47.

55 H.D. Dickenson, 'Contemporary Marxist Economics', New Left Review, no. 21, October 1963, pp. 30–6; A. Barjonet, Economie et politique, June/July 1963; L. Laurat, Le Contrat social, May/June 1963; M. Rubel, L'Année sociologique, 1963; R. Supek, Praxis, 1966, no. 2; M. Dobb, The Morning Star, 2 January 1969.

56 A. Renard to E. Mandel, 4 June 1962, E. Mandel Archives.

57 O. Lange to E. Mandel, 23 May 1963, E. Mandel Archives.

58 R L. Heilbroner, 'Marxism: For and Against', New York Review of Books, vol. XII, no. 11, 5 June 1969, pp. 14–17.

59 R. Rosdolsky to O. Morf, 11 August 1962; 17 April 1963, R. Rosdolsky Archives, folder 299.

60 K. Korsch, M. Buckmiller, M. Prat and M.G. Werner, eds, Briefe 1908–1958, vol. 2, Amsterdam, 2001, p. 1527.

61 I. Deutscher to R. Rosdolsky, 14 April 1962, I. Deutscher Archives, folder 87.

62 E. Mandel to R. Rosdolsky, 13 January 1964, E. Mandel Archives, folder 22.

63 R. Rosdolsky to E. Mandel, 18 January 1964, E. Mandel Archives, folder 22. 'His third volume' refers to volume three of Deutscher's Trotsky trilogy, The Prophet Outcast: Trotsky 1929–1940.

64 Ibid.

65 Ibid.

66 E. Mandel to R. Rosdolsky, 25 February 1964, E. Mandel Archives, folder 22.

67 E. Mandel to E. Federn, 15 July 1949, E. Mandel Archives, folder 677.

68 E. Mandel to E. Federn, 4 June 1951, E. Mandel Archives, folder 677. W.

Gebhardt [E. Mandel], *Die Wissenschaft der Entschleierung: Eine Erwiderung auf Prof. Carlo Schmid's Entschleierung der Wissenschaft*, Berlin, 1952.

69 J.-P. Sartre, *The Communists and Peace, With A Reply to Claude Lefort*, New York, 1968. A. Cohen-Solal, *Sartre 1905–1980*, Paris, 1985, p. 432. I. Birchall, *Sartre against Stalinism*, New York, 2004, pp. 147–50.

70 M. van der Linden, 'Socialisme ou Barbarie: A French Revolutionary Group (1949–65)', *Left History*, 5.1, 1998. pp. 7–37; J.-P. Sartre, *The Communists and Peace, with A Reply to Claude Lefort*.

71 M. Merleau-Ponty, *Adventures of the Dialectic*, Evanston, 1973.

72 C. Lefort, 'Le Marxisme et Sartre', *Les Temps Modernes*, no. 89, April 1953. J.-P. Sartre, 'Réponse à Lefort', *Les Temps Modernes*, no. 89, April 1953; C. Lefort, 'De La Réponse à la question', *Les Temps Modernes*, no. 104, July 1954. In early 1949 Lefort, Cornelius Castoriadis, François Lyotard and Daniel Mothé had left the Fourth International in dissatisfaction over what they saw as its Stalinophile perspective on the USSR and Stalinism. They established the periodical *Socialisme ou Barbarie* (Socialism or Barbarism) and the group of the same name, which disbanded in 1966.

73 E. Mandel, 'Lettre à Jean-Paul Sartre, 9 January 1952', *Quatrième Internationale*, vol. II, no. 2, April 1953. Also in E. Mandel, *La Longue marche de la Révolution*, Paris, 1976, pp. 83–125.

74 J.-P. Sartre, *The Communists and Peace*, pp. 107–8.

75 E. Germain, 'On pouvait prendre le pouvoir en 1944–1945', *La Vérité des Travailleurs*, October 1952.

76 J.-P. Sartre, *The Communists and Peace*, p. 113.

77 E. Mandel, 'Lettre à Jean-Paul Sartre'. E. Mandel, *La Longue marche de la Révolution*, p. 88.

78 In his memoirs Charles de Gaulle wrote about the appearances of the PCF leader Maurice Thorez, 'To those – and they were numerous – of the workers, particularly the miners, who listened to his speeches, he continually urged a maximum of work effort and production at any cost as national watchwords. Was this out of patriotic instinct or political opportunism? It was not my job to unravel his motives. It sufficed that France was served.' C. de Gaulle, *The Complete War Memoirs of Charles de Gaulle*, New York, 1968, pp. 782–3.

79 E. Germain, 'On pouvait prendre le pouvoir en 1944–1945'.

80 E. Bloch, *The Principle of Hope*.

81 J.-P. Sartre, *Situations VIII: Autour de 68*, Paris, 1972, pp. 212–3.

In the Fourth International

1 *Cahiers Léon Trotsky*, no. 57, March 1996. G. Marquis, 'Michel Pablo: un marxiste critique, un révolutionnaire', *Utopie critique: revue internationale pour l'autogestion*, no. 8, 1996. M. Najman, 'Michel Raptis, un dirigeant trotskiste hérétique', *Le Monde*, 20 February 1996. 'Der Prozess von Amsterdam', *Die Internationale* (stencilled), August 1961.

2 A. Stinas, *Mémoires, un révolutionnaire dans la Grèce du XXe siècle*, Preface by Michel Pablo, Paris, 1990, p. 9.

3 A. Stinas, *Mémoires*, p. 192.

4 *Cahiers Léon Trotsky*, no. 57, March 1996.

5 C. Nick, *Les Trotskistes*, Paris, 2002, p. 328.

6 M. Pablo, 'Where Are We Going?' in Socialist Workers Party (USA) *International Information Bulletin*, March 1951; also in *Towards a History of the Fourth International*, part 3, vol. 1, New York, 1973, p. 5.

7 Ibid.

8 M. Bleibtreu, 'Where is Comrade Pablo Going?', June 1951, *Towards a History of the Fourth International*, part 3, vol. 1, pp. 9–18.

9 M. Pablo, 'Where Are We Going?'.

10 C. Nick, *Les Trotskistes*, p. 357.

11 'What Should Be Modified and What Should Be Maintained in the Theses of the Second World Congress of the Fourth International on the Question of Stalinism? (Ten Theses)', Socialist Workers Party (USA) *International Information Bulletin*, April 1951; *Towards a History of the Fourth International*, part 4, vol. 1, pp. 16–24. Mandel held fast to the opinion that Stalinists could not lead revolutions. The fact that revolutions had occurred in Yugoslavia and China, which he acknowledged in 1948 and 1949, was proof for Mandel that the Yugoslav and Chinese Communists were not Stalinists. For decades this difference of opinion separated him from Pablo, on the one hand, and the US Socialist Workers Party (which maintained that the Yugoslav and Chinese CPs were Stalinist parties that had been forced to overthrow capitalism by popular uprisings), on the other.

12 M. Bleibtreu, 'Where is Comrade Pablo Going?', p. 71.

13 C. Nick, *Les Trotskistes*, p. 24. Bleibtreu's father was a vehement defender of the French Jewish officer Alfred Dreyfus, who had been condemned for treason in 1894. The evidence had been fabricated, but the military top brass refused to review the verdict and put all their energies into a cover-up.

14 Mandel chose unity above fighting for his own opinions. According to Michel Lequenne, Mandel and Pierre Frank were among the first to criticize Pablo's views. When Mandel returned to Pablo's camp, he told Bleibtreu that he would rather serve unity than get his own way. C. Nick, *Les Trotskistes*, p. 366.

15 E. Mandel to E. and H. Federn, 1 March 1951, E. Mandel Archives, folder 677.

16 M. Lequenne, 'A Propos de la crise et de la scission de la section française (1951–1952)', R. Prager, op. cit. L. Maitan, 'Une Nécessaire mise au point', R. Prager, op. cit.

17 S. Santen, *Adiós compañeros: politieke herinneringen*, Amsterdam, 1974, p. 56.

18 'SI [International Secretariat] à comité centrale du PCI', 14 January 1952, *Bulletin intérieur du SI*, no. 4, R. Prager Archives, folder 40 A.

19 Resolution on the French section, adopted by the tenth plenum of the International Executive Committee, R. Prager Archives, folder 40 B. In these minutes Mandel's pseudonym was Albert.

20 Circular from the International Secretariat to the sections of the Fourth International, July 1952, R. Prager Archives, folder 40 A.F. Charpier, *Histoire de l'extrême gauche trotskiste, de 1929 à nos jours*, Paris, 2002, p. 186.

21 Their way led to the International Communist Organization (OCI), founded in the mid-1950s. In 1947 Lambert, then in his thirties, was instrumental in establishing the trade union organization Workers' Force (FO), a split-off from

the Communist General Confederation of Labour (CGT). Agreement over entryism and an orientation towards the PCF and CGT would have undermined his position in FO.

22 M. Lequenne, 'Personnification du trotskysme', *Pour un portrait de Pierre Frank: écrits et témoignages*, Paris, 1985, p. 69.

23 After the 1953 split the SWP had between 400 and 500 members. A. Wald, *The New York Intellectuals: The Rise and Decline of the Anti-Stalinist Left from the 1930s to the 1980s*, Chapel Hill, 1987, p. 300.

24 C. Lotz and P. Feldman, *Gerry Healy: A Revolutionary Life*, London, 1994, p. 211. J. Callaghan, *The Far Left in British Politics*, Oxford, 1987, p. 61. Gerry Healy (1913–1989), Irish by birth, was head of a group of British Trotskyists that had been working in the Labour Party since 1947. The small, stout, unprepossessing Healy led his 'Club' out of the International with a heavy hand and a shrill voice. See his description in E. Germain, *Marxism vs. Ultraleftism: Key Issues in Healy's Challenge to the Fourth International*, Paris, 1967; and the chapters 'The Healy Group', 'The Socialist Labour League' and 'The SLL-WRP' in R. Alexander, *International Trotskyism, 1929–1985: A Documented Analysis*, Durham, 1991, pp. 471–81; also T. Wohlforth, *The Prophet's Children: Travels on the American Left*, Atlantic Highlands, NJ, 1994.

25 J. Cannon to Gabe, Ernest and Pierre, 17 February 1950, cited in R. Hansen, *James P. Cannon As We Knew Him*, New York, 1976, pp. 251–2.

26 H. Braverman, *Labour and Monopoly Capital*, New York, 1974. P. Arestis and M. Sawyer, *A Biographical Dictionary of Dissenting Economists*, Aldershot, 1992, pp. 59–67. Braverman began his career as a coppersmith. In the 1970s he made a name for himself as the author of *Labor and Monopoly Capital*, a sociological-historical study of the degradation of work in the twentieth century. In the 1960s he was the business manager of Monthly Review Press.

27 J. Hansen to I. Deutscher, 21 July 1964, I. Deutscher Archives, folder 50.

28 This accusation was first made in a letter from Cannon (Jim) to S. Gordon (Tom) dated 4 June 1953 and reprinted in *Bulletin interieur du secrétariat international de la IVe Internationale*, November 1953.

29 E. Germain to G. Breitman, 9 December 1953, *Towards a History of the Fourth International*, Education for Socialists, New York, 1974–1978, p. 206; E. Germain to G. Breitman, 15 November 1953, *Towards a History of the Fourth International*, p. 196.

30 E. Mandel, 'A Tribute', G. Breitman, P. LeBlanc and A. Wald, *Trotskyism in the United States: Historical Essays and Reconsiderations*, Atlantic Highlands, NJ, 1996, p. 286.

31 E. Germain to G. Breitman, 9 December 1953, *Towards a History of the Fourth International*, p. 204.

32 Ibid.

33 J. Cannon to F. Dobbs, 7 December 1953, *Towards a History of the Fourth International*, p. 215.

34 G. Breitman to E. Germain, 15 January 1954, *Towards a History of the Fourth International*, p. 212.

35 J. Cannon to G. Breitman, 1 March 1945, *Towards a History of the Fourth International*, p. 218.

36 J. Cannon, 'Trotsky or Deutscher?', *Fourth International*, winter 1954. Breitman

wrote an abridged version of the same witch-hunting review, *The Militant*, March/April/May 1954.

37 E. Germain, 'La Discussion sur la question syndicale dans le parti bolshevik (1920–1921)', *Quatrième Internationale*, vol. 13, no. 1/3, March 1955.

38 I. Deutscher to Pierre Frank, 18 May 1955, I. Deutscher Archives, folder 18.

39 Author's interview with Karl Manfred, 21 May 2002.

40 P. Bloch, 'Wie ich das Pogrom erlebte', G. Kößler, A. Rieben and F. Gürsching, eds, . . . *dass wir nicht erwünscht waren: Novemberpogrom 1938 in Frankfurt am Main*, Frankfurt on Main, 1993, p. 141.

41 K. Manfred, 'Mémoires d'un militant des années quarante', *Brood en Rozen: Tijdschrift voor de Geschiedenis van Sociale Bewegingen*, Ghent, 2001, no. 3.

42 K. Manfred to E. Mandel, 26 May 1950, E. Mandel Archives, folder 1.

43 K. Manfred to E. Mandel, 5 January 1957, E. Mandel Archives, folder 480.

44 E. Mandel to K. Manfred, 21 January 1957, E. Mandel Archives, folder 480.

45 E. Mandel to P. Frank, 1 July 1956, E. Mandel Archives, folder 480.

46 I. Deutscher to P. Frank, 8 October 1956, I. Deutscher Archives, folder 22. Deutscher said the slogans were no accident: 'The movement began as a proletarian demonstration and it rapidly was taken over by the nationalist and anti-Semitic petty bourgeoisie who assumed the lead . . . In truly revolutionary movements, workers often march in the first phase of the development under the leadership of the petite bourgeoisie and emancipate themselves from that leadership in the final phase. In Poznan the opposite happened: they came out with revolutionary slogans in the first phase and allowed themselves to be led by their class enemy in the final phase.'

47 E. Mandel to 'Chers amis', 22 September 1956, E. Mandel Archives, folder 480.

48 E. Mandel to 'Chers amis', 28 October 1956, E. Mandel Archives, folder 480.

49 L. Hass, 'Against All Odds – True to the Ideals of His Youth: a Tribute to Kazimierz Badowski', *Revolutionary History*, vol. 6, no. 1, winter 1995–6. 'Kazimierz Badowski (1906–1990)', *Cahiers Léon Trotsky*, no. 46, July 1991.

50 W. Jedlicki, 'Ludwick Hass', *Revolutionary History*, vol. 3, no. 1, summer 1990.

51 G. Soltysiak, 'The Hass Group', *Revolutionary History*, vol. 6, no. 1, winter 1995–6.

52 'Es Lebe die selbständige, demokratische ungarische Räterepublik! Aufruf der Vierten Internationale (Trotzkisten) an die ungarische Arbeiter, arme Bauern und Intellektuellen' (Long live the independent, democratic Hungarian council republic! Call by the Fourth International (Trotskyists) to the Hungarian workers, poor peasants and intellectuals), E. Mandel Archives, folder 480.

53 E. Mandel to 'Lieber Freund', 30 October 1956, E. Mandel Archives, folder 480.

54 E. Mandel to 'Lieber Freund', 31 October 1956, E. Mandel Archives, folder 480.

55 E. Mandel, 'La Grève générale sera-t-elle victorieuse en Hongrie?', *Le Peuple*, 12 November 1956.

56 *Le Peuple*, 5, 6, 7, 8, 9 and 12 November 1956.

57 E. Mandel to M. Kolodziejczyk, *Zycie Warszawy*, 25 October 1956, E. Mandel

Archives, folder 1. In January 1957 a report consisting of 10 articles appeared in *Le Peuple*: *Le Peuple*, 3, 4, 5, 8, 9, 10, 11, 12, 15 and 16 January 1957.

58 E. Mandel to 'Chers amis', November 1956, E. Mandel Archives, folder 480.

59 E. Mandel, journal written during his 1956 trip to Poland, E. Mandel Archives, folder 239.

60 In the 1930s Oskar Lange interpreted Marx's labour theory of value as a static theory of general economic equilibrium. Oskar Lange, 'Marxian economics and modern economic theory', *Review of Economic Studies*, June 1935. Mandel opposed this interpretation, which could at best be applied to simple production of goods in a pre-capitalist society. E. Mandel, 'The Labor Theory of Value and Monopoly Capitalism', *International Socialist Review*, July/August 1967.

61 L. Kolakowski to J.W. Stutje, 30 October 2003.

62 E. Mandel to R. Rosdolsky, 1 January 1957, E. Mandel Archives, folder 480.

63 E. Mandel to 'Chers amis', 25 December 1956, E. Mandel Archives, folder 480.

64 Ibid.

65 E. Mandel to S. Brodzki, 1 March 1957, E. Mandel Archives, folder 1.

66 E. Mandel to T. van Tijn, 12 January 1957, E. Mandel Archives, folder 480.

67 For Kolakowski's later perspective on Trotskyism, see: L. Kolakowski, *Main Currents of Marxism: Its Rise, Growth and Dissolution*, vol. 3, Oxford, 1978.

68 L. Kolakowski to J. W. Stutje, 30 October 2003; L. Kolakowski to E. Mandel, 5 April 1958, 12 June 1958, E. Mandel Archives, folder 5. In 1966 Kolakowski was expelled from the Polish Communist Party. Two years later he left Poland, making short stays in Canada and the US (Berkeley), on his way to England, where he became a fellow of All Souls College, Oxford.

69 E. Mandel to L. Maitan, 27 January 1957, E. Mandel Archives, folder 480.

70 Author's interview with G. Dobbeleer, 11 February 2003. Ludovic to 'Chers amis', 6 July 1957, E. Mandel Archives, folder 480. E. Mandel to Michel and Pierre, 4 July 1957, E. Mandel Archives, folder 480. E. Mandel to Michel, 9 August 1957, E. Mandel Archives, folder 480.

71 Ludovic to 'Cher amis,' n.d. [late 1957], E. Mandel Archives, folder 480.

72 Author's interview with G. Dobbeleer, 11 February 2003. G. Dobbeleer, 'Mémoires d'un révolutionnaire qui n'a pas vécu de révolution', unpublished manuscript, pp. 16–19.

73 S. Santen to 'Lieber Walter', 20 April 1960, S. Santen Archives.

74 K. Modzelewski and J. Kuron, *Solidarnosc, the Missing Link: A New Edition of Poland's Classic Revolutionary Socialist Manifesto: Kuron and Modzelewski's Open Letter to the Party*, London, 1982. J. Kuron, *Glaube und Schuld: Einmal Kommunismus und zurück*, Berlin-Weimar, 1991, p. 329.

75 Author's interview with G. Dobbeleer, 11 February 2003.

76 J. Kuron, *Glaube und Schuld,* p. 346.

77 G. Dobbeleer 'Mémoires d'un révolutionnaire', p. 210.

78 J. Kuron, *Glaube und Schuld,* p. 360.

79 G. Dobbeleer to K. Modzelewski, 24 June 1991, E. Mandel Archives, folder 543.

80 Author's interview with G. Dobbeleer, 11 February 2003.

81 P. Frank to I. Deutscher, 29 April 1966, I. Deutscher Archives, folder 58.

82 E. Germain, 'La Lettre ouverte de Karol Modzelewski et Jacek Kuron au Parti ouvrier polonais', *Quatrième Internationale*, vol. 24, no. 29, November 1966. Another version of Modzelewski and Kuron's 'Open Letter' was brought out in Paris by the Polish publisher-in-exile Kultura.

83 E. Mandel to 'Dear George [Novack]', 3 May 1956, E. Mandel Archives, folder 480. Walter to 'Liebe Freunde', 20 February 1957, E. Mandel Archives, folder 480.

84 A. Wald, *The Revolutionary Imagination: The Poetry and Politics of John Wheelwright and Sherry Mangan*, Chapel Hill, 1982, p. 225.

85 N. Moreno to A. Wald, 30 June 1977, E. Mandel Archives, folder 60.

86 E. Mandel to S. Mangan, 25 March 1961, E. Mandel Archives, folder 483.

87 S. Mangan to J. Epstein, 21 October 1956, cited in A. Wald, *The Revolutionary Imagination*, p. 225.

88 M. Pablo to E. Mandel, 30 April 1957, E. Mandel Archives, folder 480; S. Mangan to M. Pablo, 24 April 1957, cited in A. Wald, *The Revolutionary Imagination*, p. 226.

89 E. Mandel, *Die EWG und die Konkurrenz Europa-Amerika*, Frankfurt on Main, 1968, p. 14.

90 With Guy Mollet as prime minister, the social democratic SFIO shared responsibility for the war in Algeria. That was also true of the Communists, who had voted Mollet a blank cheque in 1956.

91 H. Harmon and P. Rotman, *Les Porteurs de valises: la résistance française à la guerre d'Algérie*, Paris, 1979. G. Perrault, *Un Homme à part: biographie d'Henri Curiel*, Paris 1984. S. Pattieu, *Les Camarades des frères: Trotskistes et libertaires dans la guerre d'Algérie*, Paris, 2002.

92 M. Pablo, internal document of the French section (PCI), November 1954, cited in S. Pattieu, 'Le "camarade" Pablo, la IVe Internationale, et la guerre d'Algérie', *Revue Historique*, vol. 125, no. 619, July/September 2001.

93 *Wilaya* is the Arabic word for 'province'. Algeria consisted of six provinces, and France was called the Seventh Wilaya because of the large number of Algerians living there.

94 H. Harmon and P. Rotman, *Les Porteurs de valises*, p. 57.

95 M. Harbi, *Une Vie debout: Mémoires politiques*, vol. 1: 1945–62, Paris, 2001. S. Pattieu, *Les Camarades des frères*, p. 76.

96 A. Wald, *The Revolutionary Imagination*, p. 229.

97 J. Doneux and H. Le Paige, *Le Front du Nord: des Belges dans la guerre d'Algérie (1954–1962)*, Brussels, 1992.

98 Author's interview with F. Vercammen, 24 June 2004.

99 G. Dobbeleer, 'Mémoires d'un révolutionnaire' p. 122. The Committee for Peace in Algeria was founded 21 April 1958, following a demand signed by thirty-two people. The committee secretary was Jean Godin.

100 J. Doneux and H. Le Paige, *Le Front du Nord*, p. 69.

101 P. Le Grève, *Souvenirs d'un marxiste anti-stalinien*, Paris, 1996, p. 56.

102 E. Mandel to 'Georg', 3 April 1960, E. Mandel Archives, folder 482. E. Mandel to S. Santen, 26 March 1960, S. Santen Archives, folder 71.

103 *Georg Jungclas: 1902–1975, Von der proletarischen Freidenkerjugend im Ersten Weltkrieg zur linken der siebziger Jahre: eine politische Dokumentation*, with an afterword by E. Mandel, Hamburg, 1980.

104 C. Leggewie, *Kofferträger: das Algerien-projekt der Linken im Adenauer-Deutschland*, Berlin, 1984, p. 115.

105 M. Harbi, *Une Vie debout: Mémoires politiques*, p. 225.

106 Ibid., p. 229.

107 Author's interview with G. Dobbeleer, 11 February 2003.

108 M. Harbi, *Une Vie debout: Mémoires politiques*, p. 228.

109 Author's interview with J. Moneta, 20–21 June 2000. J. Hinzer, H. Schauer and F. Segbers, eds, *Perspektive der Linken: Ein kämpferisches Leben im Zeitalter der Extreme*, Hamburg, 2000, p. 103. S. Pattieu, *Les Camarades des frères*, p. 121.

110 W. Röder and H. Strauss, eds., *Biographisches Handbuch der deutschsprachigen Emigration nach 1933*, vol. I: *Politik, Wirtschaft, Öffentliches Leben*, Munich, 1980. J. Moneta, 'Lebenslauf', unpublished typescript dated 8 September 1975.

111 M. Pablo, 'Pages d'histoires de la révolution algérienne: les fermes du soleil', *Sous le drapeau du socialisme*, no. 4, April 1964. A. Haroun, *La 7e Wilaya: La guerre du FLN en France 1954–1962*, Paris, 1986, pp. 212–3.

112 Author's interview with M. Plekker, 27 December 2001.

113 Ibid. C. Leggewie, *Kofferträger: das Algerien-projekt der Linken*, p. 120.

114 Author's interview with M. Ferares, 9 September 2003. I. Cornelissen, *Alleen tegen de wereld: Joop Zwart, de geheimzinnigste man van Nederland*, Amsterdam, 2003.

115 Pablo defined the de Gaulle regime as 'a Bonapartist dictatorship based on the military, which will tend to evolve into a fascist dictatorship'. International Secretariat minutes, 17 June 1958, M. Ferares Archives, folder 4. In *La Gauche* of 24 May 1958, Mandel criticized the Gaullist operation with more restraint under the heading, 'De La Lutte contre la liberté du peuple algérien à la lutte contre la liberté du peuple français' (From the War Against the Freedom of the Algerian People to the War Against the Freedom of the French People).

116 Sherry Mangan, under the pseudonym Patrice, had prepared a report on Rome as the place for relocation: Patrice, 'Report on Rome', 23 September 1958, E. Mandel Archives, folder 481. The Italian section was the second strongest in Europe and would have had no trouble supporting the International Secretariat in word and deed.

117 Author's interview with L. Maitan, 17 October 2002. S. Santen, *Adiós compañeros!*, pp. 120–21.

118 Author's interview with L. Maitan, 17 October 2002. L. Maitan, *La strada per corsa: dalla resistenza ai nuovi movimenti: Lettura critica e scelte alternative*, Bolsena, 2002.

119 Author's interview with L. Maitan, 17 October 2002.

120 S. Mangan to M. Pablo, 12 January 1959, S. Santen Archives, folder 101; Walter [E. Mandel] to Livio, 23 June 1958, E. Mandel Archives, folder 481. L. Maitan to 'Camarades du SI', 14 July 1958, E. Mandel Archives, folder 481.

121 Corrected translation of V.I. Lenin, 'Better Fewer But Better', *Collected Works*, vol. 33, Moscow, 1965.

122 E. Mandel to Willy [Boepple], 15 January 1959, E. Mandel Archives, folder 481.

123 Ibid.

124 E. Mandel to P. Frank, 23 January 1959, E. Mandel Archives, folder 481.

125 P. Frank to E. Mandel, 15 October 1959, E. Mandel Archives, folder 481.

126 E. Mandel to L. Maitan, 11 December 1959, E. Mandel Archives, folder 481.

127 E. Mandel to 'Membres du SI', 13 November 1959. M. Pablo to 'Membres du SI', 20 November 1959, E. Mandel Archives, folder 481.

128 E. Mandel to 'Membres du SI', 22 November 1959, E. Mandel Archives, folder 481.

129 Sherry Mangan saw this conflict as primarily psychological and personal: Patrice [S. Mangan] to E. Mandel, 6 March 1959, E. Mandel Archives, folder 481.

130 P. Frank to 'Membres du SI', 20 November 1959, E. Mandel Archives, folder 481.

131 A. Gilly to J.W. Stutje, 2 December 2003.

132 E. Mandel to A. Wald, 31 December 1976, E. Mandel Archives, folder 58.

133 E. Mandel to S. Mangan, 9 May 1960, E. Mandel Archives, folder 70.

134 A. Wald, *The Revolutionary Imagination,* p. 233.

135 I. Cornelissen, *Alleen tegen de wereld,* p. 173.

136 Author's interviews with M. Ferares, 7 January 2002; 9 September 2003.

137 Ibid.

138 Author's interview with L. Maitan, 17 October 2002. S. Pattieu, *Les Camarades des frères,* p. 180.

139 Author's interview with L. Maitan, 17 October 2002.

140 These were Pablo's justifications for involvement with the counterfeiting when Maitan asked him about it in 1961 in Rabat after his release. Author's interview with L. Maitan, 17 October 2002.

141 M. Harbi, *Une Vie debout: Mémoires politiques,* p. 349. A. Haroun, *La 7e Wilaya*, p. 331. S. Pattieu, *Les Camarades des frères,* p. 179.

142 Besides the Dutch political investigation department, the West German and French authorities were keeping track of the affair. The East German Stasi was also aware of it. Helmut Schneeweiss, the Osnabrück printer, provided East Berlin with information regularly from 1954 until his arrest in June 1960. He was known to the Stasi as a secret informant under the name Kurt Hartmann. Cf. G. Wernicke, 'Operativer Vorgang (OV) Abschaum', Andres Graf, ed., *Anarchisten gegen Hitler,* Berlin, 2001, pp. 291–2. For Helmut Schneeweiss, see A. Schüle, *Trotzkismus in Deutschland bis 1933,* Cologne, 1989, pp. 153–4.

143 P. Frank to E. Mandel, 17 July 1960, E. Mandel Archives, folder 482.

144 Ibid.

145 P. Frank to 'Chers amis', 18 July 1960, E. Mandel Archives, folder 482.

146 M. Pablo to 'Vous tous, camarades de l'Internationale', 21 July 1960, E. Mandel Archives, folder 482.

147 L. Maitan, 'Manuscript memoirs', Paris, n.d., p. 20. A conversation that Maitan had with Pablo in Rabat soon after his release made clear how intimately Pablo felt bound to Hélène. He accused some in the leadership of having attacked his wife: 'You attacked my Achilles heel. Hélène helps me cope with the dog's life we've had to lead. We are one and the same person.'

148 Jack [Mandel] to 'Friends', 14 October 1960, E. Mandel Archives, folder 482. P. Frank to 'Dear comrades', 15 October 1960, E. Mandel Archives, folder 482. 'The financial question is becoming, with [Pablo's] absence, critical, and will become ever more critical.' Benedict [S. Mangan] to P. Frank, 2 August 1960; 6 August 1960, E. Mandel Archives, folder 482.

149 A. Wald, *The Revolutionary Imagination*, p. 186.

150 Walter to 'Albert and Paul', 31 May 1962, E. Mandel Archives, folder 484.

151 'Posadista Fourth International', R. Alexander, *International Trotskyism*, pp. 659–65, see also pp. 332–4. 'Communiqué de la IVe Internationale-Posadiste sur le décès du camarade J. Posadas', paid announcement in *Le Monde*, 25 June 1981. His German followers published a pamphlet titled 'Informationsbulletin über den Tod des Genossen J. Posadas', n.p. [Frankfurt on Main], 1981.

152 Author's interview with L. Maitan, 17 October 2002.

153 L. Maitan to 'Membres du SI', 19 February 1962, E. Mandel Archives, folder 484.

154 E. Mandel to S. Mangan, 10 June 1961, E. Mandel Archives, folder 483.

155 S. Mangan to E. Mandel, 20 June 1961, E. Mandel Archives, folder 483.

156 A. Wald, *The Revolutionary Imagination*, p. 239.

157 S. Mangan to E. Mandel, 20 June 1961, E. Mandel Archives, folder 483.

158 Jack [E. Mandel] to Albert [L. Maitan] and Paul [P. Frank], 30 June 1961, E. Mandel Archives, folder 483.

159 L. Maitan to 'Jack' and 'Paul', 4 July 1961, E. Mandel Archives, folder 483.

160 A. Wald to E. Mandel, 18 July 1978, E. Mandel Archives, folder 171.

161 From prison Pablo wrote a moving portrait, dated 6 August 1961: M. Pablo, 'Notre ami Sherry, notre camarade Patrice (l'homme et le militant)', *Quatrième Internationale*, no. 16, July 1962.

162 M. Ferares, *Moussebilines (Vrijwilligers voor de dood)*, Arnhem, 2007, p. 78. Author's interview with M. Ferares, 26 November 2003. Author's interview with F. Tichelman, 17 January 2002. I. Cornelissen did not mention Jacques van der Meulen, later a professor on the legal faculty of the University of Amsterdam, as being concerned. He incorrectly stated that the box of documents was kept by Lies Knolle in West Amsterdam. I. Cornelissen, *Alleen tegen de wereld*, pp. 178–9.

163 Jack [E. Mandel] to 'Dear Friends', 26 July 1961, E. Mandel Archives, folder 483.

164 H. Raptis to 'Chère Costa', 2 August 1961, M. Ferares Archives.

165 Jack to 'Bureau du SI', with a copy to Joan [H. Raptis], 23 August 1961, E. Mandel Archives, folder 483.

166 Walter to Georg [Jungclas], 6 September 1961, E. Mandel Archives, folder 483.

167 According to a statement Hélène Raptis made to Mandel, Yugoslavia was also willing to grant Pablo asylum under certain conditions. 'Jack' to 'Albert and Paul', 21 May 1961, E. Mandel Archives, folder 483.

168 S. Santen to J. Beard, 14 November 1961, S. Santen Archives.

169 S. Santen to 'Political Bureau', 2 July 1963, M. Ferares Archives.

170 M. Raptis to S. Santen, 27 March 1983, M. Ferares Archives. Author's interview with M. Ferares, 9 September 2003.

171 M. Pablo, 'Open letter to comrades of the Latin American Bureau, section leaderships and members of our Latin American sections', 30 January 1962, M. Ferares Archives.

172 E. Germain to Toichi, 22 September 1962, E. Mandel Archives, folder 483.

173 E. Germain to 'Bravo and Serrano', 8 December 1961, E. Mandel Archives, folder 483.

174 E. Mandel to the National Committee of the Socialist Workers Party, 22 October 1958, E. Mandel Archives, folder 481.

175 K. Manfred to E. Mandel, 23 September 1960, E. Mandel Archives, folder 482.

176 E. Mandel to K. Manfred, 1 October 1960, E. Mandel Archives, folder 482.

177 K. Manfred to E. Mandel, 31 January 1961, E. Mandel Archives, folder 483.

178 'Jack' to 'Albert and Paul', 21 May 1961, E. Mandel Archives, folder 483.

179 E. Mandel to K. Manfred, 3 June 1961, E. Mandel Archives, folder 483.

180 K. Manfred to E. Mandel, 14 July 1961; 15 July 1961, E. Mandel Archives, folder 483.

181 K. Manfred to E. Mandel, 13 October 1961, E. Mandel Archives, folder 483.

182 E. Mandel to C. Bourdet, 28 December 1961, E. Mandel Archives, folder 12.

183 K. Manfred to E. Mandel, 14 November 1961, E. Mandel Archives, folder 483.

184 E. Mandel to K. Manfred, 4 March 1962, E. Mandel Archives, folder 484.

185 'Jack' to 'Albert and Paul', 4 April 1962, E. Mandel Archives, folder 484.

186 J. Hansen to E. Mandel, 30 May 1962, E. Mandel Archives, folder 485.

187 C. de Bloom, 'Fourth International revival being watched', *Columbus Dispatch*, 15 May 1962.

188 F. J. Donner, *The Age of Surveillance*, New York, 1981, p. 137. N. Blackstock, *Cointelpro: The FBI's Secret War on Political Freedom*, New York, 1988. The FBI's SWP Disruption Program got under way in October 1961, because, according to a secret FBI memorandum, the SWP 'had been openly espousing its line on a local national basis through running candidates for public office and strongly directing and/or supporting such causes as Castro's Cuba and integration problems . . . in the South', p. 6.

189 Through Livio Maitan at the Seventh World Congress in 1963, the leadership of the International defended the positions of China on both anti-colonial revolution and the methods of struggle in the developed, capitalist countries as more realistic than those of Moscow. Maitan's conclusion: 'The Chinese have arrived at a conception very close to ours on the key question of identifying the fundamental factor in the transition to socialism on a world scale. For Khrushchev the decisive element will be peaceful competition, with mass revolutionary combat throughout the world ultimately playing a mere supporting role. For the Chinese it's the other way around.' L. Maitan, 'Manuscript memoirs', Paris, n.d., p. 8.

190 Ibid.

191 M. Pablo to I. Deutscher, 13 February 1962, I. Deutscher Archives, folder 43.

192 F. Moreau, *Combats et débats de la IVe Internationale*, Hull, 1993, p. 177.

193 Edward, Livio, Pierre and Walter, response to Pablo, 4 June 1962, E. Mandel Archives, folders 484–5.

194 M. Pablo to 'Giovanna and Marco', 14 March 1962, S. Santen Archives, folder 55.

195 'Jack' to 'Albert and Paul', 21 May 1961, E. Mandel Archives, folder 483.

196 E. Mandel, 'A Socialist Strategy for Western Europe', *International Socialist Journal*, no. 10, February 1965, pp. 440–41.
197 Ibid.

The Worlds of Politics and Scholarship: An Odyssey

1 The foreword to the second French edition of *Marxist Economic Theory* (1969) notes that the book had already been published in dozens of languages and reviewed in about fifty publications.
2 E. Mandel, *Trattato di economia marxista*, Rome, 1965.
3 E. Mandel, 'The Economics of Neo-Capitalism', R. Miliband and J. Saville, eds, in *The Socialist Register 1964*, London, 1964. M. Newman, *Ralph Miliband and the Politics of the New Left*, London, 2002. E. Mandel, 'L'Apogée du néo-capitalisme et ses lendemains', *Les Temps Modernes*, vol. 20, no. 219/220, August/September 1964.
4 E. Mandel to C. Bourgois, 31 October 1963, E. Mandel Archives, folder 278. E. Mandel to 'Cher ami', 3 December 1963, E. Mandel Archives, folder 20.
5 E. Mandel, *Late Capitalism,* London, 1978.
6 See, for example, the Afterword to the second French edition of Mandel's *Marxist Economic Theory*.
7 E. Mandel, *Initiation à la théorie économique marxiste*, Les cahiers du centre d'études socialistes, no. 39/41, Paris, February/March 1964.
8 E. Mandel, 'The Economics of Neo-Capitalism', pp. 57–65. E. Mandel, *Introduction to Marxist Economic Theory*, New York, 1967.
9 E. Mandel, *Marxist Economic Theory*, London, 1968, vol. 1, pp. 342–63.
10 Parvus [Israël Lazarevitsj (Alexander) Helphand], *Die Handelskrisis und die Gewerkschaften*, Munich, 1901.
11 J. van Gelderen [J. Fedder], 'Springvloed: Beschouwingen over industrieele ontwikkeling en prijsbeweging', *Nieuwe Tijd*, vol. 18, nos. 4–6, April/May/June 1913, pp. 253–77, 369–84, 445–64. C. Freeman, ed., *Long Wave Theory*, Aldershot, 1996. H. Buiting, *De Nieuwe Tijd, Sociaaldemokratisch Maandschrift 1896–1921: Spiegel van socialisme en vroeg communisme in Nederland*, Amsterdam, 2003. F. Kalshoven, *Over marxistische economie in Nederland, 1883–1939*, Amsterdam, 1993.
12 N. Kondratieff, *The Long Wave Cycle*, New York, 1984.
13 L. Trotsky, 'Report on the World Economic Crisis and the New Tasks of the Communist International', *The First Five Years of the Communist International*, New York, 1945, vol. 1, pp. 174–226. L. Trotsky, 'The Curve of Capitalist Development', *Problems of Everyday Life*, New York, 1973, pp. 273–80.
14 J. Schumpeter, *Business Cycles*, New York, 1939.
15 F. Louçã, 'Ernest Mandel and the Pulsation of History', *The Legacy of Ernest Mandel*, G. Achcar, ed., London 1999, p. 104. V. Barnett, *Kondratiev and the Dynamics of Economic Development: Long Cycles and Industrial Growth in Historical Context*, Basingstoke, 1998.
16 E. Mandel, 'The Economics of Neo-Capitalism', p. 63. In 1965, Mandel, under the pseudonym Ernest Germain, published an article titled 'De Gaulle

Doesn't Know It, but the Golden Days of World Capitalism Are Gone Forever', *World Outlook*, vol. 3, no. 7, 19 February 1965.

17 E. Mandel, *Marxist Economic Theory*, vol. 1, pp. 373–6.

18 This problem was theoretically broached in a section devoted to the falling tendency of the average rate of profit. Ibid., p. 168.

19 Ibid., pp. 368–71. For such theorists of underconsumption as Karl Kautsky and Rosa Luxemburg, the lack of effective demand causes economic crises. Disproportionality theorists like Rudolf Hilferding and Michael Tugan-Baranowski, on the other hand, maintain that such crises occur when the equilibrium between Department I (production of means of production) and Department II (production of consumer goods) is disturbed.

20 R. Rosdolsky to E. Mandel, 12 March 1964, E. Mandel Archives, folder 24.

21 E. Mandel, 'The Economics of Neo-Capitalism'. E. Mandel, 'After Imperialism', *New Left Review*, no. 25, 1964. E. Mandel, 'Westeuropäische Arbeiterbewegung im Neokapitalismus', *Neokapitalismus, Rüstungswirtschaft, Westeuropäische Arbeiterbewegung*, Frankfurt on Main, 1966. E. Mandel, *The Formation of the Economic Thought of Karl Marx: 1843 to 'Capital'*, New York, 1971. E. Mandel, 'Surplus Capital and Realization of Surplus Value', *International Socialist Review*, vol. 29, no. 1, 1967. E. Mandel, 'The Labor Theory of Value and Monopoly Capitalism', *International Socialist Review*, vol. 28, no. 4, 1967. E. Mandel, 'International Capitalism and Supra-Nationality: The Common Market', *Socialist Register*, 1967. E. Mandel, 'Kritik der Wachstumtheorie im Geiste des Kapitals', W. Euchner and A. Schmidt, eds, *Kritik der politischen Ökonomie heute 100 Jahre 'Kapital'*, Frankfurt on Main, 1968. E. Mandel, 'Die Marxsche Theorie der ursprünglichen Akkumulation und die Industrialisierung der Dritten Welt', *Folgen einer Theorie: Essays über Das Kapital von Karl Marx*, Frankfurt on Main, 1967. E. Mandel, *Die EWG und die Konkurrenz Europa-Amerika*, Frankfurt on Main, 1968. E. Mandel, *Die Deutsche Wirtschaftkrise: Lehren der Rezession 1966/1967*, Frankfurt on Main, 1969. E. Mandel, 'Althusser Corrects Marx', *International Socialist Review*, vol. 31, no. 5, 1969. E. Mandel, 'The Laws of Uneven Development', *New Left Review*, no. 59, 1970.

22 L. Goldmann to E. Mandel, 1 October 1962, E. Mandel Archives, folder 278.

23 E. Mandel to L. Goldmann, 30 August 1965, E. Mandel Archives, folder 278. L. Goldmann to E. Mandel, 17 January 1966, E. Mandel Archives, folder 278.

24 E. Mandel to F. Maspero, 8 November 1966, E. Mandel Archives, folder 278. E. Mandel, *The Formation of the Economic Thought of Karl Marx*.

25 Ibid., pp. 40–5.

26 *La Pensée* opened the debate with a special issue, *La Pensée*, no. 114, 1964. For a critique of the interpretations of Maurice Godelier, Jean Chesneaux, Jean Suret-Canale and P. Boiteau, participants in the debate in *La Pensée*, see: E. Mandel, *The Formation of the Economic Thought of Karl Marx*, pp. 124–8; M. van der Linden, *Western Marxism and the Soviet Union: A Survey of Critical Theories and Debates Since 1917*, Leiden, 2007.

27 In a 1919 lecture at Sverdlov University Lenin said, 'The development of all human societies for thousands of years . . . reveals a general conformity to law . . . so that at first we had a society without classes . . . then we had a society based on slavery . . . This form was followed in history by another –

feudalism . . . Further, with the development of trade, the appearance of the world market and the development of money circulation, a new class arose within feudal society – the capitalist class. From the commodity, the exchange of commodities and the rise of the power of money, there derived the power of capital . . . This fundamental fact – the transition of society from primitive forms of slavery to serfdom and finally to capitalism – you must always bear in mind.' V. I. Lenin, 'The State: A Lecture Delivered at the Sverdlov University' (11 July 1919), *Collected Works*, Moscow, 1972, vol. 29, pp. 470–88. In 1938 Stalin codified a schema of fixed stages – primitive society, slavery, feudalism, capitalism, socialism – in the *History of the Communist Party of the Soviet Union (Bolsheviks): Short Course*. Marx's concept of the Asiatic mode of production then disappeared from discussion for two decades until Karl August Wittfogel gave it new attention in his monumental *Oriental Despotism: A Comparative Study of Total Power*, New Haven, 1957.

28 The Asiatic mode of production was seen as originating particularly where large public works, like irrigation systems, were needed. The dispersed village communities without private ownership of land were not equipped to construct such systems, so strong, centralized institutions were formed for the purpose. These institutions appropriated the social surplus, creating a powerful and stable social layer in the society, a system known as 'Oriental despotism'. G. Sofri, *Über asiatische Produktionsweise*, Frankfurt on Main, 1972. P. Anderson, *Lineages of the Absolutist State*, London, 1974.

29 M. Godelier, 'Bibliographie sommaire des écrits de Marx et d'Engels sur le mode de production asiatique', *La Pensée*, April 1964. M. Godelier, 'La notion de mode de production asiatique et les schémas marxistes de l'évolution des sociétés', *Cahiers du centre d'études et de recherches marxistes*, 1969.

30 Marx developed his ideas about the Asiatic mode of production particularly in his *Grundrisse: Foundations of the Critique of Political Economy*, London, 1973.

31 Mandel believed that no one could answer this question without relying on Wittfogel's 'masterpiece' *Wirtschaft und Gesellschaft Chinas*, Leipzig, 1931. E. Mandel, *The Formation of the Economic Thought of Karl Marx*, p. 129.

32 Ibid., p. 137

33 Mandel cited examples of non-capitalist modes of production that were increasingly integrated into the capitalist world market over more than a century, such as West Indian plantations between 1650 and 1800, the southern United States between 1650 and 1850, the economy of much of Southern and Eastern Europe in the eighteenth century, and the Chinese economy in the nineteenth century. E. Mandel, 'Postface', *Traité d'économie marxiste*, Paris, 1969, vol. 2, p. 432.

34 R. Luxemburg, *The Accumulation of Capital*, New York, 1964.

35 E. Mandel, *Traité d'économie marxiste*, pp. 430–31.

36 Mandel believed that the Third World could only free itself from its under-development by radically changing its internal and external exploitive relation-ships. This would require a revolution that would enable these countries to break with the capitalist world market. E. Mandel, 'The Industrialization of Backward Countries', A.R. Desai, ed., *Rural Sociology in India*, Bombay, 1969, pp. 925–38.

37 During the controversy, regular references were made not only to Marx and Engels's *Economic and Philosophical Manuscripts of 1844* and *The German Ideology*, but also to Marx's *Poverty of Philosophy* and *Grundrisse*. In 1983 Jürgen Rojahn demonstrated, in a famous article in the 1983 *International Review of Social History (IRSH)*, that Marx's early writings did not form a philological unity.

38 L. Althusser, *For Marx*, London, 2005. L. Althusser, *Reading Capital*, London, 1970. According to Mandel, more than a hundred writers took part in the debate (E. Mandel, 'The Marxist Theory of Alienation' in E. Mandel and G. Novack, *The Marxist Theory of Alienation*, New York, 1970).

39 The concepts of alienation and alienated labour were elaborated by Hegel in G.W.F. Hegel, *The Science of Logic*, London, 1969, and G.W.F. Hegel, *The Phenomenology of Spirit*, Oxford, 1977.

40 E. Mandel, *The Formation of the Economic Thought of Karl Marx*.

41 Mandel counted among this first group socialist writers such as Erich Fromm and Maximilian Rubel, Catholic scholars of Marx like R.D. Bigo and J.-Y. Calvez and also the Communist Palmiro Togliatti.

42 According to Mandel, the second group included Heinrich Popitz, Heinrich Weinstock, Jacob Hommes, Karl Löwith and, to some extent, Herbert Marcuse and Hendrik de Man.

43 In his *Formation of the Economic Thought of Karl Marx* (p. 169), Mandel approvingly cites Habermas: 'Materialist dialectics means, therefore, understanding the dialectical logic that starts from the context "labor", from the metabolism of men with nature, without conceiving labor in a metaphysical way (either theologically, as being necessary for salvation, or anthropologically, as being necessary for survival).' (J Habermas, *Theorie und Praxis*, Neuwied, 1963, pp. 318–9.)

44 On Althusser, see: L. Althusser, *The Future Lasts a Long Time* and *The Facts*, London, 1993; G. Elliott, *Althusser: The Detour of Theory*, London/New York, 1987; R. Resch, *Althusser and the Renewal of Marxist Social Theory*, Berkeley, 1992; E. Kaplan and M. Sprinker, eds., *The Althusserian Legacy*, London/New York, 1993.

45 Representatives of this last group were Wolfgang Jahn, Auguste Cornu, Emile Bottigelli, Manfred Buhr and Louis Althusser.

46 E. Mandel, *The Formation of the Economic Thought of Karl Marx*, p. 158.

47 Ibid.

48 One critic noted, 'All in all, *The Formation of the Economic Thought of Karl Marx* is one of those books which everyone concerned with the contemporary problems of Marxist theory must acquire.' A. Hernandez, 'The Development of Marx's Economic Thought' and E. Mandel, 'Reply', *New Left Review*, no. 72, March/April 1972.

49 H. Lefebvre, *Critique of Everyday Life*, London, 1991, vol. 1, p. 64. The first complete edition of the *Manuscripts* appeared in the Soviet Union in 1956.

50 E. Mandel to P. Anderson, 20 July 1967, E. Mandel Archives, folder 37.

51 P. Anderson to E. Mandel, 5 January 1965, E. Mandel Archives, folder 435.

52 E. Mandel, 'Althusser Corrects Marx', *International Socialist Review*, vol. 31, no. 5, 15 December 1969. The article was reprinted in French (E. Mandel, 'Althusser corrige Marx') in Denise Avenas et al., *Contre Althusser, Pour Marx*, Paris, 1999.

53 Ibid.

54 Examples include Sartre's existentialism; the structuralism of Claude Lévi-Strauss, Roland Barthes and Louis Althusser and the work of Adorno, Marcuse, Habermas and Ernst Bloch. According to Perry Anderson, the defeat of the workers' movement after the Russian Revolution explains the shift in Marxism from the terrain of political economy to that of philosophy. P. Anderson, *Considerations on Western Marxism*, London, 1976.

55 In the 1920s the Soviet Union saw a blossoming of economic theorization, with E. Preobrazhensky and the school of I.I. Rubin.

56 Rosdolsky stressed the influence of the *Grundrisse* in his 'Einige Bemerkungen über die Methode des Marxschen Kapital und ihre Bedeutung für die heutige Marxforschung', W. Euchner and A. Schmidt, eds., in *Kritik der politischen Ökonomie heute 100 Jahre 'Kapital'* p. 12. *Rosdolsky's posthumously published 1968 study of the Grundrisse, The Making of Marx's 'Capital'*, London, 1992, was very influential. See also J. Albarracín and P. Montes, 'Late Capitalism: Mandel's Interpretation of Contemporary Capitalism' in G. Achcar, ed., *The Legacy of Ernest Mandel*, pp. 38–74.

57 E. Mandel to R. Rosdolsky, 26 July 1967, E. Mandel Archives, folder 38.

58 R. Rosdolsky to E. Mandel, 29 July 1967, E. Mandel Archives, folder 38.

59 E. Rosdolsky to E. Mandel, 30 September 1967, E. Mandel Archives, folder 38.

60 For different evaluations of Mandel's remarks and Rosdolsky's contribution, see *Neues Deutschland*, 20 September 1967; *Frankfurter Allgemeine*, 27 September 1967.

61 E. Mandel to R. Rosdolsky, 9 October 1967, E. Mandel Archives, folder 38. W. Euchner and A. Schmidt, eds, *Kritik der politischen Ökonomie heute 100 Jahre 'Kapital'*, pp. 69–71.

62 Roman Rosdolsky died on October 20, 1967.

63 E. Rosdolsky to E. Mandel, 22 October 1967, E. Mandel Archives, folder 38.

64 Rosdolsky called himself a 'Marxist philologist', a researcher specializing in the question of what Marx meant with this or that passage or concept. However his *Making of Marx's 'Capital'* showed that Rosdolsky did not limit himself to philological questions. His book was not only an analysis of the *Grundrisse* but also a detailed evaluation of Marx's development in the 1850s and a defence of Marxist economic theory against critics in the workers' movement and in academic circles.

65 R. Rosdolsky to O. Morf, 25 August 1967, R. Rosdolsky Archives, folder 299.

66 On October 9, 1967, Ernesto 'Che' Guevara was killed in a remote Bolivian village.

67 E. Mandel to E. Rosdolsky, 22 November 1967, E. Mandel Archives, folder 38.

68 E. Mandel to E. Rosdolsky, 22 November 1967, E. Mandel Archives, folder 38. Above all, this meant the publication of Rosdolsky's analysis of Marx's *Grundrisse*. The Europäische Verlagsanstalt in Frankfurt on Main published Rosdolsky's magnum opus posthumously in 1968. R. Rosdolsky, *Zur Entstehungsgeschichte des Marxschen Kapital*. Pluto Press published an English translation in 1971 as *The Making of Marx's 'Capital'*. R. Rosdolsky, *Zur nationalen Frage: Friedrich Engels und das Problem der 'geschichtslosen' Völker*

(reprint, with a Foreword by Emily Rosdolsky), Berlin, 1979. Emily Rosdolsky noted, 'I think that of Roman's books, he thought this one best; and I think it best reflects his true internationalist outlook and his love for his own people.' E. Rosdolsky to E. Mandel, 8 December 1967, E. Mandel Archives, folder 38.

69 E. Germain [E. Mandel], 'Roman Rosdolsky (1898–1967)', *Quatrième Internationale*, April 1968.

70 E. Mandel, 'Kritik der Wachstumstheorie im Geiste des Kapitals' in W. Euchner and A. Schmidt, eds, *Kritik der politischen Ökonomie heute 100 Jahre 'Kapital'*, pp. 239–57.

71 K. Marx, *Capital*, vol. 3. E. Mandel, 'Kritik der Wachstumstheorie im Geiste des Kapitals', p. 245. Because of the unequal development of technological innovation, some employers and branches of industry can realize excess profits at the expense of others. These are also forced to higher levels of investment by the threat of ruin, thus contributing to an overheated economy.

72 Ibid., p. 248.

73 In 1971, in connection with his study *Late Capitalism*, Mandel asked himself if it was possible to make an algebraic-parametric formula for a system of variables, independent in the sense that none is definite or set, but rather interconnected; that is, they partially and mutually determine each other. He asked Urs Müller Plantenberg, a sociologist and Latin America specialist, to consider this question. E. Mandel to U. Müller-Plantenberg, 4 September 1971; U. Müller-Plantenberg to E. Mandel, 17 September 1971, E. Mandel Archives, folder 46.

74 Varying combinations of these factors also explain why three different phases developed in the social-economic history of capitalism since the nineteenth century: laissez-faire capitalism; classic imperialism and, since the Second World War, late, or neo-capitalism.

75 Otto Bauer and Nikolai Bukharin had pointed out the need to research multiple fundamental contradictions and their interconnections in order to understand the dynamic of the system, but neither gave this a systematic development. See N. Bukharin's *Imperialism and World Economy*, New York, 1973; O. Bauer's 'Marx' Theorie der Wirtschaftskrisen', *Die Neue Zeit*, 1904; *The Question of Nationalities and Social Democracy* Minneapolis, 2000; 'Die Akkumulation des Kapitals', *Die Neue Zeit*, 1913; and *Zwischen zwei Weltkriegen?*, Bratislava, 1936.

76 H. Grossmann, *Das Akkumulations- und Zusammenbruchsgesetz des kapitalistischen Systems (zugleich eine Krisentheorie)*, Leipzig, 1929. A variant of Grossmann's thesis can be found in the work of Michal Kalecki, a Polish-English economist. See M. Kalecki, *The Theory of Economic Dynamics*, London, 1954.

77 R. Luxemburg, *The Accumulation of Capital*, London, 1951. P. Baran and P. Sweezy, *Monopoly Capital*, New York 1966, and P. Sweezy, *The Theory of Capitalist Development*, New York, 1956. For a debate on their position, see E. Mandel's critique, 'Surplus Capital and Realization of Surplus Value', *International Socialist Review*, January/February 1967, D. Horowitz's response to Mandel, 'The Case for a Neo-Marxist Theory', *International Socialist Review*, July/August 1967, and Mandel's reply to Horowitz, 'The Labor Theory of

Value and "Monopoly Capitalism"', *International Socialist Review*, July/August 1967.

78 R. Hilferding, *Finance Capital: A Study of the Latest Phase of Capitalist Development*, London, 1981.

79 M. Kidron, *Western Capitalism Since the War*, London, 1962.

80 R. Rosdolsky to E. Mandel, 18 January 1964, E. Mandel Archives, folder 22. R. Rosdolsky, 'Einige Bemerkungen über die Methode des Marxschen Kapital und ihre Bedeutung für die heutige Marxforschung' in eds W. Euchner and A. Schmidt, *Kritik der politischen Ökonomie heute 100 Jahre 'Kapital'*, p. 10.

81 E. Mandel, *Long Waves of Capitalist Development: A Marxist Interpretation*, London, 1995, p. 11.

82 E. Mandel, 'Partially Independent Variables and Internal Logic in Classical Marxist Economic Analysis' in U. Himmelstrand, ed., *Interfaces in Economic & Social Analysis*, London, 1992, pp. 33–50. Mandel reiterated this number in his article 'Marx, Karl Heinrich (1818–1883)' in J. Eatwell, M. Milgate and P. Newman, eds, *The New Palgrave: A Dictionary of Economics*, London, 1988, vol. 3: K to P, pp. 367–83.

83 E. Mandel, 'Partially Independent Variables and Internal Logic in Classical Marxist Economic Analysis', *The New Palgrave: A Dictionary of Economics*, p. 36.

84 Ibid., p. 37

85 Ibid., p. 39.

86 This semi-autonomy can be illustrated by the fact that there is no simple synchronization between the business cycle and the cycle of class struggle. Class-consciousness is rather a function of what has taken place in the struggle between classes in a period fifteen to twenty years previously, rather than the specific economic situation of the moment. See E. Mandel, *Trotsky: A Study in the Dynamic of His Thought*, London, 1979, pp. 38–42.

87 P. Arestis and M. Sawyer, eds, *A Biographical Dictionary of Dissenting Economists*, Aldershot, 1992, pp. 336–341. F. Louçã, 'Ernest Mandel and the Pulsation of History', G. Achcar, ed., *The Legacy of Ernest Mandel*, pp. 110–3.

88 P. Arestis and M. Sawyer, *A Biographical Dictionary of Dissenting Economists*, p. 341.

89 E. Mandel to R. Rosdolsky, 9 October 1967, E. Mandel Archives, folder 38.

90 Author's interview with E. Altvater, 17 March 2004.

91 This coalition of the largest parliamentary parties was formed in 1966, made up of the Christian Democrats (CDU/CSU) and the Social Democrats (SPD), led by Kurt Georg Kiesinger (CDU) with Willy Brandt (SPD) as vice chancellor.

92 The German translation of Mandel's *Introduction to Marxist Economic Theory* was published in 1967 by the then-SDS publisher Neue Kritik. There were twenty-five printings with a total of 120,000 copies. Suhrkamp of Frankfurt on Main published the translation of *Marxist Economic Theory* the following year. Also in 1968 Mandel's *Die EWG und die Konkurrenz Europa-Amerika: Eine Antwort auf Servan Schreibers Amerikanische Herausforderung* was published by Frankfurt's European Publishing House, as was his *Formation of the Economic Thought of Karl Marx*.

93 E. Mandel, *Die deutsche Wirtschaftskrise: Lehren der Rezession 1966/1967*, Frankfurt on Main, 1969.

94 Ibid., pp. 49–50.
95 E. Mandel, 'The Economics of Neo-Capitalism'. This prognosis can be found in four publications from 1968–9: E. Mandel, *Die deutsche Wirtschafts-krise*, pp. 49–50; E. Mandel, 'Workers Under Neo-Capitalism', *International Socialist Review*, vol. 29, no. 6, November/December 1968, p. 3; E. Mandel, *Die EWG und die Konkurrenz Europa-Amerika*, pp. 85–93; 'Resolution on [the] New Rise of the World Revolution', *World Congress of the Fourth International: Documents, Intercontinental Press*, vol. 7, no. 26, 14 July 1969 (This thesis was prepared for the Ninth World Congress; Mandel's prognosis is laid out in the third chapter, 'The End of the Long Imperialist Boom', pp. 672–4).
96 In December 1959 Mandel spoke on Marx's critique of bourgeois economics at the SDS federal seminar in Dörnberg, near Kassel. On other occasions he spoke on such subjects as 'The Western European Workers' Movement, from Adaptation to Neo-Capitalism to Socialist Awakening'. W. Kraushaar, *Die Protest-Chronik 1949–1959: Eine illustrierte Geschichte von Bewegung, Widerstand und Utopie*, Hamburg, 1996, vol. 3, p. 2, 348. W. Albrecht, *Der Sozialistische deutsche Studentenbund (SDS): Vom parteikonformen Studentenverband zum Re-präsentanten der Neuen Linken*, Bonn, 1994, p. 315. E. Mandel to E. Bessau, 24 November 1965, E. Mandel Archives, folder 36.
97 Author's interview with B. Morawe, 13 July 2005.
98 Author's interview with E. Altvater, 17 March 2004.
99 G. Scholtz to 'K. en E. Bloch', 16 January 1977; G. Scholtz to K. Bloch, 5 December 1981, E. Bloch Archives.
100 U. Chaussy, *Die drei Leben des Rudi Dutschke: Eine biographie*, Darmstadt-Neuwied, 1983, pp. 158–62.
101 E. Altvater to E. Mandel, 20 November 1967, E. Mandel Archives, folder 37. K. Meschkat to G. Meschkat, 18 June 1966, E. Mandel Archives, folder 650. Using the pseudonym Paul Sering, Löwenthal, who held left-wing views before the war, wrote *Jenseits des Kapitalismus: Ein Beitrag zur sozialistischen Neuorientierung*, Lauf bei Nürnberg, 1947.
102 E. Mandel to H.-D. Mayer, 2 February 1970, E. Mandel Archives, folder 45.
103 H.-D. Mayer to E. Mandel, 7 May 1970, E. Mandel Archives, folder 44. Mandel was offered professorships at the universities of Constance (1971–2), Bremen (1972) and Frankfurt (1972). From 1966 he lectured regularly at the universities of Turin and Liège and at the Bologna extension of Johns Hopkins. H. Sontag to E. Mandel, 12 November 1971, E. Mandel Archives, folder 46. I. Fetscher to E. Mandel, 12 February 1972, E. Mandel Archives, folder 47.
104 In a report of the committee on 'Principles and Application of Marxist Economics' Marcel Liebman pointed out that 'in the faculty meeting certain professors also used political arguments against Mr E. Mandel'. E. Mandel file, Archives of the Free University of Brussels.
105 E. Mandel to L. Goldmann, 15 September 1970, E. Mandel Archives, folder 45.
106 E. Mandel to Lucien Goldmann, 29 September 1970, E. Mandel Archives, folder 44. On 10 February 1967, Mandel received his master's degree from the Sorbonne for his thesis 'The Economic Conceptions of Karl Marx before "Capital" – A Genetic Study', supervised by Liebman. His diploma was signed

by professors Lucien Goldmann, André Marchal and Charles Bettelheim. E. Mandel, 'Lebenslauf' (Curriculum Vitae), 31 January 1972, E. Altvater Collection.

107 This did not put an end to his problems. Lucien Goldmann, Mandel's thesis supervisor at the Sorbonne (the Paris Practical School of Higher Studies) died unexpectedly in the autumn of 1970. This added new complications to the process of securing Mandel's position at the University of Brussels. He valued a permanent position above all for political reasons, as he informed comrades: '. . . as you can imagine I'm not at all interested in an academic career. But I think – and the comrades think – that a formal, regularly appointed professorship, even for a very short course that will hardly cost me any time, will improve our legal cover and raise the price that our enemies would have to pay for repression. And sooner or later repression will inevitably come.' E. Mandel to 'Cher ami', 13 October 1970, E. Mandel Archives, folder 45. But Mandel soon relinquished these modest goals. It was not long before he was teaching full time, and he seemed not to consider his academic position purely as a means to other ends. B. Coppieters to J.W. Stutje, 8 February 2006.

108 In addition to a series of formal lectures on Marxist economics, Mandel taught three courses on political structure, one about developing countries, a second on Western Europe and the United States and a third on the so-called socialist countries. The textbooks that he wrote for these different courses are available in the library of the Free University of Brussels.

109 E. Mandel to H. Braverman, 30 July 1970, E. Mandel Archives, folder 283.

110 H. Gollwitzer to E. Mandel, 22 April 1971, E. Mandel Archives, folder 47.

111 E. Mandel to K. and E. Bloch, 16 November 1970, E. Mandel Archives, folder 44.

112 R. Dutschke to G. and E. Mandel, 15 September 1970, cited in K. Bloch and W. Schröter, eds, *Lieber Genosse Bloch . . . Briefe von Rudi Dutschke, Gretchen Dutschke-Klotz und Karola Bloch, 1968–1979*, Mössingen-Talheim, 1988.

113 Rudi Dutschke died at his home in Aldershvile, near Aarhus in Denmark, on Christmas night 1979, after an epileptic attack, a consequence of the April 1968 assault.

114 G. Mandel to R. Dutschke, 17 September 1970, R. Dutschke Archives. G. Mandel to E. and K. Bloch, 8 September 1970, E. Bloch Archives. *Le Monde*, 11 September 1970.

115 According to Terrence Mcdonough, Mandel's theory of the stage of late capitalism was 'directly inspired by Lenin's theory of the era of classical imperialism'. Like Lenin, Mandel wanted to surmount the crisis in Marxist theory, the consequence of an unanticipated period of capitalist prosperity. T. Mcdonough, 'Lenin, Imperialism, and the Stages of Capitalist Development', *Science & Society*, vol. 59, no. 3, Fall 1995.

116 E. Mandel, 'Vorlesung Theorie des Spätkapitalismus (Bewegungsgesetze und Etappen der kapitalistischen Produktionsweise)', E. Mandel Archives, folder 252.

117 Mandel listed the following six fundamental variables: the organic composition of capital in general and in the two departments (productive capital and consumer goods); the distribution of constant capital between fixed and circulating capital; the development of the rate of surplus value; the devel-

opment of the rate of accumulation (the relation between productive surplus value and unproductively consumed surplus value); the development of capital's turnover time; the relations of exchange between the two departments. E. Mandel, *Late Capitalism*, p. 39.

118 Ibid., p. 41.

119 As additional explanations for the rising rate of profit in the period from 1940 to 1966, Mandel mentioned cheaper raw materials and machines, and the third technological revolution – automation, electronics, nuclear power, etc., which was made possible by the accelerated accumulation of capital.

120 See Perry Anderson, *Considerations on Western Marxism*.

121 Mandel grouped the four departments as follows: I. Production of constant capital; II. Production of raw materials; III. Production of consumer goods; IV. Production of luxury goods. E. Mandel to H. Chester, 1 September 1972, E. Mandel Archives, folder 237.

122 Traces of Mandel's attempt to do this can be found in his correspondence. See E. Mandel to H. Krivine, 29 September 1970, E. Mandel Archives, folder 45. In later years, Mandel corresponded extensively about the problem. See E. Mandel to H. Chester, 1 September 1972; E. Mandel to G. Hodgson, 1 September 1972; E. Mandel to E. Mommen, 1 September 1972, E. Mandel Archives, folder 237. See also H. Chester to E. Mandel, 25 September 1972, E. Mandel Archives, folder 49.

123 Harry Chester gives technological innovation as an example. In an environment with a strong trade union movement, innovation leads to rising real wages; in the opposite context it leads to unemployment and has a negative impact on the development of real wages. H. Chester to E. Mandel, 25 September 1972, E. Mandel Archives, folder 49.

124 E. Mandel, *Late Capitalism*, p. 39.

125 Michael Krätke, 'On the History and Logic of Modern Capitalism: The Legacy of Ernest Mandel', *Historical Materialism*, vol. 15, no. 1, 2007.

126 For the English edition of *Late Capitalism*, Perry Anderson recommended 'a somewhat *longer* prefatory explanation of the *structure and the order* of the book . . . I think that you should take more trouble to explain just what the lay-out of the book is . . . The transitions from chapter to chapter are often quite abrupt.' P. Anderson to E. Mandel, 13 April 1973, E. Mandel Archive, folder 50.

127 E. Altvater, 'Kritik zu Ernest Mandels *Der Spätkapitalismus*', 27 July 1972, E. Mandel Archives, folder 332. Bob Rowthorn makes a similar critique in 'Late Capitalism'(*New Left Review*, no. 98, July/August 1976, p. 61).

128 The outline of late capitalism itself only comprises four pages. E. Mandel, *Late Capitalism*, pp. 557–61.

129 Mandel argues that even his controversial thesis of the dual rate of profit – one rate for the monopolized sector and one for the non-monopolized sector – applies to the entire period of monopoly capitalism, including classical imperialism. Ibid., p. 542.

130 M. Krätke, 'On the History and Logic of Modern Capitalism'. P. Mattick, *Kritik der Neomarxisten*, Frankfurt on Main, 1974, pp. 146–9. B. Rowthorn, 'Late Capitalism', pp. 61–2. Krätke says of the 'six basic variables' whose interaction needs to be investigated, 'Obviously, Mandel is referring to the

overall development of one 'basic variable' of capitalist economies again – to the general or average rate of profit . . . So one might accuse him of making exactly the same mistake as his predecessors.' Not only do critics reproach Mandel with taking refuge in a monocausal explanation, a practice he had himself strongly deprecated in his predecessors, they also doubt his explanation of the falling rate of profit. Rowthorn argues that Mandel underestimates the importance of rising real wages. He suggests, for example, that the 1970 recession resulted from a falling share of profits in production and not from 'a high capital value in the production process'. Similarly, A. Glyn and B. Sutcliffe, in *British Capitalism, Workers and the Profits Squeeze* (Harmondsworth, 1972), express doubts about Mandel's emphasis on the organic composition of capital. They argue that Mandel should include variable capital as well as constant capital in his accounting of production costs.

Mandel warned many times against an analysis in which the rate of profit is taken as the alpha and omega. He avoided the implication that a new expansive wave would take off spontaneously once a certain level of profitability had been attained. The rate of profit, he thought, is merely an indicator in which many underlying phenomena are manifested. Michel Husson argues that in the current recessive phase the rate of profit returned after 1982 to pre-1974–5 crisis levels without there being any comparable recovery of accumulation and growth (M. Husson, 'After the Golden Age: On Late Capitalism', G. Achcar, ed., *The Legacy of Ernest Mandel*, p. 96).

131 J. Albarracín and P. Montes, 'Late Capitalism: Mandel's Interpretation of Contemporary Capitalism' in G. Achcar, ed., *The Legacy of Ernest Mandel*, p. 48.

132 Mandel rejected every monocausal explanation of the crisis that began in the 1970s, including Andrew Glyn and Bob Sutcliffe's 'profit squeeze' theory and Sweezy's theory of inadequate surplus absorption (P. Sweezy and P. Baran, *Monopoly Capital*).

133 E. Mandel, *Late Capitalism*, pp. 408–37. The subject is also addressed in Mandel's introductions to the three volumes of the Penguin edition of Marx's *Capital* (London 1976) and in E. Mandel and W. Wolf, *Ende der Krise oder Krise ohne Ende?* (Berlin, 1977) and *Börsenkrach & Wirtschaftskrise*, Frankfurt on Main, 1988.

134 For an overview of the debate, see L. Colletti and C. Napoleoni, *Il futuro del capitalismo: Crollo o sviluppo?*, Bari, 1970.

135 E. Mandel, *Late Capitalism*, p. 140. Seven years after *Late Capitalism*, in his *Long Waves of Capitalist Development*, Mandel adds, 'The existence of the long waves in capitalist development can hardly be denied in the light of overwhelming evidence . . . [and in the light of] all statistical data available' (pp. 1–2).

136 Mandel's long-wave theory, as presented in *Late Capitalism*, was further developed in the Alfred Marshall lectures that Mandel gave at the invitation of the University of Cambridge in 1978. The lectures were published as *Long Waves of Capitalist Development: A Marxist Interpretation*, Cambridge, 1980; revised edition, London, 1995. In 1989, together with Alfred Kleinknecht and Immanuel Wallerstein, Mandel organized a conference on long waves in Brussels. See: A. Kleinknecht, E. Mandel and I. Wallerstein, eds, *New Findings in Long Wave Research*, London, 1992.

137 Parvus, *Die Handelskrisis und die Gewerkschaften.* J. van Gelderen [J. Fedder], 'Springvloed'.

138 N. Kondratieff, 'Die Preisdynamik der industriellen und landwirtschaftlichen Waren', *Archiv für Sozialwissenschaft und Sozialpolitik,* vol. 60, no. 1, 1928. This article is also included in N. Makasheva, W. Samuels and V. Barnett, eds, *The Works of Nikolai D. Kondratiev,* vol. 1, London, 1998. For a profound critique of Kondratiev, see: G. Garvy, 'Kondratieff's Theory of Long Cycles', *Review of Economics and Statistics,* November 1943, pp. 203–20. For a critical treatment of Mandel's views on Kondratiev, see: R. Day, 'The Theory of Long Waves: Kondratiev, Trotsky, Mandel', *New Left Review,* no. 99, September/October 1976. Mandel responded to these critics in his *Long Waves of Capitalist Development* (revised ed.), pp. 104–5. For a discussion of Trotsky's critique of Kondratiev, see: V. Barnett, 'Trotsky, Kondratiev, and Long Waves', *Journal of Trotsky Studies,* vol. 2, 1994, pp. 1–15.

139 J. Schumpeter, *Business Cycles.* J. Schumpeter, *The Theory of Economic Development,* New York, 1961.

140 For an overview of modern explanations – Wallerstein, Baran, Sweezy, Dupriez, etc. – see D. M. Gordon, 'Stages of accumulation and long economic cycles' in T. Hopkins and I. Wallerstein, eds, *Processes in the World-System,* Thousand Oaks, CA, 1980.

141 E. Mandel, 'The Economics of Neo-Capitalism'.

142 E. Mandel, *Late Capitalism,* p. 122.

143 L. Trotsky, 'The Curve of Capitalist Development', p. 277.

144 In the revised edition of *Long Waves of Capitalist Development,* Mandel formulated the paradox as follows: 'Is it possible, with the conceptual tools of Marxist economic analysis, to explain long-term upsurges in the average rate of profit at certain historical turning points, in spite of the cyclical downturn of that same rate of profit at the end of each industrial cycle, and in spite of the secular decline pointing to the historical limit of the capitalist mode of production? Our answer to this question is a categorical: Yes.'

145 Mandel listed the exogenous factors that provoked prolonged increases in the average rate of profit: the 1848 revolution and simultaneous discovery of the California gold fields; the rapid increase in capital investment in the colonies (imperialism) and the discovery of the South African gold fields after 1893; and the cumulative impact of fascism and war around 1940 in the US and Britain and from 1948–9 in Western Europe and Japan.

146 F. Louçã, 'Ernest Mandel and the Pulsation of History', p. 113. E. Mandel, *Long Waves of Capitalist Development* (revised ed.), p. 76.

147 Ibid., p. 82.

148 E. Mandel, *Late Capitalism,* p. 9.

149 David Gordon remarks that Mandel 'pays full attention to all strands of transformation from one stage to another; he falls short nonetheless, because he fails to articulate a full methodological foundation for his interesting analysis of successive stages in the world capitalist economy.' D. Gordon, 'Stages of Accumulation and Long Economic Cycles' in T. Hopkins and I. Wallerstein, eds, *Processes in the World-System,* p. 39, note 10.

150 The origin of the term 'late capitalism' is not entirely clear. According to Fredric Jameson, it originated in Frankfurt School circles: 'It is everywhere in

Adorno and Horkheimer, sometimes varied with their own synonyms (for example, "administered society").' F. Jameson, *Post-Modernism, or, the Cultural Logic of Late Capitalism*, Durham, 1999, p. xviii.

151 Mandel and the members of the Fourth International were not the only Trotskyists who tried to explain the peculiarities of postwar capitalism. In 1944 Walter J. Oakes developed the theory of the 'permanent arms economy' ('Towards a Permanent Arms Economy?', *Politics*, February 1944). Oakes argued that the US in particular would continue to have a war economy. T.N. Vance took up this interpretation in 'After Korea What? An Economic Interpretation of U.S. Perspectives', *New International*, November/December 1950. Vance argued that there was an irreconcilable contradiction between capitalism in general, and that of the US in particular, on the one hand and Soviet bureaucratic collectivism on the other. Tony Cliff (Ygaël Gluckstein) summed up the same idea once more in his article 'Perspectives of the Permanent War Economy', *Socialist Review*, May 1957. Michael Kidron, a co-thinker of Cliff's, reformulated the theory, which until then had been more Keynesian than Marxist, in his essay 'Reform and Revolution: Rejoinder to Left Reformism', *International Socialism*, no. 7, Winter 1961. Kidron elaborated the theory in *Western Capitalism Since the War*, London, 1968. Cf. M. van der Linden, *Western Marxism and the Soviet Union*.

152 P. Arestis and M. Sawyer, eds, *A Biographical Dictionary of Dissenting Economists*, p. 337.

153 R. Rosdolsky to E. Mandel, 18 January 1964, E. Mandel Archives, folder 22.

154 E. Mandel, *Late Capitalism*, p. 10.

155 P. Sweezy to H. Riese, 6 January 1972, E. Mandel Archives, folder 201.

156 Der Senator für Wissenschaft und Kunst (Senator for Science and Culture, *Rätesystem, Revolution und Grundgesetz: Warum Ernest Mandel nicht berufen werden konnte*, 22 February 1972, E. Mandel Archives, folder 201.

157 E. Altvater to E. Mandel, 1 February 1972, E. Mandel Archives, folder 49.

158 'Verklaring: Der Bundesminister des Innern teilt mit' (Declaration: The Minister of the Interior informs you), 28 February 1972, W. Abendroth Archives, folder 99. Verwaltungsgericht des Saarlandes, Aktenzeichen: 1 K 231/72, Urteil in dem Verwaltungsrechtstreit des Hochschullehrers Dr Ernest Mandel gegen die Bundesrepublik Deutschland (Judgement in the case of Prof. Ernest Mandel vs. the Federal Republic of Germany). *Protokoll des Deutschen Bundestags* (Proceedings of the West German Federal Assembly), 1 March 1972.

159 J. Améry, 'Revolutionär ohne Ungeduld: Ergebnis eines Gesprächs mit Ernest Mandel', *Frankfurter Rundschau*, 3 June 1972.

160 Statement by Wolfgang Abendroth, 7 March 1972. E. Mandel Archives, folder 202.

161 Komitee zur Aufhebung des Einreiseverbots gegen Ernest Mandel (Committee for the Revocation of the Ban on Ernest Mandel's Entry into Germany).

162 Kongress gegen politische Unterdrückung an der Freien Universität vom 24.–26.4.1972, 'Referate und Diskussionen', n.p., 1972, cited by J. Moneta in his obituary for Ernest Mandel, 29 September 1995 (manuscript), J. Moneta Collection.

163 S. Luria to H.-D. Genscher, 23 May 1972, E. Mandel Archives, folder 206.
164 Author's interview with E. Altvater, 17 March 2003. E. Altvater to E. Mandel, 22 July 1972.
165 Mandel's diploma was signed by Prof. Dr Hartmut Jäckel, chair of the faculty of political science at the Free University of Berlin, on 25 August 1972. The same Hartmut Jäckel defended Mandel's ban from teaching at the University in an article in *Die Zeit*, 10 March 1972, co-signed by Countess Dönhoff.
166 J. Moneta to E. Mandel, 17 July 1972, E. Mandel Archives, folder 332.
167 M. Salvati to E. Mandel, n.d., E. Mandel Archives, folder 332.
168 E. Altvater to E. Mandel, 27 July 1972, E. Mandel Archives, folder 332. E. Mandel to E. Altvater, 30 July 1972, E. Mandel Archives, folder 48.
169 'E. en K. Bloch' to E. Mandel, 1 March 1973, E. Mandel Archives, folder 51.
170 J. Miermeister, *Ernst Bloch, Rudi Dutschke*, Hamburg, 1996, p. 34. R. Dutschke to K. Bloch, 9 August 1974, *Lieber Genosse Bloch . . . Briefe von Rudi Dutschke, Gretchen Dutschke-Klotz und Karola Bloch, 1968–1979*, K. Bloch and W. Schröter, eds, pp. 95–6.
171 K. Bloch to R. Dutschke, 8 February 1975, *Lieber Genosse Bloch . . .*, K. Bloch and W. Schröter, eds, pp. 99–100.
172 K. Bloch to R. Dutschke, 23 March 1977, *Lieber Genosse Bloch . . .*, K. Bloch and W. Schröter, eds, pp. 112–3.
173 Ibid.
174 E. Bloch to Koch, 17 March 1976, E. Mandel Archives, folder 207.
175 R. Dutschke to K. Bloch, 10 May 1977, *Lieber Genosse Bloch . . .*, K. Bloch and W. Schröter, eds., pp. 115–6.

Love and Revolution

1 *Collected Works*, vol. 25, Moscow, 1977, p. 497.
2 P. Anderson, *In the Tracks of Historical Materialism*, London, 1983. P. Anderson, *Considerations on Western Marxism*, London, 1977.
3 E. Mandel, *Marxist Economic Theory*, vol. 2, London 1968, pp. 605–53.
4 E. Mandel, 'Introduction' in E. Préobrazenskij, *La Nouvelle économie (Novaia Ekonomika)*, Paris, 1966. P. Naville to E. Mandel, 20 May 1962, E. Mandel Archives, folder 278. A. Erlich analyzed Preobrazhensky's work in *The Soviet Industrialization Debate, 1924–1928*, Cambridge, MA, 1960. C. Samary, *Plan, Market, Democracy*, Amsterdam, 1988.
5 P. Naville to E. Mandel, 17 September 1960, E. Mandel Archives, folder 318.
6 E. Mandel, 'Introduction', *La Nouvelle économie*, E. Préobrazenskij, p. 35.
7 M. Löwy, *The Marxism of Che Guevara: Philosophy, Economics, and Revolutionary Warfare*, New York, 1973.
8 'Interview with Che Guevara', *L'Express*, 25 July 1963, cited in: E. Guevara, *Ecrits d'un révolutionnaire*, Paris, 1987, p. 9.
9 E. Guevara, *Socialism and Man in Cuba*, Sydney, 1988, p. 5.
10 Jack [E. Mandel] to 'Chers amis', 18 October 1960, E. Mandel Archives, folder 70. E. Germain [E. Mandel] to 'Cher camarade', 1 July 1961, E. Mandel Archives, folder 483.
11 Ibid.

12 G. Arcos Bergnes [Cuban ambassador] to E. Mandel, 12 September 1962, E. Mandel Archives, folder 16.

13 Using the pseudonym David Alexander, Zayas Pazos published a book about Cuba in 1967: *Cuba: la via rivoluzionaria al socialismo*, Rome. He also wrote letters signed with the pseudonym Emile.

14 H. Gadea, *Che Guevara: Años decisivos*, Mexico, 1972. P. Kalfon, *Che, Ernesto Guevara: Une légende du siècle*, Paris, 1997.

15 N. Zayas to P. Frank, 20 October 1963, E. Mandel Archives, folder 23.

16 N. Zayas to 'Cher camarade', 25 October 1963, E. Mandel Archives, folder 21.

17 A. Mora, 'En torno a la cuestión del funcionamiento de la ley del valor en la economia cubana en los actuales momentes', *Comercio Exterior*, June 1963. Translated as: A. Mora, 'Zur Frage des Funktionierens des Wertgesetzes in der cubanischen Wirtschaft zum gegenwärtigen Zeitpunkt' in C. Bettelheim et al., *Wertgesetz: Planung und Bewusstsein: die Planungsdebatte in Cuba*, Frankfurt on Main, 1969. Alberto Mora was the Cuban minister of foreign trade.

18 E. Guevara, 'On value' (1963) in J. Gerassi, ed., *Venceremos! The Speeches and Writings of Che Guevara,* London, 1969, pp. 280–5.

19 N. Zayas to 'Cher camarade', 25 October 1963, E. Mandel Archives, folder 21.

20 N. Zayas to E. Germain, 16 January 1964, E. Mandel Archives, folder 22.

21 E. Mandel, 'Le grand débat économique à Cuba', *Partisans*, no. 37, 1967. Reprinted in E. Guevara, *Ecrits d'un révolutionnaire*, Paris, 1987.

22 E. Mandel, letter fragment, n.d. [1964], E. Mandel Archives, folder 26.

23 E. Mandel to R. Blackburn, 12 February 1964, E. Mandel Archives, folder 28. E. Mandel to N. Zayas, 12 February 1964, E. Mandel Archives, folder 21.

24 Nelson to Germain, 16 February 1964, E. Mandel Archives, folder 19.

25 E. Mandel to 'cher ami' [L. Maitan], 3 March 1964, E. Mandel Archives, folder 22.

26 E. Mandel to L. Maitan, 7 March 1964, E. Mandel Archives, folder 22.

27 L. Maitan, manuscript memoirs (unpublished), Paris, n.d., pp. 3, 19–20.

28 E. Mandel to L. Maitan, 10 June 1964, E. Mandel Archives, folder 24. 'Che Guevara was Energetically Devoted to Anti-Imperialist Solidarity', interview with M. Piñiero, *The Militant,* 24 November 1997.

29 *La Gauche*, 9 May 1964.

30 E. Mandel to Paul [Clerbaut], 7 May 1964, E. Mandel Archives, folder 23.

31 Mandel anticipated that he would soon see *Marxist Economic Theory* published in Cuba, 'obviously' without the chapter on the Soviet economy ('There is no need for us to embarrass the Cubans.'). E. Mandel to Paul [Clerbaut], 7 May 1964, E. Mandel Archives, folder 23. Mandel wrote to his French publisher, 'The president of the Republic [Osvaldo Dorticos] himself is interested in the work and would like to publish it in Spanish in Cuba.' E. Mandel to C. Bourgois, 28 May 1964, E. Mandel Archives, folder 278.

32 E. Mandel to Paul [Clerbaut], 7 May 1964, E. Mandel Archives, folder 23.

33 Ibid.

34 C. Bettelheim, 'Forms and Methods of Socialist Planning and the Level of Development of the Productive Forces', *The Transition to a Socialist Economy*, Atlantic Highlands, NJ, 1975, pp. 121–38.

35 J. Cormier (in collaboration with H. Guevara Gadea and A. Granado Jimenez), *Che Guevara*, Monaco, 1995, pp. 291–2.

36 E. Mandel, 'Mercantile Categories in the Transition Stage', in B. Silverman ed., *Man and Socialism in Cuba: The Great Debate,* New York, 1971, pp. 63–6. S. de Santis, 'Bewußtsein und Produktion: Eine Kontroverse zwischen Ernesto Che Guevara, Charles Bettelheim und Ernest Mandel über das ökonomische System in Kuba', *Kursbuch* 18, October 1969.

37 E. Mandel, 'Mercantile Categories in the Transition Stage', in B. Silverman ed., *Man and Socialism in Cuba,* p. 82. R. Massari, *Che Guevara: Pensiero e politica dell'utopia*, Rome, 1987.

38 E. Mandel, 'Mercantile Categories in the Transition Stage', *Man and Socialism in Cuba,* p. 82 (italics in original).

39 E. Mandel, 'Las categorias mercantiles en el periodo de transición', *Nuestra Industria*, June 1964.

40 J. Habel, 'Le sens que nous donnons au combat du Che Guevara' (I), *Rouge*, 13 October 1977.

41 E. Mandel to A. Eguren, 5 August 1964, E. Mandel Archives, folder 25.

42 F. Buyens, *Een mens genaamd Ernest Mandel*, film, Brussels, 1972.

43 E. Mandel, 'Il y a dix ans, l'assassinat du Che, Les positions du Che Guevara dans le grand débat économique de 1963–1965', *Rouge*, 11 October 1977.

44 Ibid.

45 E. Mandel to 'Paul [Clerbaut]', 7 May 1964, E. Mandel Archives, folder 23.

46 E. Mandel to 'Emile' [N. Zayas], 26 May 1964, E. Mandel Archives, folder 24.

47 E. Mandel to A. Eguren, 5 August 1964, E. Mandel Archives, folder 25.

48 E. Mandel to 'Lieber Freund' [G. Jungclas], 22 May 1964; E. Mandel to K. Coates, 10 May 1964, E. Mandel Archives, folder 23.

49 Emile to E. Mandel, 5 July 1964, E. Mandel Archives, folder 25.

50 Emile to E. Mandel, 13 August 1964, E. Mandel Archives, folder 25.

51 E. Mandel to 'Cher ami' [N. Zayas], 12 October 1964, E. Mandel Archives, folder 25.

52 E. Mandel to A. Eguren, 25 September 1964, E. Mandel Archives, folder 25.

53 Emile to E. Mandel, 27 September 1964; E. Mandel to Emile, 11 November 1964, E. Mandel Archives, folder 26.

54 E. Mandel to J. Vazquez Mendez, 2 November 1964, E. Mandel Archives, folder 26.

55 E. Guevara, 'At the Afro-Asian Conference', *Che Guevara Speaks*, New York, 1967, pp. 108, 114.

56 P. Kalfon, *Che, Ernesto Guevara: Une légende du siècle*, p. 402.

57 Ibid. Also: P. Robrieux, *Notre génération communiste 1953–1968*, Paris, 1977, pp. 316–7.

58 E. Mandel to L. Maitan, 10 June 1964, E. Mandel Archives, folder 24.

59 E. Mandel to 'Dear friend' [I. Tabata], 19 May 1965, E. Mandel Archives, folder 31.

60 E. Mandel to 'Pierre', 1 March 1965, E. Mandel Archives, folder 30.

61 P. Robrieux, *Notre génération communiste 1953–1968*, p. 317.

62 E. Guevara, 'Vietnam and the World Struggle for Freedom', *Che Guevara Speaks*, p. 159.

63 E. Mandel to A. Eguren, 5 August 1964, E. Mandel Archives, folder 25.

64 E. Mandel to E. Federn, 18 February 1962, E. Mandel Archives, folder 677.
65 'Bundesverdienstkreuz für dr Scholtz', *Mühlacker Tagblatt*, 11 October 1968. Author's interview with K. Meschkat, 10 September 2004.
66 On Gottfried Benn, see H. Lethen, *Der Sound der Väter: Gottfried Benn und seine Zeit*, Berlin, 2006.
67 Author's interview with B. Morawe, 13 July 2005.
68 K. Meschkat, *Die Pariser Kommune von 1871 im Spiegel der sowjetischen Geschichtsschreibung*, Berlin, 1965.
69 U. Chaussy, *Die drei Leben des Rudi Dutschke: Eine Biographie*, Darmstadt, 1983. M. Karl, *Rudi Dutschke: Revolutionär ohne Revolution*, Frankfurt on Main, 2003.
70 S. Freud, *The Ego and the Id*, London, 1949. P. Gay, *Freud: A Life for Our Time*, New York, 1988.
71 G. Scholtz to E. Mandel, 13 June 1965, G. Scholtz Archives. Of the correspondence between Gisela Scholtz and Ernest Mandel during these years, only the letters from Gisela to Ernest could be found in the archives. His letters could not be located.
72 G. Scholtz to E. Mandel, 10 June 1965; G. Scholtz to E. Mandel, 13 August 1965, G. Scholtz Archives.
73 K. Meschkat to G. Scholtz, 17 June 1965, G. Scholtz Archives.
74 G. Scholtz to E. Mandel, 10 June 1965, G. Scholtz Archives.
75 K. Meschkat to G. Scholtz, 14 July 1965, G. Scholtz Archives.
76 Author's interview with K. Meschkat, 10 September 2004.
77 K. Meschkat to G. Scholtz, 21 September 1965, G. Scholtz Archives.
78 G. Scholtz to E. Mandel, 25 July 1965, G. Scholtz Archives.
79 G. Scholtz to E. Mandel, 30 July 1965, G. Scholtz Archives.
80 G. Scholtz to E. Mandel, 5 August 1965, G. Scholtz Archives.
81 G. Scholtz to E. Mandel, 10 September 1965, G. Scholtz Archives.
82 G. Scholtz to E. Mandel, 13 September 1965, G. Scholtz Archives.
83 G. Scholtz to E. Mandel, 17 September 1965, G. Scholtz Archives.
84 Ibid.
85 G. Scholtz to E. Mandel, 8 December 1965, G. Scholtz Archives.
86 G. Scholtz to E. Mandel, 12 December 1965, G. Scholtz Archives.
87 G. Scholtz to E. Mandel, 24 December 1965, G. Scholtz Archives.
88 G. Scholtz to E. Mandel, 28 January 1966, G. Scholtz Archives.
89 G. Scholtz to E. Mandel, 18 February 1966, G. Scholtz Archives.
90 Ibid.
91 E. Mörike, *Werke in einem Band*, Munich, 1993.
92 G. Scholtz to E. Mandel, 25 March 1966, G. Scholtz Archives.
93 M. Mauke, *Die Klassentheorie von Marx und Engels*, with an Afterword by K. Meschkat, Frankfurt on Main, 1970.
94 G. Scholtz to E. Mandel, 18 March 1966, G. Scholtz Archives.
95 G. Scholtz to E. Mandel, 20 March 1966, G. Scholtz Archives.
96 M. Karl, *Rudi Dutschke: Revolutionär ohne Revolution*.
97 S. Lönnendonker, B. Rabehl and J. Staadt, *Die antiautoritäre Revolte: Der sozialistische deutsche Studentenbund nach der Trennung von der SPD*, vol. 1: *1960–1967*, Wiesbaden, 2002, p. 299.
98 *Berliner Zeitung*, 21 December 1966. J. Miermeister, *Rudi Dutschke*, Hamburg, 1986, p. 73. U. Chaussy, *Die drei Leben des Rudi Dutschke*.

99 R. Dutschke, *Jeder hat sein Leben ganz zu leben: Die Tagebücher 1963–1979*, Cologne, 2003, 20 December 1966. S. Lönnendonker, B. Rabehl and J. Staadt, *Die antiautoritäre Revolte*, p. 299.

100 1966 marriage register, no. 737.

101 R. Debray, 'Latin America: The Long March', *New Left Review*, no. 33, September/October 1965, pp. 17–58. In 1965 Debray published a follow-up article in the Cuban periodical *Casa de las Américas* (no. 31, July/August 1965). This article was also published as 'Problems of Revolutionary Strategy in Latin America' in *New Left Review*, no. 45, September/October 1967, pp. 13–41.

102 The idea that a revolutionary party would form 'in the natural course of the liberation struggle', as it had in Cuba, was an illusion. Mandel held that Cuba was an exception and that to hope for spontaneous party formation was to idealize empiricism and pragmatism. Perry Anderson, the editor of *New Left Review*, agreed with this criticism, though unlike Mandel he thought this difference of opinion with the twenty-four-year-old Debray was minor. E. Mandel to P. Anderson, 21 January 1966, E. Mandel Archives, folder 32.

103 Ibid.

104 University of Texas: Fidel Castro speech database. The conference took place 3–15 January 1966. Its official title was 'First Afro-Asian-Latin American Peoples' Solidarity Conference'. The Fourth International's response appeared in *Quatrième Internationale*, February 1966.

105 Miguel to 'Dear Friends', 1 March 1966, E. Mandel Archives, folder 32.

106 E. Mandel to E. Federn, 1 July 1967, E. Mandel Archives, folder 37.

107 G. Mandel to K. Meschkat, 12 June 1967, cited in R. Debray, F. Castro, G. Mandel and K. Karol, *Der lange Marsch: Wege der Revolution in Lateinamerika*, Munich, 1968, pp. 257–61.

108 Ibid.

109 E. Mandel, 'Cuba 1967 et la première conférence de l'OLAS', *La Gauche*, 9 September 1967.

110 G. Scholtz to K. Meschkat, 29 June 1967, cited in R. Debray, F. Castro, G. Mandel and K. Karol, *Der lange Marsch*, pp. 261–9.

111 T. Szulc, *Fidel: A Critical Portrait*, London, 1987, p. 497.

112 M. Kenner and J. Petras, eds, *Fidel Castro Speaks*, New York, 1969, pp. 145–63.

113 E. Mandel to P. Refflinghaus, 17 July 1967, E. Mandel Archives, folder 38.

114 E. Mandel to G. Horst, 26 October 1967, E. Mandel Archives, folder 38.

115 'L'exemple de "Che" Guevara inspirera des millions de militants par le monde', *La Gauche,* 21 October 1967. ' "Che" est mort', *La Gauche*, 28 October 1967.

116 *Le Monde*, 27 October 1967.

117 D. Bensaïd, *Une Lente impatience*, Paris, 2004, p. 75.

118 Ibid., p. 76. Also: H. Hamon and P. Rotman, *Génération,* vol. 1: *Les années de rêve*, Paris, 1987, p. 384.

119 D. Bensaïd, *Une lente impatience*, p. 76.

120 E. Guevara, 'Vietnam and the World Struggle for Freedom', op. cit., p. 159.

121 E. Guevara, 'Notes on Man and Socialism in Cuba', in *Che Guevara Speaks*, p. 136. J. Miermeister, *Ernst Bloch, Rudi Dutschke*, Hamburg, 1996, p. 144.

122 R. Debray, F. Castro, G. Mandel and K. Karol, *Der lange Marsch*.

123 Author's interview with K. Meschkat, 10 September 2004.

124 R. Dutschke, *Jeder hat sein Leben ganz zu leben*, p. 62. H.-J. Krahl, *Konstitution und Klassenkampf: Zur historischen Dialektik von bürgerlicher Emanzipation und proletarischer Revolution*, Frankfurt on Main, 1977.

125 R. Dutschke and H.-J. Krahl, 'Das Sich-Verweigern erfordert Guerilla-Mentalität, Organisationsreferat auf der 22, Delegiertenkonferenz des SDS, September 1967', R. Dutschke, *Geschichte ist Machbar*, Berlin, 1980. T. Fichter and S. Lönnendonker, *Macht und Ohnmacht der Studenten: Kleine Geschichte des SDS*, Hamburg, 1998, pp. 158–66.

126 In November 1967 Mandel held a three-day discussion about the student movement with Dutschke and others. G. Mandel to R. Dutschke, 2 October 1967; E. Mandel to R. Dutschke, 23 October 1967, E. Mandel Archives, folder 42.

127 S. Lönnendonker, B. Rabehl and J. Staadt, *Die antiautoritäre Revolte*, p. 354.

128 K. Meschkat to G. Mandel, 18 July 1967, E. Mandel Archives, folder 650.

129 E. Mandel to R. Dutschke, 7 April 1969, E. Mandel Archives, folder 42.

130 D. Bensaïd, *Une Lente impatience*, pp. 54–60. G. Filoche, *68–98: Histoire sans fin*, Paris, 1998, pp. 33–4. F. Charpier, *Histoire de l'extrême gauche trotskiste: De 1929 à nos jours*, Paris, 2002, pp. 228–30. P. Robrieux, *Notre génération communiste 1953–1968*, p. 328.

131 C. Den Hond interview with A. Krivine, in *Ernest Mandel – A Life for the Revolution*, C. Den Hond, DVD, 2005.

132 E. Mandel to R. Dutschke, 23 November 1967, E. Mandel Archives, folder 37.

133 J. Miermeister, *Rudi Dutschke*, pp. 85–90. M. Karl, *Rudi Dutschke: Revolutionär ohne Revolution*, pp. 130–6. U. Chaussy, *Die drei Leben des Rudi Dutschke*, pp. 210–2.

134 U. Chaussy, *Die drei Leben des Rudi Dutschke*, p. 218. W. Kraushaar, K. Wieland and J. Reemtsma, *Rudi Dutschke, Andreas Baader und die RAF*, Hamburg, 2005, pp. 22–9.

135 G. Mandel to 'Dear comrade ' [S. Kolpe], 13 November 1967, E. Mandel Archives, folder 651.

136 *Internationaler Vietnam-Kongreß, Februar 1968 Westberlin: Der Kampf des vietnamesischen Volkes und die Globalstrategie des Imperialismus*, West Berlin, 1968 (reprinted Hamburg, 1987).

137 T. Ali, *Street Fighting Years: An Autobiography of the Sixties*, London, 1987, pp. 166–72. D. Bensaïd, *Une Lente impatience*, pp. 78–80.

138 G. Filoche, *Histoire sans fin*, pp. 31–2. *La Gauche*, 22 October 1966. Author's interview with F. Vercammen, 23–4 June 2004.

139 There were eleven participating organizations, including the JCR (France); the Socialist Party of Proletarian Unity (PSIUP) and the Trotskyists around the paper *Falce Martello*, or Hammer and Sickle (Italy), the SJW (Belgium), the Dutch student organization Politeia, and the youth organization of Britain's Labour Party. Support came from Jean-Paul Sartre, Bertrand Russell, Ernst Bloch, Herbert Marcuse, Luchino Visconti, Eric Hobsbawm, Luigi Nono, Pier Paolo Pasolini, Peter Weiss and Alberto Moravia. T. Fichter and S. Lönnendonker, *Macht und Ohnmacht der Studenten*, p. 170.

140 T. Ali, *Street Fighting Years*, p. 169.

141 *Internationaler Vietnam-Kongreß, Februar 1968 Westberlin*, pp. 133–4. The reference to Marx is from *Capital*, vol. 1, London, 1976, ch. 31, p. 926.

142 The Zengakuren, or All-Japanese Federation of Students' Self-Governing Associations, was a movement of over 300,000 students with a strong left-Communist and Trotskyist wing. It played a leading role in the anti-imperialist mobilizations of the mid 1960s.

143 *Internationaler Vietnam-Kongreß,, Februar 1968 Westberlin*, p. 130.

144 Author's interview with F. Vercammen, 23–4 June 2004.

145 U. Chaussy, *Die drei Leben des Rudi Dutschke*, pp. 210–4. S. Lönnendonker, B. Rabehl and J. Staadt, *Die antiautoritäre Revolte*, p. 501. R. Dutschke, *Geschichte ist Machbar*.

146 D. Bensaïd, *Une Lente impatience*, p. 131.

147 Ibid., p. 79.

148 H. Hamon and P. Rotman, *Génération*, vol. 1: *Les Années de rêve*, pp. 411–5.

149 J. Miermeister, *Rudi Dutschke*, pp. 90–3.

150 Ibid. Also: M. Karl, *Rudi Dutschke: Revolutionär ohne Revolution*, pp. 208–11.

151 R. Dutschke, *Mein langer Marsch: Reden, Schriften und Tagebücher aus zwanzig Jahren*, Reinbek, 1980, p. 128.

152 T. Ali, *Street Fighting Years*, p. 188.

153 H. Hamon and P. Rotman, *Génération*, vol. 1: *Les années de rêve* , p. 435. D. Bensaïd, *Une Lente impatience*, p. 81.

154 R. Dutschke, *Tagebuch*, March 1968, cited in J. Miermeister, *Ernst Bloch, Rudi Dutschke*, p. 165. R. Dutschke, *Jeder hat sein Leben*, p. 70.

155 K. Ross, *May '68 and its Afterlives*, Chicago, 2002. A. Marwick, *The Sixties: Cultural Revolution in Britain, France, Italy and the United States, c.1958–c.1974*, Oxford, 1998. A. Krivine and D. Bensaïd, *Mai si! 1968–1988: Rebelles et repentis*, Montreuil, 1988. D. Bensaïd, *Moi la revolution: Remembrances d'une bicentenaire indigne*, Paris, 1989. G. Arrighi, T. Hopkins and I. Wallerstein, *Antisystemic Movements*, London, 1989. C. Harman, *The Fire Last Time: 1968 and After*, London, 1988. A. Artous, *Retours sur Mai*, Paris, 1988.

156 In March 1968 Dutschke had travelled to Prague to enjoy the Prague Spring. R. Dutschke, *Aufrecht Gehen: Eine fragmentarische Autobiographie*, Berlin, 1981. U. Chaussy, *Die drei Leben des Rudi Dutschke*, pp. 224–8.

157 R. Dutschke, 21 August 1968 (Marino near Rome), *Jeder hat sein Leben*, p. 79.

158 G. Mandel to R. Dutschke, 22 August 1968.

159 P. Kaplan [US vice-consul] to E. Mandel, 29 July 1968, E. Mandel Archives, folder 40. G. Mandel to S. Kolpe, 8 November 1968, E. Mandel Archives, folder 651.

160 G. Scholtz to K. Bloch, 18 September 1970, E. Bloch Archives.

161 R. Mandel to E. Mandel, 17 September 1968, E. Mandel Archives, folder 41.

162 R. Mandel to E. Mandel, 26 September 1968, E. Mandel Archives, folder 41.

163 R. Dutschke, *Aufrecht Gehen*, p. 101.

164 G. Horst to E. Mandel, 10 October 1967, E. Mandel Archives, folder 38.

165 E. Mandel to G. Horst, 26 October 1967, E. Mandel Archives, folder 38.

166 T.M., 'Un commencement', *Les Temps Modernes*, vol. 23, no. 264, May/June 1968.

167 V.I. Lenin, 'The State and Revolution', *Collected Works*, vol. 25, Moscow 1977, p. 497.

168 For moderate critics, the absence of a military or economic catastrophe proved that any resolution other than a reformist one was utopian. For critics from the left, a revolution remained bound to the outbreak of a crisis like those of 1914–7 or 1929.

169 E. Mandel, 'A Socialist Strategy for Western Europe', *International Socialist Journal*, no. 10, pp. 440–41.

170 Ibid.

171 E. Mandel, 'De la faillite du neocapitalisme à la lutte pour la révolution socialiste', *La Gauche*, 1 June 1968; 'Leçons du mouvement de mai', *Les Temps Modernes*, vol. 24, August/September 1968; 'Lessons of May', *New Left Review*, no. 52, November/December 1968 Also: 'Mai 1968: Première phase de la revolution socialiste française', *Quatrième Internationale*, special no., July 1968.

172 For an impressive analysis of May 1968, see: K. Ross, *May '68 and its Afterlives*.

173 *La Gauche*, 1 June 1968.

174 H. Hamon and P. Rotman, *Génération*, vol. 1: *Les Années de rêve*, pp. 476–9. C. Nick, *Les trotskistes*, Paris, 2002, pp. 465–7.

175 H. Hamon and P. Rotman, *Génération*, vol. 1: *Les Années de rêve*, p. 479.

176 G. Mandel, 'Pariser Mai: Die rote Nacht des Quartier Latin', *Extra*, n.d., reprinted in *Dokumentation Paris Mai 1968*, Munich, 1968, pp. 5–19. C. Den Hond interview with A. Krivine in C. Den Hond, *Ernest Mandel – A Life for the Revolution*.

177 H. Hamon and P. Rotman, *Génération,* vol. 1: *Les Années de rêve*, p. 478. N. Poulantzas to E. Mandel, n.d. [May 1968], E. Mandel Archives, folder 40. E. Mandel to P. Anderson, 15 May 1968, E. Mandel Archives, folder 39.

178 G. Filoche, *68–98: Histoire sans fin*, p. 73. D. Bensaïd, *Une Lente impatience*, p. 83.

179 P. Seale and M. McConville, *Red Flag/Black Flag: French Revolution, 1968*, Harmondsworth, 1968, p. 87.

180 R. Blackburn, 'The Unexpected Dialectic of Structural Reforms' in G. Achcar, ed., *The Legacy of Ernest Mandel*, London, 1999, p. 19.

181 Interior Ministry, 'Direction Générale de la Sûreté nationale, Procès verbal de notification' (Dept of the Sûreté, Official Report of Notification), no. 993, 6 July 1968.

182 E. Mandel to Comité pour la Liberté et contre la Répression, Laurent Schwartz, 23 July 1968, E. Mandel Archives, folder 199.

183 G. Mandel to R. Dutschke, 22 August 1968. R. Dutschke Archives.

184 C. Bonnet [Minister of the Interior] to Y. Jouffa, 2 February 1981; Y. Jouffa to E. Mandel, 11 February 1981; J. Chevènement to E. Mandel, 4 March 1968, E. Mandel Archives, folder 211.

185 In *Antisystemic Movements*, Giovanni Arrighi, T. Hopkins and I. Wallerstein called 1968 – the May revolt, the Prague Spring, the Têt offensive in Vietnam – the second world revolution after 1848. The revolution failed but changed the world radically. See also: M. van der Linden, 'The Aftermath of "1968": Interactions of Workers', Youth and Women's Movements', *Transnational Labour History: Explorations*, Aldershot, 2003. The influence of May 1968 was also felt in Africa, Latin America and elsewhere. See: A. Bathily, *Mai 68 à Dakar ou la révolte universitaire et la démocratie*, Paris, 1992, and J.

Brennan, *The Labor Wars in Córdoba, 1955–1976: Ideology, Work and Labor Politics in an Argentine Industrial City*, Cambridge, MA, 1994.

186 E. Mandel, 'The Lessons of May 1968', *New Left Review*, no. 52, November/ December 1968. E. Mandel, 'Leçons du movement de mai', *Les Temps Modernes*, vol. 24, August/September 1968.

187 E. Mandel, 'The Economics of Neo-Capitalism', *The Socialist Register*, 1964, London. E Mandel, 'A Socialist Strategy for Western Europe', *International Socialist Journal*, no. 10. E. Mandel, *Die deutsche Wirtschaftskrise: Lehren der Rezession 1966/67*, Frankfurt on Main, 1973. E. Mandel, *The Formation of the Economic Thought of Karl Marx: 1843 to 'Capital'*, New York, 1971.

188 Mandel said that the vanguard, a group of between 15,000 and 20,000 young people, students and young workers, was big enough to launch effective actions. E. Mandel, 'Note politique: La nouvelle montée révolutionnaire en France', 23 May 1968, E. Mandel Archives, folder 533.

189 E. Mandel to P. Anderson, 16 December 1968, E. Mandel Archives, folder 42.

Hope and Despair

1 E. Bloch to E. Mandel, n.d. [1974], E. Mandel Archives, folder 55.

2 E. Mandel, 'The Social, Economic and Political Background of the Czecho-slovak Crisis' in K. Coates, ed., *Czechoslovakia and Socialism*, Nottingham, 1969, pp. 51–73.

3 T. Szulc, *Fidel: A Critical Portrait*, London, 1986, pp. 497–505.

4 G. Desolre, 'Fidel Castro et la Tchécoslovaquie', *La Gauche*, 7 September 1968.

5 On 4 January, 1969, for the tenth anniversary of the Cuban revolution, *La Gauche* offered 'congratulations and the affirmation of our militant solidarity with the people of Cuba and their revolutionary government'.

6 Mandel considered that the failure of the 1970 *zafra*, or sugar harvest, which should have yielded 10 million tons, marked the decisive moment in Cuba's growing dependency on the Soviet Union. E. Mandel, *Revolutionary Marxism Today*, London, 1979, p. 103. In preparatory documents for the Tenth World Congress of the Fourth International, Mandel noted that Cuba was beginning to turn away from 'their strategic orientation toward overthrowing the bourgeois state in Latin America. The question is whether they are abandoning their most important strategic advance to return to a neo-reformist and neo-Stalinist variant of revolution by stages.' E. Germain [E. Mandel] and M. Knoeller [G. Scholtz], 'The Strategic Orientation of the Revolutionists in Latin America', *International Internal Discussion Bulletin*, vol. 8, no. 2, January 1971.

7 On Schoenman's stay in Bolivia, see E. Mandel to Sibylle Plogstedt, 4 May 1969, E. Mandel Archives, folder 155. Also: R. Schoenman, 'How I Was Deported from Britain', *London Bulletin*, no. 8, Bertrand Russell Peace Foundation, February/March 1969. On Schoenman's Trotskyist sympathies, see R. Schoenman to E. Mandel, 6 October 1969, E. Mandel Archives, folder 43.

8 R. Schoenman to E. Mandel, 28 August 1968, E. Mandel Archives, folder 40.

9 T. Ali, *Street Fighting Years: An Autobiography of the Sixties*, London, 1987, pp. 48–50.

10 Stockholm Conference on Czechoslovakia, 'Agenda', organized by the Bertrand Russell Peace Foundation, 1–2 February 1969, *London Bulletin*, no. 9, Bertrand Russell Peace Foundation, April 1969.

11 *Paese Sera*, 25 August 1968, cited in R. Hyman, *Sartre: A Biography*, New York, 1987, p. 429.

12 J.-P. Sartre, *Situations*, vol. 8, p. 212. I. Birchall, *Sartre Against Stalinism*, New York, 2004, p. 212.

13 See Chapter 4.

14 R. Schoenman, report on meeting with Sartre and Garaudy, 5 October 1968, E. Mandel Archives, folder 43.

15 Mandel did contribute a paper for discussion at the conference, 'The Social, Economic and Political Background of the Czechoslovak Crisis', op. cit.

16 E. Mandel to W. Carrobio, 14 November 1968, E. Mandel Archives, folder 40.

17 'Konstitutives Manifest der HRM (Hnuti revolucni mldeže-Bewegung der revolutionären tschechoslowakischen Jugend)', *Management und Selbstverwaltung in der CSSR: Bürokratie und Widerstand*, M. Borin and V. Plogen, Berlin, 1970, pp. 118–20.

18 'Petr Uhl: Un destin tchécoslavique', *L'Humanité*, 20 November 1999. Jan Malewski, 'Das Volk hat angefangen sich selbst zu organisieren': interview with P. Uhl, *Inprecor*, 426, July/August 1998.

19 S. Plogstedt to E. Mandel, 29 April 1969, E. Mandel Archives, folder 155.

20 S. Plogstedt, *Im Netz der Gedichte: Gefangen in Prag nach 1968*, Berlin, 2001, p. 39.

21 E. Mandel to S. Plogstedt, 5 June 1969, E. Mandel Archives, folder 155.

22 *Rudé Právo*, 2 August 1969.

23 E. Mandel to S. Plogstedt, 23 July 1969, E. Mandel Archives, folder 155.

24 Fourth International United Secretariat, Eastern Commission, 'Note aux directions de sections', 18 January 1970. E. Mandel Archives, folder 155.

25 S. Plogstedt, *Im Netz der Gedichte*, 'Dix-neuf "trotskystes" jugés à Prague pour avoir attaqué la "dictature de la bureaucratie"', *Le Soir*, 16 March 1971. Interview with S. Plogstedt, *Intercontinental Press*, 28 June 1971.

26 F. Charpier, *Histoire de l'extrême gauche trotskiste: De 1929 à nos jours*, Paris, 2002, p. 298.

27 S. Plogstedt, *Im Netz der Gedichte*, p. 38.

28 Walter [E. Mandel] to the leadership of the sections, 20–21 March 1971, E. Mandel Archives, folder 156.

29 *Was Tun*, March 1971.

30 E. Mandel to E. Federn, 17 June 1982, E. Mandel Archives, folder 677.

31 E. Nowotny to E. Federn, 12 June 1984, E. Mandel Archives, folder 157.

32 The West Berlin branch of the International Marxist Group (GIM), the German section of the Fourth International, was deeply involved with Eastern Europe.

33 M. Sabrov, ed., *Skandal und Diktatur: Formen öffentlicher Empörung im NS-Staat und in der DDR*, Göttingen, 2004, p. 178.

34 Havemann's lectures on 'Philosophical Aspects of Scientific Problems in

Materialism and Natural Science' were published in West Germany as R. Havemann, *Dialektik ohne Dogma?*, Reinbek, 1964. T. Klein, W. Otto and P. Grieder, *Visionen, Repression und Opposition in der SED (1949–1989)*, Frankfurt on Oder, 1997, p. 355. S. Müller and B. Florath, eds, *Die Entlassung: Robert Havemann und die Akademie der Wissenschaften 1965–66*, Berlin, 1996.

35 R. Havemann, *Questions, Answers, Questions: From the Biography of a German Marxist*, Garden City, NY, 1972. H. Laitko, 'Robert Havemann, der Weg in die Dissidenz (1961–1965)', *Berlinische Monatsschrift*, vol. 6, 2001. W. Olle to E. Mandel, 17 August 1971, E. Mandel Archives, folder 156. S. Müller and B. Florath, eds, *Die Entlassung*, pp. 22–4, 27–31.

36 W. Olle to E. Mandel, 17 August 1971, E. Mandel Archives, folder 156.

37 E. Mandel to W. Olle, 26 August 1971, E. Mandel Archives, folder 156.

38 E. Mandel, 'The Leninist Theory of Organization', reprinted in R. Blackburn, ed., *Revolution and Class Struggle: A Reader in Marxist Politics*, Glasgow, 1977, p. 81.

39 E. Mandel, *On Bureaucracy*, London, 1973. E. Mandel, 'The Leninist Theory of Organization', pp. 99–101, 111–4.

40 E. Mandel, *Power and Money: A Marxist Theory of Bureaucracy*, London, 1992.

41 R. Michels, *Political Parties: A Sociological Study of the Oligarchical Tendencies of Modern Democracy*, Glencoe, IL, 1949.

42 E. Mandel, 'The Leninist Theory of Organization', p. 105. E. Mandel, *Revolutionary Marxism Today*, London, 1979, p. 60.

43 The classic theories of the party were developed by V.I. Lenin in *What Is To Be Done?* and in *Left-Wing Communism: An Infantile Disorder*; by Rosa Luxemburg in *Organizational Questions of Russian Social Democracy*; by Karl Kautsky in his polemics against Bernstein, Luxemburg and the Bolsheviks; and by Otto Bauer in *Die illegale Partei*. All of these are rather polemical. The theory is more abstractly handled in youthful works by Georg Lukács: *History and Class Consciousness* and *Lenin: A Study of the Unity of His Thought*; also in Antonio Gramsci's work from the early 1920s, collected in his *Political Writings*.

44 I. Deutscher, *The Prophet Outcast: Trotsky, 1929–1940*, London, 1963. According to Mandel, Trotsky changed his position on the relationship between class and party at least five times. See E. Mandel, 'Über das Verhältnis Selbstorganisation der Klasse-Vorhutpartei' in T. Bergmann and G. Schäfer, eds, *Leo Trotzki: Kritiker und Verteidiger der Sowjetgesellschaft: Beiträge zum internationalen Trotzki-Symposium, Wuppertal 26–29 März 1990*, Mainz 1993, pp. 64–78.

45 E. Mandel, *Trotsky: A Study in the Dynamics of his Thought*, London 1979. E. Mandel, *Trotsky as Alternative*, London, 1995. E. Mandel, *The Leninist Theory of Organization*, London, 1971.

46 Mandel joined with Lenin – not the Lenin of *What Is To Be Done?* or *One Step Forward, Two Steps Back*, who counterposed with spontaneity – but the post-1914 Lenin, who understood organization not merely as something functional but as something substantive. The Lenin of *Left-Wing Communism* no longer defended the position that the party had to propagandize to create class-consciousness in the working class. Instead, now that the epoch of 'the actuality of revolution' had arrived, the task of the revolutionary vanguard was to develop revolutionary consciousness among the most class-conscious workers. Thus, by uniting the program of the socialist revolution with the

experiences of struggle among the majority of these workers, a revolutionary workers' party could be established.

47 E. Mandel, *Contrôle ouvrier, conseils ouvriers, autogestion*, Paris, 1970, p. 36. E. Mandel, 'Alle Macht den Räten, Bekenntnis eines notorisch-unbeirrbaren Linken' in W. Jüttner and H. Peter, eds, *Zwischen Rätesozialismus und Reformprojekt: Lesebuch zum 70. Geburtstag von Peter von Oertzen*, K. Benz-Overhage, Cologne, 1994, pp. 19–27.

48 R. Luxemburg, *Rosa Luxemburg Speaks*, New York, 1970, p. 391.

49 E. Mandel, 'Trotzki's Theorie über das Verhältnis Selbstorganisation der Klasse-Vorhutspartei', 15 November 1989, E. Mandel Archives, folder 269.

50 G. Elliott, *Perry Anderson: The Merciless Laboratory of History*, Minneapolis, 1998, p. 56.

51 P. Sedgwick, 'Tragedy of the Tragedian: An Appreciation of Isaac Deutscher', *International Socialism* (first series), no. 31, Winter 1967–8, pp. 10–17. P. Anderson, *Arguments Within English Marxism*, London, 1980, p. 155.

52 N. Krassó, 'Trotsky's Marxism', *New Left Review*, no.44, July/August 1967, pp. 64–86. E. Mandel, 'Trotsky's Marxism: An Anti-Critique', *New Left Review*, no. 47, January/February 1968, pp. 32–51. N. Krassó, 'Reply to Ernest Mandel', *New Left Review*, no. 48, March/April 1968, pp. 90–103. E. Mandel, 'Trotsky's Marxism: A Rejoinder', *New Left Review*, no. 56, July/August 1969, pp. 69–96. In 1969, these articles appeared in French in three issues of *Les Temps Modernes*. Publication in book format followed in Argentina (*El marxismo de Trotski*, Córdoba, 1970), Italy (*Il marxismo di Trockij*, Bari, 1970), Sweden (*Trotskijs Marxism: Kritik, antikritik, kritik*, Stockholm, 1972) and the United States (N. Krassó, ed., *Trotsky: The Great Debate Renewed*, St Louis, 1972). P. Anderson to E. Mandel, 26 September 1967, E. Mandel Archives, folder 37. For a disdainful report on the debate by L. Kolakowski, see *Partisan Review*, no. 4, fall 1972.

53 G. Elliott, *Perry Anderson: The Merciless Laboratory of History*, p. 56.

54 K. Marx, 'Author's Preface to the Second Edition' (1869), *The Eighteenth Brumaire of Louis Napoleon*, New York, 1963, p. 8.

55 E. Mandel to C. Landauer, 19 August 1977, E. Mandel Archives, folder 60.

56 L. Trotsky, *The Revolution Betrayed: What Is the Soviet Union and Where Is It Going?*, New York, 1945.

57 N. Krassó, 'Trotsky's Marxism', *New Left Review*, no. 44, p. 86.

58 P. Blackledge, *Perry Anderson, Marxism and the New Left*, London, 2004, pp. 51, 57.

59 G. Elliott, *Perry Anderson: The Merciless Laboratory of History*, p. 59. R. Blackburn, 'A Brief History of *New Left Review, 1960–1990*', *Thirty Years of 'New Left Review': Index to Numbers 1–184 (1960–1990)*, New Left Review, London, 1992. P. Anderson, *Arguments within English Marxism*, p. 109, note 25. Mandel spoke of Anderson as an editor 'who has become a close sympathizer'. E. Mandel to L. Maitan, 6 January 1970, E. Mandel Archives, folder 511.

60 *Europe Versus America* (1970); *The Formation of the Economic Thought of Karl Marx* (1971); *Late Capitalism* (1975); *From Stalinism to Eurocommunism* (1978); *The Second Slump* (1978); *Revolutionary Marxism Today* (1979); and *Trotsky: A Study in the Dynamic of his Thought* (1979). From 1963 Mandel published nineteen articles in *New Left Review*.

61 P. Anderson, *Arguments within English Marxism*, p. 156.

62 P. Anderson, *Considerations on Western Marxism*, London, 1976, p. 100.

63 E. Hobsbawn, 'Look Left', *New Statesman*, 24 September 1976, pp. 408–11. This was a review of P. Anderson, *Considerations on Western Marxism*, cited in G. Elliott's *Perry Anderson: The Merciless Laboratory of History* (p. 105).

64 'NLR, 1975–1980', an unpublished memorandum of 1980, cited in *Perry Anderson: The Merciless Laboratory of History*, p. 139.

65 Jean-Paul Sartre, *The Communists and Peace with A Reply to Claude Lefort*, New York, 1968.

66 E. Mandel to P. Anderson, 1 September 1983, E. Mandel Archives, folder 130.

67 B. Anderson, *Language and Power: Exploring Political Cultures in Indonesia*, Ithaca, NY, 1990. P. Anderson, *Spectrum: From Right to Left in the World of Ideas*, London 2003, pp. 343–89.

68 Lin Chun, *The British New Left*, Edinburgh, 1993. D. Dworkin, *Cultural Marxism in Postwar Britain: The New Left and the Origins of Cultural Studies*, Durham, NC, 1997. For a critique of Anderson's interpretation of Trotsky's theory of Stalinism, see M. Cox, 'The Revolutionary Betrayed: The *New Left Review* and Leon Trotsky' in H. Ticktin and M. Cox, eds, *The Ideas of Leon Trotsky*, London, 1995, pp. 289–305.

69 E. Mandel to P. Anderson, 3 June 1978, E. Mandel Archives, folder 129.

70 E. Mandel, 'Revolutionary Strategy in Europe: A Political Interview', *New Left Review*, no. 100, November 1976/January 1977, pp. 97–138. E. Mandel, 'On the Nature of the Soviet State', *New Left Review*, no. 108, March/April 1978. E. Mandel, 'Sur la nature de l'URSS: Entretien avec E. Mandel', *Critique Communiste*, no. 18/19, Paris, 1977, pp. 2–35. E. Mandel, 'Sur la stratégie révolutionnaire and Europe occidentale', *Critique Communiste*, no. 8/9, Paris, 1976, pp. 135–76.

71 P. Anderson to E. Mandel, 5 February 1978, E. Mandel Archives, folder 61.

72 E. Mandel, *Trotsky: A Study in the Dynamics of His Thought*, London, 1979. P. Anderson to E. Mandel, 22 May 1979, E. Mandel Archives, folder 293. G. Lukács, *Lenin: A Study on the Unity of His Thought*, London, 1970.

73 P. Anderson to E. Mandel, 4 September 1967, E. Mandel Archives, folder 37. J. Halliday to E. Mandel, 26 January 1968, E. Mandel Archives, folder 39.

74 E. Mandel, 'Die Marxsche Theorie der ursprünglichen Akkumulation und die Indutrialisierung der Dritten Welt', *Folgen einer Theorie: Essays über 'Das Kapital' von Karl Marx*, Frankfurt on Main, 1967. E. Mandel, 'Kritik der Wachstum theorie im Geiste des "Kapitals" ', *Kritik der politischen Ökonomie heute 100 Jahre 'Kapital'*, Frankfurt on Main, 1968.

75 E. Mandel, *The Formation of the Economic Thought of Karl Marx: 1843 to Capital*, New York, 1971.

76 E. Mandel to P. Anderson, 26 October 1967, E. Mandel Archives, folder 37.

77 J. Halliday to E. Mandel, 29 December 1967, E. Mandel Archives, folder 37. J. Halliday to E. Mandel, 26 January 1968, E. Mandel Archives, folder 39.

78 D. Fernbach to E. Mandel, 14 January 1970, E. Mandel Archives, folder 283. The three introductions were published in Spanish in *El Capital: Cien años and torno a la obra de Karl Marx*, E. Mandel, México, 1985. In 1991 they were published in German and provided with an afterword: E. Mandel, *Kontroversen um 'Das Kapital'*, Berlin, 1991.

79 E. Mandel, 'Introduction', K. Marx, *Capital*, vol. 2, London, 1978, pp. 33–5.
80 Ibid., pp. 31–8.
81 E. Mandel, 'Introduction', K. Marx, *Capital*, vol. 3, London, 1981, pp. 21–9.
82 Ibid., pp. 29–39.
83 E. Mandel, 'Introduction', K. Marx, *Capital*, vol. 2, pp. 39–46.
84 E. Mandel, *Long Waves of Capitalist Development: A Marxist Interpretation, Based on the Marshall Lectures Given at the University of Cambridge* (second, revised ed.), London, 1995.
85 *Frankfurter Rundschau*, 19 October 1978. E. Mandel to Weisskirchen, 23 September 1978, E. Mandel Archives, folder 61.
86 *Frankfurter Rundschau*, 25 August 1978.
87 Author's interview with F. Vercammen, 25 November 2004. P. Verbraeken, 'De worsteling van Ernest Mandel', *Vlaams Marxistisch Tijdschrift*, vol. 29, no. 4, 1995, p. 33.
88 G. Filoche, *68–98: histoire sans fin*, Paris, 1998, p. 140. H. Harmon and P. Rotman, *Generation 2: Les Années de poudre*, Paris, 1988, p. 353.
89 *Le Monde*, 22 April 1972. T. Ali, *Street Fighting Years*, p. 257.
90 G. Van Sinoy and F. Dekoninck to 'Chers camarades', 29 July 1995.
91 C. Bonnet to Monsieur le Médiateur [Yves Jouffa], 2 February 1981; J.-P. Chevènement to E. Mandel, 4 March 1981, E. Mandel Archives, folder 211.
92 R. Miles to E. Mandel, 20 August 1969, E. Mandel Archives, folder 199. R. Schoenman to E. Mandel, 23 September 1969, E. Mandel Archives, folder 43.
93 R. Miles to E. Mandel, October 1979, E. Mandel Archives, folder 429.
94 E. Mandel to A. Fowler [US consul], 30 October 1969, E. Mandel Archives, folder 199. According to this document, the State Department had already decided in 1962 that Mandel was not qualified for a visa, for political reasons. Yet in 1962 and 1968 he was tacitly given one.
95 E. Mandel to R. Miles, 7 October 1969, E. Mandel Archives, folder 199.
96 K. Chamberlane to N. Middleton, 23 October 1969, E. Mandel Archives, folder 283.
97 *The New York Times*, 29 October 1969.
98 *The New York Times*, 20 October 1969.
99 *Wall Street Journal*, 13 July 1970.
100 E. Mandel to E. Glinne, 13 April 1970, E. Mandel Archives, folder 44. M. Morris to G. Mandel, 11 April 1970, E. Mandel Archives, folder 655.
101 'Heksenjachtwet hield Gisela Mandel vast op Zaventem', *De Standaard*, 16 April 1970. 'Visa Guilt by Marriage?', *The New York Times*, 18 April 1970. 'La Sabena est-elle aux ordres du consulat des Etats-Unis?', *La Gauche*, 18 April 1970.
102 E. Glinne, written parliamentary question (under art. 71) to the ministers of foreign affairs and communications, 16 April 1970.
103 'The Terrorist International', *Newsweek*, 18 September 1972. 'Le Terrorisme en voie d'internationalisation', *La Libre Belgique*, 16 October 1972. The Belgian daily asked rhetorically 'what the particular contribution might be of the Trotskyist Fourth International to the unsavoury brew of the international terrorist fraternity'.
104 'Trotskyite Terrorist International: Hearing before the Subcommittee to Investigate the Administration of the Internal Security Act and Other Internal

Security Laws of the Committee on the Judiciary, United States Senate, Ninety-Fourth Congress, First Session', 24 July 1975, p. 42.

105 'The Age of Suspicion, Still Ticking', *The New York Times*, 24 February 1977.

106 T. Ali, *Street Fighting Years*, p. 245.

107 G. Filoche, *68–98: Histoire sans fin*, pp. 106–10.

108 E. Mandel, 'The Place of the Ninth World Congress in the History of the Fourth International', *Internal Information Bulletin*, no. 5, New York, 1977.

109 E. Mandel, 'Imperialism and National Bourgeoisie in Latin America', *International*, vol. 1, no. 5, 1971, pp. 7–17.

110 J. Hansen, 'Assessment of the Draft Resolution on Latin America' (February 1969), *International Internal Discussion Bulletin: Discussion on Latin America (1968–1972)*, New York, 1973, pp. 17–28. In 1970 Hugo Blanco, who had fought with guerrillas and was in prison during the congress, associated himself with the minority that was opposed to armed struggle.

111 D. Bensaïd, *Une Lente impatience*, Paris, 2004, p. 135.

112 L. Maitan to 'Cher ami', 1 September 1971, E. Mandel Archives, folder 511.

113 'Minutes of the United Secretariat Meeting', 25–6 September 1971, E. Mandel Archives, folder 492.

114 F. Charpier, *Histoire de l'extrême gauche trotskiste*, p. 274. G. Filoche, *68–98: Histoire sans fin*, p. 133. Others involved were Janette Habel, Jean Michel Krivine and, on behalf of the International leadership, Livio Maitan.

115 'Argentinien: Kommunique no. 4 der ERP, 24 März, Mittags', *Inprekorr: Internationale Pressekorrespondenz der IV. Internationale*, no.14, 15 April 1972.

116 G. Filoche, *68–98: Histoire sans fin*, p. 142.

117 Shortly afterwards, an elegantly dressed man in his fifties turned up at the heavily barricaded, three-storey LC office at Impasse Guéménée 10 in Paris, between the Bastille and the St-Paul quarter. He came to negotiate on behalf of the multinational with 'your Argentine friends' about immunity for Fiat executives from future kidnappings. D. Bensaïd, *Une Lente impatience*, p. 146.

118 M. Tolksdorf to E. Mandel, 14 April 1972; E. Mandel to M. Tolksdorf, 21 April 1972, E. Mandel Archives, folder 207.

119 'Eine elementare Menschenpflicht: Ein Brief Ernest Mandels an Prof. Tolksdorf', *Berliner Liberale Zeitung*, 20 April 1972.

120 M. Tolksdorf to E. Mandel, 14 April 1972, E. Mandel Archives, folder 207.

121 Mandel argued that the ERP's tactics were not in conflict with the traditions of the workers' movement in his 'Lutte de classe et lutte armée and Argentine', *La Gauche*, 21 April 1972.

122 'LSA on Argentine Kidnapping', *Labor Challenge*, 10 April 1972. 'SWP Statement on Argentine Kidnapping', *The Militant*, 14 April 1972.

123 'Minutes of the United Secretariat', 23–5 September 1972 (statement by Ramon), E. Mandel Archives, folder 492.

124 'Minutes of the United Secretariat', 15–16 April 1972, E. Mandel Archives, folder 492.

125 'Minutes of the International Executive Committee', 2–6 December 1972, E. Mandel Archives, folder 492.

126 Author's interview with H. Krivine, 25 May 2005.

127 E. Méndez, *Santucho: Entre la inteligencia y las armas*, Buenos Aires, 1999, pp. 79–83. 'Una vida al servicio de la revolución', in M. Santucho, *Poder burgués y poder revolucionario*, Buenos Aires, 1988, pp. 47–54. '7 jours qui secouèrent l'Argentine', *Rouge*, 2 September 1972.

128 M. Diana, *Mujeres Guerrilleras: La militancia de los stenta and el testimonio de sus protagonistas femeninas*, Buenos Aires, 1996, pp. 308–70.

129 D. Bensaïd, *Une Lente impatience*, p. 162.

130 Walter to 'Chers camarades', 11 December 1968, E. Mandel Archives, folder 652.

131 D. Bensaïd, *Une Lente impatience*, p. 140.

132 Ibid., p. 151. G. Filoche, *68–98: Histoire sans fin*, pp. 144–6. Author's interview with F. Vercammen, 23–4 June 2004. In the spring of 1972 Bensaïd, along with three other members of the LC, signed a text that raised the question of armed revolutionary violence in France. It was published in *Bulletin Intérieur* no. 30.

133 D. Bensaïd, *Une Lente impatience*, p. 152.

134 'Trotskyite Terrorist International: Hearing before the Subcommittee', p. 116.

135 M. Knoeller, 'Balance Sheet of the international minority on Bolivia – in the harsh light of the facts', *International Internal Discussion Bulletin*, vol. 10, no. 24, December 1973.

136 Author's interview with F. Vercammen, 31 May 2005.

137 G. Scholtz to L. Maitan, 12 March 1969, E. Mandel Archives, folder 653.

138 G. Scholtz to 'Ray', 13 March 1969, E. Mandel Archives, folder 652.

139 G. Scholtz to Socialistisk Ungdoms Forum, 4 February 1969, E. Mandel Archives, folder 652.

140 G. Scholtz to C. Bolduc, 11 February 1969, E. Mandel Archives, folder 652.

141 JGS [SJW], 'A Nous d'ouvrir un nouveau front de lutte contre l'imperialisme', *La Gauche*, 15 March 1969.

142 Handwritten notes on meetings of the United Secretariat, 1968–72, E. Mandel Archives, folder 492.

143 K. Meschkat to E. Mandel, 11 August 1971, E. Mandel Archives, folder 47.

144 E. Mandel to K. Meschkat, 22 March 1969, E. Mandel Archives, folder 42. E. Germain and M. Knoeller, 'L'Orientation stratégique des révolutionnaires en Amérique Latine', *Bulletin Intérieure*, no.17, November 1970. M. Knoeller, 'Le Bilan de la minorité sur la Bolivie – à la lumière cruelle des faits'; M. Knoeller, 'Balance Sheet of the International', E. Mandel Archives, folder 666.

145 G. Scholtz to K. Bloch, 10 November 1970, E. Bloch Archives.

146 K. Meschkat to G. Scholtz, 11 August 1971, E. Mandel Archives, folder 47.

147 E. Mandel to E. Krippendorf, 14 October 1971, E. Mandel Archives, folder 288.

148 G. Scholtz to K. Bloch, 10 November 1970, E. Bloch Archives.

149 K. Bloch to E. Mandel, 25 March 1974, E. Bloch Archives.

150 E. Bloch, *Experimentum mundi: Frage, Kategorien des Herausbringens, Praxis*, Frankfurt on Main, 1975.

151 G. Scholtz to K. Bloch, 18 September 1970, E. Bloch Archives. K. Bloch to G. and E. Mandel, 8 November 1970, E. Mandel Archives, folder 44.

152 E. Mandel to K. and E. Bloch, 21 May 1973, E. Bloch Archives.

153 F. Engels, 'The True Socialists' in K. Marx and F. Engels, *Collected Works*, vol. 5, New York, 1976.

154 G. Scholtz to K. Bloch, 28 March 1977, E. Bloch Archives.

155 G. Scholtz to E. Mandel, 8 October 1971, E. Mandel Archives, folder 289.

156 G. Scholtz to E. Mandel, 17 October 1971, E. Mandel Archives, folder 46.

157 Ibid.

158 Author's interview with J. Habel, 14 July 2005.

159 G. Scholtz to E. Mandel, 11 September 1974, E. Mandel Archives, folder 53.

160 C. Breckhoff to E. Mandel, 15 October 1975, E. Mandel Archives, folder 55.

161 E. Mandel to C. Breckhoff, 20 October 1975, E. Mandel Archives, folder 55.

162 G. Scholtz to E. Mandel, 21 and 22 October 1976, E. Mandel Archives, folder 57. Mandel was convinced that Gisela had a tumour. He wrote to Tariq Ali's wife, Jane, 'the pain from the tumour [is] becoming worse and worse and the doctors [are] giving her strong painkilling drugs which upset her very much'. E. Mandel to 'Jane', 8 May 1975, E. Mandel Archives, folder 128.

163 Michèle and Philippe Julliard.

164 Author's interview with B. Morawe, 13 July 2005.

165 G. Scholtz to E. and K. Bloch, 28 December 1976, E. Bloch Archives.

166 Ibid.

167 G. Scholtz to E. and K. Bloch, 16 January 1977, E. Bloch Archives.

168 E. Mandel to C. Samary and H. Krivine, 18 April 1978, E. Mandel Archives, folder 61.

169 K. Bloch to R. Dutschke, 23 March 1977 in K. Bloch and W. Schröter, eds, *Lieber Genosse Bloch . . . Briefe Rudi Dutschkes an Karola und Ernst Bloch*, Mössingen-Talheim, 1988. E. Mandel to E. and K. Bloch, 17 March 1977, E. Bloch Archives.

170 K. Bloch to G. Scholtz and E. Mandel, 17 May 1977, E. Mandel Archives, folder 60.

171 E. Mandel, 'Anticipation and Hope as Categories of Historical Materialism', *Historical Materialism*, vol. 10, 2002. Mandel also paid tribute to Bloch on 19 April 1985, at the Goethe Institute in Brussels, with 'Ernst Bloch, der Marxist' and on 8 October 1985, in Hamburg, at a gathering organized by the periodical *Spuren* marking the 100th anniversary of Bloch's birth.

172 R. Alexander, *International Trotskyism, 1929–1985: A Documented Analysis*, Durham, NC, 1991, pp. 710–23.

173 G. Filoche, *68–98: Histoire sans fin*, p. 220.

174 *Oeuvres Complètes de Saint-Just*, vol. 1, Paris, 1908, p. 414.

175 According to the 1975 Portuguese edition (*Iniciação a Teoria Económica Marxista*, third edition, no publisher given), a first edition of the work had already appeared in 1967 titled *Iniciação a Teoria Económica*. Robert Steigerwald, a leading theoretician of the German Communist Party, told Manuel Kellner that before Salazar's fall, the Portuguese Communist Party had used a Mandel text for training in critical political economy. Mandel's name apparently gave less offence than books and brochures published in Moscow (Communication from Wilfried Dubois).

176 C. Den Hond interview with F. Louçã in *Ernest Mandel – A Life for the Revolution*, C. Den Hond, DVD, 2005.

177 D. Bensaïd, *Une Lente impatience*, p. 146. Among others, Charles-André Udry,

Charles Michaloux and Michael Löwy were active in Portugal on behalf of the Fourth International. D. Bensaïd, C. Rossi [Löwy] and C.-A. Udry, *Portugal: La révolution en marche*, Paris, 1975.
178 E. Mandel to K. Bloch, 17 May 1976, E. Mandel Archives, folder 57.
179 Ibid.
180 G. Scholtz to K. Bloch, 18 June 1977, E. Bloch Archives.
181 Author's interview with F. Vercammen, 31 May 2005.
182 E. Mandel, *Ende der Krise oder Krise ohne Ende*, Berlin, 1977. E. Mandel, *The Second Slump*, London, 1978. E. Mandel, *La Crise 1974–1978: Les faits, leur interpretation marxiste*, Paris, 1978. Mandel discussed the crisis in other publications as well, such as E. Mandel and W. Wolf, *Weltwirtschaftsrezession und BRD-Krise 1974/75*, Frankfurt on Main, 1976.
183 D. Bensaïd, *Une Lente impatience*.
184 R. Meyer-Leviné, *Leviné: The Life of a Revolutionary*, Farnborough, 1973.
185 R. Dutschke, 'Ermordetes Leben: Im Gedanken an die Genossin Elisabeth Käsemann', *Chili Nachrichten*, no. 50, 1 July 1977.
186 W. Biermann, 'Rudi Dutschke', *Kritik*, no. 24, p. 176.
187 According to Winfried Wolf, Dutschke remained close to the Fourth International: 'Naturally we can't win him soon for the Fourth, but, unlike any other prominent leftist in the Federal Republic, he displays solidarity and interest towards us.' W. Wolf to E. Mandel, 3 April 1978, E. Mandel Archives, folder 112.
188 E. Mandel to R. Dutschke, 8 May 1975, E. Mandel Archives, folder 53. R. Dutschke, *Versuch: Lenin auf die Füße zu stellen*, Berlin, 1974.
189 T. Ali, *Street Fighting Years* , p. 265.
190 R. Dutschke to Minister of the Interior Maihofer, 8 August 1974, E. Mandel Archives, folder 53.
191 E. Mandel to R. Dutschke, 18 August 1974, R. Dutschke Archives.
192 E. Mandel and A. Krivine, 'Seine Sache war die Befreiung der Ausgebeutenen', *Was Tun*, no. 10, January 1980.
193 In 1974 Mandel wrote a critical evaluation of Duschke's *Versuch, Lenin auf die Füße zu stellen* (An Attempt to Stand Lenin on His Feet), Berlin, 1974, for the *Frankfurter Rundschau*. He wrote an expanded critique in 'Lenin auf die Füsse gestelt?' (Lenin Stood on His Feet?) for *Die Internationale*, April 1975, pp. 103–9. Dutschke responded in a letter to Mandel, 'I will learn from your critique.' (R. Dutschke to E. and G. Mandel, 27 November 1974, E. Mandel Archives, folder 53). He also wrote, 'It makes me very glad, dear Ernest, to get a critical review from you in the FR [*Frankfurter Rundschau*].' (R. Dutschke to E. and G. Mandel, 19 August 1974, E. Mandel Archives, folder 111.) Mandel's review article appeared in November 1974, titled 'Lenin hätte sich über Dutschke geärgert und gefreut: das Buch des ehemaligen Anführers der Studentenbewegung aus trotzkistischer Sicht' (Lenin would have been exasperated and pleased at Dutschke: a Trotskyist view of the book by the former student movement leader), *Frankfurter Rundschau*, 9 November 1974.
194 E. Mandel to 'Lieber Freund', 28 August 1978, E. Mandel Archives, folder 64. G. Mandel to K. Bloch, 15 January 1979, E. Bloch Archives.
195 G. Scholtz to E. Mandel, 17 February 1977, E. Mandel Archives, folder 60.
196 G. Mandel to K. Bloch, 12 February 1978, E. Bloch Archives.

197 Author's interview with J. Malewski, 26 May 2005.
198 G. Mandel to E. Mandel, 17 August 1980, E. Bloch Archives.
199 G. Mandel to K. Bloch, 21 January 1982, E. Bloch Archives.
200 Ibid.
201 *Le Soir*, 22 February 1982. Also: *Rouge*, 19 February 1982; *La Gauche*, 5 March 1982; *Was Tun*, 4 March 1982.
202 E. Mandel to K. Bloch, 24 February 1982, K. Bloch Archives.
203 Author's interview with B. Morawe, 13 July 2005. H. Arendt, *Rahel Varnhagen: The Life of a Jewess*, Baltimore, 1997.

Revolution Deferred

1 Author's interview with C.-A. Udry, 23 June 2005.
2 D. Bensaïd, *Une Lente impatience*, Paris, 2004, p. 364. Author's interview with D. Bensaïd, 12 July 2005.
3 Author's interview with C.-A. Udry, 23 June 2005.
4 E. Mandel, 'Trotsky the Man', *Trotsky as Alternative*, London, 1995, p. 166.
5 'The Last Words of Adolf Joffe: A Letter to Leon Trotsky', *Leon Trotsky, the Man and His Work, Reminiscences and Appraisals*, New York, 1969, p. 126. The letter begins 'Dear Leon Davidovich, we are bound together by ten years of work in common and, I hope, of personal friendship, and that gives me the right to tell you, at the moment of farewell, what seems to me to be a weakness of you.
   'I have never doubted the correctness of the way you have pointed out . . . But I have always thought that you lacked the inflexibility, the intransigence of Lenin, his resolution to remain at the task alone, if need be, in the road that he had marked out.'
6 Walter to 'Chers camarades', 3 April 1986, E. Mandel Archives, folder 509.
7 C.-A. Udry to E. Mandel, 10 April 1986, E. Mandel Archives, folder 509.
8 Author's interview with C.-A. Udry, 23 June 2005.
9 A. Gorz, *Farewell to the Working Class: An Essay on Post-Industrial Socialism*, London, 1982. L. Colletti, *Le Déclin du marxisme*, Paris, 1984.
10 Author's interview with C.-A. Udry, 24 July 2005. In 1978 Mandel wrote to André Gunder Frank that a revolution in Europe was 'both possible and unavoidable' in the medium or long term. 'We are deeply convinced . . . that May 68 of France, the 'creeping' May of 69 of Italy and Portugal 1975 will repeat themselves several times in several countries.' E. Mandel to A. Frank, 28 February 1978, E. Mandel Archives, folder 129.
11 'Resolution on Europe' in *1979 World Congress of the Fourth International, Major Resolutions and Reports*, January 1980. A year earlier Mandel had informed Perry Anderson that there were doubts in the International about perspectives in Europe: 'While we believe that the possibility of a sudden revolutionary crisis in South-West Europe remains as real as before, we have to notice that the *credibility* of such a crisis has become much more controversial in the extreme-left and even in our own ranks – not to speak about broader masses – than in the years 1975–1976.' E. Mandel to P. Anderson, 3 June 1978, E. Mandel Archives, folder 129.

12 Author's interview with D. Bensaïd, 12 July 2005. Author's interview with J. Habel, 14 July 2005. Author's interview with C.-A. Udry, 23 June 2005.

13 Author's interview with H. Krivine, 25 May 2005. Mandel considered the evasion of critical assessments justified by the struggle with the US SWP.

14 D. Bensaïd, *Une Lente impatience*, pp. 178–98.

15 Author's interview with D. Bensaïd, 12 July 2005.

16 H. Ticktin to E. Mandel, 25 January 1980, E. Mandel Archives, folder 63. Author's interview with C.-A. Udry, 24 July 2005.

17 A. Nove, *An Economic History of the USSR*, Aylesbury, 1972.

18 A. Nove, *The Economics of Feasible Socialism*, London, 1983. Mandel responded with 'In Defence of Socialist Planning', *New Left Review*, no. 159, September/ October 1986, pp. 5–37. Nove answered with 'Markets and Socialism', *New Left Review*, no. 161, January/February 1978, pp. 98–104. In his reply 'The Myth of Market Socialism', *New Left Review*, no. 169, May/June 1988, Mandel concluded: 'Our controversy turns only around two questions: whether socialism as conceived by Marx – i.e. a society ruled by freely associated producers, in which commodity production (market economy, social classes and the state) have withered away – is *feasible*, and whether it is *desirable*.' p. 108.

19 E. Mandel, *Revolutionary Marxism Today*, London, 1979, pp. 114–61.

20 'In the initial phases of each dynasty, the objective function of the bureaucracy was to protect the state and the peasantry from the encroachment of the landed nobility (gentry) in order to permit expanded reproduction . . . [But] the bureaucrat remains *dependent on the arbitrariness of the state, never secure in his position* . . . Therefore, in the second half of each dynastic cycle, an integration of the landed nobility (gentry) and the bureaucracy often took place. Bureaucrats became private property owners, first of money and treasure, and then of the land . . .' E. Mandel, 'Marx and Engels on Commodity Production and Bureaucracy' in S. Resnick and R. Wolff, eds, *Rethinking Marxism: Struggles in Marxist Theory. Essays for Harry Magdoff and Paul Sweezy*, New York, 1985, p. 240. Something comparable occurred in the Soviet Union.

21 Ibid., pp. 241–2.

22 One exception was Charles Bettelheim. See his *Les Luttes de classes en URSS*, Paris, 1974–83, 4 vols.

23 Author's interview with F. Vercammen, 25 November 2004. Author's interview with D. Bensaïd, 12 July 2005.

24 O. Cabezas, *Fire from the Mountain: The Making of a Sandinista*, New York, 1985.

25 In 1981 Mandel spoke optimistically about an imminent 'fundamental transformation of the Western European workers' movement', and the emergence of a workers' vanguard, over which 'the SPs, CPs and union bureaucracies would no longer have the degree of control they did before 1968'. It was time for 'a fundamental questioning of the classical reformist strategy of elections, parliamentarism and strikes for higher wages'. E. Mandel to W. Wolf, 11 December 1981, E. Mandel Archives, folder 115.

26 D. Bensaïd, *Une Lente impatience*, p. 362.

27 Author's interview with J. Moneta, 20 June 2000.

28 W. Wolf, 'Gefährlicher Marxist und Visionär: Zum zehnten Todestag von Ernest Mandel. Kein Nachruf', *Junge Welt*, 20 August 2005.

29 Author's interview with C.-A. Udry, 24 June 2005.
30 Ibid.
31 E. Mandel to Perry [Anderson] and Tariq [Ali], 11 March 1984, E. Mandel Archives, folder 130.
32 Author's interview with C.-A. Udry, 23 June 2005.
33 Author's interview with F. Vercammen, 31 May 2005. A. Mandel-Sprimont to J.W. Stutje, 9 February 2006.
34 Author's interview with A. Mandel-Sprimont, 21 April 2005.
35 P. Depondt and P. de Moor, 'De misdaadroman is voor mij de alcohol of de tabak van de geest', *Vrij Nederland/Boekenbijlage*, 30 March 1985.
36 E. Mandel to 'Chers camarades', 3 April 1986, E. Mandel Archives, folder 509.
37 Author's interview with A. Mandel-Sprimont, 10 July 2001.
38 Because of the uncertain social and political circumstances in which they found themselves, many Jews converted their savings into easily portable stamps or diamonds.
39 P. Depondt and P. de Moor, 'De misdaadroman is voor mij de alcohol of de tabak van de geest'
40 E. Mandel, *Delightful Murder: A Social History of the Crime Story*, London, 1984. The book was published in French in 1986 and in Dutch and German in 1987.
41 E. Mandel to A. Wald, 4 February 1983, E. Mandel Archives, folder 346.
42 'Marx en Misdaad: Jef Geeraerts in gesprek met Ernest Mandel', *Nieuw Wereld Tijdschrift*, November 1984.
43 J. Michael, 'E. Mandel, *Delightful Murder: A Social History of the Crime Story*', *Modern Language Notes*, vol. 102, no. 5.
44 'Kein schöner Mord: Ernest Mandels einäugige Sozialgeschichte des Kriminalromans', *Frankfurter Allgemeine Zeitung*, 17 November 1987.
45 J. Jansen van Galen, 'Trotzkist als Thrillerkenner', *NRC Handelsblad*, 2 March 1985.
46 P. Siegel, 'E. Mandel, *Delightful Murder: A Social History of the Crime Story*', *Clio*, vol. 15, no. 3, 1986, pp. 328–30.
47 Author's interview with C.-A. Udry, 24 June 2005. Author's interview with F. Vercammen, 11 January 2006.
48 E. Mandel, 'De opkomende vierde stand in de burgerlijke omwentelingen van de Zuidelijke Nederlanden (1565–1585, 1789–1794, 1830)', in *Arbeid in Veelvoud: Een huldeboek voor Jan Craeybeckx en Etienne Scholliers*, Brussels, 1988, pp. 172–81.
49 E. Mandel, *The Meaning of the Second World War*, London, 1986.
50 E. Mandel, *Revolutionary Marxism Today*, London, 1979, p. 164.
51 E. Mandel, *The Meaning of the Second World War*, p. 45.
52 Ibid., pp. 64–5.
53 H. Reichman, 'Beyond the Good War: The Left, the Soviet Union, and the Nature of World War II', *Radical History Review*, issue 40, 1988.
54 P. Anderson, 'Comments on EM's The Meaning of World War II', E. Mandel Archives, folder 294.
55 Y. Thanassekos to E. Mandel, 28 March 1994, E. Mandel Archives, folder 82.
56 Author's interview with C.-A. Udry, 23 June 2005.
57 E. Mandel, *The Meaning of the Second World War*, pp. 89–95.
58 E. Traverso, *The Marxists and the Jewish Question: The History of a Debate 1843–1943*, Atlantic Highlands, NJ, 1994.

59 E. Traverso, *Understanding the Nazi Genocide: Marxism after Auschwitz*, London, 1999, p. 43.

60 M. Horkheimer and T. Adorno, *Dialectic of Enlightenment: Philosophical Fragments*, Stanford, 2002. H. Marcuse, *Eros and Civilization: A Philosophical Inquiry into Freud*, Boston, 1955. H. Marcuse, *One-Dimensional Man*, Boston, 1964. G. Anders, *Besuch im Hades: Auschwitz und Breslau 1966, nach dem 'Holocaust'*, Munich, 1985. A. Leon, *The Jewish Question: A Marxist Interpretation*, Mexico City, 1950.

61 M. Jay, *The Dialectical Imagination: A History of the Frankfurt School and the Institute of Social Research 1923–1950*, Boston, 1973. R. Wiggershaus, *Die Frankfurter Schule: Geschichte, theoretische Entwicklung, politische Bedeutung*, Munich, 1988.

62 E. Traverso, *Understanding the Nazi Genocide*, p. 46.

63 'The fury of Nazism, which was bent on the unconditional extermination of every Jewish man, woman, and child within its reach, passes the comprehension of a historian, who tries to uncover the motives of human behaviour and to discern the interests behind the motives. Who can analyse the motives and the interests behind the enormities of Auschwitz? . . . We are confronted here by a huge and ominous mystery of the degeneration of the human character that will forever baffle and terrify mankind.' I. Deutscher, *The Non-Jewish Jew and Other Essays*, London, 1968, pp. 163–4.

64 See Mandel's introduction to Trotsky's *The Struggle Against Fascism in Germany*, New York, 1971. His essay deals with the social causes and class structure of fascism. The Holocaust is scarcely mentioned. On 2 February 1964 Mandel gave a lecture titled 'Fascism as a Social Phenomenon' as part of the 'Fascism Study Days' organized by the Flemish Philosophical Society. Mandel also examined fascism in his book *Trotsky, A Study in the Dynamic of His Thought*, London, 1979, but once again ignored the Shoah. Only in passing did he mention Trotsky's 1938 warning about the destruction of the Jews in the approaching war.

65 A. Léon, *La Conception materialiste de la question juive* (revised ed. with original preface by E. Germain [E. Mandel]), Paris, 1968. Mandel's Afterword is also absent from E. Mandel and N. Weinstock, *Zur jüdischen Frage: Beiträge zu Abraham Léons Judenfrage und Kapitalismus*, Frankfurt on Main, 1977.

66 E. Traverso, *The Marxists and the Jewish Question*, Chapter 9.

67 M. Postone, 'Anti-Semitism and National Socialism: Notes on the German Reaction to "Holocaust"', *New German Critique*, no. 19, Winter 1980, pp. 97–117. Rudolf Augstein et al., *'Historikerstreit': Die Dokumentation der Kontroverse um die Einzigartigkeit der nationalsozialistischen Judenvernichtung*, Munich, 1987. R. Kosiek, *Historikerstreit und Geschichtsrevision*, Tübingen, 1987. E. Nolte, *Das Vergehen der Vergangenheit: Antwort an meine Kritiker im sogenannten Historikerstreit*, Berlin, 1987.

68 E. Mandel, *The Meaning of the Second World War*, London, 1986. E. Mandel, 'Zum Historikerstreit: Ursprung, Wesen, Einmaligkeit und Reproduzierbarkeit des Dritten Reiches', *Der Zweite Weltkrieg*, Frankfurt on Main, 1991, pp. 209–45. E. Mandel, 'Material, Social and Ideological Preconditions for the Nazi Genocide' in G. Achcar, ed., *The Legacy of Ernest Mandel*, London, 1999. This had first appeared as E. Mandel, 'Prémisses matérielles, sociales et

idéologiques du génocide nazi' in Y. Thanassedos and H. Wismann, eds, *Révision de l'histoire totalitarisme: crimes et génocides nazis*, Paris, 1990, pp. 169–74.

69 'The Nazis' systematic dehumanization of the Jews is not an isolated phenomenon in history. Comparable phenomena arose in respect to slaves in Antiquity, midwives ('witches') during the fourteenth and seventeenth centuries, the American Indians, Blacks sold in slavery, and so forth. Victims of these phenomena can be counted by the millions, including women and children.' E. Mandel, 'Material, Social and Ideological Preconditions for the Nazi Genocide', *The Legacy of Ernest Mandel*, p. 225.

70 E. Mandel to 'Branka, Neil and Perry', 3 September 1985, E. Mandel Archives, folder 294. E. Mandel, *The Meaning of the Second World War*, p. 92.

71 Ibid., pp. 91–2.

72 Mandel reproached Theodor Adorno for not seeing that technology had no application apart from human will: 'In the final analysis Auschwitz and Hiroshima were not products of technology but of *relationships of social forces.*' E. Mandel, *Late Capitalism*, London, 1975, p. 506.

73 E. Mandel, 'Material, Social and Ideological Preconditions for the Nazi Genocide', *The Legacy of Ernest Mandel*, p. 230.

74 E. Mandel, *Late Capitalism*, London, 1975, p. 508. E. Mandel, 'Material, Social and Ideological Preconditions for the Nazi Genocide', *The Legacy of Ernest Mandel*, p. 227.

75 E. Mandel, *The Meaning of the Second World War*, p. 91. E. Mandel, 'Zum Historikerstreit', p. 240–42.

76 E. Mandel, 'Material, Social and Ideological Preconditions for the Nazi Genocide', *The Legacy of Ernest Mandel*, p. 230.

77 N. Geras, 'Marxists before the Holocaust: Trotsky, Deutscher, Mandel', *The Legacy of Ernest Mandel*, p. 200.

78 E. Mandel, 'Material, Social and Ideological Preconditions for the Nazi Genocide', *The Legacy of Ernest Mandel*, p. 226.

79 Moishe Postone also rejected the idea that the death camps could only be understood 'as instances of imperialist (or totalitarian) mass murder in general'. That was to deny the specificity of National Socialism. M. Postone, 'Anti-Semitism and National Socialism', op. cit., p. 102.

80 E. Mandel, 'Material, Social and Ideological Preconditions for the Nazi Genocide', *The Legacy of Ernest Mandel*, p. 227.

81 E. Mandel, 'Zum Historikerstreit', *The Legacy of Ernest Mandel*, p. 230.

82 N. Geras, 'Marxists before the Holocaust: Trotsky, Deutscher, Mandel', *The Legacy of Ernest Mandel*, p. 202.

83 I. Deutscher, 'The Jewish Tragedy and the Historian', *The Non-Jewish Jew*, p. 164.

84 P. Anderson, 'Comments on EM's *The Meaning of World War II*', E. Mandel Archives, folder 294. In a footnote to the essay 'Zum Historikerstreit', Mandel criticized a similar thesis of the German historian Ulrich Herbert. E. Mandel, 'Zum Historikerstreit', *Der Zweite Weltkrieg*, p. 225.

85 E. Mandel to 'Branka, Neil and Perry', 3 September 1985, E. Mandel Archives, folder 294.

86 On the economic rationality of the genocide, see S. Heim and G. Aly, 'Die Ökonomie der Endlösung: Menschenvernichtung und wirtschaftliche

Neuordnung', *Sozialpolitik und Judenvernichtung: Beiträge zur nationalsozialistischen Gesundheits- und Sozialpolitik*, vol. 5, Berlin, 1987, pp. 11–90. S. Heim and G. Aly, 'Wider die Unterschätzung der nationalsozialistischen Politik: Antwort an unsere Kritiker', in W. Schneider, ed., *Vernichtungspolitik: Eine Debatte über den Zusammenhang von Sozialpolitik und Genozide im nationalsozialistischen Deutschland*, Hamburg, 1991, pp. 165–75.

87 E. Mandel to 'Branka, Neil and Perry', 3 September 1985, E. Mandel Archives, folder 294.

88 R. Luxemburg to E. and M. Wurm, 16 February 1917, in S. Bronner, ed., *The Letters of Rosa Luxemburg*, Atlantic Highlands, NJ, 1993, p. 180.

89 L. Trotsky, *The Struggle Against Fascism in Germany*, New York, 1971, p. 45, note 51.

90 E. Mandel, 'The Role of the Individual in History in the Light of the Second World War', in L. Van Langenhove, J. De Waele and R. Harré, eds, *Individual Persons and Their Actions*, Brussels 1986. E. Mandel, 'The Role of the Individual in History: The Case of World War Two', *New Left Review*, no. 157, May/June 1986.

91 G. Plekhanov, 'On the Question of the Individual's Role in History', *Selected Philosophical Works*, Moscow, 1976.

92 Ibid., p. 312.

93 I. Deutscher, *The Prophet Outcast: Trotsky, 1929–1940*, Oxford, 1963.

94 Trotsky wrote in his diary: 'Had I not been present in [St] Petersburg in 1917, the October Revolution would still have taken place – *on the condition that Lenin had been present and in command*. If neither Lenin nor I had been present in Petersburg, there would have been no October Revolution . . .' L. Trotsky, *Diary in Exile, 1935*, Cambridge, MA, 1958, p. 46.

95 I. Deutscher to R. Rosdolsky, 29 June 1962, I. Deutscher Archives. 'If neither Lenin nor Trotsky had been there someone else might have come to the fore. The fact that among the Bolsheviks there was apparently no other man of their stature and reputation does not prove that in their absence such a man would not have emerged.' I. Deutscher, *The Prophet Outcast*, p. 245.

96 E.H. Carr, *What Is History?*, London, 1961, p. 91.

97 Ibid., pp. 101–2.

98 R. Rosdolsky to O. Morf, 15 January 1963, R. Rosdolsky Archives, folder 299.

99 This manuscript was posthumously published as 'Die Rolle des Zufalls und der "Großen Männer" in der Geschichte', R. Rosdolsky, in *Kritik der politischen Ökonomie, Beiträge des internationalen Marxismus*, vol. 5, no. 14, 1977, pp. 67–95. R. Rosdolsky to O. Morf, 26 November 1963; R. Rosdolsky to O. Morf, 22 January 1964; O. Morf to R. Rosdolsky, 23 February 1964; R. Rosdolsky Archives, folder 299. P. Mattick to R. Rosdolsky, 2 February 1964, R. Rosdolsky Archives, folder 11. R. Rosdolsky to P. Mattick, 7 February 1964, R. Rosdolsky Archives, folder 9.

100 Marx and Engels wrote about chance and necessity in a number of works. See: K. Marx and F. Engels, *The German Ideology*; K. Marx, *Grundrisse*; K. Marx, *Capital*, vol. 3; and F. Engels, *The Origin of the Family, Private Property and the State*.

101 R. Rosdolsky, 'Die Rolle des Zufalls', p. 75.

102 F. Engels, *Ludwig Feuerbach and the End of Classical German Philosophy*, in K. Marx and F. Engels, *Selected Works in One Volume*, New York, 1968, p. 620.

103 L. Trotsky, *My Life: An Attempt at an Autobiography*, (1930) Harmondsworth, 1975, p. 422.

104 R. Rosdolsky, 'Die Rolle des Zufalls', p. 81.

105 In his 1967 biography, *Winston Churchill* (London, 2005), Sebastian Haffner resolutely upheld the proposition that without Churchill Hitler would have won the war.

106 E. Mandel, 'The Role of the Individual in History: The Case of World War Two', *New Left Review*, no. 157, p. 62.

107 Ibid.

108 Minutes of the European Parliament, 10 December 1985, Series A, document A21-160/85/annex 4. Y. Thanassekos to E. Mandel, 11 April 1985, E. Mandel Archives. E. Mandel, 'Prémisses matérielles, sociales et idéologiques du génocide nazi', *Révision de l'histoire totalitarisme* , pp. 169–74.

109 E. Mandel, 'Folter und der Kampf gegen die Folter: kurzer geschichtliche Abriß' (Torture and the Struggle Against Torture: A Short Historical Synopsis), June 1986, E. Mandel Archives, folder 234.

110 The advisory board was composed of Jan Philipp Reemtsma, Helmut Dahmer, Ernest Mandel, Margarete Mitscherlich-Nielsen, Jakob Moneta and Alice Schwarzer. E. Mandel, 'Die Krise unserer Zeit', *Hamburger Institut für Sozialforschung*, März, 1984.

111 J. Reemtsma to E. Mandel, 2 March 1995, E. Mandel Archives, folder 88.

112 P. Broué, *Trotsky*, Paris, 1988, pp. 763, 770.

113 F. Breth to E. Mandel, 22 March 1977; F. Breth to E. Mandel, 15 May 1977, E. Mandel Archives, folder 60.

114 E. Mandel to F. Breth, 1 June 1977, E. Mandel Archives, folder 60.

115 E. Mandel to P. Verbraeken, 19 November 1982, E. Mandel Archives, folder 68. E. Mandel to P. Verbraeken, 18 January 1983, E. Mandel Archives, folder 72.

116 E. Corijn, 'Op zoek naar de subversieve rede: Politiek in memoriam Paul Verbraeken', *Vlaams Marxistisch Tijdschrift*, vol. 38, no. 2, June 2004.

117 E. Mandel, *De economische theorie van het marxisme*, 2 vols, Bussum, 1980.

118 *Veelzijdig marxisme, I: Ekonomie, staat en recht, II: Geschiedenis, moraal, psychologie en actuele problemen: Acta van het colloquium 'De actualiteit van Karl Marx' gehouden van 24 tot 26 November 1983 aan de Vrije Universiteit Brussel*, Brussels, 1988.

119 E. Mandel to N. Steinberger, 8 March 1983, E. Mandel Archives, folder 116.

120 E. Mandel, *Marxist Economic Theory*, London, 1968, vol. 1, p. 20.

121 P. Sraffa, *Production of Commodities by Means of Commodities: Prelude to a Critique of Economic Theory*, Cambridge, 1960. M. Morishima, *Marx's Economics: A Dual Theory of Value and Growth*, Cambridge, 1973. I. Steedman, *Marx after Sraffa*, London, 1977. I. Steedman et al., *The Value Controversy*, London, 1981. NB, Sraffa himself said nothing about the labour theory of value.

122 Mandel had already written about the problem in his introduction to the third volume of the Penguin edition of *Capital*, London, 1981, pp. 21–9.

123 L. von Bortkiewicz, 'Zur Berichtigung der grundlegenden theoretischen Konstruktion von Marx im dritten Band des Kapitals', *Jahrbücher für Nationalökonomie und Statistik*, 1907.

124 Shortly before his death Langston had been deeply occupied with Sraffa's critique of Marx. He had drawn up mathematical comparisons for the transformation of value into prices.

125 E. Mandel and A. Freeman, eds., *Ricardo, Marx, Sraffa: The Langston Memorial Volume*, London, 1984. Mandel's contribution was titled 'Gold, Money, and the Transformation Problem.'

126 For the connection between neo-Ricardian theory and the policies the Italian Communist Party, for example, see E. Mandel, *From Stalinism to Eurocommunism: The Bitter Fruits of 'Socialism in One Country'*, London, 1978.

127 E. Mandel to B. Langston, n.d. [1979], E. Mandel Archives, folder 171.

128 Desai, Fine, Himmelweit, Mohun, Hodgson, general comments, E. Mandel Archives, folder 474.

129 W. Boerboom, 'Ekonomie anders bekeken: Ernest Mandel, 1923–1995', *Solidariteit*, no. 70, August 1995.

130 E. Mandel to NLB/Verso Books, 14 January 1983, E. Mandel Archives, folder 465.

131 E. Mandel to N. Levine, 31 December 1976, E. Mandel Archives, folder 58.

132 E. Mandel, *From Stalinism to Eurocommunism*. The book was translated into Spanish, Portuguese, Italian, German, Dutch and English. E. Mandel, 'A Critique of Eurocommunism', *Marxist Perspectives*, vol. 2, no. 4, Winter 1979/1980, pp. 112–42.

133 The Communist parties of Australia, Japan and Mexico had undergone the same development.

134 E. Mandel, 'A Critique of Eurocommunism', *Marxist Perspectives*, p. 136.

135 E. Mandel to P. Anderson, 3 June 1978, E. Mandel Archives, folder 129. E. Mandel, *Les Tres dimensiones del 'eurocommunismo'*, Barcelona, 1977. E. Mandel, *Austerità come modello di sviluppo: la proposta economica del PCI*, Milan, 1977. E. Mandel, *Réponse à Louis Althusser et Jean Elleinstein*, Paris, 1979. *Debat Thio (CPN)- Mandel (4ᵉ Int.): Een verslag van het debat tussen Boe Thio en Ernest Mandel op 29 March 1982*, Amsterdam, 1982. E. Mandel and L. Althusser at the symposium 'Marxism Today', 11–15 August 1980. E. Mandel to R. Bahro, 1 March 1980, E. Mandel Archives, folder 68.

136 E. Mandel to R. Garaudy, 3 June 1975, E. Mandel Archives, folder 121. Mandel had read Garaudy's manuscript *Le projet espérance*, Paris, 1976. Garaudy had mediated in a secret meeting of the French section with Santiago Carillo, General Secretary of the Spanish Communist Party. Of all the Eurocommunists, Carillo went the furthest in his criticisms of the Soviet Union. A. Krivine to E. Mandel, 12 May 1975, E. Mandel Archives, folder 121.

137 E. Mandel and J. Agnoli, *Offener Marxismus: Ein Gespräch über Dogmen, Orthodoxie und die Häresie der Realität*, Frankfurt on Main, 1980, p. 105. Mandel made a contribution on the theory of the state in 'Methodisches zur Beseitigung der Klassennatur des bürgerlichen Staats' in E. Bloch, ed., *Marxismus und Anthropologie: Festschrift für Leo Kofler*, Bochum, 1980, pp. 213–33.

138 In 1979 Mandel first mentioned his intention 'to formulate a general theory of the working class, the workers' movement, the socialist revolution, and socialism'. E. Mandel, *Revolutionary Marxism Today*, London, 1979, p. 59. E. Mandel to F. Vercammen, 7 October 1994, F. Vercammen Archives. E. Mandel to M. Löwy, 6 October 1994, E. Mandel Archives, folder 88.

139 C.-A. Udry, 'Le Début D'une ère nouvelle', *Inprecor/Intercontinental Press*, no. 84, 11 September 1980. D. Bensaïd, 'L'Explosion polonaise et ses lendemains', *Quatrième Internationale* (third series), vol. 38, no. 2, October/November/December 1980.

140 Author's interview with J. Malewski, 30 May 2005.

141 *Rouge*, 29 September 1976.

142 G. Filoche, *68–98: Histoire sans fin*, Paris, 1998, p. 264.

143 *Rouge*, 14 February 1980.

144 C. Smuga [J. Malewski], 'Pologne: Le recit des grèves', *Rouge*, 11 July 1980.

145 Author's interview with J. Malewski, 26 May 2005.

146 *L'Humanité*, 22 August 1980. The Italian Communist Party made a more positive evaluation.

147 Walter [E. Mandel], on behalf of the Bureau of the United Secretariat, to the leadership of the sections and sympathizing organizations, 15 September 1980, E. Mandel Archives, folder 157.

148 Author's interview with J. Malewski, 26 May 2005.

149 In 1990 a bookseller told Jan Malewski that between 1982 and 1984 he had reprinted several thousand copies of Polish *Inprekor* (probably no. 3 through no. 7/8). Articles seem also to have been reprinted in various Poznan publications. J. Malewski to J.W. Stutje, 13 October 2005.

150 Z. Kowalewski, *Rendez-nous nos usines: Solidarnoœ dans le combat pour l'autogestion ouvrière*, Paris, 1985.

151 T. Garton Ash, *The Polish Revolution: Solidarity*, London, 1991, p. 265. Z. Kowalewski, 'De la Tactique de la grève active: la position du comité régional de Lodz de Solidarité', *Inprecor/Intercontinental Press*, no. 110, 12 October 1981.

152 G. Sanford, ed., *The Solidarity Congress, 1981: The Great Debate*, London, 1990.

153 Author's interview with C. Samary, 25 May 2005.

154 Ibid.

155 E. Mandel and W. Wolf, *Ende der Krise oder Krise ohne Ende? Bilanz der Weltwirtschaftsrezession und der Krise in der Bundesrepublik*, Berlin, 1977.

156 W. Wolf, *Polen: Der lange Sommer der Solidarität*, 2 vol., Frankfurt on Mains, 1981. W. Wolf to E. Mandel, 15 November 1981, E. Mandel Archives, folder 115.

157 E. Mandel to N. Steinberger, 11 February 1981, E. Mandel Archives, folder 114.

158 'Une Avancée de la revolution politique en Pologne', *Inprecor/Intercontinental Press*, no. 109, 28 September 1981.

159 *The Financial Times*, 18 September 1981. *Trybunu Ludu*, 2 November 1981.

160 T. Garton Ash, *The Polish Revolution: Solidarity*, p. 259.

161 Z. Kowalewski, 'Solidarnoœ on the Eve', *Labour Focus on Eastern Europe*, vol. 5, no. 1/2, Spring 1982, p. 25. Z. Kowalewski, 'Solidarnoœ pour le pouvoir aux travailleurs: Contribution d'un membre de la direction régionale de Lodz de Solidarité', *Inprecor/Intercontinental Press*, no. 19, 22 February 1982.

162 E. Mandel, 'Les Racines de la crise économique', *Inprecor/Intercontinental Press*, no. 19, special issue on Poland, 22 February 1982.

163 G. Scholtz to K. Bloch, 21 January 1982, E. Bloch Archives.

Socialism or Death

1 'Révolution et contre-révolution politiques en Pologne', Resolution adopted by the United Secretariat of the Fourth International, 8 January 1982, *Inprecor/Intercontinental Press*, no. 117, 25 January 1982. J. Allio [J. Heinen], 'Résister sous la botte de la dictature bureaucratique: Après le premier traumatisme, les travailleurs reprennent leurs espoirs et leur luttes', *Inprecor/Intercontinental Press*, no. 119, 22 February 1982. C. Smuga [J. Malewski], 'Echos de la résistance, Manifestations, tracts et bulletins clandestins témoignent de la résistance aux bureaucrates', *Inprecor/Intercontinental Press*, no. 121, 22 March 1982.

2 'Leçons de Pologne', *Quatrième Internationale* (third series), vol. 40, no. 8, April/May/June 1982.

3 'Révolution politique et contre-révolution en Pologne', Resolution of the International Executive Committee of the Fourth International, 27 May 1982, *Inprecor/Intercontinental Press*, no. 130, 12 July 1982.

4 'Revolution and Counter-Revolution in Poland', *International Viewpoint*, special issue: 'Resolutions of the Twelfth World Congress of the Fourth International', 1985.

5 E. Mandel to 'Jacqueline' [Heinen], 19 December 1982, E. Mandel Archives, folder 157.

6 Z. Kowalewski to J.W. Stutje, 19 October 2005. The accusation was originally made by Bogdan Lis, a member of the TKK.

7 Author's interview with H. Krivine, 24 May 2005.

8 H. Krivine to E. Mandel, 3 June 1984, E. Mandel Archives, folder 157.

9 Z. Kowalewski to J.W. Stutje, 19 October 2005.

10 E. Mandel to H. Krivine, 9 May 1984, H. Krivine Archives.

11 E. Mandel to H. Krivine, 25 May 1984, H. Krivine Archives.

12 H. Krivine to E. Mandel, 26 June 1984, H. Krivine Archives.

13 Sandor [H. Krivine] to E. Mandel, 16 May 1984, E. Mandel Archives, folder 157.

14 Author's interview with J. Malewski, 26 May 2005.

15 Author's interview with C.-A. Udry, 24 June 2005.

16 A. Wilkins and C. Smuga, 'Quatre ans après le coup d'état de Jaruzelski: Les courants de l'opposition en Pologne', *Inprecor*, no. 208, 2 December 1985.

17 These papers were *Front Rabotniczy* (Workers' Front), *Sprawa Rabotnicza* (Workers' Cause), *Glosno* (A Step Further) and *Wolny Robotnik* (The Free Worker). The last two were distributed in Upper Silesia, *Wolny Robotnik* (edited by Eugeniusz Kondraciuk, pseudonym Kowal), and primarily in Gliwice. J. Malewski to J.W. Stutje, 19 October 2005.

18 Bureau of the United Secretariat to leaders of the sections, 12 May 1987, H. Krivine Archives.

19 *Inprecor*, 2 November 1986.

20 Author's interview with J. Malewski, 26 May 2005. E. Mandel to H. Krivine, 21 February 1991, H. Krivine Archives.

21 Simon [a pseudonym], 'Report on the Poland Discussion', 27 December 1986.

22 D. [Duret: Udry], S. [Sandor: H., Krivine] W. [Walter: Mandel] to A. [Arthur: Kowalewski], Al. [Allio: Heinen] and S. [Smuga: Malewski], 31 June 1986, E.

Mandel Archives, folder 157. Two months later a response was received from Poland in which the position of D., S. and W. was called 'a model example of organizational conservatism'. Letter to three comrades in the Bureau (complete manuscript transcription), n.d., E. Mandel Archives, folder 157.

23 C.-A. Udry to François [Vercammen], 16 November 1986, E. Mandel Archives, folder 75. H. Krivine to the Bureau of the United Secretariat, 8 November 1986, H. Krivine Archives.

24 H. Krivine to E. Mandel, 13 November 1986, H. Krivine Archives. H. Krivine to 'Chers camarades', 22 November 1986, H. Krivine Archives.

25 [J. Heinen] to 'Chers camarades', 23 June 1985, E. Mandel Archives, folder 157.

26 C.-A. Udry to 'François' [Vercammen], 16 November 1986, E. Mandel Archives, folder 75.

27 H. Krivine to E. Mandel, 4 November 1986, H. Krivine Archives.

28 Duret [Udry] to Claudio [L. Maitan], 19 December 1986, E. Mandel Archives, folder 75.

29 Kowalewski's books include *Antropología de la guerrilla (hacia la cienca social del tercer mundo)*, Caracas, 1971; and *Guerilla Latyno-ameryka'nska: szkize z dziejów rewolucyjnych walk partyzanckich XX wieku*, Wroclaw, 1978.

30 Z. Kowalewski to J.W. Stutje, 19 October 2005.

31 Duret, 'Déclaration à la commission d'enquête et au SU' (Testimony to the Investigating Committee and to the United Secretariat), 12 June 1987, E. Mandel Archives, folder 75.

32 Author's interview with H. Krivine, 25 May 2005. Duret to Claudio, 19 December 1986, E. Mandel Archives, folder 75. Kowalewski, writing as Arthur, defended himself in 'A proposito de encuesta secreta del C. Duret: Sobre mi trayectoria "tercermundista" anterior a la adhesión a la Cuarta Internacional y mi artículo sobre el PRT argentine' (Concerning [Udry's] secret investigation: About my 'third-worldist' past before joining the Fourth International and my article on the Argentinean PRT), E. Mandel Archives, folder 75.

33 E. Mandel to 'cher Charles' [Udry], 20 December 1986, E. Mandel Archives, folder 177.

34 Author's interview with C.-A. Udry, 24 June 2005.

35 'Motion préalable au débat Pologne' (Preliminary motion for the debate on Poland) [submitted to the United Secretariat by J. Heinen], Bureau meeting 15 December 1986, note by E. Mandel, E. Mandel Archives, folder 75.

36 Z. Kowalewski to J.W. Stutje, 20 October 2005.

37 C.-A. Udry to W. van Miert, 1 January 1987, W. van Miert Collection.

38 Z. Kowalewski to J.W. Stutje, 20 October 2005.

39 Arthur to the Bureau of the United Secretariat, 26 January 1987, E. Mandel Archives, folder 75. W. van Miert to Z. Kowalewski, 17 January 1987, W. van Miert Collection.

40 See: Arthur Wilkins [Z. Kowalewski], 'La stratégie du FSLN nicaraguayen: l'insurrection populaire prolongée', *Quatrième Internationale* (third series), vol. 41, no. 12, 1 December 1983. Kowalewski chose the pseudonym Wilkins in honour of his Uruguayan friend, Hugo Wilkins, a former Tupamaro known as Chico. Z. Kowalewski to J.W. Stutje, 24 October 2005.

41 JS [Piekarczyk], 'Salut!', February 1987.
42 Author's interview with J. Malewski, 26 May 2005.
43 Bureau of the United Secretariat to the leaders of the sections, 12 May 1987, H. Krivine Archives.
44 H. Krivine, 'Projet de Rapport bilan Pologne SU' (Draft Report to the United Secretariat on the Balance Sheet of the Polish Work), March 1988, H. Krivine Archives.
45 Verla [Samary], Klein, Sandor [H. Krivine], 'La résolution Pologne ou comment un texte "qui ne pose aucun problème" n'en résoud aucun' (On the Balance Sheet of the Polish Work, or, How a Document that 'Isn't a Problem' Doesn't Solve a Single One), H. Krivine Archives.
46 H. Krivine, 'Projet de Rapport bilan Pologne SU'.
47 E. Mandel to H. Krivine, 21 February 1991, H. Krivine Archives.
48 Z. Kowalewski to J.W. Stutje, 19 October 2005.
49 E. Mandel to Arthur, 21 January 1986; E. Mandel to Arthur, 16 March 1986, E. Mandel Archives, folder 158.
50 Z. Kowalewski to J.W. Stutje, 19 October 2005.
51 H. Krivine to E. Mandel, 27 February 1991, E. Mandel Archives, folder 543.
52 Author's interview with H. Krivine, 24 May 2005.
53 E. Mandel to H. Krivine, 10 November 1986; E. Mandel to H. Krivine, 21 February 1991, H. Krivine Archives.
54 Author's interview with J. Malewski, 26 May 2005.
55 Author's interview with J. Habel, 14 July 2005.
56 E. Mandel to H. Krivine, 21 February 1991, H. Krivine Archives.
57 Sandor to E. Mandel, 27 February 1991, E. Mandel Archives, folder 543.
58 Sandor to E. Mandel, 25 October 1991; E. Mandel to H. Krivine, 27 October 1991, E. Mandel Archives, folder 81.
59 Author's interview with C.-A. Udry, 24 June 2005.
60 Duret, 'Déclaration à la Commission d'enquête et au SU' (Testimony to the Investigating Committee and to the United Secretariat), 12 June 1987, E. Mandel Archives, folder 75.
61 C.-A. Udry to E. Mandel, 15 June 1986, E. Mandel Archives, folder 75.
62 At that time the largest sections were the French LCR and Spanish LCR, each with several thousand members, the Mexican Revolutionary Workers Party (PRT), with 1,500, the US SWP (1,000), the Swedish (500) and the Belgian, Swiss and British sections, each with 200. By the early 1990s the Brazilian Socialist Democracy (DS) in the Workers Party, with 1,600 members, had also become a major section. In late 1989 Mandel claimed that the Fourth International was present in almost fifty countries, with between 35,000 and 40,000 active members, around 100,000 organized sympathizers and something like 2 million voters. E. Mandel to A. Handlok, 15 October 1989, E. Mandel Archives, folder 159. At the end of the 1980s the Belgian section (SAP) had about 700 members. (Thanks to Steve Bloom and Alan Wald for information on US SWP membership.)
63 G. Kilden, 'Tom Gustafsson (1947–1987): A Strong Link Has Been Broken', International Viewpoint, no. 114, 23 February 1987.
64 E. Mandel, 'Mémorandum sur le fonctionnement et l'avenir du centre'

(Memorandum on the Centre's Functioning and Future), 28 March 1983, E. Mandel Archives, folder 508.

65 E. Mandel, *Trotsky As Alternative*, London, 1995, pp. 26–30.

66 E. Mandel to J. Moneta, 14 January 1988, E. Mandel Archives, folder 78.

67 L. Trotsky, 'The Class Nature of the Soviet State', *Writings of Leon Trotsky (1933–1934)*, New York, 1975, p. 115.

68 M. van der Linden, *Western Marxism and the Soviet Union: A Survey of Critical Theories and Debates Since 1917*, Leiden, 2007, Chapter 7.

69 In the 1950s Mandel had written, 'The plan in fact shows that the Soviet Union is maintaining a more or less steady pace of economic growth, plan after plan and decade after decade . . . Growth rates averaging around 10 % over a half-century will provide definitive, irrefutable proof of the historical superiority of the socialized mode of production by comparison with every social form of production that humanity has known until now.' E. Germain [E. Mandel], 'Le 6e plan quinquennal', *Quatrième Internationale*, vol. 14, no. 1/3, 1956, p. 17.

70 E. Mandel, 'The Significance of Gorbachev', *International Marxist Review*, vol. 2, no. 4, 1987, pp. 7–39.

71 E. Mandel, 'Marx and Engels on Commodity Production and Bureaucracy', *Rethinking Marxism, Struggles in Marxist Theory: Essays for Harry Magdoff and Paul Sweezy*, in S. Resnick and R. Wolff, eds, New York, 1985, p. 242.

72 E. Mandel, *Beyond Perestroika: The Future of Gorbachev's USSR*, London, 1989, pp. xv–xvi. The title of the French edition, *Où va l'URSS de Gorbatchev* (Where is the USSR of Gorbachev Going?), alludes to the subtitle of Trotsky's 1936 book *The Revolution Betrayed: What Is the Soviet Union and Where Is It Going?*

73 E. Mandel, *Revolutionary Marxism Today*, London, 1979, p. 150.

74 E. Mandel, *Beyond Perestroika*, p. xvi.

75 L. Trotsky, *Revolution Betrayed*, New York, 1972, pp. 287–90.

76 E. Mandel, *Beyond Perestroika*, p. 195.

77 E. Mandel to J. Kircz, 30 June 1989, J. Kircz Archives.

78 E. Mandel to J. Boewe, 13 September 1989; E. Mandel to A. Handlok, 15 October 1989, E. Mandel Archives, folder 159.

79 E. Mandel, 'Moves to Rehabilitate the Moscow Trial Defendants', *International Viewpoint*, no. 128, 26 October 1987, pp. 11–16.

80 BstU, Archiv der Zentralstelle (Stasi archives), MfS – HA XX, no. 10209.

81 BstU Zentralarchiv (Stasi archives), MfS – ZAIG, no. 14547.

82 B. Coppieters to J.W. Stutje, 23 January 2006. The organization was in the hands of the political scientist Bruno Coppieters, on behalf of the Free University of Brussels, and philosophy professor Gerd Irrlitz, on behalf of Humboldt University.

83 Author's interview with A. Mandel-Sprimont, 1 October 2005. W. Richter to E. Mandel, 10 October 1989, E. Mandel Archives, folder 192.

84 B. Coppieters to J.W. Stutje, 23 January 2006.

85 E. Mandel, 'The Political Revolution and the Dangers That Threaten It', *International Viewpoint*, no. 174, 27 November 1989, p. 5.

86 E. Mandel, 'The Rebirth of East German Socialism', *The Village Voice*, 21 November 1989, pp. 20–22.

87 D. Bensaïd, *Une Lente impatience*, Paris, 2004, p. 371.

88 E. Mandel to A. Handlok, 4 December 1989, E. Mandel Archives, folder 159.

89 Author's interview with J. Malewski, 26 May 2005.

90 For a discussion, see http://www.dradio.de/dkultur/sendungen/laenderreport/421153/

91 E. Mandel to J. Boewe, 27 December 1989, E. Mandel Archives, folder 159.

92 D. Bensaïd, *Une Lente impatience*, p. 371.

93 Mandel liked to cite this passage from Marx's *Contribution to the Critique of Hegel's Philosophy of Law*: 'The criticism of religion ends with the teaching that *man is the highest being for man*, hence with the *categorical imperative to overthrow all relations* in which man is a debased, enslaved, forsaken, despicable being . . .' K. Marx and F. Engels, *Collected Works*, vol. 3, New York, 1975, p. 182. See also M. Löwy, 'Ernest Mandel's Revolutionary Humanism', in G. Achcar, ed., *The Legacy of Ernest Mandel*, London, 1999, p. 29.

94 E. Mandel, 'Die zukünftige Funktion des Marxismus', H. Spatzenegger, ed., *Das verspielte 'Kapital'? Die marxistische Ideologie nach dem Scheitern des Realen Sozialismus*, Salzburg, 1991, p. 173.

95 Mandel used this formulation first in a 1985 essay, 'The Actuality of Socialism', published by the 1985 Cavtat Conference, *Socialism on the Threshold of the Twenty-first Century*, London, 1985.

96 United Secretariat of the Fourth International, 'The Situation in the GDR and Our Tasks', *International Viewpoint*, no. 181, 26 March 1990, pp. 23–4.

97 *Neues Deutschland*, 26 May 1990. 'Gysi-Mandel: Streitgespräch', *Neues Deutschland*, 28 May 1990. *International Viewpoint*, no. 187, 18 June 1990.

98 E. Mandel, 'Situation et avenir du socialisme', *Le Socialisme du Futur: Revue de Débat Politique,* vol. 1, no. 1, 1990.

99 E. Mandel, *Karl Marx: Die Aktualität seines Werkes*, Frankfurt on Main, 1984, p. 80.

100 M. Löwy, 'Ernest Mandel's Revolutionary Humanism', in G. Achcar, ed., *The Legacy of Ernest Mandel*, p. 33.

101 E. Mandel, *Power and Money: A Marxist Theory of Bureaucracy*, London, 1992, p. 246.

102 E. Mandel, 'The Paris Conference for Another Europe', 15 June 1993, F. Vercammen Archives.

103 'Een Strijdershart dat bloedt', *Markant*, vol. 2, no. 24, 11 June 1993.

104 G. Achcar, 'Ernest Mandel (1923–1995): An Intellectual Portrait', *The Legacy of Ernest Mandel*, p. 9.

105 Mandel had previously published a short study, *On Bureaucracy*, London, 1973.

106 E. Mandel, *Power and Money*, p. 5.

107 E. Mandel, *October 1917: Coup d'état or Social Revolution? The Legitimacy of the Russian Revolution,* Amsterdam, 1992.

108 E. Mandel, *Power and Money*, pp. 103–53.

109 E. Mandel, *Trotsky As Alternative*, London, 1995, pp. 81–4.

110 Among these critics were Jan Malewski, Joost Kircz and Ken Lewis. Kircz was a Dutch physicist working for a large scientific publisher, and Lewis a lawyer from Miami who had emigrated to Sweden in the 1960s to avoid military service at the time of the Vietnam war.

111 E. Mandel to the Bureau, 20 December 1992, E. Mandel Archives, folder 81.

112 E. Mandel to members of the United Secretariat, 6 July 1994, F. Vercammen Archives.
113 Author's interview with F. Vercammen, 25 November 2004.
114 Author's interview with J. Malewski, 26 May 2005. Author's interview with J. Kircz, 25 October 2005.
115 F. Vercammen to E. Mandel, 10 June 1991, F. Vercammen Archives.
116 E. Mandel to F. Vercammen, 3 July 1991, F. Vercammen Archives.
117 Among other activities, Mandel attended a gathering of the São Paulo Forum. There he met with Daniel Ortega and Victor Tirado Lopez, leaders of the Nicaraguan Sandinista Front.
118 E. Mandel to Gabriel [C. Jacquin], 13 May 1992, E. Mandel Archives, folder 81.
119 C.-A. Udry to E. Mandel, 24 March 1992, E. Mandel Archives, folder 83.
120 Author's interview with J. Kircz, 24 October 2005. E. Mandel to Bureau, 11 February 1994, J. Kircz Archives.
121 Author's interview with A. Mandel-Sprimont, 23 September 2005.
122 E. Mandel to J. Reemtsma, 20 April 1995, E. Mandel Archives.
123 E. Mandel to Beloni, 13 February 1995, E. Mandel Archives, folder 70.
124 E. Mandel to Members of the United Secretariat, 6 July 1994; E. Mandel to L. Maitan, 16 July 1994, E. Mandel Archives, folder 88.
125 E. Mandel to Beloni, 13 February 1995, E. Mandel Archives, folder 70.
126 E. Mandel to C.-A. Udry, 7 May 1994, E. Mandel Archives, folder 87.
127 E. Mandel to F. Vercammen, 7 October 1994, F. Vercammen Archives.
128 E. Mandel to C.-A. Udry, 23 March 1995, E. Mandel Archives, folder 88.
129 S. Bloom to E. Mandel, 13 April 1993, E. Mandel Archives, folder 82. A. Wald to E. Mandel, 27 April 1995, E. Mandel Archives, folder 88.
130 Bureau of the United Secretariat to E. Mandel, 9 November 1994, E. Mandel Archives, folder 510.
131 E. Mandel to Bureau, 19 November 1994, E. Mandel Archives, folder 510.
132 *New York Newsday*, 12 November 1994.
133 E. Mandel, 'Sectarisme dogmatique contre marxisme révolutionnaire', 4 February 1995, E. Mandel Archives. E. Mandel, 'World Socialist Revolution Today: Sectarianism vs. Revolutionary Marxism', *Bulletin in Defence of Marxism*, no. 125, May/June 1995, pp. 18–41.
134 A. Wald to E. Mandel, 27 April 1995; J. Kircz to E. Mandel, 15 May 1995; M. Löwy to E. Mandel, 8 May 1995, E. Mandel Archives, folder 88.
135 E. Mandel to Yvan, 30 June 1995, E. Mandel Archives.
136 E. Mandel, *Trotsky as Alternative*, London, 1995, p. 175.
137 Author's interview with C.-A. Udry, 24 June 2005.
138 Author's interview with F. Vercammen, 11 November 2005.
139 E. Mandel, 'World Socialist Revolution Today', *Bulletin in Defence of Marxism*, no. 125, p. 32.
140 E. Mandel to M. Pablo [M. Raptis], 11 March 1993, E. Mandel Archives, folder 82.
141 A. Gilly, *Pasiones cardinales*, Mexico, 2001, p. 76.
142 *Rouge*, 5 October 1995.
143 E. Mandel, 'Testament', E. Mandel Archives.

144 From a recollection by L. Apostel, 'Ernest Mandel 1923–1995: A Life for the Revolution', *Rood*, vol. 28, no. 15/16, 1 September 1995.

Conclusion

1 E. Mandel, *Trotsky As Alternative*, London, 1995, p. 165.
2 C. Den Hond, *Ernest Mandel – A Life for the Revolution*, DVD, 2005.
3 E. Mandel, 'Situation et avenir du socialisme', *Le Socialisme du Futur: Revue de Débat Politique*, vol. 1, no. 1, 1990.
4 'Framing not only relates to the generalization of a grievance, but defines the "us" and "them" in a movements conflict structure. By drawing on inherited collective identities and shaping new ones, challengers delimit the boundaries of their prospective constituencies and define their enemies by real or imagined attributes and evils.' S. Tarrow, *Power in Movement: Social Movements and Contentious Politics,* Cambridge, 1998, pp. 21–2.
5 E. Mandel, 'Anticipation and Hope as Categories of Historical Materialism', *Historical Materialism,* vol. 4, no. 10, 2002, pp. 245–59.
6 E. Germain [E. Mandel], '20 août 1940–20 août 1952: La victoire de Léon Trotsky', *Quatrième Internationale*, vol. 10, no. 5/10, October 1952.
7 'Transitional Programme of the Fourth International', *Documents of the Fourth International,* New York, 1973, pp. 181–2.
8 In Marxist circles the stagnation thesis was defended by Zinoviev, the young Bukharin and Luxemburg.
9 Mandel cited as an example Lenin's theory of the labour aristocracy: 'One can say that Lenin was politically and tactically correct in searching for a socio-logical explanation of reformism (in the social-democratic bureaucracy). But that did not justify the incorrect theory of the "labour aristocracy", which led to serious mistakes in the approach to social democracy in the 1930s and later.' E. Mandel to F. Vercammen, 4 September 1985, F. Vercammen Archives.
10 G. Myrdal, *The Political Element in the Development of Economic Theory*, London, 1953.
11 B. Coppieters to J.W. Stutje, 19 January 2006. In the 1980s Coppieters worked together with Mandel at the Free University of Brussels. My thoughts on the nature of Mandel's scholarly work emerged from an exchange of views with Coppieters.
12 D. Bensaïd, *Une Lente impatience*, Paris, 2004, p. 365.
13 In a conversation with the German political scientist Johannes Agnoli, Mandel explained, 'One cannot arbitrarily pull two or three pillars out of this attempt at a scientific explanation of the history of human societies as a whole and still imagine that the rest will be left standing.' E. Mandel and J. Agnoli, *Offener Marxismus: Ein Gespräch über Dogmen, Orthodoxie und die Häresie der Realität*, Frankfurt on Main, 1980, p. 13.
14 E. Mandel, 'Memoir Fragment', E. Mandel Archives.
15 S. Bloom, memorial meeting for Ernest Mandel, 21 August 1995, E. Mandel Archives, folder 212.
16 R. Blackburn, 'The Unexpected Dialectic of Structural Reforms', in G. Achcar, ed., *The Legacy of Ernest Mandel*, London, 1999, p. 19.

17 J. Geeraerts to A. Sprimont-Mandel, n.d., E. Mandel Archives, folder 212.

18 Author's interview with A. Sprimont-Mandel, 23 September 2005.

19 M. van der Linden, *Western Marxism and the Soviet Union: A Survey of Critical Theories and Debates since 1917*, Leiden, 2007.

20 M. van der Linden, 'Ein flämischer Internationalist jüdischer Herkunft: Ernest Mandel, 1923–1995', *Analyse und Kritik*, 1995, no. 381, p. 5.

21 E. Mandel, *Trotsky as Alternative*, London, 1995, p. 171. Also: E. Mandel, 'Why I Am a Marxist', in G. Achcar, ed., *The Legacy of Ernest Mandel*, p. 243.

22 E. Mandel, 'Die zukünftige Funktion des Marxismus', H. Spatzenegger, ed., *Das verspielte 'Kapital'? Die marxistische Ideologie nach dem Scheitern des realen Sozialismus*, Salzburg, 1991, p. 173.

23 L. Trotsky, 'The USSR in War', *In Defence of Marxism*, New York, 1973, p. 9.

24 M. Löwy, 'Ernest Mandel's Revolutionary Humanism', in G. Achcar, *The Legacy of Ernest Mandel*, p. 27.

25 Ibid., p. 34.

26 P. Verbraeken, 'De worsteling van Ernest Mandel', *Vlaams Marxistisch Tijdschrift*, vol. 29, no. 4, 1995, pp. 33–46.

27 E. Mandel, 'Situation et avenir du socialisme', *Le Socialisme du Futur , p. 89*.

28 E. Mandel, *Long Waves of Capitalist Development: A Marxist Interpretation*, London, 1995, p. 38.

29 E. Mandel, *Karl Marx: die Aktualität seines werkes*, Frankfurt on Main, 1984, p. 32. The absolute number of wage earners and their proportion among the total working population grew sharply with the beginning of industrialization. In 1977 more than 90 per cent of the working population in the US, Britain and Sweden belonged to the working class.

30 J. Mooser, 'Auflösung der proletarischen Milieus: Klassenbindung und In-dividualisierung in der Arbeiterschaft vom Kaiserreich bis in die Bundesrepu-blik Deutschland', *Soziale Welt*, vol. 34, no. 3, 1983, pp. 305–6. Mooser rejects the thesis of the embourgeoisement of the working class: 'The workers took their leave of the proletariat in a sense, but without being absorbed into a comparably coherent economic, social and political stratum. The break in working-class continuity is thus open-ended, and does not constitute the widely discussed "bourgeoisification of the workers".'

31 C. Harman, 'The Workers of the World', *International Socialism*, Autumn 2002, pp. 23–4. In various African countries waged work declined in absolute terms in the 1980s. In Latin America the proportion of the informal sector combined with wage labour in the smallest companies grew from 40 per cent in 1980 to 53 per cent in 1990. Also in India, Pakistan and Bangladesh, job growth was primarily in the informal sector. In some of the world's largest cities, permanent waged work is drowning in an endless sea of the unemployed, day labourers, contract workers and casual labourers.

32 In 2001 Raymond-Pierre Bodin remarked, 'It has become commonplace nowadays to speak of the development of atypical forms of work in the Western economies . . . Works highlighting the erosion of the Fordist standard of employment embodied in the permanent full time contract as the main way of organising labour markets and integration into social life are now innumerable.' R.-P. Bodin, 'Wide-Ranging Forms of Work and Em-ployment in Europe: Review and Challenges for the Players', paper for the

Conference on the Future of Work, Employment and Social Protection, Annecy, 18–19 January 2001.

33 M. van der Linden, 'Normalarbeit – das Ende einer Fiktion: Wie der Proletar verschwand und wieder zurück kehrte, *Fantômas* 6, November 2004. M. van der Linden, 'Nieuwe inhoud arbeidersinternationalisme nodig', in H. Boot, ed., *Om de vereniging van de arbeid: Globalisering en vakbeweging*, Amsterdam, 2005, pp. 133–43.

Bibliography

The archives consulted for this bibliography are mostly located in libraries and documentation centres that are open to the public. Ernest Mandel's 20-metre-long archive at the International Institute for Social History in Amsterdam is no exception, although only part of the extensive collection is accessible to the public. The restrictions on it mainly concern Mandel's correspondence in his capacity as a leader of the Fourth International. This is not an insuperable obstacle for research, because Mandel's extensive scholarly and personal correspondence, the heart of the collection, is freely accessible. There are also no restrictions on the papers of Mandel's first wife, Gisela Scholtz, which are in an annex to the main collection, or on the papers of Henri Mandel.

Archival research has been done at the following institutions:

- AMSAB – Institute for Social History (Ghent)
Archives:
  - Belgian section of the Fourth International (BAVI)
  - Emile van Ceulen
  - Guy Cudell
  - Stichting Léon Lesoil
  - Jean van Lierde
  - RAL/SAP-POS
  - A. De Smet

- Archive der BStU / Ministerium für Staatssicherheit (Ministry for State Security) (Berlin)
  - Ernest Mandel's file

- Ceges/Soma, Studie- en documentatiecentrum oorlog en hedendaagse maatschappij (Centre for Historical Research and Documentation on War and Contemporary Society) (Brussels)
- Jours de Guerre Collection
- *Het Vrije Woord.* Verschijnt, tegen wil en dank van Den Bezetter, te Antwerpen en elders [published by Vrank en Vrij, edited by Henri Mandel] - Antwerp.
- *Vrank en Vrij.* Verschijnt - tegen wil en dank van Den Bezetter - te Brussel en elders [edited by Henri Mandel] - [Brussels].
- *Das Freie Wort.* Sonderausgabe für deutsche Soldaten und Wehrmachtsangehoerigen in Belgien [published by Vrank en Vrij, Brussels].
- Leo Lejeune Archive

- Dienst voor de oorlogsslachtoffers (Office for War Victims) (Brussels)
- Ernest Mandel's file
- Henri Mandel's file
- Camille Loots's file
- Abraham Wajnsztock's file

- Ernst-Bloch-Archiv (Ludwigshafen)
- Ernst and Karola Bloch's correspondence with Ernest Mandel and Gisela Scholtz

- Hamburg Institute for Social Research (Hamburg)
- Rudi Dutschke Archive

- Hoover Institution (Palo Alto)
- B. Nicolaevsky Collection

- Houghton Library (Cambridge, Massachusetts)
- Trotsky Collection

- International Institute for Social History (Amsterdam)
Archives:
- Wolfgang Abendroth
- Joe Baxter
- Wim Boerboom
- Communistische Partij Nederland
- Yvan Craipeau
- Isaac Deutscher
- Georges Dobbeleer

- Maurice Ferares
- Fourth International, International Secretariat
- André Gunder Frank
- Sania Gontarbert
- Karl Korsch
- Ligue Communiste Révolutionnaire
- Jean Malaquais
- Ernest Mandel
- Henri Mandel
- Paul Mattick
- Max Plekker
- Rodolphe Prager
- Revolutionair Communistische Partij
- Roman Rosdolsky
- Catherine Samary
- Sal Santen
- Georg Scheuer
- Gisela Scholtz
- Henk Sneevliet
- Lev Davidoviè Trockij (Hoover Institution Archives / Houghton Library)
- Georges Vereeken

• Free University of Brussels (Brussels)
- Ernest Mandel's personnel file

• Private collections
Walter Besser
Bruno Coppieters
Joost Kircz
Hubert Krivine
Henri Mandel
Anne Mandel-Sprimont
Wilbert van Miert
Jakob Moneta
Catherine Samary
Rudi Segall
François Vercammen

Interviews and correspondence

I have interviewed or consulted the following people, in many cases more than once. The dates of the interviews are mentioned in the footnotes.

Gilbert Achcar, Elmar Altvater, Daniel Bensaïd, Peter Bloch, Bruno Coppieters, Helmut Dahmer, Guy Desolre, Jan Debrouwere, Rik De Coninck, Georges Dobbeleer, Rudi van Doorslaer, Peter Drucker, Wilfried Dubois, Ernst Federn, Hilde Federn, Maurice Ferares, Maurice Fischer, Adolfo Gilly, Janette Habel, Willy van der Helst, Chris den Hond, Joost Kircz, Victor Klapholz, Gretchen Klotz-Dutschke, Leszek Kolakowski, Zbigniew Kowalewski, Hubert Krivine, Jean van Lierde, Jan Malewski, Livio Maitan, Anne Mandel-Sprimont, Michel Mandel, Klaus Meschkat, Wilbert van Miert, Jakob Moneta, Sigi Moneta, Bodo Morawe, Hendrick Patroons, Herman Pieterson, Max Plekker, Catherine Samary, Rudi Segall, Fritjof Tichelman, Charles-André Udry, François Vercammen, Robert Went and Els Witte.

Periodicals consulted

Against the Current, New York
Avant-Garde: une revue marxiste revolutionnaire, Brussels
Bulletin in Defense of Marxism, New York
Les Cahiers du centre d'études socialistes, Paris
Cahiers Léon Trotsky, Paris
Cahiers marxistes, Brussels
Courrier hebdomadaire, Centre de Recherche et d'Information Socio-Politiques (CRISP-Brussels)
Critique Communiste, revue de la Ligue Communiste Révolutionnaire, Paris
Critiques de l'économie politique, Paris
Dinge der Zeit: Zeitschrift für inhaltliche Demokratie, London
Fourth International: English-language edition of the theoretical organ of the International Executive Committee of the Fourth International, Paris/Amsterdam/Rome
France Observateur, Paris
Das Freie Wort, Brussels
Funken: Aussprache-Hefte für internationale sozialistische Politik, Stuttgart
La Gauche: organe de combat socialiste, Brussels
Inprecor: International Press Correspondence, fortnightly information organ of the United Secretariat of the Fourth International, Brussels/Montreuil
Inprekorr: Internationale Pressekorrespondenz der IV. Internationale:
Informationsbulletin des Vereinigten Sekretariats der IV Internationale, Stuttgart
Intercontinental Press, New York
International Marxist Review: published under the auspices of the United Secretariat of the Fourth International in conjunction with the French language *Quatrième International*, Montreuil

International Socialism: journal for socialist theory: monthly journal of the International Socialists, London

International Socialist Journal: a bi-monthly review, Milan

International Socialist Review, New York

International Viewpoint: fortnightly review of news and analysis published under the auspices of the United Secretariat of the Fourth International, Montreuil

Konkret, Hamburg

Kritik: Zeitschrift für sozialistische Diskussion, Berlin

Kursbuch, Frankfurt on Main

Labour Focus on Eastern Europe: a socialist defence bulletin on Eastern Europe and the USSR, London

Links: voor een strijdend socialisme, Ghent/Brussels

Lutte de classe: *revue de la section belge de la Quatrième Internationale*, Brussels

La Lutte ouvrière: *organe du Parti Communiste Internationaliste (Trotskyste)*, section belge de la Quatrième Internationale, Gilly

The Militant: a socialist newsweekly published in the interests of working people, New York

Monthly Review: an independent socialist magazine, New York

New Left Review, London

Partisan Review, Boston

Perspectiva Mundial, New York

Le Peuple: *organe quotidien de la democratie socialiste*, Brussels

Pro und Contra: Beiträge zur Zeit. Diskussionsblätter für demokratischen Sozialismus, Berlin

Quatrième Internationale: *Organe du Comité Exécutif International de la IVe Internationale*, Paris

Review: a journal of the Fernand Braudel Center for the study of economics, historical systems and civilizations, Binghamton (NY)

Revolutionary History, London

Revue Internationale du Socialisme, Milan

Rood: newspaper of the Socialistische Arbeiders Partij [before 1985 of the Revolutionaire Arbeiders Liga], Brussels

Rouge: *hebdomadaire de la Ligue Communiste Révolutionnaire (IV Internationale)*, Montreuil

Science and Society: an independent journal of Marxism, New York

Le Socialisme du Futur: *revue de débat politique*, Paris

Socialisme ou Barbarie: *organe de critique et d'orientation révolutionnaire*, Paris

The Socialist Register: a survey of movements and ideas, London

Sous le Drapeau du Socialisme: *organe de la tendance marxiste revolutionnaire de la 4e Internationale*, Paris

Sozialistische Politik, Cologne

Les Temps Modernes: *revue mensuelle*, Paris

Toestanden: *socialistisch theoretisch tijdschrift*, Antwerp

La Vérité des Travailleurs, Paris

Vlaams Marxistisch Tijdschrift, Ghent

Vrank en Vrij, Brussels

Het Vrije Woord, Antwerp

La Wallonie, Liège

Was Tun, Mannheim/Frankfurt on Main
World Outlook Perspective Mondiale: A labour press service – Paris/New York

Books consulted

Articles and contributions to books and anthologies are not included here; they are cited in the footnotes.

Multiple titles by the same author are arranged in chronological rather than alphabetical order. Only the first place of publication mentioned is given. The year in parentheses after the year of publication indicates the year of initial publication.

Rare pamphlets and unpublished works can be found at the following institutes: AMSAB (Ghent), CEGES/SOMA (Brussels), IISH (Amsterdam), the Ernest Mandel Archives at the IISH, or the author's own library.

For a bibliography of Ernest Mandel's works, see: "Ernest Mandel Bibliography: An Indexed and Cross-referenced List of Publications by and about Ernest Mandel (1923–1995)", compiled and edited by Wolfgang and Petra Lubitz. It can also be consulted on the Internet: http://www.trotskyana.net/Trotskyists/Ernest_Mandel/Ernest_Mandel_Bibliography.html.

Aaron, Daniel, *Writers on the Left: Episodes in American Literary Communism*, New York 1992 (1961).
Abbas, Ferhat, *Autopsie d'une guerre: l'aurore*, Paris 1980.
Achcar, Gilbert, ed., *The Legacy of Ernest Mandel*, London 1999.
Adorno, Theodor and Horkheimer, Max, *Dialektik des Aufklärung* (1947), Frankfurt on Main 1969. (*Dialectic of Enlightenment: Philosophical Fragments*, Stanford 2002)
Agnoli, Johannes and Mandel, Ernest, *Offener marxismus: Ein Gespräch über Dogmen, Orthodoxie und die Heresie der Realität*, Frankfurt on Main 1980.
Albrecht, Willy, *Der Sozialistische Deutsche Studentenbund (SDS): von parteikonformen Studentenverband zum Repräsentanten der neuen Linken*, Berlin 1994.
Alexander, David H. [Nelson Zayas Pazos], *Cuba: la via rivoluzionaria al socialisme*, Rome 1967.
Alexander, Robert, *Trotskyism in Latin America*, Stanford 1973.
———. *International Trotskyism, 1929–1985: A Documented Analysis of the Movement*, Durham 1991.
Algemeen Belgisch Vakverbond, ed., *Holdings en Economische Democratie*, n.p. 1956.
Ali, Tariq, *Street Fighting Years: An Autobiography of the Sixties*, London 1987.
———. *Redemption*, London 1990.
Ali, Tariq and Watkins, Susan, *1968: Marching in the Streets*, London 1998.
Alles, Wolfgang, *Zur Politik und Geschichte der deutschen Trotzkisten ab 1930*, Frankfurt on Main 1987.
Althusser, Louis, *Pour Marx*, Paris 1965. (*For Marx*, London 2005)
———. *Lire le capital*, 2 vol., Paris 1965. (*Reading Capital*, London 1970)
Anders, Günther, *Besuch im Hades: Auschwitz und Breslau*, Munich 1979.

Anderson, Benedict, *Language and Power: Exploring Political Cultures in Indonesia*, Ithaca 1990.

Anderson, Perry, *Lineages of the Absolutist State*, London 1974.

———. *Considerations on Western Marxism*, London 1977.

———. *Arguments within English Marxism*, London 1980

———. *In the Tracks of Historical Materialism*, London 1983.

———. *English Questions*, London 1992.

———. *A Zone of Engagement*, London 1992.

———. *Spectrum: From Right to Left in the World of Ideas*, London 2005.

Arbeid in Veelvoud: Een huldeboek voor Jan Craeybeckx en Etienne Scholliers, Brussels 1988.

Arendt, Hannah, *Rahel Verhagen: Lebensgeschichte einer deutschen Jüdin aus der Romantik*, Munich 1962.

Arestis, Philip and Sawyer, Malcolm, eds, *A Biographical Dictionary of Dissenting Economists*, Aldershot 1992.

Arnsberg, Paul, *Die Geschichte der Frankfurter Juden seit der Französische Revolution*, Darmstadt 1983.

Arrighi, Giovanni, Hopkins, Terence K. and Wallerstein, Immanuel, *Antisystemic Movements*, London 1989.

Artous, Antoine, *Retours sur Mai*, Paris 1988.

Augstein, Rudolf et al., *'Historikerstreit': Die Dokumentation der Kontroverse um die Einzigartigkeit der nationalsozialistischen Judenvernichtung*, Munich 1987.

Avenas, Denise, ed., *Contre Althusser, pour Marx*, Paris 1999 (1974).

Bahro, Rudolf, *Die Alternative: Zur Kritik des real existierenden Sozialismus*, Cologne 1977. (*The Alternative in Eastern Europe*, London 1978)

Baran, Paul and Sweezy, Paul, *Monopoly Capital: An Essay on the American Economic and Social Order*, Harmondsworth 1975.

Barjonet, André and Mandel, Ernest, *Qu'est-ce que l'économie marxiste (à propos du 'Traité d'économie marxiste' d'E. Mandel)*, Brussels 1963.

Barnett, Vincent, *Kondratiev and the Dynamics of Economic Development: Long Cycles and Industrial Growth in Historical Context*, Basingstoke 1998.

Bathily, Abdolaye, *Mai 68 à Dakar ou la révolte universitaire et la démocratie,* Paris 1992.

Bauer, Otto, *Die Nationalitätenfrage und die Sozialdemokratie*, Vienna 1907. (*The Question of Nationalities and Social Democracy*, Minneapolis 2000)

———. *Die illegale Partei*, Frankfurt on Main 1971 (1939).

Bauer, Yehuda, *The Holocaust in Historical Perspective*, Seattle 1978.

Bellis, Paul, *Marxism and the USSR: The Theory of Proletarian Dictatorship and the Marxist Analysis of Soviet Society*, London 1979.

Bensaïd, Daniel, Rossi, Carlos [Michael Löwy] and Udry, Charles-André, *Portugal: La révolution en marche*, Paris 1975.

Bensaïd, Daniel, *Moi, la Révolution*, [Paris], 1989.

———. *Walter Benjamin: Sentinelle messianique à la gauche du possible*, Paris 1990.

———. *La Discordance des temps: Essais sur les crises, les classes, l'histoire*, Paris 1995.

———. *Résistances: Essai de taupologie générale*, Paris 2001.

———. *Passion Karl Marx: Les hieroglyphs de la modernité*, Paris 2001.

———. *Les trotskysmes*, Paris 2002.

———. *Une Lente impatience*, Paris 2004.

Bergmann, Theodor and Schäfer, Gert, eds, *Leo Trotzki: Kritiker und Verteidiger des*

Soujetgesellschaft: Beiträge zum internationale Trotzki-Symposium, Wuppertal 26–29 März 1990, Mainz 1993.

Bergmann, Theodor, Schaffer, Gert and Selden, Mark, eds, *Bukharin in Retrospect*, New York 1994.

Besser, Fritz, *Meine Überlebnisse*, London n.d.

Bettelheim, Charles et al., *Wertgesetz: Planung und Bewußtsein, die Planungsdebatte in Cuba*, Frankfurt on Main 1969.

Bettelheim, Charles, *Les Luttes de classe en URSS*, 4 vol., Paris 1974–83. (*Class Struggles in the USSR*, New York 1978)

Birchall, Ian H., *Sartre against Stalinism*, New York 2004.

Blackledge, Paul, *Perry Anderson, Marxism and the New Left*, London 2004.

Blackstock, Nelson, *Cointelpro: The FBI's Secret War on Political Freedom*, New York 1976.

Bloch, Ernst, *Das Prinzip Hoffnung*, 3 vols, Frankfurt on Main 1959 (1954, 1955) . (*The Principle of Hope*, Cambridge, MA 1986)

————. *Vom Hasard zur Katastrophe: Politische Aufsätze (1934–1939)*, Frankfurt on Main 1972.

————. *Experimentum Mundi: Frage, Kategorien des Herausbringens, Praxis*, Frankfurt on Main 1975.

————. with Garstka, Dietrich and Seppmann, Werner, eds, *Marxismus und Anthropologie*, Bochum 1980.

Bloch, Karola, *Aus mein Leben*, Mössingen-Talheim 1995 (1981).

————. and Reif, Adelbert, eds, *'Denken heißt Uberschreiten': In memoriam Ernst Bloch 1885–1977*, Cologne 1978.

Bloch, Peter and Steen, Jürgen, *'Auf wundersame Weise dem Tode entronnen . . .': Peter Bloch (New York) im historischen Museum*, Frankfurt on Main 1994.

Boepple, Willy, *Gegen den Strom: Texte von Willy Boepple (1911–1992)*, Cologne 1997.

Bogdanor, Vernon and Skidelsky, Robert, eds, *The Age of Affluence, 1951–1964*, London 1970.

Boggs, Grace Lee, *Living for Change: An Autobiography*, Minneapolis 1998.

Boot, Hans, ed., *Om de vereniging van de arbeid: Globalisering en vakbeweging*, Amsterdam 2005.

Borin, Max and Plogen, Vera, *Management und Selbstverwaltung in der CSSR: Bürokratie und Widerstand*, Berlin 1970.

Bornstein, Sam and Richardson, Al, *The War and the International: A History of the Trotskyist Movement in Britain 1937–1949*, London 1986.

Boyer, Robert, *La Théorie de la régulation: Une analyse critique*, Paris 1987.

Braverman, Harry, *Labour and Monopoly Capital*, New York 1974.

Breitman, George, Le Blanc, Paul and Wald, Alan, *Trotskyism in the United States: Historical Essays and Reconsiderations*, Atlantic Highlands, NJ 1996.

Brennan, James P., *The Labor Wars in Córdoba, 1955–1976: Ideology, Work, and Labor Politics in an Argentine Industrial City*, Cambridge, MA 1994.

Brepoels, Jaak, *Wat zoudt gij zonder 't werkvolk zijn?: Anderhalve eeuw arbeidersstrijd in België*, Leuven 1977–81.

Briem, Jürgen, *Der SDS: Die Geschichte des bedeutendsten Studentenverbandes der BRD seit 1945*, Frankfurt on Main 1976.

Brossat, Alain and Klingberg, Sylvia, *Le Yiddishland révolutionnaire*, Paris 1983.

Broué, Pierre, *L.D. Trotsky*, Paris 1988.

Bubke, Hermann, *Der Einsatz des Stasi- und KGB-Spions Otto Freitag im München der Nachkriegszeit*, Hamburg 2004.

Bucharin, Nikolai, *Der Imperialismus und die Akkumulation des Kapitals*, Vienna 1926. (*Imperialism and World Economy*, New York 1929)

Buiting, Henny, *De Nieuwe Tijd, sociaaldemokratisch maandschrift, 1896–1921: spiegel van socialisme en vroeg communisme in Nederland*, Amsterdam 2003.

Bunzl, John, *Klassenkampf in der Diaspora: Zur Geschichte der jüdischen Arbeiterbewegung*, Vienna 1975.

Buyens, Frans et al., *Vechten voor onze rechten, 60–61: de staking tegen de Eenheidswet*, Leuven 1985.

Cabezas, Omar, *La montaña es algo más que una inmensa estepa verde*, Managua 1983. (*Fire from the Mountain: The Making of a Sandinista*, New York 1985)

Callaghan, John, *British Trotskyism: Theory and Practice*, Oxford 1984.

———. *The Far Left in British Politics*, Oxford 1987.

Callari, Antonio, Cullenberg, Stephen and Biewener, Carole, eds, *Marxism in the Postmodern Age: Confronting the New World Order*, New York 1995.

Campinchi, Philippe, *Les Lambertistes: Un courant trotskiste français*, Paris 2000.

Cannon, James P., *Notebook of an Agitator*, New York 1985.

Carr, Edward Hallett, *What is History?*, London 1961.

Cassart, Jean-Pierre, *Les Trotskystes en France pendant la deuxième guerre mondial*, Paris n.d. [ca 1981].

Castoriadis, Cornelius, *L'experience du movement ouvrier, 2: Proletariat et organisation*, Paris 1974.

———. *Political and Social Writings*, vol. I, 1946–1955, Minneapolis 1988.

Charpier, Frédéric, *Histoire de l'extrême gauche trotskiste: De 1929 à nos jours*, Paris 2002.

Chaussy, Ulrich, *Die drei Leben des Rudi Dutschke*, Darmstadt/Neuwied 1983.

Claussen, Detlev, *Grenzen der Aufklärung: Zur gesellschaflichen Geschichte des modernen Antisemitismus*, Frankfurt on Main 1987.

Cliff, Tony, *Neither Washington nor Moscow: Essays on Revolutionary Socialism*, London 1982.

———. *Trotskyism after Trotsky: The Origins of the International Socialists*, London 1999.

Coates, Ken, ed., *Czechoslovakia and Socialism*, Nottingham 1969.

———. ed., *Détente and Socialist Democracy: A Discussion with Roy Medvedev*, Nottingham 1975.

Cohen-Solal, Annie, *Sartre 1905–1980*, Paris 1985.

Colletti, Lucio, *From Rousseau to Lenin: Studies in Ideology and Society*, New York 1972 (1969).

Colletti, Lucio and Napoleoni, Claudio, eds, *Il futuro del capitalismo: Crollo o sviluppo?*, Bari 1970.

Colletti, Lucio, *Le Déclin du marxisme*, Paris 1984.

Copfermann, Emile, *David Rousset, une vie dans le siècle: Fragments d'autobiographie*, Paris 1991.

Corijn, Eric et al., eds, *Veelzijdig marxisme: Acta van het colloquium 'De actualiteit van Karl Marx' gehouden van 24 tot 26 november 1983 aan de Vrije Universiteit Brussel*, 2 vols, Brussels 1988.

Cormier, Jean, *Che Guevara*, Monaco 1995.

Cornelissen, Igor, *Alleen tegen de wereld: Joop Zwart, de geheimzinnigste man van Nederland*, Amsterdam 2003.

Craipeau, Yvan, *Le Mouvement trotskyste en France: Des origines aux enseignements de mai 68*, Paris 1971.

———. *Contre vents et marées: Les révolutionaires pendant la deuxième guerre mondiale*, Paris 1977.

———. *Mémoires d'un dinosaure trotskyste: Secrétaire de Trotsky en 1933*, Paris 1999.

Crosland, Anthony, *The Future of Socialism*, London 1956.

CSSR: Fünf Jahre 'Normalisierung': 21.8.1968/21.8.1973, Dokumentation, Hamburg 1973.

Dazy, René, *Fusillez ces chiens enrages . . .: Le génocide des trotskistes*, Paris 1981.

DeBeule, Nadya, *Het Belgisch trotskisme 1925–1940*, Ghent 1980.

Debray, Régis, *Strategy for Revolution: Essays on Latin America*, London 1970.

Debrouwere, Jan, ed., *Stappen naar de Verte, Leo Michielsen: leraar, marxist*, Leuven 1997.

Degee, Jean-Luc, *L'Évolution des luttes ouvrières en Belgique*, Liège 1980.

De Gaulle, Charles, *Mémoires de guerre: Le salut, 1944–1946*, Paris 1959. (*The Complete War Memoirs of Charles de Gaulle*, New York 1968)

Desai, A.R., ed., *Rural Sociology in India*, Bombay 1969.

Desolre, Guy, ed., *50 Ans de débuts sur le controle ouvrier*, Brussels 1970.

Deutscher, Isaac, *Russia after Stalin*, London 1953.

———. *The Prophet Armed, Trotsky: 1879–1921*, London 1954.

———. *The Prophet Unarmed, Trotsky: 1921–1929*, London 1959.

———. *The Prophet Outcast, Trotsky: 1929–1940*, London 1963.

———. *The Non-Jewish Jew and Other Essays*, Cambridge 1968.

———. *Marxism in Our Time*, London 1970.

Devleeshouwer, Robert, *Henri Rolin 1891–1973: Une voie singulière, une voix solitaire*, Brussels 1994.

De Winter, Dick, *Franz Holz: Kunstenaar op de vlucht voor Hitler*, Breda 2001.

Diana, Marta, *Mujeres guerrilleras: La militancia de los setenta en el testimonio de sus protagonistas femeninas*, Buenos Aires 1996.

Diner, Dan, ed., *Ist der Nationalsozialismus Geschichte? Zu Historisierung und Historikerstreit*, Frankfurt on Main 1987.

Dobbeleer, Georges, *Memoires d'un révolutionnaire qui n'a pas vécu de révolution*, n.p. 2005.

———. *Sur les traces de la révolution: Itinéraire d'un trotskiste belge*, Paris 2006.

Doneux, Jean L. and Le Paige, Hugues, *Le front du Nord: Des Belges dans la guerre d'Algérie (1954–1962)*, Brussels 1992.

Dreyfus, François G., *Histoires des gauches en France 1940–1974*, Paris 1975.

Drucker, Peter, *Max Shachtman and his Left: A Socialist Odyssey through the 'American Century'*, Atlantic Highlands, NJ 1994.

Dutschke, Rudi, ed., *Der lange Marsch: Wege der Revolution in Lateinamerika*, Munich 1968.

———. *Versuch, Lenin auf die Füße zu stelle: Uber den halbasiatischen und den westeuropäischen Weg zum Sozialismus: Lenin, Lukács und die Dritte Internationale*, Berlin 1974.

———. *Mein langer Marsch: Reden, Schriften und Tagebücher aus zwanzig Jahren*, Reinbeck 1980.

————. *Geschichte ist machbar: Texte über das herrschende Falsche und die Radikalität des Friedens*, Berlin 1981.

————. *Aufrecht gehen: Eine fragmentarische Autobiographie*, Berlin 1981.

————. *Jeder hat sein Leben ganz zu leben: die Tagebücher 1963–1979*, Cologne 2003.

Dworkin, Dennis L., *Cultural Marxism in Postwar Britain: The New Left and the Origins of Cultural Studies*, Durham 1997.

Eastman, Max et al., *Leo Trotzki 1879–1940: In den Augen von Zeitgenossen*, Hamburg 1979.

Eatwell, John, Milgate, Murray and Newman, Peter, eds, *The New Palgrave: A Dictionary of Economics*, London 1988.

Eckstein, Susan Eva, *Back from the Future: Cuba under Castro*, Princeton 1994.

Elliott, Gregory, *Althusser: The Detour of Theory*, London 1987.

————. *Perry Anderson: The Merciless Laboratory of History*, Minneapolis 1998.

En défense de Michel Raptis (Pablo) et Sal Santen emprisonnés en Hollande pour leur soutien à la lutte de libération nationale du peuple algérien, Suresnes 1961.

Engels, Friedrich, 'Der Ursprung der Familie, des Privateigentums und des Staats', in *Marx-Engels Werke*, vol. 21, Berlin 1981. ('The Origin of the Family, Private Property and the State', in Marx, Karl and Engels, Friedrich, *Collected Works*, vol. 26, Moscow 1990)

————. 'Ludwig Feuerbach und der Ausgang der klassischen deutschen Philosophie', in *Marx-Engels Werke*, vol. 21, Berlin 1981. ('Ludwig Feuerbach and the End of Classical German Philosophy', in Marx, Karl and Engels, Friedrich, *Collected Works*, vol. 26, Moscow 1990)

Erlich, Alexander, *The Soviet Industrialization Debate, 1924–1928*, Cambridge, MA 1960.

Essel, André, *Je voulais changer le monde*, n.p. 1985.

Euchner, Walter and Schmidt, Alfred, eds, *Kritik der politischen Ökonomie heute, 100 Jahre 'Kapital': Referate und Diskussionen vom Frankfurter Colloquium im September 1967*, Frankfurt on Main 1968.

Evans, Les, ed., *James P. Cannon as We Knew Him*, New York 1976.

Evans, Mary, *Lucien Goldman: An Introduction*, Brighton 1981.

Fac-similé de La Vérité clandestine (1940–1944), Paris 1978.

Feaux, Valmy, *Cinq semaines de lutte sociale: La grève de l'hiver 1960–1961*, Brussels 1963.

Federn, Ernst, *De terreur als systeem: Het concentratiekamp, achter de schermen van de propaganda, Buchenwald in zijn ware gedaante*, Antwerp 1945.

————. *Witnessing Psychoanalysis: From Vienna back to Vienna via Buchenwald and the USA*, London 1990.

————. *Ernst Federn – Versuche zur Psychologie des Terrors*, Gießen 1999.

————. *Ein Leben mit der Psychoanalyse: Von Wien über Buchenwald und die USA zurück nach Wien*, Gießen 1999.

Feltrinelli, Carlo, *Senior Service*, New York 2001 (1999).

Ferares, Maurice, *De valsemunters*, n.p. 2005.

Ferrero, Ernesto, ed., *Primo Levi: Un antogia della critica*, Turin 1997.

Fetcher, Iring, ed., *Marxisten gegen Antisemitismus*, Hamburg 1974.

Fichaut, André, *Sur le point: Souvenirs d'un ouvrier trotskiste breton*, Paris 2003.

Fichter, Tilman and Lönnendonker, Siegward, *Macht und Ohnmacht der Studenten: Kleine Geschichte des SDS*, Hamburg 1998 (1977).

Fields, A. Belden, *Trotskyism and Maoism: Theory and Practice in France and the United States*, New York 1988.

Filoche, Gérard, *68–98: Histoire sans fin*, Paris 1998.

Fischer, George, ed., *The Revival of American Socialism: Selected Papers of the Socialist Scholars Conference*, New York 1971.

Flechtheim, Ossip K., ed., *Marx heute: Pro und contra*, Hamburg 1983.

Foitzik, Jan, *Zwischen den Fronten: Zur Politik, Organisation und Funktion linker politischer Kleinorganisationen im Widerstand 1933 bis 1993/40 unter besonderer Berücksichtigung des Exils*, Bonn 1986.

Frank, Pierre, *Le Stalinisme*, Paris 1977.

―――. *The Fourth International: The Long March of the Trotskyists*, London 1979 (1969).

Freeman, Christopher, ed., *Long Wave Theory*, Aldershot 1996.

Frey, Michèle, *Een joodse solidariteitsbeweging te Antwerpen: De Centrale, 1920–1940*, Ghent 1975.

Freyssat, Jean-Marie, Dupré, Michel and Ollivier, François, *Ce qu'est l'OCI*, Montreuil 1977.

Frölich, Paul, *Rosa Luxemburg: Gedanke und Tat*, Berlin 1990 (1939). (*Rosa Luxemburg: Her Life and Work*, London 1940)

Gadea, Hilda, *Che Guevara: Años decisivos*, Mexico City 1972.

Galbraith, John Kenneth, *The Great Crash, 1929*, Boston 1955.

―――. *The Affluent Society*, London 1962.

―――. *The New Industrial State*, Boston 1967.

Galle, Marc and Loccufier, Sylvain, eds, *Facetten van 100 jaar politieke, economische en sociale geschiedenis: Herdenking van de geboorte van Achiel Van Acker, 1898–1998*, Brussels 2000.

Garton Ash, Timothy, *The Polish Revolution: Solidarity*, London 1991 (1983).

Gavi, Philippe, *Che Guevara*, Paris 1970.

Gay, Peter, *Freud: A Life for Our Time*, New York 1988.

Gebhart, Walter [Ernest Mandel], *Die Wissenschaft der Entschleierung*, Berlin 1952.

Gellrich, Günther, *Die GIM: Zur Politik und Geschichte der Gruppe Internationale Marxisten 1969–1986*, Cologne 1999.

Georg Jungclas 1902–1975, Von der proletarischen Freidenkerjugend im Ersten Weltkrieg zur linken der siebziger Jahre: Eine politische Dokumentation, Hamburg 1980.

Gerard-Libois, Jules and Gotovitch, José, *La Belgique occupée: L'An 40*, Brussels 1971.

―――. *Leopold III, de l'an '40 à l'effacement*, Brussels 1991.

Gerard-Libois, Jules and Lewin, Rosine, *La Belgique entre dans la guerre froide et l'Europe (1947–1953)*, Brussels 1992.

Geras, Norman, *The Legacy of Rosa Luxemburg*, London 1976.

Gerassi, John, *Fidel Castro: A Biography*, New York 1973.

Germain, E. [Ernest Mandel], *Problèmes économiques de l'URSS: La société soviétique vue dans le miroir du dernier article de Staline*, Paris 1953.

Gide, André, *Retour de l'URSS*, Paris 1936.

Gilly, Adolfo, *Inside the Cuban Revolution*, New York 1964.

―――. *Pasiones cardinales*, Mexico 2001.

Glotzer, Albert, *Trotsky: Memoir and Critique*, Buffalo 1989.

Gluckstein, Daniel and Lambert, Pierre, *Itineraires*, Monaco 2002.

Glyn, Andrew and Sutcliffe, Bob, *British Capitalism, Workers and the Profit Squeeze*, Harmondsworth 1972.

Gorz, André, *Adieux au proletariat*, Paris 1980. (*Farewell to the Working Class: An Essay on Post-Industrial Socialism*, London 1982)

Gotovich, José, *Du Rouge au tricolore: Les communistes belges de 1939 à 1944*, Brussels 1992.

Gottdiener, M. and Koninos, Nicos, eds, *Capitalist Development and Crisis Theory: Accumulation, Regulation and Spatial Restructuring*, Basingstoke 1989.

Gottraux, Philippe, *'Socialisme ou barbarie': Un engagement politique et intellectuel dans la France de l'après-guerre*, Lausanne 1997.

Govaerts, Bert and Van Poele, Herman, eds, *De meesters van de westerse filosofie: Hegel, Marx, Nietzsche, Wittgenstein, Heidegger, Sartre, Levinas*, Brussels 1988.

Graf, Andreas G., ed., *Anarchisten gegen Hitler: Anarchisten, Anarcho-Syndicalisten, Rätekommunisten in Widerstand und Exil*, Berlin 2001.

Gramsci, Antonio, *Scritti politici*, Rome 1973. (*Selections from Political Writings 1910–1920*, London 1977, and *Selections from Political Writings 1921–1926*, London 1978)

———. *Passato e presente*, Rome 1977.

Grisoni, Dominique, ed., *Histoire du marxisme contemporain*, 5 vols, Paris 1979 (1973).

Grossmann, Henryk, *Das Akkumulations- und Zusammenbruchsgesetz des kapitalistischen Systems: Zugleich eine Krisentheorie*, Leipzig 1929.

Guevara, Ernesto Che, *Brief an das Exekutivsekretariat van OSPAAL*, Berlin 1968 (1960/1967). (*Che Guevara Speaks*, New York 1967)

———. *Oeuvres III: Textes politiques*, Paris 1968.

———. *Ecrits d'un révolutionnaire*, Montreuil-sur-Bois 1987. (Gerassi, John, ed., *Venceremos! The Speeches and Writings of Che Guevara*, London 1969)

———. *Der neue Mensch: Entwürfe für das Leben in der Zukunft*, Bonn 1997 (1984). (*Socialism and Man in Cuba*, Sydney 1988)

Habel, Janette, *Ruptures à Cuba: Le castrisme en crise*, Montreuil. (*Cuba: The Revolution in Peril*, London 1991)

Haffner, Sebastian, *Winston Churchill*, Reinbeck 1967. (*Winston Churchill*, London 2005)

Hamburger Institut für Sozialforschung 1984, Hamburg 1984.

Hamon, Hervé and Rotman, Patrick, *Les Porteurs de valises: La résistance française à la guerre d'Algérie*, Paris 1979.

———. *Génération*, vol. 1: *Les années de rêve*, Paris 1987.

Hamon, Hervé and Rotman, Patrick, *Génération*, vol. 2: *Les années de poudre*, Paris 1988.

Hansen, Joseph et al., *Leon Trotsky: The Man and His Work: Reminiscences and Appraisals*, New York 1969.

———. et al., *Portugal: L'Alternative*, Paris 1975.

Harbi, Mohammed, *Une Vie debout: Mémoires politiques*, Paris 2001.

Harman, Chris, *The Fire Last Time: 1968 and After*, London 1988.

Haroun, Ali, *La 7e Wilaya: La guerre du FLN en France, 1954–1962*, Paris 1986.

Havemann, Robert, *Dialektik ohne Dogma? Naturwissenschaft und Weltanschauung*, Hamburg 1964.

———. *Fragen Antworten Fragen*, Munich 1970. (*Questions, Answers, Questions: From the Biography of a German Marxist*, Garden City, NY 1972)

Hayman, Ronald, *Sartre: A Biography*, New York 1987.

Hemmerijckx, Rik, *Van verzet tot koude oorlog, 1940–1949: Machtsstrijd om het ABVV*, Brussels 2003.

Hilferding, Rudolf, *Das Finanzkapital: Eine Studie über die jüngste Entwicklung des Kapitalismus*, Vienna 1910.

Himmelstrand, Ulf, ed., *Interfaces in Economic and Social Analysis*, London 1992.

Hinzer, Jürgen, Schauer, Helmut and Segbers, Franz, eds, *Perspektiven der Linken: Ein kämperisches Leben im Zeitalter der Extreme*, Hamburg 2000.

Hippe, Oskar, *. . . Und unsere Fahn ist rot: Erinnerungen an sechzig Jahre in der Arbeiterbewegung*, Hamburg 1979.

Hodgson, Geoffrey M., *Trotsky and Fatalistic Marxism*, Nottingham 1975.

Hopkins, Terence K. and Wallerstein, Immanuel (eds), *Processes of the World-System*, Beverly Hills 1980.

Horowitz, David et al., *Het monopoliekapitaal: Beschouwingen over de opvattingen van Baran en Sweezy*, Amsterdam 1970.

Horowitz, David, ed., *Isaac Deutscher: The Man and His Work*, London 1971.

Hunter, Bill, *Lifelong Apprenticeship: The Life and Times of a Revolutionary*, London 1997.

James P. Cannon, 1890–1974: A Political Tribute, New York 1974.

Jameson, Fredric, *Late Marxism: Adorno, or the Persistence of the Dialectic*, London 1990.

———. *Postmodernism, or, the Cultural Logic of Late Capitalism*, Durham 1999.

Jaspers, Karl, *Die Schuldfrage*, Heidelberg 1946. (*The Question of German Guilt*, New York 2000)

Jay, Martin, *The Dialectical Imagination: A History of the Frankfurt School and the Institute of Social Research 1923–1950*, Boston 1973.

Jeanson, Francis, *Notre guerre*, Paris 2001.

Jenkins, Peter, *Where Trotskyism Got Lost: The Restoration of European Democracy after the Second World War*, Nottingham 1977.

Joffe, Adolf Abramovic, *The Last Words of Adolf Joffe: A Letter to Leon Trotsky*, Colombo 1950.

Journès, Claude, *L'extrême gauche en Grande-Bretagne*, Paris 1977.

Jünke, Christoph, ed., *Am Beispiel Leo Koflers: Marxismus im 20. Jahrhundert*, Münster 2001.

Just, Stéphane, *Der Kampf für den Wiederaufbau der IV Internationale (1953–1980)*, Dortmund 1980 (1978/1979).

Kahn, Lothar, *Insight and Action: The Life and Work of Lion Feuchtwanger*, New Jersey 1975.

Kalecki, Michal, *Theory of Economic Dynamics: An Essay on Cyclical and Long-Run Changes in Capitalist Economy*, London 1954.

Kalfon, Pierre, *Che: Ernesto Guevara, une legende du siècle*, Paris 1997.

Kalshoven, Frank: *Over marxistische economie in Nederland, 1883–1939*, Amsterdam 1993.

Kaplan, E. Ann and Sprinker, Michael, eds, *The Althusserian Legacy*, London 1993.

Karl, Michaela, *Rudi Dutschke: Revolutionär ohne Revolution*, Frankfurt on Main 2003.

Keizer, Madalon de, *Het Parool 1940–1945: Verzetsblad in oorlogstijd*, Amsterdam 1991.

Keller, Fritz, *In den Gulag von Ost und West: Karl Fischer Arbeiter und Revolutionär*, Frankfurt on Main 1980.

Kellner, Manuel, *Kapitalismusanalyse, Bürokratiekritik und sozialistische Strategie bei Ernest Mandel*, Marburg 2005.

Kende, Pierre and Pomian, Krzysztof, eds, *1956: Varsovie-Budapest: La deuxième revolution d'octobre*, Paris 1978.

Keyes, Roger, *Echec au Roi: Leopold III 1940–1951*, Paris 1986.

Kidron, Michael, *Western Capitalism Since the War*, London 1968.

———. *Capitalism and Theory*, London 1974.

Klein, Thomas, Otto, Wilfriede and Grieder, Peter, *Visionen: Repression und Opposition in der SED (1949–1989)*, 2 vols, Frankfurt on Oder 1997.

Kleinknecht, Alfred, Mandel, Ernest and Wallerstein, Immanuel, eds, *New Findings in Long Wave Research*, Houndmills 1992.

Kolakowski, Leszek, *Main Currents of Marxism: Its Rise, Growth and Dissolution*, Oxford 1978.

Kößler, Gottfried, Rieben, Angelika and Gürsching, Feli, eds, *. . . dass wir nicht erwünscht waren: Novemberpogrom 1938 in Frankfurt am Main*, Frankfurt on Main 1993.

Kondratieff, Nicolai Dimitrievitch, *Les Grands cycles de la conjuncture*, Paris 1992.

———. *The Works of Nikolai D. Kondratiev*, vol. 1: *Economic Statics, Dynamics and Conjuncture*, London 1998.

Korsch, Karl, *Briefe 1908–1939*, Amsterdam 2001.

———. *Briefe 1940–1958*, Amsterdam 2001.

Kowalewski, Zbigniew M., *Guerrilla estratégica: Vanguardia y método de movilización campesina*, Caracas 1971.

———. *Guerrila latyno-ameryka'nska: Szkize z dziejów rewolucyjnych walk partyzanckich XX wieku*, Wroclaw 1978.

———. *Rendez-nous nos usines! Solidarnosc dans le combat pour l'autogestion ouvrière*, Montreuil 1985.

Kowalewski, Zbigniew M. and Sobrado, Miguel, *Antropología de la guerilla: Hacia la ciencia social der Tercer Mundo*, Caracas 1971.

Krahl, Hans-Jürgen, *Konstitution und Klassenkampf: Zur historischen Dialektik von bürgerlicher Emanzipation und proletarischer Revolution*, Frankfurt on Main 1977 (1971).

Kraushaar, Wolfgang, *Die Protest-Chronik 1949–1959: Eine illustrierte Geschichte von Bewegung, Widerstand und Utopie*, 3 vols, Hamburg 1996.

Kraushaar, Wolfgang, ed., *Frankfurterschule und Studentenbewegung: Von der Flaschenpost zum Molotowcocktail, 1946–1995*, 3 vols, Frankfurt on Main 1998.

———. *1968: das Jahr, das alles verandert hat*, Munich 1998.

———. *1968 als Mythos, Chiffre und Zäsur*, Hamburg 2000.

Kraushaar, Wolfgang, Wieland, Karin and Reemtsma, Jan Philipp, *Rudi Dutschke, Andreas Baader und die RAF*, Hamburg 2005.

Krauss, Christine and Küchenmeister, Daniel, eds, *Das Jahr 1945: Brüche und Kontinuitäten*, Berlin 1995.

Krivine, Alain and Bensaïd, Daniel, *Mai si!: 1968–1988, rebelles et repentis*, Montreuil 1988.

Krivine, Alain, *Ça te passera avec l'âge*, Paris 2006.

Kröhnke, Karl, *Lion Feuchtwanger – Der Asthet in der Sowjetunion: Ein Buch nicht nur für seine Freunde*, Stuttgart 1991.

Kuron, Jacek, *Glaube und Schuld: Einmal Kommunismus und zurück*, Berlin 1991.

Kurowski, Lutz [Leszek Kolakowski], *Buch der Freunde: Geburtstag von Harry Schulze-Wilde*, Ottobrunn 1969.

Kuschey, Bernhard, *Die Ausnahme des Überlebens: Ernst und Hilde Federn: Eine biographische Studie und eine Analyse der Binnenstrukturen des Konzentrationslagers*, 2 vols, Gießen 2003.

Lagrou, Pieter, *The Legacy of Nazi Occupation: Patriotic Memory and National Recovery in Western Europe 1945–1965*, Cambridge 2000.

Lambilliotte, Maurice, *André Renard et son destin*, Brussels 1971.

Lambrechts, Danielle, *Sluikpers in de provincie Antwerpen tijdens de Tweede Wereldoorlog*, 1977.

Landes, David S., *The Unbound Prometheus: Technological Change and Industrial Development in Western Europe from 1750 to the Present*, Cambridge 1969.

Lange, Oskar, *À propos de certaines questions concernant la voie polonaise du socialisme,-* Varsovie 1957.

Die lange Wellen der Konjunktuur: Beiträge zur Marxistischen Konjunktur- und Krisentheorie, Berlin 1972.

Laqueur, Walter, *The Terrible Secret*, London 1980.

Last, Jef, *Mijn vriend André Gide*, Amsterdam 1966.

Latteur, Nicolas, *La Gauche en mal de la Gauche*, Brussels 2000.

Lefèbvre, Henri., *Critique de la Vie Quotidienne*, vol. 1: *Introduction*, Paris 1958 (1947). (*Critique of Everyday Life*, 3 vols, London 2008)

Lefèbvre, Renaud, *Dauge et le daugisme: Un page de l'histoire du mouvement ouvrier dans le Borinage*, Brussels 1979.

Lefort, Claude, *Elements d'une critique de la bureaucratie*, Geneva 1971.

Leggewie, Claus, *Kofferträger: das Algerien-Projekt der Linken im Adenauer-Deutschland*, Berlin 1984.

Le Grève, Pierre, *Souvenirs d'un marxiste anti-stalinien*, Paris 1996.

Lenin, Vladimir I., *Keuze uit zijn werken*, 3 vols, Moscow 1975. (*Collected Works*, 38 vols, Moscow 1964)

————. *Revolution und Politik*, Frankfurt on Main 1970.

Lentin, Albert-Paul, *La Lutte tricontinentale: Impérialisme et révolution après la conférence de la Havane*, Paris 1966.

Léon, Abraham [Abraham Wajnsztock], *La Conception matérialiste de la Question Juive*, Paris 1968 (1942/1946). (*The Jewish Question: A Marxist Interpretation*, Mexico City 1950)

Le Paige, Hugues and Delwit, Pascal, eds, *Les Socialistes et le pouvoir: Gouverner pour reformer?*, Brussels 1998.

Lequenne, Michel, *Le Trotskisme: Une histoire sans fard*, Paris 2005.

Lethen, Helmut, *Der Sound der Väter: Gottfried Benn und seine Zeit*, Berlin 2006.

Levi, Primo, *Se questo è un uomo*, Turin 1958. (*If This Is a Man*, New York 1959)

Liebman, Marcel, *Né Juif: Une famille juive pendant la guerre*, Paris 1977.

Liebman, Marcel, Gotovitch, José and Van Doorslaer, Rudi, *Een geschiedenis van het Belgische kommunisme, 1921–1945*, Ghent 1980.

Lin, Chun, *The British New Left*, Edinburgh 1993.

Lönnendonker, Siegward, Rabehl, Bernd and Staadt, Jochen, *Die anti-authoritäre Revolte: Der Sozialistische Deutsche Studentenbund nach der Trennung von der SPD*, Wiesbaden 2002.

Lorenz, Einhart, *Willy Brandt in Norwegen: Die Jahre des Exils 1933 bis 1940*, Kiel 1989.

Lorneau, Marcel, *Contribution à l'Histoire du mouvement trotskyste belge 1939–1960*, 4 vol, Liège 1982–3.

Lotz, Corinna and Feldmann, Paul, *Gerry Healy: A Revolutionary Life*, London 1994.

Louçã, Francisco, *Turbulence in Economics: An Evolutionary Appraisal of Cycles and Complexes in Historical Processes*, Cheltenham 1997.

Löwy, Michael, *La Pensée de Che Guevara*, Paris 1970.

———. *The Marxism of Che Guevara: Philosophy, Economics and Revolutionary Warfare*, New York 1973.

———. *Pour une sociologie des intellectuels révolutionnaires: L'évolution politique de Lukács 1909–1929*, Paris 1976. (*Georg Lukács: From Romanticism to Bolshevism*, London 1979)

———. *Marxisme et romantisme révolutionnaire: Essais sur Lukács et Rosa Luxemburg*, Paris 1979.

———. *Rédemption et Utopie: Le judaïsme libertaire en Europe centrale*, Paris 1988. (*Redemption and Utopia: Jewish Libertarian Thought in Central Europe: A Study in Elective Affinity*, London 1992)

———. ed., *Marxism in Latin America from 1909 to the Present: An Anthology*, Atlantic Highlands, NJ 1993.

———. *On Changing the World: Essays in Political Philosophy, from Karl Marx to Walter Benjamin*, London 1993.

Lukács, Georg, *Geschichte und Klassenbewusstsein*, Berlin 1923. (*History and Class Consciousness: Studies in Marxist Dialectics*, Cambridge, MA 1971)

———. *Lenin: Studie über den Zusammenhang seiner Gedanken*, Vienna 1924. (*Lenin: A Study of the Unity of His Thought*, London 1970)

Lustig, Michael M., *Trotsky and Djilas: Critics of Communist Bureaucracy*, New York 1989.

Luxemburg, Rosa, *Die Akkumulation des Kapitals: Ein Beitrag zur ökonomischen Erklärung des Imperialismus*, Berlin 1913. (*The Accumulation of Capital: An Anti-Critique*, New York 1972)

———. *Rosa Luxemburg Speaks*, New York 1970.

———. *Gesammelte Briefe*, 5 vols, Berlin 1984. (*The Letters of Rosa Luxemburg*, Boulder 1978)

Maddison, Angus, *Ontwikkelingsfasen van het kapitalisme*, Utrecht 1982.

———. *Dynamic Forces in Capitalist Development: A Long Run Comparative View*, Oxford 1991.

Maitan, Livio, Blanco, Hugo and Mandel, Ernest, *Réformisme militaire et lutte armée en Amérique Latine*, Paris 1971.

Maitan, Livio, *La strada percorsa: Dalla resistenza ai nuovi movimenti: Lettura critica e scelte alternative*, Bolsena 2002.

[Mandel, Ernest], *Only Victorious Socialist Revolutions Can Prevent the Third World War!* New York 1946.

Mandel, Ernest, *Traité d'économie marxiste*, 2 vols, Paris 1962 (revised edition, 4 vols, Paris 1969). (*Marxist Economic Theory*, 2 vols, New York 1968)

———. *Vive Cuba: Impressions de Cuba*, Toronto 1964.

———. *Initiation à la théorie économique marxiste*, Paris 1964. (*Introduction to Marxist Economic Theory*, New York 1967)

————. *Die Bürokratie*, Frankfurt on Main 1976 (1965, 1967/1970). (*On Bureaucracy*, London 1973)

————. *La Formation de la pensée économique de Karl Marx, de 1843 jusqu'a la rédaction du 'Capital': Etude génétique*, Paris 1967. (*The Formation of the Economic Thought of Karl Marx: 1843 to 'Capital'*, New York 1971)

————. *Die EWG und die Konkurrenz Europa-Amerika*, Frankfurt on Main 1968.

————. *Die deutsche Wirtschaftskrise: Lehren der Rezession 1966/1967*, Frankfurt on Main 1969.

————. *The Marxist Theory of the State*, Bombay 1979 (1969).

————. and Novack, George, *On the Revolutionary Potential of the Working Class*, New York 1970.

————. *Contrôle ouvrier, conseils ouvriers, autogestion: Anthologie*, Paris 1970.

————. *Contrôle ouvrier et stratégie révolutionnaire*, Brussels 1970.

————. *Europe versus America? Contradictions of Imperialism*, London 1970.

————. and Novack, George, *The Marxist Theory of Alienation*, New York 1970.

————. *The Leninist Theory of Organization: Its Relevance for Today*, London 1971 (1970).

————. *Die Rolle der Intelligenz im Klassenkampf*, Frankfurt on Main 1975 (1970).

————. *Der Spätkapitalismus, Versuch einer marxistischen Erklärung*, Frankfurt on Main 1972. (*Late Capitalism*, London 1978)

————. *Vervreemding en revolutionaire perspectieven: Zes essays*, Amsterdam 1973.

[Mandel, Ernest], *Von der soziale Ungleichheit zur klassenlosen Gesellschaft*, n.p. [Zurich?] n.d. [1973]. (*From Class Society to Communism: An Introduction to Marxism*, London 1977)

————. *Kontroversen um 'Das Kapital'*, Berlin 1991 (1976, 1978, 1981).

————. *La Longue marche de la Révolution*, Paris 1976.

————. and Wolf, Winfried, *Weltwirtschaftsrezession und BRD-Krise 1974/75*, Frankfurt on Main 1976.

————. *Austerità come modello di sviluppo: La proposta economica del PCI*, Milan 1977.

————. *Ende der Krise oder Krise ohne Ende? Bilanz der Wirtschaftsrezession und der Krise in der Bundesrepublik*, Berlin 1977.

————. *Las tres dimensiones del 'eurocommunismo': Santiago Carillo y la naturaleza de la URSS*, Barcelona 1977.

————. and Weinstock, Nathan, *Zur jüdischen Frage: Beiträge zu Abraham Léons Judenfrage und Kapitalismus*, Frankfurt on Main 1977.

————. *La Crise 1974–1978: Les faits, leur interpretation marxiste*, Paris 1978.

————. *Critique de l'eurocommunisme*, Paris 1978. (*From Stalinism to Eurocommunism: The Bitter Fruits of 'Socialism in One Country'*, London 1978)

————. *Long Waves of Capitalist Development: The Marxist Interpretation*, London 1980 (1978) (revised edition, with subtitle *A Marxist Interpretation*, 1995)

————. *Revolutionäre strategien im 20 Jahrhundert*, Vienna 1978.

————. *The Second Slump: A Marxist Analysis of Recession in the Seventies*, London 1978.

————. *Réponse à Louis Althusser et Jean Ellenstein*, Paris 1979.

————. *Revolutionary Marxism Today*, London 1979.

————. *Trotsky: A Study in the Dynamic of His Thought*, London 1979.

————. *De economische theorie van het marxisme*, 2 vols, Bussum 1980.

————. *Revolutionärer Marxismus heute*, Frankfurt on Main 1982.

————. *Delightful Murder: A Social History of the Crime Story*, London 1984.

————. *K. Marx: Die Aktualität seines Werkes*, Frankfurt on Main 1984.

————. and Freeman, Alan, eds, *Ricardo, Marx, Sraffa: The Langston Memorial Volume*, London 1984.

————. *The Meaning of the Second World War*, London 1986.

————. and Radek, Karl, *Rosa Luxemburg: Leben, Kampf, Tod*, Frankfurt on Main 1986.

————. and Wolf, Winfried, *Börsenkrach & Wirtschaftskrise*, Frankfurt on Main 1988.

————. and Wolf, Winfried, *Cash, Crash and Crisis: Profitboom, Börsenkrach & Wirtschaftskrise*, Hamburg 1989.

————. *Où va l'URSS de Gorbatchev*, Montreuil 1989. (*Beyond Perestroika: The Future of Gorbachev's USSR*, London 1989)

————. *October 1917: Coup d'état or Social Revolution? The Legitimacy of the Russian Revolution*, Amsterdam 1992.

————. *Power and Money: A Marxist Theory of Bureaucracy*, London 1992.

————. *Trotzki als Alternative*, Berlin 1992. (*Trotsky As Alternative*, London 1995)

————. *Revolutionary Marxism and Social Reality in the 20th Century: Collected Essays*, New York 1994.

Marcuse, Herbert, *Eros and Civilization: A Philosophical Inquiry into Freud*, Boston 1955.

————. *One-Dimensional Man*, Boston 1964.

Marie, Jean-Jacques, *Le Trotskysme*, Paris 1970.

————. *Trotsky, le trotskysme et la Quatrième Internationale*, Paris 1980.

————. *Le Trotskysme et les trotskystes*, Paris 2002.

Marrus, Michael R., *The Holocaust in History*, London 1987.

Marwick, Arthur, *The Sixties: Cultural Revolution in Britain, France, Italy and the United States c.1958–c.1974*, Oxford 1998.

Marx, Karl, 'Zur Kritik der Hegelschen Rechtsphilosophie: Einleitung', in: Marx, Karl and Engels, Friedrich, *Werke*, vol. 1, Berlin 1956 (1844). ('Contribution to the Critique of Hegel's Philosophy of Law: Introduction', in Marx, Karl and Engels, Friedrich, *Collected Works*, vol. 3, New York 1975)

————. *Das Elend der Philosophie: Antwort auf Proudhons 'Philosophie des Elends'*, Stuttgart 1921 (1847/1885). (*The Poverty of Philosophy: Answer to the Philosophy of Poverty by M. Proudhon*, in Marx, Karl and Engels, Friedrich, *Collected Works*, vol. 6, New York 1976)

————. *Grundrisse der Kritik der politischen Ökonomie: Rohentwurf, 1857–1858*, 2 vols, Berlin 1953 (1939/1941). (*Collected Works*, vols 28–9, New York 1986–7)

————. and Engels, Friedrich, *Kleine ökonomische Schriften*, Berlin 1955.

————. *Capital: A Critique of Political Economy*, 3 vols, London 1976–81.

Massari, Roberto, *Che Guevara: Politik und Utopie, das politische und philosophische Denken Ernesto Che Guevaras*, Frankfurt on Main 1987.

Mattick, Paul, Rabehl, Bernd, Tynjanow, Juri and Mandel, Ernest, *Lenin: Revolution und Politik*, Frankfurt on Main 1970.

Mattick, Paul, *Kritik der Neomarxisten*, Frankfurt on Main 1974.

Mauke, Michael, *Die Klassentheorie von Marx und Engels*, Frankfurt on Main 1970.

Mayer, Hans, *Außenseiter*, Frankfurt on Main 1975.

Méndez, Eugenio, *Santucho: Entre la inteligenzia y las armas*, Buenos Aires 1999.

Merleau-Ponty, Maurice, *Les Aventures de la dialectique*, Paris 1955. (*Adventures of the Dialectic*, Evanston 1973)

Merlier, Michel [Auguste Maurel], *Le Congo: De la colonisation belge à l'independence*, Paris 1992 (1962).

Meschkat, Klaus, *Die Pariser Kommune von 1871 im Spiegel der soujetische Geschichtschreibung*, Berlin 1965.

Mesnil, Christian, *La Question royale: Textes et photographies*, Brussels 1978.

Meyer-Leviné, Rosa, *Leviné: Leben und Tod eines Revolutionärs: Erinnerungen*, Munich 1972. (*Leviné: The Life of a Revolutionary*, Farnborough 1973)

Meynaud, Jean, Ladière, Jean and Perin, François, *La Décision politique en Belgique: Le pouvoir et les groupes*, Paris 1965.

Meynen, Alain, *Van Praag 1948 tot Vilvoorde 1954: Politieke biografische gesprekken met Louis van Geyt*, Brussels 2001.

Michels, Robert, *Zur Soziologie des Parteiwesens*, Stuttgart 1989 (1911). (*Political Parties: A Sociological Study of the Oligarchical Tendencies of Modern Democracy*, Glencoe, IL 1949)

Miermeister, Jürgen, *Rudi Dutschke mit Selbstzeugnissen und Bilddokumenten*, Reinbek 1986.

———. *Ernst Bloch, Rudi Dutschke*, Hamburg 1996.

Minguet, Simone, *Mes années Caudron: Caudron-Renault, une usine autogerée à la liberation (1944–1948)*, Paris 1997.

Modzelewski, Karol and Kuron, Jacek, *Lettre ouverte au Parti Ouvrier Polonais*, 1966. (*Solidarnosc, the Missing Link: A New Edition of Poland's Classic Revolutionary Socialist Manifesto: Kuron and Modzelewski's Open Letter to the Party*, London 1982)

Mohl, Ernst Theodor et al., *Folgen einer theorie: Essays über 'Das Kapital' von Karl Marx*, Frankfurt on Main 1967.

Moneta, Jakob, *Mehr Macht für die Ohnemächtigen: Reden und Aufsätze*, Frankfurt on Main 1991.

Moreau, François, *Combats et débats de la IVe Internationale*, Québec 1993.

Morf, Otto, *Geschichte und Dialektik in der politischen Ökonomie: Zum Verhältnis von Wirtschaftstheorie und Wirtschaftsgeschichte bei Karl Marx*, Frankfurt on Main 1970.

Morishima, Michio, *Marx's Economics: A Dual Theory of Value and Growth*, Cambridge 1973.

Müller, Silvia and Florath, Bernd, eds, *Die Entlassung: Robert Havemann und die Akademie der Wissenschaften 1965/66*, Berlin 1996.

Münster, Arno, *L'Utopie concrète d'Ernst Bloch: Une biographie*, Paris 2001.

Myers, Constance Ashton, *The Prophet's Army: Trotskyists in America, 1928–1941*, Westport, CT 1977.

Myrdal, Gunnar, *The Political Element in the Development of Economic Theory*, London 1953 (1930/1932).

Naville, Pierre, *Le Nouveau Leviathan*, vol. 1: *De l'alienation à la jouissance, la genese de la sociologie du travail chez Marx et Engels*, Paris 1957.

Nedava, Joseph, *Trotsky and the Jews*, Philadelphia 1972.

Negt, Oskar, *Achtundsechzig: Politische Intellektuelle und die Macht*, Göttingen 1995.

Nelson, Cary, *Repression and Recovery: Modern American Poetry and the Politics of Cultural Memory, 1910–1945*, New York 1989.

Neuville, Jean and Yerna, Jacques, *Le Choc de l'hiver 60–61: Les grèves contre la loi unique*, Brussels 1990.

Newman, Michael, *Ralph Miliband and the Politics of the New Left*, London 2002.

Nick, Christophe, *Les Trotskistes*, Paris 2003.

Nicolaus, Martin, *Die Objektivität des Imperialismus: Anti-Mandel /* Mandel, Ernest, *Die Wiedersprüche des Imperialismus*, Berlin 1971.

Nikolic, Milo, ed., *Socialism on the Threshold of the Twenty-First Century*, London 1985.

1979 World Congress of the Fourth International: Major Resolutions and Reports, 1980.

Nolte, Ernst, *Das Vergehen der Vergangenheit: Antwort an meine Kritiker im sogenannten Historikerstreit*, Berlin 1987.

Norden, Jan, *Yugoslavia, East Europe and the Fourth International: The Evolution of Pabloist Liquidationism*, New York 1993.

North, David, *Gerry Healy and his Place in the History of the Fourth International*, Detroit 1991.

Novack, George, *Understanding History: Marxist Essays*, New York 1972.

Nove, Alec, *An Economic History of the USSR*, Aylesbury 1972 (1969).

————. *The Economics of Feasible Socialism*, London 1983.

Paris Mai 1968, Munich 1968.

Parvus [Israël Lazaarevich (Alexander) Helphand], *Die Handelskrisis und die Gewerkschaften*, Munich 1901.

Pattieu, Sylvain, *Les Camarades des Frères: Trotskistes et libertaires dans la guerre d'Algérie*, Paris 2002.

Perrault, Gilles, *Un Homme à part: Biographie d'Henri Curiel*, Paris 1984.

Plänkers, Thomas and Federn, Ernst, *Vertreibung und Rückkehr: Interviews zur Geschichte Ernst Federns und der Psychoanalyse*, Tübingen 1994.

Plekhanov, Georgii Valentinovich, *Selected Philosophical Works*, 5 vols, Moscow 1976.

Plenel, Edwy, *Secrèts de jeunesse*, Paris 2001.

Plogstedt, Sibylle, ed., *Internationaler Vietnam-Kongress: Februar 1968, West-Berlin*, Hamburg 1987 (1968).

————. *Im Netz der Gedichte: Gefangen in Prag nach 1968*, Berlin 2001.

Pluet-Despatin, Jacqueline, *Les Trotskistes et la guerre 1940–1944*, Paris 1980.

Poretsky, Elisabeth K., *Our Own People: A Memoir of 'Ignace Reiss' and His Friends*, London 1969.

Posadistische Kommunistische Partei, *Informationsbulletin über den Tod des Genossen J. Posadas*, Frankfurt on Main n.d. [ca. 1981].

Pour un portrait de Pierre Frank: Ecrits et témoignages, Paris 1985.

Prager, Rodolphe, ed., *Les Congrès de la Quatrième Internationale: 1, Naissance de la IVe Internationale: (1930–1940)*, Paris 1978.

————. ed., *Les Congrès de la Quatrième Internationale: 2, L'Internationale dans la guerre (1940–1946)*, Paris 1981.

————. ed., *Les Congrès de la Quatrième Internationale: 3, Bouleversement et crises de l'après-guerre (1946–1950)*, Paris 1988.

————. ed., *Les Congrès de la Quatrième Internationale: 4, Menace de la troisième guerre mondiale et tournant politique (1950–1952)*, Paris 1989.

Préobrajenskij, Eugène, *La Nouvelle économique*, Paris 1966 (1926).

Prévan, Guy, *Benjamin Péret: Révolutionnaire permanent*, Paris 1999.

Prowizur-Szyper, Claire, *Conte à rebours: Une resistante juive sous l'occupation*, Brussels 1979.

La Question coloniale et la section française de la IVe Internationale: De la création de la IVe Internationale à la guerre d'Algérie, Paris 1973.

Rabehl, Bernd, *Feindblick: Der SDS im Fadenkreuz des 'Kalten Krieges'*, Berlin 2000.

——. *Rudi Dutschke: Revolutionär im geteilten Deutschland*, Dresden 2002.

Les Réformes de structures: 10 ans après le Congrès extraordinaire de la FGTB, Liège 1965.

Reisner, Will, ed., *Documents of the Fourth International: The Formative Years (1933–40)*, New York 1973.

Renard, André, *Vers le socialisme par l'action*, Liège 1958.

Resch, Robert Paul, *Althusser and the Renewal of Marxist Social Theory*, Berkeley 1992.

La Résistance et les Européens du Nord, vol. 1, Brussels 1994.

Resnick, Stephen and Wolff, Richard D., eds, *Rethinking Marxism: Struggles in Marxist Theory, Essays for Harry Magdoff and Paul Sweezy*, New York 1985.

Resolutions of the Twelfth World Congress of the Fourth International, Montreuil 1985.

Revolt in France, May-June 1968: On-the-Spot Reports and Interviews, Articles and Analyses, New York 1968.

Richardson, Al, ed., *A Paradise for Capitalism? Class and Leadership in Twentieth-Century Belgium*, London 1998.

Rioux, Lucien, *Le Nouvel Observateur: Des Bons et des Mauvais Jours*, Paris 1982.

Roberti, Jean-Marie, *Dossier Ernest Glinne*, Chenée 1974.

Robrieux, Philippe, *Notre generation communiste 1953–1968*, Paris 1977.

——. *Histoire intérieure du Parti communiste*, 4 vols, Paris 1980–4.

Rosdolsky, Roman, *Untertan und Staat in Galizien: Die Reformen unter Maria Theresia und Joseph II*, Mainz 1992 (1939/1962).

——. *Zur nationalen Frage: Friederich Engels und das Problem der 'geschichtlosen' Völker*, Berlin 1979 (1964).

——. *Zur Entstehungsgeschichte des Marxschen 'Kapital': Der Rohentwurf des 'Kapital' 1857–1858*, Frankfurt on Main 1968. (*The Making of Marx's Capital*, London 1977)

Rosenthal, Gérard, *Avocat de Trotsky*, Paris 1975.

Ross, Kristin, *May '68 and its Afterlives*, Chicago 2002.

Rousset, David, *L'Univers Concentrationnaire*, Paris 1946.

——. *Les Jours de notre mort*, Paris 1947.

Rubin, Isaak Iljitsch, *Studien zur Marxschen Werttheorie*, Frankfurt on Main 1973 (1928/1972).

Sabrov, Martin, ed., *Skandal und Diktatur: Formen öffentlicher Empörung im NS-Staat und in der DDR*, Göttingen 2004.

Saerens, Lieven, *Vreemdelingen in een wereldstad, een geschiedenis van Antwerpen en zijn joodse bevolking (1880–1944)*, Tielt 2000.

Samary, Catherine, *Le Marche contre l'autogestion: L'experience yougoslave*, Paris 1988.

——. *Plan, Marché, Démocratie: L'Expériences des pays dits socialistes*, Amsterdam 1988. (*Plan, Market, Democracy: The Experience of the So-Called Socialist Countries*, Amsterdam 1988)

Sandford, George, ed., *The Solidarity Congress, 1981: The Great Debate*, Basingstoke 1990.

Santen, Sal, *Adiós compañeros! Politieke herinneringen*, Amsterdam 1974.

——. *Dapper omdat het goed is: Brieven uit de cel*, Amsterdam 1993.

Santucho, Mario Roberto, *Poder burgés y poder revolucionario*, Buenos Aires 1988 (1974).

Sartre, Jean-Paul, *Réflexions sur la question juive*, Paris 1946. (*Anti-Semite and Jew*, New York 1970)

———. *Situations, VI: Problèmes du marxisme, 1*, Paris 1964.

———. *Situations, VII: Problèmes du marxisme, 2*, Paris 1964.

———. *Situations, VIII: Autour de 68*, Paris 1964.

Scheurer, Georg, *Nur Narren fürchten nichts: Szenen aus dem dreißigjährigen Krieg, 1915–1945*, Vienna 1991.

Schneider, Wolfgang, ed., *'Vernichtungspolitik': Eine Debatte über den Zusammenhang von Sozialpolitik und Genozid im nationalsozialistischen Deutschland*, Hamburg 1971.

Schneiders, Paul, *Het Larense geval: Een vluchtelingen affaire*, Amsterdam n.d.

Schreiber, Jean-Philippe, ed., *Dictionnaire biographique des Juifs de Belgique: Figures du judaïsme belge, XIX–XXe siècles*, Brussels 2002.

Schüle, Annegret, *Trotzkismus in Deutschland bis 1933: 'Für die Arbeitereinheitsfront zur Abwehr des Faschismus'*, Cologne 1989.

Schumpeter, Joseph A., *The Theory of Economic Development: An Inquiry into Profits, Capital, Credit, Interest, and the Business Cycle*, New York 1961 (1934/1912/1926).

———. *Business Cycles: A Theoretical, Historical and Statistical Analysis of the Capitalist Process*, New York 1939.

Seale, Patrick and McConville, Maureen, *Red Flag/Black Flag: French Revolution, 1968*, Harmondsworth 1968.

Sering, Paul [Richard Löwenthal], *Jenseits des Kapitalismus: Ein Beitrag zur sozialistischen Neuorientierung*, Lauf bei Nürnberg 1946.

Silverman, Bertram, ed., *Man and Socialism in Cuba: The Great Debate*, New York 1971.

Slaughter, Cliff, ed., *Trotskyism versus Revisionism: A Documentary History*, 6 vols, New York 1974.

Sofri, Gianni, *Über asiatische Produktionsweise: Zur Geschichte einer strittigen Kategorie der Kritik der politischen Ökonomie*, Frankfurt on Main 1972 (1969).

Sonntag, Heinz Rudolph, ed., *Che Guevara und die Revolution*, Frankfurt on Main 1968.

Soziale oder sozialistische Demokratie? Beiträge zur Geschichte der Linken in der Bundesrepublik: Freundesgabe für Peter von Oertzen zum 65. Geburtstag, Marburg 1989.

Spatzenegger, Hans, ed., *Das verspielte 'Kapital'? Die marxistische Ideologie nach dem Scheitern des realen Sozialismus*, Salzburg 1991.

Sraffa, Piero, *Production of Commodities by Means of Commodities: Prelude to a Critique of Economic Theory*, Cambridge 1960.

Stedman Jones, Gareth, Löwy, Michael et al., *Western Marxism: A Critical Reader*, London 1977.

Steedman, Ian, *Marx after Sraffa*, London 1977.

Steedman, Ian et al., *The Value Controversy*, London 1981.

Steehaut, Wouter, *De Unie van Hand- en Geestesarbeiders: Een onderzoek naar het optreden van de vakbonden in de bezettingsjaren*, 3 vols, Ghent 1982–3.

Steinberg, Maxime, *L'Étoile et la fusil: La question juive 1940–1942*, Brussels 1983.

———. *L'Étoile et la fusil: 1942: Les cent jours de la déportations des juifs de Belgique*, Brussels 1984.

Stengers, Jean, *Leopold III et le gouvernement: Les deux politiques belges de 1940*, Paris 1980.

Stinas, Agis, *Mémoires: Un Révolutionnaire dans la Grèce du XXe siècle*, Paris 1990.

Stock, Ernst and Walcher, Karl, *Jacob Walcher (1887–1970): Gewerkschaftler und Revolutionär zwischen Berlin, Paris und New York*, Berlin 1999.

Stutje, Jan Willem, *De man die de weg wees: Leven en werk van Paul de Groot 1899–1986*, Amsterdam 2000.

Sweezy, Paul M., *The Theory of Capitalist Development: Principles of Marxian Political Economy*, London 1946 (1942).

Sweig, Julia E., *Inside the Cuban Revolution: Fidel Castro and the Urban Underground*, Cambridge, MA 2002.

Syré, Ludger, *Isaac Deutscher, Marxist, Publizist, Historiker: Sein Leben und Werk 1907–1967*, Hamburg 1984.

Szulc, Tad, *Fidel: A Critical Portrait*, London 1987.

Tablada Perez, Carlos, *Che Guevara: Economics and Politics in the Transition to Socialism*, New York 1990.

Tarrow, Sidney, *Power in Movement: Social Movements and Contentious Politics*, Cambridge 1998.

Thalmann, Clara and Thalmann, Paul, *Revolution für die Freiheit: Stationen eines politischen Kampfes*, Grafenau-Döffingen 1987 (1974).

Thanassekos, Yannis and Wismann, Heinz, eds, *Révision de l'Histoire: Totalitarisme, crimes et génocides Nazis*, Paris 1990.

Thio, Boe and Mandel, Ernest, *Debat Thio (CPN) – Mandel (4e Int.): Wie betaalt de crisis?*, Amsterdam, n.d. [ca. 1982.]

Thirty Years of New Left Review (1960–1990), London 1992.

Thompson, Edward P., *The Making of the English Working Class*, London 1963.

Ticktin, Hillel and Cox, Michael, eds, *The Ideas of Leon Trotsky*, London 1995.

Tilly, Pierre, *André Renard: Biographie*, Brussels 2005.

Tourish, Dennis and Wohlforth, Tim, *On the Edge: Political Cults Right and Left*, Armonk 2000.

Towards a History of the Fourth International, 2 vols, New York 1973–1978.

Traverso, Enzo, *Lev Davidovich Bronstein (Trotsky): The Itinerary of a Non-Jewish Jew*, n.p. n.d.

———. *Les Marxistes et la question juive: Histoire d'un débat (1843–1943)*, Paris 1997 (1990). (*The Marxists and the Jewish Question: The History of a Debate (1843–1943)*, Atlantic Highlands, NJ 1994)

———. *Pour une critique de la barbarie moderne: Écrits sur l'histoire des juifs et de l'antisemitisme*, Lausanne 1996.

———. *L'Histoire déchirée: Essai sur Auschwitz et les intellectuels*, Paris 1997.

———. *Understanding the Nazi Genocide: Marxism after Auschwitz*, London 1999.

Trotsky, Leon, *The First Five Years of the Communist International*, 2 vols, New York 1945/1953 (1924).

———. *My Life: An Attempt at an Autobiography*, Harmondsworth 1975 (1930).

———. *Tagebuch in Exil*, Munich 1962 (1935/1958).

———. *The Revolution Betrayed: What is the Soviet Union and Where is it Going?*, New York 1945 (1936/1937).

———. *Transitional Programme for Socialist Revolution*, New York 1983 (1938).

———. *In Defense of Marxism*, New York 1973 (1942).

————. *Leon Trotsky and the Jewish Question*, New York 1973 (1970).

————. *Schriften über Deutschland*, 2 vols, Frankfurt on Main 1971.

————. *The Struggle against Fascism in Germany*, New York 1971.

————. *Writings of Leon Trotsky (1929–1940)*, 12 vols, New York 1972–9.

————. *Problems of Everyday Life and Other Writings on Science and Culture*, New York 1973.

————. *Oeuvres*, 27 vols, Paris 1978–89.

Tucker, Robert, ed., *Stalinism: Essays in Historical Interpretation*, New York 1977.

Uyttebrouck, André and Despy-Meyer, Andrée, *Les cent cinquante ans de l'Université Libre de Bruxelles (1834–1984)*, Brussels 1984.

Van den Enden, Hugo and Abicht, Ludo, *Marxisme van de hoop – hoop van het marxisme? Essays over de filosofie van Ernst Bloch*, Bussum 1980.

Van der Linden, Marcel, *Het westers marxisme en de Sovjet Unie, hoofdlijnen van structurele maatschappijkritiek (1917–1985)*, Amsterdam 1989. (*Western Marxism and the Soviet Union: A Survey of Critical Theories and Debates since 1917*, London 2006)

Van der Velde, C.A., *De A.N.D.B.: Een overzicht van zijn ontstaan, ontwikkeling en zijne beteekenis*, Amsterdam 1925.

Van Doorslaer, Rudi, *De K.P.B. en het Sovjet-Duits niet-aanvalspakt*, Brussels 1975.

Van Doorslaer, Rudi, *Kinderen van het ghetto: Joodse revolutionairen in België, 1925–1940*, Antwerp 1995.

Van Duijn, Jacob J., *De lange golf in de economie: Kan innovatie ons uit het dal helpen?*, Assen 1979.

Van Lierde, Jean, *Un Insoumis*, Brussels 1998.

Van Langenhove, Luk, De Waele, Jean M. and Harré, Rom, eds, *Individual Persons and Their Actions*, Brussels 1986.

Vereeken, Georges, *The GPU in the Trotskyist Movement*, New York 1976.

Wald, Alan M., *The Revolutionary Imagination: The Poetry and Politics of John Wheelwright and Sherry Mangan*, Chapel Hill 1983.

————. *The New York Intellectuals: The Rise and Decline of the Anti-Stalinist Left from the 1930s to the 1980s*, Chapel Hill 1987.

————. *The Responsibility of Intellectuals: Selected Essays on Marxist Traditions in Cultural Commitment*, London 1992.

————. *Writing from the Left: New Essays on Radical Culture and Politics*, London 1994.

Weber, Hermann, ed., *Unabhängige Kommunisten: Der Briefwechsel zwischen Heinrich Brandler und Isaac Deutscher 1949 bis 1967*, Berlin 1981.

————. and Herbst, Andreas, *Deutsche Kommunisten: Biographisches Handbuch 1918 bis 1945*, Berlin 2004.

Weber, Joseph, *'Dinge der Zeit': Kritische Beiträge zu Kultur und Politik*, Hamburg 1995.

Weinstock, Ulrich, *Das Problem der Kondratieff-Zyklen: Ein Beitrag zur Entwicklung einer Theorie der 'langen Wellen' und ihrer Bedeutung*, Berlin 1964.

Weiss, Peter, *Die Ästhetik des Widerstands*, Frankfurt on Main 1982–1984.

Widgery, David, ed., *The Left in Britain 1956–1968*, Harmondsworth 1976.

Wiggershaus, Rolf, *Die Frankfurter Schule: Geschichte, theoretische Entwicklung, politische Bedeutung*, Munich 1988.

Witte, Els, ed., *Vooruitlopen op het Vlaamse socialisme: 25 jaar links*, Leuven 1984.

————. et al., *Politieke geschiedenis van België*, Antwerp 1990.

————. with Burgelman, Jean-Claude and Stouthuysen, Patrick, eds, *Tussen restauratie en vernieuwing: Aspecten van de Belgische na-oorlogse politiek (1944–1950)*, Brussels 1990.

Wittfogel, Karl A., *Oriental Despotism: A Comparative Study of Total Power*, New Haven 1957.

Wohlforth, Tim, *The Prophet's Children: Travels on the American Left*, Atlantic Highlands, NJ 1994.

Wolf, Markus, *L'Oeil de Berlin: Entretiens de Maurice Najman avec le ex-patron des services secrets est-allemands*, Paris 1992.

Wolf, Winfried, *Polen: Der lange Sommer der Solidarität*, 2 vols, Frankfurt on Main 1981.

Wolter, Ulf, ed., *Die Sozialismusdebatte: Historische und aktuelle Fragen des Sozialismus*, Berlin 1978.

Wreszin, Michael, *A Rebel in Defense of Tradition: The Life and Politics of Dwight Macdonald*, New York 1994.

Young, Michael, *The Rise of the Meritocracy, 1870–2033: An Essay on Education and Equality*, London 1958.

Zeller, Fred, *Trois points c'est tout*, Paris 1976.

————. *Témoin du siècle*, Paris 2000.

Zwischen Rätesozialismus und Reformprojekt: Lesebuch zum 70. Gerburtstag von Peter von Oertzen, Cologne 1994.

DVDs

Buyens, Frans, *Un Homme nommé Ernest Mandel*, 2005 (1972).

Den Hond, Chris, *Ernest Mandel: A Life for the Revolution*, 2005.

Website

Vandenbroucke, Johan, 'De sportziel van De Satan', http://www.brakkehond.be/67/brouc2.html

Index

EM refers to Ernest Mandel. Pseudonyms are in parentheses.